A Social History of England, 900-1200

The years between 900 and 1200 saw transformative social change in Europe, including the creation of extensive town-dwelling populations and the proliferation of feudalized elites and bureaucratic monarchies. In England these developments were complicated and accelerated by repeated episodes of invasion, migration and changes of regime. In this book, scholars from disciplines including history, archaeology and literature reflect on the major trends which shaped English society in these years of transition and select key themes which encapsulate the period. The authors explore the landscape of England, its mineral wealth, its towns and rural life, the health, behaviour and obligations of its inhabitants, patterns of spiritual and intellectual life and the polyglot nature of its population and culture. What emerges is an insight into the complexity, diversity and richness of this formative period of English history.

JULIA CRICK is Associate Professor in the Department of History, University of Exeter. Her research interests include property, power and gender before 1100, aspects of palaeography and the transmission of texts in the Middle Ages, monastic culture and the uses of the past. Her publications include *The Uses of Script and Print 1200–1700*, edited with Alexandra Walsham (2004) and *Charters of St Albans* (2007).

ELISABETH VAN HOUTS is Lecturer in Medieval History at Emmanuel College, Cambridge and Affiliated Lecturer in the Faculty of History, University of Cambridge. She has published extensively on Anglo-Norman history and the history of gender in the Middle Ages. Her recent publications include *Exile in the Middle Ages* (2004) with Laura Napran and *Medieval Writings on Secular Women in the Middle Ages* (2011) with Patricia Skinner.

Horse harness pendants, *c.* 1200

Numerous pendants have been unearthed in recent years with metal detectors. They are difficult to date, because they were presumably lost from horses on the move and are not usually found in datable layers of archaeological sites. The earliest pendants sometimes have the kind of decoration which was incorporated into early heraldry and which might be interpreted as armorial; but heraldry itself was in its infancy and it is impossible to be certain that personal association was intended. These examples (and photographs) are from the collection of Sir John Baker (JHB) and they are reproduced with his kind permission.

1 *Chequy or and [tincture].* This may represent the arms of Warenne (*Chequy or and azure*), though in later times a chequered field would be represented with more squares. Warenne shield-pendants become common in the thirteenth century, the incised squares being filled with blue enamel. From a Yorkshire collection. JHB 512

2 *A cross.* The cross is indicated merely by raised lines, incised in the mould, and there is no cutting away for enamel as in later times. A cross occurs in numerous early coats of arms, but could perhaps have religious significance. Found in East Anglia. JHB 268

3 *Bendy of fourteen argent and azure.* These arms were on the seal of Amaury de Montfort (d. 1213), count of Evreux, earl of Gloucester *jure uxoris*, the same tinctures as here being recorded in thirteenth-century rolls: *Dictionary of British Arms*, ii. 125–7. Found at North Owersby, Lincs., in 1999. JHB 465

4 *Argent, a cross formy azure.* These arms are not recorded. There appear to be traces of whitish enamel in the field, and of blue in the cross. Found in Yorkshire. JHB 510

5 *Or, a fret [tincture].* The fret was used as an armorial device by several early families, but it may not here be heraldic. This example retains much of the gilding. Found at Great Wakering, Essex. JHB 543

6 *Barry of six, a bordure.* These arms occur on the seal of Reynold, count of Boulogne: *Dictionary of British Arms*, ii. 194. Found in Essex. JHB 126

A SOCIAL HISTORY OF ENGLAND, 900–1200

EDITED BY

JULIA CRICK
AND
ELISABETH VAN HOUTS

CAMBRIDGE UNIVERSITY PRESS
Cambridge, New York, Melbourne, Madrid, Cape Town,
Singapore, São Paulo, Delhi, Tokyo, Mexico City

Cambridge University Press
The Edinburgh Building, Cambridge CB2 8RU, UK

Published in the United States of America by Cambridge University Press, New York

www.cambridge.org
Information on this title: www.cambridge.org/9780521713238

First published 2011

Printed in the United Kingdom at the University Press, Cambridge

A catalogue record for this publication is available from the British Library

Library of Congress Cataloguing in Publication data
A social history of England, 900–1200 / [edited by] Julia Crick, Elisabeth van Houts.
p. cm. – (A social history of england)
ISBN 978-0-521-71323-8 (pbk.)
1. England–Social conditions. 2. England–Economic conditions. I. Crick, Julia C.,
1963– II. Van Houts, Elisabeth M. C. III. Title. IV. Series.
HN398.E5S627 2011
306.0942'09021–dc22
2010052184

ISBN 978-0-521-88561-4 Hardback
ISBN 978-0-521-71323-8 Paperback

Contents

Figures

Maps and tables

MAPS

TABLES

Contributors

ANNA SAPIR ABULAFIA, Lucy Cavendish College, Cambridge
JULIA BARROW, School of History, University of Nottingham
STEPHEN BAXTER, Department of History, King's College, London
MARTHA BAYLESS, Department of English, University of Oregon
RICHARD BRITNELL, Department of History, University of Durham
PETER CLAUGHTON, Department of Archaeology, University of Exeter
JULIA CRICK, Department of History, University of Exeter
ROBIN FLEMING, Department of History, Boston College
DAVID GRIFFITHS, Department for Continuing Education, University of Oxford
D. M. HADLEY, Department of Archaeology, University of Sheffield
SARAH HAMILTON, Department of History, University of Exeter
PAUL ANTONY HAYWARD, Department of History, University of Lancaster
JOHN HUDSON, School of History, University of St Andrews
NICHOLAS KARN, School of Humanities, University of Southampton
TOM LICENCE, School of History, University of East Anglia, Norwich
BRUCE O'BRIEN, Department of History, University of Mary Washington
ANDY ORCHARD, Trinity College, Toronto
DAVID A. E. PELTERET, Independent Scholar
OLIVER RACKHAM, Corpus Christi College, Cambridge
CAROLE RAWCLIFFE, School of History, University of East Anglia, Norwich
STEPHEN RIPPON, Department of Archaeology, University of Exeter
ELAINE TREHARNE, English Department, Florida State University
ELISABETH VAN HOUTS, Emmanuel College, Cambridge
CARL WATKINS, Magdalene College, Cambridge
TERESA WEBBER, Trinity College, Cambridge
CHARLES WEST, Department of History, University of Sheffield

Acknowledgements

During the preparation of the volume our contributors have been unfailing in their willingness to respond to our original brief. We owe particular thanks to Dr Sarah Hamilton and Professor Stephen Rippon for additional help and advice in the preparation of the volume. We are also indebted to Professor Sir John Baker, Dr Oliver Creighton, the Reverend Stephen Day, Professor Stephen Rippon and Mr Mike Rouillard for permitting us to publish photographs and illustrations in their possession. We should, however, add that some of the photographs and illustrations are the choice of the editors, and not the authors. We have received encouragement from successive history editors at Cambridge University Press: Simon Whitmore, Michael Watson, Elizabeth Friend-Smith and their staff, amongst whom Gillian Dadd was particularly helpful. We would like to acknowledge the constructive comments and criticism of the anonymous referees who read our proposal and final typescript. We acknowledge use of the *Prosopography of Anglo-Saxon England* database, the *Patrologia Latina* database and the *Oxford Dictionary of National Biography.*

Abbreviations

ANS	*Anglo-Norman Studies*
ASC	Anglo-Saxon Chronicle
ASE	*Anglo-Saxon England*
BHL	*Bibliotheca Hagiographica Latina, Antiquae et Mediae Aetatis*, Subsidia Hagiographica 6 (2 vols., Brussels, 1898–99); with *Novum Supplementum*, H. Fros, ed. (Subsidia Hagiographica 70; Brussels, 1986)
BL	British Library
Councils and Synods	D. Whitelock, M. Brett and C. N. L. Brooke, eds. *Councils and Synods with Other Documents Related to the English Church*, vol. I, *A.D. 871–1204*, (2 vols., Oxford, 1981)
DB fol.	Domesday Book, (A. Williams, G. H. Martin, eds., *Domesday Book. A Complete Translation. Alecto Historical Editions*, (London, 2002))
EcHR	*Economic History Review*
EEA	*English Episcopal Acta*
EETS	Early English Text Society
EHD	Dorothy Whitelock, ed. *English Historical Documents*, vol. I, (2nd edn; London, 1967); David Douglas and George Greenaway, eds., vol. II (London, 1968)
EHR	*English Historical Review*
JEH	*Journal of Ecclesiastical History*
JMH	*Journal of Medieval History*
ODNB	H. C. G. Matthew and Brian Harrison, eds., *Oxford Dictionary of National Biography: From the Earliest Times to the Year 2000* (60 vols.; Oxford, 2004; online edn 2004)

OMT	Oxford (formerly Nelson's) Medieval Texts (Oxford, 1950–)
PL	J. P. Migne, ed., Patrologia Latina (221 vols.; Paris, 1844–64)
P&P	*Past and Present*
PRO	Public Record Office (The National Archives)
RS	Rolls Series (London, 1858–96)
Sawyer, Anglo-Saxon Charters	P. H. Sawyer, *Anglo-Saxon Charters: An Annotated List and Bibliography*, (London, 1968)
TRHS	*Transactions of the Royal Historical Society*

Map 1 England and its neighbours

Map 2 England 900–1200

CHAPTER I

Introduction

Julia Crick and Elisabeth van Houts

> Master: What shall we say of the cook? Do we need his craft in any way?
>
> The 'Cook' says: If you expel me from your society, you'll eat your vegetables raw and your meat uncooked; and you can't even have a good broth without my art.
>
> Master: We don't care about your art; it isn't necessary to us, because we can boil things that need boiling, and roast the things that need roasting, for ourselves.
>
> The 'Cook' says: However, if you drive me out so as to do that, then you'll all be servants, and none of you will be lord. And without my craft you'll still not be able to eat.[1]

So the Englishman, Ælfric of Eynsham (*c.* 950–*c.* 1010), writing a thousand years ago, exposed a basic truth. Lords cannot maintain their status unaided, even for a day. Without subordinates to prepare food 'you'll all be servants, and none of you will be lord' and without skilled labour 'you'll still not be able to eat'.[2] Lordship, kingship, the actions of the elite, many of the facets of human behaviour captured in our historical sources, beg a multitude of questions, not least about what sustained them. These are questions usually tangential to the concerns of the writers who composed narratives and drafted documents in the tenth, eleventh and twelfth centuries, to the extent that when we encounter exceptions, most famously Domesday Book, historians have difficulty distinguishing the novel from the normal.[3] For this period answering questions about how

[1] *Ælfric's Colloquy*, in M. T. Swanton, ed. and trans., *Anglo-Saxon Prose* (London, 1993) p. 174.

[2] On the workers invoked by Ælfric see John Ruffing, 'The labor structure of Ælfric's Colloquy', in A. J. Frantzen and D. Moffat, eds., *The World of Work: Servitude, Slavery and Labor in Medieval England* (Glasgow, 1994), pp. 55–70.

[3] For a recent study of the complexity of this source see Alan Cooper, 'Protestations of ignorance in Domesday Book', in R. F. Berkhofer, Alan Cooper and A. J. Kosto, eds., *The Experience of Power in Medieval Europe, 950–1350* (Aldershot, 2005), pp. 169–81.

individuals conducted their lives and what their environments looked like, even about the labour and resources which sustained them, almost always involves going beyond what written sources will readily tolerate. As a consequence reconstruction risks failure: just as nineteenth-century visions of Alfredian democracy reveal nothing about the ninth century, so early reconstructions of pre-Conquest village life are now treated as an artefact of Victorian intellectual history.[4] In the absence of written evidence, or with evidence distributed very unevenly, historians of early England have had three courses of action: to scrutinize with great care surviving sources but to create necessarily tentative or lacunose accounts; to generalize from the particular; or to use projections from relatively limited sets of data. These have naturally been precarious and much criticized, and many historians have chosen not to engage in necessarily speculative and controversial reconstruction.

In the last century, particularly the last half-century, opportunities for examining questions of ranking and resources have multiplied. Archaeological discoveries, methods and technologies have transformed our understanding of the economy and demography of early England. Searchable databases are allowing the manipulation of historical data in new and powerful ways. The long-dominant interpretative model, of transformation by conquest in 1066, which has shaped historical writing about the period for four centuries, is yielding ground to other models of explication (see Chapter II.2). It will be the purpose of this introduction to explain our approach and to sketch a little of its historiographical context.

A SOCIAL HISTORY

England's semi-insular location as part of the British Isles with its exposed coastline made it vulnerable to attacks from overseas. More than any other country in medieval Europe, England suffered from repeated invasions and conquests. Even before the period covered by this volume (900–1200) Britain was subject to substantial foreign incursion, first by the Romans and then in the fifth and sixth centuries by Germanic migration from continental Europe. Against this backdrop the repeated battering by Vikings in the tenth and early eleventh centuries, followed by the Danish and Norman conquests, turned the history of Britain into

[4] S. Keynes, 'The cult of Alfred', *ASE*, 28 (1999), 225–356; J. W. Burrow, 'The village community and the uses of history in late nineteenth-century England', in N. McKendrick, ed., *Historical Perspectives: Studies in English Thought and Society in Honour of J. H. Plumb* (London, 1974), pp. 255–84.

a well-worn historiographical narrative of an island under threat of attack, as a result both of warfare and of incipient migration. From Bede, via the Anglo-Saxon Chronicle, to the works of twelfth-century historians such as William of Malmesbury and Henry of Huntingdon, the recurrence of seaborne attacks, defeat in the face of foreign naval strength, and settlement of new 'nations' (*nationes*) is a leitmotiv of English chronicles. For each wave of historians complaining of foreign invasion, the constituency of native and newcomer was, of course, different, even though from Bede onwards the natives were English. By the mid-1140s a chronicler in northern England, Alfred of Beverley, distinguished six nations prominent in the history of the island, of which the English were one. He added the Flemish as a new group to the Britons (that is, Welsh), the Picts, the Scots, the Normans and, of course, the English.[5] The process whereby newcomers turned into natives is one of which these chroniclers were well aware. It is up to modern historians to identify and trace the processes that were at work in early England. A word of caution is needed to remind ourselves that where natives and newcomers are distinguished in national groups, suggesting clear-cut lines of distinction, identifying them on the ground, so to speak, is often an impossible task. Moreover, many such statements recorded localized perceptions. For Alfred at home in Beverley in the northeast of England the Flemish were a substantial, identifiable group, whereas they were not so for, say, William at Malmesbury in the southwest.

Repeated attacks by foreigners, which in their brutality are themselves reminiscent of modern terrorism, the disastrous loss of life after battle (especially in 1066), the massive destruction of land in countryside and cities and above all the exploitation of natives by new elites compel us to realize that twelfth-century historians looked back on the preceding centuries in a way not dissimilar to how we now look back on the twentieth century, an era deeply scarred by two world wars. Then, as now, political turmoil, war and small-scale ethnic cleansing resulted in many deaths, displacement of large numbers of people – some forced from homes as a result of conquest, others propelled from homesteads in search of jobs – and the rebuilding of lives stretching across several generations. Looking at the history of central medieval England from the perspective of late twentieth- and early twenty-first-century experience inspires us to ask fresh questions from well-known sources and also to explore information that was not

[5] T. Hearne, ed., *Aluredi Beuerlacensis Annales, siue Historia des gestis Regum Britanniae* (Oxford, 1716), p. 10.

available to our predecessors. This new quest for deeper understanding of old (and new) historical problems is particularly clear in areas such as ecology, landscape history, archaeology, migration, ethnicity and gender.

In our model we have deliberately allowed ample consideration of the political dimension of 'the social' in social history, a position to which Patrick Joyce has recently lent support.[6] We have taken it as axiomatic that social history cannot be written without paying close attention to the actions of kings, their regional deputies such as ealdormen (later earls), sheriffs and reeves, or indeed minor household officers. In a period in which Britain and Ireland were under constant pressure from political and economic predators, those living in England had to work together to protect their own interests and to accommodate newcomers, whether they liked it or not. Although most resources were in the hands of a warrior elite (whether English, Danish or Norman) this relatively small group of potentates could collect and exploit their resources only through co-operation with or coercion of local people, rich and poor, by adopting existing networks of power and shaping them into new ones. Therefore, it is essential to interpret the 'social' in our title in a sense wide enough to encompass the political and the economic world of rulers and labourers. Moreover, our volume also fully embraces the material world as an essential part of the historical story. For it is only through reciprocity that the men and women of England living in their villages and towns acted the way they did, not only to keep themselves alive but also their animals and their crops, as well as to keep in good order the things they manufactured.[7] All these together form the ingredients for our view of a social history of England for the years 900 to 1200. However, beside the question of what is social in our historical investigation, there is for England also the question of its relationship with the European continent.

ENGLAND AND EUROPE

England between 900 and 1200 developed from an aspiration with little territorial expression to an intensively governed state extending into modern Wales (and Scotland). Its written record develops concomitantly, with the intensification of royal government demonstrated in and recorded by the record-keeping offices of the twelfth-century state. Its history in these three centuries has usually been told in terms of conquest and control,

[6] P. Joyce, 'What is the social in social history?', *P&P*, 206 (2010), 213–48 at 232–44.

[7] C. P. Lewis, 'The new Middle Ages?', *History Workshop Journal*, 63.1 (2007), 303–11; Joyce, 'What is the social', 231–2.

and for good reason, because three of the major ruling regimes of England in this period – the West Saxon, the Danish (from 1016) and the Norman (from 1066) – established themselves through conquest and, at least for a time, were able to live off the political fat of territorial aggrandizement. Conquest continued as the dual impetus of social mobility and political ambition pushed English and later Norman nobles into experimental forays into Wales, Ireland and Scotland, later followed by permanent plantation.[8] Indeed, the apparatus of the English state grew in response to the threat and reality of invasion. Alfred and Edward the Elder's emergency measures against Danes, both those attacking and those later resident in England, left a legacy of burghal towns and mint-centres, the locus of centralizing royal administration of the tenth century which generated much of the cash which, even at the start of our period, lubricated political and economic relationships and which later yielded the tens of thousands of pounds of currency extorted from the West Saxon dynasty in payment to the Danes.[9] Another consequence of invasion was England's position as a satellite kingdom – an appendage to political interests which lay elsewhere, in Denmark (from 1016), or Normandy (after 1066) and later Anjou (after 1154).

To a significant extent, then, it makes sense to understand England's history in our period in terms of attack, resistance and subordination. This is what the narrative sources dictate and where, consequently, the oldest historiographical paths lead. Indeed, these three centuries have been cloven in two by the historiographical chasm of 1066 around which the historiography of the two halves, pre- and post-, has accumulated over perhaps four centuries.[10] Since the nineteenth century, moreover, the fragmentary historical record of the pre-Conquest period, in particular, has been subjected to the equally powerful gravitational pull of teleology: the expectation that these centuries form a beginning, and so encapsulate in embryonic or inchoate form developments of future centuries.[11]

[8] R. R. Davies, *The First English Empire: Power and Identities in the British Isles 1093–1343* (Oxford, 2000) traced the process in the post-1066 era, but the phenomenon is exemplified in the behaviour of all three major *eorlisc* dynasties before the Norman Conquest (Harold Godwinesson and Leofric in Wales and Siweard in Scotland): see further K. L. Maund, *Ireland, Wales and England in the Eleventh Century* (Woodbridge, 1991).

[9] Note, for example, the volume of English currency in the 40-kg-haul of silver deposited in the Viking hoard at Cuerdale, Lancs., *c.* 905: J. Graham-Campbell, ed., *Viking Treasure from the North West: The Cuerdale Hoard in Its Context* (Liverpool, 1992).

[10] Hugh MacDougall, *Racial Myth in English History: Trojans, Teutons, and Anglo-Saxons* (London, 1982), chs. 3 and 5.

[11] For discussion of teleology and its implications see the contributions to P. Stafford, J. L. Nelson and J. Martindale, eds., *Law, Laity and Solidarities: Essays in Honour of Susan*

Aware of the conceptual traps of Anglocentrism, historians specializing in Anglo-Saxon England have long been willing to look across the Channel to the Continent to analyse reciprocal influences. Patrick Wormald, heir to the comparative method of his teacher, Michael Wallace-Hadrill, both historians obviously at home in both Francia and England, identified the profound debt of English royal legislation to the Carolingian kings.[12] Other Anglo-Saxon historians have made seminal contributions.[13] Carolingian specialists, too, have always had an open mind about cross-Channel contacts, foremost amongst them Janet Nelson in her Royal Historical Society lectures 'England and the continent in the ninth century', whose title is directly inspired by that important work by Wilhelm Levison, *England and the Continent in the Eighth Century*.[14] But she, too, acknowledges the relatively limited post-war participation of British scholars in studies of early Continental history, an involvement which is going to be hampered by a lack of foreign-language skills in the early twenty-first century.[15] Much wider comparative studies embrace Britain. Chris Wickham's *Framing the Early Middle Ages 400–800* despite its title covers the period up to the first millennium and firmly includes Anglo-Saxon England, while Thomas Bisson in his recent study of power in feudal Europe has treated Norman and Angevin England as something of a significant exception.[16] However, it is also clear that for the period

Reynolds (Manchester, 2001). For recent reflection on insular historiography see P. Stafford, 'Historiography', in P. Stafford, ed., *A Companion to the Early Middle Ages: Britain and Ireland c. 500–1100* (Oxford, 2009), pp. 9–22; W. Davies, 'Introduction', in W. Davies, ed., *From the Vikings to the Normans, 800–1100* (Oxford, 2003), pp. 1–8.

12 P. Wormald with D. Bullough and R. Collins, eds., *Ideal and Reality in Frankish and Anglo-Saxon Society. Studies Presented to J. M. Wallace-Hadrill* (Oxford, 1983), esp. pp. ix–xi; and of course his *The Making of English Law: King Alfred to the Twelfth Century*, vol. 1, *Legislation and Its Limits* (Oxford, 1999), esp. part 1, ch. 2, pp. 29–108.

13 J. Campbell, 'The significance of the Anglo-Norman state in the administrative history of western Europe' and 'England, Flanders and Germany in the reign of Ethelred II: some comparisons and connections', in J. Campbell, *Essays in Anglo-Saxon History* (London and Ronceverte, 1986), pp. 171–90, 191–208; L. Abrams, 'England, Normandy and Scandinavia', in C. Harper-Bill and E. van Houts, eds., *A Companion to the Anglo-Norman World* (Woodbridge, 2003), pp. 43–62.

14 J. L. Nelson, 'Presidential address. England and the continent in the ninth century: I. Ends and beginnings; II. The Vikings and others; III. Rights and rituals', in *TRHS* 6th ser., 12 (2002), 1–22; 13 (2003) 1–28; and 14 (2004), 1–24; W. Levison, *England and the Continent in the Eighth Century* (Oxford, 1947). A companion study is in press: David Rollason, Conrad Leyser and Hannah Williams, eds., *England and the Continent in the Tenth Century* (Turnhout, 2010).

15 Nelson, 'Presidential address. England and the continent: I. Ends', 10 n 31.

16 C. Wickham, *Framing the Early Middle Ages. Europe and the Mediterranean, 400–800* (Oxford, 2005), pp. 306–26, 339–51, 428–34, 502–4, 805–14. Thomas M. Bisson, *The Crisis of the Twelfth Century: Power, Lordship, and the Origins of European Government* (Princeton and Oxford, 2009), esp. pp. 378–97.

of our volume Anglo-Continental relations have not received sustained attention.[17]

Naturally, there is no shortage of work on facets of this history; indeed, in studies of the tenth-century reform movement, the Danish and Norman Conquests and the twelfth-century renaissance, England in a Continental context has received its share of attention.[18] The *Anglo-Norman Studies* series offers a truly cross-Channel perspective for Anglo-Continental research in the eleventh and twelfth centuries. Important, though much more focused, studies were written by Karl Leyser and Timothy Reuter on political and cultural comparisons and contrasts between England and Germany.[19] And there are of course other important individual scholars who looked to both sides of the Channel, as Janet Nelson has recently reminded us for Henry Loyn, who pointed out that Domesday Book did have parallels (on a smaller scale) on the Continent.[20] Or very welcome is the appreciation by David Crouch and Kathleen Thompson of the crucial contribution to England's history in a pan-Norman context by David Bates, whose own Ford lectures given at the University of Oxford in 2010 stress just this theme.[21] But this is nothing like the Levison–Nelson integrated approach that is badly needed.

Foreign-born scholars, some of whom work and live in anglophone areas, are as a matter of innate interest more willing to give England a European context. K. Van Eickels (Bamberg, Germany) weaves English

[17] There is no series of lectures on Anglo-Continental history for the tenth, the eleventh or the twelfth centuries. For the thirteenth century there is an annual publication primarily focused on England/Britain which contains the occasional cross-Channel contribution: *Thirteenth-Century England* I (1986) (Woodbridge, 1987).

[18] D. Bullough, 'The continental background of the reform', in his *Carolingian Renewal. Sources and Heritage* (Manchester, 1991), pp. 272–96; C. Cubitt, 'The tenth-century Benedictine reform in England', *Early Medieval Europe*, 6 (1997), 77–94; C. W. Hollister, ed., *Anglo-Norman Political Culture in the Twelfth-Century Renaissance. Proceedings of the Borchard Conference on Anglo-Norman History, 1995* (Woodbridge, 1997).

[19] K. Leyser, 'England and the Empire in the early twelfth century', in his *Medieval Germany and Its Neighbours, 900–1250* (London, 1982) and T. Reuter, 'The making of England and Germany, 850–1050', in T. Reuter, ed. J. Nelson, *Medieval Polities and Modern Mentalities* (Cambridge, 2006), pp. 284–99.

[20] J. L. Nelson, 'The Henry Loyn Memorial Lecture for 2006. Henry Loyn and the context of Anglo-Saxon England', *Haskins Society Journal*, 19 (2007), 154–70.

[21] 'Introduction', in D. Crouch and K. Thompson, eds., *Normandy and Its Neighbours, 900–1250. Essays Presented to David Bates* (Turnhout, 2011), forthcoming. Amongst David Bates's publications the following are particularly important for our purpose: D. Bates, 'Britain and France and the year 1000', *Franco-British Studies*, 28 (1999), 5–22; D. Bates, 'England and the feudal revolution', in *Il Feudalesimo nell'alto medioevo* (*Settimane di Studio del Centro Italiano di studi sull'alto medioevo*, 47; 2 vols.; Spoleto, 2000), pp. 611–46.

and French diplomatics together in his book on political ritual.[22] Bjorn Weiler (Aberystwyth) views the reigns of Stephen and Henry III from a pan-European perspective.[23] Viewed from the eastern side of the Channel, England, and the British Isles, belong quite naturally to the history of the Continent.[24] Some concerted efforts are made to force historians to confront unspoken biases or involuntary insular views, not only in Great Britain. The heritage of nationalist historiography going back to the late nineteenth century is still alive, not only in university curricula but in publishers' views of what textbooks should look like. Gerd Althoff, Johannes Fried and Patrick Geary brought together American and German scholars on medieval history with a view to learn from one another's approaches across national boundaries. The resulting book, despite the plea by its editors, is a collection of essays, each with a strong nationalistic focus. Interestingly for us, there is nothing in it on England![25] Clearly whereas writing parallel histories of countries, or an analysis of relationships between countries, are preferred by these scholars, the results do not amount to truly comparative history.[26]

One of the reasons why medievalists from the Continent may on occasion have seemed intimidated by the history of England, and skirted an integral Continental view of it, is the problem of England's common law. If Patrick Wormald is right that the common law roots in fact go back to

[22] K. Van Eickels, *Vom inszenierten Konsens zum systematisierten Konflikt. Die englisch-französischen Beziehungen und ihre Wahrnehmung an der Wende vom Hoch- zum Spätmittelalter* (Mittelalter-Forschungen, 10; Stuttgart, 2002) and a shorter version in French limited to the twelfth century, 'L'hommage des rois anglais et leurs héritiers aux rois français au XIIe siècle: subordination imposée ou reconnaissance souhaitée?', in M. Aurell and N.-Y. Tonnerre, eds., *Plantagenêts et Capétiens: confrontations et heritages* (Histoires de famille. La parenté au Moyen Age, 4; Turnhout, 2006), pp. 377–86.

[23] B. Weiler, 'Kingship, usurpation and propaganda in twelfth-century Europe: the case of Stephen', *ANS* 23 (2000), 299–326; B. Weiler, *Henry III of England and the Staufen Empire 1216–1272* (Woodbridge, 2006); B. K. U. Weiler and I. W. Rowlands, eds., *England and Europe in the Reign of Henry III (1216–1272)* (Aldershot, 2002).

[24] E. M. C. van Houts, *History and Family Traditions in England and the Continent, 1000–1200* (Variorum Collected Studies; Aldershot, 1999); E. M. C. van Houts, ed., *The Normans in Europe* (Manchester Medieval Sources Series; Manchester, 2000); E. M. C. van Houts with C. Harper-Bill, eds., *A Companion to the Anglo-Norman World* (Woodbridge, 2003); E. M. C. van Houts, 'The vocabulary of exile and outlawry in the North Sea around the first millennium', in L. Napran and E. van Houts, eds., *Exile in the Middle Ages* (International Medieval Research, 13; Turnhout, 2004), pp. 13–28.

[25] G. Althoff, J. Fried and P. J. Geary, 'Introduction', in G. Althoff, J. Fried and P. J. Geary, eds., *Medieval Concepts of the Past. Ritual, Memory, Historiography* (Publications of the German Historical Institute; Cambridge, 2002), pp. 1–17.

[26] C. Wickham, *Problems in Doing Comparative History.* The Reuter Lecture 2004 (University of Southampton, 2005), esp. pp. 1–9.

the tenth century (if not before), the unique legal development of England, especially after 1066, hampers comparisons across the Channel.[27] There is on occasion also the hint of suspicion within the medieval community on either side of the Channel that the common law's uniqueness is the exclusive property of English legal historians.[28] The only central medieval historian who thus far has met the challenge head-on by looking at the common law from a comparative perspective is, interestingly, Flemish, Raoul van Caenegem.[29]

One of the challenges for all contributors to this volume concerned the fault line of '1066' that runs through English history and its modern historiography. No other country in central medieval Europe witnessed an invasion followed by occupation on the scale of the Norman conquest of England. The nearest rupture of that magnitude might be in France (and some of its neighbouring countries) before and after the French Revolution and the rule of Napoleon. With this in mind historians writing about medieval social and economic development in continental Europe do not have to cope with a caesura based on political events. How then do they structure their discussion of central medieval social life for our period? Some do so thematically, as we have done for the period from 900 to 1200 as a whole, for example in the case of a recent textbook for medieval history by Wim Blockmans and Peter Hoppenbrouwers.[30] Or if they prefer a chronological approach they discuss the period on a century-by-century basis, the clearest example (from the USA) being W. C. Jordan's *Europe in the High Middle Ages*, which is divided into four parts each devoted to a hundred years.[31] Thomas Bisson, in his recent pan-European study, has reasserted the importance of the Norman Conquest as the moment when coercive lordship, a phenomenon developing across the European continent and infringing public power, was imported wholesale into England.[32]

[27] P. Wormald, *Lawyers and the State: The Varieties of Legal History*. Selden Society Lecture 2001 (London, 2002).

[28] J. Hudson on Maitland's acid remarks about German legal historians who dabbled in English legal history, though acknowledging the massive contribution by Friedrich Liebermann's edition of the legal texts, J. H. G. Hudson, *F. W. Maitland and the Englishness of English Law*. Selden Society Lecture 2006 (London, 2007).

[29] R. C. van Caenegem, *Legal History. A European Perspective* (London and Rio Grande, OH, 1991).

[30] W. Blockmans and P. Hoppenbrouwers, trans. I. van den Hoven, *Introduction to Medieval Europe 300–1550* (London and New York, 2002), where the central Middle Ages occupy pp. 128–52 (ch. 8 on religious renewal), pp. 153–85 (ch. 9 on early kingdoms and territorial principalities 900–1200), pp. 186–216 (ch. 10 on eastern Europe), pp. 217–40 (ch. 11 on towns) and pp. 241–70 (ch. 12 on thinking about man and the world).

[31] W. C. Jordan, *Europe in the High Middle Ages* (London, 2001).

[32] Bisson, *The Crisis*.

But whether historians are interested in European (Continental) history or in history across the whole of the European canvas, they all grapple with the same perennial problem of a patchy source base.

SOURCES

In our case, nowhere is the divide of '1066' more obvious than in the discussion of the spread of sources across our period. Its unevenness hampers historians in any comparative approach across three centuries of English history, so they continuously have to be aware that bounty in one period almost inevitably means scarcity in another. Here again, the situation can be understood both as the product of historical processes and as more than a local phenomenon. Historians have discussed how record-keeping advanced in tandem with acquisitive lordship in England and on the Continent and can be understood as a product of mistrust.[33] Boundaries and political relationships needed to be articulated in an age of ecclesiastical reform when the Church sought to define its relationship with secular authority.[34] The composition and keeping of written records may consequently signal political stress as much as educational attainment.

As far as narrative sources are concerned, we have a good selection of saints' lives and miracles from Anglo-Saxon and Anglo-Norman England, but in terms of chronicles – despite the existence of the Anglo-Saxon Chronicle in its various versions – the post-Conquest period provides the bulk of annals, chronicles and histories. Many were written in the early twelfth century as part of a campaign to record in writing knowledge from before the Norman Conquest that would otherwise disappear and to make sense of the new political and social order. Besides there is poetry in Old English, Latin and Old French that provides a wealth of information on social stratification. Any discussion of documentary sources must of course begin with Domesday Book, compiled on the basis of the Domesday survey of 1086, a survey of the king's resources in wealth (land, tax and moveables) for three key dates: January 1066 (the time of King Edward's death), late 1066 (the time of the Norman arrivals) and 1086 (the date of the survey). Although therefore the data straddle the '1066' divide they do so only just. It is always tempting to extrapolate

33 Bisson, *The Crisis*, pp. 28, 316–49. M. T. Clanchy, *From Memory to Written Record: England, 1066–1307* (2nd edn; Oxford, 1993) p. 5; see also below, Chapter VI.2.

34 P. Hyams, 'Homage and feudalism: a judicious separation', in N. Fryde, P. Monnet and O. G. Oexle, eds., *Die Gegenwart des Feudalismus* (Göttingen, 2002), pp. 13–49; Bisson, *The Crisis*, p. 494.

from its richness further back in time or further into the future, or even onto the continent of Europe, but the legitimacy of such stretching of evidence is highly questionable. There is no comparable source in the whole of western Europe, so as a unique collection of data it is as fantastically informative as it is frustrating in what it omits to explain to us.[35] A rare example of imbalance in source material tipped in favour of the tenth and eleventh centuries concerns wills, most in Old English, with very few surviving from after the Norman Conquest. Some would argue that the same applies for the survival of law codes, but any conclusion depends very much on one's definition of what a law code is. As elsewhere in Europe, as a result of the increased use of the written word more twelfth-century charters were composed (and have survived) than are known from the previous two centuries. Archaeological evidence and material sources have transformed our knowledge of the period, as will be clear throughout most chapters, but nevertheless thanks to the nature of the finds such information is usually very localized and does not lend itself easily to extrapolation, either chronologically or geographically. If we compare the source material on which this volume is based with that of volume II of *A Social History of England* for the later Middle Ages, one is struck by the immense imbalance between the period before and after 1200. For our period there are no manorial or household accounts, no manorial or household surveys, no detailed tax records from town or countryside, the narrative sources (richer in comparison with the pre-Conquest period) are relatively poor, as is the surviving material culture. Hence there are vast areas of research that cannot be conducted for our period that are included in the second volume. However, there is one rule that applies to both periods and that pertains to the groups in society covered by the sources. Before and after 1200 they privilege information about the top layers of society, the men and women who held land, offices or jobs and whose transactions were recorded in writing. For the lower ranks of society we depend mostly on indirect references in the written texts or material objects and archaeological remains.

[35] J. McN. Dodgson and J. J. Palmer, eds., *Domesday Book. A Survey of the Counties of England*, vol. XXXVII, *Index of Persons* (Chichester, 1992), pp. 272–3. For suggestions of Continental examples, all on a much smaller scale, see R. H. C. Davis, 'Domesday Book: continental parallels', in J. C. Holt, ed., *Domesday Studies. Papers Read at the Novocentenary Conference of the Royal Historical Society and the Institute of Geographers, Winchester 1986* (Woodbridge, 1987), pp. 15–39 and Nelson, 'Henry Loyn and the context of Anglo-Saxon England', pp. 166–9.

FRAMEWORK FOR THIS VOLUME

The Social History of England commissioned by Cambridge University Press includes two volumes for the Middle Ages. *A Social History of England, 1200–1500*, edited by Rosemary Horrox and W. Mark Ormrod, was published in 2006, and the present volume, *A Social History of England, 900–1200*, lies before you now.[36] Its status as a companion means that in our volume we have tried to keep in line with patterns put in place by our colleagues. However, the specificity of problems connected with a discussion of our period has meant that we have needed to follow a path of our own. Perhaps the most striking difference between our volumes lies in the question of periodization: our centuries bridge a major historiographical divide, the Norman Conquest. Therefore, our most important and innovative task was to build a platform for discussion created from two mostly separate historiographies, one Anglo-Saxon and one Anglo-Norman. Our brief to the contributors asked them not simply for a synthesis of recent research in both fields but encouraged them to provide fresh thinking on social history and to prepare the ground for further exploration from scratch.

Readers of this first volume of *A Social History of England* will find a deliberately collaborative, interdisciplinary and diverse collection of contributions. Our guiding principle has been to expose the reader to insights and approaches from across anglophone historiography and to bring into discussion a broad range of sources and disciplines. Archaeologists, literary scholars and historians of all complexions have contributed their vision from their particular disciplinary standpoints. Synthesis has of course been necessary, and is provided in the longer, more synthetic and discursive discussions which begin each chapter, but we depend on the cumulative effect of shorter paratactic contributions written from a diverse range of disciplines and standpoints. Our purpose is pedagogic: to inform and to direct students to read further and to read differently, most particularly by broadening the range of subject matter at their disposal. The main chapters aim to provide an introduction to the period by sketching the main historical issues at stake, and any development over time, for readers without any previous knowledge of the period. Chapter I on land and people discusses the geography and resources of England's lands and the basic living

[36] R. Horrox and M. Ormrod, eds., *A Social History of England, 1200–1500* (Cambridge, 2006).

conditions of its people. In Chapter II on authority and community the rules according to which the people organized their lives and communities are discussed in terms of conventional (and confrontational) dichotomies such as rich and poor or fighters and labourers, but crucially also according to notions of collaboration and mutual dependence. Chapter III on towns focuses on the dense conglomerations of men and women living closely together, partly for protection against outside attack, partly for mutually beneficial employment in trade and industry and also crucially to provide centres for royal administration. Chapter IV on invasion and migration analyses the impact of foreign predators and conquerors attracted by England's wealth and the process by which they insinuated themselves into its society, either piecemeal by gradual migration or by force, resulting at times in major changes to the distribution and exploitation of that wealth. Chapter V on religion and belief explores how the men and women in England coped with the force of nature and lifecycle through religion and various belief systems. Finally, Chapter VI on learning and training discusses how the English organized their knowledge and skills, both practical and intellectual, in order to pass their collective experience on to the next generations.

In a co-authored volume there will inevitably be some measure of disagreement amongst its contributors as to how they assess certain developments and changes. In the same way that we as editors have encouraged debate with published opinion so, too, have we accommodated historical debate within the volume. On purpose we have refrained from intervention and thus have not reconciled conflicting opinions. As far as editorial and technical matters are concerned, we have encouraged the use of referencing to sources in translation as far as is possible. Where available we refer to *English Historical Documents* (*EHD*), vols. I and II, even though on occasion this means that it is not the most recent edition or translation that is being referred to. For further information on persons we expect that readers will consult the databases of the *Oxford Dictionary of National Biography* (*ODNB*) and the *Prosopography of Anglo-Saxon England*.[37] Otherwise, we have not imposed a strict rule on the use of specific editions and translations, so the annotation and bibliography show a variety. We imposed strict limits on the amount of annotation our contributors could use, and as a rule we have allowed notes

[37] *Prosopography of Anglo-Saxon England* database, www.pase.ac.uk.

only for specific quotations or opinions. References within legal texts are to clauses (not page numbers), unless otherwise indicated. Where sections are not annotated, all examples can be found in the bibliographical section for each chapter. The bibliography contains booklists for further reading arranged per chapter, including its sub-chapters. A selection of frequently used technical terms can be found in a glossary.

CHAPTER I.I

Land use and people

Robin Fleming

In order to come to grips with the land of England and the people who inhabited it in the centuries on either side of the Norman Conquest, it is necessary to consider a period broader than the basic chronological time-frame of this volume. Indeed, as we shall see, the extraordinary transformations of landscape and people which so mark the central Middle Ages began not in the tenth century, but rather in the generations before AD 800. Although the West Saxon conquest of the Danelaw in the tenth century, the conquests of England by Cnut the Great and William the Conqueror in the eleventh and the problems of Stephen's reign and their resolutions in the twelfth century were the ruination of many landholders and the making of others, the major changes concerning land use and people described in this chapter had little to do with grand politics. Instead, they were determined by the ways many hundreds of thousands of people came to farm and pay what they owed their betters, and by the sorts of communities in which they chose or were told to live. These things changed dramatically over the course of the central Middle Ages, and they transformed the look of the land and the lives of the people who made their livings from it. Indeed, as people during this period remade the landscape, the landscape came to remake them.

Before AD 800 most men, women and children in England lived in small, straggling hamlets inhabited by a handful of families, each in possession of a house and a few outbuildings, and all engaged in farming. People living in settlements like these had a vested interest in the lands they farmed, but most were nonetheless beholden to more powerful men – to kings or their most distinguished followers, or to monks – groups who, by the turn of the ninth century, had long had rights to a share of hamlet-dwelling families' herds, harvests and labour. By this date it was traditional for great men to claim rights over large tracts of land and their populations, and these men's reeves, over the generations, had overseen their organization into big, loose-jointed territories, entities historians sometimes call 'multiple estates'. As a result, these territories had come to be orientated, both socially and economically, towards powerful secular or religious households, and by AD 800 families across the length and breadth of England not only resided in them but rendered agricultural surplus to their masters. Farmers, however, did not give over their swine or wheat because they were tenants who owed rents to their landlords, but rather because great men had come to rule them, and one of the obligations of the ruled in the early Middle Ages was the payment of tribute.[1]

Scattered evidence suggests that free farmers during this period, as a matter of course, would have held single hides of land, which, so the eighth-century historian Bede tells us, was the amount needed to support a single household.[2] By Bede's day the hide was both old and ubiquitous, and we find evidence that elites had come to use it as a means of assessing tribute on individual families within their territories, many of which comprised 300 hides or more. We have a list of tribute, preserved in the laws of King Ine (688–726), which gives some indication of the kinds and amounts of tribute farmers were obliged to render to their lords, and the types of dues, in turn, that the masters of such places could expect. Our list asserts that the people settled in hamlets scattered across a 300-hide territory would have been obliged each year to provide something of the order of 300 vats of honey, 9,000 loaves of bread, 360 ambers of Welsh ale and 900 ambers of clear ale, 60 full-grown cows or 300 castrated rams, 300 geese, 600 hens, 300 cheeses, 30 ambers of butter, 150 salmon, 600 pounds of fodder and 3,000 eels.[3] At first reading, this seems like a daunting amount of food, and it is clear that this level of tribute would have enabled great men and their familiars to enjoy an endless cycle of feasting. Still, in good years provisioning at this level would have created little hardship for the people who actually gave over such mountains of food. After all, if 300 farm families lived within a 300-hide territory, each, in the end, would have owed something of the order of 30 loaves of bread, a sheep, a goose and 2 hens, a cheese and a vat of honey, along with a few other items, hardly a ruinous level of tribute. There was, moreover, often little point for lords to extract more from their dependants, since thoroughgoing networks of local trading centres had yet to develop in which to exchange these by-and-large perishable goods. So, although a tiny minority controlled vast tracts of

[1] R. Faith, *The English Peasantry and the Growth of Lordship* (London, 1997), p. 4.

[2] B. Colgrave and R. A. B. Mynors eds., *Bede's Ecclesiastical History of the English People*, (Oxford, 1969), i, 25.

[3] *Laws of Ine*, 70.1, translated in *EHD*, i, no. 32 pp. 398–407.

land *c.* 800, their agricultural subordinates were not always pushed to produce larger surpluses, and the lordship under which most people lived was extensive rather than intensive.

The items on our list also provide us with some sense of the kinds of activities in which farmers engaged during this period. Although these dues make it obvious that people spent considerable energy cultivating a range of cereal crops so that their lords might eat bread and drink ale, farmers were also clearly occupied with their livestock. Thus, farmers before 800 were hardly cereal-producing specialists, a state of affairs underscored by the findings of archaeologists. Faunal and botanical remains recovered from the early and middle Saxon settlement at Gamlingay, in Cambridgeshire, for example, have revealed a group of people who raised foodstuffs similar to those on our tribute list. They had a granary in which to store their cereal crops, but they also kept sheep and cattle, pigs, geese, chickens and ducks; and they milked cows, made cloth, smithed and crafted combs from the antlers of roe deer.[4]

Animal bones recovered from high-status sites, on the other hand, provide glimpses of the kinds of beasts local farmers drove into tribute centres to discharge their obligations. Most of the livestock given over at Flixborough, in Lincolnshire, for example, was walked onto the site, rather than butchered elsewhere and then carted in as meat, and the majority of these animals had long served the farmers who owned them. Many, for example, were old, arthritic oxen – castrated males who had worked for years as draught animals. Flocks of elderly ewes were also offered up as tribute, and they had probably been milked as younger animals. The rarity of two- to eight-year-old sheep at Flixborough, moreover, hints that farmers were keeping back their best wool-producers at tribute time.[5]

By 800 whole archipelagos of places like Gamlingay had been stitched together into ingeniously administered units of production, in order to provide for high-status households like the one that controlled Flixborough. In order for this to have happened, elite households must have expended considerable energy, over the course of the seventh and eighth centuries, transforming generalized notions of obligation into thoroughgoing systems of renders, systems which could guarantee that dependants provided their lords with the entire range of necessities, not

[4] J. Murray with T. McDonald, 'Excavations at Station Road, Gamlingay, Cambridgeshire', *Anglo-Saxon Studies in Archaeology and History*, 13 (2005), 173–330.

[5] K. Dobney, D. Jaques, J. Barrett and C. Johnstone, *Farmers, Monks and Aristocrats: The Environmental Archaeology of Anglo-Saxon Flixborough*, (Excavations at Flixborough, 3; Oxford, 2007), pp. 116–89.

just meat and wheat, but goods as diverse as cheese, fodder and honey. Our late seventh-century tribute list, however, cannot have contained all the goods given over to great men. In order for high-status households to function, they would have also needed commodities like wood for burning and building, oats for horses and pigs for hams and bacon. They would have required, as well, more specialized renders – things like salt, iron and lead – from special, production-orientated communities. In order to meet this variety of needs, leading households gradually constructed what Rosamond Faith has called 'landscapes of obligation', in which farmers and the communities in which they lived came to be orientated towards the production of particular kinds of goods and services rendered to lords at specific moments in the year.[6] This necessitated highly choreographed agricultural regimens, traces of which are occasionally preserved in the names of places once tied to high-status centres. *Hunatun*, for example, was a place where the lord's hounds were raised; Linacre and Flaxley were where his flax grew. The inhabitants of Shipton and Swanscombe rendered sheep and swine, and Chiswick and Buttermere cheese and butter.[7] Place-names like these are often impossible to date, but some appear in early land grants and clearly reflect leading households' efforts to rationalize the agrarian activities of the people living within their territories. Of course, the inhabitants of such places raised the full range of crops and animals that they, themselves, needed to survive each year – communities in a period without a well-developed market system could not live on hunting-dogs or butter alone – but such place-names suggest local landscapes managed with an eye towards tribute time.

Excavated animal bones from a handful of low-status settlements also occasionally hint at particular communities' specializations. We can see the people of Pennyland, in Buckinghamshire, for example, putting more of their efforts into raising cattle than farmers in other places, and the people living at Quarrington, in Lincolnshire, beginning to concentrate their efforts on pig rearing.[8] Such moves towards specialist production would have required considerable effort on the part of lords and their reeves. Some elite households may have needed more organized renders

[6] Faith, *English Peasantry and the Growth of Lordship*, p. 10.

[7] H. E. Hallam, 'England before the Norman Conquest', in H. E. Hallam, ed., *The Agrarian History of England and Wales*, vol. II, *1042–1350* (Cambridge, 1988), pp. 1–44.

[8] R. Williams, *Pennyland and Hartigans: Two Iron Age and Saxon Sites in Milton Keynes* (Buckinghamshire Archaeological Society Monograph, 4; 1993), pp. 148, 153; G. Taylor, *et al.*, 'An early to middle Saxon settlement at Quarrington, Lincolnshire', *Antiquaries Journal*, 83 (2003), 231–80.

because of the particular tasks in which they were engaged. At the beginning of the eighth century, for example, we know that Ceolfrith, abbot of Monkwearmouth and Jarrow, oversaw the making of three great bibles. The lone survivor, the *Codex Amiatinus*, was written on the skins of 515 calves, so the abbot's great project could have been undertaken only if his community insisted upon and got large numbers of calves from those who owed it tribute.[9] Other lords may have become more attentive in the management of their dues so that they might exchange particular kinds of surplus with traders, who, from the beginning of the seventh century onwards, could be found in both temporary and permanent trading enclaves.[10] It was perhaps by employing this strategy that the master of Flixborough and the abbot of Eynsham were both able to enliven the standard tribute diet of old mutton and hard-worked beef with tastier fare, like porpoise, crane, oysters and ray.[11] Whatever the case, over the course of a couple of generations such centrally directed efforts, developed to meet the needs of elite households or the people with whom they traded, came to bind all of a territory's farmers together and in some ways co-ordinate their production.

It is probably a mistake, however, to see these territories as exclusively the handiwork of elites, ruthlessly imposing their will on the countryside. Rather, the people, woodlands, springs and flocks enmeshed in local landscapes of obligation were often both geographically dispersed and diverse. Above all else, it is clear from the few early territories we can still trace on the ground that they made ecological sense, and that they tended to be knitted together by ancient droveways, some of which had been in use since the pre-Roman Iron Age. In western Surrey, for example, the territories that centred on Woking and Godalming included lands in the distant sandy heaths running along the borders of Hampshire and Berkshire, probably because farmers' herds fed on the good grazing found there.[12] Thus, millennia-old patterns of transhumance, which linked far-flung

[9] P. Fowler, *Farming in the First Millennium AD: British Agriculture between Julius Caesar and William the Conqueror* (Cambridge, 2002), p. 238.

[10] R. Fleming, 'Elites, boats and foreigners: rethinking the rebirth of English towns', in *Città e campagna nei secoli altomedievali* (*Settimane di Studio del Centro Italiano di studi sull'alto medioevo*, 56; Spoleto, 2009), pp. 1–33.

[11] C. Loveluck, *Rural Settlement, Lifestyles and Social Change in the Later First Millennium AD: Anglo-Saxon Flixborough in Its Wider Context* (Excavations at Flixborough, 4; Oxford, 2007), p. 93; P. Booth, A. Dodd, M. Robinson and A. Smith, *The Thames through Time. The Archaeology of the Gravel Terraces of the Upper and Middle Thames: The Early Historical Period AD 1–1000* (Oxford Archaeology Thames Valley Landscape Monograph, 27; Oxford, 2007), p. 341.

[12] John Blair, *Early Medieval Surrey: Landholding, Church and Settlement before 1300* (Stroud, 1991), p. 35.

summer and winter pastures, helped dictate the extent and shape of early territories. In short, these territories were in some sense organic and must have been determined in some ways by the needs of farm families, whose survival necessitated a broad mix of resources that could only be had if they had access to distant and distinct resources. It appears, therefore, that both surplus-grabbing lords and resource-seeking farmers participated in the organization of the landscape. Both elite interventions, then, and the agency of farm families came together to create England's great 'multiple estates'.

What about the settlements within these territories where both great and little men lived? Tiny hamlets like Gamlingay, where the vast majority of people who farmed and paid tribute resided year-round, were generally not very organized collections of houses and their associated outbuildings, and they tended to drift over the generations as old structures grew ramshackle and new ones came to replace them. As a result, these settlements tended to shift over time along bands of light, well-drained soils (often in river valleys), which were relatively easy to plough and, thus, favoured by early medieval farmers; indeed, settlements in this period tended to sit on the same light soils and close by the fields their inhabitants cultivated.[13] In earlier centuries there were few boundary markers or enclosures in such places; but increasingly, from the eighth century on, farmers were building enclosures around clusters of buildings, around gardens and paddocks, and perhaps even as a way to protect infields from livestock.[14] This move hints at evolving notions of property.

Scores of hardworking little communities like Gamlingay, which were engaged in the dirty business of lambing, slaughtering and threshing, were a far cry from the settlements where more dignified households stayed. For one thing, the households of great secular lords were peripatetic, and they moved throughout the year from one tribute centre to another. The excavations of seventh-century high-status sites like Cowdery's Down, in Hampshire, and Yeavering, in Northumberland, have not only revealed the remains of substantial timber halls but have exposed a constellation of profligate practices taking place at such places – large-scale entertaining,

[13] For examples of this phenomenon, see S. E. West, *West Stow: The Anglo-Saxon Village* (East Anglian Archaeology, 24; Ipswich, 1985) and H. Hamerow, *Excavations at Mucking*, vol. II, *The Anglo-Saxon Settlement* (English Heritage Archaeological Report, 21; London, 1993). For a more general discussion of these early settlements, see H. Hamerow, *Early Medieval Settlements: The Archaeology of Rural Communities in North-West Europe 400–900* (Oxford, 2002), pp. 93–9, 120–4.

[14] A. Reynolds, 'Boundaries and settlements in later sixth to eleventh century England', *Anglo-Saxon Studies in Archaeology and History*, 12 (2003), 98–136.

the building of outsized structures, elaborate ritual practices – and they reveal sites that were geared towards consumption rather than production.[15]

Although lords stayed at central places scattered throughout their territories only as long as the food held out, small populations of slaves and reeves would have lived there year-round, in order to deal with each season's dues and renders and to safeguard the storehouses from damp, pests and pilfering. We have some idea of what the business end of tribute centres looked like in the eighth century, because archaeologists have excavated one at Higham Ferrers, in Northamptonshire, part of a complex, poly-focal settlement probably controlled by the kings of Mercia.[16] The suite of buildings excavated at Higham Ferrers seems to have acted as a tribute-gathering, processing and storage facility, servicing the king's great hall at Irthlingborough, just across the River Nene and downwind from Higham Ferrers' cattle pens and malting ovens. The compound at Higham Ferrers was surrounded by a large, keyhole-shaped enclosure, marked by a modest ditch and probably topped with a hedge or fence. The enclosure would have served as a corral for livestock driven in by local tribute payers. There were also living accommodations within the enclosure for a small, permanent workforce, as well as storage buildings, malting ovens and a mill. There is some evidence, as well, that items of high-status exchange – things like fancy pottery and the wine it contained – passed through, but were not consumed at Higham Ferrers itself. Instead, estate workers probably stored them there, but then carted them to the hall at Irthlingborough once the king and his friends had arrived.

Monastic tribute centres would have had much in common with this complex, but abbots and their communities, because of their vows of stability, lived year-round next to their stone-built churches, so the central places they controlled developed early into settlements with relatively large, permanent populations. Churches received massive endowments of land from enthusiastic laypeople, especially between *c.* 670 and *c.* 730, and during this period it is likely that the Christian rich handed over a number of tribute centres to their favourite religious communities. Such monastic central places not only had larger numbers of year-round, elite

[15] M. Millett and S. James, 'Excavations at Cowdery's Down, Basingstoke, Hampshire 1978–81', *Archaeological Journal*, 140 (1983), 151–279; B. Hope-Taylor, *Yeavering: An Anglo-British Centre of Early Northumbria* (London, 1977); C. Scull, 'Post-Roman phase 1 at Yeavering: a reconsideration', *Medieval Archaeology*, 35 (1991), 51–63.

[16] A. Hardy, B. M. Charles and R. J. Williams, *Death and Taxes: The Archaeology of a Middle Saxon Estate Centre at Higham Ferrers, Northamptonshire* (Oxford, 2007).

residents, but probably had larger populations of labourers living there as well. John Blair has argued that some monastic brethren might actually have been semi-dependent labourers, who spent their days in much the same way as lay farmers would. Thus, a large portion of the 600 or so *fratres* described in AD 716 as members of the monastic communities of Monkwearmouth and Jarrow, may, in actual fact, have laboured for and served a much smaller group of choir monks. If such men were, indeed, praying farmhands, ecclesiastical communities, in contrast to their secular counterparts, would have been freed from the endless cycle of tribute gathering engaged in by lay lords, because they would have been able to exploit their lands more directly.[17] Indeed, they may have developed inland, or core areas within their territories, early on; and because of their access to labour, they would have been able to exploit their lands more directly than secular lords to meet their households' needs.

Sometime in the eighth or ninth century the large, loose-jointed territories just described and the landscapes of obligation in which they sat began to evolve, and some started to come apart. It appears that around this time a number of kings, bishops and abbots began to feel obliged to dismantle some of the territories under their control in order to create collections of more modest parcels of 5, 10 or 20 hides, which they could then grant out to secular followers. One Worcestershire thegn in the ninth century, for example, sought just such a holding from the bishop of Worcester 'where he could live with honour and dwell in a hall there'.[18] This practice quickened over the course of the tenth and eleventh centuries, and by the eve of the Norman Conquest, thousands of English thegns (a group of landholders similar to the gentry of the later Middle Ages) had come into possession of their own small estates. These holdings were much more compact than earlier territories, and they had far fewer resources. The people behind their creation were well aware of this and appear to have taken special care, when dividing up older territories, to make each new estate a viable and self-sustaining holding. Again and again we find older territorial units split into a number of long, thin, 5-hide estates, narrow to ensure that each holding had a share of river bank, some woodland and some access to nearby trackways or roads. These new estates, moreover, were often named, by the lucky thegns who came to hold them, after themselves. To give but two from hundreds of such examples, Alverstone, in Wiltshire, means 'Alfred's estate', and Osbaston, in Leicestershire,

[17] J. Blair, *The Church in Anglo-Saxon Society* (Oxford, 2005), p. 255.

[18] A. J. Robertson, ed. and trans., *Anglo-Saxon Charters* (Cambridge, 1939), no. 4 and pp. 264–5.

means 'Osbeorn's estate'. By the time the Domesday commissioners set out in 1086 to document the wealth of England, thousands of such small, prosperous manors had come to take the place of earlier 'multiple estates', and they were presided over not by some great and distant lord, who came to the neighbourhood only at tribute time, but by country gentlemen whose whole prosperity was bound up in 5, 10 or 20 hides of land. These more modest landholders were obliged to manage their resources directly and carefully if they wished to live like lords. They were also more rooted on their lands than earlier great men, since the majority resided year-round within single neighbourhoods.[19]

So, the difficult question arises: how exactly did this evolution from large territories to smaller estates actually transpire? Clearly, the move from hundreds of large, loose-jointed territories to thousands of smaller, more compact estates required the revamping of much of the countryside; and, indeed, towards the end of these transformations in the later twelfth century, large parts of England – in a central zone running from the coasts of Dorset and Hampshire all the way north through the Midlands and into Yorkshire, Durham and Northumberland – had relatively large, nucleated villages made up of somewhere between a dozen and five dozen households, and which were populated, by and large, by semi-dependent peasants, who ploughed communally and who each held somewhere between 15 and 30 acres of land scattered throughout the fields surrounding each village, and who owed considerable labour services and rents to their lords. And now these lords more often than not resided in dignified houses in the same villages as their peasants, and they controlled the lion's share of the communally ploughed fields.[20] Still, even at the end of the twelfth century this landscape was far from universal, and hamlets and isolated farmhouses persisted, alongside small fields and pastureland, even in regions where big villages and their open fields had come to predominate.[21] And in regions in England lying outside the central 'champion' zone, dispersed settlements remained common, although in some places, like southwest England, the particular configurations of these dispersed settlements, rather than preserving a very ancient landscape, were, themselves, the result of major remakings, which seem to

[19] C. Senecal, 'Keeping up with the Godwinesons: in pursuit of aristocratic status in late Anglo-Saxon England', *ANS* 23 (2000 (2001)), 251–66, at 254–6.

[20] C. Dyer, *Making a Living in the Middle Ages: The People of Britain, 850–1520* (London and New Haven, 2002), pp. 21–39.

[21] For some examples, see M. Costen, 'Settlement in Wessex in the tenth century', in M. Aston and C. Lewis, eds., *The Medieval Landscape of Wessex* (Oxford, 1994), pp. 97–114, at 98–100.

have taken place a bit earlier than the period when nucleated villages were being established elsewhere in England.[22]

One of the places we can see the remaking of the landscape is at Shapwick, in Somerset.[23] People living in the neighbourhood around present-day Shapwick had long been part of some larger territory, but sometime, probably in the tenth century, their scatter of small hamlets and farmsteads gave way to a single, more populous village built on the site of modern-day Shapwick. During this transformation traditional settlement sites surrounding the present-day village, along with their fields, were reorganized: hamlets and farmsteads were abandoned, and two new common fields were laid out atop the old settlement sites and their fields. We can locate the deserted farmsteads and hamlets in Shapwick's hinterland through scatters of pottery and sometimes because the old settlement names survive as the names of particular strips within the new common fields. As the landscape around Shapwick was remade, farmers whose old homes lay under the new fields apparently moved to a single village – Shapwick. This settlement was not only new, but planned. The village comprised sixteen unequal plots which a lord or his reeve had laid out between two parallel roads. Each plot was designated for one of the displaced families, the larger ones probably for higher-status peasant households, the smaller one for low-status workers, perhaps even slaves, all of whom we know eventually resettled in the village, because all the plots in Shapwick were occupied by the late Anglo-Saxon period.

Although we can see the results of the laying out of a new, planned village and common fields at Shapwick, it is harder to determine what work, exactly, went into making places like Shapwick economically and agriculturally viable. Fortunately we can discern some of the steps behind reorganizations like this by carefully considering the excavations at Yarnton, in Oxfordshire.[24] Sometime in the late eighth century, so the archaeology tells us, the people living around present-day Yarnton came to farm more intensively than had their ancestors. We know, for example, from the remains of insects found in land running along the River Thames controlled by the people of Yarnton, that over the course of

[22] S. Rippon, R. M. Fyfe and A. G. Brown, 'Beyond villages and open fields: the origins and development of a historic landscape characterised by dispersed settlement in south-west England', *Medieval Archaeology*, 50 (2006), 31–51.

[23] C. Gerrard and M. Aston, *The Shapwick Project, Somerset: A Rural Landscape Explored* (Society for Medieval Archaeology, 25; Leeds, 2007).

[24] For this and everything about Yarnton that follows, see G. Hey, *Yarnton: Saxon and Medieval Settlement and Landscape* (Thames Valley Landscapes Monograph, 20; Oxford, 2004).

this period fewer dung beetles – creatures who live on the manure of cattle and horses – resided there than in past centuries, and that this bottom land now supported the kinds of creatures found in meadow habitats. This tells us that the people of Yarnton during this period had undertaken the hard work of transforming a piece of the Thames floodplain from pastureland into hay meadow. This was no simple task, because it required them to rethink how they were going to feed their livestock, since now, probably from February until early June (when they could finally mow their hay), livestock could no longer graze along the banks of the river. Fencing was critical for this move, something emphasized in an early law code which mandated that:

> If ceorls have a common meadow or other shared land to fence and some have fenced their portion and some have not [and the cattle get in] and eat up their common crops or their grass, then those who are responsible for the opening shall go and pay compensation for the damage which has been done to the others.[25]

All of this rethinking and fencing, however, were apparently worth the trouble, since the new hay meadow would have produced dramatically more fodder than the previous agricultural regimen, and it would have allowed Yarnton's farmers to over-winter larger numbers of cattle each year. Indeed, we know that their herds were growing, because they increased the size of their livestock enclosures around this time.

More cattle meant more traction for ploughing and carting and more manure for fertilizing fields; and at some point these new resources enabled the people of Yarnton to extend their arable dramatically. The remains of seeds excavated from within the settlement of Yarnton (doubtless brought there with cereal crops at harvest time) tell us that the kinds of weeds thriving in the land around Yarnton changed with this transformation: now plough-tolerant weeds survived while their more delicate cousins did not, and the seeds of clay-loving plants were present in the settlement for the first time. These things combined suggest that farmers had come to extend their cereal fields into the heavy claylands nearby, soils that had not been tilled in this district since the fall of Rome.

The ploughs people employed to cultivate these clays were probably 'heavy ploughs' with mouldboards and asymmetrical coulters, since the simple breaking-ploughs of the early Middle Ages were not up to the job of cutting through heavy clay, mixing in manure with the soil and

[25] *Laws of Ine*, 42, translated in *EHD*, i, no. 32 pp. 398–407.

creating the deep furrows necessary for the successful cultivation of these fertile, but waterlogged, soils.[26] But these ploughs were transformative even in lighter soils, because they turned the soil over completely and thus kept weeds from choking cultivated fields. This kind of plough is probably described in Riddle 21 in the *Exeter Book*:

> I keep my snout to the ground; I burrow
> deep into the earth, and churn it as I go,
> guided by the grey foe of the forest
> and by my lord, my stooping owner
> who steps behind me; he drives me
> over the field, supports and pushes me,
> broadcasts in my wake. Brought from the wood,
> borne on a wagon, then skilfully bound,
> I travel onward; I gave many scars.
> There's green on one flank wherever I go,
> on the other my tracks – black, unmistakable.
> A sharp weapon, rammed through my spine,
> hands beneath me; another, on my head,
> firm and pointing forward, falls on one side
> so I can tear the earth with my teeth
> if my lord, behind me, serves me rightly.[27]

Both the larger fields and the clayland soils required more livestock for ploughing, hauling and manuring, and these extra animals needed to be fed. Unfortunately, the extension of arable often meant less pasture, and, therefore, less land for grazing. One way out of this bind was to raise hay, which brings us back to Yarnton's hay meadow. But new crop-rotation practices, too, were critical in solving this dilemma. With a two- or three-field system of crop rotation, plough animals could graze on the year's fallow fields, as well as on the stubble left in productive fields after the season's harvesting.

The large plough teams when yoked and ploughing often measured as much as 12 metres in length, and they were very hard to turn. Thus, men who intended to plough with large plough teams often laid out their new fields in very long strips, so that ploughmen and their yoked oxen would not have to turn more than once or twice a day. One extraordinary – and early – example of very long ploughlands is found in a series of strips, apparently laid out from scratch, in the Bourne Valley

[26] For all that follows on heavy ploughs and clay soils, see T. Williamson, *Shaping Medieval Landscapes: Settlement, Society, Environment* (Macclesfield, 2003), pp. 91–122.

[27] K. Crossley-Holland, *The Anglo-Saxon World: An Anthology* (Oxford, 1999), p. 240.

in Cambridgeshire. Here, at least seven narrow fields, each of which extended some 8 km, were apparently laid out at the behest of the lord of one of those great 'multiple estates' *before* it had begun to fragment; and traces of other 'long furlongs' have been found elsewhere in England. But these plough strips, designed to meet the needs of large plough teams, were laid out yet again, as new small estates came, in many places, to take the place of older territories. Indeed, sometime in the late Anglo-Saxon or early Anglo-Norman period, when the ancient territory encompassing the Bourne Valley was broken up into at least four smaller manors, the very long strips there were dramatically curtailed as the fields around each new manor were replanned, and as each new estate was given its own, discrete field system.[28]

What lead the people of Yarnton to institute the changes they did? It is possible that the great man to whom the people of Yarnton had traditionally given over their tribute transferred them to the monks living not far from Yarnton at the monastery of Eynsham. If so, Yarnton's farmers would have now needed to produce for an elite household permanently settled a few kilometres away, rather than for a secular lord who only occasionally resided in the neighbourhood.[29] If this were, indeed, the case, it may have meant that Yarnton's new master interfered more often in its people's lives, even insisting that they give over specialized renders or larger tributes. This scenario could explain why the people at Yarnton were producing more grain during this period, as evidenced not only by the new fields they were laying out, but by their building a new granary. It may also account for why they had apparently begun to raise more ducks, geese and chickens, as witnessed by their new fowlhouse. Then again, it may have been the people of Yarnton, themselves, who were behind these moves, since the dating of our evidence suggests that these changes were taking place before the period when 'multiple estates' were breaking apart in and around Yarnton; so the innovations we have witnessed there might have been undertaken by farmers rather than lords.

Whoever, in the end, should be credited with changes like the ones found at Yarnton, it is clear that as the countryside was remade, so, too, were agricultural practices. For one thing, people living in these transforming landscapes seem to have been producing more than their progenitors, and there is clear evidence, as well, for growing crop diversity.

[28] S. Oosthuizen, 'New light on the origins of open-field farming', *Medieval Archaeology*, 49 (2005), 165–93.

[29] Hey, *Yarnton*, p. 90.

This was certainly the case at Yarnton. By the early tenth century farmers there were growing more free-threshing wheat (for human consumption) and more oats (for both humans and for animal fodder) than their ancestors had, and it appears that they were putting more of their time and energy into arable farming. But they were also growing a more diverse set of crops, cultivating, for the first time, flax and hemp for fibre. They were also managing a series of ponds in novel ways, using them for flax and hemp retting and for watering their increasing number of livestock. They were now cultivating grapes and plums as well, so it is possible that they were managing vines and orchards, agricultural practices that had disappeared with Rome's fall.

The plant and pollen remains recovered from another Anglo-Saxon site, Market Lavington, in Wiltshire, also reveal a noticeable increase in cereal-plant pollens during the later period, which suggests, in turn, the increasing intensification of arable agriculture, as well as a growing diversification in the types of crops grown.[30] Evidence gathered at Market Lavington also argues that heathland vegetation was retreating in the face of the extension of arable farming and the institution of hay meadows; and the remains of weeds found there suggest that cultivation was now taking place on a variety of soils – not just local greensand, but on heavy clay, calcareous and dry soils. Although this intensification and diversification seem to have begun as early as the later seventh century, the pace of both increased dramatically around AD 900. Indeed, from the early tenth century on it looks as if the people of Market Lavington were cultivating a host of new crops, including rye, hemp, flax, opium poppies and grapes. As at Yarnton, however, we cannot say who was directing this activity. Was it some great lord interested in maximizing his income or one of his tenants who wished to live well off his lands, or were the first steps taken, instead, by farmers, who understood that more oxen, more manure and more fodder could transform their lives?[31]

The changes we can witness at Yarnton and Market Lavington of fields and crops had a dramatic impact, in some regions of England, on settlement sites as well. In order for the new ploughs to cut through clay soils they not only needed a skilled ploughman, as the Exeter plough riddle makes clear, but they had to be pulled by large teams of oxen, often comprising as many as eight animals. This, in turn, left many households with

[30] P. Williams and R. Newman, *Market Lavington, Wiltshire: An Anglo-Saxon Cemetery and Settlement* (Wessex Archaeology Report, 19; Salisbury, 2006), pp. 118–49.

[31] S. Rippon, *Beyond the Medieval Village: The Diversification of Landscape Character in Southern Britain* (Oxford, 2008), pp. 61–105.

the wherewithal to keep and feed no more than an ox or two but who harboured the desire to extend their fields into local claylands to club together and plough with their neighbours. Co-operative ploughers must have found it easier to harness these large, multiply owned teams when everyone supplying animals lived in close proximity, and this may have pulled people during this period away from small hamlets and isolated farmsteads and into larger village communities. But the clay soils themselves may have also drawn farmers into villages. This is because many clays are unworkably sticky when wet. Spring ploughing is especially difficult, and there is often less than a week's worth of days when such soils can be ploughed. Because of this, farmers were better off living next to the people whose oxen helped make up their teams, because this allowed them to maximize the precious hours when they could plough.[32]

Another pull towards village living came from hay meadows. Farmers who had clubbed together to created large hay meadows needed to mobilize substantial numbers of people in short order when it was time to cut the hay, because haying, like spring ploughing, is not just labour intensive, but it can take place each year on only a few perfect June days.[33] Thus, large plough teams, clay soils and the extension of hay meadows pulled many people away from scattered hamlets and farmsteads and drew them into larger villages which sat at the centre of their new, commonly ploughed fields.

Other forces behind the move from hamlet to village can probably better be described as push rather than pull factors. As thegns settled on their 5- or 10-hide estates, many laid out planned villages like the one we have seen at Shapwick, and they herded low-status labourers and slaves onto small plots of land within them. Both the enslaved and the barely free would have had little choice but to live where their lords demanded. Lords may have also sometimes provided the resources needed to lay out and exploit new fields: if so, they would have been able to extract concessions from free, but resource-strapped farmers. Because landlords probably appreciated that it was easier to control the labour of people who lived within view of their own halls, one of the concessions they might have demanded was residency within their villages.

Thegns and other lords may have also enticed the families of more well-to-do farmers to settle in new villages by providing amenities there which most farmers could not afford on their own. Thousands of lords,

[32] Williamson, *Shaping Medieval Landscapes*, pp. 91–122.
[33] Williamson, *Shaping Medieval Landscapes*, pp. 173–7.

for example, in the tenth, eleventh and twelfth centuries oversaw the building of mills, and these must have acted as powerful magnets for peasant resettlement. They allowed the processing of grain, everyone's staple, to move from hands and households to machines and specialists, and they freed scarce female labour for other tasks.[34] Lords in these centuries also founded churches near their own halls, and, increasingly, these churches not only had priests who delivered pastoral care to local families, but they had cemeteries. These things, too, may have encouraged families to leave their ancestral farmsteads. Indeed, village communities with churches and mills were being founded not just in England, but across northwestern Europe during this period, in part, one suspects, because lords and farmers alike had come to feel that village life was proper life. Indeed, one eleventh-century tract on estate management details the way good lords provided people living in their villages and working on their estates with a harvest feast after corn reaping and a drinking feast after ploughing, celebrations that would come to feel natural, even traditional, soon after families had settled into village life.[35] So, the twin phenomena of nucleation and resettlement were very widespread, and they were likely to have been driven by some combination of lordly intervention, changing agricultural practices and the shifting social preferences of rural workers.

At Yarnton and Market Lavington we are confronted with a chronology which suggests that agricultural intensification and crop diversification began taking root before great territories were broken apart, but that they quickened in the later Anglo-Saxon period, probably encouraged by the proprietors of new, small-scale estates. Nonetheless, since intensification and specialization began before the breakdown of great estates, other forces besides the breaking apart of 'multiple estates' must have stood, at least at the beginning, behind these developments. One such force was probably the new opportunities available for those with goods to trade. Once, however, the advantages of such local reorganization became clear, lords may have systematically co-opted these changes. In the tenth century, for example, the monks of Glastonbury appear to have reorganized the landscape significantly across parts of Somerset, and we can see them creating new, planned, nucleated villages and laying out new field systems on many of their estates. Elsewhere in the

[34] R. Fleming, 'Bones for historians: putting the body back in biography', in D. Bates, J. Crick and S. Hamilton, eds., *Writing Medieval Biography: Essays in Honour of Frank Barlow* (Woodbridge, 2006), pp. 29–48, at 35–8.

[35] *Rectitudines singularum personarum*, translated in *EHD*, ii, no. 172, pp. 812–16, at 816.

county, it looks as if their thegnly tenants were behind the reorganization of settlements and fields.[36] So, strategies adopted quite independently by local farming communities in the eighth century may well have become by and large the preserve of the well-to-do by the tenth, eleventh and twelfth centuries.

Landlords during these centuries, however, were not always successful in settling their workers into planned villages. At West Cotton, in Northamptonshire, for example, an ambitious proprietor laid out a new village sometime in the tenth century. In it he built a dignified compound for himself and his family alongside a mill; he also laid out a series of more or less equal plots separated by earthworks on which local workers were to settle. Apparently, however, fewer farmers could be persuaded to move to the thegn's village than he had hoped, because a number of these plots remained unoccupied.[37] Indeed, in some regions, like the area around Whittlewood, although nucleation did eventually take place, villages in the region show little sign of planning, and look, rather, to have grown up haphazardly around older settlement sites; so, there is little to suggest that farmers here were driven into planned villages by lords-on-the-make.[38]

Still, however the transformations just described transpired, many farmers – whose ancestors had once lived in small hamlets or isolated farmsteads at some distance from a tribute centre, and who had provided only limited labour services and agricultural renders to their lords – now, more often than not, drifted downwards both socially and economically. In the tenth, eleventh and twelfth centuries many, for example, came to live beside bonded tenants. In the meantime reeves, so texts describing estate management tell us, were working hard to subject higher-status workers to similar kinds of onerous labour services as those shouldered by lower-status families.[39]

Rights to an increasing share of many farmers' labour was critical for the well-being of England's emerging country gentlemen, and many

36 Aston, *The Shapwick Project*, p. 979; Rippon, *Beyond the Medieval Village*, pp. 93–5.

37 S. Parry, *Raunds Area Survey: An Archaeological Study of the Landscape of Raunds, Northamptonshire 1984–94* (Oxford, 2006), pp. 172–7.

38 R. Jones and M. Page, *Medieval Villages in an English Landscape: Beginnings and Ends* (Macclesfield, 2006), pp. 99, 104.

39 These settlements in the first generations, however, were more dispersed and less densely settled, and frontages running along each village's road were less built-up than they would be several centuries later. So, the nucleation so evident in late medieval England was often the result of long, drawn-out processes, rather than a single episode of resettlement. M. F. Gardiner, 'Late Saxon settlement', in H. Hamerow, S. Crawford and D. Hinton, eds., *A Handbook of Anglo-Saxon Archaeology* (Oxford University Press, in press).

lords moved aggressively, from the tenth century on, to increase their grip on rural workers. In one eleventh-century tract on estate management, for example, we are told that the *gebur*, one of the lord's free demesne labourers, and a person now likely to have been housed with his family on a small plot in a village in the shadow of his lord's own residence,

must perform week-work for two days each week of the year … and for three days from the feast of the Purification to Easter … And from when the ploughing is first done until Martinmas, he must plough one acre each week [for his lord], and he, himself, must present the seed to the lord's barn … When death befalls him, let the lord take charge of whatever he leaves.[40]

And in Ælfric's *Colloquy* the ploughman, when describing his work, laments:

I work very hard. I go out at daybreak driving the oxen to the field, and yoke them to the plough. Because I fear my lord, there is no winter so severe that I dare hide at home. Each day I must yoke the oxen and fasten the ploughshare to the plough. Then I must plough a full acre or more every day … I have a lad driving the oxen with a goad, who is now hoarse because of the cold and from shouting.[41]

The inescapable thrust of the two surviving eleventh-century texts which speak of estate management – *Gerefa* and *Rectitudines singularum personarum* – is that reeves should extract heavy labour services from their lords' agricultural workers.

Stories preserved in a number of eleventh-century saints' lives describe, in interesting ways, the social gulf that now lay between local landowners and their peasants, and they detail the intensity with which landholders pursued both profit and leisure. The *Life of St Kenelm* preserves the following story:

At that time the priest in Pailton, as was the custom, directed that the feast of St Kenelm should be celebrated by a break from work. When the lady [*matrona*] who presided over that village heard this, as she reclined at dinner on that very feast-day, she refuted it with arrogant pride, hurled impatient words at the saint, and commanded with haughty contempt that no work should be interrupted, 'Just because of Kenelm', she said, 'I don't know why we should lose a day's profit'.[42]

40 *Rectitudines singularum personarum*, translated in *EHD*, ii, no. 172, pp. 812–16.

41 *Ælfric's Colloquy*, in M. Swanton, ed. and trans., *Anglo-Saxon Prose* (London, 1993), p. 169.

42 *Vita Kenelmi*, in Rosalind C. Love, ed. and trans., *Three Eleventh-Century Anglo-Latin Saints' Lives* (OMT; Oxford, 1996), § 20.

In yet another of the *Life*'s stories, we hear of a notorious local man, well known for collecting usurious rents.[43] In another *vita*, this one of the eleventh-century bishop St Wulfstan, we read of a thegn who passed his summer days, not sweating in the fields alongside his peasants, but, rather, relaxing in the shade of a nut tree next to his church (doubtless built near his hall), where he sat 'dicing or feasting, or indulging in some other kind of jollification'.[44] Chess or *hnefatafl* pieces, fancy horse gear, small bells (which probably hung from the collars of hunting dogs) and the bones of a stunning of array of birds – the sad remains of the victims of goshawk-loving gentlemen – have all been excavated from high-status sites of the period.[45] These things testify to spare cash and spare time and to a carefully cultivated leisure.

There are also indications that high-status sites were developing into increasingly elaborate compounds during this period. By the early eleventh century we have a clear articulation, in *Geþyncðo*, a text ascribed to Archbishop Wulfstan of York, of the kinds of structures such establishments should include – not only 5 hides of land to support them, but a kitchen, a church, a bell-cote and a gated enclosure around the manorial site.[46] Such suites of buildings were not only common, but apparently expected. According to William of Malmesbury, one of the signs of St Wulfstan's sanctity was that, unlike other landholders, 'though he was, as I have said, skilled and energetic in the fitting out of God's churches, Wulfstan could seem almost lethargic and negligent in secular matters. He never built halls or banqueting rooms in his vills.'[47] The kinds of buildings that made up such compounds can be inferred from yet another eleventh-century text, *Gerefa*. *Gerefa* includes several long lists of implements that a reeve would need to run his lord's establishment. The tools in the text, as Mark Gardiner has pointed out, are organized by the buildings in which they were stored. Thus, *Gerefa* first details those tools kept in the kitchen, then the dairy, then the granary, the buttery, the pantry, the cattle barn and finally the bake- and brewhouse. Therefore, we

43 *Vita Kenelmi*, § 19.

44 *Vita Wulfstani*, II.17, in M. Winterbottom and R. M. Thomson, eds. and trans., *William of Malmesbury. Saints' Lives* (OMT; Oxford, 2002), pp. 94–7.

45 M. F. Gardiner, 'The origins and persistence of manor houses in England', in M. F. Gardiner and S. Rippon, eds., *Medieval Landscapes* (Macclesfield, 2007), pp. 170–82, at 172; R. Fleming, 'The new wealth, the new rich, and the new political style in late Anglo-Saxon England', *ANS* 23 (2000 (2001)), 1–22, at 5.

46 *Geþyncðo*, translated in *EHD*, i, no. 51, pp. 468–71.

47 *Vita Wulfstani*, III. 10, in Winterbottom and Thomson, *William of Malmesbury. Saints' Lives*, pp. 122–3.

can begin to see the suite of structures that came to make up a thegnly *setl*, buildings that would become ubiquitous on seigneurial farmsteads by the twelfth century.[48]

Establishments like these, hinted at in our texts, have actually been uncovered by archaeologists in places as far apart as Hampshire, Oxfordshire, Northamptonshire and Lincolnshire, and these excavations allow us to see how these sites developed and were elaborated over time. Archaeologists working at Faccombe Netherton, in Hampshire, for example, uncovered two fairly substantial buildings on the site of the manor court, built sometime between 850 and 925, but these first buildings were not enclosed by a boundary ditch the way later buildings on the site were. Sometime *c.* 940–80 they were replaced with six new structures, and around this time a church was also constructed. The compound was rebuilt yet again sometime in the very late tenth or early eleventh century. At this point the proprietor erected a large manorial hall alongside a private *camera*, doubtless the living quarters of the landholder and his family. A separate kitchen was also built, as well as a latrine. These buildings, along with the church and churchyard and almost an acre of land, were enclosed by a substantial earthen bank and ditch in the early part of the eleventh century, not for the purpose of defence, but rather as a mark of prestige.[49] The combination of a more public hall, where people could be entertained and manorial courts held, and the detached private *camera*, built as living accommodations for the lord's family, have been excavated not only at Faccombe Netherton, but at Goltho, in Lincolnshire, Cheddar, in Somerset, and Furnells, in Northamptonshire; and the 'hall and chamber' survived the Conquest and are witnessed in the excavations of a number of twelfth- and thirteenth-century manorial sites.[50]

Not only were a whole constellation of buildings now expected at manorial *curiae* (court complexes), but when landowners planned such sites, it looks as if they organized their suites of buildings in ways that were deemed particularly dignified. In some places these buildings were situated around central courtyards. Perhaps more commonly, though, thegns

[48] M. F. Gardiner, 'Implements and utensils in *Gerefa*, and the organization of seigneurial farmsteads in the High Middle Ages', *Medieval Archaeology*, 50 (2006), 260–7. The text is translated in Swanton, *Anglo-Saxon Prose*, pp. 25–7.

[49] J. R. Fairbrother, *Faccombe Netherton: Excavations of a Saxon and Medieval Manorial Complex* (2 vols.; British Museum Occasional Papers, 74; London, 1990).

[50] J. Blair, 'Hall and chamber: English domestic planning 1000–1250', in G. Meirion-Jones and M. Jones, eds., *Manorial Domestic Buildings in England and Northern France* (London, 1993), pp. 1–21; M. Audouy and A. Chapman, *Raunds: The Origins and Growth of a Midland Village AD 450–1500* (Oxford, 2009), pp. 54–5.

built them in 'long ranges', that is, as single rows of buildings, a configuration most clearly seen from the excavations of Raunds Furnells, in Northamptonshire.[51] It seems that high-status sites like these were built to impress: their long range of buildings would have presented an impressive façade to people approaching them from afar. Many of these compounds, moreover, had fancy entryways leading through their impressively banked and ditched enclosures, which were, themselves, further enhanced by posts and auxiliary ditches. Some of these sites even had gatehouses. Many sat next to churches as well – all in all, impressive ranges of buildings and enclosures. Some sites, moreover, were laid out so that activities related to farming were kept away from both the family's private quarters and their compound's impressive front entrances, and were channelled, rather, through back entrances into the enclosed area. Other sites, as they were rebuilt and elaborated, saw the removal of latrines and rubbish pits from areas near their entrances, and their relocation to the business sides of these establishments.[52]

Another token of prestige was the proprietary church, an increasingly common component of lordly residences as we move into the eleventh century. The proprietor of Clayton in Sussex, for example, built an impressive stone church near his hall and embellished it with exceptionally fine, Ottonian-inspired frescoes. Its size and decoration were dictated not by the pastoral needs of Clayton's peasant community, but by the pretensions of its lord, and those visiting his *setl* must have been impressed.[53] Or again, the Hampshire thegn, Ælfric, when he built a church at Milford just after the Norman Conquest, stipulated that 'the priest should wait for [him] before beginning the service', should dine with Ælfric, presumably for Sunday lunch, and he was to accompany Ælfric to the hundred court.[54] Thus, a proprietary church was not just a status building, but it provided its lord with a dignified little entourage.

After the Conquest thegnly *setls* often continued to serve as homes to well-to-do landholders, although it is clear that many of the sons and grandsons of William the Conqueror's followers dedicated impressive resources towards the modernization of these sites' domestic quarters. Across the late eleventh and twelfth centuries we find lords replacing the thegnly 'long ranges' which their fathers or grandfathers had 'inherited'

[51] Audouy and Chapman, *Raunds*, pp. 32–4, 54–5.

[52] Gardiner, 'Late Saxon settlement'.

[53] Fleming, 'New wealth', p. 13.

[54] P. H. Hase, 'The mother churches of Hampshire', in J. Blair, ed., *Minsters and Parish Churches: The Local Church in Transition 950–1200* (Oxford, 1988), p. 60.

from their English *antecessores* with timber-and-earth or stone-built castles or with Norman-style two-storey halls, the new status-enhancing domestic buildings of the post-Conquest period. Seigneurial sites, themselves, were often enlarged after the Conquest as well, not only to accommodate larger domestic quarters, but mottes or ring-works – sometimes even moats.[55] And under post-Conquest lords the kinds of landscape interventions which were just starting to become popular in Edward the Confessor's reign – the building of fishponds and fish-stews or the setting up of deer parks, as well as the moving of agricultural workers and functions away from the display-sides of lordly accommodations – accelerated.[56] Indeed, by the later twelfth century, wealthy men were overseeing the laying out of pleasure-gardens and hunting grounds around their great houses and carefully attending to their views.[57]

Attention to labour services also both continued and intensified after the Norman Conquest. Norman lords or their reeves came to develop a variety of estate-management strategies to help increase their holdings' production, and, therefore, their profits. Assarting, getting hold of more demesne plough teams and expanding demesne ploughlands were all happening at breakneck pace in the twelfth century. Lords during this later period worked hard, as well, to increase their rents, and many aggressively managed the labour services owed to them by their peasants.[58]

Although the Norman Conquest did not end the remaking of England's landscape and its people, many of the things we think of as quintessentially medieval – villages, open fields and lordly residences; parks and fishponds; high-living country gentlemen and a hard-working peasantry – came into being in the centuries after AD 800 and were well established, in many places, by 1066. Still, these developments continued to spread and elaborate after the Norman Conquest and into the twelfth century and beyond. Many echo changes found across the Channel in

[55] G. Beresford, *Goltho: The Development of an Early Medieval Manor* c. *850–1150* (English Heritage Archaeological Reports, 4; London, 1987), pp. 23–4.

[56] M. F. Gardiner, 'The origins and persistence of manor houses in England', in Gardiner and Rippon, eds., *Medieval Landscapes*, pp. 170–82, fig. 51; R. Liddiard *Castles in Context: Power, Symbolism and Landscape, 1066–1500* (Macclesfield, 2005), p. 28. Still, even in the twelfth century, timber halls persisted. At Furnells, for example, the late Anglo-Saxon hall was replaced, sometime around the year 1100, with a new and imposing aisled timber hall (Audouy and Chapman, *Raunds*, pp. 40–1).

[57] Liddiard, *Castles in Context*, pp. 97–121.

[58] Faith, *English Peasantry and the Growth of Lordship*, pp. 178–93; Dyer, *Making a Living*, pp. 119–45.

other parts of northwestern Europe, and few in the end can be ascribed to political events or changing dynasties. Instead, the long, slow, quiet revolution described in this chapter was the product of tens of thousands of small steps and individual actions, taken by (to us) nameless farmers, slaves, reeves and lords.

CHAPTER I.2

Water and land

Stephen Rippon

INTRODUCTION

Water, in its various forms, is one of the character-defining features of Britain's landscape. Its coast is heavily indented with estuaries that allow tidal waters to penetrate far inland, and the rivers that flow into these estuaries first cross low-lying floodplains whose permanently high water tables and vulnerability to flooding make them challenging yet ecologically productive environments in which to live. Many of these estuaries, and some stretches of open coastline, are also fringed by low-lying wetlands, mostly derived from the reclamation of what were once intertidal salt marshes, and in total wetlands once covered 8.4 per cent of England.[1] In the prehistoric period these various wetlands formed a mosaic of natural environments including unvegetated intertidal mudflats around the coasts and estuaries that were covered by the sea twice a day, and more elevated areas of mud – known as salt marshes – that had been colonized by salt-tolerant plants and may have been flooded only a few times a month at the higher spring tides. In the more extensive coastal wetlands the deposition of sediment on these marshes meant that they built up to such a height that the sea no longer reached the inland areas, or 'backfens', where freshwater peatlands developed with a range of vegetation including reeds, sedges, alder-carr woodland and sphagnum moss.

In the Roman period, the coastal marshes were extensively settled and exploited for their rich natural resources including the grazing of livestock, producing salt through heating sea water and the cutting of peat. Some wetlands were even protected from tidal inundation through reclamation: the construction of earthen embankments along the coast and major tidal rivers to keep the tides at bay and then digging ditches to drain the newly won land. At the end of the Roman period, however, a

[1] R. van de Noort, *Monuments at Risk in England's Wetlands* (London, 2002).

Figure 1 The reclaimed wetlands of the North Somerset Levels, either sides of the Congresbury Yeo river, near Weston-super-Mare. The sea walls, ditches and drainage gullies cut into the surface of the fields (known locally as 'gripes') reflect the considerable investment that the reclamation of wetland involved, which in this example occurred between the tenth and twelfth centuries. Photograph reproduced by kind permission of Stephen Rippon

failure to maintain these drainage and flood defence systems, alongside a gradually rising sea level, meant that most coastal wetlands were abandoned, reverting to their natural state. After several centuries when the wetlands around England's coast saw less human endeavour, archaeological work in areas such as Fenland shows that they started to be reoccupied around the eighth century, and Domesday Book indicates that most of the higher, coastal marshes had been extensively settled by the eleventh century. As the population continued to rise in the twelfth and thirteenth centuries more and more land was embanked and drained, both in the low-lying backfens and the intertidal marshes to seaward of the first colonizations. It was this medieval reclamation that laid the foundations of today's landscape in these wetland areas.

From the perspective of permanent settlement, the watery nature of these wetlands must have been a problem: too much water, and particularly salty water, makes agriculture difficult, and so great efforts were made to remove it from the landscape. There were, however, other great feats of medieval engineering that reflect how water was an asset both as a source of power and as a means of navigation. Like reclamation, this increasing mastery of nature started over the course of a period that historians have termed the 'long eighth century' (the late seventh to early ninth century), and that archaeologists call the 'Middle Saxon period', and continued through to the twelfth and thirteenth centuries.[2]

THE EXPLOITATION, MODIFICATION AND TRANSFORMATION OF WETLAND LANDSCAPES

It is well known that during the relatively well-documented twelfth and thirteenth centuries extensive areas of wetland were drained, and that 'reclamation and the subsequent protection of hundreds of square kilometres of dyked land had become a fine art, perhaps one of the greatest achievements of medieval technology'.[3] Archaeological research has shown how this process had started in the pre-Conquest period as the wetlands fringing England's coasts and estuaries were first exploited for their rich natural resources, then modified in order to make them more conducive to agricultural production, before finally being completely transformed through reclamation. This increasing intensity with which wetland landscapes were utilized has been described in detail elsewhere, and is supported by more recently published archaeological work in Fenland, Romney Marsh and Somerset. The best-understood sequence, in the Fenlands of Cambridgeshire, Lincolnshire and Norfolk, is likely to have been typical. Settlement in the fifth to seventh centuries was ephemeral and probably seasonal, simply exploiting the rich summer grazing that the high intertidal marshes and freshwater backfens offered. Around the eighth and ninth centuries there is an increase in the number of settlements, a shift in their location from the margins of the freshwater backfens towards the higher coastal marshes and a change in their character, with substantial ditches suggesting an attempt to modify the local environment through controlling flooding. The regular spacing of an arc of settlement in the Norfolk Marshland suggests that settlements may have been established within the context of a planned subdivision of the landscape into a series of estates. That the landscape remained intertidal at this time is shown by

[2] For general discussions of this period see L. Hanson and C. Wickham, *The Long Eighth Century: Production, Distribution and Demand* (Leiden, 2000); S. Rippon, *Beyond the Medieval Village: The Diversification of Landscape Character in Southern Britain* (Oxford, 2008); and S. Rippon, 'Landscape change during the "long eighth century" in southern England', in N. Higham, ed., *The Landscape of Anglo-Saxon England* (Woodbridge, 2010).

[3] C. Dyer, 'Medieval farming and technology: conclusion', in G. Astill and J. Langdon, eds., *Medieval Farming and Technology* (Leiden, 1997), pp. 293–312.

the palaeoenvironmental material (preserved plant and animal remains) and what appears to be evidence for salt production, although a number of salt-tolerant crops were grown such as six-row hulled barley and various legumes. A comparison of the palaeoenvironmental evidence from these 'Middle Saxon' sites with later settlements suggests that the transformation of the landscape occurred in the tenth century, when a high salt marsh that had been modified in order to make it more suitable for agriculture, but which remained intertidal, was changed into a freshwater environment that was protected from tidal inundation through the construction of a substantial sea wall. During the tenth to thirteenth centuries areas that had been protected from tidal inundation were increasingly enclosed and drained, while further land was reclaimed from the intertidal marshes to seaward of the original sea walls.

THE MASTERY OF NATURE: WATER AS A RESOURCE

Reclamation represents one way in which from around the eighth century human communities started to modify their natural environment, in this case to control excess water in the landscape. Water was not, however, always a problem, and its use as a resource in the later medieval period, most notably by monastic orders such as the Cistercians, is well known. Watermills start to appear in the documentary record in the ninth century and become increasingly common in the tenth, although the archaeological record provides significantly earlier evidence. Not surprisingly, the earliest examples are found on the estates of the landowning elite. For the kings, bishops and the emerging aristocracy, wealth was largely based upon holding landed estates, and these were managed through centres such as Kingsbury in Old Windsor (Berkshire), where an eighth-century corn mill with three waterwheels was fed by a leat over 1 km long, 6 m wide and 3.6 m deep. At Tamworth a mid-ninth-century or earlier mill, with a leat some 500 m long, was constructed at a Mercian royal vill. An even earlier horizontal mill, this time powered by tidal water, has recently been recorded at Ebbsfleet in Kent and dendrochronologically dated to 691–2.[4]

From around the eighth century onwards there is also documentary evidence for increased investment in another aspect of water management

[4] G. Astill, 'An archaeological approach to the development of agricultural technologies in medieval England', in G. Astill and J. Langdon, eds., *Medieval Farming and Technology* (Leiden, 1997), pp. 193–223; P. Rahtz and R. Meeson, *An Anglo-Saxon Watermill at Tamworth* (London, 1992), p. 1; B. Buss, 'Ebbsfleet Saxon Mill', *Current Archaeology*, 183 (2002), p. 93.

in the form of fish weirs. The earliest documented example is at Ombersley on the River Severn in Worcestershire, and although there is no physical evidence for fish traps in the Severn before the tenth century, structures of eighth- to ninth-century date have been recorded elsewhere, notably in the estuaries of Essex and Suffolk, and in major rivers such as the Trent and the Thames.[5] The increased intensity with which this food source was being exploited suggests either that a growing population was placing increasing pressure on landed resources, or that dietary tastes were changing. The ability to construct and maintain what were substantial timber structures also illustrates the resources commanded by Middle Saxon estate owners.

Another example of water engineering that started in the pre-Conquest period was the canalization of rivers. The place-name Graveney, first referred to in 812 as *grafon eah*, means 'dug river' or 'ditch stream' and so hints at the construction of a canal, or at least an improvement to an existing watercourse, but otherwise it is only in the eleventh century that there is unequivocal documentary evidence for the construction of canals, such as reference to the 'old Itchen' and 'new river' in a charter of 1012 for South Stoneham in Hampshire. A number of canalized rivers in Fenland may date to the tenth century, including the diverted River Nene that cuts across March island, though the dating is far from clear. In the Somerset Levels a short stretch of wholly artificial canal linking Glastonbury Abbey with the Brue is scientifically dated to around the tenth century, while the far larger task of diverting the Brue past Meare, along 20 km of wholly artificial canal west of Glastonbury, was completed by 1091. The former has been connected with the reform of Glastonbury under Abbot Dunstan (940x46–before 974), also credited with reorganizing some of the Abbey's landed estates, such as Shapwick, through the laying out of villages and open fields. Other water management schemes have been credited to Dunstan's fellow reformer, Æthelwold, abbot of Abingdon (*c.* 954/5-63) and bishop of Winchester (963–84), including

[5] H. P. R. Finberg, *The Early Charters of the West Midlands* (Leicester, 1961), no. 201; P. M. Losco-Bradley and C. R. Salisbury, 'A Saxon and a Norman fish weir at Colwick, Nottinghamshire', in M. Aston, ed., *Medieval Fish, Fisheries and Fishponds in England* (Oxford, 1988), pp. 329–54; S. Godbold and R. C. Turner, 'Medieval fishtraps in the Severn Estuary', *Medieval Archaeology*, 38 (1994), 19–54; A. Brown, R. Morgan, R. Turner and C. Pearson, 'Fishing structures on the Sudbrook foreshore, Monmouthshire, Severn estuary', *Archaeology in the Severn Estuary*, 18 (2007), 1–17; R. Brunning, 'A millennium of fishing structures in Stert Flats, Bridgwater Bay', *Archaeology in the Severn Estuary*, 18 (2007), 67–83; N. Cohen, 'Boundaries and settlement: the role of the river Thames', *Anglo-Saxon Studies in Archaeology and History*, 12 (2003), 9–20; R. L. Hall and C. P. Clarke, 'A Saxon inter-tidal timber fish weir at Collins Creek in the Blackwater Estuary', *Essex Archaeology and History*, 31 (2000), 125–46.

the construction of a mill leat and sewerage system at Abingdon and the diversion of the River Itchen through Winchester.[6]

PERCEPTIONS OF WETLAND BEFORE AND AFTER RECLAMATION

So far we have seen how wetland landscapes in the ninth to twelfth centuries were places of remarkable change and innovation, but how were these places perceived at the time? It is clear that extensive wetland areas were recognized as having a distinctive identity. Romney Marsh in Kent, for example, was referred to as 'the region called *Merscware*' in 774, and in 796 the Anglo-Saxon Chronicle records that King Ceolwulf of Mercia ravaged the kingdom of Kent and reached 'as far as the Marsh'; in 838, it is recorded that 'this year the alderman Herebryth was slain by the heathens [Vikings], and many men with him, amongst them Marshlanders'.[7]

In the early part of the early medieval period, before reclamation started to transform coastal wetlands, it is clear that these unusual environments were perceived in very different ways. Our surviving historical writings generally stress how wetlands were wilderness areas that were to be feared, being inhabited by demons and the like. This remoteness was, however, seen as a positive virtue by early monks, who sought out such inaccessible locations, and we must also remember that all our early written accounts were written from such a Christian perspective and as such they emphasize the symbolic parallels with deserts. In practice, however, we know that wetlands are rich in natural resources, and the recent archaeological work on sites in the Lincolnshire fens shows that local communities were extensively exploiting these environments.

Following reclamation, the perception of wetlands generally changed for the better. In the mid-twelfth century, Hugh Candidus wrote of the landscape around Peterborough that the marsh was mostly uninhabited, although the higher ground was valuable for its hay and thatch; around the same time William of Malmesbury noted that the marshes around Thorney supported rich grassland. In the mid-thirteenth century Matthew Paris contrasted the dismal fens within which Guthlac lived

[6] E. Ekwall, *The Concise Oxford Dictionary of English Place-Names* (4th edn; Oxford, 1960), p. 230; Sawyer, *Anglo-Saxon Charters*, no. 1012; chapters by C. K. Currie, J. Bond, S. Rippon and C. and N. Hollinrake in J. Blair, ed., *Waterways and Canal Building in Medieval England* (Oxford, 2007).

[7] Sawyer, *Anglo-Saxon Charters*, no. 111; M. Swanton, ed. and trans. *The Anglo-Saxon Chronicle* (London, 1996), pp. 57, 62.

with 'marvellous things' that had happened as they were transformed from an area of 'sedge, deep mud, and marshy beds of rushes, inhabited only by birds, not to mention evil spirits' into 'charming meadows, and even into arable land'.[8] The twelfth-century *Libellus Æthelwoldi* contains a panegyric to 'Dunham' or 'Little Downham', an island in the fens near Ely, that extols the virtues of reclamation in bringing about 'a delightful place, rich, fertile, glad, where ploughland freely gives fertility enough', while the twelfth-century *Liber Eliensis* similarly describes the area around Ely as fertile, fruitful and pleasant.[9] The 'Ramsey Chronicle' of *c.* 1200 also describes how that island was reclaimed from wilderness: 'before it was inhabited it was full of all sorts of trees. But now, after a long period of time, the woods are mostly gone. The land is fit for the plough with its rich, fertile earth; it is pleasant with fruits and crops.'[10]

Reclamation can be seen in very functional terms as a high-cost, high-risk but high-return strategy towards managing the landscape: high-cost in terms of the initial capital outlay on drainage and flood-defence works, and the recurrent cost of their annual maintenance; high-risk in terms of the constant threat of flooding; but high-return in terms of the increased agricultural production that is brought about. Reclamation could also be of great symbolic significance, playing a powerful allegorical role in monastic life, and becoming 'a metaphor for spiritual labour and refinement'.[11] In this view of landscape, reclamation – and the notion of a virtuous ploughman – is seen as a metaphor for improving souls. This may have been in the minds of Glastonbury's monks and their chroniclers, but it was not they who actually reclaimed the Somerset Levels; it was the local communities out on the marshland manors who undertook these great feats of engineering, and their daily concerns are more likely to have been those of subsistence and paying the rent. This is a more functional view that sees reclamation as increasing agricultural production and therefore income, and arable on the abbey's reclaimed marshland manors was more productive than on their

[8] M. Gardiner, 'The wider context', in L. Barber and G. Priestley-Bell, *Medieval Adaptation, Settlement and Economy of a Coastal Wetland* (Oxford, 2008), pp. 299–300; M. Gardiner, 'The transformation of marshlands in Anglo-Norman England', *ANS* 29, (2006 (2007)), p. 35.

[9] E. O. Blake, ed., *Liber Eliensis* (London, 1962), p. 2; C. Clarke, *Literary Landscapes and the Idea of England, 700–1400* (Woodbridge, 2006), pp. 79–82.

[10] W. Dunn Macray, ed., *Chronicon Abbatiae Rameseiensis* (RS; London, 1886); Clarke, *Literary Landscapes*, pp. 83–6.

[11] Clarke, *Literary Landscapes*, pp. 31–3; C. Clarke, 'The allegory of landscape: land reclamation and defence at Glastonbury Abbey', in M. Carr, K. P. Clarke and M. Nievergelt, eds., *On Allegory: Some Medieval Aspects and Approaches from Chaucer to Shakespeare* (Newcastle, 2008), pp. 87–103.

nearby dryland estates.[12] The return on the investment that reclamation represents is seen elsewhere. Unfortunately we do not have detailed surveys for the period covered by this volume, but later records clearly illustrate the value of reclamation. In 1311, for example, the upland parts of Battle Abbey's Barnhorne estate were valued at between 3 and 6 pence per acre, whereas reclaimed marshes on the nearby Pevensey Levels were worth 12 pence per acre; unreclaimed fen was worth 4 pence, rising to 10 pence if drained.[13]

CONCLUSION

Wetlands form an important type of landscape found all around the coasts and estuaries of England. Although extensively settled in the Roman period, most areas experienced widespread flooding in the early medieval period that saw them revert to their natural condition, and it was their reclamation in the medieval period that led to the creation of the landscape of today. Archaeological work has revealed much about the largely undocumented early stages of marshland colonization that started with the simple exploitation of natural resources, then involved modifying what remained an intertidal environment and culminated in its transformation through reclamation. The decision to intensify in the extent to which wetlands were managed in these ways reflects the contemporary perceptions of the costs, risks and benefits of this investment, although in parallel with this economic/functionalist view any landscape could also have symbolic meaning. This is certainly the case with wetlands, which in the early medieval period were perceived as the ideal location for pioneer monks to settle, being an equivalent to the deserts of early Christian history. Reclamation may also have been viewed as an allegory for improvement of the soul. The medieval period, and in particular the 'long eighth century', also saw the increasing mastery of water as a resource, for example its control and use as a source of power for milling and navigation, and its exploitation with increasing intensity as a source of food through fishing. Overall, the centuries either side of the Norman Conquest witnessed important changes in the way that wetlands were exploited – both physically and symbolically – which laid the foundations of the landscape of today.

[12] I. J. E. Keil, 'The estates of the Abbey of Glastonbury in the later Middle Ages' (unpublished PhD thesis, University of Bristol, 1964), Table A.

[13] A. J. F. Dulley, 'The level and port of Pevensey in the Middle Ages', *Sussex Archaeological Collections*, 104 (1966), 26–45.

CHAPTER 1.3

Forest and upland

Oliver Rackham

WOODLAND

Anglo-Saxon England was not a very wooded country. The original prehistoric wildwood had long since gone, and woods had been interacting with people for thousands of years. Only about half of the 13,000 estates recorded in Domesday Book possessed woodland; the area adds up to about 15 per cent of England, much more than there is now, but less than France has now. About one in thirty of the boundary features mentioned in Anglo-Saxon perambulations alludes to a wood: these are located in roughly the same areas where Domesday records woodland. Woodland can also be inferred from place-names, which, however, are difficult to date. Generally place-names indicate that the distribution of wooded and non-wooded areas, as recorded in perambulations and Domesday, was already established well before 900.

England in the period from 900 to 1200 lacked many species of tree familiar today: sycamore, horse-chestnut, most poplars and all conifers except yew and juniper. Beech and sweet-chestnut were much less widespread than now. Plantations (people planting areas of trees) begin after our period. There were, however, trees in hedges and other non-woodland places, as recorded in many boundary perambulations, and also orchards.

Woodland was very unevenly distributed. There were big concentrations in the Weald and the Chiltern plateau, and lesser concentrations in Worcestershire, north Warwickshire and east Cheshire; the southern Lake District, though outside the scope of Domesday Book, had abundant woodland as recorded in place-names. In these areas woodland predominated over non-woodland for 10–20 km at a stretch, although nowhere was altogether without habitation. Some areas, such as the Breckland, around Cambridge, and much of the east Midlands, had almost no woodland. In the rest of the country there were islands of wood in a mainly agricultural landscape. Some counties, such as Leicestershire, had little more woodland in 1086 than there is now, and a few (e.g. Devon) apparently had less.

Most of the large wooded areas of medieval England contain evidence, such as long and round barrows, that they were not all woodland in Roman or prehistoric times: they were not simply residual wildwood, but had a history of advance, retreat and management long before our period.

Woodland was negatively correlated with open-field. In the middle third of England, where open-field agriculture (see Chapter I.1) was to cover most of the landscape, woodland covered only 8 per cent in 1086. In the west, east and southeast of England, areas of predominantly ancient enclosure, woodland covered 19 per cent – even more if moorland is excluded from the reckoning.

The Old English language contains many words for what were presumably different kinds of woodland. Woods had their own individual names.

Virtually all woodland was used. There were two forms of use: coppice-wood and wood-pasture, which Domesday records separately for some counties such as Lincolnshire. Coppice-woods were a permanent self-renewing resource, making use of the capacity that most English trees have for growing again either from the stump (which becomes a *coppice stool*) or from the roots. Most of the trees were felled every few years, yielding *underwood* poles and rods, used for light construction, infill of timber-framed buildings, tools, vehicles, fences, sea-defences and especially domestic and industrial fuel. *Timber trees* would be left standing for several cycles of the underwood to provide beams, planks and table- and drinking-ware. A significant by-product was oak bark for tanning leather. It was important to define the wood boundaries and to exclude grazing animals, which would eat the new shoots.

Coppicing is widely recorded from the thirteenth century onwards: the interval between fellings was typically around seven years. Written evidence from the period from 900 to 1200 is not copious, and no record survives of the felling interval: no annual accounts are known, but charters and Domesday make casual mentions of regular supplies of underwood and timber for particular purposes.

The Anglo-Saxon and Norman way of life required huge quantities of underwood and a permanent supply of timber trees, either small enough to be easily handled or (as Damian Goodburn has shown) of a growth-form which allowed them to be split into boards. Many woodland products, such as fences, were not durable and needed frequent replacement. As yet most timber buildings were post-hole structures that did not last: it is significant that very few now survive from before 1200 but many from after. Very large trees would have been used for special purposes such as dugout boats and (after 1200) windmill posts. To supply such trees implies woodland management in every part of the country that had woodland, as well as arrangements for transport and trade to supply places that had none. Many (but not all) woodless places possessed areas of woodland up to 20 miles from the main settlement, for example in Kent or Warwickshire. As far as is known importing of timber from overseas began only *c.* 1200. To what extent there was any survival of Romano-British woodmanship or organization remains to be discovered.

Wood-pasture combined trees and grazing animals. This involves a conflict, with the shade of the trees spoiling the pasture and the animals eating the regrowth of the trees. Often there were trees widely spaced in grassland or heath which provided the pasture, a savanna-type landscape like Richmond Park or Bradgate Park (Leicestershire) today. Underwood would come from pollarding the trees, cutting them at 3–4 m above ground, so that the livestock could not eat the new shoots.

Except in thinly wooded areas wood-pasture at this stage probably covered a greater area than coppice-woods. Most woodland was private or ecclesiastical property (often valuable property), although common-rights of cutting underwood are known. It may be significant that when Ely Abbey became the seat of a bishopric in 1109 and the estates were divided, the new bishop got nearly all the manors that had woodland, leaving the monks with the woodless ones. In contrast, many wood-pastures were common land (for example the present Epping Forest).

A significant use of woodland and wood-pasture was *pannage*, the autumnal feeding of pigs on acorns and beech-mast. This appears frequently in Anglo-Saxon documents. In Domesday woodland in east and southeast England is routinely recorded in terms of swine. However, this practice would always have been undependable (for, then as now, acorns were not produced in significant quantities every year) and was probably already in decline.

Woodland, although it had a value, was a possible site for the expansion of agriculture. As population increased woodland diminished, both in the period from 1086 to 1200 and in the subsequent 150 years. Many Domesday Book woods are not heard of again. Probably there had been a preceding decrease in the late Anglo-Saxon period, although this is difficult to substantiate from surviving records. Woodland disappeared mainly from the more wooded areas, tending to even out the distribution.

As far as I am aware no Anglo-Saxon document records people digging up trees, nor does any charter mention the site of a former wood. Woodland could be destroyed by people investing labour in uprooting trees and making fields, or painlessly, even without being noticed, when animals grazing wood-pasture ate the young shoots and prevented the self-renewal of the trees. The latter happened in the twelfth century as Thorpe Wood, belonging to the bishops of Norwich, turned into Mousehold Heath.

Coppice-woods are among the most durable of medieval antiquities: many hundreds are still extant, despite losses down the centuries and especially in the third quarter of the twentieth century. About 25 per cent of the woods mentioned in Anglo-Saxon perambulations appear to be still recognizable today. Ancient woods are irregularly sinuous or zigzag in outline; they are commonly surrounded (sometimes subdivided) by great banks and ditches, the ditch being on the outside of the bank. These are usually undatable, but many are probably earlier than 1200. Woods now, as in Anglo-Saxon charters, have names of their own, some being Old Norse (such as those ending *–lund*). Ancient woods are characterized also by huge coppice stools, some of which probably date from our period, and by special plants such as wood anemone and herb paris. Examples are the Bradfield Woods near Bury St Edmunds and Hayley Wood west of Cambridge.

Wood-pastures survive much less often. They are different in shape from a wood, having straggling outlines not marked by banks and ditches; they are crossed by roads and have houses scattered round the edge. The ancient trees are pollards, now often embedded in woodland that has grown up around them. Examples are Burnham Beeches (Buckinghamshire) and The Mens (West Sussex). Some wood-pastures became Forests (e.g. Epping Forest, Hatfield Forest (Essex)) and may still retain their straggling outlines and ancient pollard trees. Others turned into parks.

FORESTS AND PARKS

Forest (with a capital 'F') in the Middle Ages meant a place of deer, which might or might not also be a place of trees. Among the novelties introduced from the Continent by William the Conqueror was the idea that the king can designate areas to be Forest, can keep deer on those areas, can kill and eat them, can institute special laws ostensibly for the benefit of the deer and can appoint officials to administer those laws.

The word and the idea are unknown in Anglo-Saxon England. Probably the best account of a royal hunt at any period is the story of how Edmund the Magnificent (Edmund I, 939–46) pursued deer from his palace at Cheddar through the sparse wood-pasture which evidently covered much of the Mendip Hills, and was saved from blundering over the cliffs of Cheddar Gorge only through the miraculous intervention of St Dunstan. However, it was not suggested that he was doing anything other than what any landowner might do.

A Forest was the supreme status symbol, at first reserved to the king. Then earls and other great magnates, including the bishops of Durham, Winchester and Ely, declared their own Forests (followed in Wales and Scotland by relatively minor magnates). Domesday Book mentions twenty-five Forests, including four belonging to the earls of Chester. Successive kings and magnates declared more Forests, until by 1200 there were over 150, about 90 of them royal. King John's further extension of Forests was one of the grievances which led up to Magna Carta (1206).

Forests were located close to where the king had lands or palaces, being especially concentrated in mid-southern England, where kings spent much of their time. The king might or might not own the land: authority to keep deer on other people's land was an important attribute of Norman royalty. They could be on almost any kind of land and were only weakly correlated with woodland. Wooded Forests included Waltham (now Epping Forest) and Hainault in Essex. Forests could be moorland (Dartmoor, Exmoor and many in the Pennines), heathland (most of the New Forest) or fenland (Hatfield Chase, Yorkshire). Usually the legal boundaries of a Forest – within which people could be prosecuted for breaking Forest law – were much more extensive than the actual Forest where the deer lived.

At first the deer were the native red and roe deer. How common they had been in the pre-Forest Anglo-Saxon countryside is unknown. Fallow deer were introduced *c.* 1100 (ultimately from Persia) and rapidly became the commonest species, except on moorland. These deer were easier to keep as semi-domestic animals, especially since Forests were not fenced and had no physical means of retaining the deer.

Forests were not 'reserved to the king for hunting': deer (native or introduced) were added to, and did not displace, whatever was already going on in the Forest. Most Forests were also common land, and had the characteristic shapes of commons, with straggling outlines, criss-crossed by roads and with houses scattered round the edges.

Norman kings indulged in hunting. William I's obituary in the Anglo-Saxon Chronicle notes with distaste his obsession with deer; William II and two of his nephews perished in hunting 'accidents' in the New Forest. However, the emphasis of Forests was soon diverted into other directions. By the twelfth century they contributed largely to the exchequer through fines for breaches of Forest law. By the thirteenth they supplied hundreds of deer – mostly fallow – caught by professional hunters for the king's feasts. Eating venison in public was a status symbol; but presumably there was very extensive poaching, otherwise deer would have proliferated as they have done in the twentieth century. At this date Forests maintained the king's prestige by enabling him to make gifts of deer (live or dead) or timber to favoured subjects, or to appoint them to honorific sinecures in the Forest bureaucracy.

If a Forest was wooded, the trees might belong to the king, or the landowner or the commoners. Wood-producing trees would need to be pollarded, as noted above, to keep the regrowth away from grazing animals, unless the commoners allowed newly fenced areas to be fenced. By the twelfth century wooded Forests were the chief source of especially long trees for great buildings, such as the oaks granted from Sherwood Forest to Lincoln and other cathedrals. By the thirteenth century sales of underwood were a useful addition to the royal exchequer.

Wooded Forests constitute one of the three branches of medieval wood-pasture, as we have noted earlier, the others being parks and wooded commons. Parks began at the end of the Anglo-Saxon period. They were private property, enclosed by a deer-proof fence called a *pale*, containing fallow deer (less often red or roe deer or wild swine). There are a few parks in Domesday Book; by the thirteenth century (when the records improve through the introduction of a system of licences to empark) parks ran into the thousands. A park was a lesser status symbol than a Forest. Most parks were, in effect, deer farms, although a few formed the landscape setting for country mansions such as Caerphilly Castle in Wales.

Forests – the few that survive – retain the characteristic shapes of wood-pasture commons. Parks were usually compact in shape, often a rectangle with rounded corners, for economy in making the expensive pale. The remnants of wooded Forests and parks (together with churchyards (see Chapter V.2)) contain most of the ancient trees that survive into modern times. Windsor Great Park inherits some of the great oaks of Windsor Forest; Staverton Park in Suffolk probably has some of the original pollard oaks from its foundation *c.* 1200. The New Forest, established

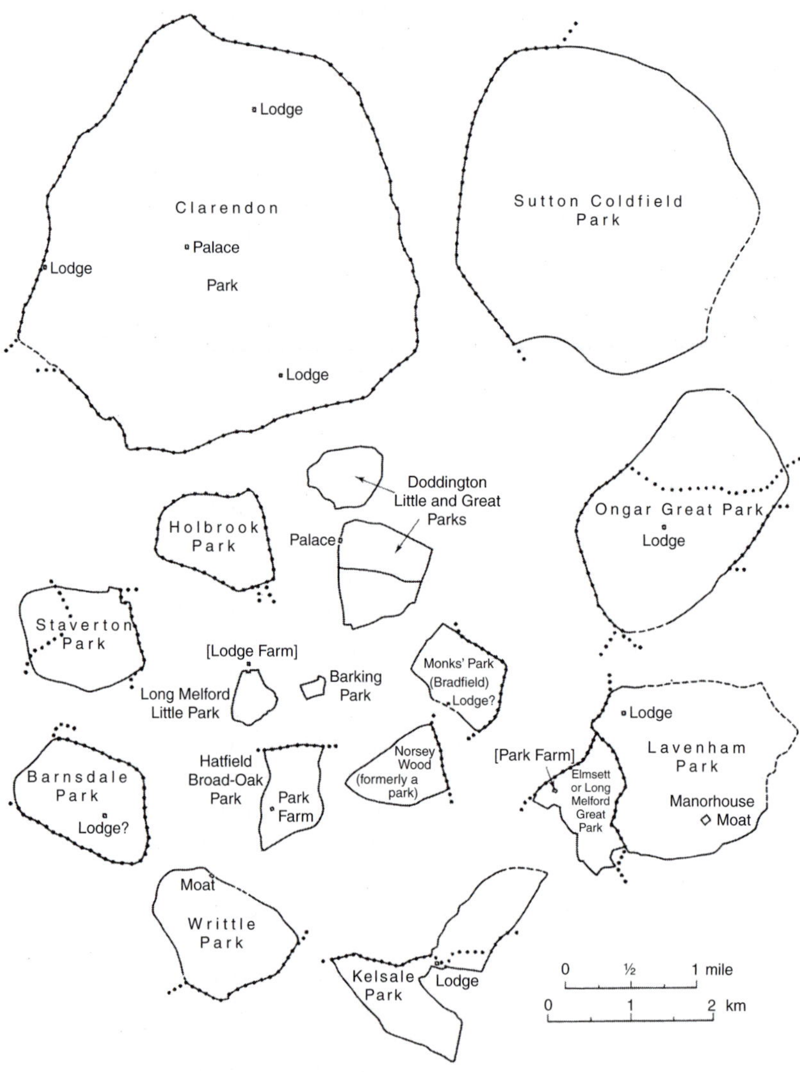

Figure 2 Outlines of some representative medieval parks, with the position of the great house (if any) and of any park lodge. Dotted lines are parish boundaries. Reproduced with the kind permission of Dr Oliver Rackham, from his *Ancient Woodland. Its History, Vegetation and Uses in England*. 2nd edn (Dalbeattie, 2003), p. 194.

by William the Conqueror, is a survival unique in Europe for its huge size and combination of wood-pasture, heath and ancient trees.

UPLAND

A great division in England is between the Highland Zone – Pennines, North Yorkshire Moors, Welsh Border, Devon and Cornwall – and the rest of the country. This goes back far into prehistory. Some features of the pre-Neolithic landscape survived into the Middle Ages and even today, such as the contrast between the predominant oakwoods of the Highland Zone and the woods of ash, lime, hazel and so forth in the Lowland Zone.

The Highland Zone is less well documented: much of it is poorly or not recorded in Domesday Book, and there are few Anglo-Saxon perambulations except in Devon and Cornwall. It seems to have been poorer and less densely populated than most of the Lowland Zone. Settlements mostly took the form of hamlets instead of villages. Parishes could be very large, including several townships, especially in northern England. Celtic languages were spoken in Cornwall (but not Devon) and south-west Herefordshire. Danish and Norwegian place-names are common in northern England, and many of them probably originated in our period, but how late the language may have lingered is not known.

Farming was not as now almost exclusively livestock: most all-year settlements, even in the highest and wettest places, grew crops as well. Agricultural infrastructure was of various kinds. Especially in Cornwall and Devon, there could be small fields with hedges and field-banks and walls. Open-field strip-cultivation (see Chapter I.1) was widely adopted, and its remains are still visible in the form of ridge-and-furrow, but it did not come to dominate the landscape on a huge scale as in the Midlands. Where settlements had access to moorland, a distinction was often drawn between *infield*, cultivated every year, and *outfield*, which was only intermittently tilled. The field-walls that are now so prominent in the Pennines are mainly of a much later date, although some of them replace earlier hedges.

As yet there was relatively little industry, although the building of Norman cathedrals and great abbeys presumably created a big demand for lead and other metals (see Chapter I.4). Abbeys themselves, such as Rievaulx and Furness, were beginning to stimulate iron-smelting. Industrial archaeology is difficult to separate from the much larger-scale works of later periods.

Woodland existed on a similar scale to lowland England: the southern Lake District had more than average, Cornwall and northwest Yorkshire much less than average. The meagre evidence indicates coppicing from at least the eleventh century. Much woodland appears to have been wood-pasture: in the Lake District and Yorkshire Dales small remnants of grassland with ancient pollard alders, ashes and elms still remain. In west Cornwall nearly all the medieval oakwoods still exist, but such a survival rate is unusual.

Moorland, then as now, was a distinguishing feature of the Highland Zone. (In the Middle Ages the word *mor* translated Latin *mons*, 'mountain', but could also be used of any wetland, even lowland fens, hence place-names such as Sedgemoor.) Most moors were covered with blanket peat from 1–10 m thick; peat was then being laid down more actively than it is now. Moorland was not necessarily at high altitudes: in Cornwall it descended almost to sea level.

All moorland was used, if only as common pasture for sheep and cattle. Dartmoor in Domesday Book is the common pasture for all Devon except Bideford and Totnes; later the central part was declared a royal Forest, although not very actively used as such. Peat was dug and used for fuel; in some areas, such as the Lizard Peninsula (Cornwall), virtually all the peat has been scraped off at one time or another. Furze, bracken or heather could also be used as fuel. Bracken was probably less abundant than now; heather was often more abundant, but fluctuatingly so. Many of the lanes and driftways between walls that lead from farms and hamlets through the farmland on to the moor probably existed at this time.

The practice of regularly burning moorland is much later: moorland fires, if they occurred at all in our period, would have been rare and accidental.

Most of the big moorland areas originated in prehistory, but were not always as extensive as now. Thus on most of Dartmoor the original forest had been turned into farmland in the Bronze Age, but this was unsustainable and became moorland. Remains of similar prehistoric farms exist locally in Swaledale. By our period the Bronze Age farms had long been forgotten. Moors (and fenlands) were the last remaining extensive areas of seemingly under-used land where there was room for expansion. There were also small moors, mostly drained and fertilized to extinction in modern times.

According to Domesday Book the vengeance of William the Conqueror depopulated much of Yorkshire in 1069–70, although this is difficult to confirm from archaeology or the pollen record. This may explain why many hamlets and villages in the area appear to have planned layouts of a kind that implies an interruption in settlement and loss of the original layout that would have resulted from gradual growth.

From then on, population pressure and the Medieval Warm Period combined to push cultivation above its present limit (see Chapter I.1). Outfields turned into extensions of the infield, and further outfields encroached on the fringes of moorland. Little farms were set up on islands of slightly better land within the moors. What had been summer pastures, known as *shields* in northern England, turned into permanent settlements. This continued beyond 1200.

In the mid-twelfth century there was a sudden phase of founding Cistercian monasteries. These were established all over England, but the biggest and most successful, from Buckfastleigh in Devon to Rievaulx in northeast Yorkshire, owned moorland as well as farmland and woodland. They set up (or took over) livestock farms in remote places, encroaching on moorland and less often woodland, and have been credited with much of the upward expansion of farmland. Most of this, however, took place after 1200, when the monks continued to acquire more land.

There were a few parks in moorland, presumably for red deer, whose massive boundary banks or walls occasionally survive; some of them may date from before 1200.

About one third of the Forests of medieval England were on moorland: there were thirty-nine such in the north of England. These were the chief source of red deer, which (then as now) was chiefly a moorland beast; they also produced revenue from fines in Forest courts and from licences for working minerals. So, for example, the red deer of Weardale Forest (Yorkshire) were slaughtered in great drives for the bishop of Durham's table. Most of the evidence is from after 1200, and it is not known whether these things were already happening in the twelfth century. Pickering Forest in Yorkshire, however, was one of two or three places in England where not only deer but wild pigs survived into the thirteenth century.

CHAPTER I.4

Mineral resources

Peter Claughton

Britain has long enjoyed a reputation for its mineral wealth. Bede, writing in the early eighth century, noted that it had 'many veins of metals, as copper, iron, lead and silver'. Henry of Huntingdon, in about 1130, added tin to that list but commented that silver was uncommon, being 'received from the neighbouring parts of Germany with which an extensive commerce is carried out by the Rhine'.

Much of the evidence for the demand and production of minerals in the period to 1200 comes from the increased generation and survival of documentary sources, in particular, during the latter part of the period, the records of English government (see Chapter VI.2). The archaeological record is at best fragmentary, and few overviews of any value have yet been published. There is, however, sufficient evidence to indicate that production increased substantially in the three centuries covered by this volume. Although metals had particular social and economic significance, other mineral resources were of equal, if not greater, practical importance. Salt was an essential of life at a period and in a climate which allowed for no other means of preserving food over the winter, ensuring a continuity of production. It was one of the resources considered here, along with limestone and chalk burned for mortar, which were totally consumed without prospect of being reused or recycled. In contrast, the ability to reuse some materials might mean that quarrying or mining was delayed until other sources were exhausted. For most purposes that position had been reached by the turn of the ninth century. The remnants of the Roman infrastructure had been turned to new uses and the existing stock had to be augmented to satisfy growing demand, drawing on skills and techniques which had survived or been re-established following the withdrawal of Roman rule, urban contraction and the subsequent collapse in demand.

By the tenth century building in stone, largely ecclesiastical in the 'Roman' style advocated from the seventh century, was gathering pace.

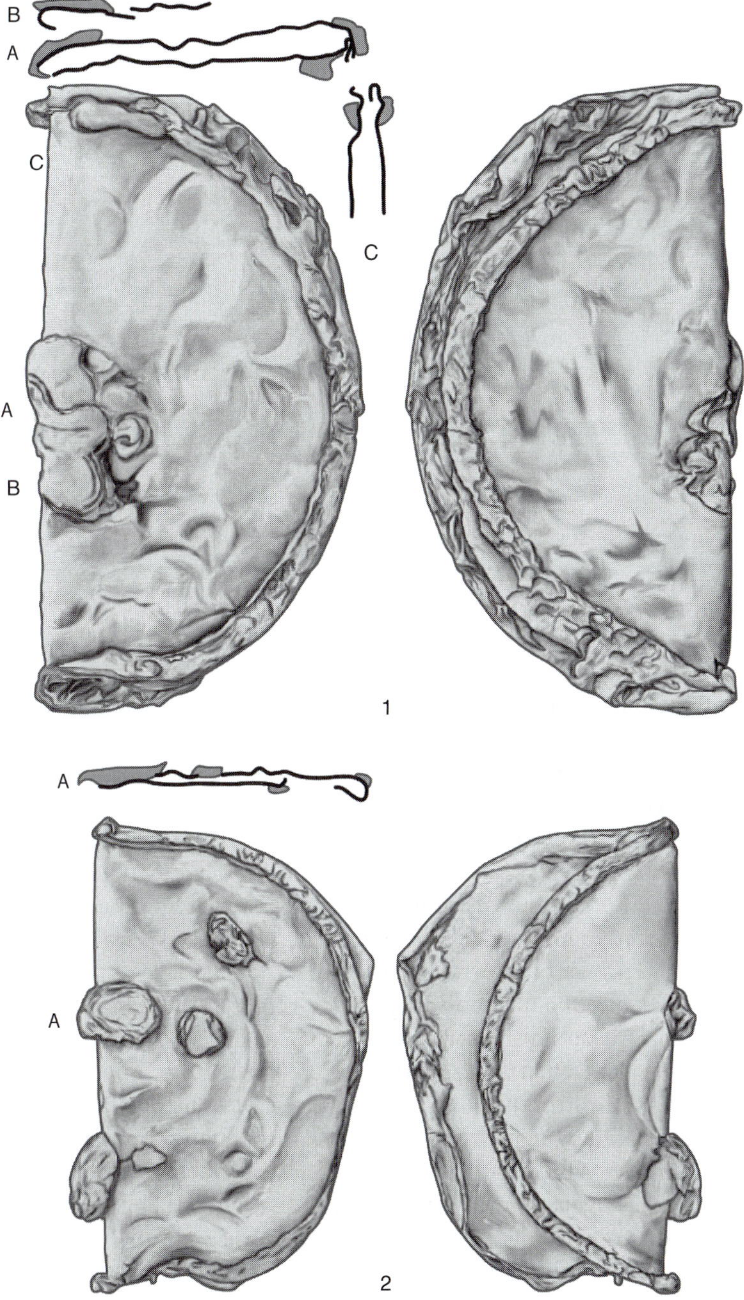

Figure 3 Lead vessel from Bottesford, Lincs. Scunthorpe (Lincs.), typical of those found on Middle to Late Saxon sites in the Trent valley
© Pre-Construct Archaeology (David Hopkins)

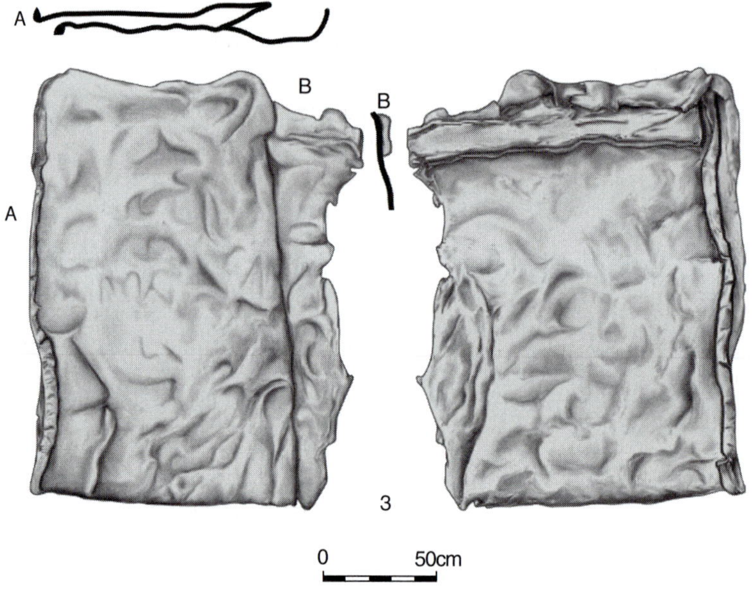

Figure 3 (*cont.*)

Early Christian buildings, such as Wearmouth and Jarrow (Co. Durham), had made use of stone recovered from structures of the Roman period. As the numbers of such buildings increased, many in areas without resources which might be easily robbed, quarrying of stone became a perquisite. Certain strata, for example the Upper Greensands in southeast England, were valued for building purposes whilst others were more specialized, for example the production of millstones. Nevertheless, quality and ease of access meant that stone was often imported from northern France up to the twelfth century.

With the increased use of stone came the requirement to provide a watertight covering over larger roof areas. Where the availability of suitable stone allowed it, that might be achieved using a combination of wood and split stone or slate but for most purposes the preferred material was lead sheet, also used in glazing and plumbing. The quantity of lead which might have survived from the Roman infrastructure is uncertain. Recycled lead, such as that recovered from a ship wrecked off Ploumanac'h on the coast of Brittany, was already being exported from Britain in the late Roman period, so it is unlikely that much remained to be reused in early church building. It would soon have to be supplemented by newly mined lead, and that had certainly begun by the ninth century in areas such as Derbyshire, where Repton Abbey controlled the mines close to Wirksworth.[1]

Tin was increasingly in demand as a component of bell metal, pewter and solders. Some continuity in production after the cessation of Roman occupation is credible, although the archaeological evidence is limited. The southwest peninsula was the only source in Britain, the major source of the metal in Europe and, as such, was to be a significant contributor to English exports from at least the twelfth century. The copper referred to by Bede was probably mined in small amounts but the evidence is scant indeed and no specific sites have been identified. The working of iron was, however, widespread throughout England, and local needs were easily met. For example, six settlements scattered across the western and southern parts of Somerset are recorded in Domesday Book as paying, or having paid, dues in iron blooms – the product of one firing of the bloomery furnace, hammered to extrude the slag and resulting in a more or less homogenous mass of malleable iron (the direct process). Other payments in iron or reference to iron working can be found in at least four other counties. Reference to specific mines is rare prior to the thirteenth century, but iron mines are identified at Lyminge (Kent) in a charter of 689, and at Rhuddlan in northeast Wales, then under English control, in 1086. There were some areas, for example the Weald of Kent and Sussex, where there is evidence for substantial and continued production from the Roman period onwards. The universal use of iron for diverse purposes, albeit generally in a multiplicity of small quantities, and the limits to which it might be recycled, ensured its continued widespread production.

Silver provides us with the best evidence for increased demand. Although there is little evidence of any continuity in the mining of silver-bearing ores up to the late tenth century, its use in coinage from the eighth century provided a stimulus for the exploitation of newly mined resources. By the mid-twelfth century it is estimated that between £30,000 and £50,000 was circulating in silver coin in England, by 1180–2 it was somewhere between £70,000 and £190,000, perhaps rising to £250,000 in 1205. In the tenth century most of the silver originated from continental European sources, drawn into an economy dependent on foreign trade, but some, and by the mid-twelfth century it was probably the greatest part, would have come from sources in England and Wales. Silver was

[1] Sawyer, *Anglo-Saxon Charters*, no. 1624.

refined from lead mined either for constructional purposes or primarily for its silver content, where the lead recovered after refining was a by-product with the malleable properties required for roofing and plumbing purposes.

Salt, on the other hand, was in constant demand and there was, without doubt, continuity in production from the Roman through into the medieval period. All the coastal counties of England had salt-works capturing seawater at exceptional high tides. The resulting salt-rich sands were then washed to extract brine, which was evaporated in pans, using wood or peat as fuel, to recover the salt. In addition to the coastal resources there were two areas of England where salt was obtained from salt-bearing rocks through the action of natural brine springs: in Cheshire, around Northwich, and in Worcestershire, at Droitwich. Unlike coastal salt-works, which were a seasonal operation governed by the tides, inland producers could continue throughout the year and, judged on the revenues itemized in the Domesday survey, were the major source in the eleventh century. Brine springs and evaporation pans at Droitwich were referred to in documents from the seventh to tenth centuries, as were the routes by which the salt was traded to a wide area in the west of England. Upwich, one of the principal springs at Droitwich, has provided archaeological evidence for continued production from at least the Roman through to the late medieval period. The springs were evidently enlarged into sizeable pits, although it was not until much later that deep shafts were sunk to directly exploit the salt-bearing strata. Particular attention is given to salt production in the Domesday survey as a source of taxable income. Many inland manors had rights to salt-works on the coast, as had manors remote from the inland salt-producing areas. Such was the importance of salt to the economy of the period that rights around Droitwich, with five springs supporting over 300 *salinae* or salt-works, included not only manors within the immediate area but some as far afield as south Gloucestershire and Buckinghamshire.

The construction of salt evaporation pans used significant quantities of lead, and they were sometimes referred to as *plumbi*, but we can only speculate as to the source of the metal. The Derbyshire Peak lead field was capable of supplying the inland salt producers by a long river/sea route, but Cheshire was much closer to northeast Wales, a known source of lead for pans later in the medieval period, and Droitwich was not too far north of the Mendip lead field in Somerset. A lead mine at Stoke Bishop on the northern edge of the Mendip field is referred to as a boundary feature in a charter of 883, but there is no evidence that it was working at that date. The

Derbyshire mines were, however, well placed to supply the east coast salt producers by way of the River Trent, and it is from the lower Trent valley and its environs that we have some of the best evidence for the use of lead in that period. Lead, in the form of fragments to complete artefacts, has been found in increasing quantities through time on sites such as Bottesford on the Trent near Scunthorpe (Lincolnshire). Archaeological investigation has revealed its use in large cylindrical vessels, tentatively identified as being used for grain storage. The form of construction suggests the use of malformed lead roofing webs. This, in turn, suggests that there was a trade in lead sheet, transported in rolled form down the Trent from Derbyshire.[2] The widespread impact of Derbyshire by the eleventh century is reflected in the definition of measures by which lead was sold/traded as being 'of the Peak'.[3] It is clear, however, that the Derbyshire Peak was not the only lead field being worked. The upland mining fields in the west and north of Yorkshire, in Wharfedale, Wensleydale and Swaledale, had equally good access to the navigable river system, entering the Humber by way of York and the River Ouse, and York Minster had been roofed with lead as early as 669.[4] Whilst we do not see documentary evidence for mining until the latter part of the twelfth century, there is palaeoenvironmental evidence for working of lead in those fields over the previous three centuries.[5]

As the pace of ecclesiastical building accelerated in the twelfth century, driven by royal patronage both north and south of the border, the demand on mineral resources increased in proportion. During the period 1135–57, in which the Scots controlled the north Pennine mines administered from Carlisle, King David I and his son endowed at least nine abbeys and monasteries, no doubt buoyed by a new-found wealth in silver and the availability of its by-product, lead, for their construction. A similar policy of generous endowment was adopted by Henry II, with gifts of lead from mines in the north Pennines, Shropshire, Derbyshire and Yorkshire being despatched to institutions in England and France as far south as Grandmont (Hte-Vienne).[6] In addition those mines were

[2] J. Cowgill, in K. Steadman, 'Excavation of a Saxon site at Riby Cross Roads', *Archaeological Journal*, 151 (1994), 212–306. I am indebted to Jane Cowgill for access to unpublished material, and discussion on the lead vessels recovered from Flixborough and other sites in the Trent valley.

[3] N. E. S. A. Hamilton, ed., *Inquisitio Comitatus Cantabrigiensis Subjicitur Inquisitio Eliensis* (RS; London, 1876), p. 191.

[4] Eddius Stephanus, *Vita Wilfridi*, 16 (trans. J. F. Webb and D. H. Farmer, in *The Age of Bede* (London, 1988), p. 122).

[5] K. A. Hudson-Edwards, M. G. Macklin, R. Finlayson and D. G. Passmore, 'Medieval lead pollution in the River Ouse at York, England', *Journal of Archaeological Science*, 26 (1999), 809–19.

[6] F. Madeline, 'Le don de plomb dans le patronage monastique d'Henri II Plantagenêt', *Archéologie médiévale*, 39 (2009), 31–52.

also supplying the works of the king at Dover, Windsor and other castles, with at least 2,000 carretas (1,470 tonnes) of lead recorded in the Pipe Rolls as being acquired by the English Crown in the forty years to 1200. By the late twelfth century there is evidence of an increased supply of lead from sources which were relatively low in silver content, such that they did not justify refining. Much of the Derbyshire production was in that category, as was that from Yorkshire from 1180 onwards, when it became the principal source for Crown acquisitions. After 1180 the output of lead as a by-product from the north Pennine mines might have been in decline but their contribution to the volume of silver circulating in England over the previous fifty years had been exceptional.

The uneven distribution and origins of stray finds of coins, thrymsas and sceattas, prior to the tenth century, with a concentration in the coastal areas of southern and eastern England, has led Dr D. M. Metcalf to conclude that monetisation in the pre-Viking Age was significantly linked with long distance and inter-regional trade. Numismatic evidence such as this provides no suggestion of the use of newly mined English silver, with a large proportion of the metal being channelled to the country by way of the Rhine valley. By the early eleventh century there is, however, some suggestion from the concentration of mints around a potential source of lead/silver on Mendip, in north Somerset, that local sources of silver were perhaps being worked. Domesday Book makes no specific reference to its production, although it is suggested by payments made in 'pure silver' from five manors in the Derbyshire lead field. For the tenth and eleventh centuries there is also an increasing amount of closely dated archaeological evidence for smelting activity in mining fields, such as the north Pennines and the Caldbeck Fells in Cumbria, which were associated with silver production from the twelfth century onwards.

Clear documentary evidence for silver mining is not available until 1130, when the £40 due for the farm of a silver mine, later referred to as 'the mine of Carlisle' (from where it was administered) was entered into the Pipe Roll of the Exchequer. Also entered in the roll was the 100s paid by the burgesses of Carlisle for the 'old' farm of the silver mine (*de Veti firma Mineirie Argi*) for the year, or years, prior to 1130.[7] These are the first in a series of entries in the Pipe Rolls which, from 1158, provide a continuous record for the 'mine'. The exploitation of silver is confirmed by Robert of Torigni, who noted that in 1133 the miners paid the Crown

[7] J. Hunter, ed., *Magnus Rotulus Scaccarii de anno 31 Henrici I* (London, 1833), p. 142.

£500 per annum to dig the metal from the bowels of the earth, although without supporting evidence the figure needs to be treated with caution. Unfortunately these early indications for the rapid exploitation of silver are interrupted by the disruption of King Stephen's reign, when the Scots moved south to occupy the border counties. Continued exploitation under the Scots is suggested by the significant amount of coin minted during their occupation and the occasional grant by David, king of Scotland, out of revenue 'from his mine of Carlisle'. It is only after the accession of Henry II and the withdrawal of the Scots that there were further returns to the exchequer.

The mines themselves, a scatter of small workings associated with Carlisle rather than a single mine, were to be found in the upland areas to the east of Carlisle, in and around the valley of the South Tyne, where the minerals were held by the Crown. To the east again, on the estates of the bishop of Durham, were further mines on which the Crown had confirmed the bishop's rights to the minerals, including silver. Unfortunately, although an archaeological landscape study is underway, we are confined to occasional reference in the chronicles of the period and the statistical evidence for the farm of the 'Mine of Carlisle' (a lease of that portion of the produce due to the Crown from the miners working the silver-bearing ores) for our assessment of the scale of production. The latter, of course, excludes the bishop's mines, on which the Crown had no call except during vacancies in the see. The interpretation of that evidence is addressed elsewhere[8] but there is enough to suggest that the 'mine of Carlisle' alone, between 1130 and 1200, could have contributed sufficient silver to account for the increase in the volume of English currency at the period. Numismatic discoveries and subsequent analyses have yet to determine the mechanism by which that silver was distributed, as insufficient dies were struck at the northern mints to account for all the coins that might have been minted.[9] There is the possibility that silver was conveyed to the rest of the country, perhaps even as far as northern France, in the form of ingots.

[8] P. Claughton, 'Production and economic impact: Northern Pennine (English) silver in the 12th century', in *Proceedings of the 6th International Mining History Congress*, Akabira City, Japan (2003) pp. 146–9; available for download at www.people.exeter.ac.uk/pfclaugh/mhinf/claugh.doc.

[9] M. Allen, 'The volume of the English currency, 1158–1470', *EcHR*, 54.4 (2001), 595–611. See also the recent work by T. C. R. Crafter, which illustrates the limited impact of north Pennine silver at mints in southern England in the late twelfth century: 'Monetary expansion in Britain in the late twelfth century' (unpublished D.Phil. thesis, University of Oxford, 2008).

By the last decade of the twelfth century, silver from the north Pennines had declined to insignificant levels. Prospecting on the Welsh borders, at Carreghwfa, and in the southwest of England during Richard I's reign failed to find new sources and the only productive mine, near Basingwerk in northeast Wales, was probably under Welsh control.[10] Thereafter, local sources of silver were to play only a secondary role in the English economy and it was tin which would dominate metal production.

The tin in veins associated with the granite emplacement in Devon and Cornwall was not worked by deep mining until at least the end of the fifteenth century. Prior to that date it was the secondary alluvial deposits found in the valley bottoms on and around the granite which were the only source of tin ore. There is archaeological evidence from prehistoric contexts for early working from finds, including smelting residues, but, although known to the Romans, tin was not worked extensively until the latter part of the occupation as an alternative to resources in northwest Spain. There is, then, sufficient evidence, particularly for the southeastern parts of Dartmoor, to indicate that some production continued after the departure of the Romans, from the fourth to eighth centuries.[11] The emergence of tin in the documentary record of the late twelfth century, with evidence for customary rights for those working and smelting the ores, along with the Crown's interest in 'coinage', a tax on the produce after a second refining smelt carried out in designated towns close to the workings, strongly suggests a well-established industry. Subsequent production figures, entered in the Pipe Rolls, also confirm the early dominance of the deposits in Devon, on and around Dartmoor.

There is no evidence of a directly managed, capital-intensive organization equivalent to that imposed by the English Crown on the Devon silver mines in the late thirteenth century.[12] Mining and quarrying was carried out by individuals or small groups. Examine any of those activities closely and you will find rights in common regulated by customs which had developed over centuries but were not codified until the thirteenth century at the earliest. Miners had access to resources in return for a portion of the produce, and rights were framed to take into account the circumstances peculiar to each mining field. In the silver-rich north

[10] Pipe Rolls Series NS 6, p. 132; NS 7, p. 20. L. Thorpe, trans., *Gerald of Wales. The Journey through Wales and The Description of Wales* (Harmondsworth, 1978), p. 196.

[11] V. R. Thorndycraft, D. Pirrie and A. G. Brown, 'Alluvial records of medieval and prehistoric tin mining on Dartmoor', *Geoarchaeology*, 19.3 (2004), 219–36.

[12] S. Rippon, P. Claughton and C. Smart, *Mining in a Medieval Landscape: The Royal Silver Mines of the Tamar Valley* (Exeter, 2009).

Pennines, those working the 'mine of Carlisle' were allowed the services of a *drivere* or refiner, ensuring an element of Crown control over the precious metal. Where a multiplicity of primary vein deposits were being exploited, as in Derbyshire, custom allocated working places in short linear sections along each vein, with only limited space on either side for ore processing and waste disposal. Tin working, on the other hand, was exploiting secondary alluvial deposits for which areas of an acre or more were allocated along with the right to water for the work and, in common with some other metal mining fields, the fuel to smelt the ore.

By the end of our period in 1200 the economy was increasingly commercialized, with a strong silver-based currency and, although the peak in English silver production had passed, the search for new resources was beginning. Large stone-built structures were becoming common features in the landscape, many of them roofed with lead mined specifically for that purpose. Tin production in the southwest of England had risen rapidly to a point where Crown income from its taxation was of real significance and its regulation had been granted formal recognition. Tin was to out-perform all other metal production in England after 1200. Its export value exceeded that of lead, and, despite the opening up of new silver mines in Devon in the late thirteenth century, it produced by far the major contribution to Crown revenues. The socio-economic importance of the expanding extractive industries was clearly in evidence across the country, a significant advance on the position some 300 years earlier.

CHAPTER I.5

Health and disease

Carole Rawcliffe

Until quite recently, historians have been obliged to rely upon documentary sources for most of their information about the health of medieval men, women and children. The most common ailments, or at least those which appeared treatable, find mention in remedy books and herbals. The lives of saints and accounts of their healing miracles likewise provide a catalogue of disease and debility, in this instance carefully chosen to reflect the superiority of spiritual over earthly medicine. Important evidence about the incidence of epidemics and famines was recorded by chroniclers, although they, in common with other medieval writers, employed a terminology that makes retrospective diagnosis difficult, if not impossible. Since the 1960s, however, advances in the study of palaeopathology (the analysis of excavated skeletal remains) have enabled us to gain a far more detailed and comprehensive picture of levels of mortality and morbidity in the years between 900 and 1200.

It is important to stress that many diseases, such as diphtheria and pneumonia, affect only the perishable soft tissue of the body, while others may prove fatal at a comparatively early stage and thus escape detection. Nor can we generalize too widely on the basis of limited data relating to particular groups of people with specific problems. Even so, skeletal evidence has proved invaluable in illuminating the lives and deaths of low-status individuals whose voices otherwise remain mute, or who are barely mentioned in the historical record.[1] Thus, for example, the excavation of one late Anglo-Saxon Norwich graveyard undertaken in the 1970s offers a fascinating insight into the living standards of a poor urban community just before the Conquest. An examination of approximately 130 individual skeletons revealed a mean age at death among the adult population of just 30 years old for males and 33 for females. Some would have perished in

[1] C. Roberts and M. Cox, *Health and Disease in Britain from Prehistory to the Present Day* (Stroud, 2003), chs. 4 and 5.

epidemics, the men being additionally exposed to industrial accidents and acts of violence, while the women risked death in childbirth. Although it is harder to determine, the rate of infant and juvenile mortality in this community may have exceeded 60 per cent, largely because insanitary conditions and malnutrition made the young especially susceptible to viral infections.[2] The case of Gurwain the tanner, who embarked on a pilgrimage to the shrine of the boy martyr, William of Norwich, a century later, in the hope of saving the only one of his six sons to survive infancy, puts flesh on these anonymous bones.[3]

The Church's emphasis upon the transitory nature of life and the inevitability of human suffering was a reflection of harsh reality. From a modern perspective, the nature of the disease burden shouldered by the population of late Anglo-Saxon and Norman England resembled that to be found today in the developing world. So, too, did the challenges faced by men and women who, at the best of times, often hovered dangerously near subsistence level and were hampered by a lack of scientific knowledge and technological expertise. Although their skills were far from negligible, medical practitioners were obliged to function without the lifelines of antisepsis, antibiotics, reliable anaesthesia and blood transfusion, which, in turn, seriously inhibited the effectiveness of even the most routine surgical procedures. To compound the problem, a testing combination of poor nutrition, low standards of personal hygiene and sanitation, physically demanding working conditions and inadequate housing took a heavy toll on the general health and life expectancy of a significant proportion of the population.

Historians and archaeologists do not always agree about the adequacy and nutritive value of the diet consumed by English men and women in this period, largely because of the striking discrepancy between the foodstuffs that were theoretically available and actual levels of production and consumption. As well as significant differences between the social classes, regional variations were pronounced. Even so, most of the rural population derived its basic calorific intake from cereals (oats, wheat and barley), legumes (beans and peas) and vegetables (especially onions, leeks and cabbage), supplemented with fruit, nuts and a wide variety of herbs. Ale made from malted barley was drunk in preference to water, wine being reserved for the elite. Meat was likewise a luxury for the great majority, although

[2] A. Stirland, 'The human bones', in B. Ayers, ed., *Excavations within the North-East Bailey of Norwich Castle, 1979*, (East Anglian Archaeology, 28; Dereham, 1985), pp. 49–58.

[3] Augustus Jessopp and M. R. James, eds. and trans., *Thomas of Monmouth, The Life and Miracles of St William of Norwich*, (Cambridge, 1896), p. 167.

Figure 4 Evidence of *cribra orbitalia* in a medieval skeleton. Reproduced by permission of MOLAS

eggs and dairy produce were more common, as were freshwater fish and molluscs, which we know from archaeological evidence to have been consumed in large quantities in towns. In good years, urban markets offered a greater choice of produce (see Chapter III.2), but were more likely to run out of supplies in times of famine. Whereas, in principle, this kind of diet would have proved sufficient to support a working adult male, seasonal shortages and fluctuating levels of agricultural productivity meant that, in practice, it would often have been impossible for even the wealthy to maintain a desirable intake of protein, calcium, folic acid, zinc and vitamins (notably A, B12, C and D). Malnutrition among the peasantry may, moreover, have been exacerbated by the consumption of so much coarse-grained bread and pottage, as excessive levels of fibre can inhibit the absorption of essential nutrients. Those who already teetered precariously on the edge of hunger were thus at the mercy of poor harvests, bad weather, warfare and the manifold diseases that affected livestock.[4]

Evidence of vitamin deficiencies such as scurvy and rickets (respectively occasioned by a lack of vitamins C and D) can be found in the surviving human remains. They also reveal that a striking proportion of the population, most notably women and children, suffered from iron-based

[4] K. L. Pearson, 'Nutrition and the early-medieval diet', *Speculum*, 72 (1997), 1–32.

anaemia. This gives rise to a condition known as *cribra orbitalia* that has, for example, been identified in 58 per cent of the eleventh- and twelfth-century children excavated in one Norwich cemetery and as many as 70 per cent in another. Well over half the adult females were similarly affected, displaying the characteristic 'honeycomb' pattern in the bone of the eye-socket.[5] The same sites reveal correspondingly high levels of hypoplasia, which produces tell-tale ridges in the enamel of developing teeth, and most commonly signifies childhood illness or malnutrition resulting from prolonged seasonal shortages or famine. Other dental problems sprang from the breakages and attrition occasioned by the stones and husks in the rough bread eaten as a dietary staple by the peasantry. Remedy books confirm that the more affluent members of society, at least, were aware of the need for oral hygiene, but many people suffered from painful disorders resulting from protracted neglect of the teeth and gums. Periodontal disease caused by untreated deposits of plaque, together with shortages of vitamin C, gave rise to abscesses and tooth loss, which in turn caused bacterial infection and digestive complaints.

None of these conditions is itself likely to prove fatal, but all will to some extent impinge upon an individual's ability to function effectively and will significantly reduce his or her resistance to infection. Anaemia can shorten life appreciably, aggravating heart problems and diseases such as pneumonia and bronchitis, while rendering even a moderate loss of blood potentially fatal. During their reproductive years, women need on average twice as much iron as men to compensate for menstrual bleeding, and even more when pregnant or lactating. Such high levels were, however, rarely available, with the result that maternal and infant health alike was seriously compromised.[6]

It is easy to see why famine and disease so often marched together. An already vulnerable population will easily succumb to infection following a season of dearth, while a sudden rise in levels of sickness and mortality among the agricultural labour force will perpetuate the cycle of poor harvests. This chain of events is vividly described by the chronicler William of Malmesbury in his account of the months before the death of William the Conqueror in 1087:

There was a great mortality both of men and beasts, severe storms and constant lightning of a violence no man had ever seen or heard of. And the year in which

[5] S. Anderson, 'Human skeletal remains', in E. Shepherd Popescu, ed., *Norwich Castle: Excavations and Historical Survey, 1987–98*, part 1, *Anglo-Saxon to* c. *1345* (East Anglian Archaeology, 132; Dereham, 2009).

[6] Vern Bullough and Cameron Campbell, 'Female longevity and diet in the Middle Ages', *Speculum*, 55 (1980), 317–25.

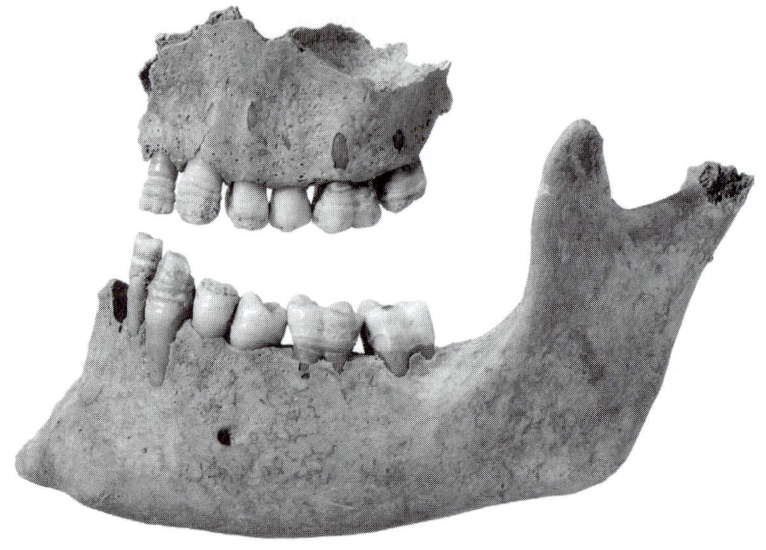

Figure 5 Evidence of hypoplasia in dental remains.
Reproduced by permission of MOLAS

he died an epidemic fever preyed on more than half the ordinary population, so severely that many succumbed to the ill effects of the disease; and then, as a result of the corrupted air, a widespread famine followed so that survivors of fever fell victim to hunger.[7]

Between 900 and 1200 over fifty food shortages and outbreaks of disease among animals and men were sufficiently serious to be recorded in the major English chronicles. Although their authors refer in only the most general terms to the various 'murrains', 'pestilences' and 'fevers' that struck at both a national and regional level, it is apparent that some decades, most notably the 980s, 1040s, 1080s, 1090s, 1100s and 1190s, were marked by successive years of crisis.[8] Many regional outbreaks were either caused or intensified by military activity, which not only had a devastating effect on productivity, but also encouraged the spread of diseases such as

[7] R. A. B. Mynors, R. M. Thomson and M. Winterbottom, eds. and trans., *William of Malmesbury, Gesta regum Anglorum* (2 vols.; OMT; Oxford, 1998–9), i, pp. 500–1.

[8] Charles Creighton, *A History of Epidemics in Britain* (2nd edn; 2 vols.; London, 1965), i, pp. 15–17; A. Hagen, *A Handbook of Anglo-Saxon Food Processing and Consumption* (Pinner, 1994), appendix D, pp. 152–5.

dysentery and typhus. In this respect, the North was especially unfortunate because of incursions by the Scots, although the greatest damage was inflicted by the Conqueror in 1070, in brutal reprisals against those who had rebelled against him (see Chapter II.2). Even allowing for the exaggeration common to medieval chronicles, the scale of devastation had a lasting impact upon the health of at least two generations of northerners.

The quality as well as the quantity of the food supply sometimes left much to be desired. Whereas levels of pollution caused by tanning, dyeing and other industrial activities were comparatively low, water supplies must often have been contaminated with human and animal waste. The processes of brewing and cooking would have eliminated many bacteria, but the large number of surviving remedies concerned with intestinal and digestive problems suggests that enteric diseases, such as dysentery and diarrhoea, were rife. Ergotism (known as St Anthony's fire), whose symptoms include gangrene and violent hallucinations, is caused by a fungus that grows on damp rye. Although they were far more common in continental Europe, outbreaks occurred in those parts of England where the cereal was cultivated, and probably gave rise to some of the more spectacular descriptions of demonic possession to be found in the hagiography of the period. The Church's ban on eating half-cooked and spoiled food probably helped to curb the spread of bacteria and parasites from unwholesome meat, as may the medical advice literature about diet that began to circulate from the mid-eleventh century onwards. Even so, internal parasites, such as ringworm, whipworm and tapeworm, were a ubiquitous problem, not least because poor sanitation encouraged their transmission from the faecal matter of domestic animals to humans. Once lodged in the gut, they would have proved a further drain on the host's nutritional resources, exacerbating any propensity to anaemia and other deficiencies.

In a predominantly rural society exposure to zoonotic diseases (those shared with, or spread by, animals) was unavoidable. Bovine tuberculosis (TB) was acquired from cattle through the ingestion of infected meat and, more commonly, milk, as well as the inhalation of airborne droplets by those who worked or lived in close proximity to animals. Since only a small percentage of cases of TB cause skeletal change, it is difficult to establish what proportion of the population may have been affected, although urban growth and improvements in diet may, ironically, have proved a catalyst in exposing far more people to the virulent pulmonary strain of the disease. The glandular variety (scrofula) is vividly described in contemporary sources as 'the King's Evil', it being a tenet of English royal propaganda from the reign of Henry I onwards that the ulcerated lesions of affected lymph nodes would respond to the sacred touch of an anointed monarch.

Infections of the liver, which figure prominently in medical works such as Bald's *Leechbook* (see Chapter VI.4), were caused by sheep fluke and tapeworms. The apparent popularity of preparations for the extermination of lice, ticks and fleas confirms that such parasites were common. Unwashed clothes and the straw used for bedding and floor covering provided an ideal breeding ground for a host of vermin, as did a propensity among the religious for ascetic practices involving unwashed hair shirts and the avoidance of regular baths. Tertian malaria, or 'spring fever', a parasitic infection spread by mosquitoes, was endemic in the low-lying and fenland areas of medieval England until the late nineteenth century. Known as *lencten adl* in Old English, it appears frequently in both the medical literature and accounts of healing miracles, in which 'agues' and 'fevers' are routinely cured by divine intervention. The disease is particularly insidious because of the attendant damage that it inflicts upon the red blood cells. Since a substantial proportion of the population already suffered from iron deficiency because of poor nutrition, we can readily appreciate why so many skeletons display the symptoms of *cribra orbitalia*.

The ubiquity of skin and eye complaints in medieval England likewise reflects the dietary and environmental problems encountered throughout society, since many ophthalmic conditions were the result of poor diet, indifferent personal hygiene, insanitary living conditions and work-related injuries. Although the scientific rationale for their effectiveness was not then apparent, antibacterial agents were used to treat infected eyes, probably with some success.[9] Many such disorders would have been aggravated, if not caused, by irritating dust or smoke, usually from the open fires common in domestic dwellings. Indeed, a remarkably high level of sinusitis occasioned by atmospheric pollutants has been detected in the skeletal evidence. An analysis of the early miracles attributed to St Thomas Becket (d. 1170) reveals that the visually impaired and leprous were among the most likely to seek and receive his assistance.[10] The former category would almost certainly have included sufferers from seasonal blindness caused by a lack of vitamin A and others with trachoma, a bacterial infection which flourishes in dirty conditions and may enter periods of remission. Most of the presumed lepers were probably

[9] M. L. Cameron, *Anglo Saxon Medicine* (Cambridge, 1993), pp. 118–22.

[10] R. Foreville, *Thomas Becket dans la tradition historique et hagiographique* (London, 1981), ch. 7.

disfigured by scorbutic sores and skin diseases such as scabies, erysipelas, psoriasis and eczema; and without proper care would have displayed distressing – if often treatable – symptoms.

Now confined to the developing world, Hansen's disease (true leprosy) was, however, endemic in England between the ninth and fourteenth centuries, and, in its most aggressive form, would invariably have proved fatal. It, too, spreads among the poor and undernourished, especially in crowded and dirty surroundings. The scale of the threat posed by this repellent disease is hard to determine because of the disproportionate attention accorded to its victims by medieval theologians and benefactors. A widespread assumption that particular spiritual merit was to be earned by assisting these 'prisoners of God' prompted the foundation of more than 300 leper hospitals between the Conquest and 1350, although many were very small and did not survive for long. Contrary to popular belief, they were regarded as places of prayer and refuge, rather than institutions for segregation and confinement.[11]

Not all medical problems sprang from malnutrition or disease. For many otherwise healthy individuals debility would have been an unavoidable consequence of hard manual labour performed without the safeguards and mechanical tools that are today a standard part of the working environment. Those engaged in heavy lifting were prone to hernias, while the eyes of masons, threshers and metalworkers were constantly at risk. Accidents were common, and more likely to prove serious in a society without antibiotics or blood transfusion. Osteoarthritis, especially of the shoulder and spine, could easily develop at an early age, being aggravated by the cold and damp working conditions so often endured by agricultural labourers. Skeletal analysis suggests that as many as half the adults engaged in manual occupations may have suffered from it, while other degenerative conditions occasioned by trauma or injury were frequent. Miracle stories abound with tales of men and women who dragged themselves for miles on crutches in the hope of relief from their manifold aches and pains.

Childbirth, the painful legacy inherited by the daughters of Eve, constituted by far the greatest challenge faced by most adult women. Once regarded as a byword for ignorance and superstition, the medieval midwife has been redeemed by much recent scholarship. Yet however competent she may have been, her role was circumscribed by the poor general health of a significant proportion of the female population, and the want

[11] C. Rawcliffe, *Leprosy in Medieval England* (Woodbridge, 2006), ch. 3.

of effective surgery. An expectant mother already weakened by anaemia and other dietary deficiencies, and perhaps physically malformed by a disease such as rickets, was clearly as much at risk as her unborn child. On the evidence of remedy books, contraception and abortion appear to have been practised, but the physical toll of repeated pregnancies remained great, increasing the likelihood of haemorrhage and other complications. Even the fittest of women had reason to fear a protracted or difficult confinement, which might easily result in permanent injury, such as uterine prolapse or fistulae of the vagina or rectum. Christ's miraculous cure of the woman with the issue of blood, replicated by many medieval saints, relates to just such an injury. Usually performed on, or just before, the death of the mother, Caesareans were intended to expose the unborn child long enough for baptism, and must often have resulted in a double fatality. The high rate of neonatal mortality, confirmed by both the written and skeletal evidence, was in part a consequence of poor maternal health, which had a profound effect upon the survival of newborn infants.

Notwithstanding the scale of the problems encountered by a significant proportion of the population, efforts were made to assist the moribund and destitute. Charity was an imperative enjoined upon all Christians, whose prospects of salvation hinged upon their readiness to feed, clothe and minister to the needy. Enshrined in the Rule of St Benedict and formally adopted in an agreement known as the *Regularis concordia* (*c.* 970), the provision of food and shelter became a significant feature of Anglo-Saxon monastic life (see Chapter II.6). Designated institutions for the care of the sick and homeless do not, however, appear to have been established before the Conquest, after which the foundation of leper houses and hospitals proceeded apace as part of a wider movement for monastic reform. Such places did not offer medical treatment in the modern sense, but through the provision of warmth, rest, basic nursing care and nourishing food constituted a valuable, if limited, resource for sick pilgrims and other vulnerable people. It is notoriously difficult to calculate the number of early hospital foundations: on a very conservative estimate, at least 250 are known to have been established in England between 1070 and 1200.[12] Many of the earliest (such as Archbishop Lanfranc's two hospitals at Canterbury) were closely associated with monasteries, but it became increasingly common for the laity and secular clergy to act independently (see Chapter III.3).

[12] Nicholas Orme and Margaret Webster, *The English Hospital 1070–1570* (New Haven and London, 1995), p. 11.

Almsgiving on a grand scale was certainly not confined to monasteries, since the conspicuous distribution of handouts occurred regularly in the households of English kings, noblemen and bishops from at least the ninth century onwards. The court of Edward the Confessor was famous for its largesse. Indeed, a readiness to tend the sick in person, however disagreeable their symptoms, became the hallmark of devout noblewomen and members of the royal family, such as St Edith (d. 984), who 'set the lepers of Christ before the sons of kings', Queen Margaret of Scotland (d. 1093) and her celebrated daughter, Matilda, the first wife of Henry I. The ad hoc and essentially indiscriminate form of almsgiving practised by the elite did not, however, constitute a proper safety net in times of real hardship, when neither the available resources nor the existing administrative structures proved adequate for the task. The bleak assumption that hunger, sickness and pain might be temporarily relieved but never eradicated seems all too understandable.

CHAPTER II.I

Authority and community

Bruce O'Brien

England between the late ninth and twelfth centuries suffered more conquests than any other western European kingdom of the period. Despite the disruption and dislocation caused by events which contemporaries perceived as catastrophes, the kingdom during these three centuries saw the development of structures of power – the state, aristocracy, families, and rural and urban customs – that shaped the lives of its inhabitants, a population numbering close to 2 million at least in 1087. These structures determined much of what the English people did not only by laying out the boundaries for action, but also by compelling it. Everywhere one looks in western Europe, kings ruled through their own agents and, by controlling their aristocracies, reached into the lives of their subjects, provoking comparable praise and complaints. Viewed close up, however, England appears remarkably distinct.

Our understanding of the actions of governments, lords, families and even slaves must rest on a broad understanding of the authority which the different elements of English society enjoyed and practices to which they were subjected. At a fundamental level, the power behind both authority and actions could work *de iure* or *de facto*. A king or lord, for example, had power to direct others to do or not to do certain things, while those so directed possessed a more limited ability to negotiate their own compliance or to resist. Power in its operation could be thus both institutional and personal: lords qua lords could control the lives of their peasants, but individual lords might do this to very different degrees, regardless of customary limits. How, or rather where, to study power, then, is a principal methodological problem, since most choices of sources, situations or social levels would cover only some of its manifestations.

Of all the evidence, however, law provides unique access to the exercise of authority. There are a number of reasons for this. First, the laws were often issued by deliberative assemblies and therefore are the best evidence we have for the kingdom's norms expressed as policy. Law-making in medieval England was reiterative and consultative. It mattered to kings and their *witan* or council to speak on matters of law and justice in almost every reign, and often much more than just once. Sources like chronicles and charters can show whether certain laws were successfully implemented or obeyed, but these sources have limited scope, addressing only those things that concerned people writing accounts of individual cases or gathered at a specific time and place to witness the resolution of a single issue. Second, the laws we have may very well be all the legislation that was ever produced by England's kings and their assemblies, while other sources were less likely to survive in anything like a representative sample. All sources, however, must be used to sketch the norms that governed behaviour, their enforcement and the responses this elicited. Third, law reveals the intentions of the powerful, the actions of their agents and the consequences to, and, at times, the response of, the people. It can also tell something of how people themselves structured their lives. Last, while law does not define all the parameters of power, nevertheless, in its creation and operation it tells us more about these parameters than any other aspect of a culture because it cuts across all the different ways of defining people: free and unfree, male and female, child and adult, tenants and lords, families and kin groups, clergy and laity, lords and agents, rulers and ruled.

This chapter, then, will approach authority and community initially from the standpoint of law. It will first address the creation of law by rulers, along with changes made over time to the system of justice responsible for applying that law. Then it will explore these enforceable and enforced norms for the elite and non-elite families in war or in peace. Next, the crucial social bonds used to ensure enforcement are surveyed. Last, the chapter assesses the spread and scope of royal power among the English.

LAW-MAKING IN ACTION: THE ASSEMBLIES AND CODES OF WOODSTOCK AND WANTAGE

With so much variety in the ideas about legal authority presented in law codes and in practice, and visible developments in these ideas over several centuries in a polity that endured several conquests, it seems wise to start with a pair of related events that typify the workings of law and spell out some crucial social norms. We begin, therefore, with two closely related law-giving assemblies that take us quickly into the exercise of power in medieval England. Both of these assemblies met very probably in the year 997. This year was untypical in that it was a rare good year in the reign of King Æthelred II (978–1016). Æthelred had survived a surfeit of bad councillors during his minority, and then the military cataclysms of the early 990s, to enjoy as a mature ruler something approaching a peaceful kingdom. Viking raiders had left after his treaty in 994 with Olaf Tryggvasson (king of Norway, 995–1000), and, except for sporadic attacks along the southwestern coast, they were not, for the time being, a menace. Æthelred had shed the bad councillors who had misled him in the 980s, and raised up others who, though relatives, were also seasoned in government and war, supporters of monastic reform and expansion and, in some individual cases, writers and patrons of writers.[1]

In 997, Æthelred summoned his *witan*, first to Woodstock, and later to Wantage, both within twenty miles of Oxford. We know little about what took place at Woodstock other than the issuance of the code enacted for *friðes bote* (public security) in areas ruled by English law.[2] We know only slightly more about the activities of the Wantage assembly. The king and his councillors not only issued similarly a code for public security, but also sought to resolve 'issues in contentious cases'.[3] The king repaired relationships strained during the bad days of his youth by, for example, returning expropriated land to the Old Minster, Winchester, in repentance for his wrongful acts in the past. It seems clear that the Wantage code was the fraternal twin of the one issued at Woodstock. It was a code that was meant to do for the Scandinavian-settled north what the Woodstock code did for southern England and western Mercia.

Together, these are typical pieces of legislation. They are not long codes, nor unusually short: combined, they are of similar size to King Edgar's (959–75) final legislation two decades before. But where Edgar's last code had attempted something more comprehensive, raising issues ranging from the obligations of tenants to pay rent to the quasi-independence of Danish-settled areas to fix their own customs, both Woodstock and Wantage codes focused on narrow points. Æthelred could very well have done the same as his father. There were certainly issues he had had to deal with over the previous five years since his last law code, his treaty with the Vikings led by Olaf. But there is nothing of geld, military service, the violence of groups or treason here.

[1] Simon Keynes, *The Diplomas of King Æthelred the 'Unready', 978–1016* (Cambridge, 1980), pp. 163–97.

[2] All citations to the Woodstock and Wantage codes are from A. J. Robertson, ed., *The Laws of the Kings of England from Edmund to Henry I* (Cambridge, 1925), pp. 52–5, 64–71.

[3] Sawyer, *Anglo-Saxon Charters*, no. 891 (K 698).

Instead, Woodstock and Wantage focused on particular problems arising from lords' relations to their men, and from all men's obligations, that mattered to the practice of justice. Its point of focus is the particular operations of royal justice that depended on the suretyship of lords over their households and the suretyship witnessing obligations between freemen. It is on these obligations that the administration of justice, and consequently the preservation of order and peace, depended. The arena where these obligations were fashioned was the assemblies called by kings; they were put into practice in England's public courts, evolving institutions during this period.

THE EXERCISE OF AUTHORITY

Assemblies summoned by kings did not just mark moments of importance in the political history of their reigns, but also served as the key fora in which broad socially significant issues, and not just law-making, were aired and resolved.[4] Not all or even most assemblies issued laws, and the law-giving ones are probably disproportionately represented among the meetings of the king's *witan* of which we know. Instead, the usual business of assemblies included judicial hearings, election of prelates, grants of land or rights, as well as discussions of events, policies and foreign relations. Such assemblies would normally have in attendance the majority of the kingdom's prelates, who presided over shire courts, as well as important abbots. Earls and thegns would be there in significant numbers. Occasionally charters give us some of the names of attendees. The importance of these meetings is that they were the principal venue for politics in a kingdom whose kings needed advice and support from their elites. Some were regular occurrences – like the three each year at which, according to later reports, the king wore his crown. Others were ad hoc – Wantage and Woodstock may fall into this category – called up to treat matters of the moment.

The impact of assembly decisions was felt in the courts, which were just emerging under royal control during this period. The tenth century starts with our having only a hazy notion of what courts folk should gather at to regulate behaviour. The courts themselves developed slowly, starting with the order of Edward the Elder (899–924) that reeves preside over their courts regularly, which most likely refers to incipient hundred

[4] Timothy Reuter, 'Assembly politics in western Europe from the eighth century to the twelfth', in P. Linehan and J. L. Nelson, eds., *The Medieval World* (London, 2001), pp. 432–50.

smoothed over time. That may have been the view of the English who attended those increasingly regular courts. From the king's perspective, however, the law changed every time he intervened. Earlier laws like Alfred's (late 880s to early 890s) had a stronger rhetorical frame than later laws, and modern historians have argued that Alfred's code in particular was part of the king's attempt to create the English as one people.[10] Alfred situated his laws in the genealogy of biblical laws and the laws of his predecessors, all to reinforce his code's authority as well as identify the English as a new Israel.[11] It is a perhaps an unanswerable question whether Alfred's royal power created not just a new chosen people, but also a new English identity, or whether he merely refashioned it, or just acknowledged its existence. It is one thing to point to the emergence of English identity in texts, and to attribute motives to the kings who issued them, and quite another to say whether such agendas mattered to anyone other than their creators.

Tenth-century laws are less rhetorical statements than some earlier and later codes, and, consequently, more descriptive of expected and actual practices. They reveal kings flexing their legislative muscles with some effect on the ealdormen, reeves and others who were meant to enforce the laws. If Alfred's laws may possibly have had great effect, his successor's laws more certainly did. One text from the reign of Æthelstan, known as the 'Judgements of the Citizens of London', looks very much like a set of local responses to royal enactments, including copies of the king's commands and his later amendments.[12] What also becomes clear in the run of legislation from Alfred to Cnut is that the king is becoming, through myriad agents, more of a necessary presence in matters of justice. By the end of the Anglo-Saxon period, there is good reason to believe that royal officials were in every court and had become critical to the workings of justice throughout the kingdom.[13]

While the Norman Conquest proved a cataclysmic event for English nobles and a catalyst for a downward slide of the peasantry, it had remarkably few consequences for the law as practised. The expectations of justice people had before 1066 continued for the most part afterwards – true for kings, lords and, to a lesser extent, peasants. This continuity was in large

[10] Patrick Wormald, '*Engla Lond*: the making of an allegiance', *Journal of Historical Sociology*, 7 (1994), 1–24; Sarah Foot, 'The making of Angelcynn: English identity before the Norman Conquest', *TRHS* 6th ser., 6 (1996), 23–49.

[11] *EHD*, i, no. 33, 408–9. [12] *EHD*, i, no. 37, 423–7 (VI As).

[13] James Campbell, 'Some agents and agencies of the late Anglo-Saxon state', in J. C. Holt, ed., *Domesday Studies* (Woodbridge, 1987), pp. 207–8 (repr. in James Campbell, *The Anglo-Saxon State* (London, 2000), pp. 210–11).

part fuelled by the desire of the new kings and lords of the land to know every aspect of the land and its resources they had conquered in order to better exploit it according to its existing rules. The earlier courts remained in operation, with occasional adjustments by the new rulers. The appearance of seigneurial and separate ecclesiastical courts followed from trends already visible before the conquest. Mid-twelfth-century treatises on the law, such as the *Laws of Edward the Confessor* and the Anglo-French *Laws of William*, reflect the fact that law and its administration, its interests and mechanisms, passed relatively unscarred over 1066 and deep into the next century.

It may be that the new nobility was less bound by whatever sense of limits had governed the behaviour of English lords before 1066. Lordship under the Normans was arguably predatory.[14] At no time was this truer than during the reign of King Stephen (1135–54). The hallmarks of the period of his reign when his right to rule was challenged – scorched fields and villages, and, most visibly on the landscape, a plague of castles – were at times the actions of armies fighting in support of the two sides to this succession dispute between Stephen and Henry I's daughter, the Empress Matilda, and her son, the future King Henry II. England was during Stephen's reign after 1139 an armed land embroiled periodically in a war of attrition. More often, however, the depredations were the result of lords seizing opportunities created by the war to grow their retinues and expand the number of estates and peasants they controlled. The author of *The Peterborough Chronicle* tells us that 'every powerful man built his castles and held them against [the king] and they filled the country full of castles'.[15] Nevertheless, during these wars, royal government continued to operate, if at a slightly impaired level. Even rebel barons produced imitations of stable royal government in the regions they had seized.[16]

Henry II (1154–89) began what historians consider a major reform of law and its administration, creating a writ-based system for litigants seeking redress for wrongs, and putting his courts and men in charge. In particular, he is credited with initiating a system of public investigation of crimes. The Assizes of Clarendon (1166) and Northampton (1176) appear to have laid out an unprecedented scheme for investigating crime and punishing its perpetrators. On issues of land and landlords, there can be little doubt about the impact of the king's reforms. Elsewhere, such as in criminal law, there appears to be more continuity with the practices of

[14] Robin Fleming, *Kings and Lords in Conquest England* (Cambridge, 1991), pp. 183–214.
[15] *EHD*, ii, no.1, 199 (ASC 1137 (E)), see Figure 6.
[16] Graeme J. White, *Restoration and Reform, 1153–1165: Recovery from Civil War in England* (Cambridge, 2000), pp. 17–49, 55–69.

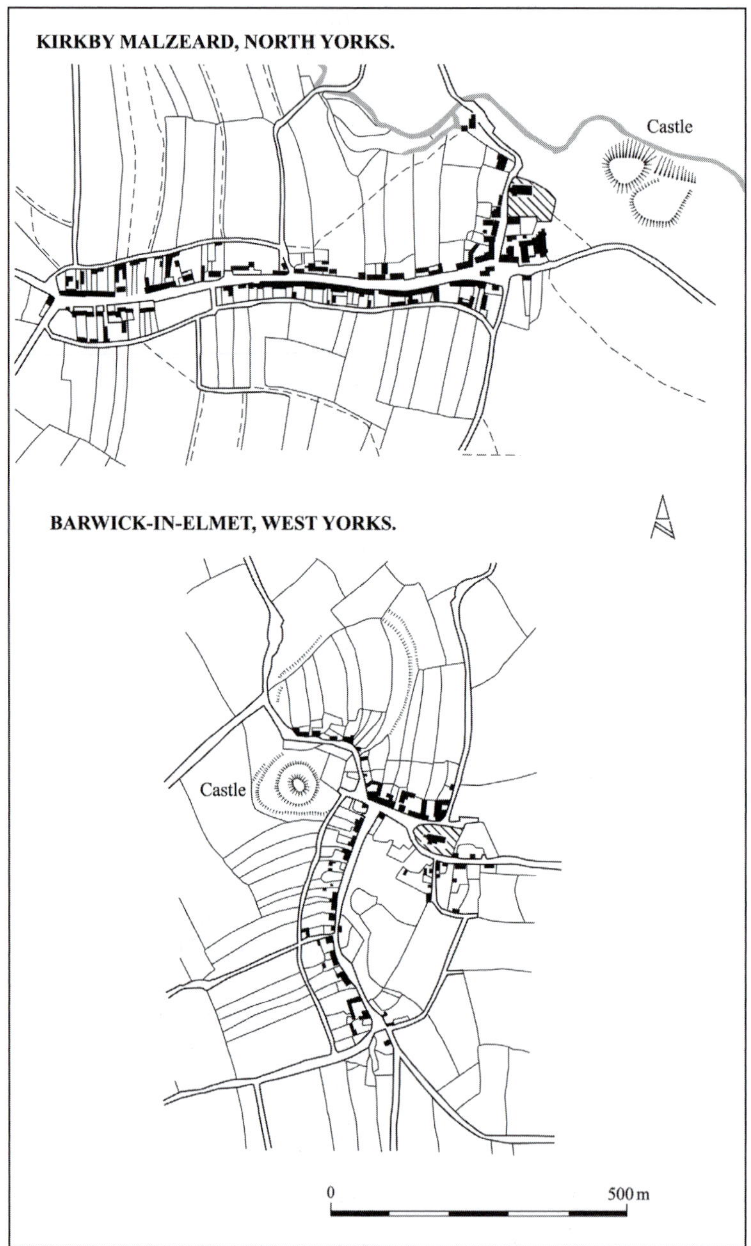

Figure 6 Examples of castles and planned lordships in Yorkshire.
© O. H. Creighton; illustration by M. Rouillard, first published in O. H. Creighton, *Castles and Landscapes: Power, Community and Fortification in Medieval England*, London, 2002

previous reigns than change to something altogether new. Even on the issue of the freeman's access to justice – that fundamental common law right – there should be some uncertainty over its scope and newness. The records of the administration of justice from before Henry II's reign were mostly private documents and were only in certain circumstances preserved, while Henry II's clerks oversaw the escalation of production of public records, many of which have survived.

LORDS AND THE REALITIES OF POWER

So far we have followed normative sources and charted structures as they were intended to operate. The reality of the people's experience of power through justice must have been rather different. Most of the English would have come into contact with the administration of justice not as suitors in courts, let alone as councillors of kings, but as law's victims or victimizers, participating in a system that could not reliably decide the guilt or innocence of the accused. Instead, courts ordered simple rituals to allow kin and friends to assert the truthfulness of both parties. Recourse to the ordeal was likely common. Almost all bishops, who often acted as judges, had books detailing how to conduct these modes of proof, and some of their texts show that both men and women were expected to undergo the terror of handling fire-heated irons or of being bound and submersed in water.[17] Execution pits must have been filled indiscriminately with the bodies of the innocent and the guilty (see Chapter II.3, Chapter II.6).[18]

During the entire period from 900 to 1200, the kingdom's lords were integral not just to the workings of justice, but also to the maintenance of the structures of English society, of which they constituted the top layer. So, those lords at the assemblies at Woodstock and Wantage who heard Æthelred's laws knew what they were about. They were the king's chief men. A charter issued at the assembly captures the elite nature of this group en masse. Both archbishops were there, along with twelve bishops, fourteen abbots, five ealdormen, and twenty-three men titled 'minister', by which the scribe meant thegn.[19] This was not everyone, just the most important, the most available and the most interested in this

[17] For example, the mid-twelfth-century bishop's pontifical, holding an ordeal manual, that is now Oxford, Magdalen College, MS. Lat. 226, esp. fols. 208–16.

[18] On execution sites used before the twelfth century, see Andrew Reynolds, *Late Anglo-Saxon England: Life and Landscape* (Stroud, 1999), pp. 105–10.

[19] Sawyer, *Anglo-Saxon Charters*, no. 891. Data on almost all of the individuals in the witness list is most easily found in the *Prosopography of Anglo-Saxon England* database, www.pase.ac.uk.

particular transaction between the king and Old Minster, Winchester. Attending assemblies like this one, and hearing kings issue laws like Æthelred's Woodstock and Wantage codes, was a normal, if not regular part of how lords helped establish the norms that governed their actions. The laws, charters, narratives of the period along with, most importantly, Domesday Book, tell us a great deal about who they were, what made them lords and what they were expected to do. Surprisingly, the stylized description of the thegn found in a text known as the *Rectitudines singularum personarum* (Rights and ranks of people), written by Wulfstan the Homilist (d. 1023), fits well enough with what is found in other sources and in excavated sites that it bears being quoted:

> Thegn's Law. The law of the thegn is that he be entitled to his book-right, and that he shall contribute three things in respect of his land: armed service, and the repairing of fortresses and work on bridges. Also in respect of many estates, further service arises on the king's order such as service connected with the deer fence at the king's residence, and equipping a guard ship, and guarding the coast, and guarding the lord, and military watch, almsgiving and church dues and many other various things.[20]

Another text written by Wulfstan tells us that someone entitled to the rights of a thegn had 'five hides of land … a bell and a castle-gate, a seat and special office in the king's hall'.[21] Some sites like Goltho in Lincolnshire were likely the estate residence of a thegn: fortified, with a gate, a hall, a chapel and more besides (see Chapter I.1).[22]

Thegns were usually royal servants, and held their status because of this. They were, then, both lords in their own right and king's men, and obligated to follow his commands. One aspect of lords' behaviour which kings regulated – included in both Woodstock and Wantage codes – was the lords' responsibility to be sureties for their men. Those in lords' households – which included everyone from simple servants and slaves to powerful but dependent landowners – could expect their lord to provide surety, which could result in the lord paying his men's wergilds if they fled rather than appear in court.[23] Such an obligation, along with its obverse of protection of his men, bound thegns and other lords tightly to those in their service. There were more and more thegns over time. Thegns in the eleventh century were becoming thicker on the ground as large estates

[20] *EHD*, ii, no. 172, p. 813. [21] *EHD*, i, no. 51, p. 468 (*Geþyncðo*).

[22] Guy Beresford, *Goltho: The Development of an Early Medieval Manor*, c. *850–1150* (English Heritage Archaeological Reports, 4; London, 1987).

[23] *EHD*, i, no. 49, p. 459 (II Cnut 31).

were broken up into smaller units consisting of land sufficient to support with tribute a single thegn and his family – usually about 5 hides or so, as we have seen. But thegns also multiplied because higher lords and especially kings found them useful. If anything, the Norman settlement increased their number.

These lords had other concerns, not mentioned in the laws. Inheritance was a matter of concern with them – if it was for others as well, there is little evidence of it. Land was one of the necessities for thegns to enjoy their status. Possession of large amounts of it was crucial for any lord who wished to have power. Before 1066, descent of property to some, or all, male and female heirs was negotiable. No favoured offspring could know what would come his or her way on a father's death. Consequently, the human geography of the elite was fluid. Even the highest members of the elite before 1066, the ealdormen, later called earls, held their earldoms at the pleasure of the king rather than as inherited titles tied to ancestral districts. Stephen Baxter's work has revealed just how precarious was the hold exercised by any earl over his earldom in the eleventh century.[24] The unpredictable nature of inheritance and office holding changed in the twelfth century, with the spread of primogeniture and the growing independence of titles from office.

Paradoxically, even as the number of lords grewed, their world was becoming increasingly circumscribed by the power of kings. Visible during the whole period is the rising power of the king, both in the nature of the power he possessed and in its expanding geographical reach. Measuring the level of royal intervention or control, and assessing how much these changed between reigns, has been the major preoccupation of historians of law and government. A question asked less frequently is what any of these intrusions and changes would have meant for the average villager. Henry II, by one report, thought his reforms would bring justice to those 'least able to help themselves', which theoretically might seem a good thing.[25] Expanded and regularized courts, along with a more intrusive administration of law through royal agents and lords, would certainly have brought peasants within reach of royal agendas. A royal reeve in a village might be the point man for policies about crime, status and obligations, and by the eleventh century there is good evidence to suggest every village had a reeve. Whether other villagers appreciated the reeve's

[24] Stephen Baxter, *The Earls of Mercia: Lordship and Power in Late Anglo-Saxon England* (Oxford, 2007), pp. 66–7 (fig. 3.2).

[25] *EHD*, ii, no. 59, p. 481 (Ralph de Diceto).

work depended very much on whether local rapacious lords or equally acquisitive kings were viewed as a greater evil.

REGULATING THE FAMILY

Royal power had its limits, though it is better to see it in some areas as a customary discretion rather than a constitutional boundary. For example, royal power rarely intruded into the family, regardless of whether it could or could not. Its dictates on marriage are mostly about where it was thought inappropriate: among the clergy. Here perhaps more important than royal regulation were the norms governing Christian clergy. The ability of the Church to shape lives was present, but limited. Its concerns were mostly about lay and clerical morality (see Chapter V.2). People, however, continued their practices of religion, relied on charms and incantations to protect them from disease and sought the magic of the land, unaffected by the contempt of high clerics or the prohibitions of Church Councils. Ælfric, writing in the 990s, may have complained about people's reliance on magic, the casting of lots and the purveyors of folk medicine, but such criticisms seem not to have affected the patterns of life and belief of non-elite Christians. Matters as common and fundamental as marriage, abortion or the birth of children and parental responsibilities receive only halting attention in canons. Although there was earlier movement in this direction, it is only in 1076 that Lanfranc, an archbishop of Canterbury with Continental training in canon law, was able to require priests to bless marriages, mostly as a check on incestuous or coerced unions.[26] The overall focus of Church canons was in the promotion of endogamy and monogamy.[27] Continental canon law, which was increasingly discussing the broader issues of marriage, came only sparingly to England before 1066.

But families were undergoing strains during the period. Fundamental aspects of the elite family were changing, as a result particularly of the inroads made by the concept of primogeniture (see Chapter II.5). This had profound effects on the maintenance of power by families. The decline of the role of family and kin in law would have a greater impact on the workings of justice in the realm. Although they were undoubtedly present as supporters of family members involved in quarrels or lawsuits,

[26] *EHD*, i, no. 50, p. 468 (*Wifmannes beweddung* 8); *Councils and Synods*, i, 670.

[27] Conor McCarthy, *Marriage in Medieval England: Law, Literature and Practice* (Woodbridge, 2004), pp. 128–30.

they are rarely named in the laws. Instead, royal attention was directed to regulating the participation of freemen by means of tithings, suretyship groups made up of anyone but slaves. Cnut's laws in the 1020s ordered every freeman who wanted the protections of the law to 'be brought, if he is over twelve years old, into a hundred or tithing'.[28] The old role of kin in disputes had been usurped by the rise of lordship and the expansion of royal power, and was in fact a critical part of that transformation by providing an analogue on which to base a more useful form of social bond. As kings increased their control of lords, so also their control of lords' dependants grew – these proved a more secure means of enacting royal will than operating through kin groups.

OBLIGATIONS OF WAR AND FEUD

Lords were also concerned with the obligations of warfare, and what they owed was spelled out with some care, principally in law codes, but also in charters, chronicles, sermons and poetry (see Chapter II.4). These obligations underwent a series of revolutionary shifts alongside gradual evolutions. In the ninth and early tenth centuries, warfare was for the elite, a standing army, rather than for peasants who became warriors when attacked. In such circumstances, those obligated to fight outside the *burhs* would have grown to recognize in one another a common bond, a bond reinforced by their general wealth and growing role in government. Kings weighed in on the obligations of war. They regulated heriots based on rank, spelled out what weapons a warrior was to have and maintained national taxes to pay for a standing army or to provide for exceptional military circumstances such as an impending invasion.[29] It is not clear how significant the changes were between the tenth century and the twelfth; for example, where earlier military service was tied to possession of an estate, later military service was directly linked to possession of a fief. One significant change lay in where war was taking place, a matter of concern to those obligated to fight. In the first half of the period, wars were principally defensive, fought by local levies against Vikings who had invaded England. In the second half, fighting was often done overseas or in Wales or Scotland, by men drawn from throughout the realm. The strains on resources and commitments caused by these expeditions were larger than those before 1066. The increasingly burdensome obligation

[28] *EHD*, i, no. 49, p. 457 (II Cnut 20).

[29] *EHD*, i, no. 49, p. 465 (II Cnut 71); ii, 416 (Assize of Arms, 1181); ii, 161 (ASC 1085 (E)).

of military service began in the twelfth century to cause serious friction between king and lords.

Of course even those who were not required to fight would on occasion be swept up in warfare, or would witness organized violence at close hand. From Danish and Norman invasions, border raids by the Scots and Welsh and the low-level endemic violence typical of England's feuding society, something like warfare touched all parts of the kingdom at least once during this time. Some periods saw warfare widespread in certain regions. It is likely that we hear about only the most egregious attacks, most destructive raids or, in some cases, insignificant fights, the reports of which might fortuitously make their way to chroniclers. Here we depend on these writers' sensibilities to assess violence. It seems clear from the absence of stories about feuds, which must have been legion, that these chroniclers were selective and purpose-driven rather than representative recorders of all events in their proper proportion or indiscriminate chroniclers fed stories by serendipity.

Public war means something different from feud to us, but in England, from the perspective of those who witnessed the violence of groups, war and feud were hardly distinguishable (see Chapter II.4). Both war and feud imposed similar obligations – legal, customary and familial – on the people. The largest military event after the Norman Conquest and English defence, the crusades, in which the English participated, were seen by contemporaries as part of a great feud, with Christian armies seeking vengeance on those who had injured the Christian kin of the English in the Holy Land. While 'feud' may stir images of family against family, in the medieval context any enmity driven by vengeance was in essence a feud. Where feuds could be ended through deaths or through negotiations along with payments to right wrongs, so also wars. Both could be started on small, personal pretexts. Both could also be stratagems for renegotiating relationships. Both could get out of hand, or remain confined to active and willing participants. The feud begun in 1016 by the murder of Uhtred, earl of the Northumbrians, consumed many of the male descendants of three generations of his and his murderer's families as well as several score of their supporters.[30] Other feuds stayed small, with often only a single killing or injury before both sides removed to the courts, where private war could be conducted by legal means.[31] England's feuds and wars continue throughout the period. What is surprising is

[30] Christopher J. Morris, *Marriage and Murder in Eleventh-Century Northumbria: A Study of* 'De Obsessione Dunelmi' (Borthwick Paper 82; York, 1992), pp. 1–5.

[31] Paul R. Hyams, *Rancor and Reconciliation in Medieval England* (Ithaca, NY, 2003), pp. 189–215.

that, despite how pervasive they appear to have been, we cannot now say what the full extent and impact of either was.

ENFORCING JUSTICE

The enforcement of justice was a particular concern of both royal government and local communities throughout the entire period (see Chapter II.3). This enforcement depended not just on the existence of courts that could issue judgements, but also on mechanisms that would compel those involved in cases to appear and accept those judgements. What complicated enforcement was the absence of anything resembling a police force to act as agents of courts. Further difficulties came from the still strong obligation of kin to support its members against their enemies in disputes, in or out of court.

Forcing accused and accuser into court required communal trust, some oversight (generally royal) and the various configurations of oath, witnessing and suretyship with which the English experimented uniquely at a kingdom-wide level. Oaths were the means by which parties asserted their facts to be true in cases, as well as accepted their obligation to act lawfully in general. Oath was central to the workings of justice, especially in the tenth and eleventh centuries. 'Each man', King Alfred commanded just before 900, 'shall keep carefully his oath and pledge.'[32] The earliest recorded oath by witnesses to the facts of a case was the Sandwich plea of 1127, when 'twenty-four wise old men full of years and having good testimony' swore that 'the toll of the port of Sandwich … [and other things] belong only to the archbishop and monks of Christchurch Canterbury'.[33] Only those in good standing in their communities were able to give oaths to either their own trustworthiness or to the facts of any matter before a court.

Acting as a witness to important events or transactions was another responsibility of all freemen in England. Witnessing provided accountability in an age without invoices to sales when theft appears to have been endemic. Æthelred's two codes of 997 dealt with this. It was already a subject treated in early laws and continued to claim a place in codes and treatises far into the twelfth century. The *Laws of Edward the Confessor*, a private treatise written just before the middle of the twelfth century, lays

[32] *EHD*, i, no. 33, p. 409 (Alfred 1).

[33] Doris M. Stenton, *English Justice between the Norman Conquest and the Great Charter* (Philadelphia, 1964), pp. 118–21.

out in detail how livestock that had been found was to be witnessed by priests, reeves and at least twelve of the 'better men' of the four nearest villages.[34] Witnessing involved popular reputation on one level, but also selection by authorities who chose to recognize that reputation. It was an act which, in the Domesday survey of 1086, many thousands of the English performed.

The last of the three mechanisms for enforcing norms, suretyship, occurred in several forms. Fundamentally, every freeman was responsible for other freemen. For practical purposes, the freemen usually were segregated into small groups who would be held responsible for their members' non-appearance in court and, in some cases, for the penalties imposed on one of its members who appeared, was found guilty but could not pay his fine. In Æthelred's Woodstock and Wantage codes, many clauses concern the regulation of suretyship. Woodstock begins with the order that 'every freeman shall have a trustworthy surety who shall hold him to the performance of every legal duty'.[35] Over the tenth and eleventh centuries, this type of suretyship developed into a system in which groups of ten or more men became a *friborh* or frankpledge, as it was later called. The concept of a suretyship group was imported into other arenas; an eleventh-century text speaks of surety groups responsible for the safe-keeping of a betrothed woman. Lords were similarly responsible: 'Every lord shall have his household in his own suretyship.'[36] This last case, however, makes visible the political aspect of suretyship, where lords could pressure courts in favour of their own men rather than merely wait for the results of a case and then fulfil any resultant financial obligation.

England was not a land with a common set of laws, even after the creation of the 'common law' in the twelfth and early thirteenth centuries. Regional or local custom mattered throughout the period. The Wantage code broadened and adjusted Woodstock's narrower precepts to apply to the situation in the Scandinavianized parts of the kingdom, known by the twelfth century as the Danelaw, conquered by Æthelred's predecessors over the previous century, regions that had never been part of any version of the kingdom of the West Saxons ruled by Alfred at his death in 899. However, for us to call northern and eastern England Scandinavian, or the Danelaw, in fact disguises our ignorance of whether the differences in social order found there had anything to do with the settlement of

[34] Bruce R. O'Brien, *God's Peace and King's Peace: The Laws of Edward the Confessor* (Philadelphia, 1999), pp. 182–5.

[35] Robertson, *Laws*, 52–3 (I Æthelred 1).

[36] Robertson, *Laws*, 54–5 (I Æthelred 1.11).

Scandinavian raiders, or were simply existing differences already found in the independent kingdoms of portions of Mercia, and all of East Anglia and Northumbria. The real differences between regions betray a kingdom where customs were local, but also where royal legislation, despite its sensitivity to these customs, attempted to intrude. Although the balance between local custom and royal law may have changed between 900 and 1200, nevertheless even at the end of the period one royalist legal writer, known commonly as Glanvill, could admit concerning common matters of criminal law, which was the most pervasive face of royal justice, that these cases 'are heard and determined according to the varying customs of different county courts', rather than under a uniform royal code.[37]

THE REGULATION OF LABOUR

The one group that had no standing in the great assemblies at Woodstock or Wantage, or for that matter at any major assembly of king and lords, were the agricultural and pastoral labourers of the kingdom, referred to collectively as the peasants. This group would have made up the overwhelming majority of the population during the entire period, but did not constitute an undifferentiated lower class. The categories into which they were divided are difficult to define. Labels like freeman or slave obscure the fact that most lived in some sort of dependent relationship with richer, more powerful people in a variety of circumstances that challenged the skills of even the Domesday commissioners, who, when tasked with their description, were able to visit the shires and ask questions of witnesses. While these commissioners were required by the king to identify only 'villagers, cottagers and slaves' in their inquest, they soon added the missing 'bordars' (*bordarii*) to their list, a group that itself made up over a quarter of the population of the shires they visited and who were domestic servants as well as part of the general peasant labour force.[38] Pre-Conquest regulations under which peasants lived do not always match up comfortably with either Domesday categories or later descriptions. A further problem of identification comes from the fact that peasants were not restricted to rural areas, but also lived in towns in a time when urban centres of all sorts maintained tight relationships with the surrounding countryside (see Chapter III.1). The best

[37] G. D. G. Hall, ed., *The Treatise on the Laws and Customs of England Commonly Called Glanvill*, (Oxford, 1993), p. 177 (xiv. 8).

[38] H. C. Darby, *Domesday England* (Cambridge, 1977), appendix 3.

approach to the problem of defining the social status of the lower classes is to set aside the towns for the moment (see Chapter II. 2) and make a general survey of the rural peasantry, those who were more free as well as less free, and to characterize them in relation to their varying burdens. As the early eleventh-century estate description called the 'Rights and Ranks of People' admitted, the burdens on peasants varied: 'at some places … it is heavier, at some places, also, lighter, because not all customs about estates are alike'.[39]

The scope of the burdens depended in part, according to one modern model, on whether the peasants lived on 'warland', land that paid a national tax, or 'inland', the land directly exploited by landlords.[40] Those living on inland were the most hobbled by custom, which burdened them with the physical work needed to run a farm. These peasants included not only those who ploughed and harvested, but also estate craftsmen and those needed in food and ale preparation. What marked them as different from warland peasants was the fact that they were bound to their estates, unable to seek new lords and fresh opportunities. One wealthy woman in tenth-century Wessex asserted that because 'she owned both stock and men', she could grant to the nuns at Shaftesbury 'the peasants [*gebura*] who dwell on the rented land', while the bondsmen [*þeowra manna*] went to her son's daughter.[41] Warland peasants, if not bound to the soil, were responsible for a number of what could be onerous obligations. Some were public burdens, like repairing and maintaining bridges and fortifications; others were of a more personal nature, such as serving lords and king in any number of ad hoc tasks like carrying messages or goods from place to place. While inland peasants paid no *gafol*, tribute, for their land, the warland peasants did. It is important to recognize, however, that much as English estates before the Norman Conquest depended on their peasant labour force to plough and harvest, these estates may, in the words of Rosamond Faith, 'have remained for a long time seigneurialized islands in a landscape still largely occupied by the holdings of independent peasant farmers'.

It took the Norman Conquest to change the relationship between authority and labouring people. The break-up of larger estates into individual manors, a remarkable growth in population and the increasing needs of the new lords to get what they could from these small estates

[39] *EHD*, ii, no. 172 p. 814.

[40] This paragraph is much indebted to Rosamond Faith, *The English Peasantry and the Growth of Lordship* (London, 1997), chs. 3 and 4. In this paragraph is from p. 177.

[41] Dorothy Whitelock, ed., *Anglo-Saxon Wills* (Cambridge, 1930), pp. 12–13 (no. III).

meant in the long run that peasants of all types, including slaves, were pushed into a more or less single class of agricultural labour which could be more easily coerced. There were checks on this reduction of the labour force: Baxter identifies the bargaining power of village communities, the force of custom and some residual mobility by peasants as the means by which peasants might resist (see Chapter II.2). This resistance, however, merely slowed the pace of change rather than reversed it. By the middle of the twelfth century, less than a century after the conquest, free peasants had been reduced in rights and found themselves fixed with new burdens, while slavery all but disappeared, assimilated into this new, relatively homogeneous peasant class. It was not runaway slaves, but all peasants whom Henry I ordered his agents early in his reign to find and bring back to the abbey of Abingdon.[42]

Regulation of slaves appears only rarely in sources (see Chapter II.6). Kings included them occasionally in their codes; the single reference to the penalties for slaves who failed the ordeal is the only place slaves appear in Æthelred's Woodstock and Wantage codes. Such inattention is typical of all normative texts from the period, and is not surprising. The legal status of slaves was not far from that of chattel at the beginning of the period, and whatever rights they acquired in the following centuries at best raised them to the level of the ever-sinking peasantry. They could own property, marry free persons, serve as guarantors of sales and, at the end of the period, merit the protection of wergild and other fines which would be imposed on their killers. These rights are recorded in prescriptive texts; in reality, the incentive to uphold them would rest not on the wishes of the kingdom's law-makers, but on their lord's calculation of their value. The early twelfth-century *Laws of Henry I* says that if a lord's slave killed another slave, the lord could either pay the wergild and fines for the slave, hand the slave over to the lord of the victim or shed financial liability by releasing the slave from service, which would likely result in the slave's death at the hands of his victim's lord or kin.[43]

One issue concerning treatment of slaves which English kings and the clergy tried to change reveals the limits of the coercive authority of both the episcopate and the state. Bishops attacked in sermons and canon law the sale of native Christian slaves out of the kingdom. Æthelred, Cnut and William I, urged on by their clergy, repeatedly banned the practice.

[42] John Hudson, ed. and trans., *The History of the Church of Abingdon* (2 vols.; OMT; Oxford, 2002–7), ii, pp. 120–3.

[43] L. J. Downer, ed., *Leges Henrici Primi* (Oxford, 1972), pp. 218–21 (70.3, 70.5a).

Nevertheless, in the late eleventh century the trade flourished, most notoriously in the port city of Bristol, where, according to one contemporary, the slave trade was so ingrained that 'neither love of God nor fear of King William had hitherto been able to abolish it'. This fear of the king may be overstatement; the same contemporary witness tells us that William I 'enjoyed a share of the profits from this traffic'.[44] Bishop Wulfstan II of Worcester (1062–95) famously fought against the Bristol trade and had some local success, abolishing it 'gradually' and even inspiring the former slavers to blind one of their number who refused to stop the trade. If stopped in Bristol, it nevertheless continued elsewhere. The Council of Westminster in 1102 banned the trade entirely, though this act had no measurable effect.[45] If kings like William I, and bishops such as Wulfstan of Worcester, tried to end the overseas trade, they did not make any attempt to abolish the institution of slavery within the kingdom. Slavery was thriving in southern England at the time of the Domesday survey and dominating the agricultural labour force in some counties (see Chapter II.6). Nevertheless, before the middle of the twelfth century, it was virtually gone. For the legal treatise writer known as Bracton, writing in the mid-thirteenth century, slavery was an academic subject, immediately followed in his treatise with a discussion of women who give birth to prodigies and babies with six fingers.

The most persuasive explanation for this disappearance is that lords found it more expensive to use slave rather than peasant labour on their estates. Slaves required upkeep and had less incentive to work hard. Peasants, on the other hand, looked after themselves – more and more the further away we move from the year 1000. While slavery might already have been in decline before 1066, this accelerated significantly once acquisitive Norman lords began to press their estates for all they could get out of them. Given these forces, a dependent labour force other than slaves was the most attractive economic option available to lords. What is striking here is that one of the signature social transformations of the period occurred, apparently, without the support or opposition of royal power.

[44] William of Malmesbury, *Life of Wulfstan*, c. 20, in M. Winterbottom and R. M. Thomson eds. and trans., *William of Malmesbury, Saints' Lives: Lives of SS. Wulfstan, Dunstan, Patrick, Benignus and Indract*, (OMT; Oxford, 2002), pp. 100–1; R. A. B. Mynors, R. M. Thomson and M. Winterbottom eds. and trans., *William of Malmesbury, Gesta Regum Anglorum*, (2 vols.; OMT; Oxford, 1998–9), i, pp. 496–9 (iii.269.2).

[45] *Councils and Synods*, i, 2, 678.

No brief survey of the role and effects of kings, lords and laws on themselves as well as on the peasantry can do justice to the complexities of the social situations in England. Major movements or trends might be invisible in some sources, and can only be teased out by detailed analysis. The following chapters will do just that.

CHAPTER II.2

Lordship and labour

Stephen Baxter

Relations between lords and peasants underwent profound change throughout northwest Europe between 900 and 1200, so one way to deepen our understanding of the nature and pace of that change in England is to consider how historians of continental Europe – especially those of France – have approached it. They have developed a model which posits radical change occurring around the year 1000: so rapid that it has been labelled the 'feudal revolution'. Its salient elements are these. In a process which began in the mid- to late tenth century and accelerated during the eleventh, the formal apparatus of Carolingian government disintegrated and collapsed. An aggressive form of seigneurial lordship filled the resulting political and judicial vacuum. Local magnates began to intercept and monopolize payments such as taxation, toll and judicial fines formerly paid to kings and found new, arbitrary and more exploitative ways of extracting surpluses from peasants: *malae consuetudines* (bad customs) such as swingeing tallages, marriage taxes and monopoly control of markets and mills. They also began to preside over private courts, thereby exercising judicial control over the peasantry and depriving them of protection from these forms of 'seigneurial piracy'. All this was sustained by violence. Magnates cultivated the support of an increasingly assertive stratum within the lesser aristocracy – *milites*, 'knights', the 'chevalerie', 'les valets du terrorisme seigneurial' – who derived their power and influence through mastery of new technologies of warfare, above all the castle, heavy cavalry and the crossbow. Competition between magnates to extend and defend territorial gains created a culture of endemic localized warfare; but violence was also used by lords to enforce the payment of novel exactions. The intensification of lordship also had a profound impact on the physical landscape, manifest in various forms: for example, the proliferation of castles, often in conjunction with a radical restructuring of the surrounding landscape; the construction of fortified, hill-top settlements where the peasantry were forced or encouraged by lords to live (a process known as *incastellamento*); and the formation of nucleated settlements, each with a church, a castle and a cluster of dependent peasants – a process known as *encellulement*, the 'cellularization' of society into intensively exploited, self-contained lordships. All this resulted in a fundamental shift in the structure of rural society, causing a sharp decline both in the number of relatively prosperous peasants with free allodial landholdings and in the number of slaves; and a commensurately sharp increase in the number of dependent peasants, who held most of their property from lords in return for heavy rents.[1]

This model of social change has proved fruitfully controversial since it was first formulated in the 1950s. Some historians have argued that it overestimates the power of royal or public authority and underestimates that of lords in the Carolingian period. Others have observed that the nature of the documentary record makes it impossible to compare rural society either side of the year 1000 with any precision: eleventh-century society may appear different from earlier periods, but that may only be because it is illuminated by new kinds of evidence; and if so, the appearance of social change may be a chimera, the product of 'documentary revelation', not a feudal revolution.[2] English-speaking historians have made important contributions to this debate,[3] but have been curiously reluctant to engage with it in relation to English social history.[4] What follows is a provisional attempt to do so. It argues that English evidence offers support for both sides of the debate, suggesting that relations between lords and peasants were determined partly by long-term developments apparent throughout the period, but also by short-term developments which caused the pace of change to accelerate sharply, usually at the peasantry's expense.

Two long-term developments were pivotal in defining relations between peasants: the evolution of the manor and changes in the balance of supply and demand for land and labour. For much of the last century, the

[1] The literature is surveyed by J.-P. Poly and E. Bournazel, *La mutation féodale, Xe–XIIe siècles* (Paris, 1980), trans. C. Higgitt as *The Feudal Transformation 900–1200* (New York, 1991).

[2] D. Barthélemy, *La mutation de l'an mil, a-t-elle eu lieu? Servage et chevalerie dans la France de Xe et XIe siècles* (Paris, 1997).

[3] See, for example, T. Bisson, 'The "feudal revolution"', *P&P*, 142 (1994), 6–42, and the ensuing debate with contributions by D. Barthélemy, S. White, T. Reuter and C. Wickham and Bisson in *P&P*, 152 (1996), 196–223 and *P&P*, 153 (1997), 177–225.

[4] Exceptions include: J. Campbell, 'Was it infancy in England? Some questions of comparison', in M. Jones and M. Vale, eds., *England and Her Neighbours 1066–1453: Essays in Honour of Pierre Chaplais* (London, 1989), pp. 1–17; repr. in his *The Anglo-Saxon State* (London, 2000), pp. 179–200; D. Bates, 'England and the "feudal revolution"', in *Il Feudalesimo nell'alto medioevo* (*Settimane di Studio del Centro Italiano di studi sull'alto medioevo*, 47; Spoleto, 2000), pp. 615–46; A. Wareham, *Lords and Communities in Early Medieval East Anglia* (Woodbridge, 2005).

prevailing view on the origin of the manor in England was that it evolved late in the Anglo-Saxon period; but recent scholarship has developed a persuasive case for thinking that large bipartite estates, which comprised an area cultivated directly for the lord's benefit (called in some documents *inland*) and an area cultivated by peasant farmers rendering tribute and service to those lords (sometimes known as *utland* or *warland*), were in fact ancient structures whose origins lie deep in the Anglo-Saxon, and perhaps prehistoric, past. Throughout the Anglo-Saxon period various forces, of which royal and lordly patronage are the most visible, caused these estates to break into smaller estates, each with their own share of *inland* and *warland*. Both the *inland* and the *warland* was settled and cultivated by peasants paying rents to lords in various forms – in labour, cash or in kind; but the tenants of *inland* tended to hold smaller holdings and pay heavier rents than the tenants of *warland*, who tended to be freer and more prosperous, though also liable to 'public' burdens such as taxation, military service and construction work (see Chapter I.1 and Chapter II.1). Such estates became known as *maneria* (manors) after the Norman Conquest. They grew in number and became more intensively exploited throughout the period between 900 and 1200, causing increasing numbers of peasants to be drawn into their orbit, and into greater levels of dependence.[5]

Demand for peasants' resources grew as kings became more powerful and nobles more numerous. The power of English kings increased as their territorial reach expanded during the tenth century and, with the possible exception of Stephen's reign, royal authority remained powerfully intrusive throughout the period. This was a mixed blessing for the English peasantry. Strong government encouraged peace and economic growth, planted judicial structures which restrained seigneurial aggression and created opportunities for some to prosper through service and patronage; but strong government also created heavy demand for taxation, military service and construction work – burdens which ultimately fell upon the peasantry, in particular the *warland* peasantry. Various forces caused the ranks of the lesser nobility to swell throughout the tenth, eleventh and twelfth centuries: kings and great lords rewarded their retainers with small estates; inheritance caused the division of large aristocratic holdings; and small landholders prospered sufficiently through trade and elite

[5] T. H. Aston, 'The origins of the manor in England', *TRHS* 5th ser., 8 (1958), 59–83; repr. with an important postscript in T. H. Aston, P. R. Cross, C. Dyer and J. Thirsk, eds., *Social Relations and Ideas: Essays in Honour of R. H. Hilton* (Cambridge, 1983), pp. 1–43; R. Faith, *The English Peasantry and the Growth of Lordship* (London, 1997).

service to enter the ranks of the lesser nobility. This placed growing pressure on the land and those who worked it, for although fashions changed, nobles always consumed conspicuously, not least since this defined their status.

Growth in elite consumption was met by growth in population and cultivation. Published estimates of the population at the time of the Domesday survey (1086) range between 1.1 and 2.5 million, but most historians would now accept that the population is unlikely to have been much lower than 2 million, and may well have been higher.[6] The rate of subsequent population growth can be estimated by comparing the number of tenancies recorded on particular manors in 1086 and later manorial surveys. Such comparisons consistently reveal evidence of steep population growth.

	Date of survey	No. of comparable manors	Tenants in 1086	Tenants at date of survey	Percentage increase from 1086
Evesham Abbey	1106	15	384	613	60
Peterborough Abbey	1125–8	25	821	1194	45
Shaftesbury Abbey	1144	10	715	982	37
Ramsey Abbey	*c.* 1160	24	729	1263	73
The church of Worcester	1182	8	412	630	53
Glastonbury Abbey	1189	23	983	1815	85
Evesham Abbey	1191	15	384	816	113
Ely Abbey	1221	3	73	152	108
St Paul's Cathedral	1222	13	306	680	122

The most comprehensive study of such data concludes that the average rate of population growth was about 70 per cent between 1086 and 1150, and about 150 per cent between 1086 and 1230.[7] The absence of comparable data makes it impossible to estimate the rate of population growth before 1086 with any precision, but it is improbable that rapid population growth was a new phenomenon after 1086: there is clear evidence that the rural landscape was filling up, becoming more densely settled and intensively exploited throughout the tenth and eleventh centuries; and this went together with economic growth manifest in the expansion of towns, long-distance trade

6 R. Bartlett, *England under the Norman and Angevin Kings, 1075–1225* (Oxford, 2000), pp. 290–2.

7 H. Hallam, 'Population movements in England, 1086–1350', in H. Hallam, ed., *The Agrarian History of England and Wales*, vol. II, *1042–1350* (Cambridge, 1988), pp. 508–93.

and the volume of coinage. These are complex phenomena, the product of various causal factors, but it would be difficult to account for them without positing significant and sustained population growth.

The growing population was fed partly through more efficient agricultural methods, such as the development of common field agriculture, and growth in the range and diversity of crops grown (see Chapter I.1), and partly through the cultivation of land recovered from woodlands, uplands, marshes and fens (see Chapter I.2, Chapter I.3). On one estimate, the arable area increased from about 8.5 million acres in 1086 to 11.5 million acres in 1300, an increase of 35 per cent. This 'drive to the margins', which began long before 1086, required a colossal labour investment; but even so, it came nowhere close to matching the rate of population growth: according to one estimate, the 'amount of arable land *per caput* roughly halved' between 1086 and 1300.[8] The population thus appears to have grown much faster than the cultivated area and lordly demand between 900 and 1200; and this shift in the balance of supply and demand strengthened the bargaining power of lords.

Short-term developments also had a major impact on relations between lords and peasants. These will be considered in four periods: the later Anglo-Saxon period (900–1066); the Norman Conquest (1066 to 1087); the rest of the Anglo-Norman period (1087–1154); and the Angevin period (1154–1215).

The late Anglo-Saxon state made heavy demands on the peasantry. Tenth- and early eleventh-century legislation adopts an almost fanatical tone concerning the payment of church dues, and there are strong grounds for thinking that tithe became a regularly observed impost during this period. If so, the social consequences of this must have been considerable, for tithe represented a 10 per cent tax on peasants' wealth. Royal taxation was another major drain on peasants' resources. It was especially onerous during the reign of King Æthelred II (978–1016): the Anglo-Saxon Chronicle records that £240,500 was raised to pay *gafol* to the Danes during his reign and in its immediate aftermath, and that another tax known as the *heregeld* was levied to pay for a standing army between 1012 and 1051: this, we are told, 'came before other taxes, which were variously paid, and oppressed people in many ways'. Allowance must be made for chroniclers' instincts for rhetorical exaggeration, but charters

[8] B. Campbell, 'Economic rent and the intensification of English agriculture, 1086–1350', in G. Astill and J. Langdon, eds., *Medieval Farming and Technology: The Impact of Agricultural Change in Northwest Europe in the Middle Ages* (Leiden, 1997), p. 225.

and coins confirm that taxation was exceptionally heavy during these decades; indeed, in some years it may have been heavier than at any other time between 900 and 1200.[9] One way of gauging the effect of long-term exposure to the late Anglo-Saxon state is to consider the distribution of free peasants in Domesday Book. They are concentrated in greatest numbers in East Anglia, the east Midlands and Yorkshire. Stenton thought that the free peasantry of the Danelaw were the descendants of Danes who had settled in England in the late ninth century, establishing a distinctively free settlement pattern. That is one possibility: there is certainly a clear positive correlation between the distribution of free peasants and Scandinavian place-names.[10] However, there remain other possible explanations; for example, it may be that the Danelaw preserved a relatively free social structure because, by comparison with southern and western England, its lords and peasants had been less heavily exposed to the burdens of late West Saxon government during the late ninth and early tenth centuries.

Were *encellulement* and the *seigneurie* present in England before the Conquest? There were undoubtedly numerous thegns and minor noblemen with small manors, many with a seigneurial centre comprising a hall, a church, a gated defensive enclosure – a *bell-hus* and *burh-geat*: the habitat of men like of King Edward's thegn, Ælfsige of Longney, who enjoyed relaxing on summer days under a nut tree beside his church (until Bishop Wulfstan of Worcester cursed the tree, causing it to wither) (see Chapter I.1).[11] Many such estates were intensively exploited within precisely delineated boundaries, closely associated with common-field agriculture and nucleated villages. These might be construed as seigneurial 'cells'. But in England the state remained able to penetrate them: almost every vill and manor recorded in Domesday Book was assessed for the purposes of taxation and other public burdens. There were unquestionably elements of private justice in England before the Conquest, but there were major differences between these and the Frankish *seigneurie*. Domesday Book proves that free landholders, *liberi homines* and sokemen, were bound to lords through commendation, a personal bond, and soke, a judicial bond. Royal grants of 'sake and soke' entitled lords to collect the profits of justice collected in public courts, but there is no clear evidence of

[9] M. Lawson, 'The collection of the Danegeld and heregeld in the reigns of Æthelred II and Cnut', *EHR*, 94 (1984), 721–38, with ensuing debate with J. Gillingham in *EHR*, 104 (1989), 373–406, and *EHR*, 105 (1990), 939–61.

[10] F. Stenton, *Anglo-Saxon England* (3rd edn; Oxford, 1971), pp. 517–25.

[11] A. Williams, *The World before Domesday* (London, 2008), pp. 85–104.

private courts from which royal officials were excluded in England before the Conquest. In addition, commendation also afforded men protection from judicial aggression. Lords undoubtedly had a financial incentive to prosecute those who owed them soke, but freemen therefore commended themselves to other lords who could provide them judicial support, for example by packing courts with oath-helpers and friendly jurors.[12] There was plenty of rough justice in late Anglo-Saxon England, but little private justice. The paradox is that the *seigneurie* was slow to evolve there, partly because of the way lordship worked.

The effect of the Norman Conquest on the English nobility was catastrophic. Domesday Book reveals that there were about 900 tenants-in-chief (lords who held land directly from the king) in 1086, but only 13 of them were English, of whom just 4 were major lords with holdings in excess of 100 hides. Many more English landholders survived at lower levels of the tenurial hierarchy: on one estimate, between 800 and 1,300 subtenants (of whom there were approximately 6,000 or 7,000 in total) were English; but between them they held less than 5 per cent of the landed wealth of England.[13] With the possible exception of the fifth century, this was the most dramatic tenurial revolution in English history. But did the Norman Conquest have any significant effects on the peasantry beyond changing the ethnicity of their lords?

There is overwhelming evidence that it did. The Anglo-Saxon Chronicle complains that in King William's time 'people had much oppression and very many injuries': taxation was heavy, English landholders were forced to buy back their land, large swathes of England were ravaged in retribution for rebellion, the new elite 'imposed unjust tolls and did many other injustices which are hard to reckon up', castles were built 'far and wide' which 'distressed the wretched folk' and left 'poor men hard oppressed'. The king treated the process of land redistribution as an opportunity for extortion: he 'sold his land on very hard terms – as hard as he could. Then came somebody else, and offered more than the other had given . . . and the king gave it into the hands of the man who had offered him most of all, and did not care how sinfully the reeves had got it from poor men.' William's followers shared in this bonanza: both the 'king and the chief men loved gain much and over-much – gold and silver – and did not care how sinfully

[12] S. Baxter, 'Lordship and justice in the early English Kingdom: the judicial functions of soke and commendation revisited', in S. Baxter, C. Karkov, J. L. Nelson and D. Pelteret, eds., *Early Medieval Studies in Memory of Patrick Wormald* (Farnham, 2009), pp. 383–419.

[13] H. Thomas, 'The significance and fate of the English landholders of 1066', *EHR*, 18 (2003), 303–33.

it was obtained provided it came to them'.[14] Such complaints might be dismissed as exaggerated laments of embittered Englishmen were it not for the fact that Domesday Book offers clamorous support for their testimony. The acquisitive culture of the new elite is enshrined in its terms of reference: the Domesday commissioners were instructed to establish whether 'more could be taken' from each estate 'than is now being taken'.[15] Domesday Book confirms that the king of England commanded a formidable machinery for taxing his subjects; that many Englishmen had been forced to buy back their land, or had forfeited their property through failure to pay geld; that much of Yorkshire and the northwest Midlands was laid waste in the winter of 1069; and that the new elite had indeed introduced new customs and exactions: for example, the burgesses of Cambridge complained that they had been accustomed to 'lend their ploughs' to the sheriff three times a year in 1066, but were compelled to do so nine times a year in 1066; and whereas they had provided neither cartage-dues nor carts in 1066, they had to do so in 1066 'because a custom has been imposed'.[16]

Anecdotal evidence of this kind could be multiplied, but the principal evidence for impact of the Conquest on the English peasantry is of three main types. First, Domesday Book reveals a drastic fall in the number of free landholders with modest holdings between 1066 and 1086. Many had been compelled to hold their lands from new lords. A certain Æthelric held 4 hides at Marsh Gibbon in Buckinghamshire freely in 1066, but 20 years later found himself holding the same 'at farm' from William fitz Ansculf 'onerously and miserably' (*graviter et miserabiliter*). The east Midland circuit reveals that the number of freemen and sokemen fell dramatically: from nearly 900 to 177 in Cambridgeshire between 1066 and 1086, from 700 to 90 in Bedfordshire, and from 250 to 43 in Hertfordshire. Second, Domesday Book proves that numerous manors were created or enlarged by absorbing land formerly held by free landholders. At Ringsfield in Suffolk, a freeman of King Edward held 1.5 carucates 'as a manor', and another 11 freemen between them held 1 carucate in 1066. By 1086, the manor was held by King William and had been transformed: 83 freemen, including those who had held there freely in 1066, had been 'added to the manor'; they 'did not pay any customary due to the manor' in 1066, but rendered £15 in 1086: 'Ælfric the reeve arranged this customary due for them in the time of Roger Bigod', we are told.

[14] ASC D *s.a.* 1066, 1069, E *s.a.*, 1083, 1087. [15] *EHD*, ii, p. 946.

[16] DB, i, fol. 189a; further references are collected by R. Fleming, *Domesday Book and the Law* (Cambridge, 1998), p. 529.

Third, Domesday Book demonstrates that many peasants were compelled to pay much higher rents in 1086 than they had done in 1066. The value of Runton in Norfolk is recorded as follows: 'Then [in 1066] and afterwards it was worth 8 shillings; it stood at 20 shillings, but could not pay it; and therefore it now [in 1086] stands for 15 shillings.'[17] Estimates of the average change in the value of non-royal estates are shown in the table.[18]

	Percentage fall between 1066 and 'later'	Percentage fall between 1066 and 1086	Percentage increase between 1066 and 1086
Kent	15	–	29
Surrey	36	–	6
Sussex	40	11	–
Hampshire (excluding the New Forest)	21	–	8
Isle of Wight	16	–	9
Berkshire	17	–	1
Buckinghamshire	24	8	–
Bedfordshire	33	24	–
Cambridgeshire	22	14	–
Hertfordshire	30	20	–
Middlesex	40	18	–
Oxfordshire	–	–	22
Warwickshire	–	–	26
Worcestershire	–	8	–
Gloucestershire	–	5	–
Herefordshire	–	–	7
Shropshire	–	–	9
Cheshire	–	35	–
Staffordshire	–	–	–
Derbyshire	–	36	–
Nottinghamshire	–	19	–
Yorkshire, West Riding	–	51	–
Yorkshire, East Riding	–	74	–
Yorkshire, North Riding	–	78	–
Lincolnshire	–	–	3
Huntingdonshire	–	–	4
Essex	–	–	20
Suffolk	–	–	21
Norfolk	–	–	38

[17] DB, i, fol. 148d; ii, fols. 184b, 282b; H. C. Darby, *Domesday England* (Cambridge, 1977), p. 63.

[18] R. Welldon Finn, *The Norman Conquest and Its Effects on the Economy 1066–86* (London, 1971), p. 35.

Values increased in fourteen shires between 1066 and 1086 – and by more than 20 per cent in six. Unsurprisingly, values fell in the shires affected by the harrying of the North: Cheshire, Nottinghamshire, Derbyshire and, most drastically, Yorkshire. Values also fell in several shires in the east Midlands, but this was probably a function of the process by which free peasants' holdings were absorbed into manors. For example, the value of Picot the sheriff's manor at Bourn in Cambridgeshire fell from £22 in 1066 to £13 in 1086. This consisted of 3 hides held by a thegn named Almær in 1066, together with 10 hides held by two priests and twenty freemen and sokemen. Almær, seven of the sokemen, eight 'villani' and four 'bordari' held land in the village in 1086, but the latter were probably either identical to, or the descendants of, the other pre-Conquest sokemen, and if so they had fallen in social status; and between them all they rendered £13 in rent to Picot in 1086 – more than half of their former income. In this case, the 'fall' in value was probably not the result of declining economic output, but of a radical redistribution of its profits, such that the indigenous landholders retained less than half of the income they formerly enjoyed from their holdings.[19] Such cases help to explain why values fell in shires where the numbers of freeman and sokemen declined: in Bedfordshire, Buckinghamshire, Cambridgeshire, Hertfordshire and Middlesex. These statistics are startling. They demonstrate that the Conquest had a profoundly deleterious effect on the peasantry.

Did the Anglo-Norman elite relax its grip on the English peasantry once these initial gains had been made? Twelfth-century manorial surveys reveal that there was a widespread tendency for lords to lease estates to estate managers at rents, and to commute demesne labour services for money rents; and some historians have interpreted this as evidence that demesne agriculture was declining during the century after Domesday, causing 'the hand of lordship' to become 'lighter'.[20] This latter view is hard to reconcile with the fact that Anglo-Norman kings and lords were consumers *par excellence*. The Pipe Roll of King Henry I for 1129–30 confirms that he was fabulously wealthy: his officials demanded £26,480 that year, of which £14,480 was paid into the exchequer, £2,531 was pardoned, £1,457 was spent and £7,942 remained owing. Roughly half of the income demanded came from land, about 20 per cent came from geld, 15 per cent from the profits of justice and 15 per cent from 'feudal incidents' such

[19] S. Baxter, 'Domesday Bourn', in D. Baxter, *Medieval Bourn: A Cambridgeshire Village in the Later Middle Ages*, (Cambridge, 2008), pp. 35–45.

[20] J. Hatcher, 'English serfdom and villeinage: towards a reassessment', *P&P*, 90 (1981), 33.

as relief, wardship and marriage agreements and from 'aids' and Forest income.[21] These figures suggest that there had been a significant shift in taxation away from the geld and towards the exploitation of feudal incidents; and since the latter were paid by nobles, it might be argued that the fiscal pressure on the peasantry had declined. However, there can be little doubt that lords sought to pass such costs on to the peasantry wherever possible: for example, several *homines* were forced to flee from their farms sometime around 1114–18, when Ranulf Flambard, bishop of Durham, attempted to extract money from them which he owed to the king. The Pipe Rolls for the early years of the reign of King Henry II establish that royal income declined sharply during Stephen's troubled reign. This perhaps brought some relief to the peasantry, but much of what they gained in reduced taxation was lost to predatory lords. According to the Anglo-Saxon Chronicle, powerful men 'oppressed the wretched people of the country severely with castle–building. When the castles were built, they filled them with devils and wicked men' who put men and women in prison and used 'indescribable torture to extort gold and silver'. 'They levied taxes on the villages every so often, and called it "protection money". When the wretched people had no more to give, they robbed and burned the villages … Wretched people died of starvation; some lived by begging for alms, who had once been rich men.'[22] Other near-contemporary writers described similar acts: precisely the combination of castellan violence and predatory lordship which some consider to have characterized the 'feudal revolution' in Francia.[23] More peaceful times brought pressures of a different kind. The Anglo-Norman nobility invested heavily in luxurious accommodation. There were probably about 500 castles in England by 1100; by 1150 many of these had stone keeps. Castles also became the focal points of new landscapes of lordship, with more spacious seigneurial centres lavishly provided with chapels, defensive works, gatehouses, deer parks, moats, fish ponds and dovecotes.[24] Investment in cathedrals and churches was greater still (see Chapter V.1). According to Holt, all this 'represented a vast capital investment, probably a greater capital investment *per capita* than this country has ever seen, at least prior to the industrial revolution of the nineteenth century'.[25]

[21] J. Green, *The Government of England under Henry I* (Cambridge, 1986), pp. 51–94, 223.

[22] ASC E *s.a.* 1137.

[23] Bartlett, *England under the Norman and Angevin Kings*, pp. 284–5.

[24] R. Liddiard, *Landscapes of Lordship: Norman Castles and the Countryside in Medieval Norfolk 1066–1200* (British Archaeological Society, British Series 309; Oxford, 2000).

[25] J. C. Holt, 'Colonial England', in his *Colonial England, 1066–1215* (London, 1997), p. 6.

The riddle of the Anglo-Norman seigneurial economy is thus to explain why demesne agriculture 'declined' in a period when lordly consumption increased. Three points help solve this riddle. First, expansion in the cultivated area helped meet growing demand. Indeed, a significant proportion of the cash-rent tenancies revealed in the twelfth-century surveys were on newly cultivated land: they were therefore the result of expansion, not contraction. Second, it is demonstrable that leasing did not necessarily cause a relaxation of seigneurial pressure: on the contrary, since estates were often leased on high fixed rents, those who managed them were compelled to exploit agrarian resources more, not less intensively.[26] Third, it now seems likely that lords were able to exploit population growth to settle increasing numbers of tenants of every kind – not just cash-rent tenants – on their estates. Domesday Book offers a plausible economic rationale for this. It reveals that manors with a low proportion of demesne and a high proportion of tenanted land tended to generate higher than average values: in other words, the more heavily a manor was tenanted, the more profitable it became. It also reveals that, on many estates, the demesne was under-capitalized whereas tenanted land was over-capitalized with ploughteams: this meant that there was scope for lords to increase the profitability of their estates by extracting more labour and plough traction from their *warland* tenants.[27] The evidence suggests that lords responded to these opportunities by increasing the number of tenants owing labour and cash rents. One way to do so was to allow slaves to become heavily dependent peasants: this helps to explain why slavery vanished from England in the late eleventh and early twelfth centuries. Another was to create new tenancies on land which had been newly acquired or released from demesne. This process, which often involved the creation of similar sized holdings based on fractions of the hide or carucate, appears to have been known as assizing, or the creation of *terra assisa*: a survey of the estates of St Paul's records how many hides were *in dominio* and how many were *terra assisa* in 1181 and in the time of Henry I and on many manors shows an increase in the latter in relation to the former.[28] According to the author of the *Dialogus*, this process began shortly after the Norman Conquest. The Conqueror's regime decreed that if native Englishmen 'had been able to acquire from

[26] A. Bridbury, 'The farming out of manors', *EcHR*, 31 (1978), 503–20.

[27] S. Harvey, 'The extent and profitability of demesne agriculture in the later eleventh century', in Aston *et al.*, eds., *Social Relations and Ideas*, pp. 45–73.

[28] R. Faith, 'Demesne resources and labour rent on the manors of St Paul's Cathedral, 1066–1222', *EcHR*, 57 (1994), 657–78.

their lords on their own merits, in a legal pact' (*pactione legitima*) this 'would be conceded to them by inviolable law' (*inuiolabili iure*) – though 'they could not claim anything for themselves by hereditary right from the time of the Conquest'. Thereafter, 'any member of the subject nation' who held property did so not 'by hereditary right, but only what he obtained by his own merits or by some contract' (*aliqua pactione*).[29] If such agreements were made in writing, none of them survive. However, the fact that the holdings of large number of freemen and sokemen were absorbed into manors between 1066 and 1086 establishes that many new tenancies were indeed created during the Conqueror's reign. The fact that several twelfth-century surveys record large numbers of yardland or half-yardland tenancies held for an identical rent lends further support to this proposition; and the uniformity of the resulting tenures is a strong indication that they were the product of collective bargains between lords and whole bodies of tenants, implemented at a stroke. There is also evidence that this process left its mark in the physical landscape, for in some villages, new tenancies appear to have been laid out in topographically discrete blocks, resulting in a major reorganization of the settlement pattern. These are not the initiatives of lax and distant lords. On the contrary, they help to explain why some lords' incomes grew rapidly in the twelfth century: for example, Peterborough Abbey's demesne estates increased in value by 70 per cent between 1086 and 1125–8; those of Ramsey Abbey increased by 90 per cent between 1086 and 1140; and those of the abbey and bishopric of Ely increased by 90 per cent between 1086 and 1171–2.[30] The evidence suggests that Anglo-Norman lords vigorously embraced effective ways of maximizing their incomes.

The main factors affecting relations between lords and peasants in the Angevin period (1154–1216) were increasing fiscal pressure, inflation, a shift back to demesne farming and the development of the law of villeinage. Those who had suffered at the hands of predatory lords in Stephen's reign may have welcomed the recovery of royal authority under the Angevin kings, but this came at the cost of high taxation. In some years, the incomes of Henry II and Richard I were in the region of £24,000, similar to that of Henry I in 1130; but in his bid to recover

[29] E. Amt, ed. and trans., *Richard fitz Nigel, Dialogus de Scaccario: The Dialogue of the Exchequer*, (OMT; Oxford, 2007), pp. 82–3.

[30] E. King, *Peterborough Abbey: A Study in the Land Market* (Cambridge, 1973), pp. 143–4; E. Miller, *The Abbey and Bishopric of Ely: The Social History of an Ecclesiastical Estate from the Tenth to the Early Fourteenth Century* (Cambridge, 1951), p. 94; J. Raftis, *The Estates of Ramsey Abbey: A Study in Economic Growth and Organization* (Toronto, 1957), pp. 56–9.

Normandy in the years after 1204, John's revenues more than doubled, averaging £49,000 a year between 1207 and 1212. Among the initiatives which made this possible was the imposition of a great 'aid' or tax of 13 per cent of the value of everyone's moveable wealth, which raised £60,000 in 1207.[31] The intensity of John's fiscal exaction was prominent among the causes of the baronial resentment which led to civil war and the making of Magna Carta; and if it was sufficient to cause barons to rebel, it presumably caused much hardship for peasants, too. The rate of inflation was such that prices approximately doubled between about 1180 and 1220. The chronology of this was uneven: prices rose rapidly in the years either side of 1180, dropped back to earlier levels in the 1190s but then soared in the five years after 1200; and although some falls in prices followed, they never came close to earlier levels.[32] This represented a major challenge for lords, since a large proportion of their income was by then derived from fixed leases and cash rents whose real value declined rapidly. Many responded by withdrawing from lease arrangements in favour of direct management and placing greater emphasis on demesne faming and labour rent.[33]

During the same period, profound changes in judicial administration caused sharper legal distinctions between peasants considered to be 'free' and 'unfree' to emerge. A range of legal procedures known collectively as 'the common law' developed during the reign of Henry II (see Chapter II.3 and Chapter II.4). Crucial among these were procedures which simplified and speeded up the process of litigation over land in royal courts; but since these were restricted to those who held their land 'freely', it became essential to differentiate free and unfree tenants and tenancies with greater precision. A body of law – the law of 'villeinage' – evolved to address this problem: peasants were considered unfree if it could be shown that they were unable to leave the manor on which they were born; if their chattels were considered to belong to their lord; if they had themselves been bought or sold like chattels; if the labour services they owed were unfixed and uncertain, such that they did not 'know in the evening the service to be rendered in the morning'; or if they were liable to servile exactions such as 'tallage' or 'aid', *merchet* (a payment made on the marriage of a daughter or son), heriot (an inheritance tax) and *gersuma* (a payment made on entering an unfree tenancy). The extent to which these

[31] N. Barratt, 'The revenue of King John', *EHR*, 111 (1996), 835–55.

[32] P. Latimer, 'The English inflation of 1180–1220 reconsidered', *P&P*, 171 (2001), 3–29.

[33] M. Postan, 'The chronology of labour services', *TRHS* 4th ser., 20 (1937), p. 186.

changes reflect an intensification of lordly pressure on the peasantry is debatable. Some regard them as an unintended by-product of legal developments which had their own logic, and argue that they were not intended to suppress the peasantry, whose social and economic condition remained largely unchanged throughout the twelfth century.[34] Others consider that the development of the law of villeinage constituted a sudden depression in the condition of the peasantry following a period of relative freedom and prosperity, which provoked a sharp reaction: Hilton used the evidence of the early Plea Rolls to show that many peasants protested against the imposition of villein status, as if responding to a 'feeling of immediate loss'.[35] More persuasive is the view that, although the process did constitute an important phase in the extension of seigneurial power, this followed a lengthy period during which lordship had grown, not diminished; and with this in mind, the law of villeinage looks less like a 'judicial by-product of legal change, more like a response to much that had already happened in rural society'.[36] Manorial records certainly support the view that servile payments and services were exacted with greater frequency, for they are rarely recorded in earlier twelfth-century surveys, but *are* recorded in surveys of the late twelfth and early thirteenth centuries. They remained an important source of income for lords thereafter: thirteenth-century manorial court records reveal that they constituted a significant fraction – usually at least a tenth and often more – of manorial incomes.

The thrust of this chapter has been to suggest that several factors enabled lords to place increasing pressure on the peasantry, but there were undoubtedly forces working in the other direction. It is always necessary to remember that peasants were small farmers who would do anything they could to protect the land, livestock and labour on which their prosperity depended; for that reason alone, it can never have been easy for lords to demand higher rents. The formation of village communities strengthened the bargaining powers of groups of peasants vis-à-vis their lords. Manor courts were not unremitting instruments of seigneurial oppression; they also served valuable social functions as small-claim courts for settling disputes between tenants and provided vehicles for communal action against lords. The force of custom made it difficult for lords to impose new demands on the peasantry: as Bracton put it, 'the authority

34 P. Hyams, *King, Lords and Peasants in the Middle Ages: The Common Law of Villeinage in the Twelfth and Thirteenth Centuries* (Oxford, 1980).

35 R. H. Hilton, 'Freedom and villeinage', *P&P*, 31 (1965), 3–19.

36 Faith, *The English Peasantry and the Growth of Lordship*, p. 246.

of custom and long use is not slight'.[37] Although the law placed restrictions on peasant mobility, many peasants seized opportunities to migrate, especially into the margins of Britain, where opportunities to colonize new land on more attractive terms became numerous in the twelfth century. A significant proportion of newly cultivated land was reclaimed by the initiative of peasants. Economic growth opened up possibilities for social advancement, as did the patronage of lords. When Glanvill discussed the position of a former serf who had become a knight after being freed, he was echoing observations on social mobility made a century and a half earlier.[38]

Further research is needed to quantify the net effect of these forces. However, it is certain that the number of manorial tenants increased rapidly between 900 and 1200, and that the rate of population growth exceeded the rate of new land cultivation; it is therefore probable that the average size of peasant holdings fell. It is also probable that the terms of tenancy became harsher; that peasants on average paid a much higher rent per acre in 1200 than they had done in 900; and that the number of relatively free and prosperous peasants fell between these dates as the number of heavily dependent peasants grew. Systematic comparison of Domesday Book and later surveys would make it possible to test these hypotheses.

Did England experience a 'feudal revolution' such as that posited for Francia? Both similarities and differences can be discerned. Royal authority did not retreat in England during the tenth and eleventh centuries – quite the reverse. One effect of this was that the *seigneurie* was slow to evolve in England. Manors existed at the outset of our period, and multiplied thereafter, drawing increasing numbers of peasants into their orbit; but private justice took a long time to emerge in England, and when it did so it was integrated within a mature system of public justice. Like all medieval nobilities, the English nobility was a society organized for war, and heavily armed members of the lesser nobility – thegns, knights, gentlemen and thugs – became an increasingly assertive element in society; but localized civil warfare was rare in England, which is why it shocked the chroniclers of Stephen's reign. In England as on the Continent, social and economic change had a major impact on the landscape, as large territories fragmented into smaller units, filled

[37] G. Woodbine, ed., S. Thorne, rev., *Bracton, De legibus et consuetudinibus Angliae* (Cambridge, MA, 1968), ii, p. 22.

[38] G. Hall, ed., *The Treatise on the Laws and Customs of the Realm of England Commonly Called Glanvill* (OMT; Oxford, 1965), v. 5, p. 58.

up with nucleated villages, *burhs*, castles and churches, and became more intensively exploited. This was *encellulement* of a sort. It also went together with the growth of lordship, for although seigneurial demand, the area of cultivated land and the population all grew rapidly, the rate of population growth was fastest of all, an imbalance which strengthened the bargaining power of lords over the *longue durée*. As a result, in England as in Francia, the numbers of relatively free peasants and slaves declined and the number of heavily burdened peasants increased. By 1200, many more peasants had been drawn into the manorial nexus, were considered legally unfree and were probably paying heavier rents than had been the case 300 years earlier. These were all long-term, almost glacial-paced developments, which could be taken to lend comparative support for those who contend that social change in Francia occurred at an evolutionary, not revolutionary pace. That would be accurate, up to a point. But the English evidence also demonstrates that the pace of change could and did accelerate sharply for short periods of time, with profound social consequences: this probably happened in England during the Viking wars, Stephen's reign and during the period of seigneurial retrenchment either side of the year 1200. It certainly happened between 1066 and 1086. Domesday Book establishes beyond reasonable doubt that a French-speaking elite made deep inroads into the resources of a nation's peasantry in a very short space of time. That this happened in England makes it all the more probable that something similar happened in France.

CHAPTER II.3

Order and justice

John Hudson

THE PROBLEM OF DISORDER

According to Richard fitz Nigel, the royal treasurer, writing in the late 1170s,

> because of the innumerable riches of this kingdom, and also because of the natives' innate tendency to drunkenness which is always accompanied by lust, theft often occurs either openly or secretly, and also homicides and other sorts of crime; and the criminals are egged on by loose women, so that there is nothing that they will not dare or attempt when they listen to their counsels.[1]

This diagnosis receives support from anecdotal evidence, for example from a near-contemporary story recounted by hagiographers of Thomas Becket.[2] A peasant named Ailward lived on the royal manor of Westoning in Bedfordshire. His neighbour owed him a penny for ploughing that Ailward had performed, but the neighbour refused to pay, claiming that he could not afford it. However, he did have enough money to go to the tavern. The writer points out that 'it was the custom of the English on feast days to indulge in banqueting and getting drunk, and to watch their enemies and mock their observance of the holy days'. Still the neighbour refused to pay the debt, even when Ailward demanded only half of it, allowing them each to spend a halfpenny on drinking. Ailward then took matters into his own hands. He broke into his neighbour's house and seized various goods, including a whetstone. These goods, we are told, were barely worth a penny. His drunken burglary was spotted by his neighbour's children, who alerted their father. He caught up with Ailward,

> wrung the whetstone from him and launched it against his head, thus breaking the whetstone on his head and his head with the whetstone. Drawing also the

[1] E. Amt, ed. and trans. *Richard fitz Nigel, Dialogus de Scaccario*, Bk ii. c. 7, (OMT; Oxford, 2007), p. 131.

[2] R. C. van Caenegem ed. *English Lawsuits from William I to Richard I*, (2 vols.; Selden Society, 106, 107; London 1990–1), no. 471.

sharp knife that he was carrying, he pierced his arm, got the better of him and took the miserable man in fetters as a thief, robber, and burglar to the house into which he had broken.

Only now did an official become involved, for the neighbour went to the royal reeve. On his advice, further goods were loaded on Ailward, so that his alleged theft appeared more serious. Ailward was brought before the sheriff and the county court. He was then kept in custody at Bedford until judgement might be made before the royal justices at Leighton Buzzard. There he denied theft, stating that he had only taken goods as security for a debt. Nevertheless, he was eventually put to trial by water. This he failed, and 'was led away to the place of execution', where 'a not inconsiderable crowd of people had gathered to see the spectacle, whether compelled by public authority or moved by curiosity'. The neighbour and the royal reeve then put out his eyes and castrated him. The voyeuristic can still see a pictorial account in a stained-glass window at Canterbury Cathedral.

The story of Ailward illustrates many of the problems of order in the medieval period. Self-help and vengeance were often the response to a perceived wrong. Such self-help might be accepted, might be channelled through communal activity, or might be considered an offence, as conducted in an improper fashion or for an unjust cause. Thus it was laid down in the tenth century that 'if anyone tries to avenge a slain thief, or show enmity to any of those who slew him, then he shall be the enemy of the king and all his friends'.[3]

Ailward's case also shows how disputes between neighbours in small communities might easily arise and might rapidly escalate, fuelled perhaps by underlying quarrels and certainly by alcohol. Ailward got away with just a cracked head and a wounded arm in the initial struggle, but the routine carrying of knives made severe wounding and death very likely, particularly given the possibility of mortality from infected wounds. Less common, but of notoriety, were crimes of passion. Again in a *Life* of Becket we are told that the mother of one of the saint's murderers had been

ardently in love with a young man called Litulf, but he rejected adultery. So she asked by some extraordinary female trickery that he should bring her horse forward and draw his sword as if to play a game. As he did this, she (in the language of the country) exclaimed to her husband who was in front of her: 'Hugh

[3] II Æthelstan, 20. 7: F. L. Attenborough, ed., *The Laws of the Earliest English Kings* (Cambridge, 1922), pp. 138–9.

de Morville, Litulf has drawn his sword, beware, beware, beware.' Therefore the innocent man was condemned to death and boiled in hot water.[4]

A more widely feared problem may have been the outsider who committed a crime and then vanished, or the local troublemaker who trusted in his power to intimidate. Tenth-century regulations from a London guild, the purpose of which was to maintain the peace, stated that 'if it happens that any group of kinsmen ... is so strong and powerful that it blocks our justice and stands up in defence of a thief, we shall ride out against them in full force with the reeve in whose district the offence takes place'.[5]

Thirteenth-century sources suggest an approximate annual homicide rate of one killing per twenty villages. Lesser violence between men must have been much more common than homicide, and sometimes have been accepted as a routine part of life, particularly if no shedding of blood were involved. Assaults on women might lead to compensation or punishment: a twelfth-century text states that 'if anyone assaults a woman, he shall suffer castration as a penalty. If anyone throws a woman to the ground in order to offer violence to her, the compensation to her lord for the breach of his protection shall be ten shillings.'[6] Petty theft must have been common, but of particular concern was cattle stealing. Cattle might constitute a large part of a person's capital, their theft disastrous to the owner, potentially extremely profitable to the thief. Considerable regulation of cattle sales existed in order to ensure that ownership was clear. Meanwhile, arson may have been particularly feared, in a world where buildings were highly flammable, all too vulnerable to the shamefully stealthy arsonist.

PREVENTION AND POLICE

It would be several centuries before professional police forces appeared in England, and in the tenth to twelfth centuries prevention and policing were primarily the responsibility of local communities. The major problem was actually to catch offenders, so the emphasis was upon either deterring offences or catching miscreants red-handed. Thereafter, as we saw in Ailward's case, public punishment would be used to deter others.

[4] van Caenegem, ed., *English Lawsuits*, no. 330.

[5] VI Æthelstan, 8. 2: Attenborough, ed., *Laws*, pp. 162–3.

[6] Leis Willelme, 18: A. J. Robertson, ed., *The Laws of the Kings of England from Edmund to Henry I* (Cambridge, 1925), pp. 262–3.

Ties of neighbourhood, family or lordship might restrain potential offenders whilst protecting the community's members. A twelfth-century charter for the burgesses of Bury St Edmunds states that

> it is their custom to find eight men per year for the four wards to guard the town at night and on the feast of St Edmund sixteen men for the four gates, two during the day and two during the night and similarly during the twelve days following the birth of the Lord. They shall also find four gatekeepers per year for the four gates, the fifth gate being the east gate and in the abbot's hand.[7]

Lords were responsible for the behaviour of their own households. Another twelfth-century text tells us that 'barons had their knights and their own servants, namely stewards, butlers, chamberlains, cooks, and bakers under their own *friborg*, and these men had their esquires and other servants under their *friborg*'.[8] The term *friborg* is the same as the more familiar 'frankpledge', which is usually used of communal rather than lordship responsibilities. The system known as frankpledge may well predate the Norman Conquest, and certainly key elements existed in Anglo-Saxon England. A group known as a 'tithing' was made up of ten or twelve men, or sometimes all the men of a settlement, who were mutually responsible for their behaviour. They acted as sureties that the tithing's members would not commit offences, and had to produce the offender if a wrong was done. Failure to do so left them owing a monetary penalty to the king. There was thus a clear incentive both to prevent offending and to capture perpetrators.

Yet misdeeds were still done, and it seems likely that miscreants not caught swiftly were often not caught at all. Fugitives who had committed serious offences were outlawed, that is they were put outside the protection of the law. Such men were said by the English to bear the 'wolf's head'.[9] An outlaw should be killed if he resisted arrest or immediately his outlawry had been proved.

TRIAL AND PUNISHMENT

If the accused had been captured, he might be able to arrange a settlement, probably through payment to the wronged party and quite possibly to a local official. Otherwise he faced accusation in court. The accusation

[7] van Caenegem, ed., *English Lawsuits*, no. 295.

[8] *Leges Edwardi*, 21: Bruce R. O'Brien, *God's Peace and King's Peace: The Laws of Edward the Confessor* (Philadelphia, 1999), p. 180.

[9] *Leges Edwardi*, 6. 2a: O'Brien, *God's Peace and King's Peace*, pp. 164–5.

normally would be brought by the victim or, in cases of homicide, a relative of the dead victim. However, as we shall see, accusations might also be made by royal officials or, at least in certain periods, by groups of sworn men from the locality. Some cases might be settled by common knowledge of the facts, whilst in others physical evidence was used. A man named Helmstan

> stole the untended oxen at Fonthill … and drove them to Cricklade, and there he was discovered, and the man who tracked him rescued the traced cattle. Then he fled, and a bramble scratched him in the face; and when he wished to deny it, that was brought as evidence against him.[10]

In the absence of obvious guilt, the accused would seek to clear himself by compurgation, that is by swearing an oath denying the accusation and by a group of oath-helpers swearing that his word should be trusted. In other cases the accused might have to go to ordeal by water or iron, whilst after the Conquest trial by combat, between accuser and accused, became a common form of proof.

The convicted faced the consequence of their wrongdoing. For minor offences, compensation to the victim and monetary penalty to the authorities would be the norm. However, physical punishment was also of importance, both before and probably increasingly after the Norman Conquest. We know of the use of the death penalty from written and archaeological sources. About twenty cemeteries, it has been suggested, may have characteristics of judicial execution sites. The skeletons that they contain in some cases display evidence of decapitation different from that probably suffered in combat, whilst others have hands tied behind the back and may have suffered hanging.

DISORDER AND ROYAL CLAMPDOWNS

So far the period has been treated very much as a whole, but there are indications of particular times of disorder. In the Anglo-Saxon period evidence for crime is particularly plentiful from Æthelred the Unready's reign (978–1016). This may result from the unusually frequent mention of crimes in royal charters, but also could relate to the diminution of order linked to the Viking attacks. Cases again show resort to self-help, the turning to royal authority and problems arising from the actions of royal officials.

[10] Sawyer, *Anglo-Saxon Charters*, no. 1445.

There were three brothers sharing a certain establishment, one of whose men, named Leofric, stole a bridle at the instigation of the devil. When it was found in his bosom, those who had lost the bridle, and the three brothers, the masters of the aforesaid thief, rose up hurriedly and fought with one another. Two of the brothers, namely Ælfnoth and Ælfric, were killed in the fight and the third, Æthelwine, barely escaped along with the aforesaid robber, entering the church of St Helen [at Abingdon].[11]

Such men should have been denied Christian burial, for crime and sin were closely associated. However, Æthelwig, the king's reeve of Buckinghamshire, together with the reeve of Oxford gave the brothers Christian burial. Ealdorman Leofsige of Essex, whose interest in the case is not entirely clear, reported the reeves' misdeed to King Æthelred, but the king, as a favour to Æthelwig, allowed the Christian burial to remain.

The other major breakdown of authority in our period is associated with the succession dispute and civil war of King Stephen's reign. We hear much in contemporary chronicles of the oppressions carried out by holders of castles, but it is a later source, from the early thirteenth century, which provides one of the best stories of everyday wrongdoing:

In the war of King Stephen, it happened that a knight named Warin of Walcote was an honest itinerant knight and he fought in the war and at length he passed through the dwelling of Robert of Shuckburgh … And Robert had a daughter named Isabel whom Warin loved and took, so that he asked Robert to give him his daughter, and he could not have her, both because of Robert and his son William who was then a knight. At length William went out to fight and was killed in the war. Hearing this, Warin came with a multitude of men and took Isabel away by force and without the assent and will of Robert her father and of Isabel herself, and he held her for a long time.

He then entered upon a life of violence and theft, until the time of Stephen's successor, Henry II. At this point, the records tell that:

he fell into poverty because he could not rob as he used to do, but he could not refrain from robbery and he went everywhere and robbed as he used. And King Henry, having heard complaints about him, ordered that he should be taken. Eventually he was captured, brought before the king, and Henry, that he might set an example to others to keep his peace, by the counsel of his barons, ordered Warin to be put in the pillory, and there he was put and there he died.[12]

[11] S. E. Kelly ed., *Charters of Abingdon Abbey*, (2 vols.; Oxford, for the British Academy, 2000–1), no. 125.

[12] D. M. Stenton, ed., *Rolls of the Justices in Eyre, 1221–2* (Selden Society, 59; London, 1940), pp. 167–9.

As this case shows, there were not just breakdowns of authority but also periods of particular royal effort against disorder. One such may have come in the reign of King Æthelstan (924–39). Certainly his legislation is marked by particular ferocity. If a thief takes flight:

> he shall be pursued to his death by all men who are willing to carry out the king's wishes, and whoever shall meet him shall kill him. And he who harbours him shall forfeit his life and all that he has as if he were a thief himself, unless he can prove that he was not aware of any theft or crime for which the fugitive's life was forfeit. In the case of a free woman, she shall be thrown from a cliff or drowned. In the case of a male slave, sixty and twenty slaves shall go and stone him. And if any of them fails three times to hit him, he shall himself be scourged three times.[13]

How effective such measures were we cannot tell, but we do also hear Æthelstan complaining that 'I have learned that the public peace has not been kept to the extent either of my wishes or of the provisions laid down at Grateley. And my councillors say that I have suffered this too long.'[14]

Another particular effort may have come under Henry I (1100–35), soon after his death, famed as the Lion of Justice. He was able at least to take successful measures against what appears to be a large criminal gang:

> In the course of [1124] after St Andrew's day [30 November], before Christmas, Ralph Basset and the king's thegns held a council at 'Hundehoge' in Leicestershire, and hanged there more thieves than had ever been hanged before; that was in all forty-four men in that little time; and six men were blinded and castrated.[15]

In this case Ralph Basset may be a justice specially dispatched by the king, but Henry also had a powerful local intelligence and prosecution network. Thus we hear of

> a certain minister of King Henry [I], who was more particularly a servant of the devil with wolf-like fangs ... He was nicknamed *Malarteis*, from the Latin meaning 'ill-doer'. The name was well deserved, for he seemed to have no function except to catch men out. All men, I repeat: monks and clerks, knights and peasants, men of every order, whether living under a religious vow or otherwise ... He accused all equally whenever he could, striving with all his might to harm everyone ... If he could find no valid reason for condemning them, he became an inventor of falsehood and father of lies through the devil who spoke in him.[16]

[13] IV Æthelstan, 6. 3–5: Attenborough, ed., *Laws*, pp. 148–51.
[14] V Æthelstan, Prologue: Attenborough, ed., *Laws*, pp. 152–3.
[15] van Caenegem, ed., *English Lawsuits*, no. 237.
[16] van Caenegem, ed., *English Lawsuits*, no. 204.

However, it is particularly with Henry I's grandson, Henry II, that we associate royal efforts against disorder. Key measures were taken in the mid-1160s, with the Assize of Clarendon. Juries of twelve lawful men were chosen from each of the administrative units called 'hundreds', and of four lawful men from each village. These men made 'presentments' to royal justices travelling on circuits, that is they jointly made public accusations on oath as to 'whether there be in their hundred or village any man accused or notoriously suspect of being a robber or murderer or thief, or any who is a receiver of these'. The suspects went to ordeal by water, and if found guilty were punished by the loss of a foot, and forced to leave the realm within forty days. Even if acquitted, 'if they have been of ill repute and openly are disgracefully spoken of by the testimony of many and that of lawful men', they were to leave the realm within eight days.[17] Co-operation between local officials was enforced:

> if any sheriff shall send word to another sheriff that men have fled from his county into another county, on account of robbery or murder or theft or the harbouring of them … let [the second sheriff] arrest them; and also if he knows of himself or through others that such men have fled into his county, let him arrest them and guard them until he has taken safe pledges for them.[18]

The king was willing to spend money on enforcement, and we have a record of the allowance to the sheriff of Wiltshire of 5 shillings for ordeal pits for the judgement of robbers and 20 shillings for payment of the priests who blessed them.[19] At the same time, it was the king who was to receive the profits arising from the new procedures:

> concerning those who are taken by the oath of this Assize, none are to have court or justice or chattels except the lord king in his court in the presence of his justices, and the lord king will have all their chattels. Concerning those who are taken other than by this oath, let it be as is accustomed and proper.[20]

Such a provision, together with the emphasis on cases being heard before itinerant royal justices in courts that were seen very much as the king's court, show a new pattern of central control characterizing Henry II's clampdown on crime.

[17] Assize of Clarendon, 14: *EHD*, ii, pp. 442–3.
[18] Assize of Clarendon, 17: *EHD*, ii, p. 443.
[19] PR 12 Henry II (Pipe Roll Society, 9; 1888), p. 72; see also, e.g., p. 117, which mentions blessing of a pit and also work on Oxford gaol.
[20] Assize of Clarendon, 5: *EHD*, ii, p. 441.

CONCLUSION

It seems unfair to leave the peasant Ailward in his mutilated state. Why was his punishment so graphically illustrated in the Canterbury glass? Because his devotion to St Thomas Becket led to miraculous intervention, and he was almost fully cured. First his eyes were restored, although one of them now was black rather than multicoloured. Then he set off to walk to Canterbury: 'having walked about four thousand paces he started to scratch with his hand the itching scrotum of his testicles and discovered that he had recovered those organs which although still very small were growing all the time; nor did he object to anyone wanting to touch them'. His story thus spread, providing an example of devotion to the saint but surely also a warning to those who in drunk and disorderly fashion sought to take law into their own hands.

CHAPTER II.4

War and violence

John Hudson

Historians have often separated their treatments of war and of other forms of violence. They have done so mainly on two related criteria, the status of the leading participants and the scale of the violent activities; wars are large scale and the parties are obedient to opposing rulers or certainly leaders of high status. People in the tenth to twelfth centuries, however, used words such as '*guerra*' both of conflicts between rulers and between parties of much lower status. At the same time, they, too, made distinctions, not only as to scale but also, for instance, as to legitimacy. Although churchmen made efforts to lay down strict canons of legitimacy, in practice judgment was very much in the eye of the beholder; the use of force by others might be seen as improper, and in turn require a forceful response. Thus Jordan Fantosme has Henry II of England state:

> My lords, give me your counsel! My son is wronging me, it is right that you should be aware of this, for he wants to win by force revenues from my lands; I do not think it right that they should be made over to him; such revenues have never been extorted from one in my strong position. What is taken or achieved by force has no title in right or reason; that has often been decided. Harsh things are said about me because I stand up for my rights … yet there is no reason why we should suffer further harm. I pray you, my lords, to unite in aiding me; prove your strength in the heat of battle, and exert all your efforts on my behalf.[1]

CHIVALRY

No doubt all levels of society had their own notions of the proper conduct of violence in their own lives and in society, but we know most about the aspirations of the aristocracy, about the values that historians at least of post-Conquest England refer to as chivalry. These values were instilled from a young age. As a child King Alfred listened day and night to

[1] R. C. Johnston, ed. and trans., *Jordan Fantosme's Chronicle*, (OMT; Oxford, 1981), lines 212–24.

'Saxon poems', and retained them in his memory; these were presumably heroic verses, perhaps resembling *Beowulf*.[2] When Simon of Senlis, earl of Huntingdon (d. 1153), was a little boy, he 'used to collect branches and brushwood to build a castle and, mounting a toy-horse as his steed and brandishing a branch like a lance, would, with other boys of his own age, undertake the guard and defence of this imaginary play-castle, imitating the ways of knights'.[3] The values might need particular reinforcement before battle. Thus the mid-twelfth-century poet Wace, in his *Roman de Rou*, pictures events before the Battle of Hastings, a century earlier:

> Taillefer, a very good singer, rode before the duke on a swift horse, singing of Charlemagne and Roland and of Oliver and the vassals who died at Rencesvals. When they had ridden until they drew close to the English, Taillefer said: 'My lord, I pray you! I have served you for a long time and you owe me a debt for all my service. Discharge your debt to me today, if you please. As my only reward I beseech you and want to beg you earnestly for this. Grant me, and let me not fail in it, the first blow in the battle.' The duke replied: 'I grant it.' Taillefer spurred his horse impetuously and positioned himself before all the others. He struck an Englishman and killed him beneath his feet, passing his lance right through his belly. He laid him out dead on the ground. Then he drew his sword, struck another knight, then cried: 'Come on, come on! What are you doing? Strike, strike!'[4]

At least ideally, chivalry was a matter both of song and deed.

At the same time, impetuosity might be a vice, in particular in those who had responsibility for the safety of others. The relative values of bravery and prudence must have been a matter of discussion amongst at least some of those who listened to the *Song of Roland*, with its debate between Oliver and Roland as to whether to sound the horn, the Oliphant, in order to obtain aid for the Frankish rearguard. An alternative model of good rulership is presented by William of Malmesbury in his portrayal of Henry I: the king 'was capable in administration and obstinate in defence, striving to avoid wars as long as he honourably could; but once he had decided that a situation could no longer be supported, he became insupportable himself in the quest for revenge, armed with resolution like a shield to beat down the dangers in his path'.[5]

[2] *Asser, Life of Alfred*, § 22, in S. Keynes and M. Lapidge trans. *Alfred the Great*, (London, 1983), p. 75.

[3] *Jocelin of Furness, Vita S. Waldevi*, in *Acta Sanctorum*, August 1 (Antwerp, 1733), p. 251.

[4] G. S. Burgess, A. J. Holden and E. M. C. van Houts, eds. and trans., *Wace, The Roman de Rou*, (Jersey, 2002), lines 8013–38.

[5] R. A. B. Mynors, R. M. Thomson and M. Winterbottom, eds. and trans., *William of Malmesbury, Gesta regum Anglorum*, Bk v. §. 411, (2 vols.; OMT; Oxford, 1998–9), i. 742–3.

ARMIES

The literary texts present the waging of war very much as a collaborative activity involving leader and followers, rather than a matter of service that had to be performed. Crucial probably to the audience of such literature and to the conduct of campaigns were the lords' military retinues, the *huscarls* of the Anglo-Scandinavian kings, the household knights of the Norman rulers. These might be composed of some of the lord's relatives and of other men, often young and seeking reward for their service.

On occasion it might be hard to distinguish sharply between household troops and mercenaries, although the latter might have a shorter-term connection to their employer. In any case, paid troops were of considerable importance throughout our period, and at times might amount almost to a standing army. The Anglo-Saxon Chronicle records the English paying £48,000 tribute to the Danes in 1012: 'When that tribute was paid and the oaths of peace were sworn, the Danish army then dispersed as widely as it had been collected. Then forty-five ships from that army came over to the [English] king, and they promised him to defend this country, and he was to feed and clothe them.' Later the Chronicle states of Harold Harefoot (1035–40) that 'in his time 16 ships were paid for at eight marks for each rowlock [presumably each oarsman], just as had been done in Cnut's time'.

In addition there were obligations to provide military service. It seems plausible that throughout the period there was a requirement that all freemen be prepared to serve, at least in time of particular emergency. The Anglo-Saxon Chronicle for 893 may well be referring to men serving on such a basis when it states that King Alfred 'had divided his army into two, so that always half its men were at home, half on service, apart from the men who guarded the boroughs'. In 1181 Henry II specified the arms and armour to be had not only, for example, by every holder of a knight's fee, but also every free layman; such freemen and burgesses were to have 'quilted doublets and a headpiece of iron and a lance'.[6]

Also needed were methods of raising more elite troops. Before 1066, this seems to have been done on a hidage basis, as suggested, for example, by a Domesday Book entry for Berkshire: 'if the king sent an army anywhere, only one knight went from five hides, and for his food or pay from each hide four shillings were given to him for two months. They

[6] Assize of Arms, 3: *EHD*, ii, no. 27.

did not send this money to the king but gave it to the knights.'[7] After the Conquest, service came to rest on quotas set for the king's tenants and then by such men for their own followers. Often, rather than actual service, the king took a commutation payment known as scutage, based on the quotas, with which he could then pay other troops.

There was also a need for troops to garrison fortifications. These appear to have been gathered on a similar variety of bases: household retainers, paid troops, those owing service. The document known as the Burghal Hidage shows such an obligation existing at the start of our period, for the garrisoning of the *burhs* of the kings of Wessex: 'for the maintenance and defence of an acre's breadth [22 yards] of wall, sixteen hides are required; if every hide is represented by one man, then every pole [five and a half yards] can be manned by four men'.[8]

In many encounters the numbers involved may have been small, tens or hundreds. In the largest battles, notably Hastings, numbers certainly reached thousands, and it has even been argued that both armies may have been well into five figures.[9] Armies on such a scale must have caused immense logistical problems. Even if the Conqueror's army had only 3,000 war-horses, it has been calculated that they would have required each month about 600 tons of grain and the same of hay.[10]

BATTLE TACTICS

Anglo-Saxon forces seem to have fought on foot, even if they travelled to battle by horse. The poetic account of the Battle of Maldon gives a good sense of the close-ranked tactics and of the variety of weapons employed:

> There, ready to meet the foe, stood Brihtnoth and his men. He bade them form the war hedge with their shields, and hold their ranks stoutly against the foe. The battle was now at hand, and the glory that comes in strife ... They let the spears, hard as files, fly from their hands, well-ground javelins. Bows were busy, point pierced shield; fierce was the rush of battle, warriors fell on either hand, men lay dead. Wulfmær was wounded, he took his place among the slain; Brihtnoth's kinsman, his sister's son, was cruelly cut down with sword.[11]

[7] DB, i, fol. 56v. [8] Keynes and Lapidge, trans., *Alfred the Great*, p. 194.

[9] M. K. Lawson, *The Battle of Hastings 1066* (Stroud, 2002), pp. 163–71.

[10] Lawson, *The Battle of Hastings*, p. 166; A further problem was the potential squalor and sickness threatened by the equine production of up to 5 million pounds of excreta and 700,000 gallons of urine.

[11] *EHD*, i, no. 10 pp. 294–5 (old edn).

The classic contrast with such infantry tactics is the Norman cavalry charge, as best depicted on the Bayeux Tapestry. Often, however, the kings and knights of post-Conquest England fought on foot, sometimes in co-operation with horsemen. Orderic Vitalis tells us that, at the Battle of Tinchebray in 1106, on the Duke of Normandy's side:

Ralph of Bayeux commanded the first column, Robert count of Meulan the second and William of Warenne the third … [On the other side] the king [Henry I] himself kept the English and Normans with him, dismounted, and posted the Manceaux and Bretons some distance away under Count Helias … When the two armies clashed, and the troops of Count William were trying to cut down Ralph's force, they were so closely crowded together and were brought to a halt with their weapons so closely locked that it was impossible for them to strike one another, and all in turn struggled to break the solid lines. As shouts and cries sounded from both sides Helias suddenly charged with his men, attacked the duke's helpless foot-soldiers on the flanks, and cut down two hundred and twenty five of them in the first onslaught.[12]

In addition there were troops, most notably archers, who fought only on foot.

It is disputable how much control a leader had over his army in battle. William of Poitiers suggests the use of sophisticated, highly disciplined tactics at Hastings:

When the Normans and the troops allied to them saw that they could not conquer such a solidly massed enemy force without heavy loss, they wheeled round and deliberately feigned flight. They remembered how, a little while before, their flight had brought about the result they desired. There was great jubilation among the foreigners [i.e. King Harold's men], who hoped for a great victory. Encouraging each other with joyful shouts, they heaped curses on our men and threatened to destroy them all forthwith. As before, some thousands of them dared to rush, almost as if they were singed, in pursuit of those they believed to be fleeing. The Normans, suddenly wheeling round their horses, checked and encircled them, and slaughtered them to the last man.[13]

However, some are sceptical that a manoeuvre requiring such tight control could have been executed amidst the chaos of battle, so well evoked in the description of the Battle of Maldon quoted above. What is clear, though, is that commanders did exercise considerable control in the period leading up to battle, through use of intelligence. For a year before

[12] M. Chibnall, ed. and trans., *Orderic Vitalis, The Ecclesiastical History of Orderic Vitalis*, (6 vols.; OMT; Oxford, 1969–80), vi. 88.

[13] R. H. C. Davis and M. Chibnall, eds. and trans., *William of Poitiers, The Gesta Guillelmi of William of Poitiers*, (OMT; Oxford, 1993), p. 132.

he moved against Robert de Belleme, Henry I had him watched by men called in the Latin source '*privati exploratores*', surely translatable as 'secret agents'.[14]

SIEGE

Attacks on fortifications were of considerable importance both before and after the Norman Conquest, although the Norman introduction of castles to England clearly increased the importance of sieges. Faced by Henry I's imminent attack, Robert de Belleme had the walls and ramparts of his castles strengthened. Henry responded by besieging Robert's castle at Arundel, against which he built siege-castles. Eventually the occupants surrendered, and the king received them kindly and gave them gifts, thereby encouraging a further surrender at another castle.[15] As castles became stronger, a larger proportion being built of stone, more powerful siege engines were needed with which to bombard the defences. These brought mixed success, as during a Scottish siege of a northern English castle in 1174:

> The king of Scots grew very angry when he saw his [men] dying and meeting with no success … and he said to his knights in his great grief: 'Bring up your catapult without delay! If the engineer speaks truly, it will batter down the gate and we shall take the bailey in no time at all.' Now … hear how the first stone that it ever hurled left the catapult: the stone barely tumbled out of the sling and it knocked over one of their own knights to the ground. Had it not been for his armour and the shield he was carrying he would never have returned to any of his relatives.[16]

When besieging Rochester in 1215 King John saw that his war engines were having little effect and had to turn to different method.

> [He] at length employed miners, who soon threw down a great part of the walls. The provisions of the besieged too failed them, and they were obliged to eat horses and even their costly chargers. The soldiers of the king now rushed to the breaches in the walls, and by constant fierce assaults they forced the besieged to abandon the castle, although not without great loss to their own side.[17]

A royal writ records the purchase of the necessary combustibles, whereby the wooden staves holding up the mine might be burnt, leading to the

[14] Chibnall, ed., *Ecclesiastical History of Orderic Vitalis*, vi. 20–1.

[15] Chibnall, ed., *Ecclesiastical History of Orderic Vitalis*, vi. 20–3.

[16] Johnstone, ed., *Jordan Fantosme's Chronicle*, lines 1235–47.

[17] H. O. Coxe ed. *Roger of Wendover, Flores historiarum*, (4 vols.; London, 1841–4), iii. 334.

collapse of the tower: 'with all speed, by day and night, send to us forty bacon pigs of the fattest and least good for eating, to bring fire beneath the tower'.[18]

RAVAGING, FEUD AND OTHER VIOLENCE

If sieges and open battles were the most spectacular manifestations of violence, much more common was ravaging. This could be part of a wider military strategy. We are told that in 1149 King Stephen

> deliberated on the most effective means of shattering his opponents and the easiest way of checking the continual disorder that they fomented in the kingdom. Different people gave advice of different sorts, but at last it seemed to him sound and judicious to attack the enemy everywhere, plunder and destroy all that was in their possession, set fire to the crops and other means of supporting human life, and let nothing remain anywhere, that under this duress, reduced to the extremity of want, they might at last be compelled to yield and surrender.[19]

On other occasions, ravaging aimed at simply gaining resources or at exercising local control.

Feuds, particularly those involving the killing of participants, appear to have been uncommon in England, at least from the mid-tenth century. Orderic Vitalis, writing in Normandy, commented that 'waging war in England and burning the lands of neighbours is an unaccustomed crime in that country and can be atoned only by a very heavy penalty'.[20] An exceptional period was the reign of Stephen. Probably in the 1170s, Richard de Clare, earl of Hereford, recalled that in Stephen's reign, a certain Stephen de Dammartin

> unjustly and against reason occupied the land of Pitley, which belonged to William the reeve of Bradfield and his heirs, in such a way that he cruelly and unjustly caused one of William's sons to be killed, since he knew and understood him to be nearer to his father's inheritance in regard to possessing that land.[21]

There are no contemporary indications of homicide rates, but thirteenth-century records may suggest a rough annual average of one killing per twenty villages.[22] Some probably arose from sudden quarrels that turned

[18] T. D. Hardy, ed., *Rotuli Litterarum Clausarum* (2 vols; Record Commission, 1833–44), i. 238b.

[19] K. R. Potter ed., R. H. C. Davis, intr., *Gesta Stephani*, (Oxford, 1976), p. 219.

[20] Chibnall, ed., *Ecclesiastical History of Orderic Vitalis*, vi. 18–19.

[21] F. M. Stenton, *The First Century of English Feudalism, 1066–1166* (2nd edn; Oxford, 1961), pp. 82, 270.

[22] See J. B. Given, *Society and Homicide in Thirteenth-Century England* (Stanford, CA, 1977), pp. 40, 189.

fatal in a society where weapons were readily available. Others stemmed from underlying disputes, for example over land, as is suggested by the presence of charters in the following case from early in John's reign. Simon 'Clericus' accused Thomas son of William, together with several accomplices, of killing Simon's father John 'Cusin' or 'Monachus'. John was dragged from his meal to his chamber, placed on a bed, had his face and beard set fire to, and his tongue pulled out. Next they broke into his strongboxes, removed several charters and burnt two of these on John's face. Finally they chopped off John's head.[23] Other killings are presented simply as aristocratic loutishness, as when the chronicler Roger of Howden tells us that in Henry II's reign

it was said to be the custom in London that a hundred or more sons and relations of the nobles of the city carried out nocturnal raids on the houses of the rich and plundered them, and if they found someone wandering through the streets at night they immediately killed him without any mercy, so that few dared to walk in the city at night out of fear of them.[24]

CONCLUSION

Despite all this evidence of violence, it does appear that for most of our period England was relatively free of internal disorder compared with large areas of continental Europe. There was not the acceptance that a wrongdoer might have a right to protection from his lord, such as appears in an 1186 edict of the Emperor Frederick Barbarossa:

c. 1.16 If an arsonist in his flight comes to a castle and the lord of the castle happens to be his lord or vassal or relative, then he need not hand him over to his pursuers, but will help him to leave the castle for the forest or some other place that he deems safe. But if he is neither his lord, vassal nor relative, he should hand him over to the pursuers or he will be guilty of the same crime.[25]

Both modern historians and men at the time associated such relative peace with the strength of royal rule. According to Suger of Saint-Denis:

'In his days' gold was being squeezed by Henry I 'from the lily', referring to monastic clergy of good behaviour, and 'from the nettle', referring to troublesome laymen. He had in mind that, just as he worked for the profit of all, so all should serve him. For there is more safety in the land if one man profits from

[23] F. Palgrave, ed., *Rotuli Curiæ Regis*, (2 vols.; Record Commission, 1835), ii. 245, *Curiæ Regis Rolls* (HMSO, 1922–), i. 395, *Pipe Roll 3 John*, pp. 31–2.

[24] R. C. van Caenegem, ed., *English Lawsuits from William I to Richard I*, (2 vols.; Selden Society, 106, 107; London, 1990–1), no. 493; note that the troublemakers were prosecuted in the end.

[25] *Monumenta Germaniae Historica*: *Legum*, §iv, *Constitutiones*, i. 451.

all in order to defend all, than for all to perish if this one man fails to make his profit. 'Silver will flow from the hooves of mooing cattle' means that a safe countryside made the barns full, and full barns supplied an abundance of silver for his full coffers.[26]

Like twelfth-century popes who wished to prevent unjust violence within Christendom in order to allow a crusade, Henry I clearly saw the link between maintaining internal peace and waging successful war.

[26] R. C. Cusimano and J. Moorhead, trans., *Suger, The Deeds of Louis the Fat*, c. 16, (Washington, DC, 1992), pp. 70–1. The words in quotation refer to the Prophecies of Merlin.

CHAPTER II.5

Family, marriage, kinship

Elisabeth van Houts

In the early twelfth century, Adam, an Englishman, together with his widowed mother Sagiva (Old English Sægifu) gave to the nunnery of Barking part of his tithe at Lindsey (Suffolk) for his sister Edith, possibly on the occasion of her entrance there as a nun. The location of the land enables us to identify Adam as Adam of Cockfield, mentioned elsewhere as the tenant of the monastery of Bury St Edmunds, who was confirmed in the holding of land at Cockfield and Lindsey as his father Leofmær held it, and at Lindsey, as his grandfather Wulfric of Groton had it. The abbot also let it be known that Adam's heir in due course would inherit these lands. Together the evidence from Barking and Bury St Edmunds suggests that this native family, whose ancestry stretches back to pre-Conquest times, had been able to hold on to their land despite the arrival of the Normans and would be allowed to pass it on to the next generation.[1] The grant to Barking, however, reveals a more complicated picture, for it is witnessed by Adam's half-brothers Fulco and Roger, sons of one Robert, who had married Sagiva after the death of her first husband, and Robert's brother Roger. Robert's absence from the documents suggests that he had already died. Given that their names are Norman, we have here an English widow with land who had remarried a Norman newcomer. As a result of this marriage, Sagiva's second husband's family in the person of her brother-in-law and her sons by Robert had to agree to the disposal of land by the English members of the family.

The case of Adam of Cockfield illustrates that living in a nuclear family consisting of a couple and their children was the norm in the Anglo-Saxon and Anglo-Norman periods, even though his case highlights the fact that in his family one nuclear arrangement was followed by another with seemingly good relations between the two sets of siblings. Normative

[1] C. R. Hart, 'An early charter of Adam of Cockfield, 1100–1118', *EHR*, 71 (1957), 466–9; *EHD*, ii, no. 250, p. 925.

texts, such as laws, illustrate the predominance of the nuclear unit in the case of inheritance, for example II Cnut 70 stipulates that land belonging to a man who died without leaving a will went to his widow, his children and close kin. And wergild, a fine to exonerate a blood relation who had committed a crime under Anglo-Saxon law, was paid in the first instance to the near kin of the person killed: their children, brothers and paternal uncle (*Wer* 5). When in 1014×16 Archbishop Wulfstan in his *Sermon of the Wolf* decried the decline in the social responsibility of kin (wider and narrow), his outrage was marginally greater for the lack of support within the narrow family: father and son, brothers, or as in a case of insults by strangers where he reproached a thegn for not defending the honour of his wife, daughter or close kinswoman.[2]

Wulfstan's despair at the failings of the wider kin came after a century of its decline as a result of the increased control over kin by lords and kings. Yet historians have long considered the wider kin to be more important than the nuclear family. Legal codes from the seventh century onwards have been interpreted as suggesting that the wider kin was the social agent through which society imposed law and order on its members. The importance of kin, the wider group of an individual's blood relations going back to a common ancestor on the mother's or the father's side, was seen as prominent thanks to the many references that stipulate mutual responsibility for paying fines or acting as oath helper in case of the individual's misdemeanour. Many of these early texts were preserved in later law codes, and the question arises what their practical applicability was and how it declined over time. Also, how are we to understand the workings of the wider kin in practice? To what extent did any one individual know his father's kin and his mother's kin in his own time, and how exactly could anyone call on any of them in times of crisis? Influenced by sociological and anthropological research, modern scholars began to question a view based primarily on a reading of legal codes and the normative picture derived from them.[3] An obligation to help pay wergild should not be interpreted to mean that all cousins are always liable to pay such fines under all circumstances, nor that such norms signify actual and frequent contact between all members of the

[2] *EHD*, i, no. 49, p. 465; no. 240, pp. 931, 932; H. R. Loyn, 'Kinship in Anglo-Saxon England', *ASE*, 3 (1973), 197–209.

[3] P. Stafford, 'La mutation familiale: a suitable case for caution', in J. Hill and M. Swan, eds., *The Community, the Family and the Saint: Patterns of Power in Early Medieval Europe. Selected Proceedings of the International Medieval Congress, University of Leeds, 4–7 July 1994, 10–13 July 1995* (International Medieval Research, 4; Turnhout, 1998), pp. 103–25.

same kin. Although legal texts continue to incorporate references to presumed action by members of the wider kin for the protection and defence of individual members and imposition of fines payable by kin, there is consensus amongst historians that the responsibility of the wider kin decreased with the rise of lordship and royal government, both of which took over many of the tasks of mutual protection and regulation of crime and violence (see also Chapter II.3).

From the tenth century onwards two things are changing. First, we see a change from horizontal obligations between cousins of various degrees both agnatic and cognatic, to a more vertically organized group. Second, we can trace an increase in the interest of the paternal side of the family.[4] Land was handed down the generations privileging the male members, as we have seen in Adam of Cockfield's case; he had greater control over bequests and gifts than the women. Significantly, a third of surviving Anglo-Saxon wills are issued in the names of female testators, yet the scope for women to freely give land as they wished was severely limited, because most of their 'wishes' had been dictated by earlier (male) members of their families. This is not to say that an heiress or widow could never exercise any initiative to give away land without a trace of coercion: some did give land to kinsfolk, as in the case of the Hereford woman who bypassed her son (see below), or to family monasteries.[5] They were, however, freer in bequeathing their moveable possessions such as garments, jewellery, bedclothes or other utensils. Such gifts, too, illustrate that amongst the aristocracy, after gifts to the king and queen, the most valuable ones went to sons and daughters, brothers and sisters and only thereafter to cousins and members of a household.[6] After the Norman Conquest the structure of the family as a patrilinear descent group intensified, as suggested by the incidence of primogeniture, whereby land went to the eldest son, at the expense of other siblings, and the attachment of patronymics (usually based on toponyms themselves often related to castle sites) to such groups.[7] The effect on women was that more than ever

[4] A. Wareham, 'The transformation of kinship and the family in late Anglo-Saxon England', *Early Medieval Europe*, 10 (2001), 376–7, 396–9.

[5] J. Crick, 'Women, posthumous benefaction and family strategy in pre-conquest England', *Journal of British Studies*, 38 (1999), 399–422; J. Crick, 'The wealth, patronage and connections of women's houses in late Anglo-Saxon England', *Revue Bénédictine*, 109 (1999), 155–85.

[6] J. Crick, 'Women, wills and moveable wealth in pre-conquest England', in M. Donald and L. Hurcombe, eds., *Gender and Material Culture in Historical Perspective* (Manchester, 2000), pp. 17–37.

[7] J. Holt, 'Presidential address: feudal society and the family: notions of patrimony', *TRHS* 5th ser., 33 (1983), 193–220.

they were absorbed in the families they married into, resulting in a potential loosening of ties with agnatic kin.

The size of the nuclear family in our period seems to have remained fairly static. Sources studied for the purpose present problems: the commemoration books (with their known over-representation of men), wills (though they cease for the period after 1066 and do not resurface in significant numbers until the end of the thirteenth century) or government tax records such as The *Rolls of the Ladies, the Boys and the Girls* (1185). The latter list contains the widows and (minor) children of deceased royal tenants in twelve counties with a view to providing the king with information about the potential to marry off any widow (preferably of childbearing age) and give in wardship the young boys and girls.[8] The average family consisted of a father, mother and three to five children. Research by John Moore suggests an average of four to five children per family household in the twelfth century, which is slightly under that cited in comparative research on the Carolingian period on the Continent, which gives an average of about five children, and comparable to that cited by Peter Laslett for the early modern period.[9] Given the spotlight nature of the sources, in the sense that they often highlight the size of a family at one particular moment in time, it is always possible that older children had left the household or that younger children had not yet been born. The *Rolls of the Ladies, the Boys and the Girls*, which recent research has shown under-reported the incidence of children, reveals larger than average families. For example, seven widows had five children, six had six children and ten had seven children, and there were also six widows whose children ranged in number from ten to thirteen.[10] Amongst the aristocracy large families were thus not exceptional. A problem with the source material is that we know of families and their size because they had land and its transactions were recorded in writing. The landless and dispossessed leave very little trace, and the information, for example, about slaves in households has not permitted any clear conclusions (see Chapter II.6). In any aristocratic household there would be more people living under one roof than the nuclear family of the owner because there would be servants

[8] J. H. Round, ed., *Rotuli de dominabus et pueris et puellis de XII comitatibus* (Pipe Roll Society, 35, 1913); J. Walmsley, trans., *Widows, Heirs and Heiresses in the Late Twelfth Century: The Rotuli de dominabus et pueris et puellis* (Medieval and Renaissance Texts and Studies, 308; Tempe, AZ, 2006); and for commentary, see S. Johns, *Noblewomen, Aristocracy and Power in the Twelfth-Century Anglo-Norman Realm* (Manchester, 2003), pp. 165–93.

[9] J. S. Moore, 'The Anglo-Norman family: size and structure', *ANS* 14 (1992), 153–96.

[10] Johns, *Noblewomen*, p. 175.

such as nursemaids, chaplains and stewards. Aristocratic houses therefore might host groups of ten for a modestly landed family to about fifty for a wealthy baronial one.[11]

Fostering other people's children was not uncommon in medieval England. In some cases the foster-mother was the nurse who had breastfed the child, a situation which explains the closeness between the foster-brothers Richard Lionheart and Alexander of Neckham, who were suckled together by the latter's mother, Hodierna. Richard remembered his nurse with great affection when as king he granted her a generous pension.[12] At aristocratic level we find various instances of children, mostly boys, who on purpose were brought up in the households of other lords. King Æthelstan (924–39) was godfather and foster-father to Alain of Poher, son of the Breton count Mathuedoi, who spent several years at the English court, and reputedly also fostered Hakon, son of King Harald Fairhair of Norway. Another Continental nobleman, St Simon (d. 1088), previously count of the Vexin and godchild of Queen Matilda I, was brought up at the court of William the Conqueror, while King Stephen as a young man lived at the court of his maternal uncle, Henry I.[13] Such arrangements were mutually beneficial: the birth family normally was of (slightly) lower status and accepted opportunities of a court education as a means of preferment for their sons, while from the court's perspective the guests provided company for resident children, who together received tuition in learning, military training and hunting exercises. The cases of Alain of Poher and St Simon reveal that arrangements could be tied in with religious responsibilities of godparenthood. Whereas in the case of boys the fostering or stays with another family were a temporary affair, girls changed homes permanently as a result of engagement or marriage. Underage aristocratic girls would spend time abroad to acclimatize, learn the language and customs of the country and be weaned off their homeland so as to prepare them for their new role as mother of a future ruler. Empress Matilda was eight when in 1110 she left England to go to Trier, where she lived in the household of the archbishop to be educated in the language and customs of Germany before in 1114 she married Henry V. Her language training involved Latin and probably Italian as well.[14] While

11 Moore, 'The Anglo-Norman family', 185.

12 For Hodierna, nurse to Richard and mother of Alexander, see J. Gillingham, *Richard I* (New Haven and London, 1999), p. 17, and J. Goering, 'Alexander Neckham', *ODNB*.

13 S. Foot, 'Æthelstan (893/4–939), king of England', *ODNB*; J. P. Migne, ed., *Vita beati Simeonis*, *PL* 156, cols. 1215, 1222; D. Crouch, *The Reign of King Stephen 1135–1154* (Harlow, 2000), p. 12.

14 E. M. C. van Houts, ed. and trans., *The Gesta Normannorum Ducum of William of Jumièges, Orderic Vitalis and Robert of Torigni* (2 vols.; OMT; Oxford, 1992–4), ii, pp. 216–19.

we are well informed about high-status families, we know very little about families lower down the social scale, where fostering in particular must have been common as a result of death in childbirth of women (see Chapter I.5).

Between 900 and 1200 arrangements for marriage in England, as elsewhere in Europe, underwent considerable change because of the increasing involvement of the Church. Marriage was a social contract arranged between families which exchanged women and land in the process of agreeing unions between men and women. At the beginning of our period, for which details are sparse, we learn about some of its negotiations from the early eleventh-century vernacular tract 'Concerning the betrothal of a woman', as well as from two marriage agreements for high-status couples.[15] Details about the dowry or morning gift, the gift by the bride's family to her husband's which remained in the woman's possession even after her husband's death, as well as the husband's provisions for his widow (dower), were agreed beforehand. That many arrangements failed to solve all issues that could be foreseen at the time a marriage was contracted is clear from the many charters, particularly from the period after the Norman Conquest, that record disputes about dower and dowries. At high aristocratic level the king may have had some involvement, particularly in the case of widows (see below), but generally in the Anglo-Saxon period marriage was a private matter. As is discussed in Chapter IV, the circumstances of conquest in 1016 and 1066 gave kings an opportunity to coerce some English women into marriage with foreigners. Patrick Wormald's observation that the manuscript tradition of the tract 'Concerning the betrothal of a woman' positions it in a possible Anglo-Danish context is particularly suggestive. Important, though, in the same tract are references to the presence of the priest to bless the couple, which increasingly became the confirmation that marriage was indissoluble, as well as advice that the couple should not be too closely related in blood. The increasing involvement of the Church in the contracting (and dissolving of) marriages especially in the twelfth century resulted in a variety of ecclesiastical texts, such as episcopal letters, saints' lives or canon law documents, detailing conflict of one sort or another. What normal marriages were like is difficult to establish. The legal age of marriage for girls was twelve and for boys fourteen, even though other

[15] *EHD*, i, no. 50, pp. 467–8, and commentary in P. Wormald, *The Making of English Law: King Alfred to the Twelfth Century* (Oxford, 1999), pp. 385–7; Sawyer, *Anglo-Saxon Charters*, nos. 1459 and 1461 = *EHD*, i, nos. 128 and 130, pp. 593, 596–7.

evidence suggests that most girls did not marry until fourteen or fifteen, once their childbearing capacity had been well established. The nearest we come to details based on historical reality is the case of Christina of Markyate, a merchant's daughter from Huntingdon, whose marriage negotiations *c.* 1115 are known in great detail from her saint's life written by an anonymous author on the basis of her own information some forty years later. As she adamantly refused to accept the Englishman, Burthred, chosen for her by her parents, we hear that both lay (her parents and parents-in-law) and Church authorities (local priest, bishop of Lincoln, hermits) were involved in an attempt to make her change her mind, but to no avail.[16]Apart from marriage, there were many living arrangements between men and women that although socially sanctioned were not formal legal contracts. Although since 1054 the Church had forbidden marriage amongst clergy, the majority of secular priests, deacons and bishops had women in their households who functioned as wives or concubines. Christina of Markyate's maternal aunt Alveva (Old English Ælfgifu) was one of them. She was the concubine of Ranulph Flambard, bishop of Durham (1099–1128), who on his regular visits to London used to stop off at Huntingdon to lodge with her. Later he married her off to one of his protégés.[17] That bishops did not limit themselves to their concubines is clear from Christina's own tale that one day, when he stayed at her aunt's house, he requested her to come to his room, on her own. She refused, even when afterwards he tried to bribe her with precious silk brought back from London.

Increasingly from the tenth century kings extended their authority into the sphere of marriage. As early as King Æthelred II's reign the king supported the freedom of widows to choose whether to remarry one year after the death of their husbands, while his successor Cnut added that upon remarriage women would forfeit the dowry of their first marriage.[18] However, Cnut's explicit order that women could not be forced into marriage or sold into it sounds like a statement that may well be tied up with the incidence of intermarriage after conquest. Interestingly, these royal intentions seemed to have clashed with reality judging by Wulfstan's complaint in his *Sermon of the Wolf* (1014×16) that widows are wrongfully forced into marriage and too many are reduced to poverty and greatly

[16] P. L' Hermite-Leclercq and A.-M. Legras, eds. and trans., *Vie de Christina de Markyate* (2 vols.; Paris, 2007) and the recent collection of essays devoted to her: *Christina of Markyate, a Twelfth-Century Holy Woman*, S. Fanous and H. Leyser, eds. (Abingdon, 2005).

[17] L' Hermite-Leclercq and Legras, eds., *Vie de Christina*, i, pp. 80–3.

[18] For the next section, see also Chapter IV.3.

humiliated. From the conqueror-kings Cnut and William to John and the Magna Carta, the king's ambivalent position as protector of widows and as exploiter of their monetary value remained an urgent problem. The 1185 *Rolls of the Ladies, the Boys and the Girls* lists 108 widows across 12 counties, ranging from the underage widow, ten-year-old Matilda de Bidune, to the very elderly Beatrice de Say, who was in her eighties. Of the seventy-three widows whose ages are given only twenty are under forty years of age.

But what do we know about emotion and sentiment within the family? Marriage was often a contractual affair, where landed interest had priority over sentiment. Marital affection and love did, of course, exist, although on the few occasions when it is explicitly mentioned historians have argued that this might be evidence of its rarity. In the *Life of Edward*, commissioned by King Edward the Confessor's wife Edith, she is described as warming his feet in her lap, a sign of intimacy that reveals affection.[19] And William the Conqueror's lack of bastards has been interpreted as evidence for an affectionate relationship with his wife, which was not undermined as far as we know by her monetary support of their eldest son Robert during the row with his father. Heartbreak did occur, as when Empress Matilda's second son, William, left England having been refused the hand of Isabel, widow of William IV of Warenne, and sought solace with his mother in Normandy, as movingly described by Stephen of Rouen in his poem 'Draco Normannicus'.[20] A family's grief for the death of a father is nowhere so beautifully penned as in the *Life of William of Marshall*, celebrating one of the great patriarchs of the Anglo-Norman aristocracy in the first vernacular biography of a lay nobleman. With relatively few explicit expressions of affection in documents one wonders how much sentiment we may read into the fact that the atheling Æthelstan (d. 25 June 1014) in his will remembered his grandmother Queen Ælfthryth, 'who brought me up'.[21] Yet the trope of (grand)motherly love is not universal. Some mothers did not get on with their sons for one reason or another. The Hereford Gospel report of a family dispute in Cnut's reign shows us a woman irreconcilably broken with her son, who claimed land from her. In public before witnesses she angrily cast him aside in

19 F. Barlow, ed. and trans., *The Life of King Edward Who Rests at Westminster* (OMT; Oxford, 1992), pp. 118–19.

20 R. Howlett, ed., 'The "Draco Normannicus" of Etienne de Rouen', in *Chronicles of the Reigns of Stephen, Henry II and Richard I* (4 vols.; RS; London, 1884–9), ii, p. 676.

21 Sawyer, *Anglo-Saxon Charters*, no. 1503.

favour of a kinswoman (see also Chapter V.6).[22] But as the case of William and Robert Curthose intimated, the father–son relationship was also one of rivalry and competition. For fathers who were kings (or for that matter earls or barons) like William and Henry II, their longevity caused their eldest sons to become impatient at not being able to exercise control over their patrimony. Both Robert Curthose and Henry the Young King rebelled for significant periods at the time. Duby's model of the 'jeunes', the unmarried aristocratic men without inheritance who lead an aimless life, often in bands with other similar friends, remains a perceptive study of a social group that was potentially destabilizing for society.[23]

[22] *EHD*, i, no. 135, p. 602.

[23] W. Aird, 'Frustrated masculinity: the relationship between William the Conqueror and his eldest son', in D. M. Hadley, ed., *Masculinity in Medieval Europe* (Manchester, 1999), pp. 39–55, and G. Duby, 'Youth in aristocratic society. Northwestern France in the twelfth century', in G. Duby, *The Chivalrous Society*, trans. C. Postan (London, 1977), pp. 112–22.

CHAPTER II.6

Poor and powerless

David A. E. Pelteret

> [Geatflæd] gave freedom for the love of God and for their souls' need, that is, Ecceard smith and Ælfstan and his wife and all their offspring, born and unborn, and Arcil and Cole and Ecgferth, Aldhun's daughter, and all those people whose head she took in return for their food in those evil days.
>
> Durham *Liber Vitae*, c. XXXX[1]

Slavery is a legal status whereby people are denied freedom by being defined as chattels subject to the ownership of another person or institution. In societies that have permitted slavery usually only criminals have had a lower status. As the human possessions of others, slaves would seem to represent the essence of powerlessness. There were slaves in Anglo-Saxon England from the time of our earliest texts and the institution survived the Anglo-Saxon period, only disappearing from English records in the first half of the twelfth century. From a modern perspective, this was a social change of momentous significance; for the English of the time the disappearance of slavery elicited no comment at all. This gulf in perception should arouse the curiosity of anyone who examines the period from 900 to 1200.

The document from the Durham *Liber Vitae* quoted above records a manumission, the legal act of freeing a slave. Its wording and the context in which it is found permit us imaginatively to grasp the position of those who were slaves and at the same time to explore the social contradictions inherent in a status that sought to classify certain members of society as powerless, so devoid of the right of ownership that some Anglo-Saxon laws required them to be beaten when found guilty of a wrong, since their

[1] David and Lynda Rollason, eds., *The Durham 'Liber Vitae': London, British Library, MS Cotton Domitian A.VII*, (3 vols.; London, 2007), i, p. 138. The text, which probably dates from 1070×5, is found in London, British Library, MS Cotton Domitian A.VII, fol. 47r. The translation is my own. For a detailed discussion see David A. E. Pelteret, 'The manumissions in the Durham *Liber Vitae*', in Rollason and Rollason, eds., *The Durham 'Liber Vitae'*, i, pp. 66–72.

skin was the sole possession that they could offer in reparation. In a legal system that sought to uphold the personal honour of the free by providing redress for physical injuries, no more signal act of dishonour can be imagined.[2] The manumission reveals to us that 'poor' and 'powerless' were not necessarily synonymous with being a slave. The unnamed persons whom the manumittor freed were evidently so poor that they had exercised the only power they possessed as free people: to bow their heads in submission, thereby becoming slaves of the woman who ultimately freed them. In return they received food. The status of slave was humiliating, but when times were harsh it could be more desirable than being destitute.

Since the time of Constantine the Great (AD 306–37) people were encouraged to release slaves as a pious act, especially in church. Significantly the first English manumission document, dating from AD 924, is recorded in a Gospel book. Many of these texts state that the act was usually (unlike here) 'for the good of the soul' of the manumittor, a phrase that should not be interpreted as a hollow legal formula. By the late tenth century, English wills are declaring that 'all my men are to be free'. It is difficult to believe that such manumissions were contrary to the wishes of the testators' beneficiaries or led to the testators' estates being deprived of a labour force. Piety and economic advantage (a more flexible use of labour for a perceived lower outlay) may well have marched hand-in-hand.[3]

At the time of Domesday Book slaves were still ubiquitous, however, forming anything from 10 to 25 per cent of the recorded population. Forty years later one is hard-pressed to find mention of slaves at all. The growing control over the land and seas round England may have brought to an end the acquisition of slaves by razzias (such as the lines of young men and women brought to Bristol for export to Ireland during the lifetime of Bishop Wulfstan of Worcester (d. 1095)), but this will hardly account for the change. It is difficult to explain the disappearance of slaves unless one posits that the Normans had a different attitude towards those who peopled their estates from the Anglo-Saxon overlords whom they supplanted.[4] The Anglo-Saxon classifications of those who occupied land on

[2] Pelteret, 'The manumissions'; David A. E. Pelteret, *Slavery in Early Mediaeval England from the Reign of Alfred until the Twelfth Century* (Studies in Anglo-Saxon History 7; Woodbridge, 1995).

[3] See Pelteret, *Slavery in Early Mediaeval England*, chaps. 4 and 5, for slavery in Anglo-Saxon wills and manumission documents; the latter are listed on pp. xiv–xvi.

[4] John Gillingham, 'Conquering the barbarians: war and chivalry in twelfth-century Britain', *Haskins Society Journal*, 4 (1993 for 1992), 67–84, esp. 81–2, has some thoughtful words on this change.

a manorial estate were foreign to the Normans; now all those on an estate were in a sense the overlord's people, though the concept of being 'free' remained important to the peasantry involved. As the eleventh century drew to a close the Anglo-Saxon legal distinction between a slave (Old English *theow*) and a freeman became irrelevant to the new masters and the native word for a slave died out. Many male slaves had been ploughmen: now they were designated by their occupation (Latin *bovarius*) or by the cottages they occupied (*cotset* or *cotarius*). Masked behind such terms former slaves may still be discerned on manorial demesnes in the twelfth century.[5] The situation was to change dramatically at the end of the twelfth century.

Those who had yielded up their freedom in the *Liber Vitae* document are unnamed. It brings to the forefront of the attention of anyone wishing to study the poor and powerless a significant problem. History cannot be written without evidence, written or archaeological. The poor and the powerless in most periods of human history have possessed neither the education to describe in writing their situation nor the kinds of possessions that might survive to illustrate the nature of their lives. It was no different between AD 900 and 1200. Only if their lives impacted in some way on the powerful were they likely to receive written recognition. Their anonymity has carried over into modern times. Historians especially have been drawn to those well attested in written sources. Archaeologists have been more eclectic in the study of those who left material evidence of their existence, but only in very recent years have the latter sought to exploit and develop technological means to learn more about those whose sole legacy to the twenty-first century has been the evidence of their body, usually surviving just in skeletal form and sometimes even only as a three-dimensional shadow in the earth (see Chapter I.5).

The *Liber Vitae* manumission reminds the attentive reader that the poor and powerless were very much part of a wider society and shared in its mores. Ecceard was a smith, a skilled occupation that was very important in a predominantly agrarian society. Ælfstan had a wife and children; Ecgferth's father was known by name. They were owned by a woman of sufficient influence that the record of their freeing could be placed in a volume that was a treasured possession of the church of Durham; no more public a document was conceivable at this time. The nameless ones had suffered because of 'evil days', an infuriatingly vague description to

[5] Pelteret, *Slavery in Medieval England*, pp. 237–8.

which we shall return, but one that implies a period of misfortune that had a wide social impact.

The poor and powerless thus cannot be examined without considering the nature of the wider society and how that society changed over the centuries. These changes were significant, but their precise nature, geographic scale and chronology are as yet not fully understood. Because of their social and economic impact it is important to recall them here, even though their influence on the poor and powerless cannot be precisely evaluated in the current state of scholarship.

Throughout the period England remained a predominantly agrarian society. Historians are generally agreed that by the tenth century the former great multiple estates were becoming fragmented into units whose viability demanded changes in their underlying economic organization (see Chapter I.1). At the same time a growing nucleation of settlement becomes evident in a great swathe of the country extending from the northeast through the Midlands to the southwest, frequently accompanied by a reorganization in peasant landholdings to form so-called 'open fields'. The process took place over several centuries, and it is probably misguided to try to explain this as initiated by either landlords or the peasantry: an element of economic fashion may have played its part. The manner in which the land was farmed is equally elusive.

What is clear is that great landlords such as monasteries were already taking note of who among the lower peasantry had been occupying their land in the tenth century. A list of serfs from lands under the abbey of Ely's control records persons classified as *geburas*, 'boors', with ties to its estates going back five generations, i.e. to the ninth century.[6] An eleventh-century text, probably from Worcester, the so-called *Rectitudines singularum personarum* (Rights and ranks of people), notes that *geburas* owed particularly onerous labour dues in return for the land they occupied. On the other hand, *cotarii* (people occupying little more than a cottage with attached gardens) owed very few labour dues. This does not make much sense unless one posits a large labour market of hirelings, paid either in cash or in kind. *Geburas* must have employed family members or others to work their land or supply the labour services. The *cotarii* are the obvious ones to have provided the labour.[7]

[6] David A. E. Pelteret, 'Two Old English lists of serfs', *Mediaeval Studies*, 48 (1986), 470–513, at 472–4 (text and translation).

[7] *English Historical Documents 1042–1189*, ed. David C. Douglas and George W. Greenaway (English Historical Documents 2; 2nd edn; London and New York, 1981), pp. 875–9, at p. 876 (no. 172).

The increase in the valuation of various manors in Domesday Book between 1066 and 1086 suggests that Norman landlords were often extracting greater dues in labour services and in kind from their peasantry than had been the case under their Anglo-Saxon predecessors.[8] Rent-payers, or *censarii*, already find mention, however, in records from Burton, Staffordshire, in the late eleventh century; as the twelfth century advanced many landlords found it convenient to convert services in labour and kind into cash payments and to farm out their demesnes. When inflation hit the country in the closing decades of the twelfth century, those paying rent now found themselves at an advantage – but landlords then started shifting back to managing their own lands or attempting to change from a rent-paying regime to one based on labour services. Landlords employed their economic and social power in the courts to argue that those owing labour services were 'unfree', a group without legal redress against them. It was a process that was to continue into the thirteenth century and beyond.[9]

Throughout the period one needs always to be aware of the fragility of rural existence for the peasantry, their vulnerability to misfortunes that could easily be seen by all as 'evil days' (see Chapter I.5). In 900 the risk of Scandinavian raids from the Midlands southwards remained omnipresent; they recurred in the late tenth century in the reign of Æthelred the Unready. Then, in the years following 1066 William the Conqueror brutally put down dissent in the northeast of the country. Social historians should always try to visualize in concrete terms the consequences of this kind of mayhem rather than simply masking its effects under an abstraction such as 'the harrying of the North'. Though the degree of the devastation may have been exaggerated by twelfth-century writers,[10] for those who lived off the land burnt crops and houses meant poverty and an early death. The widespread disruption during the reign of Stephen must also have had dire consequences for peasants who were unfortunate enough to live in areas where the troubles occurred.

To the problems created by human unrest should be added the vagaries of the weather. It has been assumed that the period saw an improvement

[8] Rosamond Faith, *The English Peasantry and the Growth of Lordship* (London, 1997).

[9] J. F. R. Walmsley, 'The *censarii* of Burton Abbey and the Domesday population', *North Staffordshire Journal of Field Studies*, 8 (1968), 73–80; P. D. A. Harvey, 'The English inflation of 1180–1220', *P&P*, 61 (November 1973), 3–30; R. H. Hilton, 'Freedom and villeinage in England', *P&P*, 31 (July 1965), 3–19.

[10] D. M. Palliser, 'Domesday Book and the "harrying of the north"', *Northern History*, 29 (1993), 1–23.

in the climate, but this now is understood to be a much more complex issue. The weather in England and on the Continent, and even within different parts of England, can vary widely during a single season. Exogenous events such as volcanic eruptions far removed from the country can also play their part, as historians are now beginning to realize.[11] Here the details of the sources should take precedence over abstractions such as 'the medieval warm period'. The Peterborough version of the Anglo-Saxon Chronicle records several instances of turbulent weather around the turn of the eleventh century, with the year 1103 being particularly harsh: corn and fruit-trees were ruined and on 11 August a windstorm created havoc with crops; to all this another disaster, cattle disease, was added. Until the sources have been combed, one should not assume that the weather patterns of 1103 extended beyond the east Midlands, but for those upon whom they impacted the consequences must have been dire. In a society dependent upon arable land, one need only contemplate the loss of plough oxen.

This brings us back to the Durham manumission with its focus on the need for food. The study of consumption of food in the Middle Ages is in its infancy. The Anglo-Saxon Chronicle makes much of the way the Normans restricted the hunting of game in forests, but the reality is that most of the rural peasantry are likely to have subsisted on cereals in various forms (see Chapter I.5). They may have owned chickens and pigs, and *Rectitudines* states that a *metecu* ('a cow for food') should be given to an *esne*, a class of person who appears to be a slave. Where an estate was in the vicinity of a town with a market, possessors of such birds and animals will have been tempted to sell rather than eat them.[12]

The tenth century saw the development of towns, whose origins lay in the ninth century, if not earlier (see Chapter III.1). With towns came trade and growing specialization in occupations. Increasing monetization becomes evident, especially in the reign of Edgar and his successors, leading to what has been termed the 'commercialization' of the economy. Rural people were presented with a growing market for their produce in the new towns. The towns themselves (and, in the twelfth century, major monasteries) provided opportunities for specialist occupations such as

[11] J. C. Diaz and M. K. Hughes, 'Was there a medieval warm period and if so, where and when?', in J. C. Diaz and M. K. Hughes, eds., *The Medieval Warm Period, Climatic Change*, 26 (1994), 109–42;. Michael McCormick, Paul Edward Dutton and Paul A. Mayewski, 'Volcanoes and the climate forcing of Carolingian Europe, A.D. 750–950', *Speculum*, 82 (2007), 865–95.

[12] See the various essays in C. M. Woolgar, D. Serjeantson and T. Walldron, eds., *Food in Medieval England: Diet and Nutrition*, (Oxford, 2006).

tanners and shoemakers. But with the growth of occupations divorced from the production of food, risk of impoverishment through upheaval or personal misfortune grew. Thus the creation after the Conquest of castles in urban settlements such as London or Oxford, often with the destruction of tenements, must have ruined many, and there was an ever-present risk of fire in dwellings that were still in this period built of wood, wattle and daub. Domesday Book's report on one of the largest Anglo-Saxon towns, Norwich, is telling: in the time of King Edward there were 1,320 burgesses; in 1086 there were only 665 English burgesses 'and 480 bordars who, because of their poverty, pay no customary dues'.[13]

How did the desperately poor respond to their plight? For women in modern societies prostitution offers an escape from complete impoverishment; for men criminal activity provides a solution when other employment appears not to be available. There is little unambiguous evidence that prostitution as known today (i.e. the sale of sexual services) existed. Medieval sources tend to be more concerned about female promiscuity than about the commercialization of sex, and words that might be interpreted as 'prostitute' might equally mean 'loose woman'. At most one can suggest that as towns such as London and Norwich grew during the period, they presented the anonymity, floating population and monetary economy whereby prostitution could flourish. By *c.* 1230 Oxford had a *Gropecuntelane* (euphemized to Grove Lane, now Magpie Lane) and the City of London barred prostitutes by 1266×7: the activity suggested may have existed long before it finds mention in the records.[14]

Of the existence of criminality there is no doubt. Æthelstan brought in a range of laws that provided for capital punishment, including for theft by anyone over the age of twelve. Theft seems to have been a particular problem during the reigns of Edgar, Æthelred and Cnut, and robbery during the reign of the latter two kings, if one can judge from the

[13] D. M. Metcalf, *An Atlas of Anglo-Saxon and Norman Coin Finds*, c. *973–1086* (Royal Numismatic Society special publication 32; London, 1998), especially pp. 283–4; Richard H. Britnell, 'Commercialisation and economic development in England, 1000–1300', in Richard H. Britnell and Bruce M. S. Campbell, eds., *A Commercialising Economy: England 1086*–c. *1300*, (Manchester, 1995), pp. 7–26.

[14] Julie Coleman, 'Prostitution', in Michael Lapidge, John Blair, Simon Keynes and Donald Scragg, eds., *The Blackwell Encyclopaedia of Anglo-Saxon England*, (Oxford and Malden, MA, 1999), p. 380; Ruth Mazo Karras, 'Prostitution in medieval Europe', in Vern L. Bullough and James A. Brundage, eds., *Handbook of Medieval Sexuality*, (New York and London, 1996), pp. 243–60; Keith Briggs, 'OE and ME *cunte* in place-names', *Journal of the English Place-Name Society*, 41 (2009), 26–39; Eilert Ekwall, *Street-Names of the City of London* (Oxford, 1954), p. 165; J. B. Post, 'A fifteenth-century customary of the Southwark stews', *Journal of the Society of Archivists*, 5 (1974–7), 418–28, at 428.

frequent mention of these crimes in their laws. One notes that this was a period of great social change – and also one where coins, a tempting prize for the thief and robber, had become more prevalent.

Wealthier thieves were likely to escape capital punishment through their power or influence; poor persons would have lacked such protection. The latter were decapitated or, more usually, hanged. Here archaeological excavations have been particularly enlightening. Twenty so-called 'execution cemeteries' from the late Anglo-Saxon period have been identified so far; almost all are located on a hundred boundary. The location seems to have been a deliberate strategy to deny burial in consecrated land to those who were deemed to be criminals and instead symbolically marginalize them from the community. The process seems to have started in the tenth century. A particularly poignant burial is that of a hanged man at Stockbridge Down, Hampshire, who had secreted under his armpit a bag containing six coins. Did he lack the resources to purchase his life by paying his wergild – or were the coins concealed by him because they had been stolen and perhaps were themselves the grounds for his execution? It is interesting to see that the location for the burial of apparent criminals changed in the latter half of the eleventh century. Rather than exclude criminals from the community as the Anglo-Saxons had done, the Normans displayed their power over the conquered by incorporating the executed within the community. St Margaret's parish church in Norwich (described as St Margaret's 'where those who have been hanged are buried') presents a number of burials that point to execution. The leper hospital of St Nicholas in Lewes, East Sussex, contains burials of persons with their hands tied behind their backs and, in one instance, with an iron manacle on the leg. The gallows, too, ceased to be on the margins: castles might possess them and in the twelfth century even monasteries.[15]

The destitute had one other option: to seek the charity that those better off might grant them. At this period, this was channelled through the institution of the Church, though the form that charity took changed and developed over the centuries. By giving a charitable gift, donors were encouraged by the Church to expect a counter-gift after their death. Such

15 Andrew Reynolds, *Later Anglo-Saxon England: Life and Landscape* (Stroud, 1999), pp. 105–10; Andrew Reynolds, 'Burials, boundaries and charters in Anglo-Saxon England: a reassessment' and Christopher Daniell, 'Conquest, crime and theology in the burial record: 1066–1200', in Sam Lucy and Andrew Reynolds, eds., *Burial in Early Medieval England and Wales* (Society for Medieval Archaeology monograph 17; London, 2002), pp. 171–94 and 241–54; Alexander Murray, 'Money and robbers, 900–1100', *JMH*, 4 (1978), 55–94.

pious benefactions formed the basis of the landed wealth of the Church since the latter was not mortal. Acts of charity to the poor were fundamental to the monastic Rule of St Benedict since monks themselves took a vow of poverty. Mid-tenth-century England underwent a monastic revival that led to the adoption in *c.* 973 of a customary entitled *Regularis concordia*. Following the injunction (*mandatum* or Maundy) of Christ in John 13:1–2, the *Regularis* prescribed the daily washing of the feet of three poor persons, to whom should also be given the same food eaten by the brethren.

That according to the *Regularis* 'poor strangers' should also receive Maundy at the abbot's discretion and where possible be provided with victuals on their departure hints at another group who were often without means and dependent on charity. The devout had for centuries been drawn to Rome as a place of pilgrimage, but there were also local pilgrimage sites in the tenth century such as the tomb of St Swithun in Winchester. His *Life* mentions no less than three incidents where slaves sought their freedom at his tomb. Pilgrimage as a phenomenon increased considerably as the eleventh and twelfth century progressed. To the new local cult centres such as Waltham Abbey (Harold II in the eleventh century) and Canterbury (Thomas Becket in the late twelfth) should be added the Holy Land, following the preaching of the crusades at the end of the eleventh and during the twelfth centuries. Poor pilgrims included both the improvident and those who fell victim to theft and robbery.[16]

As with the poor and powerless in modern societies, the treatment of the sick and destitute in early medieval England was marked by ambivalence. Already by the end of the Anglo-Saxon period lepers were being marginalized by being interred on the edges of a cemetery, as in the case of a mid-tenth-century burial at Raunds, Northamptonshire, and thirty-five inhumations of lepers on the northern side of a cemetery beyond the city gates in Norwich. Skeletal evidence indicates that medieval people correctly identified Hansen's disease but its aetiology was not understood, which encouraged contradictory interpretations as to its causation: to some, lepers, like the suffering Job of the Old Testament, were especially blessed by God; to others, leprosy was caused by sexual excess (see Chapter I.5). The hospitals were customarily located on the edge of towns, frequently near bridges and watercourses. The provision of water

[16] Thomas Symons, ed. and trans., *Regularis concordia Anglicae nationis monachorum sanctimonialiumque/The monastic agreement of the monks and nuns of the English nation*. Thomas (London, 1953), pp. 61–2; Michael Lapidge, *The Cult of St Swithun* (Winchester Studies 4.ii; Oxford, 2003), pp. 288–91, 302–5 and 332–3.

must have been both a curse and a blessing: an ample supply for ablution, but also noisome and damp. A suburban location encouraged the giving of alms by those coming on business to a town; it also marginalized the sufferers. Healing of the soul was a fundamental dimension of the hospital, so it was staffed by religious. The rise of lay piety in the twelfth century led many *leprosaria* to be endowed by laypersons, whose act of charity might receive both religious commemoration by the ecclesiastical staff in this world as well as the promise of blessings after death. As has perhaps always been the case, marginal folk were needed by the rich and powerful.[17]

Yet the poor and powerless were no less human than the person who is reading this chapter; they merit more attention. Only by the careful assembling of incidental references in saints' lives, chronicles, charters, custumals and the records of monasteries and towns will it be possible to fully celebrate their existence.

[17] Christina Lee, 'Changing faces: leprosy in Anglo-Saxon England', in Catherine E. Karkov and Nicholas Howe, eds., *Conversion and Colonization in Anglo-Saxon England* (Essays in Anglo-Saxon Studies 2; Tempe, AZ, 2006), pp. 59–81; Max Satchell, 'The emergence of leper-houses in medieval England, 1100–1250' (unpublished D.Phil. thesis, University of Oxford, 1998), which contains a gazetteer of medieval English *leprosaria*; Carole Rawcliffe, 'The earthly and spiritual topography of suburban hospitals', in Kate Giles and Christopher Dyer, eds., *Town and Country in the Middle Ages: Contrasts, Contacts and Interconnections, 1100–1500* (Society for Medieval Archaeology monographs 22; Leeds, 2007), pp. 251–74, for the suburban location of *leprosaria*. Lee and Rawcliffe discuss attitudes towards leprosy; see also Saul Nathaniel Brody, *The Disease of the Soul: Leprosy in Medieval Literature* (Ithaca, NY, 1974), and Sally L. Burch, 'Leprosy and law in Béroul's *Roman de Tristan*', *Viator*, 38.1 (2007), 141–54.

CHAPTER III.1

Towns and their hinterlands

David Griffiths

THE SEARCH FOR DEFINITIONS

The growth of urban life is one of the most important features of English society in the period 900–1200. A small number of places in England arguably displayed urban characteristics before 900, but these were tiny in number and scope compared with the spread of towns visible in 1200. The traditional definition of what constituted a town, common in urban history prior to the 1970s, was taken directly from historical legal status based on founding charters and privileges. Archaeology, which began to reveal widespread traces of medieval occupation in English towns and cities in the third quarter of the twentieth century and has continued to do so since, has contributed a perspective which stresses the living conditions of ordinary people and the organic complexity of urban occupation. This led to a questioning of traditional historical definitions. Attempts were made, such as that by Martin Biddle,[1] the excavator of medieval Winchester, to break down the essence of urbanization into a series of individual characteristics, such as a dense population, market functions, defences and evidence of planning – where conformity to all or some of which would qualify a place for urban status. Most historians, geographers and archaeologists still readily accord with the timeless and elegant definition provided by Susan Reynolds in 1977, namely that a town is 'a permanent and concentrated non-agricultural settlement, supported by agricultural production located elsewhere, and maintaining a sense of social separateness from the countryside'.[2] Few more succinct ways could be found of expressing the urban/rural contrast.

Yet there still seems something unsatisfactory about conventional urban definitions. Suburban development in the medieval period,

[1] M. Biddle, 'Towns', in D. M. Wilson, ed., *The Archaeology of Anglo-Saxon England* (Cambridge, 1976), pp. 99–150.

[2] S. Reynolds, *An Introduction to the History of English Medieval Towns* (Oxford, 1977).

although tiny in comparison with later sprawls, nevertheless existed. Organic ribbon developments of housing and industry along major roads, and surrounding extensive extra-mural markets, such as St Giles at Oxford or Wigford at Lincoln, undermine the claim of intra-mural areas alone to urban status. Beyond the outer peripheries of towns, the countryside was profoundly affected by their presence. Far from being a monolithic 'other' against which towns can be contrasted and defined, countryside is at least as diverse in its complexity. There is an equally vast and marked difference between remote, wild countryside of sparse population dominated by subsistence agriculture and relative inaccessibility to urban markets, and a more densely populated, organized countryside dominated by intensive agriculture and dependent on urban markets for the disposal of its productive surplus. Differences in geology, soils, vegetation and weather caused regional imbalances in production which were, to some extent, corrected in distributional terms by inter-regional trade. The balance of arable cultivation and pastoral husbandry varied considerably across the English landscape. Forestry, hunting, wildfowling and fishing were all of lesser or greater importance in different regions. Much early medieval mining and industrial activity remained rural, and shipping and harbours made use of the natural advantages of tidal estuaries and coastal havens. By the eleventh century many landowners and abbeys had the resources and manpower to tame and straighten watercourses, equipping them with weirs and mills (see Chapter I.2). These activities created and sustained complex networks of social and economic interdependence across the countryside, yet were essential in creating and supporting urban economy and society.

Medieval towns have received a wealth of recent scholarly attention, perhaps most significantly in the first volume of *The Cambridge Urban History of Britain*.[3] This covered the hierarchy of towns from large to small, and included topographic, social and economic aspects. The introduction to a recent key collection of papers looking at town and country in the period 1100–1500 describes the question 'what is a town?' as 'hackneyed and old-fashioned',[4] although the very fact that it is still visible suggests that it remains impossible completely to dispose of it. The purpose of the conference which gave rise to the 'Town and Country' collection was to break down the dichotomy between town and country and to promote a

[3] D. M. Palliser, ed., *The Cambridge Urban History of Britain*, vol. 1, *600–1540* (Cambridge, 2000).

[4] K. Giles and C. Dyer, eds., *Town and Country in the Middle Ages, Contrasts, Contacts and Interconnections 1100–1500* (Society for Medieval Archaeology Monograph, 22; Leeds, 2005).

sense of interconnection and shared inquiry in historical, archaeological and geographical approaches and methods.

There has of course always been an understanding that a town could not prosper, or even in most cases exist, without reliance on its immediate rural environs to service it with people, goods and raw materials, and to reabsorb its outputs ranging from profit to rubbish. Yet in contrast to the prolonged and now perhaps outmoded debate about what constitutes a town, there have been fewer attempts to describe or quantify what its hinterland might be, and those have been largely couched in purely economic terms.[5] The extent of a town's political territory, which eventually came to find permanent expression in city and country boundaries, is a first point of recourse. The historical English shires, the extents of which survived relatively unscathed until the early 1970s, are a case in point, in most cases bearing the name of their shire town; these may seem to provide an easy answer as to the extent of their hinterlands. Yet many questions remain as to how the geographic configurations of these territories arose – were they amalgams of ancient estates governed by previous political geographies, a grand design dictated by an early medieval central planning authority, or economic and demographic catchment areas which found their expression and limits in competition for resources, or a combination of all of these? Techniques of economic geography, such as central place theory, seek to predict the extents of hinterlands in proportion to the size of town populations and equivalence in their demand on resources across geographic areas, and tend to produce generally mutually exclusive zones of influence. Sometimes these hypothetical distributions do accord strikingly with the extent of known political boundaries.[6] However we might seek to map hinterlands as coherent or discrete economic or political provinces, we remain at the surface of a complex depth of town–country relationships which extended far beyond simplistic definitions. Towns were not monolithic consuming entities, but collections of individuals and groups often with discordant interests and external affiliations. Town–country relationships were driven by social connection, political allegiance and interdependence of individual estates and specific markets. Zones of influence were multidimensional, overlaid upon each other and often discontinuous. It was possible that a rural estate, a fishery or a saltern could be linked to supplying an urban market well away

[5] J. Galloway 'Urban hinterlands in later medieval England', in Giles and Dyer, eds., *Town and Country in the Middle Ages*, pp. 111–30.

[6] D. Hill, *An Atlas of Anglo-Saxon England* (Oxford, 1981), fig. 217.

from the nearest and apparently most obvious one, entirely because of the exigencies of ownership links and transport preferences. When historical sources begin to fill out individual details of proprietorships and their often surprisingly long-distance allegiances and interdependencies from the twelfth century onwards, their complexity becomes clear. It is therefore dangerous for us to infer for earlier centuries lacking such a detailed documentary record that relationships between town and country were in any way less complex, unpredictable and quirky. In many ways these relationships were personal and familial, rather than commercial. Commerce (see Chapter III.2) had not yet succeeded in completely supplanting an older tradition of reciprocal obligations, dues and service.

THE EARLIEST ENGLISH TOWNS

The riverside trading enclaves known as the *wics*, which had arisen in the later seventh or early eighth century, but most of which did not continue after the mid-ninth century, had marked something of a false start in English urbanization. The most important were Lundenwic (London) and Hamwic (Southampton), with Eoforwic (York) and Gipeswic (Ipswich) as smaller but nonetheless important regional centres. Debate on the extent of the *wics* has encompassed the additional possibility of Canterbury and its Kentish satellites such as Fordwich, Sarre and Sandwich, together with Norwich.[7] The especially informative evidence excavated at Hamwic (which was located in the St Mary's district, to the northeast of the centre of modern Southampton) shows not only the high-status trade links with the Continent in terms of large quantities of Frankish and German pottery and glass, but also the settlement's dependence on its hinterland. This was, by later standards, a curious and one-sided dependency. Most animals consumed in the riverside trading settlement were older beasts, suggesting that there was a concerted (and hence to a great extent uncommercial) system of supply. Human burials from this period within the associated cemeteries show a bias towards adult males, implying that the population was not permanent but based on specialist occupations – the diversity of gender, age and wealth which would characterize later towns was not present to the same degree. Lundenwic's core was at Covent Garden and Aldwych – 'the old wic' – beside the Strand, west of the

[7] R. Hodges, *Dark Age Economics* (London 1982); D. Hill and R. Cowie, eds., *Wics. The Early Medieval Trading Centres of Northern Europe* (Sheffield, 2001).

Roman city.[8] Early eighth-century London was described by Bede as 'a mart of many nations coming to it by land and sea'.[9]

The *wics*, however, were by no means the only loci of trade in pre-tenth-century England. A charter reference of 857 to the bishop of Worcester holding property in London indicates that a hierarchy of markets may have existed, with smaller inland centres developing links with international markets. Smaller, non-urbanized markets also existed. Some of these were coastal, such as Sandtun (Kent) and Meols (Wirral, Cheshire).[10] *Sceatta* coins, minted in some of the *wics*, and the ninth-century Northumbrian derivative *stycas* are found in varying combinations with pins, other dress items and more utilitarian items such as lava querns and fishhooks. Inland, metal-detectorists have discovered vast quantities of middle and later Anglo-Saxon metalwork and coins, often at entirely rural and remote sites in fields, and alongside lanes and small rivers. These have been termed 'productive sites' by archaeologists, for want of a better term. Displaying their instinct to classify and categorize without fully understanding a phenomenon, commentators (this author included) have speculated about systems of rural markets, trade hierarchies and regional redistribution.

The social dimension of the urban and rural distribution of traded material needs more extensive and discriminating research. Nevertheless, it does seem that the Church played a greater role in the circulation of wealth in the countryside than previously suspected, and many of the items found at the productive sites (and to a lesser extent the coastal markets) are also found at contemporary high-status sites of monastic character, such as Flixborough and Jarrow/Wearmouth[11] The minsters of Anglo-Saxon England, which provided the template for the pastoral parish, remained an essential factor in generating urban characteristics in the tenth and eleventh centuries (see Chapter V.2). The convergence of people upon the minsters required servicing and resourcing, and as their numbers increased, so did the opportunities for buying and selling.

[8] G. Malcolm, D. Bowsher and R. Cowie, *Middle Saxon London, Excavations at the Royal Opera House 1989–99* (London, 2003).

[9] *EHD*, i, no. 151, p. 662 (Bede) and also compare no. 92, p. 529.

[10] M. Gardiner, R. Cross, N. Macpherson-Grant, I. Riddler *et al.*, 'Continental trade and non-urban ports in mid-Anglo-Saxon England: excavations at Sandtun, West Hythe, Kent', *Archaeological Journal*, 158 (2001), 161–290; D. Griffiths, R. A. Philpott and G. Egan, *Meols: The Archaeology of the North Wirral Coast* (Oxford, 2007).

[11] C. Loveluck, *Rural Settlement, Lifestyles and Social Change in the Later First Millennium AD: Anglo-Saxon Flixborough in Its Wider Context* (Oxford, 2007); R. Cramp, *Wearmouth and Jarrow Monastic Sites* (2 vols.; Swindon, 2005–7).

Pilgrimage traffic is also an important, if largely unquantifiable, factor in long-distance movement of people and in attracting associated economic activity around the church. Archaeologically attested examples of proto-urban development around minsters include Northampton (Northamptonshire), North Elmham (Norfolk), Bampton (Oxfordshire) and at Steyning (West Sussex), where clusters of rural-style buildings and small-scale manufacturing grew up around the minster of St Cuthman.[12]

The importance of minsters in generating population and market growth has been attributed by John Blair to their static presence in the landscape, attracting permanent communities around them, in an age when royal and secular authority was still to a great extent itinerant. In Blair's point there is an echo of a wider and more basic observation familiar to prehistoric archaeologists and ethnographers: mobile, hunter-gathering or nomadic populations tend not to accumulate extensive property – they take their herds and people with them and consume in relation to their immediate supply. Settled and static communities construct, store and curate resources as well as consume them, giving rise to permanent architecture, a more elaborate material culture and ultimately to specialized occupations serving 'lifestyle' above the level of mere subsistence. This 'process' is the driver behind structured settlement and ultimately urbanization, and may explain why in terms of material culture it is often the higher-status objects we find in urban excavations – the poorer and less free people even in the Middle Ages were still to an extent nomadic in that they came and went in seasonal migrations from the countryside, especially at harvest time. Small-scale manufacturers and pedlars of simple objects such as pins, combs and baskets were also itinerant between town and country, as were drovers, carters, sailors, quacks and soothsayers. Many of the poor and unfree owned and therefore left behind little or nothing. Their presence is to an extent visible in their meagre contribution to the consumption of resources, their occasional mentions in legal documents and in the mostly anonymous disposal of their bodies.

FROM *BURHS* TO BOROUGHS: URBAN INNOVATION AND CONSOLIDATION

The tenth century saw a resurgence in urbanization in England, which is attested in historical documents and in archaeological evidence. As

[12] J. Blair, 'Small towns 600–1270', in Palliser, ed., *Cambridge Urban History*, pp. 245–70; comment on minsters' static presence: p. 250.

we have seen, the later ninth century marked something of a nadir in urban life. As the century progressed the *wics* were no longer able to function without rudimentary defences, and subsequently lost their influence altogether and became derelict. The kingdoms of Northumbria, Mercia and East Anglia, which had begun the century in conditions of reasonable stability, fell prey to internal dynastic weaknesses and external pressure. The Welsh and Scots were an ever-present threat at the western and northern borders, and they were joined from 855 by the Danish 'great army' which threw first Kent (a satellite of Mercia), then Northumbria, East Anglia, midland Mercia itself and subsequently Wessex into yet greater chaos. There are archaeological indications that the Mercian centres of Hereford, Winchcombe, Tamworth and Bedford developed defences in the ninth century; although still very small-scale by later standards, they do seem at this time to have begun to provide fortified regional foci for people and resources in a pattern which would be replicated elsewhere.

The reigns of Alfred 'the Great' of Wessex (871–99) and his son Edward 'the Elder' (899–924) saw a turning point in the long struggle to return Wessex, and subsequently the rest of England, to some measure of unity and stability. A document of the early tenth century known to historians as the 'Burghal Hidage', which is simply a list made up of several near-contemporaneous versions, reveals a hierarchy of named fortified places with their 'hidage' – literally the number of households (later meaning an area of land) upon which they could call for the people and resources to maintain their defences.[13] The largest, Winchester and Wallingford, had 2,400 hides, whereas the smallest, Lydford and Lyng in the south-west, had 140 and 100, respectively. Amongst the places named were former Roman towns and fortresses such as Winchester, Bath, Exeter and Portchester; places with existing monasteries such as Malmesbury and Oxford; larger foundations on largely new, open sites such as Wallingford and Cricklade; and smaller defended enclaves on strategic bends in rivers such as 'Sashes' on the Thames in Berkshire, or reused Iron Age hillforts such as Chisbury in Wiltshire.

The 'Burghal Hidage' gives us above all a glimpse of a systematic strategy for civil defence in a time of threatened invasion, which linked defended places across the landscape by means of herepaths (military roads), beacons and look-outs. This was essential in a successful long-term military and political campaign which gradually extinguished the

[13] D. Hill and A. R. Rumble, *The Defence of Wessex: The Burghal Hidage and Anglo-Saxon Fortifications* (Manchester, 1996).

influence of Danish warlords first from the south and southeast under Alfred (London was retaken in 886), then the Midlands and northwest under Edward, who absorbed the remnants of independent Mercia into the West Saxon kingdom in 918. It is highly doubtful, as some historians have claimed, that the places mentioned in the 'Burghal Hidage', and their immediate successors in the southeast Midlands and northwest such as Hertford, Buckingham, Bakewell and Chester, were planned as towns from the start. Barely any archaeological evidence for anything but defensive banks and ditches exists for their earliest phases, nor does archaeology give anything approaching a convincing picture of urban occupation before, at the earliest, 920 and in many cases the mid-tenth century onwards. There were apparently some early efforts to reconfigure former Roman topography such as at Winchester, but detailed urban planning such as residential and market streets, burgage plots and intramural parishes (see Chapter III.3) was something which would largely take place as conditions evolved in later decades.

By no means all of the 'Burghal Hidage' places subsequently developed into towns, and mostly those that did already had good reason to do so, in terms of an existing centre of population (such as a monastery) or a strategic location on networks of routeways, rivers or with access to the sea, which gave them an advantage in market terms. Furthermore, this very limited document does not include anywhere outside Wessex or on its immediate borders (the *burhs* of Mercia established by Æthelflæd and Edward the Elder are mentioned in a slightly later addendum to the Anglo-Saxon Chronicle known as the 'Mercian Register'.[14] London, known to the middle Saxons as Lundenwic, was renamed Lundenburh after its conquest by Alfred in 886 but, like Canterbury, does not appear in the 'Burghal Hidage'). It also misses out a number of smaller centres, mostly of ecclesiastical importance, which were probably beginning to develop some urban and market characteristics at that time, such as Sherborne, Avebury, Abingdon and Dorchester-on-Thames. Nevertheless, there is an undeniable connection, not just in etymological but also in functional and political terms, between the *burhs* and later boroughs. The *burhs* with their territorial dependence on their set quotas of hides were integral to the process of shiring, whereby counties composed of groups of hundreds (of hides) were defined, named and linked for the first time into a central place. Justice and administration, still based at the local rural level on the earlier Anglo-Saxon tradition of moots or hundred meeting

[14] *EHD*, i, no. 1, pp. 208–19.

places, became focused in its higher manifestation on town-based assizes. As urban development took off in the tenth century, military, political and judicial obligations took on an economic and social character as people and goods gravitated towards growing urban markets.

The process by which trade and markets became concentrated in the shire centres was promoted and assisted by legislation. The laws of Alfred issued in the later ninth century make no reference to towns (perhaps another indication that Alfred was not planning any systematic urban innovation) But from Æthelstan (924–39) onwards, a succession of royal decrees limiting trade to 'ports' (towns), backed up by severe penalties for non-compliance, were issued. The Grateley Decrees issued by Æthelstan in the late 920s[15] limit transactions over twenty pence to towns, and there is a complex set of rules and stipulations governing the minting of coins, including the precise numbers of moneyers permitted in Canterbury (seven), of which four were of the king, two of the bishop and one of the abbot, London (eight), Winchester (six), Lewes, Wareham, Southampton, Exeter, Shaftesbury (all two), Hastings, Dorchester (Dorset) and 'the other boroughs' (all one). Although important mints elsewhere, such as Chester, which numismatic evidence has shown was thriving in the 920s, were not mentioned here, the extent of royal control of coinage is clearly evident. Minting was, as the unusual detail provided for Canterbury shows, a lucrative royal privilege and restricted to the king's own representatives together with only the most senior and loyal ecclesiastical authorities. Moneyers enjoyed affluence and prestigious professional status, albeit subject to savage retribution in the form of amputation or the ordeal of hot iron should they infringe the rules by cheating. Money in the form of hammered silver pennies made from a strictly controlled supply of dies, mostly bearing a bust of the king on the obverse, gradually ousted non-monetary conventions of exchange and the use of silver bullion by weight, together with the remnants of the poorer cast silver coinages of previous centuries. The extensively-supervised gathering in of taxation payments in kind from the townspeople and the issuing of silver coin in return – always at a rate of exchange advantageous to the authorities – was a primitive but effective means of capitalizing upon revenue from economic activity.

The currency reform of Edgar in 973 took a further step towards a 'national currency' by further limiting local autonomy in standards and design of issues. As the centuries moved on towards the Norman

[15] *EHD*, i, no. 35, p. 417.

Conquest, the silver content of Anglo-Saxon coin declined during the course of repeated reissues, reaching an inflationary high during the long and troubled reign of Æthelred II 'the Unready' (978–1016). Indeed, amidst the resurgence of Danish attacks and instability, coupled with the drain on the country's finances caused by extortionate 'Danegeld' payments (which led to Scandinavia, not England, becoming the richest depository of English coinage of the late tenth and early eleventh century), in desperation Æthelred staged the only known revival of the Alfredian *burh* policy. His forces constructed new *burhs* with mints in defended Iron Age hillfort enclosures at South Cadbury (Somerset) and Old Sarum (Wiltshire) when the neighbouring lowland towns of Ilchester and Wilton appeared too vulnerable. The stone enclosure wall is still evident at South Cadbury, although traces of Æthelredan occupation were found to be extremely slight during excavations between 1966 and 1972, suggesting the new *burh* lasted a very short time.[16] Old Sarum survived the Norman Conquest as the political and ecclesiastical centre of Wiltshire, only to be supplanted by the new foundation of Salisbury in 1220.

The West Saxon realm and its growing annexations in the southeast and Midlands were not the only areas of England which experienced impulses towards urbanization, shiring and the production of coinage in the early tenth century. The impact of Viking attacks was felt most strongly in the north. Northumbria, the first of the major English kingdoms to flourish and the first to fail, was already on its knees in the middle of the ninth century. A Danish war-band entered York in 866, putting an end to its long Anglian heritage as the political and ecclesiastical successor of Roman *Eboracvm*; its more shortlived period of economic advance during the growth of Eoforwic was already more or less finished, although a debased successor coinage to the sceat, the *styca*, continued to be produced until the 860s. The Danes under Halfdan returned to rule the city in 876, whereupon the Anglo-Saxon Chronicle tells us that he 'shared out the lands of the Northumbrians and they proceeded to plough and to support themselves'. No clearer evidence is needed to point towards the interdependence of town and country – it was not enough to conquer a city: to establish a secure long-term occupation, its hinterland had to be captured, too, and the two made to work in tandem.

Archaeological evidence from numerous excavations in York has confirmed that the broken-down Roman fortress and colonia, within which had sheltered the churches and palace of the Anglian city, oversaw a major

[16] L. Alcock, *Cadbury Castle, Somerset: The Early Medieval Archaeology* (Cardiff, 1995).

urban revival from the early tenth century.[17] A dense neighbourhood of narrow lanes fronted by tenements and industrial workshops grew up, focused on the point of land formed by the confluence of the rivers Ouse and Foss. Fires were common, and the buildings were rebuilt numerous times in gradually more elaborate styles of architecture throughout the tenth to twelfth centuries. Once established, however, property boundaries proved more impervious to generational change. Behind the street-facing wooden buildings (which in the later tenth century progressed from single to double storey in height), narrow tenement yards enclosed subsidiary buildings, wells, cesspits, animal pens and middens. Exceptional levels of waterlogged organic preservation (paralleled in the British Isles only by the Wood Quay excavations of Viking Age Dublin) revealed timber, wattles, reeds, charcoal, textiles, grain, fruit stones, nuts, animal, bird and fish bone, all indicative of extensive supply networks in the countryside and trade and redistribution in urban markets. The physical evidence is graphic, but we know much less about the complex social relations which underlay its supply and distribution.

Excavations have revealed that life in early medieval York was short, harsh and squalid for many of the inhabitants. Rubbish and sewage were deposited and redeposited in wells, pits and yard middens in close proximity to human occupation and water supplies. Human burials, such as those excavated from the churchyard of St Helen on the Walls, reflect an increase in the urban population during the tenth century coupled with an overall decrease in life expectancy, and palaeopathological studies of the bones together with excavated evidence for insect larvae, rodents and preserved remains of intestinal parasites show the prevalence of disease and the generally overcrowded and filth-ridden domestic life of the inhabitants. The most revealing insights to date occurred in large-scale excavations at 16–22 Coppergate in 1977–82, but smaller excavations throughout the ancient core of the city since the 1960s and continuing today have revealed a similar picture – yet strangely, perhaps, the old site of Eoforwic southeast of the Foss/Ouse confluence remained comparatively underdeveloped in the tenth century, only eventually recolonized by suburban development in the later eleventh and twelfth centuries, and by a Gilbertine priory founded *c.* 1200. York's archaeological record is particularly informative as a result of unusually good *in situ* preservation of deposits, but life in medieval York must have been similar to that in larger towns elsewhere – indeed age-at-death profiles of burials from St Nicholas

[17] R. A. Hall, ed., *Aspects of Anglo-Scandinavian York* (York, 2004).

Shambles, London, suggest very similar conditions prevailed there.[18] The vibrant but dangerous and disease-prone nature of urban communities can only have increased their constant call on the countryside for their supply of people, animals, raw materials and agricultural produce.

Halfdan took his part of a Viking force which had overwintered in 873–4 on the Trent at Repton (Derbyshire) northeast to York; another force under Guthrum headed towards East Anglia and thence towards eventual confrontation with Alfred's forces at Edington, Wiltshire, in 878. The Treaty of Wedmore of 886 created English and Danish spheres of influence, divided east and north of London by the rivers Lea and Ouse, and by the Roman road, known to the Anglo-Saxons as the Watling Street, which leads northwest across the Midlands towards Staffordshire and Cheshire. The 'Danelaw', as it later became known, was a short-lived entity in terms of its claim to political independence (the southern Danelaw and much of East Anglia was conquered by Edward the Elder, and the independent Viking kingdom of York was defeated by Eadwig in 954), but its right and special status under English law lasted a good deal longer. There were some differences in the systems of judicial administration and land tenure between the two sides, with the 'sokes' being a particularly Danelaw feature, but the functions of 'carucates' and 'wapentakes' are a reasonable approximation to that of the English hides and hundreds. First mentioned in 954, but almost certainly earlier in foundation, are the so-called 'Five Boroughs of the Danelaw' – namely Lincoln, Nottingham, Stamford, Derby and Leicester. Archaeological finds from these have thus far been less rewarding than at York, but evidence of a townscape of wooden workshops with glass- and bronze-working evidence was found at the Flaxengate site, Lincoln, in the 1970s.[19] Ribbon development around and south of the river-wharf in the Wigford area south of the former Roman lower town also grew, attested today by the magnificent surviving pre-Conquest church towers of St Mary Le Wigford and St Peter at Gowts. Added to these were towns in East Anglia such as Thetford, Norwich, Dunwich and Ipswich, which maintained some urban functions in the tenth, eleventh and twelfth centuries. Stamford was a centre of iron working, and became a centre of pottery manufacture in the tenth to twelfth centuries, the latter, 'Stamford Ware', becoming

[18] J. D. Dawes and J. R. Magilton, *The Cemetery of St Helen on the Walls, Aldwark* (The Archaeology of York 12/1; York, 1980); W. White, *Skeletal Remains from the Cemetery of St Nicholas Shambles* (London and Middlesex Archaeological Society, special paper 9; London, 1988); R. Holt, 'Society and population 600–1330', in Palliser, ed., *Cambridge Urban History*, pp. 79–104.

[19] D. Perring, *Anglo-Scandinavian Occupation at Flaxengate, Lincoln* (London, 1981).

near-ubiquitous in the east Midlands with outlying exports being found as far away as Dublin. Thetford also produced pottery; another smaller pottery centre in the east Midlands, Torksey on the Trent near Lincoln, may also have been a borough at this time.

In those towns which attracted increased trade and rising populations, space was increasingly in short supply. The main streets were an early and probably centrally planned feature, whereas it is more probable that the laying out and subdivision of burgage plots, most commonly with narrow street frontages and long yards behind connected to the street by narrow alleys, occurred mostly piecemeal as the result of the development of individual blocks and the settlement of disputes. Commercial and domestic premises, which had been simple and single storey in the tenth century, acquired cellars and in some cases upper storeys. Churches and monastic houses became more elaborate, as did their associated burial grounds. Public buildings, such as guildhalls, and grander and sometimes palatial town residences of lords also started to appear. Sections of towns under ecclesiastical liberties were exempt from civil administration, and increased population and sub-division meant that complex patterns of often tiny, interlocking parishes arose. Danish, French and, later, Jewish people often occupied their own 'ghetto' district in towns – the Danes of Oxford for instance were probably concentrated in St Clement's parish, on the eastern outskirts across the River Cherwell, prior to the horrific events of 1002, and there are numerous references to French boroughs in Domesday, such as at Nottingham, Southampton and Norwich (see Chapter III.3).[20] Marginalized and stigmatized people, such as the chronically sick and infirm, began to gravitate towards monastic and charitable hospitals, which were commonly found on the urban periphery.

Market specialization was already evident in London before the Norman Conquest, where there were dedicated markets such that which arose for the fish trade at Billingsgate (establishing a tradition which survived *in situ* until the 1970s), and by this time Cheapside in the city of London had become a bustling shopping street of international renown. In London, as in other major port-towns around England, people of widely differing language, ethnicity and geographical origin interacted in the pursuit of profit and service. German merchants from the Rhine, whose trading role enjoyed protected status, bought and sold with Londoners; drovers or ironmongers from Wessex or the Welsh border encountered weavers and

[20] H. M. Thomas, *The English and the Normans: Ethnic Hostility, Assimilation and Identity 1066–c. 1220* (Oxford, 2003), p. 190.

potters from the north and east Midlands, or fishermen, shipwrights and millers from the Thames Estuary, Kent and Essex. Transient pilgrims and Scandinavian, Flemish, French or Spanish merchants added to the cacophony. For those who resided in towns especially, exposure to an energetic and acculturative mix of other cultures prompted experimentation in new fashions, further emphasizing their urban status in relation to the relative conservatism of the countryside.

The eleventh century, at least in the fifty years between the accession of Cnut in 1016 and the Norman Conquest, saw a considerable, if temporary, stabilization of political and economic life in England. Outside London, the gathering impetus and aspiration towards urban status in the eleventh century is marked by the grants of port and market privileges (almost certainly a retrospective recognition of existing practice) to small ecclesiastical towns such as Pershore, Tewkesbury and Evesham. The shire structure was already largely in place in midland and southern England, although it was still tentative and under-developed north of the Mersey–Humber line, where more local independence and administrative variation existed. In the aftermath of the Conquest, the taxable assets of the defeated kingdom were assessed by the new authorities. From this we are fortunate still to have a relatively systematic, if partial, record of towns and their associated counties and rural resources. Domesday Book (1086) is not universal or even in its coverage, but it contains enough information to map a broad picture of urban development, recorded as it existed in 1066 and its somewhat damaged post-Conquest state in 1086. London was excluded from the 'Great Domesday', and Winchester was apparently not recorded in comparable terms until the 'Winton Domesday' composed in the early years of the twelfth century. It is not the purpose of this chapter to address the many and manifold weaknesses, idiosyncrasies, biases and lacunae evident in the Domesday survey (although it has these shortcomings in common with most if not all contemporary historical sources). Nevertheless, when its evidence on towns is reviewed, nowhere in England south of Cheshire and Yorkshire, or east of Dartmoor, can be shown to be more than 40 miles from a town of appreciable size (denoted here by a population of over a thousand). In some areas, most notably the south and west Midlands, the density of towns was a good deal higher, with more smaller market towns such as Droitwich, Tewkesbury, Winchcombe and Warminster filling the gaps between the bigger centres of Warwick, Oxford, Bath and Shaftesbury. In the east Midlands – a former area of the Danelaw – fewer small towns existed between the larger centres, suggesting that rural markets to an

Figure 7 The more important towns in 1086.
D. M. Palliser, ed., *The Cambridge Urban History of Britain*, vol. 1, *600–1540* (Cambridge, 2000), map 3.1

extent persisted, and recognition of smaller centres as towns was slower to take place. Further, probably minor, differences existed – *iudices civitatis* (city justices) are recorded in the Danelaw Boroughs and at Chester, but not elsewhere.

North of the Midlands, towns remained far fewer and further apart, with only York being of any great size in national terms. In the north-west, Æthelflæd of Mercia's *burh* of 907 at Chester had developed into a regional urban centre with strong links to the Viking-dominated Irish Sea.[21] It acted as the lynchpin of a string of tiny *burhs* founded in the early tenth century, from Manchester westwards to *Cledemutha* (Rhuddlan) in northeast Wales, which came under Welsh control for a period in the early to mid-eleventh century. In the far north, Durham grew up initially in the shadow of the great Northumbrian monastery on a precipitous bend in the River Wear. Both depended on rural hinterlands composed of prosperous estates and increasingly nucleated villages, in the Dee and Clwyd valleys in the case of Chester, and along the Wear and Tees in the case of Durham. Archaeological evidence has pointed to the existence of urban tenements in both cases well before 1066. These northern outposts bore the brunt of William the Conqueror's harsh depredations following the Conquest – for example, Chester lost 40 per cent of its houses as recorded in Domesday for 1066 and 1086. Elsewhere, towns suffered in the aftermath of the Conquest. Oxford, Ipswich and Thetford lost over half of their tenements, the latter suffering a reverse in importance from which it never recovered in comparative terms, its see subsequently moved to Norwich in the 1090s. These losses were paralleled in the country, particularly in the north, where the values of estates declined between 1066 and 1086, and much productive land in 1066 was recorded as 'waste' in 1086. After the Conquest there was no overall consistency of recovery: some of the *burhs* which were originally planned on an ambitious scale, such as Cricklade and Wallingford (almost a quarter of which was subsumed by Robert D'Oilly's massive Norman castle), did not prosper and expand after the Conquest, as did others of similar size and pre-Conquest importance, such as Winchester and Oxford.

To the Normans, military conquest and establishing a secure occupation were higher immediate priorities than maintaining civic prosperity. Remaining pockets of resistance from the old order and subsequent rebellions and attempts at invasion were put down with unremitting severity. The construction of new town castles and cathedral precincts, which in many cases obliterated existing streets and tenements, occurred in towns all over England and probably explains the loss of such huge numbers of houses between 1066 and 1086 in places such as Chester

[21] D. Griffiths, 'Exchange, trade and urbanization', in W. Davies, ed., *From the Vikings to the Normans* (Short Oxford History of the British Isles; Oxford, 2003), pp. 73–104.

and Oxford. Concomitant with the Conquest was a major reordering of landed authority, although the local territorial structure of estates were apparently largely kept intact. The secular nobility of the defeated kingdom was dispossessed or downgraded in favour of incoming Norman lords, and freemen were required to adopt new political allegiances, in some cases driving ahead new fashions by adopting more Continental lifestyle traits and French-sounding names. The religious houses of Normandy were given extensive lands and properties in England, and in many English towns the existing Anglo-Saxon minsters and cathedrals were razed to make way for new Romanesque replacements, some of which, such as at Durham, were of staggering scale and ambition. The huge demands of these new castle and cathedral construction projects in terms of labour, building stone and timber injected some energy back into the shocked and stagnant English economy in the later eleventh and twelfth centuries.

The Norman system of military occupation began with the construction of vast numbers of temporary earthwork castles, many of which were later converted into permanent stone structures. Attached to many were small service settlements, initially little bigger than an outer bailey, but which developed into small towns. 'Planted settlements', a theme which emerges particularly in the twelfth century, has preoccupied many archaeologists and historians of this period. Defended urban enclaves grouped around castles began to acquire borough status, and in some cases, such as Newcastle upon Tyne and Cardiff, were positioned in proximity to such mineral wealth and good harbourage that significant future urban growth was almost inevitable. In areas where suspicions remained about the depth of loyalty to the Normans, such as East Anglia, planned defended boroughs such as Pleshey, Essex, and New Buckenham, Norfolk, were imposed. The Welsh border was even more densely militarized by the Normans. Aspects of Norman civic governance were imported, as in the case of the privileges of Breteuil being applied to Hereford and Shrewsbury.[22] Building on a strategy already to an extent in place before the Conquest, castle-boroughs such as Richard's Castle, Ludlow and Wigmore held the western edges of the English lowlands, whereas tiny forward-situated boroughs in the remoter hilly interior of the Marches, such as Ewias Harold, Kilpeck, Brecon and Abergavenny, provided points of strength and security for new lords in a generally uneasy and hostile

[22] M. W. Beresford, *New Towns of the Middle Ages: Town Plantation in England, Wales and Gascony* (London, 1967, repr. Stroud, 1988).

landscape. Their newly won estates were linked into these, gaining economic advantage from their exclusive trading privileges.

The Norman practice of creating defended towns and linking these to estate hinterlands as an instrument of strategic power was far more extensive and successful than anything seen previously. In the twelfth century, as the Norman influence extended across Wales, and, after 1170, to Ireland, new walled towns such as Carmarthen and Pembroke, and re-establishments of former Hiberno-Norse trading enclaves such as Cork and Wexford, became a means of securing the landscape. Twelfth-century Anglo-Normandom was still an extensively militarized society, and the influence of domestic civil war and the crusades (which began in 1095/6) maintained this far beyond the point where the Conquest itself was a distant and dying memory. In Wales, the well-proven military–urban strategy reached its apogee under Edward I (1272–1307) with the foundation of planned and massively defended castle-boroughs on harbours at Flint, Rhuddlan, Conwy, Caernarfon, Beaumaris, Harlech and Aberystwyth. It was also a highly influential strategic model in the development of state power in twelfth-century Scotland, where David I (1124–53) and Malcolm IV (1153–65) founded *burhs* with associated shires at Berwick, Roxburgh, Edinburgh, Dunfermline and Perth, and the total of burgh foundations in the Scottish kingdom had reached thirty-eight by 1200. In England, there was a slackening of urban foundations during the mid-century civil and political upheavals known as 'the Anarchy' during the interrupted reign of Stephen (1135–41 and 1145–54), but resurged during the subsequent and somewhat more successful reign of Henry II (1154–89), when there was a rise once again in the chartering of smaller town markets such as Chelmsford, Epping and Witney, promoted by local medium-ranking noble and ecclesiastical interests. Seaports such as Southampton, Hull, (King's – formerly Bishop's) Lynn, Boston and Bristol also expanded at this time.

The rash of thirty charters bestowed upon towns by Henry II was described by James Campbell as indicating a concerted political will,[23] and as documentary sources improve in their coverage of detail at this time, it gradually becomes clear to us how complex and contested the various relationships were between king, nobility and townspeople. The king borrowed money extensively from urban merchants in both England and France to finance his military campaigns, a dependence which constrained his power. Indeed the creation of small money-markets within

[23] J. Campbell, 'Power and authority 600–1300', in Palliser, ed., *Cambridge Urban History*, p. 66.

their fiefdom which could be used to raise cash revenue seems also to have been an important stimulus for lords to found new small towns, in a diminutive echo of royal and episcopal practice.

However, freedoms hard won by townspeople were jealously and increasingly assertively guarded from the king, bishops and lords. The twelfth century in particular saw increasing pressure for economic, and to some extent political, independence on the part of burgesses. Concessions to towns to reap their own tolls (the 'fee farm') proliferated in the reign of Henry II. Once created and in growth, a town became too complex and energized an organism for any long-term expectation of political docility. Although key to the strategic control of the countryside, towns also became the most heated centres of popular strife and rebellion. Towns sometimes competed against each other, as in the case of Newcastle upon Tyne in the early twelfth century trying to prevent outsiders from buying cloth.[24] Internal disputes arose between guilds, Jews were singled out for persecution and sources emerging in the twelfth century such as Pipe Rolls record the creation of seditious communes in Gloucester and York. In these turbulent and disputatious events it is not difficult for historians to see the developing patterns of upcoming clashes in the reigns of Henry's sons and successors, Richard I and John, and to trace their contribution en route towards eventual legal constraint on royal power in the Magna Carta.

AGRICULTURE AND THE REORGANIZATION OF THE COUNTRYSIDE

Domesday Book's textual record of population (divided into different categories from freemen to slaves), boroughs, vills, ploughlands, mills, fisheries and industries has been mapped and transformed into a graphic historical geography of – most of – England in the later eleventh century, most notably by H. C. Darby.[25] Notwithstanding the caveats outlined above on the extent and depth of Domesday's coverage, Darby's distribution maps provide an unparalleled insight into the concentrations of people and resources. These serve to raise as many questions as they answer. Perhaps most strikingly, the free population is concentrated towards the east coast, which by the same measure is an area of fewer,

[24] C. M. Fraser, 'Medieval trading restrictions in the north-east', *Archaeologia Aeliana* 4th ser., 39 (1961), 135–50; R. H. Britnell, *The Commercialisation of English Society, 1000–1500* (2nd edn; Manchester, 1996), p. 26.

[25] H. C. Darby, *The Domesday Geography of England* (Cambridge, 1977).

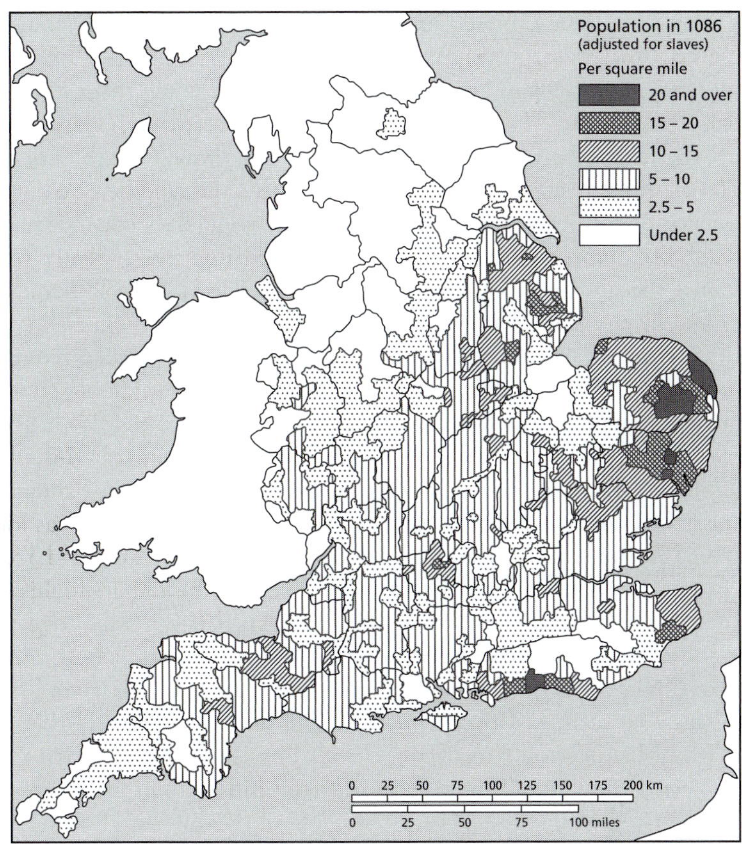

Figure 8 Domesday population.
H. C. Darby, *The Domesday Geography of England* (Cambridge, 1977), fig. 35

larger towns as compared with the Midlands and west (Figure 8). Dyer subsequently drew attention to the cottars and bordars mentioned in Domesday.[26] These humble classes of inhabitant were probably mostly smallholders, and were concentrated in and around towns. They swell further our impression of the urban population – Dyer estimated that up to 10 per cent of people lived in towns in 1086.

Darby's mapping of 'urban fields' (which he classed as vills with contributory burghers (*burgenses*), houses (*domus*) and enclosures (*hagae* or

[26] C. Dyer, *Everyday Life in Medieval England* (London 2000), pp. 242–54; estimate of percentage of people living in towns, p. 252.

mensurae) also gives an impression of the spread of urban–rural tenurial ties in the English landscape. Significant concentrations of fisheries and mills surrounded towns such as London, Gloucester and Chester; the seven mills at Battersea, on the Thames a short distance upstream of London, were worth the huge sum of £42 9s 8d. The corn they milled for the London market would have come in from the Surrey, Kent and Middlesex countryside, much of it probably coming along the Thames on flat-bottomed boats. William fitz Stephen's description of London written in the early 1170s described the town fields as like 'the fat Asian plains that yield luxuriant crops and fill the tillers' barns with the sheaves of Ceres'.[27]

The increase in urban population and spread of urban markets required not only a steady and reliable supply of defensive manpower, food, civilian labour and raw materials from the countryside; such centres also became increasingly dependent on the rural population to consume urban-derived or urban-finished products and services. Before the Norman Conquest, the principal concentrations of wealth and production in most counties remained in the large rural estates, but lords increasingly sought residential properties in towns in order to participate in the opportunities for profit and status there. These linkages increased urban–rural interdependence and in time even people of modest rank came to possess both urban and rural properties. In Domesday, Bedford's entry has a separate list of burgesses who possessed rural estates. In the twelfth century in the tiny borough of Launceston (Cornwall), the leading families drew upon their possession of rural estates to exert prestige and influence in the town, and the wealthy Christina of Markyate, a resident of the town of Huntingdon, also based her elevated social status on rural landed possessions.[28] The Pipe Roll of 1130 indicates that Londoners were responsible for choosing the sheriff of Middlesex, a clear indication that townspeople's interests had become paramount in the government of London's rural fringe.[29]

A recent survey of urban hinterlands, although predominately based on sources from the fourteenth and fifteenth centuries, suggests that by the High Middle Ages towns had local trade hinterlands which 'did not vary greatly in size' for agricultural staples, whereas 'higher-order' goods (luxuries and so forth) prompted more extensive links, and these in particular were affected by the growing predominance of London.[30] Tenurial

[27] *EHD*, ii, no. 281 p. 1025; Britnell, *Commercialisation*, p. 50.

[28] Thomas, *The English and the Normans*, p. 187.

[29] J. Tait, *The Medieval English Borough: Studies on Its Origins and Constitutional History* (Manchester, 1936).

[30] Galloway, 'Urban hinterlands'.

links between urban and rural estates, court and debt pleas and patterns of rural origins of burgesses as traced in later sources do in this case seem to offer support to a broadly conceived 'central place theory' model for the rural economic influence of towns. The predominance of single shire centres had during the eleventh, but more particularly the twelfth, century been eroded and made more layered and contested by the granting of market privileges to smaller centres which had in the tenth century been rural estate centres, minsters or in some cases altogether non-existent.

The social and economic histories of medieval towns and the countryside have until recently been investigated and interpreted largely as separate phenomena. Moreover, documents and archaeological evidence have tended also to be treated separately and in relation to divergent concerns. This has given rise to a series of disconnections in theory and method which have been alleviated by the work of relatively few contemporary inter-disciplinarians such as John Blair for the earlier medieval period and Christopher Dyer for the later. A major concern in medieval archaeology and historical geography since the influential book *The Making of the English Landscape* by W. G. Hoskins, published in 1955, has been the agrarian history of the English landscape and in particular rural settlement forms and the growth of communal peasant agriculture.[31] Fifty years of intensive research, beginning with the 'deserted medieval village' research of M. W. Beresford and J. G. Hurst, and continuing in a wealth of regional and local studies, has contributed a detailed multilayered cartography of regional variation.[32] The deserted and shrunken villages are now understood to be only one aspect of medieval settlement, much of which lies beneath currently occupied villages. Of principal concern to participants in this debate have been the origins of the pattern of nucleated and dispersed villages. A broad and straggling band or 'central province' up to 100 miles wide in places, of nucleated village forms with predominantly communal open-field systems of agriculture, can be traced from the Scottish border on the east coast, south through Durham, Yorkshire and the Midlands to Hampshire and Dorset. Commonly referred to using terms first coined by John Leland, the sixteenth-century antiquarian, the 'champion' lands of the nucleated belt are on predominantly heavy soils, whereas the 'bosky' or woodland areas on either side (East Anglia, Kent, the Welsh border counties and Lancashire; see Chapter I.3) are on lighter soils for the most part and characterized by more dispersed settlement

[31] W. G. Hoskins, *The Making of the English Landscape* (London, 1955).

[32] B. K. Roberts and S. Wrathmell, *An Atlas of Rural Settlement in England* (London, 2000).

patterns of single farms and hamlets. This overall model, until recently widely accepted, is now subject to intensive revision where the monolithically nucleated status of the 'central province' is questioned, and smaller clusters of nucleated and dispersed settlement which break up and complicate the broad picture are receiving the attention of historical researchers and fieldworkers.[33] There are numerous smaller clusters of nucleated settlement outside the 'central province', such as in the environs of Canterbury, Ipswich, Chester and Carlisle: a distribution which should alert us to the influence of towns on shaping settlement forms in their rural environs. Intensive field studies in areas characterized by a particularly dominant geographic character, such as the Fenland, the Somerset Levels, the Weald or the uplands of the southwest, and by common historical identities and functions, such as the royal hunting forest of Whittlewood on the Northamptonshire–Buckinghamshire border, are contributing new data which show dramatic variation even in small areas. Moreover the relic influence of ancient prehistoric and Roman land use is shown to be more pervasive than Hoskins ever suspected or gave credit for. The forms of villages themselves are being shown to be far more complex and nuanced than previously thought, with many apparently nucleated villages having developed organically from clusters of individual or 'polyfocal' settlements, whereas others, such as the village of Shapwick (Somerset) were planned by landowners, in Shapwick's case by Glastonbury Abbey.[34]

Much of the 'central province' pattern of nucleated settlement is thought to have taken shape in the ninth to eleventh centuries, having been characterized by dispersed settlement previously (Figure 9). The widely accepted ninth-century date for the beginnings of the reorganization stems from field research done in East Anglia but above all in work by David Hall and others in Northamptonshire and its neighbouring counties bordering the Fens to the west.[35] Pottery scatters of eighth- and early ninth-century date have been found in locations away from nucleated village centres, suggesting that dispersed settlements were abandoned, and population and resources grouped together into centralized villages, subsequently deserted examples of which show evidence of pottery from

[33] C. Lewis, P. Mitchell-Fox and C. Dyer, *Village, Hamlet and Field: Changing Medieval Settlements in Central England* (Macclesfield, 1997, 2001).

[34] R. Jones and M. Page, *Medieval Villages in an English Landscape: Beginnings and Ends* (Macclesfield, 2006); C. Gerrard and M. Aston, *The Shapwick Project, Somerset: A Rural Landscape Explored* (Leeds, 2007).

[35] D. Hall, 'The late Anglo-Saxon countryside: villages and their fields', in D. Hooke, ed., *Anglo-Saxon Settlements* (Oxford, 1988), pp. 99–122.

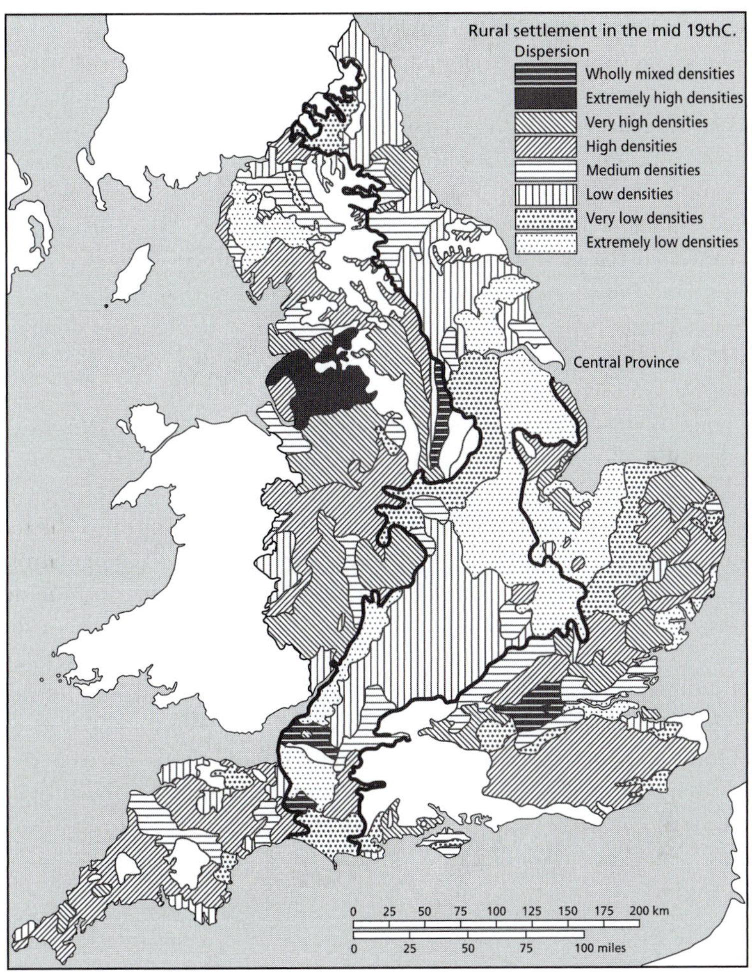

Figure 9 Zones of nucleation and dispersal.
Simplified version of B. K. Roberts and S. Wrathmell, *An Atlas of Rural Settlement in England*, London, 2000, fig. 3, based on zones of dispersion represented in nineteenth-century Ordnance Survey maps

the later eighth, ninth and tenth century onwards. The nucleated villages were mostly characterized by simple single-storey mud and wattle houses with infield-yards behind (tofts and crofts), facing onto common greens or thoroughfares – the latter still evidenced in many examples by hollow-ways. Parish churches, fishponds, mills and manorial sites which were often moated, overlooking an expanse of strip-cultivated open fields marked by extensive ridge-and-furrow, complete the 'classic' picture. Like all 'classic pictures' it is to an extent an overly normative construct, and the date of these changes in particular is now being shown to be earlier than ninth century in some individual cases, and later in others, although the broad consensus remains. The reasons for rural reorganization towards nucleation are historically obscure, but have nonetheless been the subject of fierce debate. In the 1960s the economic historian Joan Thirsk took the view that the central zone of nucleated or planned villages was more economically and socially developed than the dispersed, more heavily wooded areas on either side, and this 'developmental' view has since been upheld by other leading commentators.[36] An opposing case, voiced in particular by Tom Williamson, has laid stress on the influence of the heavy clay soils of the Midlands and emphasized the practical challenges they posed to individual farmers, which he argued led to a move to maximize returns on agricultural production by the concentration of people and resources in one place.[37] Williamson's view is convincing, but does not explain why such an extensive reorganization should have happened at the time it evidently did – surely the potential advantages of common agriculture on heavy soils were as pertinent in the eighth or even the seventh century as in the ninth or tenth? The opposing view, that the Midlands were somehow ahead of East Anglia, the southeast and the west in terms of economic development, looks decidedly shaky when compared with the Domesday maps of boroughs (see Figure 7) and the Domesday population (see Figure 8) – neither of which emphasizes the 'central province' in remotely the same way, but suggests that there was also considerable economic and demographic development in the dispersed areas, notably East Anglia.

CONCLUSION: WAYS FORWARD FOR RESEARCH ON TOWN AND COUNTRY

The increased propensity of rural estates and villages towards generating productive surplus lies at the heart of urban–rural interaction in this period. The interdependencies of towns and their hinterlands hinge upon the consequent patterns of trade, consumption and movements of people. These were a complex network of relationships, varying on a case-to-case

[36] J. Thirsk, 'The common fields', *P&P*, 29 (1964), 3–29. C. Dyer, *Making a Living in the Middle Ages: the People of Britain 850–1520* (Yale, 2002), p. 21.

[37] T. Williamson, *Shaping Medieval Landscapes: Settlement, Society, Environment* (Macclesfield, 2003).

basis between the aspiration and direction of lords, merchants, burgesses and the common interests of the peasantry. Some elements of town and village innovation were planned, others evolved organically or may have taken their cue informally from examples of successful planned reorganization elsewhere. The combination of institutional innovation and organic development in rural settlement and agriculture were mirrored in the rise of small towns in the eleventh and twelfth centuries – these were above all connected and interdependent phenomena. Recent research has demonstrated that the rise of village nucleation and common agriculture in the 'central province' was only one major manifestation of change, and that far from being more 'advanced' than other areas, it represented a particular spectrum of responses to increasing economic opportunities and imperatives conditioned by geography, soils and population. Outside the 'central province', as work on the northwest and wetland sites in the southwest has shown, significant innovation and the transformation of population and production levels were achieved without a marked increase in settlement nucleation.[38] Villages and common agriculture had deep origins in the English landscape and there were numerous variations in the forms they took. Larger villages became indistinguishable in social and economic terms from small towns, forming a series of regional hierarchies with complex and layered hinterland interdependencies.

The increased productivity of arable agriculture is marked by increases in cereal pollen in cores dated to 900–1200.[39] Palaeoenvironmental studies are especially valuable for understanding settlement and agrarian development in poorly documented regions with a generally lower circulation of pottery, such as the southwest and northwest. Patterns of animal slaughtering and consumption are similarly receiving intensive analysis.[40] These types of data reflect a more recent emphasis on palaeoenvironmental and landscape research, which as it progresses promises to add significantly to the historical and archaeological picture. Williamson is surely right that optimal forms of agriculture and social organization were conditioned by the geography and topography of different regions, but overall the

[38] N. Higham, 'Changing spaces, towns and their hinterlands in the north-west, AD 900–1500', in M. Gardiner and S. Rippon, eds., *Medieval Landscapes* (Macclesfield, 2007), pp. 57–70; S. Rippon, R. Fyfe and A. G. Brown, 'Beyond villages and open fields: the origins and development of a historic landscape characterised by dispersed settlement in south-west England', *Medieval Archaeology*, 50 (2006), 31–70; S. Rippon, *Beyond the Medieval Village* (Oxford, 2008).

[39] Rippon, Fyfe and Brown, 'Beyond villages and open fields', p. 35.

[40] U. Albarella, 'Meat production and consumption in town and country', in Giles and Dyer, eds., *Town and Country on the Middle Ages*, pp. 131–48; N. Sykes, *The Norman Conquest: A Zooarchaeological Perspective* (BAR International Series 1656; Oxford, 2007).

chronology and pattern of change are seemingly more related to urban and market innovation than has hitherto been stressed. It is surely no accident that the upsurge in rural productivity happened at periods of growth in towns, where accompanying market distribution mechanisms began to balance out regional disparities in production.

Towns and their hinterlands, together with rural settlement, estates and overland and maritime transport links, can therefore be seen as a network of linked phenomena. Research is already progressing towards a synthesis of evidence and interpretation on these: it is no longer true as perhaps it was until the 1980s that they are generally studied in isolation from each other. Studies of material culture, environment and diet have risen up the agenda and promise to unlock some of the opacities and nuances in connections between urban and rural cultures. Nevertheless huge questions remain. The influence of growing towns and urban markets on the reshaping of the countryside is a vast and as yet under-explored theme. How, for the period prior to 1200, when historical sources are so qualified and limited, can we fill out the human detail of individuals' urban–rural links and interdependencies; how can we chart the rise and fall of economic confidence, prices, and levels of consumption in relation to political upheaval, good and bad harvests, epidemics and technological breakthroughs? Seeking the answers to urban questions in the countryside, and vice versa, is a good place to start.

CHAPTER III.2

Commerce and markets

Richard Britnell

After the disasters that followed the collapse of Roman authority, trade, both international and internal, eventually grew, but its institutional infrastructure needed to be recreated. Even where towns eventually revived on old sites they operated with newly devised trading institutions and new monetary systems. During the eighth and earlier ninth centuries overseas commerce increased, especially through London, Southampton, Ipswich and York, and wider trading interests prompted currency reform as well as co-operation between the principal English monarchies. A single standard of currency established by the kings of Mercia and Wessex, together with the archbishop of Canterbury, implied a common interest in trade. But the later ninth and early tenth centuries experienced a temporary setback in parts of England as the Danish invasions of eastern England disrupted established institutions and practices.[1] The level of international trade stagnated in the *wics* through which merchandise had previously passed, and the money supply diminished. Danish rulers ultimately proved no less interested than the English kings in fostering trade, but the coins they minted were of lower quality. No common standard of currency was re-established until King Edgar's new coinage of 973. The year 900 is accordingly a useful point at which to take stock of the institutional provision for trade, before proceeding to examine the subsequent revival of commerce in the Late Saxon and Anglo-Norman periods.

COMMERCE AND MARKETS IN 900

At the end of the ninth century, as later, trade was most likely to take place where people assembled for other reasons. Three hundred years later this was almost invariably a port, an inland town or at least a larger

[1] J. R. Maddicott, 'Trade, industry and the wealth of King Alfred', *P&P*, 123 (1989), 6–12.

village. The situation in 900 is more obscure, partly because such settlements were rarer. The population of England was not only predominantly rural; it was also scattered in communities often no larger than hamlets, whose members were too few to constitute significant centres of market demand. In small settlements, people were most likely to exchange goods with neighbours. However, archaeological evidence suggests that the scattering of minsters across the countryside served as a frequent context for a more focused pattern of trade. Such churches accommodated communities of monks and priests, who not only needed provisions for their own use but were also often obliged to entertain patrons and their following. In addition, minsters drew together the inhabitants of surrounding settlements for religious observance, and so offered wider possibilities of trade than other residential neighbourhoods.[2] Though we know little about such exchanges, they were probably not normally transacted in the sort of weekly markets attached to boroughs and manors identifiable from Anglo-Norman sources. Though some minsters – like Kidderminster, Malmesbury, Ripon and Hexham – became the site of formal markets in later centuries, there is no evidence at this earlier date to suggest that gatherings there were subject to the exercise of superior lordship. Trading perhaps occurred frequently on Sundays; the scarcity of references to Sunday trading in pre-Conquest sources suggests that it was not perceived as a problem, but does not imply that it did not occur, given the absence of references to trading on specific other days. Assemblies of traders, where they had no institutional identity, could have had no legal status, though doubtless minster populations would try to limit activities they considered objectionable. Some at least of this informal exchange was conducted without the need for coinage, or any supervised system of weights and measures.

By 900, however, the encroachment of secular authorities and interests on activities at minster sites was in some places already advanced, with noteworthy implications for the extent and character of trade. The word 'borough' (Latin *burgus*; English *burg* or *burh*), once commonly used to describe a minster community, was coming increasingly to be associated with centres of secular authority, especially royal authority. This is most easily recognized in the history of Wessex, where many former minster sites from the 830s onwards became royal manors. Under Alfred and his successors, some centres attracted even more investment because

[2] John Blair, *The Church in Anglo-Saxon Society* (Oxford, 2005), especially pp. 149–52, 193–5, 251–61.

they were fortified for military defence against the Danes. The text known as the 'Burghal Hidage', dating from before 919, lists thirty-three boroughs, stretching from Lydford in Devon to Worcester, Warwick and Buckingham in the Midlands, and as far east as Southwark and Hastings. The fact that many boroughs became centres for the minting of coins at some point in the tenth and eleventh centuries, and that a high proportion of them – twenty-five out of the thirty-three boroughs in the 'Burghal Hidage' – were recognized as prescriptive markets in later centuries, suggests that normally their exceptional size and status as centres of demand for food, and of supply for services and manufactures, attracted monetized trade and served to reduce transaction costs.[3] Marketing facilities were apparently incorporated into borough plans from an early date, implying that, like their later successors, kings deliberately set out to increase opportunities for monetary exactions. The military and economic objectives of lordship nevertheless need to be considered apart; economic development was unlikely to be a prime motive for the fortification of boroughs amid the uncertainties of wartime, when money was scarce.

The prominence of western England in histories of borough formation is chiefly a matter of institutional terminology in Wessex, and is misleading as an indicator of commercial development across England as a whole. Even as late as 1086 Wiltshire and Somerset, containing 3,000 square miles, are recorded in Domesday Book as having nineteen boroughs, as against only fifteen in Lincolnshire, Norfolk and Suffolk, whose combined area was over twice as large. This cannot correspond to a real difference in the development of local commerce whether before or after 900, given the wealth and populousness of East Anglia. In later records southern and midland England are seen to have markets of unknown origin attached to manors that were either definitely early minster sites, like Barking in Essex, or that may have had early minsters, like East Dereham in Norfolk and Blythburgh, Clare, Stowmarket and Sudbury in Suffolk. The early development of these and similar markets is wholly obscure, but it had probably proceeded on lines similar to that of Wessex up to the late ninth century. Continuity between the ninth century and the eleventh or twelfth is less impressive in eastern England than in Wessex, however, so it is likely that the structure of marketing was more radically reshaped during the Late Saxon period.

[3] S. R. H. Jones, 'Transaction costs, institutional change, and the emergence of a market economy in later Anglo-Saxon England', *EcHR*, 46 (1993), 658–78.

Areas occupied by the Danes suffered exceptional disruption around the turn of the ninth century, which may have been the occasion for some such restructuring, though this was unlikely to have been a permanent setback in most instances since Danish lords were as concerned to make money as any others.

Institutional development before 900 was conspicuously slow in the North beyond York, where it is difficult to find indications of early urban nuclei, and where no English kings thought fit to mint coinage. In this region, as in East Anglia, such development as had occurred before 900 was probably disrupted by Danish invasion. Yet the relationship between minster sites and later marketing centres was here even weaker, and few trading centres of any sort seem to have had any prominence before 1100. This suggests that the value of trade associated with such centres in 900 was exceptionally low, and its organization informal.

Despite the different degrees of investment and development that central places had already attracted by 900, the regulation of trade was not an issue important enough to need regulation by kings or other lords, and our understanding of how it was organized is correspondingly poor. Documentary sources rarely supply unambiguous references to a market or market place (Latin *mercatum*, *forum*; English *ceping*, *ciping* or *cyping*). A recognized centre of trade could be called a 'port' (Latin *portus*; English *port*) as in the laws of Edward the Elder.[4] This usage is preserved in place-names at Bridport, Langport and Newport Pagnell, all recorded by 1100, as well as in later examples. Other commercial centres were known as *wics* (Latin *vicus*; English *wic*), as at Ipswich, Norwich and London's Aldwich. *Port* and *wic* describe the mercantile nature of a settlement rather than the developments upon which trade depended, and offer no institutional criteria by which such a centre might be identified. Yet there is nevertheless scattered evidence that elements of trading organization better known from later centuries were already to be found by the late ninth century in principal centres of activity. One of the commonest is likely to have been a market place. A charter of 762 records a town-house in the market place (*forum*) at Queningate in Canterbury, and another of 786 records a 'trading place' (*venalis locus*) in the same city.[5] The presence of market places of different shapes and sizes is implicit in the topography of many early Anglo-Saxon boroughs, so far as they can be reconstructed from

[4] I Edward, 1: F. L. Attenborough, ed., *The Laws of the Earliest English Kings* (Cambridge, 1922), p. 114.

[5] Sawyer, *Anglo-Saxon Charters*, nos. 125, 1182, pp. 103, 348.

cartographic and archaeological evidence.[6] Some trading areas, as in later centuries, were along a central street rather than in a more open area, as in Winchester and Colchester (see Chapter III.3). The lords of boroughs might be expected to derive some benefit from them; by agreement with Ealdorman Æthelred of Mercia and his wife, made sometime between 884 and 900, the bishop of Worcester had half of the rights to Worcester market place (*ceapstow*) in the late ninth century. According to a charter whose integrity is in some doubt, Edward the Elder in 904 recognized the right of the bishop of Winchester to *þæs tunes cyping* of Taunton, an elliptical expression for 'income from dues paid for trading in the town'.[7] In at least some early markets these rights included the exaction of tolls, though the later distinction between transit tolls and marketing tolls is not clearly defined.[8] From these examples it is likely that open trade could be restricted to particular places and times, since it would otherwise have been impossible to prevent traders from evading seigneurial dues. The trade of boroughs and ports was more likely to require coinage than informal rural trade, which is why so many boroughs came to have mints in the tenth century. Lords of more formal centres of marketing may have taken responsibility for the regulation of weights and measures. By a charter supposedly of 857, the bishop of Worcester claimed a right to possess weights and measures by virtue of a property he acquired in London from King Burgred of Mercia. Though these shreds of information show that elements of later market right were to be found in 900, they do not imply that these practices were standardized between boroughs or that they were widespread. We can rarely say with any certainty whether marketing in particular boroughs or ports was daily, weekly or less frequent, and can make even fewer surmises about how formally trade was conducted, a problem that inhibits any very refined analysis of institutional development for the whole period before 1200.

COMMERCE AND MARKETS, 900–1200

Despite the impossibility of measuring the growth either of overseas or internal trade, there is little dispute that its volume increased between

[6] For abundant evidence to this effect, see Jeremy Haslam, *Anglo-Saxon Towns in Southern England* (Chichester, 1984).

[7] Sawyer, *Anglo-Saxon Charters*, nos. 223, 373, pp. 127, 162; F. E. Harmer, '*Chipping* and market: a lexicographical investigation', in C. Fox and B. Dickens, eds., *The Early Cultures of North-West Europe* (Cambridge, 1950), pp. 342–3.

[8] Peter Sawyer, 'Early fairs and markets in England and Scandinavia', in B. L. Anderson and A. J. H. Latham, eds., *The Market in History* (London, 1986), pp. 62–3.

900 and 1200, despite interruptions caused by warfare. The best evidence is of urban development, particularly after about 970. London's growth as an international port, as a market centred on Westcheap and Eastcheap, and as a centre for the minting of coinage, put it ahead of all other English towns by the late tenth century, and the city grew rapidly thereafter. Exeter and Norwich gained ground as major regional centres from the tenth century. The strong Scandinavian connections of York and Lincoln gave them particular advantages for trade in the tenth and eleventh centuries, and they, too, continued to expand under the Normans, even though cross-Channel contacts then grew more rapidly than the northern trades. Many other boroughs come into prominence in the archaeological record of the tenth and eleventh centuries. Amongst the best evidence for growing overseas trade after 1066, probably involving wool as the most prominent export, is the multiplication of ports and coastal towns. On the east coast the new towns of Newcastle upon Tyne, Wyke upon Hull (later Kingston upon Hull), Boston and Lynn (later King's Lynn) complemented Ipswich and London as major ports. Portsmouth was founded by King Richard I towards the very end of this period, in 1194.

Monetary evidence confirms the generally expansive experience of the English economy over these 300 years. Although the amount in circulation before the reign of Henry II may never have exceeded £120,000, archaeological evidence suggests that it had increased during the previous three hundred years. During the course of the tenth century, and particularly during its last three decades, there was a spread of minting activity to new centres in the Midlands. The amount of coin in circulation was to increase further from the later twelfth century, according to the best estimates, from £130,000 ± £60,000 in 1180 to £350,00 ± £150,000 about 1210.[9] An increase in the money supply over this period, despite large exports of Danegeld to Scandinavia between 991 and 1014 – some of which presumably came from reserves rather than from currency in circulation – was partly attributable to the exploitation of native silver resources, but depended more on increasing imports (see Chapter I.4).

The expansion of internal trade stimulated the development of trading institutions. Four patterns of change deserve particular attention, even though we lack the detail that would allow them to be described except in the most sketchy manner. The first was the frequent detachment of marketing from a minster context, the second the standardization of marketing institutions, the third the spread of formal marketing to parts of

[9] M. Allen, 'The volume of the English currency, 1158–1470', *EcHR*, 54 (2001), 595–611, at 607.

England where it had previously been rare and the fourth a new identity of markets and fairs as distinct legal entities.

Though formal marketing, subject to lordship, was originally associated most strongly with places that had minsters, Domesday Book reports markets in other contexts. Some opportunities for the appropriation of marketing activities were evidently created by the maturing of hundredal organization during the tenth and eleventh centuries, since later prescriptive markets are commonly found at hundredal manors.[10] Many such manors were at former minster centres, and probably had some older tradition as centres of local trade, but this was by no means true of all, especially in the eastern counties. Attendance at a hundred court, like attendance at a church, might encourage spontaneous informal exchanges, but since these courts met only once every four weeks they could not be expected to give rise to regular weekly trade. If weekly hundredal markets were operating in the tenth and eleventh centuries they depended on the rising importance of hundredal manors as central places, with above-average concentrations of population, as well as upon deliberate enterprise by the king or the relevant franchise owner. Analogies with older royal manors were doubtless important. There is little evidence of the more widespread 'feudal' multiplication of markets and fairs before the later eleventh century, but this, too, was a Late Saxon development parallel to the establishment of numerous local churches by manorial lords and others. Domesday Book records several instances, including two markets recently established beside new castles (at Trematon and Eye).[11] The creation of boroughs and markets at centres of secular lordship became a major feature of development between 1086 and 1200, especially in northern and southwestern England. The northern market towns of Alnwick, Warkworth, Barnard Castle, Thirsk, Skipton and Richmond are all examples of seigneurial boroughs that owed little to any recorded antecedent development.

In addition to the 112 boroughs recorded in Domesday Book, Beresford identified 79 towns founded on new sites between 1071 and 1200, and this number was probably exceeded by the number created in existing settlements. Most marketing centres before 1200 enter the documentary records as 'boroughs'. Such boroughs were necessarily subject to lordship, and so were their trading institutions. The laws of Æthelred imply that

10 R. H. Britnell, 'English markets and royal administration before 1200', *EcHR* 2nd ser., 31 (1978), 183–96.

11 DB, i, fol. 122; ii, fol. 379.

the collecting of tolls of some kind was a normal responsibility of town reeves.[12] Domesday Book demonstrates that lords generally regarded a borough or market as a source of income, and in three cases explicitly mentions the exaction of tolls (at Leighton Buzzard, Luton and Titchfield). The survey also records manors whose market was on a fixed day each week (Wallingford, St Germans, Hoxne and Eye); this had probably become a normal feature of borough trade.[13] By 1200 it is reasonable to assume that a place described as a borough had a market place at or near its centre, that it had a regular market day or days and that some commercial operations were liable to the exaction of toll. The 300 years since 900 had seen an increasingly standard expectation of what a borough should provide, created partly by innovation in the larger centres, followed by imitation elsewhere. Even many markets directly descended from earlier minster gatherings must have been formalized under the aegis of either the church to which they owed their origin or that of a king or other secular lord; they would not otherwise have been recognizable in twelfth- and thirteenth-century law. Apart from the direct impact of royal enterprise in royal manors, which accounts for many early developments, the more formal markets of the twelfth century also owed something to legislation. Royal attempts to unify weights and measures between markets go back at least to the laws of Edgar.[14] Tenth- and eleventh-century legislation to enforce the witnessing of transactions had no later follow-up, but perhaps had a temporary impact on the formal conduct of trade. Regulations for particular markets were more ambitious; some towns, for example, had introduced assizes of bread and ale by 1200.[15]

Given the difficulty of identifying marketing centres with any reliability in 900, it is not possible to separate the geographical spread of formal markets from their multiplication. Nevertheless, the urban development of the tenth and eleventh centuries was largely confined to counties south of a line from York to Chester. Even at Durham Late Saxon development was restricted to a small site on the peninsula. By contrast, there was rapid development in the North during the twelfth century, when this region first obtained a network of markets such as Wessex had possessed probably by the end of the tenth century.

[12] IV Æthelred, 3: A. J. Robertson, ed., *The Laws of the Kings of England from Edmund to Henry I* (Cambridge, 1925), pp. 72–5.

[13] DB, i, fols. 39, 56v, 120v, 209 *bis*; ii, fol. 379.

[14] III Edgar, 8: *EHD*, i, p. 433 and Robertson, ed., *Laws*, pp. 28–9.

[15] Richard H. Britnell, *The Commercialisation of English Society, 1000–1500* (2nd edn; Manchester, 1996), pp. 24–8.

The last change to be considered here concerns developments in the legal status of markets and fairs, implied by the royal right to authorize new markets and fairs. This seems to have been an eleventh-century innovation, from sometime before the 1080s, probably introduced by William I by analogy with some Continental practices. Domesday Book records that there were markets held 'by the king's gift' at Kelsale and Eye in Suffolk.[16] Implicit in the royal claim was the recognition of markets and fairs as distinct franchises rather than simply as institutions incidental to particular central places – a new point of English law, though it was another hundred years before the need for a licensing charter was respected throughout the kingdom.

This account of Anglo-Saxon and Anglo-Norman trade has been pointedly sceptical of how much is known about its institutional context. The formal characteristics and customs of medieval markets and fairs are never self-evident. On the other hand, it is only by recognizing what is unknown that we can appreciate the creativeness of successive generations of lords and traders during this period. The commerce of England under King John depended upon a complex, if largely unrecoverable, earlier history of institutional innovation and adaptation.

[16] DB, ii, fols. 330v, 379. See, too, David Bates, ed., *Regesta Regum Anglo-Normannorum: The Acta of William I (1066–1087)* (Oxford, 1998), no. 195, p. 624.

CHAPTER III.3

Urban planning

Julia Barrow

Proto-urban sites of various types had been a feature of Anglo-Saxon England, especially Mercia, for some time before the late ninth century, and from the 870s to 890s, under the influence of Viking attacks, Viking settlement and an energetic fortification programme in Wessex by Alfred the Great (king of Wessex 871–99), urbanization in England became more vigorous. The sites fortified in or by the late ninth and the tenth centuries were usually based at river-crossings and also on major roads. Permanent garrison settlements, coupled with the need for regulated markets to allow rulers to tap into profits from sales, encouraged many places to become urbanized. Defences were therefore an important feature of many urban places in England in the 900–1200 period, and certainly of the larger ones, including most of the shire towns; they often helped to determine the planning of streets and other minor features within the areas they demarcated. Also significant in deciding the internal layout of towns were major churches, especially, though not only, where these preceded urban development; in particular, Anglo-Saxon minster churches and Benedictine abbeys fostered the growth of markets and towns. Sites associated with secular political authority tended to be less influential than major churches, but nonetheless could influence internal organization, especially with the need to find sites for royal castles in major towns after the Norman Conquest. Planning arrangements made in the ninth and tenth centuries were durable; later generations, especially after the Norman Conquest, tended to add on extra areas of settlement and commercial activity, or to subdivide properties within existing plot-boundaries, rather than to replan what already existed.

Urban sites in this period were usually low-lying; some Iron Age hillfort sites, such as Sarum, became boroughs but failed to flourish. River-crossing sites were the most successful; here inhabitants could benefit from the linking of road and river communications, or, even if the river was not properly navigable, could control the crossing and exact tolls. Oxford, situated on crossings over the Thames (navigable from this point downstream) and the Cherwell, and on the route from Southampton north to the Midlands, was a notable example. In the case of major river-crossings, the duty of supplying labour for bridge building and repairs was often levied on the rural population of the hinterland. Six late Anglo-Saxon shire towns (Hereford, Stafford, the first element of whose name is *stæth*, i.e. staithe, Oxford, Bedford, Hertford, Cambridge) took their names from river-crossings; several other similarly named towns (such as Stamford and Wallingford), though failing to achieve this status, were also prominent. Towns at lowest bridging points, such as London, Norwich, York, Chester and Gloucester, were well placed to become entrepôts. River-crossings and navigation took precedence, in terms of river use, over mills and fishweirs, at least theoretically.[1] At Chester, the tidal section of the Dee was separated from the non-tidal section by a weir running across the river, on which it was possible to site mills, and these, because they could use the full power of the river, were very valuable. Elsewhere, mills might be limited to sites on streams and ditches surrounding towns, as in Hereford. At York, William the Conqueror dammed the River Foss to create a great fishpond, leaving the Ouse unimpeded. Low-lying urban sites found it easier to expand in subsequent centuries and also were able to exploit surrounding land, including floodable land, as pasture for livestock to be fattened for market, for example Port Meadow at Oxford.

Defences had been a feature of some Mercian settlements (Hereford, Tamworth and Winchcombe) since perhaps the later eighth century; they consisted of earth ramparts and a ditch. This was also the format adopted by Alfred in the late ninth century when fortifying or refortifying a ring of settlements around Wessex, and also by Edward the Elder and Æthelflæd in the early tenth; however, where Roman walls existed, as at Exeter and Chester, these would be repaired. Chester's walled area was enlarged by extending the northern and eastern walls to the river in this period. But defensive layouts required a large hinterland to provide the manpower to garrison and repair them, calculated by the length of wall, as we see in the 'Burghal Hidage', a document which probably originated under Alfred, though surviving to us in a later recension dating from the reign of Edward the Elder (899–924). Only some of Alfred's sites survived as towns; his fortifications at *Eorpeburnan*, Burpham, Chisbury, Sashes and Eashing lost their significance quickly. Once towns were established,

[1] For example, a dispute between the inhabitants of Nottingham and royal officials mentioned in DB, i, fol. 280a; see also J. C. Holt, *Magna Carta* (Cambridge, 1965), pp. 324–7 (33).

however, their inhabitants might be expected to perform military service. Oxford's 'wall-houses' bore extra responsibilities for defence, and the Domesday entries for Hereford and Shrewsbury state that the sheriff could summon burgesses to accompany him on campaigns into Wales.[2] Gates might include churches built next to them or, by the end of our period, on top of them, as at Bristol and Canterbury; at Oxford, the tower of St Michael's at the North Gate was originally separate from the church and incorporated into the defences.

The extent to which members of the secular elite had lived in proto-towns, especially in the husks of old Roman urban sites, in the period before *c.* 900 is a matter of debate, though some places (Canterbury for early kings of Kent, Tamworth for Mercian rulers and, in the ninth century, Aldermanbury in London, whose name may refer to Æthelred of Mercia) clearly did contain royal residences, even though the actual sites remain to be discovered. Towns often had royal manors lying close to them, for example Kingsholm at Gloucester or Headington at Oxford, from which rulers could pay close attention to urban activities; Æthelred and Æthelflæd established their own minster in Gloucester, and Æthelred the Unready made a grant to St Frideswide's.[3] But as the shire system was extended across the Midlands and southern Northumbria in the tenth century it became necessary to create halls for earls and sometimes for kings in major centres. In Winchester, the royal palace was built near the Old Minster; at York, a large complex was built for the earl of Northumbria at Earlsburgh on the site later occupied by St Mary's Abbey, and Earl Siward (d. 1055) founded a church there dedicated to St Olave (St Olaf of Norway); a royal hall in Hereford is mentioned in Domesday. It is possible that Edward the Confessor's nephew Ralph of Mantes may have introduced French innovations at Oxford (a tower in Romanesque style) and perhaps at Hereford, where the castle, which certainly existed early in 1067, may have been built as early as the 1050s. Apart from Winchester, these sites were on the edges of towns, sometimes outside the walls.

Immediately following the Conquest, William I ordered the building of castles in major towns, especially shire towns, across England.[4] Two

[2] DB, i, fols. 154a, 179a and 252a.

[3] Carolyn Heighway and Michael Hare, 'Gloucester and the minster of St Oswald: a survey of the evidence', in Carolyn Heighway and Richard Bryant, eds., *The Golden Minster: The Anglo-Saxon Minster and Later Medieval Priory of St Oswald at Gloucester* (Council for British Archaeology, Research Report 117; York, 1999), pp. 1–29, at 3–4 and 7–12; *The Cartulary of the Monastery of St Frideswide at Oxford*, i (Oxford Historical Society, 28; 1895), pp. 2–6, dated 1004.

[4] Cf. P. McGurk ed. and trans., *The Chronicle of John of Worcester*, iii, (OMT; Oxford, 1998), iii, p. 4 (s.a. 1067), p. 6 (s.a. 1068: Nottingham, York, Lincoln 'and other places').

were built at York, on opposite sides of the Ouse; sites on bluffs overlooking rivers were favoured, for example Rochester, Chester and Worcester; at Shrewsbury the castle was placed high up on a strategic neck of land. Where riversides were overlooked by higher ground it was necessary to seek the latter, as at Nottingham, Lincoln and Cambridge. In several cases (for example Gloucester, York, Lincoln and Norwich) the building of castles necessitated the demolition of houses;[5] at Worcester, a slice of the cathedral precinct was taken over; at Winchester, the city enceinte was expanded to accommodate the castle. Although the military role of castles in shire towns was not insignificant, administration mattered rather more, which helps to explain why some of the sites chosen (for example Winchester) were not impressive. In the twelfth century, lords building their own castles often planned small seigneurial market towns next to them, with burgage plots running back from a main street, as part of the scheme (for example at Alnwick, Bridgnorth and Ludlow); at Richmond a round plan was adopted.

Street layouts were often carefully planned. In the boroughs built or refortified in the ninth and tenth centuries, a principal street system, often cross-shaped (as at Gloucester), would link up the main gateways, while back lanes would run behind the main streets, often at some depth, and minor lanes would follow the lines of the ramparts within them (and sometimes outside them as well), to provide access for defence. Even where a Roman site was being reused, the late Anglo-Saxon street plan usually made decisive alterations. At Winchester, a single principal street, the High Street, ran east–west, with back lanes parallel on either side at no great depth; at right-angles to the main street were side streets, parallel to each other at roughly 100-yard intervals, leading to the lanes running behind the walls; the streets were metalled with knapped flints (8,000 tonnes would have been required in total) by the earliest years of the reign of Edward the Elder.[6]

In the Anglo-Saxon period the crossroads at the middle of a walled town usually formed the market place, but this was not a convenient layout for livestock markets, which functioned better in a wider space, preferably with a funnel shape. Markets associated with great Benedictine abbeys began to be laid out in this way in the tenth century in a few cases, for example St Albans, but more often from the middle of the eleventh

[5] DB, i, fols. 162r, 298r, 336v and ii, fol. 116v.

[6] M. Biddle, 'The evolution of towns: planned towns before 1066', in M. W. Barley, ed., *The Plans and Topography of Medieval Towns in England and Wales* (Council for British Archaeology, Research Report 14; London, 1976), pp. 19–31, at 27.

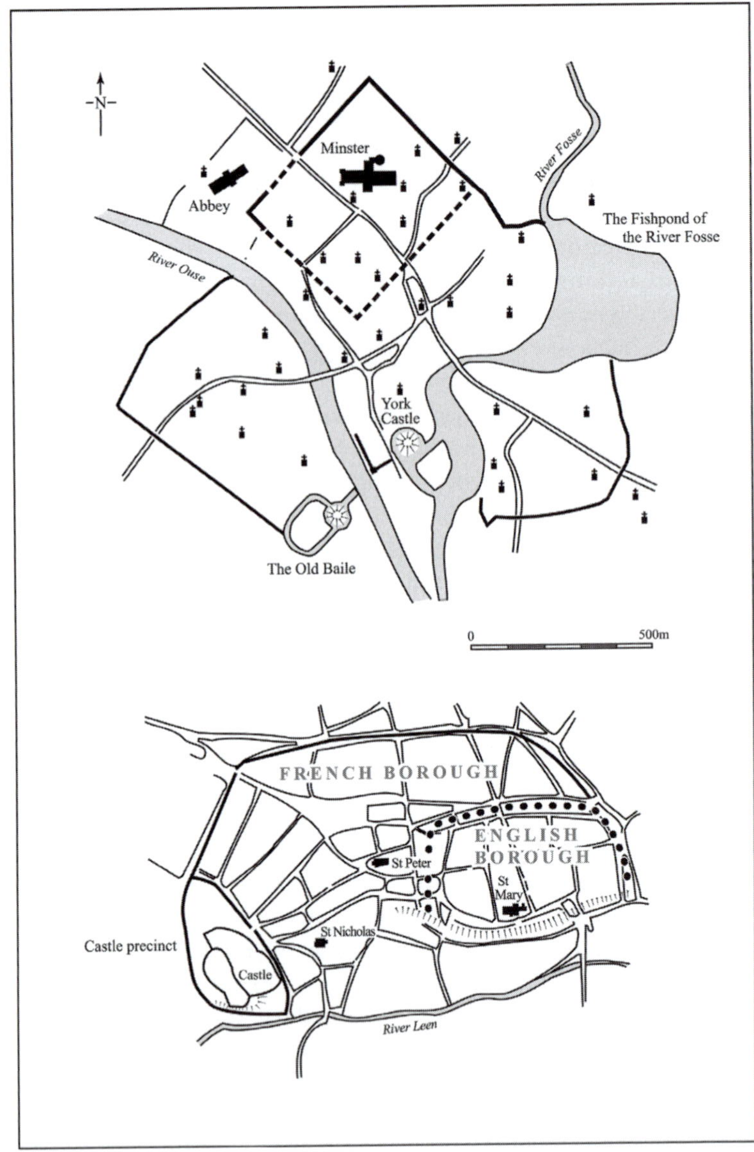

Figure 10 Urban castles at York (top) and Nottingham (bottom) © O. H. Creighton; illustration by M. Rouillard, first published in O. H. Creighton, *Castles and Landscapes: Power, Community and Fortification in Medieval England*, London, 2002

century, for example Coventry. After the Conquest, earls and sheriffs in charge of shire towns also sometimes laid out new triangular or rectangular market places on new sites, as at Hereford (under William fitzOsbern), Nottingham and Norwich. At Bristol likewise a huge rectangular market place was laid out to the north of the old Anglo-Saxon walled area. Integral to these developments were new streets, whose house-plots were sometimes earmarked for French settlers. Meanwhile the development of market sites and towns associated with Benedictine abbeys gathered pace, as for example Coventry and Bury St Edmunds, which is recorded by Domesday as having been significantly expanded in the twenty years following the Conquest.[7] As butchery began to emerge as a specialized profession butchers began to congregate in special streets (shambles); this had occurred by 996 in Winchester but not until over half a century later in York, where much animal slaughter was still being carried out by amateurs well into the eleventh century.[8] Shambles could be in prominent positions; in early thirteenth-century Oxford the butchers were congregated near Carfax on the south side of the High.

In the tenth and eleventh centuries major towns, especially shire towns, had to provide suitable places for prominent people to live in, at least for certain parts of the year; this was necessitated partly by their military role and partly to make it easier for aristocrats to attend shire courts. Thus for example we find Edgar granting a *haga* (haw, or enclosure) at Hereford to Ealhstan his thegn in 958.[9] Haws might sometimes be very large – big enough to contain warehousing and private chapels as well as domestic accommodation – and they tended to be subdivided in later developments, as in the case of the large haw at Worcester described in the agreement between Æthelred of Mercia and Æthelflæd on the one hand and Bishop Wærferth on the other in 904.[10] As a result there was some adjustment of the original property boundaries in major Anglo-Saxon towns in the century or so before the Conquest, but original arrangements can be observed where boundaries can be traced as uninterrupted lines between a pair of streets. The main unit of measurement from Anglo-Saxon times onwards was the 16½-foot unit known

[7] DB, ii, fol. 372r.

[8] A. Rumble, *Property and Piety in Early Medieval Winchester: Documents Relating to the Topography of the Anglo-Saxon and Norman City and Its Minsters* (Oxford, 2002), pp. 207–12 (Sawyer, *Anglo-Saxon Charters*, no. 889); T. P. O'Connor, *Bones from Anglo-Scandinavian Levels at 16–22 Coppergate* (The Archaeology of York, 15/3; York, 1989), p. 159. York had a shambles (*macellum*) by 1086: DB, i, fol. 298a.

[9] Sawyer, *Anglo-Saxon Charters* , no. 677.

[10] Sawyer, *Anglo-Saxon Charters*, no. 1280, discussed by N. Baker and R. Holt, *Urban Growth and the Medieval Church: Gloucester and Worcester* (Aldershot, 2004), pp. 174–8.

as the rod, pole or perch. House-plots that are very long in proportion to their width (in a more than 3:1 ratio) are reckoned by historical geographers to be pre-Conquest, and suggest that the householders used the space for gardens. Subsequent generations might develop shallow plots along the edges of markets or as infill in market places, but where possible long thin plots were preferred; until the twentieth century these boundaries were tenacious, and in many cases survived to be recorded in the great 6-inch OS series of the late nineteenth and early twentieth centuries. Groups of house-plots of a particular size and shape suggest that a particular street, a section of a street or a group of streets was laid out at one time, and historical geographers and topographers have been able to build up a picture of urban development through the disaggregation of street plans. Landowners were probably usually the principal agents of development, as has been argued in the case of Coventry. Street frontages were often densely built up; gaps between houses were narrow already in the tenth century (as in York, for example), and during the eleventh and twelfth centuries the frontages usually became continuous. Fire regulations from the eleventh century onwards suggest that street frontage was at a premium. In Chester in 1066 burgesses from whose houses fires spread were fined three oras of pennies and had to pay their neighbours 2s.[11] Stone houses, less prone to fire, were still fairly unusual by the end of our period, most substantial houses being built of timber. The long back plots made it possible for householders to get some air and light, though by the twelfth century they were being built on intensively in populous towns. Even where they survived, pollution would have been a problem, with wells easily contaminated by leakage from cesspits; poorer householders would have had to draw water from rivers or streams. Major monastic houses, such as Christ Church, Canterbury, could organize quite elaborate water systems. In London and Bristol conduits were built in the late twelfth century, but in other towns the provision of conduits came not before the thirteenth century, often thanks to the initiative of friars.

As should already have become apparent, churches were important factors, both actively and passively, in medieval town planning. Many urban settlements of the late Anglo-Saxon period and later had originated around early minster churches, for example Banbury, Beverley, Much Wenlock and Southwell,[12] and, although major urban settlements

[11] DB, i, fol. 262v.

[12] J. Blair, *The Church in Anglo-Saxon Society* (Oxford, 2005), pp. 246–90, 330–41, and note in particular p. 223 on the right of sanctuary enjoyed by minsters including Beverley and Southwell.

usually owed their status to a range of factors (shire-town status, surviving Roman walls and ninth-century fortifications), they, too, often had at least one, sometimes several, Anglo-Saxon churches as focal points. Multiple minsters in Shrewsbury and Chester resulted from divided royal and episcopal lordship; at Gloucester, an early Anglo-Saxon monastery was subsequently rivalled by a minster built by Æthelred and Æthelflæd of Mercia as their mausoleum. Cathedrals, as in Canterbury, London, Winchester, York, Worcester and Hereford, dominated the landscape in major settlements from the outset of urbanization; in smaller settlements, such as Wells and Lichfield, their impact would have been even greater. In the decades immediately following the Norman Conquest, bishops were encouraged to move their thrones from churches in minor places to walled or other significant towns (Bath and Norwich, for example); in the latter, though the new cathedrals often took over the sites of earlier churches, they would additionally require large areas previously used for housing. The positions of cathedrals within towns were not completely unchanging; over the tenth and eleventh centuries the spaces surrounding them might become more firmly demarcated, as at Winchester, and often smaller, as at Worcester, while the post-Conquest trend for rebuilding all the major churches in England in a Romanesque style could lead to the resiting of churches, though not necessarily by much. In this way the Anglo-Saxon sites of York and Hereford cathedrals have become lost to us, but at Winchester, on the other hand, we can compare the footings of the Old Minster with Walkelin's replacement.

Major churches would be surrounded by large spaces required for the accommodation of the clergy or monks serving them and their servants, and often also for minor churches, chapels or belfries, such as the now destroyed St Michael in Bedwardine at Worcester, and the church of St Michael-le-Belfrey, perhaps originally associated with a free-standing timber belfry, at York. Canons of major churches had individual houses,[13] but monks required stricter enclosure, and one of the effects of the tenth-century Benedictine reform movement was to create separate enclosed spaces within some towns. In addition, the space around a large church was used for sanctuary and as a graveyard; it was common for the oldest (or sometimes the largest) church in a town to claim a monopoly over burials within the intramural area. These rights persisted longest in western areas of England; further east the political upheavals of the ninth and

[13] Cf. DB, i, fol. 252, 263 for Shrewsbury and Chester.

tenth centuries and the development of a land market made it impossible for senior churches to maintain such rights.

Over the course of the period from the mid-tenth to the mid-twelfth century most of the larger and longer-established towns acquired numerous parish churches, usually built by landlords. Numbers were highest in the biggest towns (London had over a hundred, Norwich, Winchester, Lincoln and York between forty and sixty each by the twelfth century), but many towns had more than ten (for example Exeter, Oxford, Chester, Worcester and Gloucester). Parish boundaries were often fixed to allow householders to be parishioners of the church whose door was nearest to their property. Towns established after the mid-eleventh century usually had only one or two churches, and this was also true of towns that saw serious expansion only after that date.[14] Parish churches could be sited where they would be clearly visible, at street corners or near gateways; from the later eleventh century onwards they might actually be placed on top of gateways, as at Canterbury and Bristol, and by the twelfth century in the middle of streets, as in Gloucester and Hereford. In eastern areas of England, where minor churches often had burial rights from the tenth century, more space was required and minor churches were planned with graveyards. Down to the late twelfth century churches were usually of fairly simple plan, with nave, chancel and often a tower, but at the end of our period some were enlarged as more space was required inside for a wider range of activities, notably schools and, just beginning *c.* 1200, chantries, which encouraged the provision of aisles.

Houses of the new monastic orders that emerged at the end of the eleventh century tended to prefer rural to urban sites, but Augustinian canons liked being connected with towns, sometimes taking over Anglo-Saxon minsters within them, for example St Oswald's in Gloucester and St Frideswide's in Oxford. More often, they chose sites slightly outside them, for example Llanthony by Gloucester, Darley near Derby and Barnwell near Cambridge. Hospitals, run by brothers and sisters following a simplified monastic rule, were usually situated in towns; by *c.* 1200 most major towns already had more than one. They did not need, or perhaps were usually not able to afford, much room; a single long narrow building might suffice for a dormitory-cum-chapel, with a few outbuildings for kitchen and storehouses. Peripheral, often transpontine sites were often chosen, for example St Bartholomew's, London, and Kepyer's Hospital in

[14] R. K. Morris, *Churches in the Landscape* (London, 1989), pp. 185–9, 222–5, 338–9.

Durham. Since inmates could include travellers these were particularly appropriate; however, most inmates were elderly, often bedridden. Few hospitals took in patients suffering from infectious diseases, and leper houses, which did, were always sited at some distance from towns.

Jewish communities, a feature of most shire towns and a few other significant towns from the middle of the twelfth century onwards (and from the late eleventh century in London), were not ghettoized but nonetheless tended to live within a fairly closely defined area, often only a few streets (see Chapter IV.4). Jews were expected to live in towns with royal castles, whose officials were charged with their oversight.

CHAPTER III.4

Urban populations and associations

Charles West

In May 1147, people from across southern and eastern England gathered at the port of Dartmouth, where they took an oath. Joining forces with fleets from the Rhineland and Flanders, they sailed to besiege Lisbon, at this time under Muslim rule. Their assault, co-ordinated with the king of Portugal, eventually succeeded, and they took the city – one of the few successes of the generally disastrous Second Crusade.[1]

It may appear idiosyncratic to begin an exploration of urban populations and associations with this incident of crusading history. But it actually takes us to the issue's heart: for although from one perspective this was the work of an association of crusaders, from another it resembles nothing so much as the activities of a specially formed urban community, a town afloat. This is partly because the group consisted largely of townspeople from coastal towns including Ipswich, Southampton, Bristol and Hastings, together with representatives from Cologne and other North Sea towns – a salutary reminder that urban communities were never extrinsic to the rest of society, and that people in towns were caught up in just the same currents of history as everyone else, including the crusading movement. But more importantly, the group acted as townsmen tended to act. In the absence of pre-arranged or self-evident aristocratic leadership, a collective oath was sworn, creating an artificial community resembling those formally recorded in town archives.

Admittedly, it was rather a dysfunctional community, riven with ethnic, class and gendered tensions. Women were forbidden from going out in public, costly clothing was not to be shown and it was generally agreed that Scots were barbarous. Nevertheless, it cohered. And though the king of Portugal was disconcerted by this form of political organization – he disliked the 'shouting of the people' – he still recognized it as a corporate

[1] C. David, ed. and trans., *De expugnatione Lyxbonensi/The Conquest of Lisbon* (2nd edn; New York, 2001).

entity, granting it rights over potential spoils, much as kings in England granted their townsmen rights and privileges. Hence the Dartmouth association can, in a way, be considered as paradigmatic for how more prosaically stationary towns faced the challenges of organizing urban life. It provides clues to answering the double question with which this section is chiefly concerned: what characterized urban communities, and were they profoundly distinctive?

TOWNS AS PRIVILEGED COMMUNITIES

For earlier generations of historians, answers to these questions would have seemed both self-evident and little to do with the Dartmouth sworn oath. Pioneering historians of English towns like Charles Gross, James Tait and Frederic Maitland thought that it was legal status which determined whether a group of people formed a proper town (or 'free borough'). Legal documents, known as charters, which conferred certain privileges and rights, had been granted, usually by kings, to most sizeable urban communities by the early thirteenth century (for example, Bristol in 1155 and Ipswich in 1200, both of which sent crusaders to Dartmouth). Most were issued in the decades around 1200 in the reigns of kings Richard I and John, though William the Conqueror's 1067 charter for London (the first 'civic charter') and a fragmentary text for the otherwise obscure town of Burford before 1107 hint at earlier precedents. The three privileges typically found in such charters which these historians considered particularly significant in creating a distinctly urban community, namely burgage tenure, borough courts and merchant guilds, can be explained as follows.

The rural peasantry, free and unfree, had various obligations to the lords who owned their land, including compulsory labour and assorted personal dues (see Chapter II.2). In the early period, as Domesday Book shows, inhabitants of a town were still often bound to a rural manor. But by the twelfth century, residents of towns were not only presumed legally free after a year and a day according to the lawyer Glanvill, they also held their land from the lord in an arrangement known as 'burgage tenure', which gave considerable freedom of manoeuvre. They owed merely a fixed ground-rent, typically twelve pence a year, for the plot of land ('landgable'). Their time was their own, and they were free to pass on the plot as they wished.

Most rural settlements were under their lords' tight jurisdictional control, in the shape of manor courts. In contrast, royal charters often recognized that towns had their own semi-independent court (sometimes called a 'portmanmoot'). Closely connected to these courts were elected posts, such as those of mayor and alderman, replacing royal and seigneurial figures like the portreeve and the shadowy 'lawmen' attested in Domesday Book in Danelaw towns such as Lincoln and Cambridge. These elected officials were often entrusted with the responsibility of managing the town, particularly if the town acquired the 'borough farm' or right to collect itself revenues owed.

Finally, towns were also characterized by the presence of sworn associations, particularly guilds or fraternities. Guilds had deep roots in the Anglo-Saxon period, and pre-Conquest statutes survive from Exeter and Cambridge. However, only in the late eleventh and twelfth centuries do guilds set up for urban merchants begin to look both prominent and distinctive. They were soon sufficiently established to own buildings, like the guildhalls attested at Dover in Domesday Book (*gihalla burgensium*), at Winchester in the Winton Domesday and at Battle in the Battle Chronicle. Later royal charters commonly recognized the right of particular towns to form a merchant guild, with associated favourable trading rights within and even outside the town. To read Christina of Markyate's life, which refers to a guild in Huntingdon around 1114, guilds were largely based around alcoholic male solidarity, and though the text aimed to stress Christina's virtuous abstinence, the Winton Domesday concurs in referring to the Winchester guildhall as where the thegns 'drank their guild'. Yet merchant guilds evidently had a serious function, too, bearing some relation to early town governance.[2]

The legalist approach which stresses these three characteristics of towns appears therefore to resolve the issue: urban communities were, obviously, those with the legal status of urban communities. However, historians are no longer so certain that legal characteristics should carry so much weight. For example, concentrating on legal form may create the illusion that there was an identikit model of urban community. Admittedly, sometimes the sources themselves give this impression, since the customs and rights of one town were often imported and applied to another. The 'customs of Breteuil', deriving from an obscure town in Normandy, spread widely in western England and Wales in this period, just as those of Newcastle later spread in Scotland. In reality, though,

[2] P. L' Hermite-Leclercq and A. -M. Legras, eds. and trans., *Vie de Christina de Markyate* (2 vols; Paris, 2007); M. Biddle, ed., *Winchester in the Early Middle Ages: An Edition and Discussion of the Winton Domesday* (Oxford, 1976).

towns which enjoyed similar formal freedoms were sometimes very different places.

Moreover, to concentrate exclusively on these legal definitions excludes proper consideration of the earlier part of the period. Anglo-Saxon urban communities do not seem to have been legally privileged, as no Anglo-Saxon king or noble ever issued a formal written privilege for a town. Yet it is undeniable that, practically speaking, there were Anglo-Saxon urban communities in abundance: Domesday Book reveals over a hundred of them. It is true that we do not know for certain the absolute size of these communities, since their inhabitants are chronically under-represented in Domesday Book. But on a conservative estimate, more than 30 towns sheltered 1,000 or more permanent residents by 1086, and 17 of these contained more than 2,000 residents. These are minimal figures. Recent estimates have given Domesday Lincoln a population of up to 10,000, and London's could have been twice that.[3] Very plausibly, 10 per cent of the population already lived in towns at the time of the Norman Conquest, with the visible later growth in town size simply keeping step with general population trends.

Furthermore, not only did towns exist in material terms, they were considered legally separate from their hinterland, as shown by Anglo-Saxon legal texts, like a document on theft from London (VI Æthelstan, *c.* 930) or the 'Episcopus' treatise, *c.* 1000, which talks about *burhriht* ('town law'). Canterbury seems to have had its own city bylaws by the mid-ninth century, setting a minimum distance (2 feet) between houses.[4] Clearly historians need to find approaches which do not automatically involve judging one period in terms of another, which means abandoning a focus on legal status derived from conditions around 1200.

URBAN TENSIONS

Most historians and archaeologists have therefore turned away from defining towns in legal or constitutional terms, and now agree that what constitutes a town is 'functional diversity', which is to say that its

[3] C. Dyer, *Making a Living in the Middle Ages: The People of Britain, 850–1520* (London, 2003), p. 62. For the Lincoln estimate, M. Jones, D. Stocker and A. Vince, *The City by the Pool* (Oxford, 2003), p. 167; and for the London estimate, D. Keene, 'London from the post-Roman period to 1300', in D. M. Palliser, ed., *The Cambridge Urban History of Britain*, vol. I, *600–1540* (Cambridge, 2000), p. 196.

[4] N. Brooks, *The Early History of the Church of Canterbury: Christ Church from 597 to 1066* (London, 1984), p. 27.

inhabitants are engaged in varied economic activities. But this leaves open the question of what sort of communities inhabited these settlements. Indeed, if what defines an urban community is that everyone was doing something different, and legal arrangements should not be overemphasized, was there necessarily a functioning community at all? As we have seen, the Dartmouth crusading community seems shot through with tensions, of which two strands, those based on class and on ethnicity, merit particular attention.

That there was the potential for a class-based antagonism is clear, for towns were marked by pronounced inequalities of wealth and power. On close examination, royal charters which recognized urban communities' autonomous existence turn out to have favoured only a small fraction of the population. For example, King John's grant to Ipswich in 1200 was typical in talking loftily about the town community, but an accompanying charter issued by the town itself, describing a subsequent assembly, shows that Ipswich was very firmly controlled by a couple of dozen leading burgesses. The guilds and fraternities which dominated urban society and formed the real citizen body were by no means open to all: entry fees were required, as demonstrated by the earliest surviving guild rolls, those of Leicester from *c.* 1196. These were associations for the towns' male elites.

There are signs at the end of the period of tensions arising from this inequality. Disturbances in London in the 1190s exploited by a populist leader, William fitzOsbert, were rooted in tensions within London's urban community, sparked off by grants of authority to the ruling oligarchy. Frustrations were doubtless also expressed by the low-level violence which made all large twelfth-century towns dangerous places at night, when gangs of youths, like those in London which so appalled the chronicler Roger of Howden, terrorized worthy citizens. Nevertheless, tensions between these wealthy townspeople and the far more numerous poor – unskilled labourers, street traders and the newly arrived, Domesday Book's 'bordars' – in general remained latent. Perhaps the zoning of towns into districts, as attested in tenth-century Winchester, minimized conflict.

Alternatively, we might wonder whether networks of patronage and arbitration relieved the pressure. The marked twelfth-century growth in numbers of hermits has long been connected with rapid commercialization, the other side of the same coin: many hermits might, like Godric of Finchale (d. 1170), have been disillusioned ex-merchants and townsmen. But such hermits often lived in proximity to urban settlements (Godric lived near Durham) and provided much-needed social mediation. The rise to prominence of the solitary life perhaps reflected, and helped resolve, a growth in urban tensions.

In any case, more prominent than class-based tensions were those based on ethnicity. Towns were, almost by definition, ethnically diverse places. As centres of trade, nodes in the transfer of goods and money, the more important the town, the more foreigners it would contain, which provoked dangerously strong feeling. Most noticeable is an ugly animosity against the Jews, an intermittent but persistent feature of English urban life. Violence peaked with a number of riots and murders in 1190, particularly savage in York, but resentment was violently expressed at other times and places, too, such as mid-twelfth-century Norwich and Lincoln, where Jews were accused of the sacrificial murder of two Christian children, William and Hugh.

If such anti-Semitism is not attested in England before the Norman Conquest, that is simply because Jews arrived in English towns only subsequent to the Conquest (see Chapter IV.4). Anglo-Saxon towns had certainly known ethnic intolerance. On 13 November 1002 (St Brice's Day), King Æthelred II 'the Unready' launched a persecution against Danes resident in England, a measure which if it found a response anywhere, found it in towns. Indeed, the most detailed description of events is preserved in a charter Æthelred issued for the monastery of St Frideswide (Oxford), describing how some Oxford citizens had chased a group of Danes into the monastery's church, which they then burned down, Danes and all (Æthelred compensated the monastery; see Chapter IV.1).[5] When, after the Conquest, the Normans imported townspeople directly from France into the topographically distinct districts known as 'French boroughs' of English towns like Hereford, Norwich, Nottingham and perhaps Southampton, they were therefore merely adding another layer of ethnic tension to a potentially volatile mixture.

URBAN SOLIDARITIES

Nevertheless, even if tensions of class and ethnicity militated against the formation of durable and integrated urban communities, from an early date towns demonstrably often did think of themselves, and act, as identifiable communities. The Conqueror's Domesday commissioners recorded that many had well-established customs. Of course, town inhabitants had

[5] *EHD*, i, no. 127, pp. 590–1.

many common interests, engaged in regular interaction with one another, lived in distinctive forms of housing (combining street frontage and a cellar) and were spatially separated from the rest of the population, sometimes behind walls. But all this provided only a potential for community identity, one which required actualization. What forces, then, brought their inhabitants together?

Part of the answer is lordship. All English towns had a lord, important ones usually – unusually in the European context – the king, but sometimes a major monastery (at Bury St Edmunds), bishop (at Worcester from the tenth century) or secular aristocrat (at Leicester, controlled by its earls from the early twelfth century). These lords owned the land on which the town was built, and held other rights, too. They played a role, willingly or not, in building up urban solidarities. This should not be interpreted as primal class tension forcing self-consciousness onto oppressed burgesses. Contrary to traditional views which considered towns as alien implants in a feudal economy and so irrevocably at loggerheads with aristocrats in general, the two were not in fact always separable. Aristocrats often spent time in towns and owned urban properties, and indeed most towns, whether or not formally planted, owed their origins in some form to aristocratic or royal intervention. What disturbances there were (for example in York in 1065 against the unpopular Earl Tostig) point not to a radical dissatisfaction with lordship, but to often intense political engagement. The Londoners fought off the raiders Olaf Tryggvasson and Svein in September 994, and with the same determination they supported Edmund Ironside against Cnut in 1016, and arranged King Stephen's accession in 1135.

Rather, what mattered was that lordship over towns imposed certain obligations, which made necessary, if for no other reason, the existence of town authorities. Though shadowy in this period, towns like Canterbury appear from a very early date (perhaps the eighth century) to have had elaborate jurisdictions, divided into urban districts or wards. Also attested in post-Conquest York, those of London can be worked out in detail from a rental survey of *c.* 1127. There is also scattered evidence for towns holding communal property, even before town councils developed seals and began to act formally on behalf of their citizens (Oxford's guild-government granted land to Oseney Abbey in 1147, but possessed no seal before 1191).

Sometimes, and particularly towards the end of the period, these administrations clashed with town lords, demanding more self-government in disturbances which had something in common with movements in continental Europe. Many continental towns (most famously Laon in 1112) demanded self-governance with the cry of 'commune' and negotiated 'customs', often in the form of stereotyped confirmations of rights as held by other towns. Given the ready co-operation the urban crusaders showed at Dartmouth with their continental comrades, and their alacrity in electing chosen representatives, it would hardly be surprising if English towns participated in this movement, too. And, indeed, a commune was suppressed at Gloucester in 1170, there were rumblings of anger against the controlling abbey at Bury St Edmunds in the 1190s and London in the 1190s was briefly granted communal status. However, the communal movement never really caught on in England. The lords of English towns, most notably the Norman kings, were strong enough to make these disturbances foolhardy. King Henry I is said as a young prince to have pushed a rebellious Norman townsman from the top of Rouen's tower with his own hands, so little wonder that English town-dwellers kept quiet.

In any case, administration alone cannot have been the glue which stuck towns together: only the top echelons were directly involved, and, given the negligible evidence for urban policing, means of enforcement were lacking. This has led historians to infer that the 'essence of the medieval urban community' must lie elsewhere. The hunt for a substitute has mainly made use of more abundant later archives, particularly those of York, Coventry and London, to come to its conclusions, but some of these can, with due caution, be applied to the earlier period, too. A town's elite perhaps helped bind it together informally, through social networks, identifying and expressing common interest. Most obviously the case in terms of elite merchant guilds, this also applies to craftsman guilds, which bestowed a veneer of respectability on their members. First mentioned in the Pipe Roll of 1130, permissions to form craft guilds were granted in the later twelfth century to the bakers of Bury St Edmunds, the cordwainers of Oxford and the weavers of London. Such guilds were not universally welcomed by those in charge, who feared their potential for subversion, particularly weavers' associations. Nevertheless, as networking institutions, they helped articulate interests and provided a bond, a form of artificial kinship, connecting up disparate populations.

In later times, these guilds would be closely involved in ceremonies and processions, and the role ritual played in bringing together the town's inhabitants is already dimly visible in this period. Pre-Conquest evidence relates largely to feast-day religious processions organized by the churches around which many towns had grown (see Chapter V.4). For instance, a beautiful miniature in the Benedictional of Æthelwold, a late tenth-century liturgical manuscript from Winchester, shows townspeople ushering Christ on his donkey into town, instead of the conventional Christ's disciples, presumably reflecting a Palm Sunday procession.[6] Later evidence is more forthcoming. The twelfth-century cleric William fitz Stephen portrayed London's ceremonial life in his *Description of London* as extraordinarily energetic, ranging from religious plays to naval tournaments, reminding us of the attractions large towns offered. As he said: 'it is not fitting that a city should be merely useful and serious-minded, unless it be also pleasant and cheerful'.[7] Participating in these spectacles of religious and secular power, which affirmed the town's unity, or even just watching them go past, could have been a powerful source of urban pride, though, according to later evidence, also a potential flashpoint for conflict.

How far townspeople were persuaded of a common identity through myth is also an open question. Geoffrey of Monmouth's *History of the Kings of Britain* preserves a considerable number of legends relating to English towns. Maybe the citizens of Leicester were proud of their legendary foundation by King Lear, and those of Lincoln of King Arthur's defeat of the Saxons there. More maliciously, stereotypes about various English towns were circulating by the twelfth century, which the chronicler Richard of Devizes collated in a mildly scurrilous lampoon of some major urban centres: Ely stinks because of the fens, in Bristol everyone is a soap maker and so on.[8]

AN URBAN DIFFERENCE?

There was, in short, plenty which brought townspeople together, more fundamental than formal legal status, and which in combination transcended – most of the time – tensions deriving from towns' economic role. However, the question remains whether these communities were in some profound way different in nature from other communities of the period. And this is where the Dartmouth crusaders once again prove helpful. Their sworn oath and concern for the collective election of the leaders were certainly characteristically urban, organizational forms markedly more egalitarian than those of most crusades. Yet though townsmen predominated, there were others on this crusade, too, so it should not be

[6] M. Bedingfield, *The Dramatic Liturgy of Anglo-Saxon England* (Woodbridge, 2002), p. 104.

[7] *EHD*, ii, p. 960, also M. Kowaleski, ed., *Medieval Towns: A Reader* (Peterborough, Ont., 2006), p. 292.

[8] J. Appleby, ed. and trans., *The Chronicle of Richard of Devizes of the Time of King Richard the First* (London, 1963), pp. 64–7.

reified as the Townsmen's Crusade. And more importantly still, while sworn oaths and elected officials characterized towns, they were not actually restricted to them.

For, contrary to some traditional views, collective action of this kind was actually widespread in the period, as Susan Reynolds has demonstrated. After all, villagers, too, sometimes appointed officials, swore oaths and even set up guilds.[9] From this perspective, it would be surprising only if towns had not formed communities, using common practices like oaths and ceremonies to bind themselves together. The Dartmouth crusaders simply point to how urban life was embedded in wider society. From one perspective, they created a floating city, but similar organizational techniques could be used in all sorts of different circumstances. Organizing a crusade in this way was a pragmatic measure, just as organizing towns was, not a consequence of townsmen's instinctive proto-democracy.

So while there were undoubtedly urban communities, it is not at all clear that there was an Urban Community, essentially distinct from other forms of collective identity – unless according to precisely those legal definitions which historians now play down. In this sense, townsmen were perhaps exemplary more than exceptional in their organization. We must be careful that our preconceptions about the Middle Ages do not make towns and their inhabitants seem more exotic, peculiar or radically 'other' than they really were.

[9] S. Reynolds, *Kingdoms and Communities in Western Europe, 900–1300* (Oxford, 1984).

CHAPTER IV.1

Invasion and migration

Elisabeth van Houts

Looking back to the year 1000, the mid-twelfth-century historian Henry of Huntingdon characterized the coming of the Danes and the Normans as a divine punishment for the English comparable with the Britons' fate after the invasions by the Angles, Saxons and Jutes:

> This He brought about as if laying a military ambush. I mean that on one side the persecution by the Danes was raging, and on the other the connection with the Normans was growing, so that even if they were to escape the obvious lightning fire of the Danes, valour would not help them to escape the Normans' unexpected trick.[1]

This retrospective view by the bilingual married archdeacon, son of a Norman clerk and an English mother, whose job required him to travel around in the Danelaw, is a valuable starting point for the present chapter. Between 900 and 1200 England experienced repeated foreign invasion, culminating in three periods of extended rule. While the first resulted in settlement and occupation of much of northeast England in the late ninth and early tenth century, the latter were political takeovers by a military elite which turned the eleventh century into an era of unprecedented trauma in the history of the English people. In this chapter the elite small-scale immigration will take centre stage with subsidiary roles for the various groups of immigrants that entered the country as they have done throughout English history (mercenaries and merchants, artisans and craftsmen as well as clerks and clergy). How did English society and its leaders cope with the influx of foreigners at various levels and in different waves? What strategies for dealing with newcomers can be detected across the period a whole? How did the foreigners and their descendants themselves deal with their situation, not least in terms of cross-Channel responsibility for land and income? In addition

[1] D. Greenway, ed. and trans., *Henry, Archdeacon of Huntingdon Historia Anglorum. The History of the English People* (OMT; Oxford, 1996), pp. 338–9.

to the section on immigration, there will be one on (temporary) migration within England, which was often seasonal, but could be the result of exile or outlawry, a third will focus on emigration from England, whether intended and accidental, while a brief final section will explore the variability of moves in and out of England in ways that are not easily covered under the previous three headings. For all four sections what we would like to know best is of course the experience of individuals in these migratory movements and developments in such experience over time. Yet, if experience on an individual basis is extremely hard to elucidate, it is even more difficult to identify trends for groups of immigrants, migrants and emigrants in our period.

IMMIGRATION

With its extensive coastline and natural resources, England has always been a magnet for people from continental Europe. In our period there occurred a shift in immigration from newcomers originating in the north of Europe, Norway and Denmark especially, to regions further to the south, particularly Normandy and northern France. Around 900, many Danes had settled in what became known as the Danelaw, an area north of the Thames covering the eastern Midlands, East Anglia, Lincolnshire and Northumbria with as western border the Watling Street. The Dane Halfdan, who according to the Anglo-Saxon Chronicle came and took over Northumbria, arrived with followers to whom he handed out land for cultivation: 'and in this year [876] Halfdan came and shared out the lands of Northumbria and they were engaged in ploughing and in making a living for themselves' (see Chapter III.1). Collaboration with the English, as suggested by evidence from Chester-le-Street, a domain belonging to Durham, points to a different scenario from that of pure plundering and bloodshed by marauding invaders. A sizeable influx of Norse people, many of whom had come from Dublin and its surroundings, held sway in York. There extensive excavations in the 1970s and 1980s revealed a vibrant Scandinavian trading and artisan community from the 970s onwards. Others were men of whom nothing is known but for their names recorded in English sources centred on towns, like 'Thurcytel' in Bedford, 'Thurferth' at Northampton, 'Toli' in Huntingdon.[2]

[2] D. M. Hadley, '"Hamlet and the princes of Denmark": lordship in the Danelaw, *c.* 860–954', in D. M. Hadley and J. D. Richards, eds., *Cultures in Contact: Scandinavian Settlement in England in the Ninth and Tenth Centuries* (Turnhout, 2000), pp. 112–14.

Not all of them came on their own – some men brought families, which suggests that in places there were enough Danish (or Norse) people to provide a pool of unrelated people that could marry and keep communities going where Danish customs and language might still be passed on from generation to generation. As far as numbers for the Scandinavian influx are concerned, in the ninth and early tenth centuries we are very much in the dark, not least because there was no centralized authority in charge of these migrants, nor have they left enough trace in written records to allow us to even begin to estimate in what numbers they came.

In contrast, the Danes who arrived in the wake of well-organized and centralized royal conquest under kings Svein and Cnut look like a military elite attracted by England's wealth and determined at the highest level to exploit its fiscal resources. This could be achieved only by a political takeover of the house of Wessex and those parts of England which were (more or less) under its control. Although the indigenous nobility suffered considerable casualties at ealdorman and thegn level as a result of the intermittent fighting, the disruption was not on a scale comparable to that of sixty years later.[3] With a conqueror-king in charge of the indigenous nobility that surrendered (or was otherwise eliminated) the taxation revenues were directly under his control, which meant that he had cash to pay off most of his troops, who then left the country. King Cnut's most trustworthy and highest-ranking Danish followers were handsomely rewarded with cash, offices and land; the latter on occasion through marriage to rich English widows (see Chapter IV.3). Only one Englishman, Godwine, was admitted by marriage to the new royal family, and he certainly did well as a result. Overall, the amount of land handed over to Cnut's Danish followers was relatively modest, for example in Worcestershire and Herefordshire only twenty pre-Conquest Domesday Book landholders have Scandinavian names and between them they held relatively small amounts of land.

William the Conqueror's conquest in the autumn of 1066 was shorter and more brutal than the previous ones, but effective because of its concentration of highly trained military personnel who were immediately given land in the late winter of the following year. Most of the English male aristocracy was wiped out as a result of death in battle and military expeditions, or exile, which in turn paved the way for the Norman

[3] K. Mack, 'Changing thegns: Cnut's conquest and the English aristocracy', *Albion*, 16 (1984), 375–87.

conqueror to hand out the lands of the dead (and ignore claims from their surviving womenfolk) with unprecedented largesse (see also below, 'Emigration'). Domesday Book evidence reveals overwhelming foreign landholding. Approximately 8,000 foreigners from France (the majority of whom were Normans) received land. In terms of the categories of landholders by the value of their lands in demesne and tenanted, as established in the classic study by W. J. Corbett in 1926, the top category of just over ten landholders in class A, holding land valued between £650 and £3,240 per year, held between a quarter and a fifth of all Domesday England.[4] What happened, then, was dispossession of the native landholders, the English, on an unprecedented scale (see Chapter II.2). The colossal foreign gain could only have been realized by sheer military power and exploitation of the indigenous population by a well-organized invasion force armed to the teeth and led by a military dictator. Thus, of the three distinctive waves of immigrants in our period the immediate impact on the indigenous population in terms of scale of enterprise, numbers of people killed or dispossessed and on the social order of life, that of the Normans in 1066 was the most profound and was therefore long remembered as a traumatic event.

Yet this seemingly neat division of our period, into distinct waves of immigrants-settlers, proposed by Henry of Huntingdon, can mislead: it should not obscure the fact that pretty much continuously from 900 to 1200 a stream of immigrants arrived in England, of whom a significant number stayed on and settled. Amongst them must be counted merchants, sailors, moneyers, royal servants and landholders, male and female, who originated from Scandinavia and (northern) France (especially Normandy, Brittany, Flanders and Picardy), the same countries of origin as the immigrants discussed above.[5] And when the lands of the Norman kings expanded so did the area from which individual immigrants arrived, including from the 1150s Anjou, Poitou and Aquitaine. Added to the laymen were the many clergymen who came as part of the Europe-wide travelling of monks, chaplains and scholars. Early on in our period in *c.* 940 a certain Fredegaud, who became known under his anglicized name of Frithegod, settled for a while in Canterbury, where he worked for Archbishop Oda (d. 958), but then returned to France, where

[4] W. J. Corbett, 'The development of the duchy of Normandy and the Norman conquest of England,' in J. R. Tanner *et al.*, eds., *The Cambridge Medieval History* v (1926), pp. 481–520, esp. 508–16; D. Carpenter, *The Struggle for Mastery: Britain 1066–1284* (London, 2003), pp. 82–3.

[5] S. Jayakuma, 'Some reflections on the "foreign policies" of Edgar the "Peaceable"', *Haskins Society Journal*, 10 (2001), 17–37, at 25; C. P. Lewis, 'The French in England', *ANS* 17 [(1994 (1995))], 125–7.

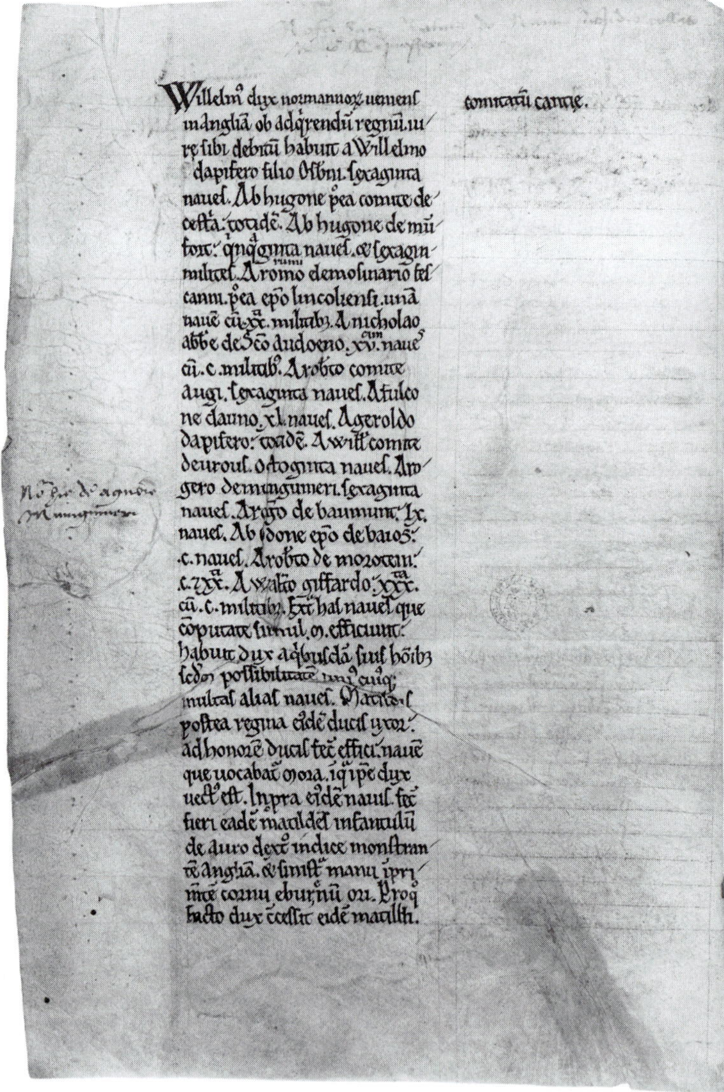

Willelm̄ dux normannorum ueniens
in angliā ob adq̄rendū regnū iu
re sibi debitū habuit a Willelmo
dapifero filio Osberni. sexaginta
naues. Ab hugone postea comite de
cestra: totidē. Ab hugone de mū
fort: quinquaginta naues. et sexagin
ta milites. A remigio elemosinario fes
canni. postea epō lincoliensi. unā
nauē cum .xx. militibꝫ. A nicholao
abbē de sc̄o audoeno. xv. naues
cū .c. militib. A roberto comite
augi. sexaginta naues. A fulco
ne dauno. xl. naues. A geroldo
dapifero: totidē. A will'mo comite
deurous. octoginta naues. A ro
gero demungumeri. sexaginta
naues. A rogero de baumunt. lx.
naues. Ab odone epō de baios:
.c. naues. A roberto de morotein:
.c. xx. A waltero giffardo: xxx
cū .c. militib. Ex hıs naues que
cōputate simul. m. efficiunt.
habuit dux a quibusdā suis hoībꝫ
secundum possibilitatem uniuscuiusque
multas alias naues. Matildis
postea regina eidē ducis uxor:
ad honorē ducis fecit effici nauē
que uocabat' mora. in qua ipse dux
uect' est. In prora eiusdē nauis fecit
fieri eadē matildis infantulū
de auro dext' indice monstran
tē angliā. et sinist' manu inpri
mentē cornu eburnū ori. Pro quo
facto dux concessit eidē matildi

comitatū cantie.

Figure 11a The ship list of William the Conqueror, probably written at Fécamp (Normandy) after 13 December 1067 or *c.* 1072; this manuscript from Battle Abbey was copied in the period 1130–60.
Oxford, Bodleian Library MS E Museo 93, fol. 8v (p. 16); reproduced with kind permission of The Bodleian Libraries, University of Oxford

Figure 11b Portrait of William the Conqueror, from the *Gesta Normannorum Ducum*, autograph manuscript of Orderic Vitalis, *c.* 1113.
Rouen, Bibliothèque municipale, MS. Y 14 (1174), fol. 116r; published with kind permission of Collections de la Bibliothèque municipale de Rouen

he lived at Brioude (Auvergne). A few decades later Lantfred, probably a monk from Fleury, worked at Winchester. From the mid-1050s several Flemish monks from Saint-Bertin at Saint-Omer (Flanders), e.g. Goscelin and Folcard, settled in England, where after 1066 the latter became abbot of Thorney. What these men have in common is a superb command of Latin, which made them attractive as skilled hagiographers. Around the same time a string of Lotharingian clergy found employment under Edward the Confessor, a tendency that was strongly continued under William the Conqueror, so that by the time of his death in 1087 virtually all bishops and abbots were foreign born.

Amongst the laity, however, the largest pool of steady immigrants across the whole period was formed by mercenaries. They were male and ranged in social rank from younger aristocratic sons, who were professionally armed knights, to ex-peasants, urban workers or other poor men, who brought only their physical body-power with them. Almost invariably they came if not at the invitation of England's rulers then at least with their strong encouragement. In the early part of our period no Scandinavian soldier or sailor would have arrived in the service of the English kings, especially south of the Watling Street, if it had not been for the initial settlement of Danes and Norse in various regions across Britain. Contemporary evidence is unambiguous that foreign fighters arrived as early as 917 and were employed under Æthelstan (924–39), in increasing numbers under Edgar (957–75) and especially in the second half of the reign of Æthelred (978–1016).[6] Under Cnut and William the evidence for foreigner soldiers is self-evidently overwhelming because of the presence of armies of occupation which had been recruited from Denmark and northern France, respectively. In the early part of the period the majority came, not surprisingly, from Scandinavia, and Denmark in particular, but enough Frisians and Flemings are mentioned to warn us not to underestimate immigration from immediately across the Channel. After the Norman Conquest we see the reverse, with a sharp decline in Danes taking service and instead many men coming from France, especially from Flanders, particularly its urban areas, and Brittany. Also after 1066 substantial numbers of mercenaries from other parts of the British Isles, especially Wales and Scotland, fought for the Norman kings. Records for royal recruitment pick up again in Henry I's reign. From this period we have a series of diplomatic treaties

[6] Jayakumar, 'Some reflections', pp. 26–7; for Flemish immigration in the late tenth century, see also S. Vanderputten, 'Canterbury and Flanders in the late 10th century', *ASE*, 35 (2007), 219–44.

between the kings of England and the counts of Flanders dating from 1101, 1110, 1163 and 1197 (and others now lost in 1175, 1180 and 1182) in which the king of England would offer an annual sum, usually £500, in return for which the count of Flanders would provide 1,000 mercenaries for royal campaigns in England.[7] The treaties reveal that the recruitment in Flanders was probably delegated to the guarantors of the treaties, many of whom were castellans, comital officials, with expertise in recruitment, especially from the southeast of the county. This raises the question as to the recruitment in other areas and periods under discussion. We must assume that in the days of the Anglo-Saxon kings royal officials would be charged with the task of engaging these men. The English kings, cash-rich as a result of their efficient taxation collection regime, could afford to maintain foreign fighters. Moreover, Henry II's Pipe Rolls reveal incidental payments to Flemish men, who may or may not have been recruited as a result of the treaties. Common sense suggests that before and after 1066 contacts existed in Danish, Flemish and Breton communities between the settlers and incoming mercenaries, though such contacts may have been easier amongst the higher ranks of society than for the poor. By the nature of their jobs mercenaries were male but not necessarily single; some at the top end of the social scale brought their wives and children with them. In King Æthelred's reign the Danish nobleman Pallig came with his royal wife Gunhild (sister of King Svein Forkbeard) and at least one child, while under King Stephen, William of Ypres, leader of the Flemish mercenaries, was for many years based in Kent, presumably with his Burgundian wife. Across our period the presence of strangers in England, whether conqueror-settler or fighter-mercenary, caused at times considerable ethnic tension.

Royal legislation designed to deal with such unrest can be roughly divided into three categories. First there is legislation that acknowledges ethnic groups and issues laws for each of these groups to protect royal supporters against guerrilla attacks from the indigenous population in immediate post-conquest situations. Second, there is legislation that acknowledges ethnic groups and provides for each of these in the hope that individually tailored legislation allows the various groups to coexist peacefully. Third, there is legislation against specific groups of foreign origin, issued by kings at times of crisis and aimed at removing them.

[7] I gratefully acknowledge permission to use E. Oksanen, 'The relations between England and Flanders, 1066–*c.* 1200 with special reference to the Anglo-Flemish treaties' (unpublished Ph.D. thesis, University of Cambridge, 2007).

Although all three types of law were aimed at quelling ethnically inspired unrest, only one was not aimed at privileging one group over the other. As far as the first type is concerned, the conquerors Cnut and William had to protect their followers against English guerrilla warfare. After Cnut's accession legislation was put in place in the form of the *murdrum* fine, which was aimed at protecting Danes in royal service against attacks from English in revenge mode.[8] This same legislation was then revived by William the Conqueror when he had to protect the French against attacks by the English resistance. It was a fine levied at the English kin of an Englishman who had murdered respectively a Dane or a Frenchman who fought at the king's command. Significantly, however, the so-called *Laws of William the Conqueror* specifically provided that 'all the Frenchmen who were in England in the time of Edward the Confessor shall be treated as English'.[9] Few instances of the *murdrum* fine, however, can be found to have been applied in practice. What has survived is twelfth century, can be found in the Pipe Rolls of Henry II and interestingly concerns the Flemish, another indication that over time royal legislation was flexible enough to be targeted at whatever minority group of immigrants was perceived as posing the greatest threat. Virtually all other royal legislation by the conqueror-kings was English and meant to treat Danes and French in the same way as the English.

As for the second type of legislation, laws designed for preserving the status quo of different ethnicities living side by side, the sole example was issued by an English king and has no equivalent for the Danish or Norman kings. It is regularly mentioned between the late tenth century and mid-eleventh century as originating with King Edgar in *c.* 970. By the mid-tenth century the Wessex kings began their conquest of the area north of the Watling Street, occupied by the Danes. In the process King Edgar, a conqueror himself, allowed the Danes to keep their customs. Who exactly these Danes were, we do not know. Were they the descendants of Scandinavians who had emigrated en masse or as an elite of warriors? Or were they, which is much more likely, the grandchildren of original Scandinavian settlers who had adapted to local regional practices thereby distinguishing themselves from the English (not only of Wessex) on both ethnic and regional counts? With any such distinctions, however, we have to bear in mind that neither the Danes nor the English would

[8] B. O'Brien, 'From *Morðor* to *Murdrum*: the preconquest origin and Norman revival of the murder fine', *Speculum*, 71 (1996), 321–57.

[9] Lewis, 'The French', p. 136.

necessarily have been purely genetically ethnic.[10] With these caveats in place we can now turn to Edgar's so-called *Wihtbordestan* code (*c.* 970), which uniquely recognizes a distinction in law and custom between clauses for the English and for the Danes:

IV Edgar 2.1: 'And it is my will that secular rights be in force among the Danes in accordance to as good laws as they can decide upon'; and IV Edgar 12: 'Further it is my will that there should be in force amongst the Danes such good laws as they can decide upon, and I have ever allowed them this and will allow it as long as my life lasts, because of your loyalty, which you have always shown me.'[11]

These laws were popular in the North, because they recognized regional politics and significantly were reissued in 1018, when Cnut came to an agreement with the English and the Danes at Oxford, and again under Edward the Confessor in 1065 after the Northumbrian rebellion. As Matthew Innes has argued, Edgar's law was the only royal legislation that recognized ethnic diversity, a development which contemporaries thought to be absolutely essential for the public good in northern England. Edgar's law was issued, it is generally agreed, for the area that would become known as the Danelaw (*Dena lage*). As 'laws of the Danes' it was a vague expression first coined by Archbishop Wulfstan II in 1008 when he revised the law known as V Æthelred for the northern country without the specificity of a geographical area.[12] Never much in use before the Normans arrived, after 1066, however, it occurs in legal treatises interested in regional custom and carried a false notion of authority that in areas to the north of the Watling Street legislation had been divided according to ethnic lines between English and Danes.

The third type of law was legislation issued against a foreign minority. The most famous case dates from King Æthelred's reign, when in 1002 he issued orders 'for all the Danish men who were in England to be slain on St Brice's Day [13 November]' (see also Chapter III.4 and Chapter IV.2).[13] Most historians argue that this royal order was aimed primarily at the small groups of recent Danish soldiers who arrived as part of the relentless Viking

[10] L. Abrams, 'King Edgar and the men of the Danelaw', in D. Scragg, ed., *Edgar, King of the English 959–975. New Interpretations* (Woodbridge, 2008), pp. 171–91 at 175–7.

[11] *EHD*, i, no. 41 pp. 434–7.

[12] M. Innes, 'Danelaw identities: ethnicity, regionalism and political allegiance', in Hadley and Richards, eds., *Cultures in Contact*, pp. 76–7; P. Wormald, *The Making of English Law: King Alfred to the Twelfth Century* (Oxford, 1999), pp. 334–5, 346, suggests that the revision makes better sense for 1018 when he worked for Cnut.

[13] S. Keynes, 'The massacre of St Brice's Day (13 November 1002)', in N. Lund, ed., *Seksogtyvende tværfaglige vikingesymposium Københavns Universitet 2007* (Aarhus, 2007), pp. 32–67.

onslaughts on England. Amongst them the most prominent female casualty was King Svein's sister Gunhild and her family. She was, as we have heard, the wife of Pallig, who had come with his ships to support King Æthelred, but then after a while defected to Svein again. The 1002 royal order was not, so it is generally agreed, aimed at the third- or fourth-generation Danish settlers who lived mostly in the Danelaw and to whom Edgar's laws applied even as late as 1018, as we have seen. Yet there are problems with an interpretation that limits the targeted victims to recent Viking male fighters. First of all there is the crucial evidence for Oxford (note its place on the Watling Street) emanating remarkably from King Æthelred himself. His royal charter of 1004 recalled the event in extraordinary detail:

> that all the Danes who had sprung up in this island sprouting like cockles amongst the wheat were to be destroyed by a most just extermination and this decree was to be put into effect even as far as death, those Danes who dwelt in the aforesaid town, striving to escape death entered this sanctuary of Christ, having broken by force the doors and bolts, and resolved to make a refuge for themselves therein against the people of the town and suburbs; but when all the people in pursuit strove, forced by necessity to drive them out, and could not, they set fire to the planks and burnt, as it seems, the church with its ornaments and its books.[14]

The argument that these Danes were none other than mercenaries is undermined by the important evidence from later chroniclers who stress the unacceptable level of unjustified royal violence against the king's (foreign) subjects (in one way or another) across the country. William of Jumièges, a Norman historian with access to Scandinavian and English sources, active from *c.* 1050, condemned the royal action as 'a detestable shocking deed defiling a kingdom' because it hit innocent Danish men, women and children who not only 'had not been charged with a crime' but 'lived peacefully and quite harmoniously throughout the kingdom and did not at all fear for their lives'.[15] Admittedly, he misplaced the event to 1013, implying that it happened after King Svein's conquest; nevertheless his explicit references to 'civilians', including families, is worth noting. In England Henry of Huntingdon reported that as a boy (presumably in the 1090s) he heard old men say 'that the king had sent secret letters to every city according to which the English either maimed all the unsuspecting Danes on the same day and hour with their swords, or suddenly,

[14] ASC 'E' 1002; *EHD*, i, no. 127, Sawyer, *Anglo-Saxon Charters*, no. 909.

[15] E. M. C. van Houts, ed. and trans., *The Gesta Normannorum Ducum of William of Jumièges, Orderic Vitalis and Robert of Torigni* (2 vols.; OMT; Oxford, 1992–5), ii, pp. 16–17.

at the same moment captured them and destroyed them by fire'.[16] Even if we allow for an element of distortion and exaggeration caused by time (several decades later), means of communication (oral testimony) and in Jumièges's case geographical distance, these accounts emphasize abhorrence about nationwide, centrally co-ordinated royal violence against unsuspecting inhabitants of foreign origin. It is important to stress that this is the only evidence – albeit persuasive – for royal violence against particular minority groups. Potentially comparable cases date from much later times. In 1136–7 during the height of tension following King Stephen's contested accession, there circulated a rumour about a secret plot in England that all French (or, in some accounts, Normans) would be killed on a fixed day and that the government would be handed to the Scots. And in 1189 rumours abounded that the king had ordered the killing of Jews in London on the day of his coronation (see Chapter IV.4). The interest for us lies in the apparent credibility to contemporaries of a story that one ethnic group could be targeted and killed on royal orders on one specific date.[17] Such evidence from elsewhere in Europe is hard to come by.

How different is Æthelred's royal order against ethnic minorities in 1002 from those aimed at exploitation or neutralizing their perceived power? The question is important in order to understand royal actions against the Flemish in the reigns of Henry I and Henry II. Around *c.* 1108 King Henry I ordered the Flemish from their homes in Cumbria or Northumbria, to south Wales, where in Pembrokeshire around Haverfordwest and Carmarthen they were forced to settle and form a bulwark against the Welsh.[18] The forced migration concerned not just Flemish men but whole families including women and children, who were of sufficient numbers to survive as a recognizable community for a long time, maintaining their language and some customs. At the end of the twelfth century Gerald of Wales visited them, and even as late as the sixteenth century it was reported that some Flemish dialect was still spoken there. The example of the Flemish is instructive because, like the Danes earlier, their numbers were swelled by mercenaries who on various occasions were recruited to help the English kings. As in previous centuries this was all very well but could become a problem when the

[16] Greenway, ed., *Henry, Archdeacon of Huntingdon Historia Anglorum*, pp. 340–1.
[17] J. Gillingham, *The English in the Twelfth Century* (Woodbridge, 2000), pp. 135–6.
[18] L. Toorians, 'Wizo Flandrensis and the Flemish settlement in Pembrokeshire', *Cambridge Medieval Celtic Studies*, 20 (1990), 99–118

soldiers were not kept under control, or if they turned against the king. Across our period royal agents in charge of maintaining law and order may not always have found it easy to distinguish between those foreigners (Flemings or Danes) who quietly went about their business and those who professionally carried arms occasionally breaking the peace. Whereas under King Stephen these Flemish were royal supporters, under his successor Henry II they were seen as a liability and, according to William of Newburgh, in 1154 by royal edict expelled from the country. Their leader, William of Ypres, had his English income confiscated in an action that again reminds us of previous occasions when Danes or French had been called in as royal supporters but were exiled when they were perceived as threatening. There is no evidence of executions, but the forced expulsion combined with the withdrawal of £440 per annum which had been at William of Ypres's disposal under Stephen gives some idea of centralized royal power that could be enforced to get rid of unwanted foreigners on a scale Continental rulers could only dream of.[19] However, in terms of the economy overall, the king recognized the importance of Flemish merchants, who, like other foreign merchants, lived under his protection with the same *murdrum* fines Cnut and William had used for the protection of their occupation armies. It is extremely interesting, therefore, that English history in our period reveals a see-sawing development of on/off royal action, and at times formal legislation, along lines of ethnicity (Edgar in 970, Æthelred in 1002, Cnut in 1018, William the Conqueror in 1066–7, Henry I in 1108 and Henry II in 1154/7). These royal decisions highlight flashpoints of acute social and political anxiety, which however were not necessarily long-lasting. Consequently, we must be careful not to extrapolate too much from these incidents and instead imagine a reality of communities often suffering from ethnic tension that posed a permanent threat to social order.

In the Middle Ages, as in our own time, there is plenty of evidence that after their arrival in England immigrants tended to live (and die) together. Unsurprisingly, such evidence comes primarily from urban areas. We have already referred to the Scandinavian settlement in tenth-century York, where they developed urban quarters predominantly non-English. There was a mid-eleventh-century Danish cemetery in London (not far from St Paul's), while the Irish seemed to have settled around St Bride's.

[19] *William of Newburgh, Historia Rerum Anglicarum*, in R. Howlett, ed., *Chronicles of the Reigns of Stephen, Henry II, and Richard I* (4 vols.; RS; London, 1884), i, pp. 101–2; R. Eales, 'Local loyalties in Norman England: Kent in Stephen's reign', *ANS* 8 [(1985 (1986))], p. 107.

In Winchester, too, there was some immigration from Danish followers of Cnut for whom Winchester became the favourite residence. After 1066 Southampton had a 'French' street running parallel to the main 'English' street. Domesday Book mentions a French community in Shrewsbury occupying one fifth of all the messuages. They paid the same rate as in King Edward's time, whereas the English burgesses on top of the tax for their own plots were made to cover the loss of income from the fifty-one messuages destroyed to make room for the Norman castle. Similarly in Hereford the French received preferential treatment compared with the English.[20] Nottingham, incidentally one of the Five Boroughs (towns in the Danelaw), imposed different legal practices on the French and English boroughs; it is unknown whether this legal distinction, perhaps for different ethnicities, predates the Norman Conquest.[21] Although the names of ethnic quarters long outlived what might initially have been segregated living, such as for example the district of 'Flammengaria' or 'Flemingate' in Beverley, they remind us of the human nature of immigrants initially to cluster together for mutual support, social customs and not least the comfort of being able to speak one's own language. However, for one group assimilation was not tolerated on religious grounds, so on the whole in England, as elsewhere in Europe, the Jews continued living in the same neighbourhoods within towns for social and religious reasons (see Chapter III.3 and Chapter IV.4).

To what extent did immigrants keep in touch with their families and friends at home? Given the distances involved, in particular to Scandinavia, and the cost of travelling, any personal visits would be relatively sporadic. Most communication presumably was through oral messages by travelling acquaintances; letters were still rare. Virtually nothing is known about any contacts that the immigrant Danes and Norse maintained in the ninth and tenth centuries. Anyone who arrived in the company of kings Svein and Cnut may have remained in touch with home as King Cnut travelled back and forth between England and Denmark at least five times between 1016 and his death in 1035. Since Cnut held together a North Sea empire, government, trade and religious contacts kept lines of communication open. Several Scandinavian rune-stones (from Denmark, Sweden and Norway) record men who went to England, with some revealing a record of burial in England, which in itself indicates that news did

[20] DB, i, fols. 252r and 179r.

[21] H. Thomas, *The English and the Normans: Ethnic Hostility, Assimilation and Identity, 1066–c. 1220* (Oxford, 2003), p. 190.

travel back home. A splendid stone from Nävelsjö parish in Nöbbelesholm (Sweden), one of thirteen to mention burial in England, records that one Gunnar, son of Hrothi, was buried by his brother Helge at Bath and that the memorial at home was erected by Gunnar's son Gunnkel.[22] During this time, too, we know that Ralph de Gael's father, also named Ralph, spent some time in Brittany on his maternal family's estates, perhaps as a result of temporary exile. The situation after the Norman Conquest was similar, with much to-ing and fro-ing across the Channel, though as the occupation of England lasted longer and longer, families who initially held land on both sides of the Channel increasingly divided their lands along geographical lines. Different branches of the same family held land exclusively either in Normandy or England, establishing a way of managing the family's estates which was practical and convenient. The 1066 veteran Robert of Beaumont (d. 1118), for example, divided his lands between his twin sons, with the Norman patrimony going to Waleran of Meulan and Robert of Leicester receiving the English estates. A study of the burial practices of Anglo-Norman families suggests that in the first generation recent immigrants to England still made plans to have their bodies returned to Normandy because that was where they had burial places reserved (and paid for) in monasteries.[23] Subsequent generations founded religious houses and churches overseas, not least to provide their children and grandchildren with a final resting place in their new home country. There are important exceptions, as in the case of William and Gundrada of Warenne, who were both buried at St Pancras, Lewes, in 1083 and *c.* 1088, respectively. The tombstone of Flemish-born Gundrada is, incidentally, the oldest surviving for a woman in medieval England (Figure 15). Immigrants were sometimes targeted by fundraisers at home. In Normandy this was a practice that had been established and perfected during the years of Norman emigration to southern Italy in the early eleventh century. In northern France, knowledge of England's wealth was widespread – it had after all been one of the prime reasons for the conquests of England – so when in 1113 a group of Laon canons travelled to southwest England in order to raise funds for the repairs to their cathedral

[22] B. Sawyer, *The Viking-Age Rune-Stones. Custom and Commemoration in Early Medieval Scandinavia* (Oxford, 2000), p. 117, plate 25, and M. Syrrett, *The Vikings in England: The Evidence of Runic Inscriptions* (Cambridge, 2002).

[23] B. Golding, 'Anglo-Norman knightly burials', in C. Harper-Bill and R. Harvey, eds., *The Ideals and Practice of Medieval Knighthood. Papers from the First and Second Strawberry Hill Conferences* (Woodbridge, 1986), pp. 35–48; E. Cownie, *Religious Patronage in Anglo-Norman England 1066–1135* (Woodbridge, 1998), pp. 212–15.

they called in on Judhael, a Norman of Breton origin, who lived in Totnes (Devon), because his wife from Picquigny was known to them.

MIGRATION

But what do we know about migration, the movement around England by its inhabitants, for temporary or permanent reasons? The king and his aristocracy, the tenants-in-chief, led itinerant lives. Kings and barons with their followers travelled from place to place in order to solve disputes, hear court cases and keep an eye on their estates. There was also an important economic reason underpinning the continuous caravanning through the countryside, because no one manor, not even large ones like royal Brampton, could provide food, drink and accommodation for a king and retinue of many hundred followers and animals (such as horses and dogs) for more than ten days or a fortnight at most (see also Chapter I.1). Stocks would need replenishing. In the tenth and eleventh centuries the royal court journeyed primarily in Wessex, where Winchester, Westminster and Woodstock near Oxford were the most popular bases. After 1066 Windsor gained in popularity, while Henry I set up in Brampton (Huntingdonshire) and Henry II Northampton; journeys further north were rare.[24] The great barons held land in various counties, where they lived in the castles associated with their honour. The Warennes, for example, divided their time between the castles in Lewes (East Sussex), Castle Acre (Norfolk) and Knaresborough (Yorkshire). Lordship in our period meant that lords had control over their peasants and tenants and would carefully control the absence, temporary or permanent, of their workforce, or those who looked after the workforce. Most people in England would live all their lives in the locality in which they were born and would move around in the immediate locality for certain special events, such as ecclesiastical processions to nearby episcopal sees or to court sessions at the hundred or shire court. Such journeys were usually undisputed and undertaken with the agreement of the local lords, especially where they concerned services for them. This is particularly true for the lower ranks of society in the countryside like peasants or slaves, or the burghers in towns. Town customs, as recorded in Domesday Book, provide evidence for regular movement from countryside to town and vice versa. The Chester customs, for example, stipulate that the town's reeve calls up one man per hide in the shire for repair duties on the walls

[24] R. Bartlett, *England under the Norman and Angevin Kings 1075–1225* (Oxford, 2000), p. 135.

and bridge in the city. Alternatively, if one wished to move (permanently) out of the town as the customs of Hereford envisage, the reeve's consent was necessary.[25] Although freedom of burghers in towns was the norm, freedom to move permanently elsewhere was restricted. Anyone with a lord, and that meant most people, had to have his or her permission to move away from their home. Runaways were chased and punished, as we learn from Burton upon Trent, where two peasants ran away from the monastery and sought shelter with Roger Poitevin in a nearby village. Burton's abbot demanded restitution from Roger when it became clear that the men refused to return home.[26] In a sense, therefore, freedom of movement as we know it now did not exist in medieval England. Clearly merchants, craftsmen and traders, by the nature of their work, travelled around under the king's protection, but anyone wanting to up sticks had to ask permission from their lord. By Henry I's time, however, formal procedures were put in place to deal with the homeless or itinerant person (*homo vagans*) with and without a lord, and it was understood that those without land might move outside the county in order to find work.[27]

The control over people's movements, leading to migration, is nowhere more clear than in the laws regulating exile and outlawry, although it ought to be noted that how these norms worked in practice is not always easy to trace. Exile and outlawry were punishments that were either imposed on an individual and his family by a court (royal, shire or hundred), or could be voluntary, or in many cases the sources do not allow us a definitive conclusion as to who instigated the expulsion.[28] Such temporary exile or outlawry, as the author of the *Life of Hereward* tells us, let 'things cool down a bit' and allowed reflection for the two parties concerned.[29] Any banning would be ended by royal decree, so for example Eadric of Laxfield was inlawed again by Edward the Confessor himself. Only in York, far away from the centre of royal authority, could a sheriff,

[25] DB, i, fols. 262 and 179r.

[26] R. Bartlett, ed. and trans., *Geoffrey of Burton, Life and Miracles of St Modwenna* (OMT; Oxford, 2002), pp. 192–7; D. Postles, 'Migration and mobility in a less mature economy: English internal migration *c.* 1200–1350', *Social History*, 25 (2000), 285–99.

[27] L. C. Downer, ed., *Leges Henrici Primi* (Oxford, 1972), 8, 4–5, pp. 102–3; Postles, 'Migration and mobility', p. 295.

[28] E. van Houts, 'The vocabulary of exile and outlawry in the North Sea area around the first millennium', in L. Napran and E. van Houts, eds., *Exile in the Middle Ages. Selected Proceedings from the International Medieval Congress, University of Leeds, 8–11 July 2002* (International Medieval Research, 14; Turnhout, 2004), pp. 13–28.

[29] 'ut interim ista tepescerent': *Gesta Herewardi incliti exulis et militis*, in T. D. Hardy and C. T. Martin, eds., *Lestorie des Engles solum la translacion maistre Geffrei Gaimar* (2 vols.; RS; London, 1888), i, p. 370.

too, give dispensation for a return. Often culprits were allowed to come back, because their presence (manpower, military know-how and family support) was deemed more advantageous than their absence, which might necessitate difficult decisions such as forfeiture of land which had then to be given to someone else at the risk of rebellion by other family members. Sometimes we hear of outlawry at the moment of the imposition of the punishment without knowing the precise details of the lawsuit. For example, in King Edgar's reign a (widowed) mother and son were found guilty of witchcraft because they had stuck pins in a wax image of Wulfstan Uccea's father Ælfsige; the mother was drowned at London Bridge, but the son escaped and, as a fugitive of the law, became an outlaw.[30] In this case although their land was forfeited and ended up in the possession first of Wulfstan and then Æthelwold, bishop of Winchester, the fate of the fugitive is unknown. Other cases of peacetime exile concern those of Earl Godwin's son Tostig and Hereward the Wake in the mid-1060s; both men fled to Flanders, where in Saint-Omer they worked in a military capacity for the count. As temporary emigrants they earned a living by using their war skills. The eleventh-century military conquests resulted in various cases of outlawry. King Cnut outlawed Ealdorman Æthelweard and Earl Thorkell the Tall, while Domesday Book testifies to a considerable number of cases after 1066. Several men connected with St Benet's Holme fled to Denmark (Abbot Alfwold, a certain Ringulf and Eadric the steersman), all of whom came back in due course, as did the other Denmark refugee, Abbot Æthelsige of St Augustine in Canterbury.[31] Skalpi, King Harold's housecarl, as an outlaw forfeited his land because he had gone to York, where he died. He is generally thought to have fought as part of the last-ditch defence of the North against the Conqueror.[32] Thus it is clear that high-status outlaws with skills, although (temporarily) dispossessed, might find a living elsewhere by doing what they did best: fighting. Foreign rulers or resistance movements would provide them with shelter and protection. The abundance of evidence for exiles fleeing abroad may be explained by the fact that the English were forbidden by law (II Cnut 13) to provide shelter to outlaws, and those who did would be outlawed themselves, as the widow Æthelflæd, sister of Leofsige, found. In 1007 the ealdorman had been accused of treason and forfeited his lands, while five years later his sister

30 Sawyer, *Anglo-Saxon Charters*, no. 1377, with translation in *EHD*, i, no. 112, p. 519.

31 F. Stenton, 'St. Benet Holme and the Norman conquest', *EHR*, 37 (1922), 225–35, at 227, 233.

32 A. Williams, *The English and the Norman Conquest* (Woodbridge, 1995), pp. 34–5.

was accused of having sheltered him and on that account lost her lands as well.[33] Bereft of indigenous support, exiles became emigrants by fleeing abroad. The twelfth-century legal tract the *Laws of Edward* elaborates on the effect of Cnut's law by explicitly stating that any murder or traitor, if granted his life and limbs, was not allowed to stay in the country, and thus in effect became a foreign exile.[34] This penalty for treason explains why a considerable number of Englishmen fled the country after the eleventh-century foreign invasions. How exactly the king or his representatives were supposed to police the migration is unknown. Life as an outlaw was potentially grim unless one had a skill that was desirable for others. The fictional image of the outlaw is that of a war hero-migrant on the run who during his adventures stands up for moral values, defending the poor and weak against the might of the lord who had dispossessed him. Inevitably the families of outlaws were caught up in their fate in one way or another. Wives could be excused if they could prove that they had not known about their spouse's action, but even if innocent they were vulnerable and loss of land occurred. In exceptional cases outlawry resulted in permanent exile overseas, which leads us to turn from migration to emigration.

EMIGRATION

In our period people left England for a variety of reasons, some political (such as escape after military defeats, permanent exile or military service) some economic (lack of land or poverty) and some social (marriage or joining family members who had emigrated) or religious. Not all departures were intended from the start as permanent emigration. Social status determined the element of freedom in the decision to leave, as we have already seen in the previous section on migration. In the Middle Ages people could not normally leave their land without permission of their lord or, ultimately, the king. Unauthorized absence was punished severely in order to prevent precious manpower (essential for labour on fields, military duty and other services) draining away. Most emigrants therefore left under unusual circumstances, when a lord's authority was weakened. Although most cases of recorded emigration concern men, if they were married they were often joined by their families.

33 Sawyer, *Anglo-Saxon Charters*, no. 916 (1007 Leofsige's outlawry), no. 926 (1012 forfeiture of Æthelflæd).

34 Bruce R. O'Brien, *God's Peace and King's Peace: The Laws of Edward the Confessor* (Philadelphia, 1999), pp. 176–7 and introduction, p. 81.

Departure as a result of defeat in combat – be it military expedition or, rarely, a full-blown battle – was common, especially after the military takeovers in the eleventh century. It is well attested for the Norman Conquest of England. A number of Anglo-Saxon men fled from Hastings and travelled down the Danube to the east. It was from their mouths probably that the annalist of the monastery of Nieder-Altaich in Bavaria took down what is one of the few eyewitness accounts of the battle. In Constantinople the men took service with the Byzantine emperor, very much like the Norse and Danes who for decades had been recruited to serve amongst the Varangians as imperial bodyguards, before ending up in a small colony at Civitot near Nicaea (modern Iznik in Turkey). These men are known only as an anonymous group, except perhaps for Wulfric of Lincoln, who in 1100 as ambassador for Emperor Alexius Comnenos to Henry I and his wife Matilda paid a visit to Abingdon. Denmark and Flanders, as we have seen, were other favourite destinations for defeated Englishmen not only in 1066 but at other times as well. King Harold's mother, Gytha, fled to Saint-Omer in 1067, where her widowed daughter-in-law, Judith (Flemish by birth), had found refuge a year earlier. They were joined by Gytha's daughter Gunhild, who led a peripatetic life, spending some time in Denmark with distant relatives before returning to Flanders, where she died and was buried at St Donat's church at Bruges, judging by a contemporary plaque containing her epitaph (Figure 12). And what about fighting abroad, especially during the crusades? Did these campaigns encourage men and women from England to emigrate permanently? Although a fair number of Englishmen went on crusade only a few can be found as permanent settlers in the Holy Land. Ernulf of Hesdin, a second-generation Continental immigrant to England, had left England as an exiled penitent, perhaps with the intention of settling in the Holy Land, but he died at Antioch *c.* 1100. Most information relates to English participation in the Third Crusade (1147–8), when we catch a glimpse of a group of English sailors and merchants who went to the Holy Land via Lisbon in 1147 (see also Chapter III.4). Some of them never returned home but seemed to have moved to the Spanish east coast, where in Tortosa from the late 1140s an English trading community prospered.[35]

Nearer to home emigrants from England settled in neighbouring principalities of the British Isles. The most interesting aspect of the evidence must be that the emigrants from England to Wales and Scotland were

[35] A. Virgilii, '*Angli cum multis aliis alienigenis*: crusade settlers in Tortosa (second half of the twelfth century)', *JMH*, 35 (2009), 297–312.

Figure 12 Gunhild (d. 1087) burial plaque. This is a lead plaque inscribed with a brief biography of Gunhild, daughter of Earl Godwine and Gytha. It was buried with her in the coffin when she died in 1087 in Flanders. The object is now in the Cathedral of St Salvator, Bruges (Belgium).
Photograph by Jean-Luc Elias (2005), published by permission of the Royal Institute for Cultural Heritage Belgium, © KIK-IRPA, Brussels, object number 144772 and cliché number Z011814

frequently recent arrivals in England themselves. Often they were younger sons of first-generation Continental immigrants to England who were lured to more distant pastures. As Robert Bartlett and Geoffrey Barrow have pointed out, the ones who went to Scotland came at the invitation of the kings, keen to install them as landholders in the border areas.[36] The royal aim was twofold. These men brought with them practical knowledge of the manorial economy and would provide valuable services to the king such as overseeing the building of castles, recruiting soldiers and serving from time to time in the king's household. Amongst the earliest emigrants to Scotland were the dynasties of the Brus and Stewart. Robert I de Brus (d. 1141), lord of Brix and Cleveland (North Yorkshire) received Annandale in *c.* 1124; after his death his English lands went to his eldest son and his Scottish land to the younger, also called Robert. The Stewarts descended from Walter, third son of the Breton Alan fitzFlaad, who in *c.* 1136 became steward of King David of Scotland. Others were younger sons of Norman families settled in England who benefitted from the patronage of Malcolm IV, such as John of Vaux (near Rouen), who became lord of Dirleton in East Lothian; Robert de Quincy took his name from a place near Béthune in French Flanders, received land in East Lothian and Fife and was responsible for the import of several countrymen. A Flemish colony in the 1150s had established itself in Clydesdale. From William de Lion's reign dates the arrival along a similar route of Philip de Valognes and Philip de Mowbray. Ultimately of Continental origin, these men came without, it seems, their own peasants, but settled as Englishmen.

The situation in Wales was different, because only the southern and most eastern fringe fell (intermittently) under the control of the kings of the English, from the early eleventh century, who from then on consistently used the marcher areas as a springboard for further inroads into the principality. The primary strategy was to colonize the march from Herefordshire in the south to Cheshire in the north with men whose royal rewards of land (in fact land robbed from the Welsh) would bind them to the English throne. Under Cnut we find several important Danish followers such as Hakon and Hrani in the area, followed under Edward the Confessor by Norman settlers, such as Richard fitzScrob, his son Osbern fitzRichard, Alfred of Marlborough and Earl Ralph, the king's nephew, in Herefordshire.[37] By the time of the Norman Conquest, these men – although legally English (as all pre-Conquest Frenchmen were) – held on

[36] G. W. S. Barrow, *The Anglo-Norman Era in Scottish History. The Ford Lectures Delivered in the University of Oxford in Hilary Term 1977* (Oxford, 1980); Bartlett, *England under the Norman and Angevin Kings*, pp. 80–8.

[37] M. K. Lawson, *Cnut. The Danes in England in the Early Eleventh Century* (Harlow, 1993), pp. 165–6; C. P. Lewis, 'The Norman settlement of Herefordshire under William I', *ANS* 7 [(1984 (1985))], 195–213.

to their marcher estates and were joined in the north around Chester by Hugh of Avranches and later Arnulf of Montgomery. By then, however, the landed wealth of these men meant that their marcher possessions on the whole were less important than their estates elsewhere in England and Normandy. Amongst the earliest foreign earls after the Norman Conquest was the Fleming Gerbod at Chester, who left in 1070, and after a hiatus of forty years we find in the Welsh borderlands the Flemish colony moved by Henry I from Cumbria to Pembrokeshire.

The story of emigration to Ireland is a more recent one for the landed classes. For it was from Wales in the 1170s that Ireland was conquered, and many Cambro-Norman younger sons benefitted from land grants by Henry II which enabled them to set up estates across the Irish Sea. As the *Song of Dermot*, a vernacular Old French poem on the conquest of Ireland, tells us, the early settlers can be found along the eastern border of Ireland, especially in the counties of Leinster and Meath. Other emigration to Ireland consisted not of landholders but of traders and artisans from western England attracted by job opportunities in Dublin, some as early as the tenth century (see below, 'Maritime migrations'). As Robert Bartlett has shown, the earliest part of a list of Dublin tax payers, dating to *c.* 1175–1205, lists a total of 2,800 people, of whom just under half are men with toponymics as surnames. Clusters of more than thirty surnames each bear witness to emigration from south Wales, the area between Hereford and Gloucester, London and Glasgow, and clusters of between sixteen and thirty names reveal origins from Winchester, the Midlands and the Welsh borders.[38] They were taxpayers, and consequently their income suggests that their departure from England was an economic success and that as burghers of Dublin they flourished.

Marriage was another reason why English women, and occasionally men, left England, usually those at the upper end of the social scale. Empress Matilda (1102–67), daughter of King Henry I and Edith-Matilda, spent a few years in Trier before she married in order to be educated in German language and customs. After one and a half decades as queen consort to Henry V (d. 1126), she returned as widow but soon remarried and became countess of Anjou, bearing her husband three sons in quick succession. Between 1139 and 1147 she was back in England, the country of her childhood, in order to lay claim to the royal throne. Unsuccessful in this quest, she retired to Normandy, where she spent the

[38] R. J. Bartlett, *The Making of Europe* (Harmondsworth, 1993), pp. 181–3, with map 7 showing the geographical spread.

last twenty years of her life. Her granddaughters, daughters of Henry II and Eleanor, all followed in her footsteps and married abroad: in 1168 Matilda (1156–89) married Henry, duke of Saxony, in 1176 Eleanor (1161–1214) married Alphonso of Castile and the next year Joan (1165–99) married King William II of Sicily and two decades later Raymond VI, count of Toulouse. If their young age upon departure from home, at respectively twelve, fifteen and eleven years old, seems shocking to us now, the girls were still more mature than their grandmother, Empress Matilda, who had been eight when she said goodbye to her parents. Not since King Æthelstan (924–39) had sent his sisters abroad to the Holy Roman Empire and Flanders were English princesses (and their lavish dowries) so sought after on the Continent. Yet, whereas the tenth-century girls knew Old English and perhaps a smattering of Latin, their younger counterparts were fluent in French, probably well versed in Latin, yet may have known only a few words of English. Unlike royal women, aristocratic women and those lower down the social scale usually stayed nearer to home.

Amongst the clergy it was quite normal to travel extensively, though emigration as such was less common. When these men left England they may never have anticipated that they would spend the rest of their lives away from the country, in which case emigration was not a move that was consciously planned. For unknown reasons, though perhaps forced by events in the aftermath of the Norman Conquest, the monk Ælnoth of Canterbury (d. *c.* 1122) lived in Odense (Denmark), where after twenty-four years, as he tells us, he wrote a biography of King Cnut IV (d. 1085). His younger contemporary Robert of Ely followed in his footsteps by writing a *Life* of King Lavard (killed in 1131). Whereas once Frankish and Flemish hagiographers had come to England to offer their literary services, now England exported this same skill to countries only recently interested in having indigenous traditions recorded in Latin. Others left England in pursuit of foreign administrative employment. In the early twelfth century the secular clerk Nicholas Breakspear went to the Continent never to return. First he became abbot of St Hug in Arles (Provence), then cardinal-bishop of Albano and lastly in Rome the first, and thus far only, English pope, Adrian IV (1154–9). The historian Gervase of Tilbury, author of the *Otia Imperialia*, written for Emperor Otto IV, was a secular clerk, too, who – like Henry of Huntingdon – was married. He began his Continental career at the University of Bologna and spent some time at the courts of Henry II and William II of Sicily before ending up (like Nicholas Breakspear before him) in Arles. There the archbishop, Imbert d'Aignières, gave him a job as judge and married him off to one of his relatives. After the death of his wife Gervase became a Premonstratensian canon and died *c.* 1222, either in Marseilles or England.[39]

MARITIME MIGRATIONS

The imposition of foreign rule in England, either in specific areas, such as York in the tenth century, or countrywide, as after the Danish and Norman conquests in the eleventh century, resulted in multiple maritime migrations between the settlers' homelands and England, manifesting themselves as flows and counter-flows. Apart from the landed aristocracy, we can trace such movements particularly amongst specific groups of skilled workers, such as moneyers and precious metalworkers.[40] An English moneyer called Godwine was active in Denmark under Svein Forkbeard (d. 1014) striking coins modelled on those in England, while the lid of a pen case found in Lund (Sweden) bears the name of Leofwine, who is thought to have been another minter. Archaeological evidence has revealed English moneyers also at work at Viborg. From both places we now have English-style brooches and dress hooks as well as some ivory work with English names 'Eadrinc' and 'Hikuin' inscribed on combs. In the early twelfth century a moneyer called Ansketil worked for King Niels of Denmark (d. 1134) as a goldsmith in charge of the royal administration of mints. After the king's death we find him as a monk at St Albans, where he instructed Salomon of Ely, a royal goldsmith. The 'English' expertise in working gold and minting, however, in itself owed much to the input of eleventh-century German immigrants to London. The most famous amongst them was Otto 'the goldsmith', who married an English widow, Leofgifu, was a benefactor of Bury St Edmunds and decorated William the Conqueror's tomb in 1087. Their descendants were hereditary moneyers at London. From Caen came the moneyer Ranulf, whose eldest son, Waleran, set up as a minter in Colchester; a younger son, Richard, and his issue remained in Normandy.[41]

39 S. E. Banks and J. W. Binns, eds. and trans., *Gervase of Tilbury, Otia imperialia, Recreation for an Emperor* (OMT; Oxford, 2002), pp. xxvi–xxxviii.

40 E. Roesdahl, 'Denmark–England in the eleventh century: the growing archaeological evidence for contacts across the North Sea', in N. Lund, ed., *Seksogtyvende tværfaglige vikingesymposium Københavns Universitet 2007* (Aarhus, 2007), pp. 14–19. E. van Houts, 'Nuns and goldsmiths: the foundation and early benefactors of St Radegund's priory in Cambridge', in D. Abulafia, M. Franklin and M. Rubin, eds., *Church and City 1000–1500. Essays in Honour of Christopher Brooke* (Cambridge, 1992), p. 69.

41 DB, ii, fol. 107v.

Trading contacts meant that merchants travelled round, and having seen opportunities abroad decided to stay, often if finances allowed, building up trade on both sides of the sea. Gilbert, the father of Thomas Becket, was a modest merchant, possibly from Rouen, who by the 1120s had settled in London. The family was prosperous but nevertheless took lodgers, such as the learned brothers Eustace and Baldwin from Boulogne. From these contacts we can surmise that the Beckets did business with men in harbours along the Channel coasts. Little did anyone then know that Thomas would be martyred and that his tomb in turn would be frequented by pilgrims, amongst whom were merchants from as far away as Cologne. From this Rhine town in the late twelfth century, Arnold, one such merchant, and his wife, Ode, travelled to England, where they paid their respects at Thomas's shrine in Canterbury. They also visited London, liked the city and decided to stay. We know of their decision from the autobiography of their grandson, Arnold Fitzthedmar of London (d. 1274/5), son of their daughter, Juliana, who had married a fellow German emigrant, Thedmar of Bremen. Arnold became a prosperous and distinguished burgher of London, who as 'alderman of the Germans' was involved in the Baltic trade.[42] An older contemporary, William Cade, the Flemish moneylender who bankrolled many of King Henry II's military enterprises, also held properties in England and Flanders. And grandfather Arnold's younger contemporary, Thierry Teutonicus ('the German'), also from Cologne, managed to make himself indispensable at the court of King John and his son Henry III, while at the same time making trade profits in London, King's Lynn, Boston and Stamford.[43] Not only men but women were actively engaged in trans-maritime trade. The great Rouen matriarch Emma the 'vicecomitissa' (viscountess) created during a career of forty years (1158–98) a trading empire which at times comprised the farm of Southampton as well as the *vicomté de l'eau* (all tolls of transport across the River Seine) at Rouen, and who used her own silver to provide loans to others, including the English kings. As she can be traced as holding (and living in) properties in both cities it is clear that cross-maritime work required residency in both countries. The Abbotstone family on both sides of the Irish Sea provides an interesting parallel, even though their wealth ranked them lower than Emma. The growing links between southwest England and Ireland from the

[42] J. P. Huffmann, *Family, Commerce, and Religion in London and Cologne. Anglo-German Emigrants, c. 1000–c. 1300* (Cambridge, 1998), pp. 189–96.

[43] N. Fryde, *Ein mittelalterlicher deutscher Grossunternehmer. Terricus Teutonicus de Coloniania in England, 1217–47* (Stuttgart, 1997) and Huffmann, *Family*, pp. 180–8.

1170s onwards are exemplified in William of Abbotstone, who together with his daughter Dionysia held trading interests and houses in Bristol and Dublin. Property management established by Emma and Dionysia in turn enabled their sons to continue their mother's business acumen.[44] This evidence testifies to creation of wealth by maritime trade in family businesses where men and women collaborate side by side (and down generations) through arrangements whereby delegation of authority to make decisions was required. Having discussed invasions and migration by exploring the various comings and goings in England, there remain three specific aspects of English migration that need discussion in greater detail in three subchapters: the problem of ethnicity and acculturation, the role of intermarriage and the experience of the Jews.

[44] For Emma, see L. Delisle, ed., *Recueil des actes de Henri II* (Paris, 1909), pp. 212–17; for William of Abbotstone and Dionysia, see J. Crick, 'The Irish in England from Cnut to John: speculations on a linguistic interface', in E. Tyler, ed., *Conceptualizing Multilingualism, 800–1250* (Turnhout, in press).

CHAPTER IV.2

Ethnicity and acculturation

D. M. Hadley

Over the last twenty years the constructed nature of ethnic identity has been extensively discussed, and both historians and archaeologists have explored the processes – often dubbed 'ethnogenesis' – by which ethnic groups came into existence, were transformed and, in some cases, disappeared. This branch of scholarship has mainly focused on the societies of the early post-Roman centuries, but studies of later periods have more recently begun to address similar issues. Drawing on both historical and archaeological evidence, this subchapter explores the construction of ethnic identity and the processes of acculturation in England in the wake of successive invasions and migrations during the period *c.* 900–1200. Despite the presence of various migrant groups, who were frequently in the political ascendancy and in some regions were also numerically dominant, a sense of Englishness prevailed, both politically and culturally.

For much of the twentieth century researchers of the early medieval period regarded ethnic identity as largely unproblematic, and as readily identifiable from the ascription of ethnic labels to individuals and groups in contemporary sources and from discrete distributions of material culture. Such attitudes have, however, been thrown into sharp relief by scholarly developments since the 1980s. Patrick Geary memorably described ethnic identity as 'a situational construct', liable to be modified according to circumstances, and he argued that 'early medieval ethnicity should be viewed as a subjective process by which individuals and groups identified themselves or others within specific situations and for specific purposes'.[1] The so-called 'Vienna school' of historians, among whom Walter Pohl is prominent, have taken their lead from the work of Reinhard Wenskus, who in the 1960s had argued that ethnic identity among the Germanic tribes was based on a group perception of shared characteristics,

[1] P. Geary, 'Ethnic identity as a situational construct in the early Middle Ages', *Mitteilungen der Anthropologischen Gesellschaft in Wien*, 113 (1983), 15–26, at 16.

'*Zusammensgehörigkeitsgefühl*' (literally 'a feeling of togetherness').[2] It is now appreciated that ethnic labels are not used consistently in early medieval written sources, and that groups may identify themselves differently from the ways in which outsiders describe them; thus, the application of ethnic terminology is not necessarily a reliable guide to contemporary ethnic identities. Moreover, it is salutary to note that early medieval chroniclers seldom refer to the ethnic affiliations of individuals, and that ethnic identity is particularly likely to be mentioned during times of conflict. Detailed case studies have also revealed that the diverse sources of evidence typically used to identify ethnic groups – for example, the territories associated with particular named ethnic groups, linguistic groups, political boundaries and areas characterized by distinctive assemblages of material culture – rarely coincide precisely.

Scholarship on early medieval migrations has recently begun to be influenced by research on modern migrations, which has provided new insights. Studies of contemporary migrations by social scientists and anthropologists have highlighted the wide range of reasons why individuals migrate, which typically include a range of 'push' factors (such as competition for resources in the homeland, limited opportunity for improvement of social and political circumstances, and oppression) and 'pull' factors (such as the opportunity for material gain and social and political advancement). Where migrants settle has also been shown to be informed by often extensive networks of communication between the homelands and those regions to which migrants travel. The implications of such studies are that we might expect to find that early medieval migrations were far from 'free-for-alls', instead being influenced by existing social networks and hierarchies.

It is also apparent from studies of recent migrations that the migrating population rarely mirrors exactly the communities from which it departs; the elderly and the very young are often under-represented in migrating groups, and the first waves of migration, especially in contexts of conflict, may include disproportionately large numbers of young adult males.[3] In this respect, it is notable that James Barrett has recently proposed a new model for the causes of the Viking Age, which focuses on male behaviour within Scandinavian society. Having rejected traditional arguments that

[2] See, for example, W. Pohl and H. Reimitz, eds., *Strategies of Distinction. The Construction of Ethnic Communities, 300–800* (Leiden, 1998).

[3] S. Trafford, 'Ethnicity, migration theory, and historiography', in D. M. Hadley, and J. D. Richards, eds., *Cultures in Contact: Scandinavian Settlement in England in the Ninth and Tenth Centuries* (Turnhout, 2000), pp. 17–39.

focus on technological developments in shipping and both environmental and demographic determinism, Barrett suggests that competition for wealth with which to win a bride may have created the circumstances in which participation in raiding parties became a common element of the Scandinavian male's life cycle. This deduction is supported, for what it is worth, by the later sagas, which also offer a possible explanation for this proposed competition between young males in the form of the practice of selective female infanticide within pre-Christian Scandinavian society, which would have increased the competition for a wife. Barrett takes his inspiration from recent historical research on the implications of the so-called 'youth bulge' in modern societies, in which warfare is posited as a frequent corollary of disproportionately large numbers of young males in society.[4] If migrating groups did, indeed, contain disproportionate numbers of males, then intermarriage with the host population may have been an important element of the acculturation process, as may also have been the children of such unions (see Chapter IV.3). Indeed, much recent migration theory has emphasized the importance of children as arbiters of cultural interaction. Moreover, it is notable that three of the most important commentators on the impact of the Norman Conquest – William of Malmesbury, Henry of Huntingdon and Orderic Vitalis – were products of mixed marriages, whose upbringings arguably influenced their perception of the Conquest and its effects on personal identity.

ETHNICITY IN THE PERIOD *C.* 900–1200

In England the period between *c.* 900 and 1200 is characterized by a rich array of written and archaeological sources with which we can explore ethnic identity. In the written record it is not difficult to find evidence for the perceived ethnic distinctiveness of the various migrant groups who came to England at this time. For example, in the decades after the Norman Conquest contemporary chroniclers frequently commented on the differences between the Normans and the English, focusing on language, law, military practices, hairstyles and clothing. Even religion marked out the English and the Normans as distinct, since despite having Christianity in common there were subtle, but contentious, differences in liturgical practices. However, the issue to be considered here is not whether such cultural differences existed – they certainly did – but how they were overcome, how the incomers acculturated to English society,

[4] J. Barrett, 'What caused the Viking Age?', *Antiquity*, 82 (2008), 671–85.

how the indigenous population responded to the arrival of new groups and whether, or for how long, ethnic allegiance was a determining factor in behaviour. Such matters have frequently been reduced to debates about the scale of settlement of particular groups, but this is difficult to assess in the early medieval period, and is usually only indirectly discernible, typically in the linguistic and archaeological record. Moreover, the scale of settlement cannot be regarded as a predictable factor in ethnic relations or in the processes of acculturation.

The application of ethnic labels to individuals and groups has often formed the starting point for debates about ethnicity, although the hazards of such evidence are now recognized. In the later tenth century, both Edgar and Æthelred legislated for regions that had previously been settled by Scandinavians, and their law codes have long been regarded as evidence for a kingdom riven by ethnic difference that could be objectively codified. A clause in Edgar's fourth law code (of the 960s or 970s) stipulated that 'secular rights should be in force among the Danes according to such good laws as they best decide on', while Æthelred's law code issued in 997 at Wantage (Berkshire) contains much Scandinavian terminology and has been contrasted with a broadly contemporary code issued at Woodstock (Oxfordshire) that was said to be 'according to the laws of the English'. Once regarded as evidence that the newcomers were living under separate legal provision, this legislation has more recently been interpreted as indicative of the limitations regional interests placed on tenth-century royal authority. Patrick Wormald has argued that the Wantage code was drawn up by men local to the north Midlands and that it is a product of regional preoccupations; it is English law, but reflects local practices.[5] Indeed, ethnic difference was rarely articulated in the tenth century. The term 'Danes', for example, was scarcely used in contemporary sources between 920 and 990, and was typically reserved for periods of conflict. As Susan Reynolds has observed of the attitudes of tenth-century chroniclers, 'Danes were invaders and enemies, not subjects of the kingdom'. Finally, although Edgar may have legislated for 'the Danes', tenth-century kings, including Edgar himself, conceived of the realm in their charters as consisting of 'Anglo-Saxons', 'Northumbrians', 'Mercians', 'Britons' and 'pagans', a mixture of ethnic, regional and religious identities, among which 'Danishness' is notably absent.[6]

[5] P. Wormald, 'Æthelred the law-maker', in D. Hill, ed., *Æthelred the Unready. Papers from the Millenary Conference* (British Archaeological Reports British Series, 59; Oxford, 1978), pp. 47–80, at 61–2.

[6] S. Reynolds, 'What do we mean by "Anglo-Saxon" and "Anglo-Saxons"?', *Journal of British Studies*, 24 (1985), 406–10, at 409 for the quotation.

Early eleventh-century events are often scrutinized for evidence of the enduring legacy of the Scandinavian settlements of a century or so earlier. For example, in 1002 King Æthelred II ordered the killing of 'all the Danish men who were in England', apparently fearing an attack on his life and his kingdom (see Chapter IV.1), which has been interpreted as evidence for the lasting ethnic distinctiveness of the descendants of earlier settlers. However, it is more plausible that Æthelred was referring to a more immediate threat. The known victims were recent arrivals, and in contemporary sources it is only in Oxford, remote from the main regions of earlier Scandinavian settlement, that the order can be shown to have been effected. There are also reasons to doubt that ethnic loyalty influenced the behaviour of Swein Forkbeard, king of Denmark, when he landed at Gainsborough (Lincs.) on the Trent in 1013 and desisted from causing great damage until he had crossed Watling Street. Instead, political and military pragmatism probably dictated that this attempt to conquer England was launched far from the heartlands of King Æthelred's realm, where regional disaffection from the English king might be harnessed. Throughout the tenth and eleventh centuries kings of England had to find ways to handle the regional demands of their subjects, particularly of the northerners. One measure adopted was the appointment of men to positions of authority in northern England who had landed interests further south, and who might, on this basis, be expected to be loyal to kings based in southern England. Yet regional interests persisted, and the rebellions against William I in the decades after the Norman Conquest were notably most intensive in the regions that had long been in opposition to the house of Wessex. Ethnic sympathies may have been mobilized during rebellions against kings of England, but regional interests appear to have been the fundamental cause.[7]

In contrast to the situation in the wake of Scandinavian settlement, chroniclers writing in the decades after the Norman Conquest used ethnic labels frequently, and they perceived many differences between Normans and English (see above). Yet, even if contemporaries were often clear about the differences between Normans and English it is apparent that they simultaneously described the ethnic divide in fluid terms. For example, English chroniclers typically referred to the Normans as

[7] *EHD*, i, no. 1, pp. 245–6; D. Whitelock, 'The dealings of the kings of England with Northumbria in the tenth and eleventh centuries', in P. Clemoes, ed., *The Anglo-Saxons: Studies in Some Aspects of Their History Presented to Bruce Dickins* (London, 1959), pp. 70–88; M. Innes, 'Danelaw identities: ethnicity, regionalism and political allegiances', in Hadley and Richards, eds., *Cultures in Contact*, pp. 65–88, at 83–5.

'French', possibly because of the ambiguity inherent in the Old English term for the Normans – '*Normenn*'/'Northmen' – which could equally be applied to people from Scandinavia. William's followers were not, in any case, all from Normandy, and they included Bretons, Lombards and Flemings. The written sources of the century or so after the Norman Conquest demonstrate the continuing malleability of ethnic labels. For example, some Continental settlers quickly came to be described, and apparently to describe themselves, as English, such as the new archbishops, Lanfranc of Canterbury (1070–89) and Thomas of York (1070–1100), and the monk Reginald of Canterbury, who shortly after his arrival in England was able to write of '*gens Anglica nostra* (our English people).' The application of multiple ethnic labels to individuals is demonstrated by the career of Gerald of Wales (*c.* 1146–1223), who variously described himself as Welsh, English or Norman, while he described Robert Chesney, bishop of Lincoln from 1148, as 'English by birth, but Norman by ancestry'. The contrast between the identity provided by birth and that later adopted is further demonstrated by Henry of Huntingdon, who, in his account of the Battle of the Standard (1138), has Ralph, bishop of Orkney, addressing the English as 'Brave nobles of England, Norman by birth', which was reportedly well received by 'all the English'; Henry, himself of mixed ancestry, evidently conceived of the 'English' as being an amalgamation of Norman and English peoples.[8] To eleventh- and twelfth-century chroniclers, the 'English' could be both those of English birth and the inhabitants of the English realm, irrespective of birth.

We also have to allow the possibility that entirely personal experiences informed decisions about ethnic self-perception, although such factors are almost impossible to verify. Much has been made of the fact that the twelfth-century chronicler Orderic Vitalis maintained an English self-identity in his writings, despite being the son of a French immigrant and having spent most of his life in a Norman monastery. The English origins of his mother may have been relevant to his sense of Englishness, although Hugh Thomas has suggested that another factor may have been Orderic's traumatic experience of being sent to a monastery at the age of ten far from his home where, in his own words, he felt 'an exile, unknown to all, knowing no one'.[9] We cannot safely pursue such issues at this remove, but they are likely to have been relevant.

[8] H. Thomas, *The English and the Normans: Ethnic Hostility, Assimilation and Identity, 1066–*c. *1220* (Oxford, 2003), pp. 72–3; A. Williams, *The English and the Norman Conquest* (Woodbridge, 1995), p. 179.

[9] Thomas, *The English and the Normans*, pp. 81–2.

In sum, across the period *c.* 900–1200 ethnic labels are far from straightforward guides to identity, whether perceived or experienced, and the fluidity with which they were employed suggests that whatever an individual's subjective sense of ethnic identity they were able to describe themselves and others in flexible terms.

MANAGING CONQUEST AND MEDIATING ETHNIC DIFFERENCE

A crucial element in the acculturation process was the tendency for the leaders of conquering groups to present their kingship in an English fashion. Often, this took the form of respecting the laws of an earlier English king. For example, when the English and the Danes made peace at Oxford in 1018 following the conquest by Cnut they are said to have reached an agreement, which the 'D' manuscript of the Anglo-Saxon Chronicle states was 'according to Edgar's law'. The laws of Edgar had a symbolic value, allowing the chronicler to look back beyond the disastrous reign of King Æthelred, to a king who was an acknowledged success, and offering a promise of continuity with the past. Edgar was also apparently regarded as a pragmatist, and a gloss inserted into the northern recensions of the Chronicle by Archbishop Wulfstan commented, not uncritically it should be added, on his indulgence of foreigners; as Patrick Wormald has pointed out, this made Edgar an even more appropriate 'patron for an Anglo-Danish *entente*'.[10] Cnut's law codes were subsequently drawn up by Archbishop Wulfstan of York, who had previously legislated for Æthelred, and accordingly there is much in common with previous English legislation. The level of engagement Cnut had with this law-making is, however, debatable, as is the extent to which he personally adhered to its prescriptions; for example, his maintenance of a concubine was in conflict with a clause in his second law code.[11] Moreover, the promulgation of legislation in English coincided with the maintenance of a court that was culturally and linguistically Scandinavian. The Scandinavian skaldic praise poetry produced at his court notably depicts Cnut as a Dane, in the tradition of the ninth-century war leader Ivarr, the slayer of the Northumbrian king Ælla. The poets reassure the Danes that Cnut still has their interests at

[10] P. Wormald, *The Making of English Law: King Alfred to the Twelfth Century* (Oxford, 2001), pp. 131–2.

[11] M. K. Lawson, 'Archbishop Wulfstan and the homiletic element in the laws of Ethelred II and Cnut', in A. Rumble, ed., *The Reign of Cnut: King of England, Denmark and Norway* (Leicester, 1994), pp. 141–64.

heart, and references to Cnut's Christianity are combined in the poetry with allusions to paganism.[12]

During William's reign the importance of respecting the laws of King Edward the Confessor was repeatedly stressed, although no law code of the latter king survived. As a result, the testimony of Englishmen concerning the legal practices of the time of King Edward was frequently requested. In the early twelfth century several legal compilations were produced, and it is to this revival of legal writing that we owe the survival of much pre-Conquest law. Translations were produced into Latin and French, presumably to instruct those whose first language was not English in the ways of English legal custom, and some legal codes were manufactured to compensate for the absence of law codes of earlier kings. These undertakings were part of the process by which the Norman lineage was transformed into an English kingship.

The Church was consistently central to the establishment of new rulers. For example, Scandinavian kings of York repeatedly received archiepiscopal support, such as when Archbishop Wulfstan accompanied Olaf Guthfrithson as he raided the north Midlands in 939. The importance of Christianity is also reflected in the coins minted in the names of Scandinavian kings between the late ninth and mid-tenth century, which typically bear Latin inscriptions, often incorporate liturgical phrases or the names of saints and display diverse types of crosses. There was an active promotion of Christianity on this coinage, such that by *c.* 895 Scandinavian rulers were minting coins in the name of St Edmund, the East Anglian king murdered by a Viking army in 869. The minting of coins served to consolidate the image of these kings as ruling in the manner of western European, Christian rulers, not least because it was a practice scarcely known at this time in Scandinavia.

Cnut and William were both Christian when they conquered England, yet each had a complex relationship with the English Church and needed the support of prominent churchmen to legitimize their authority. Despite his accession to the throne just a few years after a Danish army had kidnapped and murdered Archbishop Ælfheah of Canterbury, Cnut was presented as a king who protected the interests of the Church through the law codes drafted for him by Archbishop Wulfstan. Cnut also vowed to protect the interests of the Church in his letters and made gifts to English churches. Indeed, the *Liber Vitae* of the New Minster, Winchester depicts Cnut and his wife, Emma, donating an altar cross, as

[12] R. Frank, 'King Cnut in the verse of his skalds', in Rumble, ed., *The Reign of Cnut*, pp. 106–24.

an angel crowns Cnut. The incapacity of the archbishop of Canterbury, Stigand, to crown William was partially resolved by the role in the coronation of Archbishop Ealdred of York, who reputedly requested that William swear an oath 'that he would treat this people as well as any king before him did, if they were loyal to him'. Within a generation of the Norman Conquest the majority of the upper echelons of the clergy were of Continental origin, yet the Church was central to the processes of acculturation. This was as a result of the integration of the Continental ecclesiastics with local churchmen, the founding and rebuilding of parish churches and monasteries by new Norman lords and the writing of histories by ecclesiastics that emphasized continuity with the pre-Conquest past. While there has been much debate about apparent initial scepticism towards English saints by the Normans, it is, nonetheless, apparent that they quickly embraced English saints, to whom they prayed and from whom they sought assistance, and that this was important to promoting a sense of belonging to Englishness and England (see Chapter V.3).[13]

Would-be conquerors rarely found local allies difficult to acquire. The raiders provided useful support in internecine disputes, while promoting the interests of one raiding group was often a means of managing the threat of conquest. In 878 King Alfred stage-managed the baptism of the leader of a defeated Viking army, Guthrum, and they subsequently forged a peace treaty, which was essential to the integration of Guthrum and his followers into English society. Guthrum subsequently minted coins that were imitative of those of Alfred before minting coins in his new baptismal name of Æthelstan.[14] The community of St Cuthbert encouraged a Viking army active in northern England in the 880s to elect one of their number, Guthred, as king. The community then presided over a ceremony with complex symbolism. King Guthred's election took place in the presence of the body of the saint at a place associated with a seventh-century Northumbrian king ('the hill called *Oswigesdune*'), and it involved the giving of a gold armlet, which was probably a Scandinavian, perhaps pagan, symbol of authority.[15] Rebellious English lords frequently seem to have found allies among the Viking raiders. For example, following the death of King Alfred, his son, Edward the Elder, faced a challenge from his cousin, Æthelwold, who was accepted as king in Scandinavian-controlled Northumbria and then garnered support in East

[13] Thomas, *The English and the Normans*, pp. 283–96.

[14] P. Kershaw, 'The Alfred–Guthrum treaty: scripting accommodation and interaction in Viking Age England', in Hadley and Richards, eds., *Cultures in Contact*, pp. 43–64.

[15] Innes, 'Danelaw identities', p. 79.

Anglia, another region of Scandinavian dominance. When he engaged in battle with King Edward shortly afterwards he was supported by various Scandinavian leaders and a member of the Mercian royalty, Brihtsige, 'son of the *atheling* Beornoth'. In the early tenth century, the English lords Esbrid and Ealdorman Ælstan received land from the Viking leader Ragnall, who had seized properties in northern England, much of it from the community of St Cuthbert. Esbrid and Ælstan had probably been rewarded for their support in battle, and local rivalries between the community of St Cuthbert and the lords of Bamburgh may lie behind this development. In sum, whatever sense of ethnic difference the incoming elite may have felt, it is apparent that their authority was typically presented in English terms, that there were English allies willing to support them in establishing their rule and that ethnicity was malleable in the face of political manoeuvring.

SETTLEMENT AND IDENTITY

The impact of successive conquests and migrations on wider society is difficult to assess, because it largely falls beyond the remit of contemporary chroniclers. Nonetheless, the Scandinavian impact on the English language and on place-names suggests that there was a sizeable Scandinavian settlement that followed the military conquests of the last quarter of the ninth century. There has, however, been considerable debate about what this reveals about the processes of acculturation. Matthew Townend has, for example, argued that the mutual linguistic intelligibility of the English and the Scandinavians helped to perpetuate the distinctiveness of the two communities. One possible indication of the separateness of the Scandinavian community is offered by those place-names formed with the characteristic Scandinavian naming element –*by*, which are overwhelmingly combined with a Scandinavian first element. It has accordingly been suggested by Lesley Abrams and David Parsons that they were coined by Scandinavian-speaking communities before linguistic assimilation had commenced.[16] However, this linguistic evidence has to be set alongside the impressions conveyed by material culture from the regions where the Scandinavians settled. In particular, the extensive corpus of metal jewellery and dress-accessories, much

[16] M. Townend, *Language and History in Viking-Age England. Linguistic Relations between Speakers of Old Norse and Old English* (Turnhout, 2002); L. Abrams and D. Parsons, 'Place-names and the history of Scandinavian settlement in England', in J. Hines, A. Lane and M. Redknap, eds., *Land, Sea and Home* (London, 2004), pp. 379–431, at 394–5.

of it retrieved by metal-detectorists from regions with dense concentrations of Scandinavian place-names, combines Scandinavian and English forms and decorative styles, suggesting significant cultural mixing in this medium. Purely Scandinavian artefacts – such as the oval brooches characteristic of Scandinavian female costume – are far less commonly found, and this has been interpreted as evidence that the newcomers speedily adopted English styles of dress.[17] Stone sculpture produced in the tenth century in the regions of Scandinavian settlement also combined English and Scandinavian motifs, even though the very medium of stone sculpture was scarcely known in Scandinavia. The sculpture, particularly those examples incorporating scenes from Scandinavian mythology, has been interpreted as serving a didactic function, in which parallels were drawn between the Christian and pagan belief systems. Thus it can be suggested that no matter how long the Scandinavian settlers and their descendants remained separate speech communities it is evident that they simultaneously acculturated to English cultural styles and had a marked impact on such English styles of material culture in the process.

Recent studies of the Norman Conquest have explored the impact of settlement on social groups beyond the leading aristocrats. For example, Cecily Clark traced the widespread adoption of Norman personal names across the social spectrum in the decades after the Conquest, and suggested that this was a significant indication of contemporary attitudes, and one perhaps more reliable than that provided by some of the chroniclers. A Bury St Edmunds' estate survey dated to *c.* 1100 reveals that the peasantry had adopted such names as Robert, William, Hubert and Richard, and Clark suggested that this reflected an 'apparent absence of any nationalistic or xenophobic reaction against the cultural patterns associated with the new rulers and settlers'.[18] Ann Williams has demonstrated that many English tenants survived the Conquest, although they were required to submit to new lords, with whatever alterations to their terms of tenure this might entail. The descendants of many of the English survivors adapted to the new cultural situation, evident, for example, in their adaptation to Continental methods of warfare and adoption of Continental personal names. This survival of a stratum of English landholders was fundamental to the transmission of English culture. In contrast, Hugh Thomas has suggested that the peasantry need not have had a

[17] G. Thomas, 'Anglo-Scandinavian metalwork from the Danelaw: exploring social and cultural interaction', in Hadley and Richards, eds., *Cultures in Contact*, pp. 237–55, at 252.

[18] C. Clark, 'Willelmus rex? vel alius Willelmus?', *Nomina*, 11 (1987), 7–33.

strong sense of English identity, and that the cultural association between Englishness and rusticity might have been as likely to have prompted the Normans to reject Englishness. This did not happen, but it serves as a reminder that the numerical supremacy of the English was no guarantee of the survival of English identity after the Conquest.[19]

CONCLUSIONS: THE PREVAILING OF 'ENGLISHNESS'

A communal English identity was constructed at the court of King Alfred, who promoted the term *Angelcynn* to describe the common identity of the peoples of his realm, and emphasized the common language (*Englisc*) in the creation of a sense of a shared past. Sarah Foot has detailed the creation of a legal structure that amalgamated the laws of the various kingdoms, and a programme of education and revival of learning at his court that she has interpreted as a conscious attempt 'to shape an English imagination'. However, the English of Alfred's conception were principally the inhabitants of Wessex, western Mercia and Kent, and Alfred's claim in his treaty with Guthrum (see above) to be supported by 'the councillors of all the English [*ealles Angelcynnes witan*]' was part of the process by which Alfred presented himself as a ruler beyond the limits of Wessex.[20] At a later date, Cnut conceived of the people he had conquered as 'the whole race of the English' (*totius gentis Anglorum*), and the Normans similarly encountered a people with a strong sense of Englishness. Yet English identity was not exclusive and could exist alongside other forms of identity, in which allegiance to kingdom and region might be particularly strongly felt. A clear sense of an English people and kingdom prevailed by *c.* 1200, despite the successive migrations and conquest, but it should not be assumed that this was either inevitable or the product of a linear progression. Ethnic identity was shaped by multiple decisions, both personal and political, along the way.

[19] Williams, *The Norman Conquest*, pp. 71–97; Thomas, *The English and the Normans*, pp. 161–80.

[20] S. Foot, 'The making of *Angelcynn*: English identity before the Norman Conquest', *TRHS* 6th ser., 6 (1996), 25–49; Kershaw, 'The Alfred–Guthrum treaty', pp. 57–8.

CHAPTER IV.3

Intermarriage

Elisabeth van Houts

Throughout history one of the consequences of immigration was marriage between indigenous people and newcomers. Intermarriage, or exogamy, is the sexual union of an indigenous person and a foreigner, sanctioned by society, with the aim to produce offspring. Exogamy can be taken as a sign for assimilation between the two groups, and it can be seen as an agent producing it.[1] In cases where immigration itself followed a military takeover there may have been, as we have seen, amongst the conquerors a surplus of young men looking to settle down with local women (see also Chapter IV.2). For our period intermarriage has been studied particularly by scholars of the Norman Conquest, amongst whom in the 1970s and 1980s Cecily Clark and Eleanor Searle dominated the historiographical debate by arguing that intermarriage after the Norman Conquest must have been substantial enough to explain the widespread change in naming patterns as well as legitimization of landholding by newcomers through marriage to English female landholders. The influential work of Cecily Clark was based on onomastic evidence which pointed to women's insular names surviving longer in the twelfth century than those of English men, who were given Continental names very soon after the Conquest. While acknowledging the absence of statistical evidence, she argued that intermarriage of foreign (French) men to indigenous English women was the most likely explanation for this pattern. In English-speaking households women were free to name their daughters according to custom, whereas their French husbands, eager to please the foreign conquerors and conform to their fashion, wished their sons to be named after them. Building upon this linguistic reasoning Eleanor Searle proposed a second argument that the Conqueror used his prerogatives of lordship to marry off English widows and heiresses to his male followers

[1] D. L. Pagnini and S. P. Morgan, 'Intermarriage and social distance amongst U.S. immigrants at the turn of the century', *American Journal of Sociology*, 96 (1990), 405–32.

in order that their offspring could legitimize the holding of land both by right of (maternal) inheritance and (paternal) conquest. While both arguments have great merit there is a danger that in combination they have taken on a canonical validity that is difficult to maintain in view of the surprisingly limited evidence for actual cases of intermarriage between the French and the English in the late eleventh and early twelfth century, as signalled tentatively by Katherine Keats-Rohan and explored at greater length by Hugh Thomas and myself. Moreover, if conquest and the demise of the Anglo-Saxon male elite opened opportunities for a stream of young foreigners onto the marriage market after 1066, it raises the question whether we can observe a similar trend half a century earlier, a period for which the topic has hardly been studied. Although I will concentrate on the eleventh century, the period of invasion and migration for which there is good evidence and recent historiography, we first have to think about intermarriage for our period as a whole. Between 900 and 1200 English men and women undoubtedly married foreigners, but as to the question of frequency, the answer seems to be, not that often. It seems likely that where exogamy took place it did so across the period, particularly in the border areas with Wales and Scotland, but also across the sea with the Irish in the west and with Continental foreigners in the east. High-status marriages are the most likely to be known because they have survived in the records, so for the tenth century the increasing presence of Scandinavian newcomers in the Danelaw led to some degree of intermarriage. In 925 King Æthelstan's sister Eadgyth married the Dane Sihtric, king of Northumbria, and in 940 Orm's daughter Aldgyth married an Olaf, while John of Worcester under the year 993 identifies three Danish men mentioned in the Anglo-Saxon Chronicle, Fræna, Godwine and Frithugil, as 'Danes on their father's side'.[2] In contrast, at the other end of our period in the second half of the twelfth century, it is much harder to speak of exogamy amongst an aristocratic elite that spread across the Angevin empire covering western France and England, while hardly any scholarly attention has been paid to the subject lower down the social scale. Whatever linguistic and cultural differences there may have been up to the middle of that century, there is plenty of evidence to suggest that acculturation predominated and that the descendants of foreigners identified themselves as English first and foremost. By the 1170s this was a fact according to Richard fitz Nigel, the author of the *Dialogue of the*

[2] *EHD*, i, no. 4, p. 283; R. R. Darlington and P. McGurk, eds., and J. Bray and P. McGurk, trans., *The Chronicle of John of Worcester* (OMT; Oxford, 1995), ii, p. 442.

Table A: *English people marrying Scandinavians (S) or Frenchmen (F)*

	1000–16	1017–41	1042–66	1067–86	1087–*c.* 1110
Men	1F	1S	4/7 F	6F	9F
Women	1F 1S	8/9S	3F	10F	34F

Exchequer, who noted that 'the nations are so mixed that today one can scarcely distinguish who is English and who is Norman'.[3] For him, past intermarriage was the reason for the successful assimilation of the English and the French.

Detailed study of the incidence of exogamy in the eleventh century suggests that overall the number of cases amongst Scandinavians and French remained relatively small, as illustrated by Table A.[4] Already in the run-up to the military takeovers there is evidence for some marriage arrangements between the foreign conqueror-to-be and the indigenous ruling class. These high-ranking unions were aimed at sealing political alliances whereby the men and women involved were more or less hostages to guarantee upholding military agreements: as early as 1016, before he was recognized as king of England, Cnut 'married' Ælfgifu of Northampton and in 1064 or 1065 William of Normandy had already promised his eldest daughter, Adelaide, in marriage to Earl Harold in the event he became king of England. In the same periods lower down the social scale, according to an early thirteenth-century St Albans tradition, foreigners courted English girls whose names have not survived. Near the top we find the king's nephew Ralph, son of his sister Godgifu and Drogo of Vermandois, who married Gytha, a woman of Midlands origin, while slightly lower down Ralph the Staller and William Malet, both half-French but living in England, married a Breton and Norman woman, respectively.

For the immediate post-Conquest periods the gender information is strikingly different between the Danish and Norman rule. In the years

[3] E. Amt, ed. and trans., *Richard fitz Nigel, Dialogus de Scaccario: The Dialogue of the Exchequer*, (OMT; Oxford, 2007), pp. 80–1.

[4] The table originates from E. van Houts, 'Intermarriage in eleventh-century England', in D. Crouch and K. Thompson, eds., *Normandy and Its Neighbours 900–1250. Essays Presented to David Bates* (Turnhout, 2011), forthcoming, which also includes an appendix listing all known cases of English exogamy with Scandinavians and French in eleventh-century England, as well as a detailed justification of the catalogue and the nature of the source material on which it is based.

of Danish occupation (1017–42) only one high-status case is known of an Englishman marrying a Danish woman, namely that of Godwine of Wessex who married Gytha, Cnut's sister-in-law, in *c.* 1019 or 1022/3, as a reward for royal service. All other eight or nine exogamous cases concern Cnut's Danish followers who married English women with land, but whether they were all (like the last case below) widows is unknown: Thurkill earl of East Anglia, whose wife was named Edith; Thurkill the White and Leofflead, who held 25 acres in Herefordshire; Toki and his wife Æthelflæd with land in Buckinghamshire; Ocea whose wife was Ealdgyth, a wealthy landholder in Gloucestershire; and the anonymous Dane mentioned in the *Ramsey Chronicle* whose unnamed English wife was the widow of a wealthy Englishman at *Athelint.* Clearly these women landholders were particularly attractive to the Danish conquerors, for whom marriage legitimized their holding of land. This phenomenon was identified by Eleanor Searle for the Norman Conquest of England, when indeed the French married English women to claim lands by right of their wives' lawful holdings as opposed to their own, which was based on conquest. Early examples are Ealdgyth, daughter of Wigot of Wallingford, who may have married Robert d'Oilly as early as the late 1060s, and well before 1075 King Harold's daughter Gunhild, so it has been argued recently, may have been snapped up by the Breton earl Alan Rufus.[5] Leofwine's daughter and heiress was given to Geoffrey of la Querche in Lincolnshire and Walter of Douai's first wife, Edeva, had been the widow of Hemming at Uffculme (Devon), which he held after her. Surprisingly, perhaps, Domesday Book provides only two explicit cases of intermarriage.[6] The first, in Gloucestershire, concerns the widow of a middle-ranking officer and a valuable plot of land in Guiting Power which between 1066 and 1086 had decreased in value from £16 to £6, and it is recorded that: 'the king gave his [sheriff Ælwen's] wife and land to a certain young man called Richard'. In the second case the foreigner was a Breton, of far lower status, who married without royal involvement a woman on land in [north or south] Pickenham (Norfolk) valued at a meagre 3s: 'and after the king came to the country Earl Ralph held that land. But a man of Wihenoc loved a certain woman on that land and he took her [in marriage] and afterwards he held that land in Wihenoc's fief without the king's grant.' The only reason that we know of these two cases of

[5] R. Sharpe, 'King Harold's daughter', *Haskins Society Journal*, 19 (2007), 1–27.

[6] DB, i, fol. 161r and DB, ii, fol. 232r.

intermarriage is because there were queries about the ownership of the land involved.

Yet Searle's conclusions need some gender correction for the immediate post-Conquest Norman period. While at least ten English women with land were indeed handed over to foreigners, William the Conqueror at the same time allowed, or intended to allow, just over half that number of Norman women to be married to his new English subjects. Very early on these were high-status affairs: in an attempt to pacify English noblemen and forestall rebellion, he betrothed his daughter Adelaide (the same one who had been promised pre-Conquest to Earl Harold) to Earl Edwin of Mercia, and his sister's daughter Judith to Earl Waltheof. As a result of Edwin's death in 1071 only the second betrothal led to marriage. Slightly later in the 1070s lower-ranking men followed: Edward of Salisbury married a French woman called Maud; Edwin the Hunter one Odelina; Æthelred of Yalding and Tierry, son of Dearmann had wives called Hawise and Maud, respectively. The famous Fenland resistance fighter Hereward the Wake, probably a thegn, had met his foreign wife Turfrida during his exile in Saint-Omer (Flanders), and if we believe his twelfth-century biography he brought her back to England after his reconciliation with the Conqueror. That some subjected Englishmen married French women implies that the Norman regime recognized their value as useful assets and associates. Given that these data suggest a contrast between the conquerors Cnut and William, one wonders whether initially William consciously followed a more conciliatory policy towards the English than Cnut. After the bloodbath at Hastings he had perhaps less to fear from the emasculated nobility than Cnut had.

As Table A reveals, from the late 1080s there is a pronounced gender imbalance amongst the English partners of mixed marriages with many more women marrying Frenchmen. At the same time we must remember that endogamous marriage remained the rule. This is nowhere more obvious than in the many names of identifiable couples listed in the commemoration books, such as the *Liber Vitae* of Newminster-Hyde at Winchester, Thorney and Durham.[7] Onomastic evidence underlines the fact that people with Continental names married each other, as did people with English names. Amongst them unambiguous cases of intermarriage are exceptional: one in Durham in the north of England, where

[7] Hyde and Thorney are conveniently listed side by side in J. S. Moore, 'Prosopographical problems of English *libri vitae*', in K. S. B. Keats-Rohan, ed., *Family Trees and the Roots of Politics. The Prosopography of Britain and France from the Tenth to the Twelfth Century* (Woodbridge, 1997), pp. 183–6.

Norman settlement was thinnest, a dozen around Thorney Abbey, the Fenland monastery with a considerable catchment area, and fifteen in Winchester, the second city of England. Yet intermarriage did attract the attention of contemporaries. On the Continent, Frutolf of Michelsberg (d. 1103) in Bavaria reported in his chronicle under 1066 that William the Conqueror forced English widows to marry foreigners. In Normandy *c.* 1120 Orderic Vitalis described the late 1070s as a period of peaceful cohabitation with foreigners and natives living side by side in *burhs* and cities, and intermarrying. Around the same time in England William of Malmesbury *c.* 1118 commented that the Normans 'of all nations are the most hospitable, they treat their strangers with the same respect as each other and they also marry those they have conquered'.[8] Orderic and William were themselves offspring of mixed marriages, which probably accounts for their distinctly rose-tinted assessments of exogamy compared with Frutolf's damning report. For the period of Danish rule we have no evidence for an upsurge for the simple reason that the foreign rule lasted not more than two and a half decades, that is just one generation.

Intermarriage and sexual relations between conquerors and conquered were by no means unproblematic, as for both periods we have contemporary evidence that betrays on the part of the rulers and their advisers anxiety over force and coercion, especially against women. Their concerns, it seems, went beyond that of peacetime lordship and matters of wardship. Widows in particular are singled out. The main author of early eleventh-century royal legislation, Archbishop Wulfstan of York (1002–23), on various occasions stressed the vulnerability of widows.[9] Yet, on behalf of (or, perhaps, despite of) Æthelred and Cnut, he was not alone in his concern for women's vulnerability; his later fellow clergymen in the Norman period had similar anxieties. The conquest of 1066 seems to have triggered an additional concern, namely that of sexual violence by men of lower rank. Initially in 1070, four years after the Battle of Hastings, the papal legate Bishop Eremfrid of Syon in clause 10 of his *Penitential Articles* legislated, seemingly on all men, that 'those who committed adulteries or rapes or fornications shall do penance as though they had thus sinned in their own country'.[10]

[8] F. Schmale and I. Schmale-Ott, eds., *Frutolfs und Ekkehards Chroniken und die Anonyme Kaiserchronik* (Darmstadt, 1972), p. 78; M. Chibnall, ed. and trans., *The Ecclesiastical History of Orderic Vitalis* (6 vols.; OMT Oxford, 1969–80), ii, pp. 256–7; R. A. B. Mynors, R. M. Thomson and M. Winterbottom, eds. and trans., *William of Malmesbury, Gesta Regum Anglorum. The History of the English Kings* (2 vols.; OMT; Oxford, 1998–9), i, pp. 460–1.

[9] *EHD*, i, no. 44, p. 445; no. 240, p. 930; no. 49, p. 465.

[10] *Councils and Synods*, ii, no. 88, p. 584.

Note, incidentally, that penance for such trespassers in England was expected to be meted out in France according to French customs. Rape and violence against women is reported by both William of Poitiers and Orderic Vitalis, with the latter being more willing to accept its reality than the former.

For the Norman Conquest there is convincing evidence that English women who had the means to do so tried to avoid marriage with Frenchmen. The Domesday Book evidence cited above reveals beyond doubt that William the Conqueror, like his predecessors, married off widows to his followers. Paying off the king to remain unattached was one defensive strategy, though evidence for it remains elusive.[11] Another tactic was to take refuge in monastic houses, as is revealed by Archbishop Lanfranc in his letter 53 to Bishop Gundulf of Rochester. Responding to the latter's query about what to do with various categories of nuns who were not living according to monastic rules, Lanfranc replied:

> But those who have been neither confessed nor presented at the altar are to be sent away at once without change of status, until their desire to remain in religion is examined more carefully. As to those who as you tell me fled to a monastery not for love of the religious life but for fear of the French, if they can prove that his was so by the unambiguous witness of nuns better than they, let them be granted unrestricted leave to depart. This is the king's policy and our own.[12]

Although the timing of the query cannot be established more precisely than the 1070s or 1080s, this period throws up one famous historical case concerning Edith-Matilda, daughter of King Malcolm III of Scotland, who through her mother Queen Margaret was a direct descendant of the Wessex royal family. In the autumn of 1100, about to be married to Henry I, Edith-Matilda recalled her time at Wilton, where her aunt was abbess:

> For, when I was quite a young girl and went in fear of the rod of my aunt Christina, whom you knew quite well, she to preserve me from the lust of the Normans which was rampant and at that time ready to assault any woman's honour, used to put a little black hood on my head and, when I threw it off she would often make me smart with a good slapping and most horrible scolding, as well as treating me as being in disgrace.[13]

[11] DB, i, fol. 74r; P. Stafford, 'Women in Domesday', in K. Bates, A. Curry, C. Hardman and P. Noble, eds., *Medieval Women in Southern England* (Reading Medieval Studies, 15; Reading, 1989), pp. 80–1.

[12] H. Clover and M. Gibson, eds. and trans., *The Letters of Lanfranc, Archbishop of Canterbury* (OMT; Oxford, 1979), pp. 166–7.

[13] M. Rule, ed., *Eadmeri Historia Novorum* (RS; London, 1884), pp. 123–4.

It seems therefore that when on various occasions male visitors, some as suitors, had arrived at the nunnery, Abbess Christina had taken the precaution of pretending that the girl was a nun.

For the early eleventh century there is no equivalent of Lanfranc's letter, and such evidence as we have is far more circumstantial. Even so, the section of Cnut's law of 1020/2 that was discussed earlier in this chapter throws up one clause that may be highly significant. Tucked away between clauses on forced marriages sits clause 73.3: 'and a widow is never to be consecrated too hastily'.[14] Normally, this clause is seen as an indication that widowed women in their first grief on occasion took the veil but in due course regretted their decision. Do we read too much into the law, and its date, to suggest that a country under foreign occupation saw an increased incidence of women taking drastic action in an attempt to avoid (inter)marriage?

Little is known about the wider family strategies surrounding intermarriage during periods of conquest and foreign occupation. One of the difficulties in assessing them is that the whole subject is already tricky enough for peacetime, as we have already seen in the chapter on family and marriage (see Chapter II.5). If increasingly rights of lordship determined the fate of women, would women themselves have experienced any difference in treatment by parents whether they were told to marry a (known) neighbour – as in the case of Christina of Markyate – or an (unknown) foreigner such as when the Norman Judith married Waltheof? The silence on the subject from the (male) offspring from mixed marriages (think of Orderic Vitalis, William of Malmesbury and Henry of Huntingdon) speaks volumes. Interestingly, Goscelin of Saint-Bertin, the Flemish hagiographer who was resident in England, is ambiguous. On the one hand he accuses widows who remarry foreigners of complicity: 'an enemy murders a husband and so "merits" to be married to the widow. The murdered man is dead and buried, trampled underfoot; the killer is loved more and more and accepted into the widow's embraces.' On the other he sympathizes with young girls forced to accept foreign husbands, contrasting 'the happiness of home' with 'barbarous customs, strange languages, subservience to fierce lords and repugnant laws that go against nature'.[15] All the signs are, however, that families acquiesced and accepted intermarriage as a variation of the (endogamous) marriage

[14] *EHD*, i, no. 49, p. 466.

[15] M. Otter, trans., *Goscelin of St. Bertin, The Book of Encouragement and Consolation (Liber Confortatorius)* (Cambridge, 2004), pp. 40, 41–2.

they knew. And if the case of Adam of Cockfield is anything to go by, the resulting family dynamics between English and Norman members of one family could be cordial (see Chapter II.5). There is, however, one exception of a different kind of exogamy in the sense of a union between people of different religions that caused tremendous uproar. The only known case of intermarriage between Christian and Jew took place in England in the 1220s between a Jewess and a deacon, who ended up being burnt as a heretic. It is to the Jews, as the one group of immigrants after 1066 not yet discussed, that we now turn.[16]

[16] F. W. Maitland, 'The deacon and the Jewess; or, apostacy at Common Law', in H. A. L. Fisher, ed., *The Collected Papers of Frederic William Maitland* (Cambridge, 1911), i, pp. 385–406.

CHAPTER IV.4

The Jews

Anna Sapir Abulafia

The Jews arrived in England in 1066 and succeeded in building up a successful livelihood. By the end of Henry II's reign some two dozen Jewish communities had come into being. By the end of the twelfth century a Jewish financial network had spread from London, where the first Norman Jews had settled after the Conquest, to Norwich and Lincoln and reached into the developing areas around York. Jewish prosperity owed much to Henry II's actions against the English moneyers and foreign Christian moneylenders like William Cade. By 1180 moneylending, rather than money changing or business in plate, had become the main financial occupation of English Jews. They enjoyed the king's backing, for rather than seek credit from them, he targeted their profits as a ready source for royal taxation.[1] The complexities and shortcomings of this backing would become obvious in the pogroms of 1189/90. Richard's 1194 Ordinance of the Jews began to put in place the stringent royal control of all aspects of Jewish business which was to become the peculiar characteristic of English Jewish life before their expulsion in 1290.

It is likely that William the Conqueror brought Jews from Rouen to London on account of their expertise in trade of luxury items and their experience in money changing and supplying moneyers with plate to mint coins. The Anglo-Saxon kings seem to have decided not to follow this route. Indeed, William may have hoped to use 'his' Jews as some kind of counterweight against the Anglo-Saxon merchant community in London. Whatever the case may be, it was through their business concerns with plate and coin that the Jews became successful. As they spilled out of London to other market and minting towns from around the middle of the twelfth century, some local lords seem to have gained rights

[1] R. C. Stacey, 'Jews and Christians in twelfth-century England: some dynamics of a changing relationship', in M. A. Signer and J. Van Engen, eds., *Jews and Christians in Twelfth-Century Europe* (Notre Dame, 2001), pp. 346–7; H. G. Richardson, *The English Jewry under Angevin Kings* (London, 1960), p. 121.

over them. But the notion that all Jews in fact 'belonged' to the king was never lost. The so-called *Laws of Edward the Confessor* made it plain that all Jews fell under royal jurisdiction and protection because Jews and all their possessions belonged to the king. By the end of the 1170s Henry II was insisting that this should be the case in practice. In 1190, for example, Abbot Samson of Bury St Edmunds received permission from Richard to expel the Jews from Bury; apart from anything else, Samson did not want people who 'belonged' to the king rather than St Edmund living within his jurisdiction.[2] John's 1201 charter to the Jews, which claimed to confirm rulings by Henry I and Henry II and which was very similar to a charter of Richard I of March 1190, lists the privileges Jews enjoyed. Jews were granted permission to reside freely and honourably in England and Normandy and were given free passage throughout these lands; their goods were to be protected in the same way royal possessions were. Jewish witnesses as well as Christian ones were used in court cases between Christians and Jews. Jews were expected to swear oaths on the Torah; allusion was made to the existence of internal Jewish judges.[3]

These privileges, in combination with the particular need for ready cash in twelfth- and thirteenth-century England and the concerted royal support Jews received in collecting their debts, without doubt helped the Jews of England become wealthier than their counterparts in northern France and Germany. Although many Jewish moneylenders dealt with small sums of money, a few leading members of the Jewish community, like Aaron of Lincoln (d. 1186), lent substantial sums to the elite of the land, which included prominent landowners, knights and religious houses.[4] However, behind this success lay the ambiguities of the notion of Jewish service and attitudes within Anglo-Norman and Angevin society towards a group of newcomers under special protection of the king, who not only continued to speak French but also used Hebrew and who, crucially, were adherents of a different religion.[5]

Bede's writings prove that Christian concern with Judaism did not rely on proximity to Jews, but the presence of Jews in post-Conquest England would seem to have put Judaism very much on the agenda. Already

[2] Stacey, 'Jews and Christians', pp. 340–54; R. C. Stacey, 'Jewish lending and the medieval economy', in R. H. Britnell and B. M. S. Campbell, eds., *A Commercialising Economy. England 1086 to c. 1300* (Manchester, 1995), pp. 78–92.

[3] J. Jacobs, ed., *The Jews of Angevin England* (New York, 1893; repr. New York, 1977), pp. 134, 212–4.

[4] Stacey, 'Jewish lending', pp. 90–7.

[5] On the use of French see Stacey, 'Jews and Christians', pp. 343–5.

by the end of the eleventh century Gilbert Crispin, Norman abbot of Westminster, had composed his widely disseminated *Disputation between a Christian and a Jew*, which he claimed to have written on the basis of discussions he had held with a Jew who had been educated in Mainz. Another even more widely disseminated and hugely influential disputation was penned by Peter Alfonsi, the Spanish Jew who was baptized in Huesca in 1106 and who travelled to England to join Henry I's entourage. Christian knowledge of Hebrew is attested by the twelfth-century manuscript of the *Ysagoge in Theologiam*, a theological compendium composed by a certain Odo in the 1140s. The text contains Hebrew versions of most of the standard texts of the Christian–Jewish debate, with Odo strongly arguing that Christians needed to learn Hebrew if they ever hoped to convert Jews.[6] Herbert of Bosham, a close associate of John of Salisbury and Thomas Becket, was one of the most accomplished Hebraists of the century. In his commentary on the Psalms Herbert quoted extensively from the biblical commentaries of Rashi, the Jewish exegetical luminary from late eleventh-century Troyes.[7] It is clear that twelfth-century English scholars with their Continental connections were important players in the Christian–Jewish debate, and it is, therefore, worthwhile to examine William of Newburgh's assessment of the role of the Jews in England by analysing his comprehensive account of the anti-Jewish riots of 1189/90.

William was an Augustinian canon at Newburgh, who wrote his *History* shortly before his death in late 1198. Although he relied heavily on Roger of Howden's *Chronicle*, he greatly enlarged on it for the topics he cared about. One of those topics was what happened to the Jews following Richard's coronation in September 1189. William's opening shot is that Henry II had cherished the Jews more than he should have on account of the profits he made from their usuries. This had allowed the Jews to act insolently towards Christians and impose hardship on them. William tells his readers that he is recording what befell the Jews as a memorial of divine judgement against that 'perfidious and blasphemous race'.

William relates how Richard had excluded the Jews from attending his coronation in London. A riot against the Jews started after a Christian lashed out at a Jew who was pushed into the palace of Westminster by the crush of people standing outside. Meanwhile, the 'most welcome' rumour circulated that the king had commanded that all the Jews be

[6] A. Sapir Abulafia, *Christians and Jews in the Twelfth-Century Renaissance* (London, 1995).

[7] D. L. Goodwin, *"Take Hold of the Robe of a Jew". Herbert of Bosham's Christian Hebraism* (Leiden, 2006).

killed, and a large group of undisciplined men from within and without London attacked the 'Jewish citizens' of London together with the Jews who had travelled to the city for the occasion. Many Jewish lives were lost. Although Richard was upset when he heard about it, he could not do much to stop the riots or bring the rioters to justice. 'Hatred for Jews and greed for plunder' had involved the large numbers attendant on the coronation: nobles with their large revenues and most of the population of London. William concludes that God used the 'absurd fervour of undisciplined, wicked men' because the Jews, who had lorded over Christians in the previous reign, needed to be humbled at the start of the new one. He proceeds to record the persecution of Jews in King's Lynn in early 1190. Lynn had attracted many Jews through its commercial advantages, and, according to William, they had become arrogant on account of their numbers, wealth and the royal protection they enjoyed. William specifically notes that the perpetrators there were young outsiders coming into the port, rather than the citizens of Lynn, who feared royal reprisal. Perhaps these were youths who had taken the cross. Omitting the riots of Norwich (and also the later riots in Bury, Colchester, Thetford and Ospringe (Kent)), William focuses next on Stamford. The perpetrators, again, were said to be young crusaders, visiting the Lenten fairs, who felt that Jews had no right to so many possessions while they who had taken the cross had so little. The inhabitants of Stamford offered the crusaders hardly any help. The Jews who survived found haven in the castle. In Lincoln, the Jews managed to escape local attack by retreating to the royal castle.

In York the Jews had no such luck. William epitomizes the York Jewry by singling out two of the wealthiest, Josce and Benedict, who had died of the wounds he received in the London riot. He had been forced to convert but the king had allowed him to return to Judaism. In William's words he was thus damned twice over as a Jew and an apostate. Josce and Benedict's houses in York are described as emulating palaces. Living as princes among their own people, they are regarded as exercising tyranny over the Christians to whom they lent money. The ringleaders of the attack on the Jews were high-ranking people who owed money to the Jews; they drew in local people of the area and crusaders who sought plunder. The young men of York itself were also drawn in but not the 'nobility of the city or the weightier citizens'. It is more than likely that feelings were running particularly high on account of Henry II's pursuit of the debts owed to the estate of Aaron of Lincoln which he had confiscated. Aaron had had extensive dealings with northern England. The Jews found refuge in Clifford's Tower but the royal castle came under siege. William then explains how a distinguished rabbinical scholar urged the others to martyr themselves rather than be murdered by Christians or be subjected to baptism. William describes the rabbi, who must have been Yom Tov of Joigny, variously as 'most famous', 'infamous', 'a mad old man' and as a portender of evil. The Jewish families who kill themselves are described as 'rational beings acting with irrational fury'. William mentions that Jews on the Continent had recently responded to persecution in this way. As for the Jews who tried to save their lives by agreeing to be baptized, they were murdered as they left the castle. William is so horrified by this that he maintains that the sincere converts among them would have been baptized by their own blood. He roundly condemns the cruelty and the deceit of those who withheld baptism from those willing to receive it. After the killings the perpetrators burnt the bonds of their Jewish debts in York Minster, where the Jews had brought them for safekeeping.

William's overall judgement is of immense interest. He points out that notwithstanding their zeal to serve God, the attackers forgot the basic Christian maxim that Jews should not be killed 'lest my people forget' (Psalm 58[9]: 12). Jews, whom he saw as the crucifiers of Christ, were allowed to live among Christians in order to remind them of Christ's Passion. But on account of their guilt for the crucifixion, Jews must *serve* Christians. Jewish service is the key concept here. However critical William was of those who persecuted the Jews in 1189/90, he did feel that the correct ordering of Christian–Jewish relations had been inverted. The *raison d'être* of Jews was to serve Christians until they converted. This meant that Christians should not be indebted to them; Jews should not be particularly successful; the king should not exacerbate this inversion by profiting from their moneylending. William implies that this inversion caused widespread resentment among Christians, especially among those indebted to Jews and those who had taken the cross. Reading William's views on the position of Jews within Christian society in this way is confirmed by his references to Jews in his commentary on the Song of Songs, which he wrote a few years before his *History*. That William read the whole Song as an allegory concerning the Virgin Mary does not concern us here. What matters is that he portrays the Synagogue as the Church's mother; through the flesh of Mary, Christ is born of the Jews. By repudiating Christ, Synagogue betrayed her Lord. William spells out that Jews are guilty of deicide and that all contemporary Jews share in this guilt because the Jews called out Christ's blood over their children. But in so doing they unknowingly served Christ because he used their evil to save the Gentiles. Christians are now the true Israelites. Hatred for Jews should not obscure the fact that salvation comes from the Jews because Christ took his flesh from them. The burden of service in this world which Jews suffer as a punishment for killing Christ will be lifted when they convert. Mary is portrayed as praying on a daily basis for this to happen. Seen in this light William's anguish at the slaughter of Jews who were prepared to be baptized is even more understandable, as is his contempt for Benedict's apostasy, not to mention his consternation at the self-martyrdom of Jews in order to avoid conversion. But the bottom line remained the in-built complexity concerning the temporal realities of the theological concept of Jewish service. Only by being successful could Jews be useful to their royal masters on a practical level. Yet on a theological level this very success could be interpreted as an inversion of the correct relationship between Christians and Jews. Having said that, the Jews could not have prospered if they had not been reasonably integrated in their Christian environment. After all, William talks about the Jewish *cives* (citizens) of London. In King's Lynn and in Stamford the locals were not the perpetrators of the riots. In York the impetus came from indebted knights from the county, not the elite of the city itself.[8]

Another aspect of the ambiguous nature of the Jewish presence in England was the emergence of accusations that Jews crucified Christian children in derision of Christ's Passion. The libel was first voiced in Norwich after the body of a boy called William was found in 1144; further accusations occurred in Gloucester in 1168 and Bury in 1181. The best-known case concerns Hugh of Lincoln in 1255. The emergence of this bizarre fiction has been explained by connecting it to internal Christian doubts about the real presence of Christ in the consecrated host, by pointing to the advantages accruing to the religious institutions establishing shrines for the alleged victims and by stressing that infanticide has always been a standard libel against people deemed to be outsiders.

[8] R. Howlett, ed., *The History of William of Newburgh*, in *Chronicles of the Reigns of Stephen, Henry II and Richard I* (RS; London, 1884), i, pp. 280, 293–322; trans. J. Stevenson, *The Church Historians of England*, vol. IV.ii (London, 1856); also ed. S. McLetchie (1999): www.fordham.edu/halsall/basis/williamofnewburgh-intro.html; J. C. Gorman, ed., *William of Newburgh's Explanatio sacri epithalamii in matrem sponsi* (Fribourg, 1960), pp. 151–3, 228, 238, 299–302, 341–2; see also M. J. Kennedy, '"Faith in the one God flowed over you from the Jews, the sons of the Patriarchs and the Prophets": William of Newburgh's writings on anti-Jewish violence', *ANS* 25 (2002 (2003)), 139–52, and R. B. Dobson, *The Jews of Medieval York and the Massacre of March 1190* (Borthwick Papers, 45; York, 1974).

Others remark on similar rumours circulating on the Continent or point to similarities between the libel and the treacherous role assigned to Jews in some Marian miracle stories. Twelfth-century England was, in fact, a centre for the dissemination of Marian stories, both in Latin and in the vernacular.[9] One only needs to think of how William of Newburgh incorporated the Jews in his Marian exegesis of the Song of Songs to imagine how explosive the portrayal of Jews committing treachery against the Virgin must have been. It is, however, also worth reflecting on the social realities prevailing in Norwich less than a hundred years after the Conquest. The influx of Normans into Norwich fundamentally altered the make-up of that market town. The Norman castle and cathedral displaced scores of Anglo-Saxon houses; a new Norman borough competed with older Anglo-Saxon institutions. The arrival of French-speaking Jews sometime before 1144 added another component to the strained heterogeneity of the city. It is indeed possible to join Jeffrey Cohen in reading into Thomas of Monmouth's *Life of William* an attempt to forge some kind of unity among the disparate Christians of Norwich.[10] It is, however, important to stress that in twelfth-century England Jews were not murdered on account of these libels, however emotive their subject matter might have been.

What about the Jews themselves? The central focus of any Jewish community would have been the synagogue. We know of at least twenty-seven synagogues from the twelfth and thirteenth centuries. Most of these would not have been particularly elaborate structures; some would even have been situated in wealthy homes. As a precautionary measure most synagogues were not immediately visible from the street. Synagogues were used for a wide range of communal activities besides religious services. Males studied Hebrew, the Hebrew Bible and Jewish law there at different levels. The Talmud was used by the scholars to legislate on all internal Jewish matters concerning food regulations, matrimonial matters, contracts and any internal disputes. They were in close contact with their counterparts in France, the so-called Tosafists, who followed in the footsteps of Rashi. Snippets of rabbinical deliberations which have survived from the twelfth century tell us, for example, that Jacob of Orleans, who was killed in the London riot of 1189, struggled – unsuccessfully one has

[9] J. A. Shea, 'Adgar's *Gracial* and Christian images of Jews in twelfth-century vernacular literature', *JMH*, 33 (2007), 181–96.

[10] J. J. Cohen, 'The flow of blood in medieval Norwich', *Speculum*, 79 (2004), 26–65.

to say – with the knotty problem of how to work round the prohibition on Jews charging each other interest on loans. Benjamin of Cambridge discussed procedural questions relating to Jews suing each other for damages following denunciation to the Christian authorities.[11] Jewish marriage contracts (*ketubbot*) protected Jewish women by guaranteeing them a sum of money if they were widowed or divorced by their husbands. Female Jewish participation in moneylending is extensively documented, and it appears that Jewish women played an active role in families' economic endeavours.[12] Although moneylending together with pawnbroking became the chief occupation within the Jewish community, one must not forget that besides moneylending Jews were active as doctors, teachers and scribes; others must have been bakers, butchers, wine traders and so forth.[13]

Most of the rich documentation concerning medieval English Jewry is financial. This derives from the fact that Jewish affairs were conducted under careful royal scrutiny. The level of scrutiny was greatly increased by Richard in 1194 in order to prevent any future loss of Jewish bonds of the sort which had occurred in the conflagration in York Minster. Everything Jews owned, from their debts to their rents and houses, would henceforth be registered. All loans would be recorded in double charters (chirographs), one half would be stored in chests (*archae*) kept in significant places like London, Lincoln and Norwich; the other half would be held by the Jewish lender as a receipt. Rolls would preserve transcripts of all these charters. These rulings led to the formalization of the Exchequer of the Jews, a special department for Jewish affairs, which had started up in connection with the collection of the debts of Aaron of Lincoln.[14] The precarious nature of Jewish life in the twelfth century would be exacerbated in the thirteenth. The Jews recovered rapidly from the crusade riots and were able to expand their business

[11] R. R. Mundill, 'The medieval Anglo-Jewish community: organization and royal control', in C. Cluse, A. Haverkamp and I. J. Yuval, eds., *Jüdische Gemeinden und ihr christlicher Kontext in kulturräumlich vergleichender Betrachtung von der Spätantike bis zum 18. Jahrhundert* (Hannover, 2003), pp. 267–75; J. Hillaby, 'Beit Miqdash Me'at: the synagogues of medieval England', *JEH*, 44.2 (1993), 182–98; H.-G. von Mutius, trans., *Rechtsentscheide Mittelalterlicher Englischer Rabbinen* (Judentum und Umwelt, 60; Frankfurt a.M., 1995), pp. 6–13.

[12] Hannah Meyer has researched the role of Jewish women in medieval England: 'Female moneylending and wet-nursing in Jewish–Christian relations in thirteenth-century England' (unpublished Ph.D. thesis, University of Cambridge, 2009).

[13] R. R. Mundill, 'England: the island's Jews and their economic pursuits', in C. Cluse, ed., *The Jews of Europe in the Middle Ages* (Turnhout, 2004), pp. 221–32.

[14] Mundill, 'Medieval Anglo-Jewish community', pp. 273–81; Jacobs, ed., *Jews*, pp. 156–9.

with considerable success. But increased royal monetary demands on the Jews indirectly exerted unwelcome pressures on their debtors, and the fate of English Jewry became a part of internal Christian politics. This, combined with continuing religious concerns about moneylending and the nature of Jewish service, eventually led to the expulsion of the Jews from England in 1290.

CHAPTER V.I

Religion and belief

Carl Watkins

By the year 900 England had already been shaped for three centuries or more by a Christian message which had spread from the north and west with Irish missionaries and from the south with the mission that arrived in 597 with Augustine of Canterbury (d. 604). That message was a meaning-rich account of existence in which a God-created world was riven by suffering and death because of the disobedience of the first human beings. That 'Fall', and the original sin which henceforth stained all born into the world, had been restored when God entered the world as Christ, a God-man who suffered and died to redeem the sins of humankind and then rose from the dead to seal his promise of eternal life. Through him, the Church taught, and through the remedies, the sacraments, which the Church offered in his name, salvation was possible for the believer. Moreover all, believer and unbeliever alike, would face Christ eventually for he would return at the end of days to judge the quick and dead, delivering the righteous into heaven and the wicked into the eternal fire. These essential messages ran like a golden thread through the conversion, into our period and beyond, but their institutional setting and detailed elaboration were subject to enormous change during the central Middle Ages. The Church itself was subject to a transformation which had major ramifications for the regions. Papal power, in particular, increased exponentially. In 900 England was little troubled by Pope Benedict IV (900–3), whose writ ran little further than the city of Rome itself, but by the end of our period, his eventual successor, Innocent III (1198–1216), wielded authority not only over bishops and abbots but even aspired to shape the religious lives of ordinary men and women in the parishes of the medieval west. Underpinning this change of papal fortunes were other important developments in theology and law. During the eleventh and twelfth centuries, European churchmen worked to turn the idea of standardized canon law enforceable across the Christian west from a pious dream into a realistic possibility. At the same time, theologians helped to crystallize the Church's teaching wherever it was inchoate – in matters such as the eucharist, the relationship of Father, Son and Holy Spirit in the Trinity, and the fate of the soul after death – laying foundations for the teaching of clear accounts of these things to the laity.

The official teachings of the Church are relatively easy for the historian to reconstruct from the rich seams of evidence that they have left behind. Far more difficult is the business of exploring the religious practices and beliefs of the ordinary laity of England, because our evidence thins the lower down the social hierarchy we look. Religious practice is easier to describe than the interior world of belief, but even in matters of praxis some very basic questions prove impossible to answer. We are, for example, in no position to work out how often ordinary people went to church. A letter written by Ælfric of Eynsham in 993×*c.* 5 stressed that 'Christian men were to go to church frequently'.[1] But what people were supposed to do is, inevitably, an inadequate guide to what they actually did. Similarly, although the legislation of 1005×8 required every priest to 'shrive and impose penance on him who confesses to him', we cannot be sure that ordinary men and women made a regular habit of this; nor can we know how often they took communion.[2] Some questions become easier to answer later in our period because evidence gets thicker on the ground. Indeed, it proliferates precisely because the Church hierarchy became more concerned with regulating the beliefs and practices of ordinary men and women and so generated texts designed to shape them – texts such as sermon materials, preaching manuals and handbooks for confessors. Despite this, the historian of the central Middle Ages never has the abundant sources that historians of the later Middle Ages possess, and we lack texts which take us in relatively unmediated ways into the lives and thoughts of the ordinary laity. We are obliged instead to rely on evidence generated by churchmen: charters describing lay donations to monasteries (but written by a clerical amanuensis), the stereotyped hagiographies which portray the lives of saints, collected stories of miracles allegedly worked by them, chronicles and annals, sermons, law codes and the legislation of Church Councils. To these we can add the witness of material culture: archaeology (especially of graveyards), traces of early wall painting in churches and clues offered by the architecture and organization of ecclesiastical spaces. In assembling these diverse sources we frequently have to estimate what people actually did using the Church's teachings about what they were supposed to do

[1] *Councils and Synods*, i, p. 217. [2] *Ibid.*, p. 335.

(and supposed *not* to do) and we are regularly forced to infer belief from fragmentary evidence of practice.

PARISH CHRISTIANITY

One thing that can be said with confidence is that the religious infrastructure of much of England underwent a dramatic transformation between 900 and 1200. Grand minsters gave way to smaller local churches. Hinterlands formerly served by minsters splintered into more compact parishes each served by its own priest (see Chapter V.2). And yet amidst the change was a thread of continuous concern among senior churchmen about the quality of the clergy tasked with ministering to ordinary men and women. For any system was only as good as its staff. Thus Ælfric of Eynsham (*c.* 955–*c.* 1010) and Wulfstan of York (d. 1023) were already striving early in the period to sharpen the priest's identity, requiring that he distinguish himself from his flock. New legislation, notably the so-called 'Northumbrian Priests' Law' of the first half of the eleventh century, laid out in some detail what was expected of a local priest.[3] It tackled the elementary mechanics of celebrating Mass, dues the priest was to collect, instruction to be given to the laity, priestly dress and general appearance (including the importance of shaving hair and beard) and the need to set a moral example. That some of this needed saying at all is perhaps telling. We learn, for example, that any priest who 'practises drunkenness or becomes a glee-man or tavern minstrel' was to pay a fine.[4]

Perhaps unsurprisingly, therefore, Lanfranc of Bec (*c.* 1005–89) still found much to fault in the English Church when he was installed as archbishop of Canterbury in the wake of the Norman Conquest. His reform drew much of its inspiration from a reinvigorated monastic life in which he himself had been prominent during his time as prior of Bec. His measures were both more intensively applied and more durable in their effects than the reform launched by Ælfric and Wulfstan. Here the underwriting that his enterprise enjoyed from a more assertive and reform-minded papacy was important and so, too, were mechanisms of enforcement in the dioceses, particularly the emergence after 1072 of archdeacons, whose courts supervised clusters of parishes and imposed the Church's increasingly standardized canon law upon them. But if the reform was more lasting it was also conceived on a narrow front. At its heart was the simple desire to separate the Church and churchmen more clearly from

[3] *Ibid.*, pp. 449–68. [4] *Ibid.*, p. 460.

a lay world thought to be absorbed in sinfulness. Lanfranc, in essence, sought a 'monasticization' of the larger Church. From this sprang two important initiatives. The first concerned local or parish churches. These were becoming too important to the Church's pastoral mission to be left in the control of the laymen and women who had originally built them and so needed to be wrested from their grasp. Reformers therefore argued that any layman or woman retaining a proprietorial interest in a church committed a grievous and ongoing sin (the sin of simony). With this argument, prelates deployed the sledgehammer of damnation to crack the age-old nut that was lay ownership of churches. These were now transferred en masse into the care of monasteries and communities of Augustinian canons. It seems very likely that the Norman baron Ralph Paynel was moved by these among other considerations when he decided to divest himself of churches in Yorkshire and Lincolnshire to help refound Holy Trinity, Micklegate as a Benedictine community in 1089.[5]

A second strand of Norman reform involved the clergy themselves. They, too, were to be 'monasticized'. They were to shun the buying and selling of ecclesiastical office, again a manifestation of simony, and they were not to marry or keep concubines (practices which were habitual through much of the period). These provisions were in part matters of pragmatic politics, because they prevented the alienation of Church property by sale or inheritance. But they were also bound up with a concerted attempt to ensure the dignity of priests as ministers of the sacraments, a special standing which required that they be separated from a sinful world which they sought to serve and save. Much here was a reprise of old legislation: priests were to wear the tonsure, dress in clerical garb and not to hunt or get drunk. Yet there were new emphases, too. Great stress was also placed on the correct performance of the liturgy, and particularly the eucharist, which was coming to have an enhanced status in the ritual of the Church. Towards the end of the period Gerald of Wales (*c.* 1146–*c.* 1223) deals with the practical ramifications of this in his manual, the *Jewel of the Church*.[6] He spelled out what should be done if a clumsy priest spilled the 'blood' (the consecrated wine) onto the altar cloth during Mass, or if he dropped the 'body' (the consecrated discs of bread) onto the floor. He even explains contingencies in the event of more dire pollution – where a mouse had nibbled negligently stored wafers, a spider

[5] J. Burton, *The Monastic Order in Yorkshire, 1069–1215* (Cambridge, 1999), pp. 46–51.

[6] J. S. Brewer *et al.*, ed., *Giraldi Cambrensis Opera* (8 vols.; RS; London, 1861–91), ii, pp. 12–13.

fell into the chalice during Mass or a communicant was unable to keep down the bread and wine.

The enhanced dignity of the priest can be traced not only in the way he was to dress and behave and the precision with which he was to perform the liturgy but also in the internal organization of the churches themselves. A 'great rebuilding' in the eleventh and twelfth centuries saw wood exchanged for stone in many local churches. It also saw chancels, the priest's distinctive space in which he would celebrate the eucharist at the high altar, first created and then steadily elongated. In Raunds church (Northamptonshire) archaeological investigations have traced the shift, the altar being moved from the end of the nave into the chancel at some point during the eleventh century. The effect of this, in concert with the other changes we have surveyed, was to alter the experience of worship. Intimate ritual enacted in a dark wooden chapel by a priest who was only subtly different from his fellow villagers yielded to a more solemn and remote rite in a bright stone church performed by a man marked out more sharply by dress and lifestyle from his peers.

But what of the lay experience of religion? Certainly by *c.* 900 at least the rudiments of Christianity seem to have been well rooted in England. Anglo-Saxon paganism was long dead. Flurries of legislation against heathen practices had attended the Viking settlements – after the second wave, the Laws of Cnut of 1020×2 re-emphasized the need to protect churches and avoid all 'worship of heathen gods … sun or moon, fire or flood, wells or stones or any kind of forest trees' – but worries about paganism seem to have been relatively short-lived.[7] Like the Anglo-Saxons before them, the Vikings seem to have converted quite rapidly to Christianity, preserving some traces of their older religion in artistic motifs and in folk beliefs and practices but absorbed now in a substantially Christian culture. If paganism was no longer seen as a serious threat by senior churchmen, 'secularization', the failure to treat sacred space and time with due reverence, did register as a significant problem. Injunctions to preserve holy places and holy days were repeated throughout the period. Ælfric of Eynsham condemned men who 'drink madly in God's house and … defile God's house with scurrilous talking'.[8] There were also ongoing battles to ensure that graveyards were fenced to keep out livestock (especially pigs, who might root out corpses) and to drive games, drinking bouts and general revelry from the church precincts. Effort was needed to defend holy days from 'secular' encroachment, too: the Northumbrian Priests'

[7] *Councils and Synods*, i, p. 489. [8] *Ibid.*, pp. 217–18.

Law prescribed a flogging for slaves and a fine for everyone else who broke Sunday observance. That as late as 1235–6 Robert Grosseteste (*c.* 1175–1253), bishop of Lincoln, was telling his archdeacons to put a stop to rowdiness and commerce in churchyards on Sundays and holy days suggests that this fight was still far from won by 1200.[9]

The Church also had evolving expectations about what the laity *should* be doing as well as what they should not be doing. The tenth century in particular seems to have witnessed two major innovations. First, the assumption that the dead must be buried in hallowed ground gathered force, being formally noticed in Æthelstan's Grateley law code (926×30), which distinguished consecrated and unconsecrated ground.[10] This had significant ramifications, because ancestral burial places such as ancient mounds and barrows were only now steadily abandoned in favour of consecrated graveyards (often leaving the old sites as places where criminals and other undesirables might be obliged to lay their bones). Second, the finances of the Church were also set on a new foundation. While distinctive dues such as 'churchscot' and 'soulscot' had long been owed by the English, the Grateley law code also moved to introduce, from the Continent, a new obligation to pay tithe. This requirement, to pay a tenth of one's income to the Church annually, became by far the most important financial payment owed by the laity to the Church in the central and later Middle Ages and seems to have been bound up from the outset with the idea that the beneficiary of the due had a pastoral responsibility for those who rendered it.

The mechanisms of Church teaching in this period are not easy to discern and their effects are still more elusive. Ælfric of Eynsham seems to have scripted vernacular homilies with a lay audience at least partly in mind, as these texts were designed to explain in Old English the contents of Gospels read in Latin during church services. How far the average priest was up to the task of delivering such teaching orally is open to serious question. Although there were certainly learned men among the ranks of local priests in the tenth, eleventh and twelfth centuries, it is uncertain how many of them were capable of preaching or catechizing. The vernacular clearly offered one way round this problem, as Ælfric's project indicates, but new vernacular texts for instructional purposes dwindled after 1066 with the advent of a Norman episcopate committed to Latin rather than Old English. Nonetheless, mechanisms were in place to allow

[9] C. S. Watkins, *History and the Supernatural in Medieval England* (Cambridge, 2007), pp. 98–9.

[10] F. Liebermann, ed., *Die Gesetze der Angelsachsen* (3 vols.; Halle, 1903–16), i, p. 164.

exposition of the rudiments of the faith. Bishops preached throughout this period – we have numerous references to them doing so and some clues that bishops could be crowd-pullers. Bishop Oswald of Worcester (d. 992) was obliged to preach outside because his cathedral church was not large enough for the congregation. We also have a large collection of sermons expounded by Herbert Losinga, bishop of Norwich (d. 1119), who in all probability aimed his words at a mixed lay and clerical audience.[11] *Regularis concordia*, a great tenth-century compendium of monastic regulations, anticipated that laymen and women might be present at Sunday masses in Benedictine monasteries and this may also have exposed them to teaching. Rather later, it was certainly the case that the energetic Samson, abbot of Bury St Edmunds (*c.* 1135–1211), was accustomed to preach to the townsfolk 'in the speech of Norfolk, where he was born and bred'.[12] Away from cathedrals and monasteries, the teaching of the Church may have been communicated in less formal ways, perhaps through the simple exhortations of less skilled local clergy and perhaps also, from the early twelfth century, by the Augustinian canons. The drama of a liturgy rich in gesture would probably have been a further important vehicle for communicating meanings about rituals such as the eucharist. Carved and painted images also decked most churches. The Bible, or at least its salient stories of the Fall, Nativity, Passion, Resurrection and Last Judgement, were painted over interiors as at Chaldon church, Surrey, where heaven, hell and the torments of the damned are still clearly visible in a twelfth-century mural. Literate laymen and women had the further luxury of reading about these things for themselves. The existence of some capable of this is revealed by guild statutes from Exeter (dating from the first half of the tenth century) which envisaged that guildsmen of ordinary rank would be able to say two Psalters for the good of the living and the souls of the dead at each of their meetings.[13]

Thus we can say with some confidence that the rudimentary teaching of priests, the preaching of bishops and heads of religious houses, the theatre of the liturgy and Bible stories communicated in paint, carved wood and stone would have guaranteed widespread exposure to the essentials of the Christian faith. That what was on offer was not, in the eyes of many reform-minded bishops of the twelfth and thirteenth centuries, good enough should come as no surprise. These men put a premium on

[11] E. M. Goulburn and H. Symonds, eds. and trans., *The Life, Letters, and Sermons of Bishop Herbert de Losinga* (2 vols.; Oxford, 1878).

[12] H. E. Butler, ed. and trans., *The Chronicle of Jocelin of Brakelond* (London, 1949), p. 40.

[13] *EHD*, i, no. 137, p. 605.

learning. But this also means that their recurrent criticisms of the quality of the local clergy might be at variance with local experience, where proper performance of saving ritual mattered more than exposition of the faith's finer points. Here there might be much greater satisfaction. And of course, the very rough-and-readiness of the Church's teaching infrastructure also had another effect, less palatable for prelates than ordinary believers, namely, the scope it offered for flexible local interpretations and articulations of official teaching.

SAVING THE BODY

But what was the faith for? The official message here was clear enough: it was the pathway to paradise, a shape in which the good life could be lived so that the believer achieved salvation. And yet medieval Christian practice did more than pave the way to heaven. It also supplied explanatory and remedial strategies which the faithful might use to counter misfortune in this world. The prevalence of man-made and natural disasters ensured that a premium was placed on these countermeasures. When Vikings again threatened England in 1009 the menace was read as a sign of divine wrath, and Æthelred II directed that 'all the nation shall fast for three days on bread and herbs and water' to cleanse its sins and abate God's anger.[14] Supernatural as well as natural forces and human agents might be instruments of God's providence: demons might tempt and test and punish human beings. Unofficial beliefs, neither sanctioned nor anathematized by the Church, twined around such teachings, adding local variation to a core of shared instincts about the invisible world. Devils in human shapes, skilled in seduction and known as *incubi* and *succubi* by learned writers, might tempt men and women into sexual sin. Morally ambiguous fairies might steal children and replace them with sickly changelings or snatch adults into fairyland, from which they might escape raving or, generations later, into an age which was not their own. The dead might return as ghosts or even, as the courtier and cleric Walter Map (1130×5–1209×10) observed, in their own flesh if God 'had given power to the evil angel of that lost soul to move about in the dead corpse'.[15]

Here then was a host of perils, seen and unseen, which needed to be resisted. Against them the Church erected a buttress. The parish

[14] *Councils and Synods*, i, p. 375; p. 379.

[15] M. R. James, ed. and trans., R. A. B. Mynors and C. N. L. Brooke, rev., *Walter Map, De Nugis Curialium, Courtiers' Trifles* (OMT; Oxford, 1983), pp. 203–4.

church would have supplied a primary focus for prayer which enclosed self, family and community. As Paul Hayward's chapter (Chapter V.3) suggests, the intercession of the saints, sought most effectively by visiting the shrines which contained their powerful bones, not only promised help in the afterlife but also held the promise of aid in this world, whether the miraculous healing of illness, the stilling of storms, ending of droughts or wondrous destruction of mortal enemies. Evil could also be turned aside with gestures, words and the use of holy things and substances. The sign of the cross, invocation of the holy names of Jesus, Mary or a saint, holy water, chrism (consecrated oil), incense and sanctified candles were all thought capable of banishing supernatural dangers. Such strategies of remedy were hallowed by long use in the Christian west and enjoyed the authorization of a Church which pressed them regularly into service. But the idea that certain things, words and gestures were invested with special power might also lead to tensions. Informal, unsanctioned strategies might develop in which the power of holy things was co-opted for purposes which the Church deemed illicit. Consecrated wafers might go unswallowed by communicants who spirited them off for use in spells. Font water might be stolen or used by diviners who gazed into the potent mix of baptismal oils and holy water to discern the future from the mysterious shapes forming there. Alarm about such magical abuses recurs in the Church's prescriptive writing and legislative enactments during the central Middle Ages, Gerald of Wales worrying in his *Jewel of the Church* that hosts could be stolen for use in magic or even that requiem masses might be celebrated for the living so that they might die.[16] And yet the causes of this sort of anxiety probably lay at least partly in the faith itself. From the vantage point of senior churchmen, invocations of holy names, sprinkling of holy water and making the sign of the cross were all essentially supplicatory: ritual acts combined with right faith made an appeal for divine aid which may, or may not, be forthcoming. Yet in practice many of the ordinary faithful (and perhaps their priests, too) probably imagined these things as possessing *inherent* power and having a compulsive effect, the utterance or act being enough to drive the devil away. Such habits of thought, which thinned the theoretical distinction between religion and magic, formed a context in which the co-option of holy things for novel purposes would have been natural to many ordinary men and women.

[16] Brewer *et al.*, eds., *Giraldi Cambrensis Opera*, ii, p. 137.

The line between sanctioned uses of the holy and magical abuses was also often more blurred in practice than it appeared in the Church's official writings. John of Salisbury (*c.* 1120–80), taking his cue from the pronouncements of Church Councils, excoriated almost all magic in his *Policraticus*, but many churchmen tolerated activities which the Church's formal strictures should have encouraged them to condemn.[17] This is nowhere more marked than in the quest for knowledge of the future. While the Church tended to set its face against prognostication, the Bible itself was littered with legible signs, and the medieval Church continued to hold that God showed portents of things to come and that these were susceptible to interpretation. Exploiting this ambiguity, we find that churchmen and laymen alike shared a desire to know what an uncertain future held. Prognostication and prophecy, in both formally sanctioned and unofficial guises, were thus deeply embedded in medieval culture. When new bishops were consecrated it was thought perfectly orthodox for prognostics of their episcopate to be taken from Bibles opened randomly while resting on their shoulders. When Lanfranc was consecrated as archbishop of Canterbury the monk-chronicler William of Malmesbury (d. *c.* 1143) tells us without blinking that his prognostic was 'Give alms and all things are open to you' (Luke 11:41).[18] Far less conventionally, in parts of twelfth-century Pembrokeshire Gerald of Wales tells us that the art of 'scapulimancy' was practised by Flemish settlers, a technique in which the future was discerned by inspecting the boiled shoulder blades of rams.[19] Gerald, an archdeacon, was cautious about the art but he did not condemn it outright.

This second example also suggests that divinatory and magical arts might be grounded in extra-ecclesial ideas as well as Christian cosmology. Notions about natural properties and occult virtues of herbs and minerals informed medieval medicine and much medieval magic. These were hardly the Church's invention, but the idea of the 'properties of things' was generally accepted by a Church which was willing, up to a point, to christianize older intuitions. Other forms of magical activity were more specialized and more dangerous in the eyes of senior churchmen. Image magic and astral magic which harnessed cosmic forces both savoured of

[17] C. C. J. Webb, ed., *Ioannis Saresberiensis Episcopi Carnotensis Policratici: sive de nugis curialium et vestigiis philosophorum libri III* (2 vols.; Oxford, 1909).

[18] G. Henderson, '*Sortes Biblicae* in twelfth-century England: the list of episcopal prognostics in Cambridge, Trinity College MS R.7.5', in D. Williams, ed., *England in the Twelfth Century: Proceedings of the 1988 Harlaxton Symposium* (Woodbridge, 1990), pp. 113–35.

[19] Brewer *et al.*, eds., *Giraldi Cambrensis Opera*, vi, p. 87.

dabbling with demonic powers and both might easily be imagined as species of necromancy – the black art which involved explicit commerce with the spirits of the dead or demons. Magic which made use of occult virtues as well as image and astral magic all seem to have been practised in England (though the extent of it is hard to establish). Indeed, at the end of the twelfth century, some such enterprises were even acquiring a measure of intellectual respectability as scientific theory seemed to offer a rationale for them, rehabilitating some magic as 'natural', while other forms were more forcefully condemned as black arts. Beyond the bounds of magic, but closely allied to divination, the twelfth century also witnessed an upsurge of interest in astrology. This, too, was a product of learned, one might say scientific, speculations. A new alertness to Arabic astrological knowledge is detectable at a number of religious houses in the late eleventh and early twelfth centuries, perhaps most notably at Worcester, where tell-tale manuscripts survive, but also at other centres such as Malvern, where the prior, Walcher, was said by the chronicler William of Malmesbury to be skilled in the art.[20] Some churchmen were distinctly edgy about a practice emanating from the east which promised knowledge of the future, but it was nonetheless starting to enter the cultural mainstream during the twelfth century – not least, perhaps, because it allowed some of its practitioners to curry favour with a political elite nervous about the future course of war and politics.

SAVING THE SOUL: THIS WORLD AND THE NEXT

The Last Judgement loomed large in the central Middle Ages, cut elaborately into the façades of some cathedrals and painted on the chancel arches of many local churches as at Clayton, West Sussex, a rare early survival dating from the second half of the twelfth century. Such images depicted Christ returning to judge the quick and the dead. The dead were resurrected and the saints, arrayed around Christ, pleaded for the salvation of souls as the saved were separated from the damned. The New Testament Book of Revelation explained the course of these terrible events but it gave few clues about when they would be enacted. As a result, people read the signs and at particular moments apocalyptic expectation grew more fevered. The return of the Vikings, falling alarmingly close to the millennium, moved Ælfric of Eynsham to meditate on the coming of

[20] R. W. Southern, *Robert Grosseteste: The Growth of an English Mind in Medieval Europe* (2nd edn; Oxford, 1992), pp. xxxiv–lv.

Antichrist, an event which would set the machinery of the Apocalypse in motion, and led him to conclude that 'men particularly require good teaching in this age which is the end of the world'.[21] His contemporary Wulfstan, archbishop of York, agreed and bleakly warned in his *Sermon of the Wolf* (1014×16) that 'the world is in haste and the end approaches; and therefore in the world things go from bad to worse'.[22] When the new millennium did not usher in the end-times, expectations of an imminent apocalypse seem to have evaporated. The twelfth-century chronicler Henry of Huntingdon even felt sufficiently confident of an extended future to address those readers of his chronicle who would be alive during the third millennium, asking them to remember him, now turned to dust, and to pray for his sinful soul.[23]

But even if the end was not imminent, it was inevitable. At some point the script of Revelation *would* be played out and the living and the dead would face terrible judgement and unerring justice. The stark promise of Revelation and its associated iconography – eternal life to the righteous; everlasting fire for the wicked – was a stimulus for many to anxiety about whether one could ever do enough during life to escape the flames of hell. For most of this period the best chance of freedom from this fear lay in renunciation of the sinful world and the vocation of monk, nun or hermit with its stress on prayer and penitence. 'No one can be saved', warned Gilbert Crispin, abbot of Westminster (d. 1117), 'unless he follows as much as he is able the life of a monk.'[24] And yet the proper pattern and appropriate disciplines of the monastic life were themselves open to discussion and debate. How could one know, even as a monk, that one's life was sufficiently committed to prayer and penance? This general question, and the apprehension it generated, was an important mechanism for efforts to perfect the lives of monk, nun and hermit. King Edgar (d. 975) sponsored one such enterprise in England. Taking his cue from earlier Carolingian legislation, Edgar presided over a reform of the religious life spearheaded by Dunstan, archbishop of Canterbury (*c.* 909–88), Æthelwold, bishop of Winchester (909–84) and Oswald, bishop of Worcester. These three churchmen sought to impose the sterner discipline of the Benedictine Rule, a pattern for monastic living imported from across the Channel, on some of the larger and more important English cathedrals and collegiate

[21] *EHD*, i, no. 239, p. 924. [22] *Ibid.*, no. 240, p. 929.

[23] D. Greenway, ed. and trans., *Henry, Archdeacon of Huntingdon Historia Anglorum, The History of the English People* (OMT; Oxford, 1996), pp. 496–501.

[24] G. Constable, *The Reformation of the Twelfth Century* (Cambridge, 1996), p. 7.

churches. The reformers' successes were trumpeted loudly in hagiography. And yet simple arithmetic tells against any claim that this reform was a triumph: the thirty reformed houses of monks and some nine or so of nuns which emerged from it must be set against the survival of hundreds of unreformed minsters.

Reform came again to the monastic life in the aftermath of the Norman Conquest. Some early stirrings had distinctively insular origins. In 1073×4 three monks left the monastery of Evesham and sought to revitalize monasticism in the north, travelling to Jarrow, Monkwearmouth, Whitby and ultimately Durham in 1083. This triumvirate drew their reformist inspiration from Bede, in whose writings about the early Church in England they found a blueprint for religious renewal. Yet the most powerful reformist impulses had their origins in the ideologies of Continental communities. Hence the advent of the Normans saw the spread of Cluniac monasticism to England, with notable foundations by the powerful Warenne family at Lewes in 1077 and Castle Acre in 1089. Their choice reflected the spiritual cachet of the mother house, the great Burgundian monastery of Cluny itself. With its strict observance of the Benedictine Rule and its promise of ceaseless prayer for a sinful world, it was advertised by Peter the Venerable, its famous twelfth-century abbot, as 'the treasury of the whole Christian republic'.[25] Much more important than Cluny in an English context were the black-habited Augustinian canons and white-robed Cistercian monks who arrived in England after *c.* 1100 and 1128 respectively. The essential mission of these 'new orders' was familiar – the restoration of the disciplines of the early Church – but they expressed this ambition in very different ways. The Cistercians sought renewal by following the Rule of St Benedict more closely and living the life of renunciation with renewed zeal. Striving to recreate the ideal of third- and fourth-century monastic communities of Palestine and Egypt, they preferred whitewashed walls over rich decoration, stripped down the liturgy and, in place of the desert, chose the Yorkshire moors for some of their earliest English houses at Rievaulx, Fountains and Jervaulx.

If the Cistercians set out to flee the sinful world, the Augustinian canons were committed to improving it. Their first houses in England emerged in the early twelfth century, among them Holy Trinity, Aldgate and a little later Nostell and Llanthony (where existing reform-minded communities took up the Rule of St Augustine as the best way to give their ambitions shape). The early canons, like the Cistercians, lived under

[25] G. Constable, ed., *The Letters of Peter the Venerable* (2 vols.; Cambridge, 1967), i, p. 264.

a Rule, but this time one attributed to St Augustine and, so they claimed, of still more ancient vintage than that of Benedict. Augustinian canons, as priests, could also administer the sacraments – baptizing, officiating at marriages, offering shrift and housel to the dying, celebrating the eucharist and hearing confessions – and their pastoral role tended to distinguish them from monks, particularly monks like the Cistercians, who had, in theory at least, no such traffic with the world. Cistercian monks and Augustinian canons were thus very different manifestations of reform but each had its origins in the idea of restoration of the Church and the search for models of the religious life in its early history and in scripture itself. Both also shared a broadly similar vision of the way to salvation. The old Benedictine monasteries, including Cluny and its dependencies, stressed the collective activity of monks, who were engaged in ceaseless corporate prayer, in securing this. The 'new orders', in contrast, emphasized the individual's conscious decision to tread the hard path to heaven and their inner life of prayer and penitence once they became members of the community. This promise of salvation, set in a context of deep anxiety about the sinfulness of the world, encouraged large numbers to convert to the religious life and contributed to the remarkable proliferation of new monasteries in twelfth-century England.

Not only men but also women were attracted to the religious life in great numbers during this period. The great difficulty in exploring this phenomenon is that nunneries have generally left far thinner records than male houses; only recently have innovative readings of this evidence revealed something of the life of women religious. After the reform of the tenth century, and prior to the Norman Conquest, there were, seemingly, only some nine nunneries in England. But recent work has shown these institutions to have been complemented by much more widespread informal arrangements whereby aristocratic 'vowesses' took the veil and committed themselves to secluded lives perhaps in their existing households. Such arrangements allowed families to meet the needs of female members who sought the religious life without the permanent loss of family lands needed to establish a nunnery. More formally constituted female religious communities multiplied after 1066, but many of these seem to have grown slowly and to have had their origins in ad hoc groupings of recluses. Here we can perhaps see the sorts of informal arrangements visible in the tenth and eleventh centuries acquiring more formal institutional shapes in the twelfth, a trend which would be consistent with a wider concern within the Church to fit new religious communities, male and female alike, into existing frameworks and Rules.

The proliferation of monasteries in the twelfth century is not explicable solely in terms of a flood of eager converts. It also depended on lay enthusiasm, too. Here the role of the members of the aristocracy was paramount because they contributed the great swathes of land necessary to sustain the new communities. Complex motives encouraged them to do this but fundamental was growing apprehension about the consequences of their sinful lives, especially lives of violence, and consequent desire for the powerful prayers of monks to redeem them. Pre-Conquest England was not insulated from such harsh messages. They are there in Cnut's laws of 1020×2 where dread of Doomsday was deployed as a stimulus for religious rectitude and fear of hellfire is evident in many wills of the Anglo-Saxon aristocracy, too.[26] The Normans seem to have suffered similar apprehensions, and these could only have been intensified by the many sins committed during the blood-soaked conquest of England. The penitential ordinance issued by the papal legate Ermenfrid in 1070 tried to reduce these anxieties to mathematical proportions, describing in meticulous detail the lengthy penances each man must perform for each wound inflicted and man slain.[27] He even calculated the penances to be undertaken by archers, who were, necessarily, unable to work out what injuries their arrows had caused. Others spelled out the danger more colourfully. Writing in the wake of the 'anarchy' of Stephen's reign, Gilbert Foliot (d. 1187), a Cluniac bishop, warned his uncle, William de Chesney, to make proper amendment for his sins because otherwise, when he stood before Christ at the day of judgement, he risked being swept to hell by the cries of orphans and widows he had oppressed during a life of violence and acquisitiveness.[28]

Penance, a subject explored at greater length in Sarah Hamilton's chapter (Chapter V.2), was a powerful antidote to sin. But it is likely that the sheer scale of penance which a military participant in the Conquest or a man like William de Chesney needed to perform made the system unworkable. The solution therefore was to 'franchise out' one's penitential obligations and engage the services of professional penitents, monks, who would lead the life of renunciation in your place. Establishing a new religious house, or endowing an existing one with new resources, supplied ways in which a warrior might thus make amends for his sins without abandoning his obligations in the world. It is likely that

[26] *Councils and Synods*, i, pp. 484–5. [27] *EHD*, ii, no. 81, pp. 606–7.

[28] C. N. L. Brooke and A. Morey, eds., *The Letters and Charters of Gilbert Foliot, Abbot of Gloucester (1139–48), Bishop of Hereford (1148–63) and London (1163–87)* (Cambridge, 1967), p. 55.

William de Chesney was already aware of his dangerous spiritual predicament before Gilbert Foliot upbraided him, and although he may not, in the monk-bishop's eyes, have done enough to save his soul he had at least entered into confraternity with a religious house and would derive benefit from the prayers and penances of its brethren.

It seems likely that anxiety about sin was fired by changes within the life of the cloister itself during the later eleventh and early twelfth centuries. As the monastic life became more ascetic and rigorous the gap between the good life, the way to salvation, which monks exemplified, and real life lived by the warrior elite grew wider. Thus the *Visio Leofrici* suggested that a late Anglo-Saxon noble might be able to take up elements of the monk's vocation – hearing Mass twice daily, fasting and praying each night – and feel that he was participating actively in the monastic life.[29] But the much stricter obligations of retreat, prayer and penitence emerging among orders like the Cistercians could not be emulated by lay men and women who were still living in the world. So their solution to the problems of worldliness and sin must, for the most part, lie in supporting monks and nuns from outside the cloister, benefitting from their prayers, enjoying rights of confraternity, perhaps hoping to join the community in old age (or even just before death) and probably anticipating eventual burial near to the monks. By these measures benefactors hoped that at the Last Judgement, when they stood before Christ clothed in new flesh, they might still reap the rewards of a monastic life they had not lived and benefit further from the intercession of their monastery's patron saint.

This 'spiritual' dynamic is a necessary but not sufficient condition in accounting for the pattern of religious foundations in twelfth-century England. An inspection of chronology reveals that relatively few religious houses were established by the Normans in the decades immediately after 1066 – Battle Abbey is a striking exception but also an unusual case because it was the Conqueror's own foundation. This pattern is perhaps surprising given the bloodshed of the Conquest, and yet the interaction of spiritual impulses with issues of identity can account for it. The first generation of conquerors were still attached emotionally to their homelands across the Channel and so tended to endow Norman monasteries

[29] A. S. Napier, 'An Old English Vision of Leofric, earl of Mercia', *Transactions of the Philological Society*, 26.2 (1907–10), 180–8; M. McGatch, 'Piety and liturgy in the Old English Vision of Leofric', in M. Korhammer, with K. Reichl and H. Sauer, eds., *Words, Texts and Manucripts: Studies in Anglo-Saxon Culture Presented to Helmut Gneuss on the Occasion of His Sixty-Fifth Birthday* (Woodbridge, 1992), pp. 159–79.

with English lands rather than build new houses in England. Only as the first generation gave way to the second did a landholding elite with more firmly Anglocentric interests and loyalties begin to take shape. Many in this next generation were born in England and many aristocratic families split their inheritances when the head of the family died, elder sons tending to receive the Norman patrimonial lands and second sons the recently acquired English properties (see Chapter IV.1). These more distinctively 'English' landholders now needed to establish new monasteries in England. Further dissection of founders' motives also suggests that the need to save the soul was not the only imperative in the foundation of religious houses. Indeed there is something of a paradox here: because general acceptance of the idea that great wealth and worldly power demanded lavish endowment to offset their effects in the afterlife, patronage of a monastery itself became a mark of high social rank. Each great family came to have its 'own' monastery, just as it had a grand castle as its principal residence. Thus the arrival of Walter Espec (d. 1147×58) in high society during the 1120s was marked not only by the building of a substantial castle at Helmsley, North Yorkshire, around 1120 but also by the establishment in 1132 of a Cistercian abbey just a few miles away at Rievaulx and a second, in 1136, at Wardon, Bedfordshire, near to his family's ancestral lands. Patronage of religious houses was also filtered through further, more specific obligations created by political loyalties and dynastic traditions. Particular trends of benefaction were often set at court. Henry I's courtiers were, for example, especially engaged in the foundation of houses of Augustinian canons, a trend initiated by the king and his queen, Matilda, who established Holy Trinity, Aldgate in *c.* 1107. Pious fashions spread down the social hierarchy, too. Barons initially set the trend in establishing new monasteries, their knightly tenants tending to offer donations to their lord's monastery. But as some knights acquired riches and a measure of political independence during the twelfth century they aspired to found their own house, frequently electing to establish a house of Augustinian canons as this would demand only a small parcel of land.

Yet even as we separate these different motives, silently labelling them 'worldly' or 'pious', we need to remember that we risk teasing apart matters which were tightly bound in the thoughts of donors. Worldly, even mercenary, motivations could coexist with spiritual impulses. Walter Espec may have patronized the Cistercians at Rievaulx and Wardon in part to mark his dizzying social rise. But it is interesting that he also made grants to Augustinian canons of nearby Kirkham, which he had founded in 1121.[30] More was at stake here than simple display, and given the pastoral role of the canons and their likely function as confessors at Henry I's court, it is possible that Walter felt a need *both* for the prayers of the Cistercians and the spiritual counsel of the Augustinians.

Similar complex motives can be observed in child oblation, a practice which saw children gifted by parents to monasteries and nunneries. This was common in the period and there are well-known examples. Eve, a nun of Wilton, was immortalized in the *Liber confortatorius* composed for her by the monk Goscelin (d. *c.* 1099); Orderic Vitalis (1075–*c.* 1142), an oblate of Saint-Evroult in Normandy, immortalized himself in his *Ecclesiastical History*, recalling in old age how he had left his Shropshire home and his father 'a weeping child' for the monk's life, never to see either again.[31] Such hard parental choices encouraged some historians to see medieval monasteries as dumping grounds for surplus children in a world in which property (for boys) and good marriages (for girls) were in relatively short supply. And yet, again, any simple mercenary explanation falls short of the mark. Families had to endow the host monastery with land when they offered a child, so this was not a cheap and easy option. More importantly, spiritual as well as economic calculations may have been in play, as the prayers of some family members leading the good life in the cloister might benefit the rest.

A greater challenge than explaining the mortuary piety of the elite is to explore the same among the ordinary faithful of town, village and farmstead. Here our evidence is exiguous in the extreme, but what survives indicates that piety of peasants and townsfolk, though different in its forms, was probably structured by similar beliefs and values to those of the elite. The life of religious renunciation was not only available to the aristocracy. The old Anglo-Saxon minsters may have recruited their communities from quite a broad range in society, and, for true spiritual athletes, there was always the option of striking out into the wilderness and embracing the life of the hermit. Although the Benedictine and Cluniac houses were quite socially exclusive, the new orders also offered a religious vocation to a wider social circle. This was especially true of the Cistercians, who recruited *conuersi* or lay brothers. These were usually peasants who followed a simplified round of prayer and glorified God principally through the work that they carried out on the monastic estates or granges.

[30] Burton, *Monastic Order in Yorkshire*, pp. 79–80, 100–1.

[31] M. Otter, trans., *Goscelin of St Bertin, the Book of Encouragement and Consolation* (Cambridge, 2004); M. Chibnall, ed. and trans., *The Ecclesiastical History of Orderic Vitalis* (6 vols.; OMT; Oxford, 1969–80), ii, pp. xiii–xiv.

For the great majority who were not prepared to embrace a life of penitence, less radical opportunities existed to salve their sinful souls. Gift-giving to monasteries at levels beneath that of the social elite was probably commonplace but would seldom have demanded records. Where these do survive in unusual detail, for example for Rochester Cathedral Priory, we find a host of very small-scale donations of property.[32] Rochester was probably unusual only in its record-keeping, and there is no reason to think such giving aberrant. For the very many who could not give even a fragment of land, smaller-scale gifts of wax or pennies might be offered at shrines along with prayer in the hope of a saint's intercession. Guilds, for which there are extant statutes from as early as the tenth century, were also probably important in the efforts of the 'middling sort' to provide for their souls. These associations, such as that found in tenth-century Exeter or the slightly later thegns' guild of Cambridge, bound the living for purposes of conviviality, politics and welfare but spiritual provisions were at their heart – the proper burial of brethren, offering of alms in their names, singing of masses by hired priests and psalms and prayers by fellow guildsmen for the good of their souls.[33] Beyond the horizons of formal institutions we must also be alert to the existence of unregulated or partially regulated prayer professionals. England in the central Middle Ages was a land full of hermits, and their numbers can hardly be explained simply in terms of the social functions which they discharged. These were surely incidental to their primary purpose of prayer and penitence, undertaken not only for their own salvation but also for the good of those who sustained them with small-scale almsgiving.

There is an important sense, then, in which the spirituality of the later eleventh and twelfth centuries was powerfully shaped by the monastic ethos. The good life was epitomized by the monastic life, and those who did not lead it themselves associated with those who did. Remarks by prominent monks such as Anselm of Canterbury (*c.* 1033–1109) suggest that the fate of ordinary lay men and women was therefore thought by Church leaders to be bleak, with the fires of hell awaiting most of them on the other side of the grave. And yet there is a complexity here, too: Anselm, for all his pessimism, never abandoned hope for the world. When he was prior of Bec he sought to spread the fruits of the monastic life beyond the cloister wall, and he was deeply committed to the pastoral care of his flock when he became archbishop of Canterbury. This tension,

[32] H. Tsurushima, 'The fraternity of Rochester cathedral priory', *ANS* 14 (1991 (1992)), 313–37.

[33] *EHD*, i, no. 136 pp. 603–5.

between pessimism about the laity's fate and energetic care of souls, can be explained by the ethics in which Anselm was immersed. As a monk, Anselm was consumed with anxiety about his own unworthiness, and this could not help but trigger further dark reflections about the fate of those outside the monastery whose lives were not subjected to its discipline. Yet this fear of divine justice was in a delicate relationship with hope for mercy. Anselm's words and acts reveal both impulses at work, stimulating an anxious monk-prelate to do what he could for a sinful world.

REDISCOVERING THE LAITY

The later twelfth century saw a strengthening of the hopeful rhetoric of mercy in the formal teachings of a Church which was increasingly keen to embrace the world, and the laity, more tightly and to create structures to aid the lay search for salvation. The Fourth Lateran Council of 1215 illustrates this evolution of thinking within the Church hierarchy.[34] It sought to strengthen the parish, stressing that all of the faithful should be baptized, married and buried in their own parishes, and it required all the faithful to make their confessions to, and receive communion from, their local priest. During the thirteenth century, the provisions laid down by the canons of this council would be fleshed out in the English dioceses as bishops promulgated their own synodal legislation. Great energy would also be invested in a 're-evangelization' of the faithful, with a new emphasis placed on preaching and catechesis, especially as the friars, religiously dedicated not only to lives of renunciation but also to evangelical activity, spread through western Europe with papal blessing. These changes lie beyond the chronological range of this essay, but many of their causes, which are European in their scale rather than peculiarly insular, are to be found in the twelfth century and so must command our attention.

In part these causes can be traced to some hard economic realities. The aristocracy's land surplus steadily dwindled during the twelfth century. In England, as the post-Conquest glut slowly dried up holy poverty became doubly appealing, and benefactors were probably moved by practical considerations as well as spiritual impulses to focus their attentions on the Augustinians and Cistercians: the former needed relatively little property; the latter actively preferred waste lands less profitable to the donor. But by

[34] N. P. Tanner, ed. and trans., *Decrees of the Ecumenical Councils* (2 vols.; Washington, DC, 1990), i, p. 245.

the late twelfth century the appetite for endowing new houses of any kind was largely sated. Most great families had acquired 'their' religious house, few had land to spare, and population increase and commercialization were rendering even the once unprofitable wastes valuable. The great age of new monastic foundations was over. A consequence of this was that the Church became increasingly dependent on compulsory dues, particularly tithes, and voluntary donations from a broader constituency. At the same time the parish was emerging as the essential context in which the Church hierarchy planned to disseminate teaching about the faith and guarantee basic pastoral care of the laity.

That desire to engage more closely with the laity was also encouraged by spiritual developments. One of these is suggested by crucifixion iconography, which reveals a growing preference in the eleventh and twelfth centuries for the depiction of Christ as a dying or dead man rather than, as the fashion had been in the early Middle Ages, a living 'God-man'. This artistic trend alerts us to deeper forces: a new affective piety which dwelt less on Christ's divinity and more on his suffering humanity emerged initially in the monasteries of northern Europe but spread more generally through the twelfth-century Church. This celebration of the suffering humanity of Christ had major ramifications, one of which was to encourage leading churchmen to see a Christlike quality in every man and woman. All, whether monks or not, became worthy of salvation. Where Anselm of Canterbury had mused at the beginning of the twelfth century on the bleak fate of those living beyond the cloister wall, Hugh, bishop of Lincoln (d. 1200) at the end of the same century argued that 'the kingdom of God is not confined only to monks, hermits and anchorites'.[35] Inner transformation, not vocation, would be the key to salvation. In that connection, theologians of Paris and other schools were also busy by this point redefining the good life, placing more emphasis on interior disposition, right intention and the saving power of the sacraments. In so doing, the Church constructed a regime which made it easier to find salvation while living in the world under its discipline, passing through rites of passage, paying tithe, attending Mass, engaging in voluntary devotion and perhaps pilgrimage, making regular confession, taking communion annually and dying the 'good death' in which one set things right with God. But the more positive valuation of the lay vocation implied by such a scheme is perhaps most clearly signalled by two other developments.

[35] D. L. Douie and H. Farmer, eds. and trans., *Adam of Eynsham, Magna Vita Sancti Hugonis, The Life of St Hugh of Lincoln* (2 vols.; OMT; Oxford, 1961–2), ii, pp. 46–7.

The first is the energy invested by the theologians in the sacramentalization of marriage (see Chapter IV.3). Marriage was not a ritual which the Church closely superintended in 900, but by 1200 it was transforming from a matter of extra-ecclesial contract into an ecclesiastical rite. More significantly, it was also defined as a means by which divine grace was communicated to ordinary men and women and thus described a way to salvation unique to the laity. The second sign of change is the Church's shifting thinking about the warrior's profession. Although the First Crusade, initiated in 1095 by Pope Urban II, drew few from England, later crusades did involve substantial English participation. Yet just as important as direct involvement was the larger cultural effect of crusading. Where violence was previously seen as sinful by a Church alarmed by internecine warfare in the tenth and eleventh centuries, it now became meritorious at least in certain conditions. The extent of this rehabilitation can be observed in the phenomenon that is the military orders, such as the Templars. These institutions, which had commanderies in England as in other parts of Europe, hybridized the ideals of knight and monk to turn out brethren living at once under a strict religious rule and committed to the defence of the Holy Land. Thus two essential characteristics of the lay estate, sex and violence, were sprinkled with holy water and made more acceptable to God.

Yet theologians also recognized that any vocation, clerical or lay, even if lived with the best intentions, must inevitably be unperfected. So the Church also began to work out more systematically how the souls of those who died in the faith, full of remorse and yet still blemished by their sins, might be cleansed after death. The idea that sin unexpiated in life through penance might be burnt away in purging fires after death was very ancient. It can be traced back through the writings of Bede (d. 735), who offered striking visions of the fate of the dead in his *Ecclesiastical History*, to those of Gregory the Great (d. 604) and Augustine of Hippo (354–430) and even, perhaps, to allusive references in scripture itself. But the Church's need to preach a consistent message about how the ordinary faithful might be saved required a sharper definition of the soul's fate after death. This came by increments through the twelfth and thirteenth centuries as theologians came to agree that purgation occurred in a space optimized for the purpose: purgatory. Although purgatory began to acquire formal definition only in 1274, the fear of purgatorial suffering was shaping mortuary piety long before this point, most obviously in elaborate provisions made by men and women to speed their souls through the purging fires. These 'suffrages' might take the form of simple prayer for the dead, almsgiving in their name or, most powerfully, masses sung for their souls. All of these measures were, of course, of great antiquity, but preaching about purgation and the conviction that most of the dead would find themselves in purgatorial fire lent them a new urgency.

BELIEF, SCEPTICISM AND LAY AGENCY

If we consider English religious culture in European perspective, we can see that the growing interest of the Church hierarchy in the laity was encouraged not only by hard economic realities and spiritual developments but also by fear of heresy. Heresy, either in the form of charismatic cults or the more durable threat of Catharism, was thought to be spreading through Europe during the eleventh and twelfth centuries. This led the Church to evangelize regions in which heresy had taken root (particularly the Languedoc and northern Italy) and also to strengthen its pastoral provision in those that were not much affected. The latter policies would have ramifications for English dioceses in the thirteenth century, pastoral agendas formulated in Rome being rolled out by the bishops, but it is striking that heresy seems never to have become established in England during the central Middle Ages. The author of the early thirteenth-century *Ancrene Wisse* was able to claim confidently that 'heresy, thank God, is absent from England'.[36] Why this was the case is not so easily explained. It may be that the robust rule of English kings made heretical proselytizing distinctly risky – a conclusion impressed on budding Cathar preachers in 1166, who were branded then whipped through the streets of Oxford on the orders of Henry II. The absence of heresy may also have owed something to the precocity of parochial religion in England. Parishes formed early and, as we have seen, their supervision by diocesan authorities was strengthened in the late eleventh and twelfth centuries with the introduction of archdeacons and the enforcement of canon law in their courts. And of course, the parishes were not the product of clerical initiative alone. They sprang originally from lay enterprise, and parishioners remained well placed throughout our period to shape their own local devotional life. The parish might thus be an institution in which there was scope for varied expressions of lay religiosity albeit within a framework of ecclesiastical supervision.

[36] H. White, trans., *Ancrene Wisse. Guide for Anchoresses* (Harmondsworth, 1993), p. 43; B. Millett, ed., *Ancrene Wisse: A Corrected Edition of the Text in Cambridge, Corpus Christi College, MS 402, with Variants from Other Manuscripts* (2 vols.; EETS, 325–6; Oxford, 2005), i, p. 33.

We can only rarely penetrate the life of the parish in this period, so ultimate conclusions about its vitality must remain tentative and hesitant. Yet there is sufficient, if scattered, evidence for lay agency to show that laymen and women were not merely passive beneficiaries of Church teaching. Anglo-Saxon guild statutes reveal that these lay associations, at least, hired and fired priests who performed spiritual services for them. Some funds for the provision of church lights were already managed by laity in the late Anglo-Saxon period. Ælfric of Eynsham envisaged learned lay readers of his homilies who would need to be convinced by his arguments, and Wulfstan in his *Sermon of the Wolf* anticipated a lay audience similarly capable of thinking for itself. Indeed, laymen and women can be glimpsed thinking for themselves about spiritual questions and working out their own answers. When the great baron William Marshal lay dying in 1219 he confessed his sins and made careful provision for his soul. But he also refused to sell livery, saying that his men must have their robes, or to restore all of the property he had seized in war. None would be saved, so he argued, if such things were a prerequisite for salvation.[37]

Independent thought and calculation can be seen in other lay responses to Church teaching, too. Doubt about, and resistance to, the Church's claims were not the most frequent reflexes of laymen and women but they certainly existed. We see them most commonly in the culting of saints (see Chapter V.3). Here most of the evidence, which comes in the form of hagiography and miracle collections cataloguing the wonders of the saint, necessarily stressed enthusiasm for the cults. Yet some cults, particularly those assiduously promoted by a monastery, clearly had to make headway against at least a measure of scepticism. The tell-tale signs here are vengeance miracles. The compilers of the miracle collections felt it necessary to advertise reprisals visited by angry saints on those who doubted their powers: miracles ascribed to St Erkenwald include one in which a drunken silversmith was struck dead for mocking the money-grubbing canons who acquired cash and gifts through the shrine. The reverse was also possible: a local community might begin to venerate a saint who was unacceptable to the Church hierarchy. One such 'false cult' grew up at Northampton in 1190 around an executed criminal whose remains allegedly worked wonders. It was ultimately suppressed, but not without effort, on the orders of Hugh, bishop of Lincoln.[38]

[37] A.J. Holden, S. Gregory and D. Crouch, eds., *The History of William the Marshal* (2 vols; Anglo-Norman Text Society; London, 2002–4), ii, p. 427; p. 437.

[38] R. Howlett, ed., *William of Newburgh, Historia Rerum Anglicarum,* in *Chronicles of the Reigns of Stephen, Henry II and Richard I* (4 vols.; RS; London, 1884–9), ii, p. 472.

The sharper definition of the faith in the twelfth century might also elicit mixed reactions. The Church was making increasingly robust claims about transubstantiation, the process during Mass whereby bread and wine mystically transformed into the body and blood of Christ, in the late twelfth and early thirteenth centuries. Although some were so enamoured of the teaching that they wanted to be buried near high altars so that they might benefit from the trickle-down effects of this daily miracle, others, probably a minority, clearly reacted less enthusiastically. Miracle stories, used by the Church in preaching, depict sceptics for whom the claim that bread and wine turned into flesh and blood at the moment of consecration was too much to swallow. As in the case of vengeful saints, such stories would scarcely have been needed if materialistic scepticism was non-existent. Still more radical forms of doubt are also occasionally to be found. King William Rufus was said to have mocked divine providence and rejected the idea that the ordeal by fire or water could deliver a true verdict in a criminal case.[39] Still more startlingly, Peter of Cornwall (1139×40–1221), prior of Holy Trinity, Aldgate, claimed in *c.* 1200 that some men did not believe in good or bad angels or that the soul lived on when the body died.[40] Both of these examples involve some colourful rhetoric (used against Rufus by hostile monastic chroniclers and used by Peter of Cornwall for shock effect), but they still reveal something of the range of thinkable thoughts. It is likely that few in practice entertained convictions as radically sceptical as these, but doubt in its more localized forms, about the credentials of a saint or the miracle of the eucharist, was clearly common enough to need rebutting. The Middle Ages might, in other words, conventionally be portrayed as an 'age of faith', but belief need not imply credulity, and piety was shot through by strands of more sceptical reflection.

[39] M. Rule, ed., *Eadmeri Historia Nouorum in Anglia et opusculo duo de uita sancti Anselmi et quibusdam miraculis eius* (RS; London, 1884), pp. 101–2.

[40] Peter of Cornwall, *Liber Revelationum*, London, Lambeth Palace, MS 51, fol. 2; and discussion in R. Bartlett, *England under the Norman and Angevin Kings, 1075–1225* (Oxford, 2000), p. 478.

CHAPTER V.2

Rites of passage and pastoral care

Sarah Hamilton

It is probably true to say that medieval churchmen in the period 900–1200 displayed rather more interest in the delivery of pastoral care than modern historians have done until very recently. Dismissed as routine, pastoral care has been overlooked in favour of the dramatic transformations unfolding in monasticism, saints' cults and the crusades in the course of these three centuries. Yet the mundane business of the cure of souls lay at the heart of all Christians' experience of the Church to which they belonged. Giles Constable has defined pastoral care as 'the performance of those ceremonies that were central to the salvation of the individual Christian and that were the primary responsibility of ordained priests working in [local] churches': the Mass, baptism, penance, the last rites and burial of the dead, that is the fundamental rites of Christian life, the *cura animarum*.[1] This chapter will focus mainly on the rites for entry into, and exit from, life and the earthly Christian community. The evidence for pastoral care ranges from the prescriptive laws, aspirational liturgical rites, model sermons and other texts to the physical remnants of buildings, ecclesiastical furnishings and interments. Whilst much of the textual evidence is the work of second-generation reformers in the late tenth century and the first decades of the eleventh century, led by Ælfric and Wulfstan I, archbishop of York and bishop of Worcester, there is sufficient testimony, especially when combined with the material evidence, to suggest pastoral care was important to both churchmen and laymen throughout this period.

In England the years 900 to 1200 witnessed such an explosion in the building of churches for local communities that it was singled out for comment at the time. Bishop Herman of Ramsbury reportedly told

[1] G. Constable, 'Monasteries, rural churches and the *cura animarum* in the early Middle Ages', in *Cristianizzazione et organizzazione ecclesiastica delle campagne nell'alto medioevo: espansione e resistenze* (Settimane di Studio del Centro Italiano di studi sull'alto medioevo, 28; Spoleto, 1982), pp. 349–89, at p. 353.

Pope Leo IX in 1049 about how England was 'being filled everywhere with churches, which daily were being added anew in new places; about the distribution of innumerable ornaments and bells in oratories; about the most ample liberality of kings and rich men for the inheritance of Christ'.[2] Three-quarters of a century later the monastic historian William of Malmesbury observed the continuation of this movement: 'You may see everywhere churches in villages, in towns and cities monasteries rising in a new style of architecture.'[3] It is impossible to quantify this building and rebuilding: the county commissioners of Domesday Book were erratic about whether they chose to record churches, and there was often a substantial lag between the architectural evidence and the earliest textual records. Nevertheless it has been suggested that by 1100 there were between 6,000 and 7,000 local churches in England.[4]

The clergy of such churches had prime responsibility for the delivery of pastoral care. In his early twelfth-century text, *De statu ecclesiae*, which, although written for an Irish audience, circulated within England, Bishop Gilbert of Limerick identified fourteen offices for priests, but only seven for bishops. The duties of the local priest were 'to preside, to serve, to pray, to offer [the Mass], to preach, to teach, to baptise, to bless, to excommunicate, to reconcile, to anoint [the sick], to communicate, to commend souls to God, to bury bodies'.[5] As Gilbert made clear, in both his text and the diagram which accompanied it, the priest was in charge of the bottom layer of a pyramidical hierarchy, that is of the lesser clergy and the laity (those who fight, plough and pray, both men and women) within his parish; he thus had prime responsibility for pastoral care but above him came the bishop, who was in charge of the priests of the various parishes (and also, at least theoretically, the monasteries) within his diocese. Above the bishop came the archbishop, above him the primate and above him the Roman pontiff. The bishop had responsibility for confirming the baptized with chrism, blessing nuns, absolving 'the people' of venial sins at the start of Lent and of serious sins on Maundy Thursday, holding a synod twice a year, attended by all the priests of the diocese, dedicating

[2] *Historia translationis sancti Augustini*, *PL* 155, cols. 13–46, at col. 32; translated by R. Gem, 'The English parish church in the eleventh and early twelfth centuries: a great rebuilding?', in J. Blair, ed., *Minsters and Parish Churches. The Local Church in Transition, 950–1200* (Oxford, 1988), pp. 21–30, at p. 21.

[3] R. A. B. Mynors, R. M. Thomson and M. Winterbottom, eds. and trans., *William of Malmesbury, Gesta regum anglorum*, iii. 246 (2 vols.; OMT; Oxford, 1998–9), i, pp. 460–1.

[4] R. Morris, *Churches in the Landscape* (London, 1989), pp. 147, 167.

[5] J. Fleming, ed., *De statu ecclesiae*, in J. Fleming, *Gille of Limerick (c. 1070–1145). Architect of a Medieval Church* (Dublin, 2001), p. 154.

new churches and altars, consecrating the items used within a church and ordaining abbots, abbesses, priests and lesser clergy. The diocesan synod should provide an opportunity for the bishop to discipline priests and hear problematic cases which were too complex or too important to be dealt with at a local level, such as those of contumacious lay sinners who refused to accept sacerdotal authority.

The reality was a much messier and more complex and fluid world of institutional exemptions from episcopal jurisdiction, and unclear and changing boundaries between both dioceses and the territories served by local churches. The structures for the delivery of pastoral care changed in this period. There were seventeen dioceses in England in both 1000 and 1200, but their centres and the areas they covered had been subject to considerable rearrangement in the intervening years. The increase in the number of local churches led to changes in structures at local level. In the early Middle Ages it seems that a community of clergy, based in a minster church, provided pastoral care to the population living in a relatively large area, going out from the minster to provide services in local chapels to widely scattered communities; the clergy of the minster church retained a monopoly over the fundamental rites of baptism and burial in this larger area. The reasons for, and the timing of, the move to the parish structure envisaged by Gilbert in which a single priest was responsible for the delivery of all the pastoral rites within a much smaller area have been the subject of a good deal of debate. Much has been made of the secular and ecclesiastical benefits for local lords to be accrued from establishing a local church with a graveyard: the accompanying tithes and fees for particular rites were lucrative, the building itself an important statement of power in the landscape. Nor was local church building the sole prerogative of individual lords and their families; local communities of merchants and wealthy farmers, acting collectively, seem to have been behind the building of some local churches in this period, especially in the eastern counties of Lincolnshire and Suffolk. Changing church provision also coincided with changing settlement patterns; this period witnessed the emergence of more nucleated villages in central England. Yet local churches were not merely sources of revenue: what went on inside them was also of central importance to the lives of everyone living in these localities. It was through the rite of baptism that people entered into the community, and through those for the anointing of the sick and the burial of the dead that they marked their passing from the community of the living to that of the dead. The presence of Romanesque fonts in many local churches in England, even if subsequently rebuilt, points to their role in baptism, the bounded graveyards surrounding them to that in death. The establishment of a cemetery alongside a local church may even in some instances have acted as an instigator for the emergence of local communal identity, rather than its establishment necessarily being a reflection of existing ties.[6]

However, the extensive repertory of texts written by and for the English pastoral clergy in the central Middle Ages omits any detailed requirement of the rites lay Christians were expected to undergo in the course of their life. This is not to say that evidence for these rites and the expectations made of lay Christians does not exist, but it has to be pulled together from episcopal guidance on the duties of local priests, liturgical prescriptions about how to administer particular rites and decrees about those whose behaviour led them to be excluded from Christian *societas*. That Christian rites should govern a person's entry into, and exit from, life was so self-evident that there was no need to spell it out. In the words of an early eleventh-century Worcester rite for the consecration of cemeteries, those buried there were those 'who had gained the grace of baptism and had persevered in the catholic faith until the end of their life'.[7] This rite is from a pontifical linked with Archbishop Wulfstan I, who, in the statutes he composed for his diocesan clergy (*c.* 1005×8), probably for a synod, was keen to set out the duties of lay Christians:

> And it is right that every man learn so that he knows the Paternoster and the Creed according as he wishes to be buried in a consecrated grave or to be entitled to the sacrament; for he who will not learn it is not truly Christian nor ought he by rights to stand sponsor at baptism or at confirmation until he learn it.[8]

The rites of baptism, communion and burial in consecrated ground were fundamental, but Wulfstan also encouraged active participation in the faith: the Christian who failed to learn the two fundamental prayers of the faith risked exclusion from Christian *societas* in this life and the next. Whilst Wulfstan's text here drew heavily on the ninth-century *capitula* originally composed by Bishop Theodulf of Orleans for his diocesan

[6] E. Zadora-Rio, 'The making of churchyards and parish territories in the early medieval landscape of France and England in the 7th–12th centuries: a reconsideration', *Medieval Archaeology*, 47 (2003), 1–19.

[7] D. H. Turner, ed., *The Claudius Pontificals (from Cotton Ms. Claudius A.iii in the British Museum)* (Henry Bradshaw Society 97; London, 1971), p. 61.

[8] 'The so-called "Canons of Edgar"', c. 22 in *Councils and Synods*, i, p. 322 (also for references to Wulfstan's sermons), citing Theodulf of Orleans, *Capitula 1*, c. 22, P. Brommer, ed., *MGH Capitula episcoporum 1* (Hannover, 1984), p. 119; see also 1 Cnut 22, *Councils and Synods*, i, pp. 483–4.

clergy, he went on to repeat this injunction in subsequent royal codes and sermons.

The reiteration of this message across liturgy, law, sermons and synodal statutes suggests it had a resonance for the audience of reforming clergy for whom it was intended. More precise injunctions in prescriptive texts allow one to test the reality of such aspirations for pastoral care. Ælfric enjoined in a letter to Bishop Wulfsige of Sherborne (d. 1002) that a local priest should possess a Psalter, the Epistles, a Gospel book, a missal, a hymnal, a 'handbook', pastoral and manual, a penitential and a lectionary.[9] Although this list echoes those in ninth-century Carolingian *capitula*, it was not merely rhetoric: attempts were sometimes made to implement these injunctions at a more local level. A mid-eleventh-century booklist records how the local church of Sherburn in Elmet in North Yorkshire possessed a sacramentary, a gradual, two Gospel books, two Epistolaries, a Psalter, an antiphonary and a hymnal. There is no mention of a manual for pastoral rites such as baptism, penance and the rites for the dying, but such texts were sometimes combined together with a sacramentary, as in the codex composed either at Sherborne or New Minster, Winchester *c.* 1061, now known as the Red Book of Darley after its sixteenth-century provenance, which includes towards the end liturgies for baptism and those for the visitation of the sick and burial of the dead. They also circulated separately, as in the codex composed at a similar date at Worcester which combined texts of the vernacular Old English Penitential and *Scriftboc* with liturgical *ordines* for visiting the sick and burying the dead, alongside other penitential texts.[10] Both manuscripts are probably the product of cathedral scriptoria and they suggest an attempt being made to realize the aspirations alluded to in more prescriptive texts. Both also include Latin pastoral rites which have been extensively rubricated in Old English, a feature which, when combined with the texts of the rites themselves, has recently led scholars to suggest that both manuscripts were composed as educational texts to train priests in the pastoral ministry.[11] They thus offer insight into how the higher clergy

[9] C. 51, *Councils and Synods*, i, pp. 206–7.

[10] Cambridge, Corpus Christi College, MS 422; Oxford, Bodleian Library, MS Laud Miscellaneous 482.

[11] H. Gittos, 'Is there any evidence for the liturgy of parish churches in late Anglo-Saxon England? The Red Book of Darley and the status of Old English', in F. Tinti, ed., *Pastoral Care in Late Anglo-Saxon England* (Anglo-Saxon Studies 6; Woodbridge, 2005), pp. 63–82; V. Thompson, *Dying and Death in Later Anglo-Saxon England* (Anglo-Saxon Studies 4; Woodbridge, 2004), pp. 57–91.

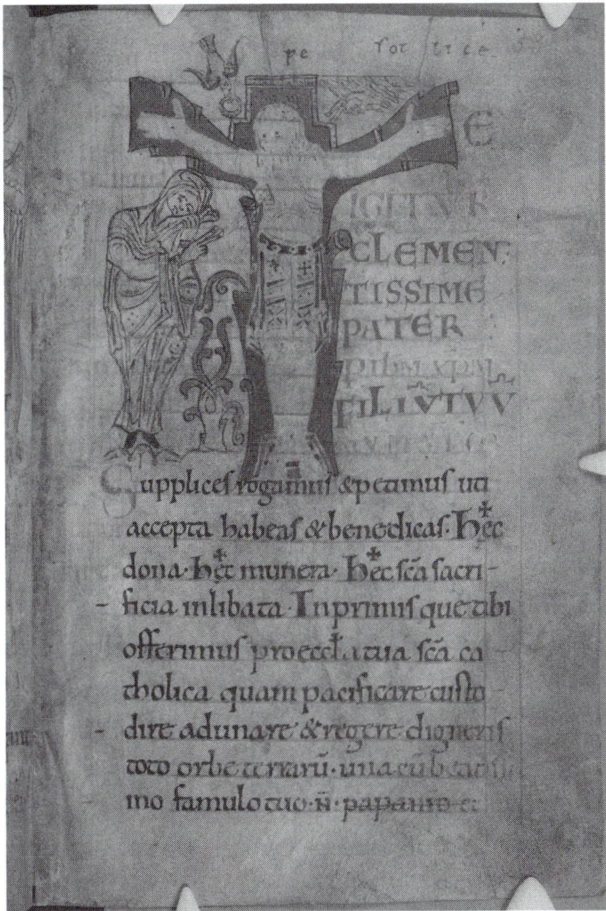

Figure 13 Liturgical compendium in Latin and Old English *c.* 1062; English. Cambridge Corpus Christi College MS 422, p. 53; picture of Crucifixion published with the kind permission of the Master and Fellows of Corpus Christi College, Cambridge

of two dioceses perceived the delivery of pastoral services outside the great churches of England, if not into what was happening at a local level.

The surviving liturgical evidence for pastoral rites when taken as a whole paints a more complex picture. Pontificals are collections of the services pertaining to a bishop made for, and used by, bishops and their cathedral communities. Some twenty-one pontificals and benedictionals (collections of the texts of episcopal blessings arranged by the liturgical year) survive from the tenth and eleventh centuries; only twelve include the occasional pastoral offices. Whilst only six pontificals survive from the twelfth century, four include rites for baptism, the administration of penance and the reconciliation of penitents, and the visitation of the sick, burial of the dead and marriage. Fewer episcopal books survive from the later period, but the proportion interested in pastoral care is higher. Such books tell us about the aspirations for practice within the grandest churches in England. The elaborate rites for baptism in the early eleventh-century Missal of Robert of Jumièges and the twelfth-century Magdalen Pontifical presume the presence of at least two acolytes, deacons and other clergy.[12] It is hard to see how they would have been used in a parish church like Haselbury in Somerset, where, we are told in the life of the anchorite attached to the church in the mid-twelfth century, the priest, Brichtric, had only his son to support him at the altar. But the rite of baptism in the Red Book of Darley makes no mention of other clergy. It is pragmatic and therefore perhaps closer to the sort of rite which might be administered by the priest of a local church.

BAPTISM

Liturgical evidence is problematic because it is inherently conservative. English churchmen inherited a rite for baptism which was resonant with tradition. In the early Church adult baptism had been the norm and baptism was confined, except in cases of imminent death, to Easter and Pentecost. In the pastoral injunctions of the tenth and eleventh centuries, following Carolingian precedents, ad hoc baptism was widely promoted. The *Scriftboc*, a tenth-century vernacular penitential, enjoined a penance of three winters' fast on parents who failed to have their child baptized, whilst if a child died unbaptized owing to the negligence of the priest, the priest should be cast out of his orders. Other texts set a time limit of seven or nine days within which a child should be baptized.[13] Yet despite the emphasis on immediate baptism in the law, the rite for baptism was normally located on Holy Saturday within liturgical books, as it was in the early eleventh-century Missal of Robert of Jumièges and the

[12] Rouen, Bibliothèque municipale, MS Y.6 (274): H. A. Wilson, ed., *The Missal of Robert of Jumièges* (Henry Bradshaw Society 11; London 1896; repr. 1994), pp. 93–100; Oxford, Magdalen College, MS 226: H. A. Wilson, ed., *The Pontifical of Magdalen College with an Appendix of Extracts from other English Mss. of the Twelfth Century* (Henry Bradshaw Society 39; London, 1910), pp. 170–9.

[13] *Scriftboc* VIII, Oxford, Bodleian Library, MS Junius 121, fol. 89v: A. J. Frantzen, *The Anglo-Saxon Penitentials. A Cultural Database* (www.anglo-saxon.net/penance/index.html); 'The so-called "Canons of Edgar"', c. 15 (seven days) and 'Northumbrian Priests' Law', c. 10.1 (nine days), both in *Councils and Synods*, i, pp. 319, 455.

twelfth-century Magdalen Pontifical. The Red Book of Darley, on the other hand, included it in a sort of pastoral supplement with the rites for the visitation of the sick, burial of the dead, burial masses and offices.

The rite for baptism which circulated in late Anglo-Saxon England was one which had been standardized by the Carolingians. The texts make provision for both collective and singular baptism, with alternative readings for boys and girls, singular and plural. They presume a one-stop service, in which the infants are exorcized, given salt, the font blessed and the child is baptized, vested in a white garment and given a light, and, only if the bishop is present, then confirmed. Often, however, it seems as if children went without confirmation. What is perhaps most striking about the usual services, as set out in the Missal of Robert of Jumièges and the Magdalen Pontifical, is that, whilst reference is made to the 'infans' no reference is made to their sponsors, the godparents. The godparents' presence has usually to be inferred from a rubric referring to the 'priest taking the child from someone holding him' but no reference is made to their role as vicarious responders on the child's behalf to the various questions. We know from the texts that we have already cited about exclusion that the institution of godparents was viewed as a form of social cement, and that eligibility for that role was integral to inclusion in Christian society. Perhaps because it had a pedagogic function, the baptismal rite in the Red Book of Darley spelled out the role of the godparents more clearly. To the questions which precede baptism – do you renounce Satan, and all his works, and his pomps – the rubrics make explicit that it is the godfather who replies '*Abrenuntio*' (I renounce).[14] Here in a practical book made for the delivery of the pastoral liturgy in the 1060s the significance attached to godparents in the earlier eleventh-century injunctions is reinforced.

It has proved easier for scholars to demonstrate that bishops were concerned with policing and reforming what was going on inside local churches than to link the textual evidence to the material evidence of the buildings themselves, their contents and their surroundings. Nevertheless it is worth exploring the material evidence for what it can reveal about the success of episcopal aspiration. One of the most prominent features of the newly built churches was that most of them acquired in the latter half of the twelfth century a permanent font in stone or lead. Whilst many surviving examples lack any form of decoration, and on others it is confined to foliate designs or formal geometric ones, many were decorated

[14] Cambridge, Corpus Christi College, MS 422, pp. 388–9; Gittos, 'Is there any evidence for the liturgy', pp. 73–4.

Figure 14 Burnham Deepdale font: this stone-carved font shows the months of the calendar year. Each month is represented by agricultural work appropriate for the time of the year except for May. Here the months May to August are represented. Photograph by the Reverend Stephen Day of Papworth Everard, Cambs.; published with his kind permission

with an iconography which hints at how these fonts may have been the focus of sacerdotal teaching, and preaching, to the local community. The baptism of Christ by John the Baptist is common, as is the rationale for baptism, that is the need to wash away original sin as represented by the Temptation of Adam and Eve in the Garden of Eden and their subsequent expulsion. Also frequent are the Annunciation, the Nativity and the Passion. Sometimes St Peter is depicted clutching the keys to heaven, alongside St Michael weighing the souls of the dead. The didactic function of such objects is made even clearer at Lullington (Somerset), where the inscription reads 'sins perish through holy washing in this font'.[15] Many fonts are decorated more intensely on two sides, suggesting that they were intended to stand in a corner by the door, as well as economy on the part of whoever commissioned them. They are standing testimony to the role of the local church as a centre for baptism within the community. That the parish was the centre for other activities as well is clear

[15] C. S. Drake, *The Romanesque Fonts of Northern Europe and Scandinavia* (Woodbridge, 2002), p. 14.

from the Burnham Deepdale font in Norfolk, which is illustrated with the 'Labours of the Months': that for May was not an agricultural task but rather a rogationtide procession. Iconography also sometimes allows the identification of small ateliers, as for six lead fonts in Gloucestershire, all of which are cast from the same mould panel, suggesting either the influence of lordship or the existence of a common atelier serving rival local communities along the River Severn; at the very least it means that by the second half of the twelfth century a permanent font was something which a local church had to have.

The popularity of infant baptism is testified to by the archaeological evidence: there is very little evidence for infant burial in pagan cemeteries, whilst children make up a significant proportion of the burials in cemeteries which can clearly be associated with churches: 20 per cent of the graves in the late Anglo-Saxon graveyard at the church of Raunds Furnell in Northamptonshire were of children, whilst children make up 45 per cent of the graves in a late Anglo-Saxon cemetery in Norwich. Their inclusion represents the success of the Church's message that unbaptized children would not achieve salvation: unbaptized children would not have been buried in such sacred space. More than anything else, their corpses testify to the reality of the Church's preoccupation with pastoral care in these centuries.

DYING

As with baptism, the compilers of ecclesiastical laws displayed little interest in ensuring the laity died and were buried in accordance with the rites of the Church, and were instead preoccupied with regulating the conduct of the clergy conducting these rites and the income from burial dues. The one exception to this seeming neglect is the provision made in penitentials and ecclesiastical and royal laws of the tenth and eleventh centuries for the exclusion of recalcitrant excommunicants from burial in Christian cemeteries as a marker of social exclusion and eternal damnation; exclusion burials, like that of a male, aged between twenty and thirty, whose right hand had been cut off, at the meeting point of the boundaries of three Cambridgeshire parishes, Burwell, Newmarket and Swaffham Prior, and execution cemeteries, like that identified at Guildown near Guildford, have been established throughout this period.[16]

[16] A. Reynolds, *Anglo-Saxon Deviant Burial Customs* (Oxford, 2009), pp. 216–17, 245.

The liturgical evidence, like that for baptism, is biased towards elite clerical communities. The sequence of liturgical rites which accompanied the dying person from the deathbed to the grave was established only in the Carolingian monasteries of the second half of the ninth century. The following account is taken from that given in the twelfth-century Magdalen Pontifical, but the liturgical rites for the dying were far from uniform in these three centuries. The rite began at the dying person's bedside; she or he was visited by a priest, accompanied by the entire community. The dying person confessed to the priest, s/he was then absolved by all present, signified by kissing all those there; s/he was then anointed with holy oil, and given communion (the *viaticum*). These preliminary rites served as a preparation for death itself. Unless death followed immediately, the majority of the community would withdraw at this point, leaving only a few members to keep watch. When s/he was about to die the brethren would be summoned by the striking of a board to mark the commendation of the soul, led by the cantor: a sequence of prayers for mercy and release of the soul from punishment, an antiphon and psalm. The corpse was then washed, dressed and placed on a bier and, after being sprinkled with holy water by the priest, carried into the church whilst chants were sung. It was placed where the brothers could walk around it on all sides, singing psalms; this implicit reference to keeping a vigil is made more explicit in monastic customaries. A Mass was said for the dead person. Then the body was carried out, whilst bells were rung, to the grave, which was sprinkled with holy water and incensed, accompanied again by chants led by the cantor. Earth was thrown on top of the grave and prayers said for the dead person and all those in the graveyard.

The rite in the Magdalen Pontifical, like most of those which survive, was written for a monastic community, probably in this case that at Christ Church, Canterbury: it requires a priest, a cantor, at least two brothers to lead the responses and the presence of the entire community at the commendation of the soul. It is far too elaborate for use in a local church. Yet an attempt was made to give this particular text a universal application: the prayers for the dying and the dead were written in the masculine singular, but feminine and plural readings were added above the line; and the initial rubrics for the last rites were written in the second person, for example: 'You shall say this. The Lord be with you. Let us pray. [*Hic dices. Dominus vobiscum. Oremus.*]'[17]. This suggests that the rite may have been recorded with a didactic purpose, to train priests how to conduct the rite.

[17] Wilson, ed., *The Pontifical of Magdalen College*, p. 190.

Here the rite echoes that for the anointing of the sick in the earlier Missal of Robert of Jumièges in which the rubrics, which are in Old English, are similarly written in the second person.

Other evidence envisages a lay audience for such rites. The rite in the eleventh-century Worcester handbook advises the priest that if the dying person does not know the Creed or the Pater Noster, he should investigate whether he 'knows what is true belief', that is belief in the Trinity and the Last Judgement.[18] The priest is also advised to differentiate how he hears last confession: whilst clerics will be accustomed to making confession, he should encourage laymen when doing so, presumably because it is an unfamiliar process for them. There are also hints in other sources that the laity had a specific role to play in these rites. The Old English penitential makes provision for those standing around a dying person's bedside; in the event the dying person is incapable of speech when the priest arrives, they may attest that he desired confession and communion; if so, the priest should carry out the rite.[19] The rubrics to the Worcester rite outline one aspect of the deathbed which is missing from many other sources: the making of the will: if the sick person is 'a layman, then the mass-priest must tell him to put his household in order, that is, that he must bequeath his things and completely reveal his sins'.[20] The rubric also refers to the laying out of the corpse by 'those who stand by', rather than specifying, as in other rites, that it should be undertaken by clerics.[21] It is clear that members of the laity sought a role in the obsequies of fellow laymen: the statutes of the mid-eleventh-century confraternity of Abbotsbury in Dorset make provision that if any member falls ill within 60 miles he is to be brought home by 15 men, and if he dies in the neighbourhood as many as possible should bring the body back to the minster and pray earnestly for the soul.[22] Later Anglo-Saxon penitentials written in the vernacular promoted lay prayer: the *Scriftboc* enjoins that whilst Mass for a dead man should be said on the third and seventh days after his death, it need not be said on the thirtieth day after his death, as was usual, 'if his kinsmen and relations fast for him and make him some offering for his soul at God's altar'.[23] The Old English Handbook

[18] V. Thompson, 'The pastoral contract in late Anglo-Saxon England: priest and parishioner in Oxford, Bodleian Library, MS Laud Miscellaneous 482', in Tinti, ed., *Pastoral Care*, pp. 106–20, at p. 116.

[19] Oxford, Bodleian Library, MS Laud Miscellaneous 482, fol. 2r; Frantzen, *The Anglo-Saxon Penitentials. A Cultural Database* (www.anglo-saxon.net/penance/index.html).

[20] Thompson, *Dying*, p. 111. [21] *Ibid.*, p. 82. [22] *Councils and Synods*, i, pp. 517–20.

[23] Oxford, Bodleian Library, MS Junius 121, fol. 96r; Frantzen, *The Anglo-Saxon Penitentials. A Cultural Database* (www.anglo-saxon.net/penance/index.html).

comments that the deathbed penance of a powerful man rich in friends was lightened with their help. Here the focus is on lay involvement in burial and prayers after death, rather than on the rites for the dying. The growth in the later eleventh and twelfth centuries in references to members of the lay nobility entering regular communities on their deathbed, becoming a *frater* or *soror ad succurrendum* in order to receive the benefit of the elaborate liturgical rites for the dying, as well as the benefit of monastic prayers for the dead, suggests that such rites had not yet spread to the lay community. Yet narrative texts hint at the normalization of the practice of the last rites outside the cloister. Written in the late 1130s, Geoffrey Gaimar's account of the death of William Rufus, who was shot whilst out hunting in the New Forest in 1100, records how the king anxiously requested that he receive communion before he died, whereupon the huntsman who was with him gave him some herbs to eat in place of the *viaticum*.[24] William of Canterbury, writing in the 1170s, recorded how a knight on Henry II's expedition to Ireland was unable to make his last confession, perhaps because he did not know the native language, and died without the *viaticum*.[25] There is, however, also evidence for practices which were interpreted as pagan by ecclesiastical authority: in particular the seemingly widespread practice of funeral wakes. Thus Ælfric warned priests against taking part 'in the heathen songs and loud laughter of the laity', and eating and drinking beer in the presence of the corpse, and recounted a miracle which took place on such an occasion.[26]

Whilst the Church all over Europe found it difficult to eradicate such secular vigils, the design of late eleventh- and twelfth-century Lincolnshire parish churches may, according to a recent case study, testify to the extension beyond the cloister of the practice of keeping a liturgical vigil over the corpse. This hypothesis suggests that because the base of the bell-tower in these churches was open to the nave it may have acted as the site for a vigil, whilst the siting of windows in the tower's upper chamber afforded the ringers the necessary view of the graveyard to time their tolling of the bells with the carrying of the bier from the church to the grave.[27] There is currently insufficient evidence to make this more than a

[24] I. Short, ed. and trans., *Geffrei Gaimar, Estoire des Engleis* (Oxford, 2009), lines 6339–46, pp. 342–3.

[25] William of Canterbury, *Miracula S. Thomae Cantuariensis*, IV.52; J. C. Robertson, ed., *Materials for the History of Thomas Becket, Archbishop of Canterbury* (7 vols.; RS; London, 1875–85), i, p. 364.

[26] Ælfric, Pastoral Letter for Wulfsige of Sherborne, *Councils and Synods*, i, p. 218.

[27] D. Stocker and P. Everson, *Summoning St Michael. Early Romanesque Towers in Lincolnshire* (Oxford, 2006), pp. 79–91.

hypothesis: it is based on a reference to the vigil being in a separate place in Lanfranc's monastic customary, which was written for Christ Church, Canterbury, but Lincoln is not known to have possessed a copy of this text, none of the surviving English liturgical rites from the period supports this reference explicitly and as the diocese of Lincoln spread as far south as the Thames, a wider study of the architecture needs to be undertaken before accepting the suggestion that Remigius, the first Norman bishop of Lincoln, successfully promoted this new practice amongst the Anglo-Norman elite who built and rebuilt local churches. More concrete is the archaeological evidence for burial, which suggests there was a move from locations which seem to have been a matter of personal choice – in the garden with the rest of the family, or in a local feature such as a barrow or hill – to locations which were defined and controlled by the Church. From the late ninth century onwards burial usually took place within bounded graveyards, often centred on a local church, as at the small manor church of Raunds Furnells (Northamptonshire) or Rivenhall (Essex). That correct burial mattered is clear from the plentiful evidence of stone and wooden monuments to mark the graves of members of the elite. Excavation at Raunds Furnells and St Mark's Wigford, Lincoln, suggests the presence of postholes for wooden markers beside the graves, and elsewhere in northern England in the tenth century, where stone was more plentiful, many graves were marked by stones decorated in a distinctive Christian Hiberno-Norse style. Whilst most graveyards contain only one or two such graves – which are usually presumed to be those of the founders of the church – the presence of up to twenty monuments in the graveyards of urban churches in Lincoln and York may testify to the desire of merchants in these towns to display their social status even in death, and emulate the burial of the lesser nobility in rural churches. Burial itself in this period was sometimes marked by the presence of foreign substances, usually charcoal, underneath the corpse in the grave, which may have signified contrition, just as ashes were used to signify contrition in the giving of penance. The corpse was sometimes buried in an elaborate container, such as a coffin, chest or sarcophagus, tiles and stones might have been used to line the grave and a canon of the legatine Council of London (1143) suggests that burial in a wood or stone coffin was the norm.[28] It has been argued by Victoria Thompson that these attempts to enclose the corpse reflect a concern in homiletic and poetic texts with having a perfect body at the time of resurrection at the Last

[28] C. 6, *Councils and Synods*, ii, p. 801.

Figure 15 Tombstone of Gundrada of Warenne (d. 1083). This tombstone dates from the mid-twelfth century, when it was made for the reburial of Gundrada and her husband William I of Warenne (d. 1088) in the newly dedicated monastery church of St Pancras at Lewes. The text of the epitaph dates from the time of her death. The tombstone, made of black Tournai marble, is now at the church of St John the Baptist at Southover (Lewes, East Sussex).
Photograph by Edward Reeves (Lewes), published by permission of E. M. C. van Houts

Judgement.[29] The inclusion of lead plaques within the grave, identifying the person within, like those found in the tombs of Earl Odda (d. 1056) and Giso, bishop of Wells (d. 1088), suggests a concern to identify the person at the Last Judgement.[30] These markers – internal and external – signify that in burial the elite conformed to ecclesiastical authority and, more importantly, to Christian theology.

The correct delivery of pastoral care was clearly important to reforming churchmen in the second half of the tenth and first quarter of the eleventh centuries, but conciliar evidence suggests it was not nearly so central to the concerns of twelfth-century churchmen. This decline in interest is particularly striking if one compares the provisions made in the law codes drawn up by Wulfstan I for kings Æthelred II and Cnut with the canons of councils held by the archbishops of Canterbury in the twelfth century. Thus v Æthelred begins:

> First, namely, that we shall love and honour one God and zealously hold one Christian faith and entirely cast off every heathen practice, and we all have confirmed both with word and with pledge that we shall hold one Christian faith under the rule of one king.

[29] V. Thompson, 'Constructing salvation: a homiletic and penitential context for late Anglo-Saxon burial practice', in S. Lucy and A. Reynolds, eds., *Burial in Early Medieval England and Wales* (London, 2002), pp. 229–40.

[30] See, for example, Figure 12.

Figures 16a, b Burial casket of Gundrada of Warenne (with close-up of her name), similar to its surviving twin for her husband, William I of Warenne (d. 1088). The lead burial caskets date from the mid-twelfth century, when the couple were reburied in the monastery of St Pancras, Lewes, and are now kept at the church of St John the Baptist at Southover (Lewes, East Sussex). Photographs by E. M. C. van Houts; published with her kind permission

He enjoins the regular payment of tithes, plough alms and other dues, sets out how feasts and fasts should be observed and enjoins that 'every man should confess frequently and freely prepare himself often and frequently for going to communion'.[31] There is a concern here with promoting and regulating lay religion. The conciliar canons of the late eleventh and twelfth centuries are much more prosaic, being concerned with procedure and regulation rather than encouraging the delivery of pastoral care: baptism must be celebrated at Easter or Pentecost unless there is a danger of death, the laity must pay tithes, no charge should be made for chrism, baptism, penance, visitation of the sick and divine unction or communion, nor for burial. There is also an absence of evidence for diocesan synods in the later period. The decline in the legal texts' preoccupation with pastoral care is accompanied by a decline in the survival of liturgical pastoral rites. There is also a decline in homiletic evidence: the final decades of the tenth century witnessed the composition of at least four vernacular sermon collections, the anonymous Vercelli and Blickling collections, and those by Ælfric and Archbishop Wulfstan; the texts of the latter were expanded upon and widely copied in the eleventh century, although the manuscript evidence suggests they were owned only by members of the clerical elite. The evidence for the twelfth century is, however, much sparser, suggesting a lack of interest amongst higher churchmen in the business of the *cura animarum*.

The early eleventh-century churchmen's preoccupation with promoting correct Christian practice has been linked, in part, to a desire to reinforce the kingdom's defences in the face of attacks by the northmen, leading in 1009 to a call for a nationwide three-day fast. Much less attention, however, has been paid to the apparent indifference to pastoral care shown by the post-Conquest clergy. In part, at least, this is because here the leaders of the Church in England were no different from their European contemporaries: higher clergy, as evidenced by the conciliar canons elsewhere, were not much interested in pastoral care. Individuals, such as Robert of Arbrissel in northwestern France and Norbert of Xanten in Flanders, were concerned to preach to the laity, but on the whole reformers seem to have directed their efforts to regulating the lives of the clergy rather than those of the laity. Local factors have also been adduced to explain the post-Conquest episcopate's apparent apathy towards the *cura animarum*. From

[31] v Æthelred 1, 22: F. Liebermann, ed., *Die Gesetze der Angelsachsen* (3 vols.; Halle, 1903), i, pp. 236–7, 242–3; *Councils and Synods*, i, pp. 344, 355.

the mid-eleventh century onwards there was an influx of Continental churchmen into higher office, exacerbated by the Conquest, and the language problems which ensued have often been thought to explain, in part, the apparent indifference to pastoral care within the twelfth-century English Church. Brichtric, the parish priest of the Somerset village of Haselbury in the mid-twelfth century, complained that the local hermit was able to converse in French with the lords and bishop, whilst his own ignorance of the language rendered him dumb when he met the bishop. Such language barriers must have existed elsewhere and probably, in the face of an ill-educated clergy, posed problems for the effective working of diocesan synods.

But the picture for twelfth-century England is not as bleak as it looks. The copying of pastoral texts, including penitentials and homilies, in the vernacular at Worcester under Bishop Wulfstan II (d. 1095) and at Exeter under Bishop Leofric (d. 1072) testify to the primacy of pastoral care for individual bishops. In the early twelfth century Bishop Gilbert of Limerick, as we have seen, outlined a more extensive list of the duties of a parish priest than anything which survives from the writings of the tenth- and early eleventh-century English reformers, and went on to specify in more detail how these various offices should be performed. Bishop Herbert Losinga (d. 1119), who moved the East Anglian see from Thetford to Norwich in 1096, left the text of fourteen sermons in Latin. Whilst it is usually assumed that these were written for a monastic audience, to be read aloud in the refectory, Martin Brett has shown that they were addressed to a mixed audience, similar to that which has been adduced for Ælfric's *Catholic Homilies*, as is demonstrated by Herbert's reference to married women in his sermon for Candlemas. Although Bishop Herbert's sermons survive in a single manuscript they point to a wider preaching tradition within the twelfth century.[32] The vernacular homilies copied at the cathedral priory of Rochester in the mid-twelfth century demonstrate a concern to instil basic catechetical precepts; these texts were copied contemporaneously with Latin texts more suited to a monastic audience, suggesting this collection was aimed at either elementary students or the lay community.[33] Two studies of twelfth-century vernacular homilies suggest that they were not mere copies of earlier texts, but rather reflected the concerns of the new pastoral theology of the parish schools; a

[32] E. M. Goulburn and H. Symonds, eds., *The Life, Letters and Sermons of Bishop Herbert de Losinga* (2 vols.; Oxford, 1878); M. Brett, *The English Church under Henry I* (Oxford, 1975), pp. 116–17.

[33] London, BL, MS Cotton Vespasian D. xiv.

collection of vernacular sermons compiled in the east Midlands in the late twelfth century denounced marital infidelity, non-payment of tithes and non-attendance at church, and seems to have been composed for public preaching at diocesan level.[34] The twelfth-century evidence is thus biased towards the higher clergy, secular and regular: Abbot Samson of Bury is reported to have preached in the vernacular. The higher clergy in this period do not seem to have shared Ælfric's earlier aspirations to provide materials for regular preaching in local churches, but it is clear they were as conscientious as pastors as their late tenth- and early eleventh-century counterparts. Their continued interest, when combined with the wider community's investment in local church building, is witness to the abiding preoccupation with the delivery of pastoral care that existed throughout these three centuries.

[34] Cambridge, Trinity College, MS B.14.52 (335): Old English Homilies Second Series: *Old English Homilies of the Twelfth Century from the Unique Ms B.14.52 in the Library of Trinity College, Cambridge*, ed. R. Morris (EETS original ser. 53; 1873).

CHAPTER V.3

Saints and cults

Paul Antony Hayward

No two cult centres in England have exactly the same history between AD 900 and 1200, but if there is a general pattern it is that the period saw three great surges of interest in saints and their cults: the first took place at the end of the tenth century, the second in the six decades between 1070 and 1130 and the third and the most diffuse during the last three decades of the twelfth century. These periods saw efforts on the part of the leading churches to introduce new cults or to renew old ones. At Thorney, for example, there was much activity during the first two phases: diverse cults were relocated to the abbey when it was founded in the 970s; several of these cults – those of Botulf, Tancred, Torhtred and Tova – were subsequently equipped with *vitae* by Folcard, the *viceabbas* whom William the Conqueror appointed in about 1069;[1] in 1098 the relics were translated to a new church built by Abbot Gunther, who had succeeded Folcard in 1085; more relics were then acquired in 1105 and 1111 – relics of Theodore the Martyr and then relics of the founder St Æthelwold himself;[2] but there is little sign that the abbey's repertoire of cults was expanded or that they were provided with further textual support during the remainder of our period. Similar narratives, marked by bursts of interest and lengthy periods of neglect, could be detailed for many cult centres in England, most of them adhering to the broad chronological contours defined above.

Exactly what these patterns of growth and recession signify is the question before this essay. It will assess the capacity to explain these phenomena of the three broad approaches to the cult of saints that have gained

[1] For Folcard and his works, see M. Lapidge and R. C. Love, 'The Latin hagiography of England and Wales (600–1550)', in G. Philippart, ed., *Hagiographies: histoire internationale de la littérature hagiographique latine et vernaculaire, en Occident, des origines à 1500* (Turnhout, 2001), vol. III, pp. 235–7; cf R. A. B. Mynors, R. M. Thomson and M. Winterbottom, eds. and trans., *William of Malmesbury, Gesta pontificum Anglorum*, iv. 186.5 (2 vols.; OMT; Oxford, 2007), i, pp. 494–5.

[2] For these translations, see the annals in Oxford, St John's College, MS 17, fol. 29v, and London, B.L., MS Cotton Nero C.VII, fol. 80v.

the greatest currency among scholars of our period: that which suggests that saints' cults were commercial enterprises, that which explains their rise and fall in relation to their political utility and that which relates their evolution to broad changes in the intellectual climate. It will suggest that although all three approaches draw attention to important developments, it is the second that can best explain the general pattern and clarify its significance.

CULTS AS COMMERCIAL ENTERPRISES

The first approach holds that cults operated like businesses. On this view, it is the income they generated, chiefly in the form of offerings left by pilgrims, which explains why religious maintained them. The service they offered was in essence a remedial one: pilgrims visited shrines in the hope of obtaining relief from adversity, typically in the form of physical ailments; they may not actually have been cured, but the shrine would at least provide them with the consolation afforded by having undergone a curative ritual. On this view, the function of hagiography was to advertise the saint's capacity to intercede with the deity by setting out his or her track record for obtaining cures – or at least to authenticate a cult by providing its subject with a certificate whose form, style and contents matched the literary memorials associated with undisputed and famous saints. In keeping with this view the way in which phases of cult promotion so often coincided with the building of churches is often explained by the theory that the pilgrimage trade was a ready source of cash that could be exploited to fund construction projects. On this view, moreover, the surges of interest in saints reflect either periods when custodian communities had greater financial need or the arrival of new ideas as to how to realize the potential of neglected assets – ideas that were often rudely introduced under the direction of foreign religious, not least those who were appointed to many bishoprics and abbacies after 1066.

There is certainly some evidence for the commercialization of cults between 900 and 1200, but chiefly in the decades after 1170, when England's culture of sanctity was much affected by the sensational martyrdom of Thomas Becket. For it was in these years that the granting of indulgences and the production of pilgrims' badges seem to have taken off. Lead ampules containing water mixed with the archbishop's blood or dust from his tomb and inscribed with the legend *Optimus egrorum medicus fit Toma bonorum* ('Thomas makes the best doctor of the worthy who are ill') were being sold to pilgrims within a few years of his death, perhaps even as early as 1171. Stories about their marvellous properties were soon being collected at Canterbury – stories alleging that those who stole them would find that Becket's water did them harm rather than good, that they were good for putting out fires as well as performing cures, that contact with the saint's body made them resistant to being remelted, and so on.[3] A practice that was soon imitated at other cult centres, the selling of souvenirs represents one of the ways in which the dramatic rise of Becket's cult alerted custodian communities to the economic potential of their cults.

There is, moreover, material which suggests that some religious felt compelled to reassert the efficacy of their cults at this time. The *Miracles of the Hand of St James* tells, for example, how the apostle appeared to a deformed girl who had crawled from Seaford to Canterbury: 'You will certainly not receive a cure here', he is supposed to have said, 'but go to Reading, to my monastery, and there you will be healed.' Insisting that St Thomas would help her, she remained in Canterbury until she had lost all her money. It was only then that she went to Reading to receive her cure.[4] This story needs to be compared with an older type of *miraculum*, a type in which two saints, a distinguished saint and the subject of the collection, would co-operate in the delivery of a cure by having the former appear to a pilgrim in a vision promising that they would be cured if he or she went to the latter's shrine. The purpose of such stories was to establish the latter saint's position in the celestial hierarchy by asserting that he or she was of sufficient standing for the greater saint to have used them as a partner. Hagiographers continued to write up stories along these lines, but the appearance of the hostile variant found in the *Miracles of the Hand of St James* points to the rise of a more competitive climate in which the fear of losing pilgrims to Canterbury was driving the promotion of some cults.

There are problems, however, with the idea that commercial considerations lay behind all of this. The evidence of the hagiographical record is much less supportive, first of all, than is often assumed. It is not just that

[3] For example, William of Canterbury, *Miracula gloriosi martyris Thomæ Cantuariensis archiepiscopi* (*BHL* 8185), iii. 54, vi. 62, 79, 81, in J. C. Robertson, ed., *Materials for the History of Thomas Becket, Archbishop of Canterbury* (RS; London, 1875–85), i, pp. 308–9, 464–5 and 477–8. The discovery of how to produce metal *ampullae* is reported in Benedict of Peterborough, *Miracula sancti Thomæ Cantuariensis* (*BHL* 8171), iii.18, in Robertson, ed., *Materials for the History of Thomas Becket*, ii, p. 129.

[4] B. R. Kemp, 'The miracles of the hand of St James', *Berkshire Archaeological Journal*, 65 (1970), 1–19, at 15.

Latin texts were hardly the best vehicles for advertising cures to a largely illiterate population that used a Germanic language. The crucial problem is that the miracle collections often celebrate *miracula* that will have damaged the economic potential of their subjects' cults. There are, for example, miracle stories which imply that offerings were *not* expected. In one such story a mother is shown abusing her son for wasting his money on doctors when all that St Oswine requires is *faith*: 'O miserable son, why is it that you, who have present the best of doctors, your lord, the holy king and martyr, Oswine, pay out all your substance to doctors? He requires of the suffering not payment but faith!'[5] Supplicants were expected, of course, to show their contrition by making an adequate sacrifice, but in many *miracula* the ordeal of reaching the shrine seems to have been sufficient. In some the sacrifice consists of thanks or praise for the saint. If the intention was to fashion pilgrims for the purpose of making money from their offerings, stories like these will have set an unhelpful example.

Another issue is that few of the churches that housed important shrines seem to have been constructed with a view to accommodating crowds of pilgrims. This point is especially true of those built in the six decades after 1066. At Canterbury, for example, Archbishop Lanfranc (1070–89) opted for a design with three parallel apses at its eastern end as opposed to one with an ambulatory, a design better suited for moving pilgrims to and from a shrine. Much the same arrangement was employed at St Albans, Lincoln and Old Sarum. But even when an ambulatory was part of the design, the needs of pilgrims seldom seem to have been the primary consideration. The cathedral erected by Bishop Walkelin (1070–98) at Winchester had such an arrangement, but the shrine of St Swithun was placed on a large platform behind the high altar to which only the monks had access, except in so far as the 'Holy Hole', a niche permitting a few supplicants to keep vigil under the shrine, was cut into its eastern face. The priority in the placement of the shrine was not to provide access for pilgrims but to create an exclusive precinct for high-status burials, chiefly those of the bishops themselves. Though Bernard of Clairvaux accused the Benedictines of erecting grandiose churches in order to raise money from pilgrims, few of England's larger churches seem to have been built with this aim in mind.

5 *Vita, inventio et miracula sanctissimi et gloriosissimi regis Deirorum Oswini* (*BHL* 6382–4), §18, in J. Raine, ed., *Miscellanea Biographica* (Surtees Society Publications 8; London and Edinburgh, 1838), pp. 1–59, at 32.

CULTS AS SOURCES OF LEGITIMACY

The second approach emphasizes the value of cults as symbols of God's esteem. On this view, their utility lay in the way in which the legends and miracles of saints could be spun to the advantage (or disadvantage) of the persons and communities with custody of their relics. The custodians were not so much interested in providing a service for pilgrims as in the oral or textual by-products of their visits – reports of cures that could be redeployed for political effect. Thanks to the explicit testimony provided by Wulfstan's *Life of St Æthelwold*, the clearest case in point is that of St Swithun, an obscure bishop of Winchester who held office from 852/3 to 862×5 (see Chapter V.5). Previously unsuspected, his sanctity was revealed by a sudden burst of miracles which began around 970, six years after Bishop Æthelwold (963–84) had ejected the secular clerks from the Old Minster, replacing them with celibate monks. Writing twenty-five years later, Wulfstan tells us that Æthelwold's preaching

> was greatly aided by the holy bishop Swithun's being *at this time* marked out by signs from heaven and gloriously translated to receive a proper burial within the church. So it was that at one and the same time two lamps blazed in the house of God, placed on golden candlesticks; for what Æthelwold preached by the saving encouragement of his words, Swithun wonderfully ornamented by display of miracles ... And so it came about ... that monasteries were established everywhere in England, some for monks, some for nuns, governed by abbots and abbesses who lived according to the Rule.[6]

That Æthelwold contrived this revelation to give the appearance of divine approval to the far-reaching changes which he had brought about at Winchester – the violent intrusion of monks at a cathedral church, reversing a long-standing trend towards the secularization of England's minsters – seems clear. With the signs of divine support provided by an active cult one could defend the indefensible.

The immense advantage of this approach is that it can account for the pattern of rising and falling interest described at the outset of this essay, for all three 'surges' coincided with periods when the English Church was in the throes of change. In the late tenth century it was reformers Æthelwold and Oswald who were driving events, imposing the Benedictine Rule on existing establishments and reorganizing local landholdings to support the refoundation of minsters which had fallen into abeyance. These

[6] M. Lapidge and M. Winterbottom, eds., and trans., *Wulfstan of Winchester, The Life of St Æthelwold* (OMT; Oxford, 1991), §§26–7, p. 43 (emphasis added) (*BHL* 2647).

changes were often justified by the need to provide for the veneration of the saints of the conversion period or by the acquisition of relics whose arrival was proclaimed as a sign of divine approval.

The post-Conquest surge is characterized by a more complex pattern. Some cults were exploited to justify sweeping change, the clearest case in point being that of St Mildburg. Her body was, so her *inventio* alleges, rediscovered at Much Wenlock in 1101, a decade or so after Roger de Montgomery, earl of Shrewsbury (d. 1094), gave this minster and its extensive endowment to the Cluniac priory of La-Charité-sur-Loire. The community thus created was a colonial establishment, populated with monks from the French mother house and threatened by the fall in 1102 of Roger's heir, Robert of Bellême. The newcomers needed signs that their presence had God's approval, signs which were supplied by the discovery of Mildburg's remains. In the six decades after 1066 cults were more often deployed, however, for the purpose of resisting rather than of legitimizing change. This much is evident, for example, at Winchester, where Swithun's cult was now being used to prevent a reversal of Æthelwold's reforms. It was around 1100, soon after the death of Bishop Walkelin in 1098, that the first *vita* of Swithun was composed, a text that presented the saint, not as the married cleric which he had almost certainly been, but as a quasi-monastic figure. The author tells us that he was always humble; that he was frugal with food; that he used to travel, not on horseback, but walking barefoot; that he permitted himself to sleep only as much as was needed to keep himself fresh for God's service; and that he was always engaged in psalmody and chant.[7] Walkelin, moreover, whom Eadmer says was only prevented from secularizing the Old Minster through the last-minute intervention of Archbishop Lanfranc, is cast in the accompanying miracle collection as an eager participant in the cult.[8] This life and its version of the *miracula* were produced, it seems, to defend the received constitution of the cathedral by reasserting the saint's preference for a monastic form of life.

Similar concerns were a factor in the late twelfth-century surge, for reform was again on the agenda in the 1180s and 1190s, and in this phase the Benedictines' difficulties were compounded by the transfer of ascetic authority to the new orders that had taken place over the previous seven decades. Becket's cult – a symbol of the liberties of the English Church

7 M. Lapidge, ed. and trans., *The Cult of St Swithun* (Winchester Studies 4.ii; Oxford, 2003), pp. 630–9 (*Vita*).

8 Lapidge, ed. and trans., *Cult of St Swithun*, pp. 648–97 (*Miracula*), esp. §52, pp. 684–7. Cf. M. Rule, ed., *Historia novorum in Anglia Eadmeri* (RS; London, 1884), p. 18.

from its inception – was invoked by both sides when Baldwin of Forde, the Cistercian who was archbishop of Canterbury from 1185 to 1190, attempted to found a college for secular canons at Hackington. This scheme implied the transfer of much influence and wealth, including half the offerings left at the shrine, from the cathedral priory to the new foundation. Baldwin justified the plan with the argument that churches dedicated to Becket were lacking; the monks cited the miracles taking place at the shrine as proof that the saint was happy with the existing arrangement. Gervase even defended their decision to refer the dispute to the apostolic see by reporting a vision in which Becket had appeared to one of the younger monks and prophesied that the sword of St Peter would smash the terrifying machine – a flame-belching Katherine's wheel – with which the archbishop was threatening to destroy the priory.[9]

The conflict between seculars and monks was a major factor in all three 'surges', but it was only one of many issues which were negotiated using saints' cults during our period. Perhaps the most important was the great rank-order dispute which broke out in earnest in the 1070s. Much was at stake in this contest. It was not just that higher rank entitled a church to a larger share of the kingdom's resources. It also granted its head access to the highest echelons of society and the right to a say in the making of policy. With their revival under Lanfranc and Anselm church councils became the decisive venue for the conduct of ecclesiastical government. A prelate's capacity to protect his church depended on his ability to assert himself at these meetings, but speaking rights were allocated according to rank, each man speaking to issues under discussion in a fixed order; and, in a crucial change from Anglo-Saxon practice, the relative importance of saints in the celestial hierarchy would now play a decisive role in settling disputes about the ranking of churches. These developments initiated a series of campaigns among the greater churches of the kingdom to enhance the standing of their patron saints – campaigns that continued into and well beyond the lull after the second of our three surges.

St Augustine's Abbey led the way with its argument that its patron was 'the apostle of the English'. The monks seem to have begun to assert their patron's claim to this title in the 1040s, inspired perhaps by recent events in Aquitaine, where the monks of Limoges had argued that their patron, St Martial, was one of the seventy-two apostles of Jesus Christ. But it was

[9] William Stubbs, ed., *The Historical Works of Gervase of Canterbury* (RS; London, 1879), i, pp. 338–43. For the context, see *ibid.*, pp. 229–31, 332–4, 337–8.

only after the Conquest that this kind of spin began to have real bite. At Lanfranc's general council in 1072 Scolland, the first Norman abbot of St Augustine's (1070–87), was seated first among the abbots, almost certainly on the basis that the patron of his church was England's apostle. Armed with a new sense of entitlement, St Augustine's went on to argue that it ought to have an exemption, much to the annoyance of its diocesan, the archbishop of Canterbury. A grander church was erected, and in 1091 Abbot Guy (1087–93) translated the abbey's saints to an array of shrines at its eastern end, an event celebrated in the monumental cycle of hagiographical texts which Goscelin of Saint-Bertin produced for the abbey. The central theme of those texts was the status which the abbey ought to have because it had the relics of England's apostle. Pope Alexander II is made, for example, to confer on Abbot Æthelsige (1062–70) the right to use a bishop's mitre and sandals, 'because of St Augustine's dignity as a Roman *alumnus* and as the apostle of the English'.[10] The response of Lanfranc and Anselm to this challenge to their authority was to reassert the traditional position that Pope Gregory the Great was the *Anglorum apostolus*, but St Augustine's was trumped far more effectively by the sustained efforts of the other great monasteries – Westminster Abbey, Glastonbury and especially St Albans.

It seems likely that St Alban was first proclaimed as 'the protomartyr of the English' – as the martyr with whose blood God had dedicated the *ecclesia Anglorum* – when the monastery was refounded in the late tenth century, but it was not until after the Conquest that this idea's potential was realized. It was probably Lanfranc who first used Alban's status to improve his abbey's position, for the house was a possession of the archbishopric during his pontificate. His aim was probably to remove the monastery from the bishop of Lincoln's jurisdiction, so that it would be subject to his spiritual lordship directly. But once St Albans had secured its independence from Canterbury, it redeployed the cult in an attempt to make itself the leading monastery in England, a position which it attained with the help of Pope Adrian IV (1154–9). With the privilege *Religiosam vitam* he granted to the abbot a primacy of rank marked by the right to use all the pontifical ornaments – namely, the mitre, the gloves, the seal and the sandals. This rank was justified, the pope declared, by the status of the abbey's saint, 'for just as the Blessed Alban is known to be a protomartyr so also the abbot of his monastery should be held forth as first among the

[10] *Historia translationis S. Augustini et aliorum sanctorum* (*BHL* 781), ii.6, in D. Papebroch, ed., *Acta Sanctorum Maii*, vi (Antwerp, 1688), pp. 411–43, at p. 433.

abbots of England in order of dignity on every occasion'.[11] St Albans had risen a long way since the 1070s, when its head had occupied a middling position among the abbots at Lanfranc's councils, thanks in large part to the ways in which the cult of its principal saint could be spun.

CULTS AS GAUGES OF CULTURAL CHANGE

On the basis of the material assembled so far it appears that the political approach has more to recommend it than the commercialist alternative. There is, however, a third way of explaining the ebb and flow of interest in saints' cults during our period, namely, by arguing that the custodians were responding to broad changes in their intellectual and cultural milieu, such as the rise of the Schools. This development, it is claimed, exposed cults to increased scrutiny by encouraging churchmen to question their authenticity and by empowering them with the mental tools – reason and dialectic – which could be used to unpick the arguments that validated them. The episode most often cited in support of this interpretation is that where Lanfranc is said to have questioned the authenticity of the cult of St Ælfheah, one of his predecessors as archbishop of Canterbury (d. 1012). He had expressed his doubts to Anselm, pointing out that the English do not deny that he had been killed 'not for the confession of Christ's name but because he would not ransom himself with money'.[12] Lanfranc's critique was answered, Eadmer tells us, partly through the reasoned arguments developed by Anselm, who was then abbot of Bec, and partly through the provision of a *historia*, a life of the saint intended not only for reading but also for singing. The life was composed by Osbern of Canterbury. This episode is often cited as though it were a decisive example of how cultural change prompted the modernization of cults, but it is hardly an unambiguous case. It is true that Lanfranc had run schools at Bec and Caen and that he had helped to defeat the eucharistic heresies preached by Berengar of Tours; but he was no ordinary schoolman. He was, at the time when he questioned Ælfheah's cult, a central figure in a colonial regime, presiding at successive synods over the deposition of English bishops and abbots so that they could be replaced with Norman churchmen. At Canterbury he was carrying out a far-reaching

[11] W. Holtzmann, ed., *Papsturkunden in England*, iii (Abhandlungen der Gesellschaft der Wissenschaften zu Göttingen: philologisch-historische Klasse, 3rd ser. 33; Berlin, 1952), no. 118.

[12] R. W. Southern, ed. and trans., *The Life of St Anselm by Eadmer* (2nd edn; OMT; London, 1972), i. 30, pp. 50–4 (*BHL* 526a).

programme of reform, and his questioning of Ælfheah's cult can be seen as an exercise in fault-finding intended to disarm opposition.

The strongest example of a hagiographical text that may have been composed in order to refute learned scepticism is Arcoid's *Miracula S. Erkenwaldi* (*BHL* 2601), a work dating from around 1140; but it is unique among English miracle collections of this period in taking so much account of this issue – a reflection perhaps of the urban setting of its subject's cult. London, a trading city of around 20,000 persons by the 1140s, may well have supported a higher level of resistance to cults. But it should not be assumed that belief was elsewhere the norm. Some degree of indifference, fairly evenly distributed amongst the laity and across the period, is implied by the continued production of certain types of *miracula*. Most collections or appendices of posthumous miracles include, for example, at least one or two stories in which persons dwelling within a cult's catchment area are punished for working on the saint's feast day, implying that non-observance of their festivals was a persistent problem. Consider, moreover, Arcoid's story of the man who satirized the pretensions of St Erkenwald. Fooling around inside the shell of a reliquary which was being made for the saint, he called out in a deep voice: 'I am the holy Erkenwald: bring me gifts; ask me for help; make me a bier of silver!' The man soon became ill and died a few days later.[13] Now this story might be interpreted as evidence for attitudes current in London when Arcoid was writing, but Ælfric of Eynsham, writing at the rural backwater that was Cerne Abbas in the 990s, attributes a similar act of vengeance to St Swithun.[14] The two episodes are instances of the same type of *miraculum*, one that seems to have been devised in order to counter the criticism that a cult was being promoted as a way of gaining lordship over others – gift-giving being one of several gestures of submission which the saint is accused of demanding. It is likely that resistance to the cult of saints was a factor long before the advent of scholasticism: the use of cults to validate claims to authority will have inspired jealousy, a problem aggravated by the likelihood that pilgrims who really wanted to be cured will often have returned home disappointed.

Yet, in most times and places, in the normal course of events, religious seem to have been content to ignore hostility of this kind and to allow their cults to suffer a kind of benign neglect. This much is apparent

[13] E. G. Whatley, ed., *The Saint of London: The Life and Miracles of St Erkenwald* (Medieval and Renaissance Texts and Studies 58; Binghamton, NY, 1989), §10, pp. 142–5 (*BHL* 2601).

[14] Ælfric, 'Life of St Swithun', in Lapidge, ed. and trans., *Cult of St Swithun*, pp. 590–609, §19.

from the record provided by the surviving miracle collections, for the vast majority provide patchy coverage of their subject's cures, even during the period after 1170 when Becket's cult became a factor. Consider, for example, the cult of St Edmund at Bury. This cult arose soon after King Edmund was martyred by the Danes in 869, yet its custodians did not think it necessary to make an extended record of his posthumous miracles until around 1100, when a collection comprising some thirty episodes was produced. Several *miracula* were added to this collection and at some point after 1139 Osbert of Clare wrote up another thirteen at the request of Abbot Anselm (1121–48); but aside from these rather pathetic efforts, there were no other attempts to record fresh events at the shrine during the twelfth century. It is true that several new books of miracles were produced in conjunction with the cult, but they are almost entirely composed not of new episodes but of stories derived from earlier compilations which have been rewritten for stylistic effect. Much the same pattern is evident at Winchester. Lantfred's *Translatio et miracula*, in which some thirty-six posthumous *miracula* (many involving groups of cures) are reported, was compiled around 974, within a few years of the revelation which established Swithun's cult. The saint was the subject of another six hagiographical texts produced over the next two centuries, but they added little to the record of his cures. The only contributors to add posthumous miracles to the dossier were Ælfric and the anonymous hagiographer who refashioned Swithun as a monk: the former added two items when he produced his Old English homily between 993 and 998, while the latter, writing after 1098, added sixteen.

There are, William of Malmesbury complained, many churches in England where only the names of the local saints were known – where their lives as well as their miracles have gone unrecorded.[15] This much was the tenth- and eleventh-century norm, and it was not much altered by the rise of the Schools in the twelfth: hagiography was produced in larger quantities, but such efforts remained spasmodic. This should not surprise us. It was the offering up of liturgical prayer on behalf of the dead and for society as a whole that was the core task of monasticism, whilst for the secular clergy it was pastoral care.

It seems best, then, to conclude that saints' cults were phenomena of intermittent importance. The one concern which seems to have led to sustained efforts to develop and promote cults was the need felt by some

[15] Thomson and Winterbottom, eds. and trans., *William of Malmesbury, Gesta pontificum*, ii. 95; ii, p. 316.

of the greatest churches of the kingdom to secure the resources and the say in the decision-making process that came with having a pre-eminent saint. But for most churches efforts to remind people of their saints and their achievements, to refurbish their *vitae* and to record their miracles and to renew the fabric of their shrines were concentrated in periods when reform and the expulsion of the unreconstructed were on the agenda. In England those periods were the late tenth century, the final decades of the twelfth and above all the six decades between 1070 and 1130. Saints' cults were often invoked at these times for the purpose of resisting change or of justifying it. At these moments shrines would become the focus of urgent activity: the need for miracle stories to support the position of the moment might lead *for a while* to the promotion of a cult among the laity. It was on these occasions that defects in the arguments used to validate cults might become a factor, to be exploited by exponents of change like Lanfranc, or to be repaired in haste by defenders of the status quo like Osbern. It was at these times that efforts were made to provide *vitae* for those cults which lacked them or to repair the texts that were available. It was the political life of the Church that did most, in short, to drive the development of the cult of saints in England between 900 and 1200.

CHAPTER V.4

Public spectacle

Tom Licence

Public spectacle, which may be defined as any orchestration of events designed to engage the minds of spectators, can inform our understanding of the social identity or prevailing mores of past cultures. Typically it evolves as a co-adapted set of devices: superficially, devices such as sights, sounds, smells, splendour and ceremony, but at a deeper level – one might say psychologically – a sense of participation; an affirmation of identity and life's meaning for the individual, as a spectator within a collectivity of his or her peers. The trick is that each spectator imagines that he or she is at one with all, most or many of the others by participating in the common response of the crowd; indeed, the most enduring forms of public spectacle in the period 900–1200 stimulated the crowd to respond in a predetermined way. In doing so they performed four main social functions. The first function of spectacle was essentially contractual: to affirm the mutual responsibilities, or the mutually profitable relationship, between different ranks of the social hierarchy (including God and the saints), or social equals. Another function was to affirm life's meaning, usually by reinforcing belief in God and in the Christian cosmology. A third function might be termed recreational. Village drama, knockabout, satire, skits and the enactment of heroic tales tackled life's big questions in engaging, allusive, fun or frivolous ways, and surely helped people come to terms with them. The fourth function of spectacle was to affirm social mores, the value of good behaviour and the rejection of its opposite. This fourfold framework may serve us as a map for exploring spectacle, interpreting its significance and reconstructing its processes of thought. We can try it out in the case of a saintly person's public funeral.

The saintly bishop Robert de Béthune was a charitable ascetic occupying the see of Hereford. He died while attending the Council of Rheims in 1148, and when his funeral procession finally entered London after its long journey back by land and sea 'there thundered from all sides bells tolling with great clamour so that deafened ears could scarce bear the tremendous roar. From all sides flocked processions from every religious order, weeping and chanting psalms.' The bishop of Winchester went before the procession on foot, weeping.[1] Replete with plangent mourners, this grand, effusive funeral served to uphold the course of a life well lived by affirming that the virtues of asceticism and charity were of value to society and were a loss rightly to be mourned.

Initially the saintly bishop's funeral should have inspired participants to approve his good conduct, before leading them to reflect on the meaning of life and on the nature of the bond between man and God. Here was a man who by service to God earned a saint's reputation and a place, no doubt, in heaven. If his funeral stimulated thoughts such as these it would have performed three of the four functions previously outlined.

The first function of spectacle was to affirm the mutual obligations between some powerful individual (such as God, a king or a saint) and those over whom he wielded power. The king or saint, for his part, required allegiance and homage. His subjects, for theirs, sought that he should exercise his power to their advantage. The ceremony of crowning a new king; crown wearings in which a king conducted business, regally attired; the procession of the relics of saints and the ritual elevation of saints' shrines (*translationes*) all made appeal to this reciprocal principle of power relationships and impressed it on participants, in a way no written contract could, through auditory, visual and olfactory mediums. In the tenth and eleventh centuries the king underwent formal election by a convention of magnates from all over the realm, not to diminish his heredity but as a symbolic transference of power by his would-be subjects. Once this was done he was invested with God's authority in the rite of consecration, when the officiating archbishop would preach before him and his assembled subjects on the king's duties to God and to his people. During the Anglo-Norman period the ritual acceptance of power was reinforced with an oath, by which the new king swore to rule justly. At no time was he more exposed to public scrutiny than at his coronation, which was sure to draw expectant crowds and generate much talk. Blunders could get his reign off to a bad start, as the historian Orderic Vitalis observed in the cases of kings Harold II and William I, who were both crowned within the space of the year 1066. Harold II (so the story goes) was consecrated surreptitiously without the magnates' consent. At William's consecration the cheering of the English crowd was mistaken for a riot, whereupon the

[1] B. J. Parkinson, 'The life of Robert of Béthune by William of Wycombe: translation with introduction and notes' (unpublished B.Litt. dissertation, University of Oxford, 1958), p. 226.

Norman garrison started a fire that soon precipitated panic.[2] These tales may be apocryphal, but they illustrate the importance of right and proper ceremony. In Orderic's opinion, its collapse in each case incurred deep feelings of betrayal, with lasting ramifications for the reign. He even identified the fiasco at William I's coronation as the reason for English loss of trust in the Normans. In Harold's case the consent of the people was not secured; in William's, the devil's antics turned goodwill into hostility. Effectively, in both, the contract was broken.

If the coronation ceremony was an affirmation of kingship, the ecclesiastical ceremony of translation, in which a saint was honoured through the removal of his or her bodily remains to a more splendid and exalted resting place, was an affirmation of sanctity. In the tenth and eleventh centuries saints were translated in recognition of miracles recently performed, as was the case with St Æthelwold at Winchester in 995, St Eadwold at Cerne Abbas in Dorset, probably in the 1020s, and St Mildthryth, from Minster-in-Thanet to St Augustine's, Canterbury, in 1030. Later (if not already), its value as a stimulus to cultic rejuvenation was the attraction of this ceremony. Like a coronation, translation signified a contract, if undertaken in expectation that the saint so honoured might subsequently redouble his miracle-working efforts. Such, indeed, was the result after the translation of St Edmund at Bury St Edmunds in 1095, or the translations of St William of Norwich in 1151 and 1154 or that of St Frideswide at Oxford in 1180, to identify but a few. The reason for this was that translation raised a saint's profile and consequently drew pilgrims who would then report more miracles. Rivalry between three of the greatest abbeys in the realm (St Swithun's, Winchester, St Augustine's, Canterbury, and St Edmund's, Bury), each of which possessed a saint with a national reputation, prompted each in the early 1090s to stage a well-publicized translation.[3] These ceremonies drew magnates, bishops, abbots and congregations of lesser clergy and laity, male and female, who thronged each church, while the monks processed in great splendour, bearing the saints to magnificent new shrines. The list of those in attendance at the translation of St Edward the Confessor in Westminster Abbey in 1163 reads

[2] M. Chibnall, ed. and trans., *The Ecclesiastical History of Orderic Vitalis* (6 vols.; OMT; Oxford, 1969–80), ii, pp. 136–8, 184. Orderic, here, makes much more of the incident than his source, William of Poitiers, for whose account see R. H. C. Davis and M. Chibnall, eds., *The Gesta Guillelmi of William of Poitiers* (OMT; Oxford, 1993), pp. 150–1.

[3] R. Sharpe, 'The setting of St Augustine's translation, 1091', in R. Eales and R. Sharpe, eds., *Canterbury and the Norman Conquest: Churches, Saints and Scholars 1066–1109* (London and Rio Grande, OH, 1995), pp. 1–13.

like a contemporary *Who's Who*, from the king and archbishop down.[4] This particular event was also a celebration of English kingship (two years before, Edward had become the first English king to be canonized by a pope). But translations generally served to reinvigorate the bonds between the saints and their supplicants. The same could well be said for relic showings and relic processions.

Herman, a senior monk at Bury St Edmunds during the 1090s, was remembered for displaying St Edmund's undergarment, punctured with arrow holes and empurpled with gore, while preaching to the Sunday congregations. On one occasion he passed it around the audience, allowing the faithful to kiss it at the modest price of tuppence a turn.[5] This was a rare stimulus to devotion, for not only did the garment illustrate the saint's manner of suffering and martyrdom in such a way as to fire the imagination; it also exuded a heavenly fragrance, as a token of authenticity, and initiated a feeling of intimacy and empathy towards the saint in the minds of those who handled it (mostly townsfolk). It was the custom at Beverley, in the early twelfth century, to elevate the relics of the local saint, St John of Beverley, at the door of the church on Ascension Day so that the clergy and congregation could pass by them on their way out. Public processions on other holy occasions, such as Rogationtide, provided opportunities for renewing one's devotion. These would have involved relic-bearing clergy dressed in white and accompanied by crowds of laity, halting for Gospel readings at established stations, which were probably marked by crosses or at nodal points in the landscape.[6] Sometimes bodies of clergy undertook singular tours, bearing relics in procession, to raise the profile of their cult and gather funds for associated building projects. In the 980s or 990s 'Pictish' clergy – they may have been Bretons – journeyed to Wilton in Wiltshire, bearing the body of St Iwi, an eighth-century saint who had retired to be a hermit in Brittany. They probably intended to employ their saint as a useful source of income, but his relics proved so popular and impressive in working miracles that the abbess of Wilton offered 2,000 shillings for them, at which Iwi and his acolytes parted company. Fund-raising tours organized by the monks of Evesham during Walter's abbacy (1077–1104), when they processed with the feretory of St Ecgwine, and by the canons of Laon Cathedral in France, who processed through England

[4] London, Lambeth Palace, MS 761, fols. 61v–65r.

[5] New York, Pierpont Morgan, MS M. 736, fols. 71r–71v and T. Licence, 'History and hagiography in the late eleventh century: the life and work of Herman the archdeacon, monk of Bury St Edmunds', *EHR*, 124 (2009), 516–44, at 530.

[6] J. Blair, *The Church in Anglo-Saxon Society* (Oxford, 2005), pp. 486–7.

in 1113 bearing relics of the Virgin, were hailed as successful operations, enabling sponsors to benefit from the saints' miracles and by commending themselves to a needy saintly patron. On other occasions relic processions functioned to enlist the saint's support, in times of drought for example. Here the saint was expected to answer his followers' prayers.

The symbolic affirmation of a contract (or mutually beneficial relationship) can be discerned in many other spectacular occasions. When King Æthelstan bestowed a lavish Gospel book upon the custodians of a shrine in Durham, or when King Cnut and members of his entourage entered into confraternity with the monks of Thorney Abbey, associated ceremonies would have impressed upon onlookers the nature of the exchange and the ensuing relationship: in return for patronage, prayers were offered. Official royal visits to any town or city could also serve as an opportunity to display the generosity incumbent upon kingly office, in order to win affection and admiration. The same was true of crown wearings. Regular crown wearings at Christmas, Easter and Pentecost were a post-Conquest innovation and a custom, particularly, of the two kings William. Great men of the kingdom would gather on these important, festive occasions for feasting, business transactions and the reception of foreign visitors.[7] As the king sat fully arrayed his subjects acknowledged his authority, while appealing to his regal generosity. Other, like forms of ceremony may have tended rather more to promulgate pretensions of grandeur than to celebrate the reciprocity of lord–subject relations; for certain kings of our period, including Æthelstan, Edgar and William I, were hailed in imperial terms. Edgar, in 973, formulated a showy inauguration ritual, presenting himself as the quasi-imperial overlord of a pan-Britannic alliance. Bath was the venue, presumably because it was redolent of imperial Rome. Afterwards, at Chester, eight sub-kings, in token of their submission, rowed Edgar up the Dee.[8] The set of eleventh-century acclamations known as the *Laudes regiae*, which began as a salutation to one of the Norman dukes, were adapted to celebrate King William I's triumph and power, and to frame his authority in imperial terms. It is not clear which categories of people these rites aimed to impress (perhaps they were aimed partly at foreign ambassadors), but as celebrations of regal prowess they should have assured the loyal *populus* or whoever was in the audience that the realm was in good hands.

[7] M. Biddle, 'Seasonal festivals and residence: Winchester, Westminster and Gloucester in the tenth to twelfth centuries', *ANS* 8 (1985 (1986)), 51–72 at 57.

[8] J. L. Nelson, 'Inauguration rituals', in P. H. Sawyer and I. N. Wood, eds., *Early Medieval Kingship* (Leeds, 1977), pp. 50–71, at 67–70.

Within the monastic or ecclesiastical context liturgical drama reminded spectators of the meaning of the Christian life. The *Visitatio sepulchri* play, an Easter enactment of the discovery of Christ's empty sepulchre, became popular in Europe (and instated in England) during the tenth century. It took place at the altar in any monastic church, where a monk waiting at the 'sepulchre' played the part of the angel, while three more monks came to anoint Christ's body. Asked whom they sought, they replied 'Jesus of Nazareth', to which the angel replied, 'He is not here. For he is risen, as the prophets foretold.' Hearing this, the three returned to choir, praising God.[9] This basic formula of seeking, discovery and adoration applied also in the Christmas play, which evolved rather later to encompass the visits of the shepherds and the Magi to Christ in his crib. It was a metaphor of the Christian life, and a reminder that the meaning of mankind's existence was to seek out, discover and worship God. These dramas may well have had a limited audience consisting mostly of monks or nuns. Yet it is easy to imagine that public plays with similar themes spread a comparable message. During the reign of King John a group of players staged a resurrection drama with words and actions in the northern part of the cemetery at Beverley. The clergyman who reported the event commented that they wore masks 'as was customary', and that a great crowd of men, women and children attended to view the spectacle.[10] On certain important days in the ritual year, panoplies of rites, sights, sounds and architecture were orchestrated with the intention of drawing religious congregations into the enactment of sacred events. By the beginning of the thirteenth century these events were carefully stage managed. Worshippers in the Palm Sunday procession, carrying their palms into Wells Cathedral through the western door, could see on the façade ahead and above them references to heaven, the Second Coming, the saints and particularly the angels. To herald Christ's triumphant entry (and the worshippers' entry to the New Jerusalem) these angels even burst into song, courtesy of a row of boy choristers concealed behind them in a hidden passage. A higher row of trumpeting angels may have masked trumpeters, to sound a fanfare. One of the angels still holds a palm, as the worshippers did themselves.[11] The intended effect upon those in the procession was the experience of transportation, in the company of the heavenly hosts, to the

[9] T. Symon, ed., *Regularis concordia* (London, 1953), pp. 49–50.

[10] S. E. Wilson, *The Life and After-Life of St John of Beverley* (Woodbridge, 2006), pp. 82, 204.

[11] C. M. Malone, *Façade as Spectacle: Ritual and Ideology at Wells Cathedral* (Boston, MA, and Leiden, 2004), p. 138.

gates of the New Jerusalem, followed by a triumphal entry: a foretaste of future blessings, in this harsh and unpredictable world.

Spectacle for the purposes of recreation and entertainment must have been a part of life throughout our period, albeit an obscure one for historians to analyse because little was written about it (it was noticed mostly when clerics wished to condemn it). Entertainers could be categorized as mimic performers (*mimi*), as professional actors (*histriones*) and as players (*lusores*), jesters (*scurrilae*) or musical performers-cum-story-tellers (*joculatores/jongleurs*), but no rigid typology is evident, and some were presumably multitalented. Knockabout humour, obscenity and satire won audiences, to the distaste of moralists and sensitive types alike (see Chapter VI.5). King Edgar, a notable patron of monasticism, complained that the clerical patronage of performers and jesters was a source of public scandal.[12] We may only guess what scandals he had in mind, but it is not improbable that the character of the drunken, lecherous cleric was as familiar in this context as he is seen to be in later centuries. Exemplary ecclesiastics disapproved of any divertissement that smacked of worldly folly. They also disapproved of actors and entertainers generally. Robert de Béthune (d. 1148), the saintly, ascetic bishop of Hereford, eschewed 'singers, mimers, players, smutty jesters and all their ilk'; and the Londoner William fitz Stephen was apparently rather proud that, instead of theatrical displays, his city could boast 'holier plays', concerned with the lives and deaths of the saints.[13] Professional players had to make a living and probably turned their hands to whatever sort of spectacle their patrons sought or the authorities deemed permissible. Fitz Stephen's observation could indicate that in London, by the early 1180s, certain public performances – perhaps the enactment of heroic tales, classical drama or skits – were discouraged or even censored. King Edgar's complaint stands in favour of this hypothesis by demonstrating that already, 200 years before fitz Stephen, the powers of the realm had an interest in suppressing irreligious spectacle. Their reach, however, extended only so far, and it can scarcely be doubted that traditional plays of the folk variety, perpetuated by village communities and acted out by their members, were inscrutably commonplace. Touring entertainers sought the largest audiences in the towns, or the patronage of the rich. Away from their circuits, the commonest form of spectacle through the English countryside may well

[12] D. Wilkins, *Concilia Magnae Britanniae et Hiberniae, 446–1717* (4 vols.; London, 1737), i, pp. 228, 246.

[13] Parkinson, 'Robert of Béthune', p. 156 (my translation); *EHD*, ii, no. 281, p. 1028.

have been the amateur variety requiring ritualistic yet creative participation, maybe year-in, year-out, on a particular occasion. Folk drama made light of life's more serious elements, notably birth, death and marriage. In tight-knit communities its licensed buffoonery, mutual name-calling and indirect parody probably functioned as a release for simmering social tensions.[14]

The last function of spectacle worthy of notice encompassed all public rituals and ceremonies that celebrated good behaviour or stigmatized social transgression. For the principal effect of these occasions (in so far as spectacle was involved) was to reinforce social mores. We have already seen how the funeral of Robert de Béthune upheld the message that here was a man whose personal cultivation of virtue benefited society. The ignominious treatment of the traitorous Earl Waltheof, beheaded before sunrise outside the walls of Winchester (in 1076) and dumped in the nearest ditch, conveyed the opposite message, that his chosen path brought only contempt and oblivion. It is not at all clear in this period whether executions were the spectacular, crowd-drawing events that they became in later centuries, or secretive, shameful ones in which taboo-breakers were removed from communities and despatched in sombre locations beyond the bounds. In the case of public penance, in which penitents atoned publicly for their sins, the spectacle began with their ritual expulsion from church, i.e. the community of the faithful, although also the building in which they gathered, at the beginning of Lent. After this, the penitents themselves constituted a sort of spectacle wherever they displayed their penitent status by wearing sackcloth, hairshirts, chains or similar penitential paraphernalia. It was claimed that King Henry II undertook a semi-public penance in 1174 for his share of blame in the murder of Archbishop Thomas Becket, allowing the monks of Canterbury to flog him in their chapter house as an admission of guilt and a catalyst for reconciliation. This form of penance also had a contractual function inasmuch as it sought forgiveness and closure in return for acknowledging a noted wrong. Any number of public or semi-public rituals, including oath-taking, ring-giving, gift exchange, the freeing of slaves, taking the cross to embark upon crusade, assuming the monastic habit and issuing a charter, functioned doubly in a similar way, in that they affirmed some worthy course of action while obliging participants in the presence of onlookers to see it through to completion. After the spectacle of taking the cross, wherein a would-be crusader might pin upon himself a cloth

[14] R. Axton, *European Drama of the Early Middle Ages* (London, 1974), p. 38.

cross in front of a great crowd of people in attendance at a sermon, it was a public shame upon the would-be warrior who later rescinded his vow. The spectacle of the judicial ordeal, in which ordeals by fire, water or combat served to determine the innocence or guilt of a defendant, betokened agreement on the part of all spectators who countenanced it that judgement in difficult cases could be given over to God, whose prompt verdicts in turn gave occasion for communal submission to the ultimate, omniscient authority.

To conclude by evolutionary analogy, it would fit well with what we have seen if the sort of spectacle that evolved and survived in our period was the sort that affirmed an individual's worth within society. To grasp this idea we should abandon any view of it as a thing that was merely experienced. Spectacle invited participation, whether in the acclamation of a king or the booing of a theatrical villain, and on these sorts of occasions the individual in the crowd perceived that others responded in the same way and were empowered to do so by common notions of the way the world should work. The corollary would be that the sort of spectacle in which a king excluded his people (say Harold's coronation, described by Orderic), in which evil triumphed over good, which expected the breaking of agreements and an abstention of responsibility, should never have evolved or survived; and indeed, it did not. If recreational spectacle seems to require a different explanation, we should recall that the label is a makeshift one for accommodating all events with no clear political, religious or social message; it does not betoken lack of meaning. Simple traditional themes such as folly or madness are subject to endless manipulation (as Shakespeare shows in Lear), and if one function of spectacle was to affirm common notions, another, perhaps, was to present things from a fresh or unusual perspective. There is a place for laughter and for silliness, and for turning the world upside-down, if only to invite a climax wherein all is put to rights. Coronations, liturgical drama and funerary processions were occasions for clear and unambiguous messages, but so were plays and other performances inasmuch as their patrons and participants wanted them to be. They even had greater scope for subtlety and archaic or incongruous components. Although there was always a possibility that the influence of tradition on any ritual or ceremony might fossilize defunct elements, so long as the spectacle fulfilled its social role this was hardly a problem. Its role, of course, was to energize the interest, sympathy and mental collaboration of the crowd.

CHAPTER V.5

Textual communities (Latin)

Teresa Webber

Latin texts played a central role in the life of all religious institutions, in a way that set them apart from the laity. Monks, nuns and clergy encountered such texts daily, through the communal performance of the liturgy and other customary observances, individual devotional reading and study. Levels of knowledge and comprehension of Latin varied considerably both within and between religious institutions. Nevertheless, the concept of a textual community, as formulated by Brian Stock, accommodates the existence of differing levels of literacy within a single such community. Membership involved a shared understanding of the contents or precepts of a text or group of texts which shaped or reinforced their ideals and identity.[1] Stock's detailed analysis focused primarily upon Continental marginal and heretical groups, but he acknowledged that textual communities also existed within the religious mainstream. England did not experience the emergence of Christian heterodox or dissident groups until the late Middle Ages, and, in all but exceptional cases, the laity's inclusion as part of a textual community required the use of the vernacular. The number of Latinate laymen was not sufficient to obviate the equation of *clericus* and *litteratus*, at a time when to be literate was understood to entail an ability to read Latin.[2]

There are two contexts in which the role of Latin texts in fostering group identity among clerics and religious is especially evident: the liturgy and the scholarly environment. The repeated rhythms of the liturgical round, in which the same texts were read, recited and chanted in communal worship on a daily, weekly or annual basis, lay at the heart of the common life. The regularity of such communal performance itself no doubt contributed to a sense of common identity among those

[1] B. Stock, *The Implications of Literacy: Written Language and Models of Interpretation in the Eleventh and Twelfth Centuries* (Princeton, NJ, 1983), pp. 90, 238, and 522.

[2] M. T. Clanchy, *From Memory to Written Record: England 1066–1307* (2nd edn; Oxford, 1993), pp. 226–30.

who participated; texts of particular local significance did so in a more obviously direct manner. Among the scholarly elite, a shared textual knowledge, particularly of those works deemed especially authoritative, was an ingredient in the emergence of new alignments. These were reinforced not only through personal and institutional contacts but also through a shared repertoire of textual allusion and quotation in newly composed or compiled works, the exchange of letters and the circulation of books.

LITURGY AND RELIGIOUS OBSERVANCE

From the ninth century onwards, the liturgy of the Mass and the daily Office (the services of Matins, Lauds, Prime, Terce, Sext, None, Vespers and Compline) included rituals and texts common to those churches of western Europe that professed adherence to a 'Roman' tradition. Such uniformity of observance proclaimed the existence of a unified ecclesiastical community. Nevertheless, there was no single liturgy, uniform in all its component texts and melodies, even within any one region or ecclesiastical province. As far as the variable elements of the liturgy are concerned (those texts that differed according to the day or the season), similarities between the practices of different religious houses were usually the result of informal contact. Movements of religious reform, however, might involve the more deliberate introduction of texts and melodies to supplement or replace the existing repertoire, yet elements of the local tradition were often retained. During the second half of the tenth century, several religious communities in southern England were reformed in accordance with a strict observance of the Rule of St Benedict. As part of the reform, a set of customs (the *Regularis concordia*) amplifying the details of the Rule was sanctioned by a Council at Winchester for implementation in all reformed houses: 'for they were united in one faith, though not in one manner of monastic usage'. The new uniform usage, however, did not extend to every element of the liturgy. The homilist Ælfric, for example, drew up a set of customs for his new abbey of Eynsham closely based upon the *Regularis concordia* (which had been compiled by his teacher, Bishop Æthelwold of Winchester). But whereas the *Regularis concordia* prescribed just one biblical reading for Matins on ordinary weekdays during the short nights of summer, Ælfric insisted upon a more rigorous requirement of three readings.[3]

[3] C. A. Jones, ed., *Ælfric's Letter to the Monks of Eynsham* (Cambridge, 1998), pp. 39–42, 149.

COMMUNION WITH THE SAINTS

The liturgical calendar of feast days followed by each religious institution indicates most clearly how membership of both a universal and a local community was affirmed through written texts. As with the liturgy as a whole, some saints, such as the apostles, were celebrated throughout the 'Roman' Church, often on the same day, recalling the unity of the whole Church with the communion of saints, as stated daily in the creed. But the commemoration of many saints was more localized. Of special importance was a community's principal saint (or saints), to whom the church might be dedicated, and in whose name it was often represented (for example, as the beneficiary of grants and privileges, or as the defender of its rights). To enhance the reputation of that saint was to enhance the prestige of the institution. Also important were those saints whose relics the community possessed. The annual celebration of the feasts of these saints was embellished by the reading and singing of special texts and chants, while the acquisition of relics or their 'translation' (their movement to a new shrine) could provide a fitting opportunity for the composition of new texts. On 15 July 971 the relics of a former bishop of Winchester, Swithun, were translated to a splendid new shrine within the cathedral. To commemorate the event, Bishop Æthelwold commissioned from Lantfred, a Frankish monk resident in Winchester, an account of the translation and the miracles that ensued. An early copy of the text from Winchester contains markings that indicate how it was to be divided up as readings in Matins, presumably on the feast of Swithun's translation, kept each year on 15 July (see also Chapter V.3).[4]

During the uncertain aftermath of the Norman Conquest, a potent mix of anxiety about the preservation of property, privilege and local tradition coupled with a climate of renewed enthusiasm for the religious life prompted several communities to promote the cult of their saints, and to enrich their commemoration with new *Lives* and accounts of miracles. A Flemish hagiographer, Goscelin of Saint-Bertin, resident in England since about 1058, was commissioned to write lives of local saints of several abbeys: for example, a life of Wulfsige for the monks of Sherborne, a life of Eadgyth for the nuns of Wilton and lives of Sexburgh and Eormenhild for Ely Abbey. Among Goscelin's commissions was an account of a

[4] London, BL, MS Royal 15.c.vii; M. Lapidge and M. Winterbottom, eds. and trans., *Wulfstan of Winchester, The Life of St Æthelwold* (OMT; Oxford, 1991), pp. l–li, cxxx; M. Lapidge, ed. and trans., *The Cult of St Swithun* (Winchester Studies 4.ii; Oxford, 2003).

spectacularly impressive liturgical event: the week-long (6–13 September 1091) ceremony of translation of the relics of the first six archbishops of Canterbury into new tombs at the east end of the newly rebuilt abbey of St Augustine's, Canterbury.[5] The event sparked miraculous occurrences at the new site, and within two or three years it had become commemorated as a feast, held one week after that marking the translation of the first and most important of the archbishops, Augustine. Goscelin's narrative, written between 1098 and 1100, recorded both the event itself and the miracles. Although the translation had been necessitated by building works, Abbot Wido's decision to mark it with such ceremony, and then subsequently have it commemorated in text and liturgy, is likely to have been a deliberate attempt to increase the prestige of his community. Rivalry with the neighbouring cathedral priory of Christ Church must have played a part, but equally important was the need to restore communal harmony following recent traumatic rupture. In 1089, the monks had rebelled against Wido, to whose appointment they were opposed. The dissenting monks were expelled and replaced by monks from Christ Church. What better way to impose unity upon the fractured community than to focus attention upon the presence of its illustrious saints and their continuing efficacy as protectors and intercessors?

It is no coincidence that the authors commissioned to write the accounts of the translations of Swithun at Winchester and the archbishops at Canterbury were both foreigners. It was not until the late eleventh century that more than a handful of communities were capable of producing skilled writers or sustaining elaborate liturgy. The Latin liturgy had survived the troubles of the ninth century in an imperfect and fragile condition. King Alfred, in his lament on the poor state of religion and learning in the Preface to his translation of Gregory the Great's *Pastoral Care*, asserted that 'Learning had declined so thoroughly in England that there were few men on this side of the Humber who could understand their divine services in English, or even translate a single letter from Latin into English'.[6] The revival was, to begin with, confined to a small number of centres, such as Winchester, Canterbury, Worcester and Glastonbury, extending, under the influence of the Benedictine reform of the second half of the tenth century, to other communities in the south,

[5] R. Sharpe, 'The setting of St Augustine's translation, 1091', in R. Eales and R. Sharpe, eds., *Canterbury and the Norman Conquest: Churches, Saints and Scholars 1066–1109* (London, 1995), pp. 1–13.

[6] S. Keynes and M. Lapidge, trans., *Alfred the Great: Asser's Life of King Alfred and Other Contemporary Sources* (Harmondsworth, 1983), p. 125.

west Midlands and east, such as Abingdon and Ramsey. Skilled cantors – the person responsible for most aspects of the performance of the liturgy, including its chant – were scarce, and, until the twelfth century, English communities often looked to men educated overseas to create new texts to embellish their festal liturgy and enhance their devotional reading: Frithegod at Canterbury in the mid-tenth century; Lantfred at Winchester and Abbo, who at Ramsey in the late tenth; Folcard at Thorney and the peripatetic Goscelin of Fleury in the late eleventh were both Flemish (see Chapter IV.1).

Local talent emerged only gradually. The tenth-century reform produced a small clutch: Wulfstan, cantor at Winchester at the end of the tenth century, turned Lantfred's prose account of Swithun's translation into Latin verse and also wrote a Latin *Life* of Æthelwold. Æthelwold's pupil Ælfric, although now best known for his writings in Old English, was also a talented Latinist, as was his younger contemporary, Byrhtferth, a monk of Ramsey. It was not until the end of the eleventh century, however, that high standards of Latin learning and composition became more widespread. By this date tastes in Latin style were changing. Much of the Latin written by both Continental and native authors in late Anglo-Saxon England was remarkably ornate and, at times, deliberately arcane in its vocabulary. The native-educated authors of Anglo-Norman England, most notable among them Eadmer, cantor at Christ Church, Canterbury, and William of Malmesbury, eschewed so florid and complex a style, preferring unadorned clarity. William did not mince his words: 'As for Æthelweard, a distinguished figure, who essayed an edition of these Chronicles in Latin, the less said of him the better; I would approve his intention, did I not find his language distasteful.' By contrast, he commended 'the careful work of Eadmer, sober and elegant in style'.[7]

COMMUNION WITH THE LIVING AND THE DEAD

The celebration of saints was not the only way in which religious institutions used texts to affirm their membership of the community of the wider Church and their own local identity. They also commemorated a continuing relationship with benefactors, deceased monks and members of other institutions with whom they had established bonds of 'confraternity'. These relationships were remembered and recalled through

[7] R. A. B. Mynors, R. M. Thomson and M. Winterbottom, eds. and trans., *William of Malmesbury, Gesta regum Anglorum* (2 vols.; OMT; Oxford, 1998–9), i, p. 15.

written record and oral delivery. The most widely attested practice is the recording of 'obits' (death notices) in a calendar or a martyrology (a collection of brief lives of the saints in calendrical order). At the daily meeting of the community in the chapter house, the relevant portion of the martyrology and the names of all those other individuals commemorated that day would be read out. Some communities also practised an additional form of commemoration, whereby lists of names were recorded in a *Liber vitae* (Book of life), placed each day on the principal altar of the church during the main Mass. A particularly splendid and evocative example survives from the New Minster at Winchester, compiled in 1031 and added to throughout the Middle Ages.[8]

LATIN LEARNING IN PRE-CONQUEST ENGLAND

The quality of the liturgy and the composition of new texts corresponded closely with standards of Latin education. In 900 these were at a low ebb, and the subsequent revival remained highly localized until the twelfth century. Until then, education in Latin at any level beyond the most rudimentary was probably confined to major ecclesiastical centres (themselves few in number until the Benedictine reform), and perhaps also the royal court, with its constant presence of leading clergy and their entourages. Direct evidence of schools and schooling in pre-Conquest England is scanty; much of our knowledge of its character has to be gleaned indirectly from surviving manuscripts and the style and content of Anglo-Latin literature (including charters).

The substance of what was taught was shaped to a great extent by the requirements of the liturgy – its correct pronunciation and comprehension. Contemporary sources, such as Wulfstan's *Life of Æthelwold*, refer to the 'liberal arts', defined in late antiquity as the three subjects of the trivium (grammar, rhetoric and logic) and four of the quadrivium (arithmetic, geometry, astronomy and music). In reality, this curriculum was not followed in full. The essential component was grammar, which, after the basic elements of the language had been grasped, was taken to a more advanced level primarily through the study of the Latin poetry of late antiquity, and in particular the Christian Latin poets, such as Prudentius, Sedulius, Juvencus and Arator. Some of the pagan poets of

[8] S. Keynes, ed., *The Liber vitae of the New Minster and Hyde Abbey Winchester: British Library Stowe 944 together with leaves from British Library Cotton Vespasian A.* VIII *and British Library Cotton Titus D.* XXVII (Early English Manuscripts in Facsimile, 26; Copenhagen, 1996).

classical Rome, such as Vergil, Persius and Statius, were also studied, as worthy of imitation in their vocabulary and style. Set against the evidence of teaching and study at the leading ecclesiastical centres in France and the Rhineland, where this curriculum was supplemented by a wider range of classical poetry and the other subjects of the liberal arts, attainments in England appear somewhat limited. However, it may have been more closely comparable to that of the majority of religious houses on the Continent.

ENGLAND AND THE TWELFTH-CENTURY RENAISSANCE

During the late eleventh and twelfth centuries, English monks and clerics became full participants in an increasingly international scholarly environment. The Norman Conquest coincided with a period of religious reform and developments in intellectual life that had a profound effect upon the range and character of the Latin literature studied throughout western Europe. The influx of monks and clerics trained on the Continent to senior positions within English cathedrals and monasteries facilitated and gave added impetus to the dissemination of these developments in England. The impact is most obvious in the rapid growth of monastic and, to a more variable degree, cathedral book collections, and, in particular, their holdings of patristic texts (the writings of the early Church Fathers).

With the exception of the Psalms, versified versions of the Bible and hymns used in the teaching of grammar, the Bible, theology and Christian doctrine were not taught systematically in the schoolroom in pre-Conquest England but through hearing the texts of the liturgy and sermons, and through private reading. From late antiquity onwards, the authoritative, orthodox guides to divine learning were acknowledged to be the Church Fathers, foremost among them Augustine, Jerome, Gregory and Ambrose. Their writings had been incorporated into the readings of the night Office from at least the ninth century, and they also were an essential component of daily devotional reading. However, with the exception of Gregory, only a limited range of their works was available in late Anglo-Saxon England. Yet in this, England was not unusual: few Continental copies of the Fathers date from the tenth or earlier eleventh centuries. From the late eleventh century onwards, there was a remarkable change of emphasis. In England, as in Normandy and elsewhere, scribal and other resources were directed towards extensive copying of patristic texts. The importance of these initiatives to religious culture was recognized by contemporary chroniclers when describing the good deeds of bishops and abbots. A twelfth-century chronicler at Abingdon Abbey, commemorating the benefits bestowed by Abbot Faricius (1100–17), recorded that he brought in six scribes to copy numerous works by Augustine, Gregory, Jerome, Ambrose and other Church Fathers.[9]

In the absence of a commercial book trade, collaboration between institutions in the circulation of exemplars (the manuscripts from which scribes made further copies of a text) was essential. Many texts were not readily available in England, and exemplars had to be imported from the Continent. These exemplars and their descendants circulated between religious houses, for copying by monks, canons or (as at Abingdon) scribes hired for the purpose. The various patterns of textual relationship between surviving copies reflect a diversity of institutional and personal connections, ranging from local proximity to specific requests that exploited personal contacts or knowledge. The distances travelled could be large, and the channels of transmission transcended institutional affiliations. One imported exemplar of Augustine's *Confessions* (from Saint-Bertin at Saint-Omer near Boulogne) lay behind copies made in Canterbury and Durham, while another (from Ghent) gave rise to a regional dissemination in the southwest, including both the secular cathedrals of Exeter and Salisbury and the Benedictine abbeys of Bath and Gloucester.[10]

Developments in the organization and content of academic study on the Continent also had a profound impact in England. Scholars travelled across Latin Europe to study with teachers who had gained an international renown. From impermanent beginnings in the eleventh-century cathedral schools of northern France, more permanent concentrations of masters and students emerged, most notably at Paris and Bologna, and, by the end of the twelfth century, Oxford, which would soon after be incorporated as universities. The liberal arts became only the first stage of academic study. From the late eleventh century onwards, masters began to lecture on what became regarded as subjects of higher study: biblical exegesis, theology, canon and civil law and medicine. They applied techniques of analysis drawn from the liberal arts to their explication of authoritative texts and their constituent topics. In Paris, these were the books of the Bible and, by the mid-twelfth century, the

[9] R. Sharpe, J. P. Carley, R. M. Thomson and A. G. Watson, eds., *English Benedictine Libraries. The Shorter Catalogues* (Corpus of British Medieval Library Catalogues, 4; London, 1996), pp. 4–7.

[10] T. Webber, 'The diffusion of Augustine's Confessions in England during the eleventh and twelfth centuries', in J. Blair and B. Golding, eds., *The Cloister and the World. Essays in Medieval History in Honour of Barbara Harvey* (Oxford, 1996), pp. 32–9.

major topics of theology, brought together as a theological compendium in Peter Lombard's *Sentences*. In Italy, attention was focused upon legal texts: the corpus of Roman (or civil) law of Justinian and a new systematically organized compilation of canon (ecclesiastical) law attributed to a master Gratian, while in the Mediterranean region a corpus of Latin translations of ancient Greek medical texts emerged, later known as the *Articella*. The textbooks, commentaries and reference tools of academic study gained an international circulation. A late twelfth-century book-list from the Augustinian abbey of Waltham, perhaps representing books acquired by one or more canons during the course of their studies on the Continent, includes several glossed books of the Bible, Peter Lombard's *Sentences*, Gratian's *Decretum*, Justinian's *Code*, *Institutes* and *Digest* and seven of the elements of the *Articella*.[11]

By the end of the twelfth century, the *Sentences* and the *Decretum* had become standard components of monastic and cathedral book collections. The largest investment, however, was directed towards acquiring the multiple volumes of the *Glossa ordinaria*: the new standard reference tool for the study of the Bible, in which the inherited wisdom of the Fathers and more recent scholarship were arranged as marginal and interlinear annotation beside the columns of biblical text. Civil law and medicine were of more restricted interest at this date than theology and canon law. The same is true of science, although here a cluster of English scholars from the west of England, such as Adelard of Bath and Daniel of Morley, played a significant role in transmitting Arabic (and thus, indirectly, Greek) scientific learning from the Iberian peninsula to northern Europe. The literature of ancient Rome also became more widely read outside the confines of the curriculum. Here, too, English scholars and scribes played a significant role in the transmission of texts. In England and elsewhere, the works of authors such as Cicero and Seneca became appreciated as more than merely useful models for Latin grammar and rhetoric but as sources of ethical and moral values. Cicero's treatise *On Friendship*, for example, informed the Cistercian Aelred of Rievaulx's treatise *On Spiritual Friendship*. The theme of friendship, variously interpreted, contributed, in its turn, to the popularity of the exchange of letters between friends (including those who had never met, but who shared spiritual ideals or literary tastes).

[11] T. Webber and A. G. Watson, eds., *The Libraries of the Augustinian Canons* (Corpus of British Medieval Library Catalogues, 6; London, 1998), pp. 428–42.

LATIN LEARNING AND NEW ALIGNMENTS

The flourishing of intellectual life and the climate of religious reform, in both of which close study of Latin texts was a key ingredient, created new alignments, formal and informal, among male and female religious during the twelfth century.

The emergence of professionally trained scholars, and the growing importance of a training in the schools, contributed to a marginalization of female communities from Latin religious and learned culture. Evidence for levels of Latin learning in female communities in the late Anglo-Saxon and Anglo-Norman periods is meagre, but the royal nunneries of southern England may have shared in the post-Viking revival of Latin. Goscelin of Saint-Bertin, for example, wrote a lengthy work of spiritual consolation in complex Latin for Eve, a former nun of Wilton, who had become a recluse in France (the *Liber confortatorius*). Queens Edith and Edith-Matilda (consorts of Edward the Confessor and Henry I), both educated at Wilton, commissioned Latin saints' lives.[12] During the twelfth century, however, while Latin continued to be the language of the liturgy, any more extensive use seems to have become increasingly the exception. Surviving non-liturgical books from female institutions from the thirteenth century onwards are overwhelmingly in the vernacular.

Newly perceived groupings also began to appear among the clergy and male religious. Those who had received training in higher learning in the Continental schools became identified as 'magistri' (masters). Their specialized knowledge and facility with language and argument were of benefit to both secular and ecclesiastical government and to monastic houses, in a period in which litigation both at home and through appeals to Rome was becoming rife. Their names appear with increasing frequency in episcopal households and in senior positions in monasteries and cathedrals. At least to begin with, such men were viewed with jealous suspicion by clerks with lesser learned expertise, to judge from John of Salisbury's complaints in his *Metalogicon*.[13] Some spiritual writers, such as the Cistercian Gilbert of Hoyland, also warned against the dangers of voracious reading and an inquisitive approach to divine learning: 'reading ought to serve our prayer … not encroach on our time and weaken our

[12] F. Barlow, ed. and trans., *The Life of King Edward Who Rests at Westminster* (2nd edn; OMT; Oxford, 1992); 'Vita Sanctae Margaretae Scotorum reginae', in J. H. Hinde, ed., *Symeonis Dunelmensis opera et collectanea* (Surtees Society, 51; London, 1868).

[13] R. W. Southern, 'The place of England in the twelfth-century renaissance', in his *Medieval Humanism and Other Studies* (Oxford, 1970), pp. 175–6.

character', concluding 'Monks should seek out silence, not conversation; quiet, not questions': a criticism, perhaps, of academic disputation.[14]

Close reading of the Bible and other fundamental texts not only fuelled demands for religious reform but also provided sources of textual authority with which to justify them. Differing interpretations enabled opponents to invoke their authority. In both Benedictine and Cistercian communities, a portion of the Rule was read aloud to the community during their meeting in the chapter house – a daily reminder of the precepts upon which their communal life was based. The Cistercians, however, claimed that their practice constituted a more faithful adherence to the letter of the Rule than that represented by the increasingly elaborate liturgy and customs with which Benedictine tradition had become amplified since the ninth century.

Texts and textual references were not only traded to highlight difference but could also evoke and stimulate shared knowledge and spiritual values across the religious spectrum. Several letters were sent from the Benedictine abbey of St Albans to the Augustinian abbey of Saint-Victor in Paris between around 1167 and 1173 in an effort to acquire a complete set of the works of the renowned teacher and theologian Hugh of Saint-Victor.[15] Also telling is the evidence provided by a late twelfth-century booklist, probably from the Augustinian priory of Bridlington in Yorkshire. The collection recorded is not very large, but it included not only works of Hugh of Saint-Victor and of the house-author Robert of Bridlington, but also lives of the great abbots of Cluny, the spiritual works of the Cistercian Aelred of Rievaulx and the life of the hermit Godric of Finchale.[16]

[14] B. Smalley, *The Study of the Bible in the Middle Ages* (3rd edn; Oxford, 1983), p. 282.

[15] R. M. Thomson, *Manuscripts from St Albans Abbey 1066–1235* (2nd edn; 2 vols.; Woodbridge, 1985), i, pp. 64–6.

[16] Webber and Watson, eds., *Libraries of the Augustinian Canons*, pp. 9–22.

CHAPTER V.6

Textual communities (vernacular)

Elaine Treharne

DEFINING THE TEXTUAL COMMUNITY

The literate, Latinate elite of Anglo-Saxon England represents specific social and intellectual groups – those men and women fortunate enough to be educated through an institutional system that was religious, and principally monastic. Many of these privileged learners would have been aristocratic, or at least freeborn, as Alfred recommends in his Preface to Gregory's *Pastoral Care*. This Preface was written by Alfred towards the end of the ninth century, when he recognized that the consolidation of the truce with the Danes would require rebuilding a country devastated by a century of strife. Part of this reconstructive process involved the conscious fostering of education, so that the rich cultural and intellectual traditions of Anglo-Saxon England could be permitted to flourish once again. In the extant manuscript, Oxford, Bodleian Library, Hatton 20, given to Wærferth, bishop of Worcester, at the end of the ninth century, Alfred reveals his educational plans to his bishop, in what has become one of the most famous passages of early English:

> Therefore it seems better to me, if it seems so to you, that we also should translate certain books, which are most necessary for all men to know, into the language that we can all understand, and also arrange it, as with God's help we very easily can if we have peace, so that all the young freeborn men now among the English people who have the means to be able to devote themselves to it, may be set to study for as long as they are of no other use, until a time when they are able to read English writing well. Afterwards one may teach further in the Latin language those whom one wishes to teach further and wishes to promote to holy orders.[1]

The textual community imagined here by Alfred is two-layered: there are those freeborn students who require a pragmatic literacy in English, in

[1] 'King Alfred's Preface to Gregory's *Pastoral Care*', in E. Treharne, ed., *Old and Middle English, 890–1400. An Anthology* (2nd edn; Oxford, 2004), p. 13.

order to benefit themselves, their households and, presumably, their local administration; then there are those talented enough for, and inclined towards, a religious life, who will go on to study Latin. From these plans, and from his own example as writer, thinker and translator, Alfred and his team thus authorized education in English, from which sprang a dynamic and unprecedented vernacular tradition of writing that is unbroken to this day.

The 'most necessary' books that Alfred had produced by his circle of scholars include not only Gregory the Great's *Pastoral Care* and *Dialogues*, but also significant works of history, such as Paulus Orosius's *Seven Books of History against the Pagans* and Bede's *Ecclesiastical History of the English People*, a work that provides us with the earliest English poem, and with an insight into an ostensibly very different form of textual community from that envisaged by Alfred.

DIVINELY INSPIRED TEXTS

Alfred's innovative concept of a nation of educated freeborn men is inspired, he tells us, by the examples of the early good and wise men in England, by the Hebrews, Greeks and Romans, who translated the word of God ('the law', as Alfred calls it) into their own language so that teachers could access it and share its potential for salvation. This inspired view of what can be achieved by committed Christians is the driving force for Alfred's reforms. In part, such inspiration lies behind Bede's very famous account of Cædmon, too: a lay brother and cowherd at Whitby Abbey, who dreams of an encounter with a musically inclined angel. Cædmon exchanges one textual community for another in this famous episode, a pair of communities whose existence is visually reinforced by the manuscripts containing the story.

Bede narrates that Cædmon 'was often in the drinking party, when there was decreed, as a cause for joy, that they should all sing in turns to the accompaniment of the harp. When he saw the harp approach him, he rose up for shame from that feast and went home to his house.' After feeding the animals, Cædmon dreamt that 'a man stood before him as if in a dream and called him and greeted him and spoke to him by his name: "Cædmon, sing me something … Sing to me about creation."' There ensues the composition of *Cædmon's Hymn*, which, in English, is a nine-line alliterative poem about God's creation of the earth. The earliest surviving manuscripts of Bede's *Ecclesiastical History*, written at his own monastery, Monkwearmouth-Jarrow in Northumberland in the

730s, illustrate well the respective textual communities of early Anglo-Saxon England in this story.[2] In both these manuscripts, the dominant text is the Latin version of the *Ecclesiastical History*. Squeezed into available space in the lower margin of the Leningrad Bede and at the very end of the Moore Bede, as if an afterthought, and certainly removed from the immediate contexts, are the less formal Old English texts of *Cædmon's Hymn*. Extrapolating from this visual indicator of the texts' relative status, with all of the concomitant cultural connotations, one can perceive the vernacular textual community of the beer-party to be one of verse sung to the accompaniment of the harp, representing an oral tradition characterized by extemporization and transience. Within the wider context of textual production and participation in early Anglo-Saxon England, the English performance is marginal to the authorized, Latinate, written, permanent and formal community of the scholars in their monastic environments. Cædmon's miraculous powers of song, though, effect a transformation of the transient oral culture of the early Anglo-Saxons into a form that could be validated by its Christian subject: the Germanic form of alliterative verse, happily for its survival, as a new medium for the dominant ideology of the Church.

THE POWER OF WRITING

The symbiotic relationship of oral and textual is reflected in the role of writing itself, which documents that which has been spoken or is to be spoken, fixing as record – if history permits its survival – what would otherwise rely on memory. Without the written evidence yielded by the thousands of manuscripts, fragments, single leaves and artefacts from the Anglo-Saxon period, scholars would have a difficult time indeed reconstructing this culture in its manifold aspects. Throughout this period, and into the High Middle Ages, the oral and the textual existed side by side, obviously: English was always the spoken language of the English, and Latin that of the learned among them; a third language, Old Norse, a cognate of Old English, was spoken by Scandinavian settlers, who had a major impact in the eastern and northern counties of England. Often, our only witness to the multilingualism of the textual community in the broadest sense comes in a line of writing here or there, inscribing information that would otherwise be lost.

[2] St Petersburg, National Library of Russia, MS lat. Q. v. I. 18 (the Leningrad, or St Petersburg, Bede) and Cambridge, University Library, MS Kk. 5. 16 (the Moore Bede); both date to the second quarter of the eighth century.

In the case of Old Norse, while it is certain the language was widely spoken in Danelaw in the ninth to eleventh centuries – and even at court under the Anglo-Scandinavian King Cnut (1016–35) and his sons – the contemporary evidence for what must have been, for many, first-language use, is minimal. It extends to the appearance of a few loanwords such as *eorl* ('ealdorman'), *lagu* ('law'), many place-names (such as Grimsby, Kirkby and Deepdale), personal names (for example, Thorkell and Svein) and remnants of runic carvings in memorial stones and a sundial, among other media (see Chapter IV.2).

Similarly, for English, while those who spoke the language numbered hundreds of thousands by the eleventh century, there are whole swathes of the country which are barely represented in the surviving written materials. English does not always appear even in the obvious places, such as Wessex, home of the major sites of textual production. Salisbury, for example, founded in 1075 when the see was moved from Sherborne, had many decades of thriving book production, but none of the manuscripts that is extant is written in English; they are all Latin. It is as if this textual community had no vernacular participants. However, a single clause in a legendary written at Salisbury has '*of Searbyrig ic eom*' (I am from Salisbury) inscribed on a flyleaf in the later eleventh century. This shows one literate manuscript user who was presumably English. One English writer does not make a textual community, but a few glosses written in English into Salisbury Cathedral 150 (the Salisbury Psalter) in the twelfth century suggest that among this predominantly Latinate community (where presumably French also featured after the Norman Conquest in 1066) were English speakers and writers, who infrequently felt empowered to write themselves into the books they used.

The power of the written word to sanction the individual, the state, Church and nation is undoubted. Extensive manuscripts and numerous documents that survive from multiple points of origin in Anglo-Saxon England bear testimony to the production and use of English as a legitimate and legitimizing phenomenon. Writing in the vernacular was clearly felt to have the potential to save souls, create emperors, rehabilitate society, validate truth, establish lineage, secure status and land and more: its intelligibility was widespread, its demographic ubiquitous.

THE WRITTEN APPARATUS OF STATE AND CHURCH

In this early period, those responsible for disseminating texts to all communities, whether private or public, were a privileged group, closely associated with the Church and, often, also the court. Alfred's Preface to Gregory's *Pastoral Care* is really an epistle, written to his bishops, without whom his educational programme would stand no chance of success. The close involvement of King Edgar (d. 975) in the tenth-century movement often called the Benedictine reform both ensured and reflected the achievements of the bishops involved. This movement greatly expanded the transmission of the vernacular in the sermons and saints' lives of the great English prose-writer Ælfric (d. 1010), monk of Winchester, and abbot of Eynsham at his death. His correspondence with other bishops, among them Wulfstan, archbishop of York (d. 1023) and Sigeric, archbishop of Canterbury (d. 994), demonstrates the establishment of what was, essentially, a national network of senior ecclesiastical preachers, teachers and, in Wulfstan's case, statesmen. This textual community, well versed in the efficacy of the vernacular for maintaining social and moral control, had a major impact on the longevity of English; Ælfric's homiletic texts, for example, were still being copied, read and adapted for pastoral purposes into the thirteenth century and beyond; the Anglo-Saxon Chronicle – record of a nation's elite – was copied in many monastic locations and continued being written until 1154.

Wulfstan I, for his part, represents perhaps the apogee of Anglo-Saxon textual involvement, expertise and foresight. Serving under two kings, Æthelred (d. 1016) and Cnut (d. 1035), Wulfstan operated as a chief adviser and ecclesiastic throughout the earlier eleventh century, when Anglo-Saxon England was threatened by Scandinavian incursions, which resulted in the accession, by conquest, of Cnut. Wulfstan left us with some of the most stirring writings to survive from the period: multigeneric texts in Latin and English, comprising law codes, letters and sermons. His firm conviction of the need for proper Christian behaviour permeates his work, and propels his rhetoric into a powerful statement against a nation's sin.

Wulfstan's textual involvement is evinced by the large number of manuscripts that survive with demonstrable links to the archbishop, some containing his own hand, showing his interventions on the page to correct and comment on the existing work. Such scribal activity might have taken place in the privacy of his archiepiscopal palace at Sherburn-in-Elmet, in North Yorkshire, where a scribe working for Wulfstan added to the back of the York Gospels sermons summarizing Wulfstan's beliefs about Christianity, about paganism and kingship and governance. The last text, 'Cnut's Letter to the English of 1020', is itself resonant of the complexity of early medieval vernacular textuality.[3] It is writ-like, opening with a cross and a call from Cnut to all his subjects, from the highest to the lowest. It declares in English the adherence of Cnut to Edgar's laws, and lays out for the Anglo-Scandinavian kingdom (but in a language some of Cnut's own countrymen would presumably struggle with) the reciprocity between king and people. Here in the York Gospels that statewide message is mediated by Wulfstan, but elsewhere, in multiple, transient and irretrievable textual communities, this was a vernacular message for every subject in the kingdom.

THE PERMANENCE OF TEXT

Wulfstan's record of 'Cnut's Letter' is an apt part of the York Gospels, since it is likely that this magnificent book was given to him by Cnut and his wife, Emma, to persuade Wulfstan to consecrate Æthelnoth as archbishop of Canterbury in 1020. The Latin Gospels, created at Christ Church, Canterbury, thus found their way north to York, where they still reside. The movement of books in this period was not at all uncommon, and it often makes tracing their origins problematic, but it is clear that the majority of books, in both Latin and English, were produced within religious establishments. The majority of English texts seem to have been compiled in monastic cathedrals during the tenth to twelfth centuries, with a notable exception being the large corpus of vernacular material produced during the episcopacy of Leofric (1050–72) at the secular cathedral of Exeter. Rather like the York Gospels and Wulfstan, the many vernacular religious texts produced in English at Exeter appear to be closely associated with Leofric himself and possibly symbolize his own tools for his pastoral work. Other books we know belonged to the cathedral after 1072, since they were famously donated by Leofric to his institution. Among these books is the Old English *Exeter Book* (one of four major volumes of vernacular verse to survive), made *c.* 970, in the west of England.[4]

The *Exeter Book* contains an extensive collection of poetry, most of it surviving uniquely in this volume. The poetry ranges from secular wisdom

[3] The manuscript is York Minster, MS 1. On this, and the latest scholarship on Wulfstan I, see M. Townend, ed., *Wulfstan, Archbishop of York: The Proceedings of the Second Alcuin Conference* (Turnhout, 2004).

[4] See P. Conner, *Anglo-Saxon Exeter: A Tenth-Century Cultural History* (Woodbridge, 1993) and E. Treharne, 'Producing a library in Late Anglo-Saxon England: Exeter, 1050–1072', *Review of English Studies*, 54 (2003), 155–72.

texts, like *The Wife's Lament* and *Wulf and Eadwacer*, to scurrilous riddles; religious poetry includes the hagiographic *Juliana*, the moving *Advent Lyrics* and the allegorical *Whale*. The potential audience for this book might have been not only those monks who created it and the canons who later owned it, but also secular participants, such as guildsmen. The Anglo-Saxon scholar Patrick Conner has plausibly suggested that this lay audience of local professional craftsmen might have heard the poems read on holy days, when they shared in the hospitality of the cathedral. But the book gives us more than an imagined audience, for within its covers now are lists of guildsmen in the Exeter diocese, manumissions declaring the release of slaves and documents about land sales. These misbound leaves belonged originally to a copy of the Old English Gospels, written during Leofric's time as bishop. The Gospels, the word of God, had the benefit of being so highly regarded that vernacular (and Latin) materials were often added into the manuscripts. These lists of names, and records of human and land transactions, bear witness perfectly to the large, often indeterminate textual community that had access to the books of the local religious institution.[5]

It was not only the religious institution that owned books, however; other textual communities, fluent and literate in the vernacular, had access to reading materials that might have been used to educate the whole household. One book does not equate to one audience member, unlike today, in many cases; the audience could be listening to the head of the family read from the lives of saints, as may have been the case with Æthelmaer and Æthelweard, ealdormen of Wessex and commissioning patrons of Ælfric's *Lives of Saints*. Indeed, sermons, too, would be read aloud to large groups of auditory participants: we know from the *Vita Wulfstani*, for example, that Wulfstan II of Worcester (d. 1095) is said to have drawn huge audiences when he preached peripatetically in churches around his diocese.

A certain example of vernacular textuality and the community it could draw can be seen in the eighth-century Hereford Gospels. This is the oldest manuscript to survive from Hereford Cathedral, remaining intact after a ferocious fire destroyed everything else in 1055. It is certain this book was of inestimable value to its community, a group of stakeholders that stretched across the whole shire of Hereford. We know this from

[5] The manuscript is Cambridge, University Library, MS Ii. 2. 11, see P. Conner, 'Parish guilds and the production of Old English literature in the public sphere', in V. Blanton and H. Scheck, eds. *(Inter)Texts: Studies in Early Insular Culture Presented to Paul E. Szarmach* (Tempe, AZ, 2007), pp. 257–73.

vernacular legal texts added in a blank space to the Latin Gospels in the mid-eleventh century, when the book's function as public repository for the entire community is demonstrated by an account of a case in which a woman, Enniaun, issued an oral will, rejecting her son as beneficiary and bequeathing her land instead to Leofflæd, wife of Thurkil the White. At the end of proceedings, we are told:

> Then Thurkil the White stood up in that [shire] meeting, and asked all the thegns to give to his wife, clear from the claim, the lands which her kinswoman had granted her, and they did so. And Thurkil rode then with the permission and witness of all the people to St Ethelbert's minster [Hereford], and had it entered in a gospel-book.[6]

One might argue that here the 'marginal' added vernacular text becomes central; that the Gospels' significance becomes contemporary and about both the present recording of text and the future assurance of land ownership. Moreover, a whole shire – from the nobility to the witnesses, canons at the minster and scribal author – participated in this enshrinement of decision-making, created and protected by the sanctity of the book and the permanence afforded by the written record.

MANY TEXTS, MANY LANGUAGES

In his groundbreaking work *From Memory to Written Record*, Michael Clanchy shows how the post-Conquest period, and the twelfth century in particular, saw a very significant increase in the production of legal and administrative texts, issued by kings and their officers to support and reflect an expanding bureaucracy. From about 1100 onwards, manuscripts and diplomata began to be written in Anglo-Norman, the dialect of French spoken by the Norman invaders, and in the twelfth century England emerged as a trilingual society, with Latin, French and English all represented in various kinds of writings, though English, of course, remained the spoken language of the vast majority of the population.

A key witness to this trilingualism is the Eadwine Psalter, a manuscript that almost defies description.[7] Written at Christ Church, Canterbury in about 1160, the volume is a vast and extraordinary testimony to the achievements of the monastic cathedral scriptorium. While its approximate

[6] Hereford, Cathedral Library, MS P. i. 2, see *EHD*, i, no. 135, p. 602 (my own translation).
[7] Cambridge, Trinity College, MS R. 17. 1.

measurements – 482 mm long × 343 mm wide and 120 mm thick when closed – indicate its vast size, perhaps the fact that each bifolium (a pair of leaves or folios) represents one animal skin best displays its physical impact and value. At 286 folios and perhaps 20 lb or more, this extensive book illustrates even at the swiftest glance the considerable resource given over to the copying and illustration of the Psalms in the mid-twelfth century. This is no simple Psalter, though; it might most usefully be conceived of as a snapshot of the period itself. Of particular note here are the two sets of complete glosses to the Psalms and Canticles in French and English. The main version – the Gallicanum – is glossed in Latin, while the Hebraicum version of the Psalms (a scholarly version never used in the liturgy) is accompanied by French word-for-word glosses and the Romanum version (used in the Anglo-Saxon Church until the eleventh century) has a contemporary English gloss. The combination of texts, and the care given over to the correctness of the volume, demonstrates unequivocally its immense significance not only to the textual community of Christ Church but also to those beyond: this is a book that represents the zenith of monastic achievement and a recognition of the sanctity and validity of the three languages in use in England in the post-Conquest period.

The Eadwine Psalter is the only complete manuscript of this period consciously designed to contain Latin, English and French *together* on the page. Other manuscripts show that, in general, specific languages functioned principally for their own respective textual communities. French manuscripts produced after 1100 tend to be written for aristocratic or scholarly patrons, who were often women and their households. Thus, for example, Benedeit's *Voyage of St Brendan* was composed in French around 1106 initially for Matilda, the first wife of Henry I; and in about 1140, Gaimar composed his *L'Estoire des Engleis* for Constance Fitzgilbert, a Lincolnshire noblewoman. For this chronicle, Gaimar reveals he used English, Latin and French historical sources, giving us evidence of the trilingualism present in scholarly circles at this time and the ways in which particular languages of composition were directed at particular communities of readers and listeners.[8]

While French, then, was the scholarly and aristocratic language, often used for literary, historical and learned works that had individual patrons as the inspiration, we have a good deal less explicit information about the function of English texts in the twelfth century. Current research

[8] I. Short, ed. and trans., *Geffrei Gaimar, Estoire des Engleis* (Oxford, 2009).

suggests that English was produced almost entirely by the monastic institutions that formed part of the pre-Conquest Benedictine reform group: Worcester; Christ Church and St Augustine's, Canterbury; Winchester; and Peterborough. The hundred and more books of sermons and saints' lives, legal documents, histories and medical compilations that survive are the tip of the textual iceberg: access to the text extended far beyond the single reader and the single book, and thus the dissemination of this material – particularly the sermons and saints' lives – must have reached far into the parishes within the diocesan and pastoral remit of these monastic establishments. In other words, the textual communities are potentially vast, but shadowy and unnamable. Yet we do know from scattered references how complex these networks of communities could be; thus, in the early twelfth-century homily on the Assumption of the Virgin Mary written by Ralph D'Escures, bishop of Rochester (1108–14) and archbishop of Canterbury (1114–22), he tells us that he delivered the homily to his chapter of monks in French (it does not survive in this language though), and that his audience liked it so much, he had it transcribed into Latin. A Latin version formed the basis for the English text contained in a mid-twelfth-century monastic manuscript which itself will have been used for preaching on the festival of the Assumption, possibly to English monks and perhaps to other native-speaking audiences.[9] Such transmission might be the result of entirely memorized delivery, each new performance effectively constituting a new (but transient) text.

NEGOTIATING COMMUNITY

It should be clear from this brief discussion that evidence for vernacular textual communities throughout the earlier medieval period needs to be very carefully negotiated. What often appears to be insignificant – yet another 'copy' of an Ælfric homily, only one surviving witness to the life of an English saint like Neot, a French history copied for a single patron, or a throwaway comment about recording a legal case in a Gospel book – can in fact represent a multilayered and multilingual network of communal literacy. Textual communities thus extended from the concerned author and his circle to the individual reader, to the learned listener in

[9] R. -N. Warner, ed., *Early English Homilies from the Twelfth-Century MS. Vesp. D. XIV* (EETS, old ser., 152; London, 1917 for 1915).

the chapter house, to the wide-eyed parishioner acquiring an intimate knowledge of the inevitability of eternal damnation for liars and adulterers. What survives in English, French and Latin in fragments, single leaves and manuscript books tells us everything we need to know, if only we knew how to listen.

CHAPTER VI.I

Learning and training

Julia Crick

In 1158, while on an embassy to the French king, Henry II's chancellor Thomas Becket took up temporary residence with the Templars in Paris, where he received among others the English scholars in the city – masters, students and the Parisian citizens from whom the evidently cash-strapped English scholars had borrowed money. By entertaining on a royal scale Becket consciously usurped the role of host, deliberately flouting the wishes of the king of France, who had tried to ensure that his guest paid for nothing, but the opportunities for social display proved irresistible. A graduate of the university himself, he embodied all the opulence and, indeed, social aggrandizement that new learning might promise. Brought up in a Cheapside residence, the son of an immigrant merchant who had himself risen socially in his adoptive town of London, the future chancellor had been educated at a priory school at Merton and later at a London grammar school, before moving to Paris and later Bologna to continue his studies. Received into the household of Archbishop Theobald of Canterbury, he had then entered royal service, and in 1158, when he embarked for France, he was almost at the summit of his career. He and his splendid entourage of 200 had set off on horseback, dressed in fur and silk and laden with gold and silver vessels, much of which material wealth he offloaded at the end of his embassy, to the distaste of his biographer, but to the considerable advantage of his French hosts and their retainers, his expatriate guests and their creditors, few of whom reportedly went home without a cloak or even a horse.[1] Within four years he was archbishop of Canterbury.

[1] Frank Barlow, *Thomas Becket* (London, 1986), pp. 11–30, 55–8; J. C. Robertson, ed., *Materials for the History of Thomas Becket* (7 vols.; RS; London, 1875–85), iii, pp. 29–33, esp. pp. 32–3. On Becket's conduct and his contravention of royal etiquette, see John Gillingham, 'The meetings of the kings of France and England, 1066–1204', in D. Crouch and K. Thompson, eds., *Normandy and Its Neighbours, 900–1250. Essays Presented to David Bates* (Turnhout, 2011), forthcoming.

Becket, though not renowned himself as a great scholar, both in his career and in his intimacy with Paris-educated contemporaries who were indeed intellectuals, illustrates the power of education to transform the fortunes of individuals and to mould a new social elite. The universities which emerged in France and Italy in the course of the twelfth century educated a cohort of graduates who staffed and directed the burgeoning bureaucracies of kings, emperors and prelates across the west. This was an age of documentation, of accounting, of litigation, and the educated elite who made these aspects of governmental control manifest could practise their skills on an international stage.[2] Increasing access to intermediate education in England via grammar schools established in cathedral cities and elsewhere ensured the presence of Englishmen in the Continental schools, and at Paris in the second half of the twelfth century not only were more than half the students reportedly English, but so were many masters.[3] It is said that Becket himself later rescued one English master from penury in France, recommending Robert of Melun for the bishopric of Hereford.[4] Extreme social mobility was in part a product of the physical mobility of graduates, and it is no accident that during Becket's period as chancellor a contemporary, Nicholas Breakspear, graduate of the French schools, friend of Becket's friend John of Salisbury, became pope (Adrian IV), the only Englishman ever to have reached this dignity (see Chapter IV.1).[5]

Dual processes of the scattering and the personal aggrandizement of this educated elite might appear familiar to students of more recent periods – English public schoolboys who administered the British empire before and after the Great War, or the international band of business-school graduates who headed later twentieth-century commercial empires – but we should be careful not to link them to the future too readily. To be sure, the new graduates illustrate the process of 'increasing

[2] M. T. Clanchy, *From Memory to Written Record: England 1066–1307* (2nd edn; Oxford, 1993); J. Gillingham, 'Some observations on social mobility in England between the Norman Conquest and the early thirteenth century', in his *The English in the Twelfth Century: Imperialism, National Identity and Political Values* (Woodbridge, 2000), pp. 259–76; S. E. Banks, 'Tilbury, Gervase of (*b.* 1150s, *d.* in or after 1222)', *ODNB*.

[3] R. M. Thomson, *England and the Twelfth-Century Renaissance* (Aldershot, 1998), XIX, pp. 7–8; J. W. Baldwin, 'Masters at Paris from 1179 to 1215: a social perspective', in R. L. Benson and G. Constable, eds., *Renaissance and Renewal in the Twelfth Century* (Cambridge, MA, 1982), pp. 138–72.

[4] William fitz Stephen, *Life of St Thomas*, §13 (in Robertson, ed., *Materials*, iii, p. 24); Barlow, *Thomas Becket*, p. 45.

[5] Christopher N. L. Brooke, 'Adrian IV and John of Salisbury', in B. Bolton and A. J. Duggan, eds., *Adrian IV, the English Pope (1154–1159): Studies and Texts* (Aldershot, 2003), pp. 3–13.

separation of education from the rest of life' which one historian of education has detected in the history of (English) education over the last millennium.[6] With some justification scholars have located in the post-Conquest era the origin of the development of structures and habits of thought familiar to us as aspects of modernity: institutional libraries, bureaucratic government, universities and urban schools, rational and sceptical deduction.[7] Indeed, the late twelfth century is taken as the point of origin for institutions whose successors survive to the present day: the University of Oxford traces an unbroken line of descent from that point. This continuity, although significant in itself, brings undoubted problems of interpretation. The details of faltering attempts to establish a Continental-style school in Oxford in the 1120s are lost to history: not only does the obsolescence of earlier traditions and forms of record-keeping tend to bring about the destruction of evidence, whether through carelessness, hostility or tidiness, but temporary or informal arrangements will not leave documentary traces at all.[8] Moreover, the products of the new education, twelfth-century graduates, were noisy witnesses, and their chatter tends to drown out the stories of those who preceded them. Educated courtiers like Walter Map (*De nugis curialium*) and Becket's friend and later companion in exile John of Salisbury (*Policraticus – De nugis curialium et vestigiis philosophorum*), writing in the last half of the twelfth century, used writing to document thoughts which two generations earlier those educated under the rod of monastic discipline might have suppressed or never have committed to the page. Some schoolsmen paraded their erudition, presumably in the competition for preferment, like Gerald of Wales who advertised his own writings through self-citation and public reading.[9]

6 N. Orme, *From Childhood to Chivalry: The Education of the English Kings and Aristocracy 1066–1530* (London, 1984), p. 237.

7 Teresa Webber, 'Monastic and cathedral book collections in the late eleventh and twelfth centuries', in Elisabeth Leedham-Green and Teresa Webber, eds., *The Cambridge History of Libraries in Britain and Ireland*, vol. 1, *To 1650* (Cambridge, 2006), pp. 109–25; N. Orme, 'Schools and society from the twelfth century to the Reformation', in *Education and Society in Medieval and Renaissance England* (London, 1989), pp. 1–21, at 21.

8 For Oxford in the 1120s see R. W. Southern, 'From schools to University', in J. I. Catto, ed., *The History of the University of Oxford*, vol. 1, *The Early Oxford Schools* (Oxford, 1984), pp. 1–36. Jaeger has attempted to reconstruct intellectual life in the face of institutional discontinuity: C. S. Jaeger, *The Envy of Angels: Cathedral Schools and Social Ideals in Medieval Europe, 950–1200* (Philadelphia, 1994).

9 Robert Bartlett, 'Gerald of Wales (*c.* 1146–1220×23)', *ODNB*; Southern, 'From schools', pp. 13–14.

Becket's career was not entirely without precedent, as it happens. More than two centuries earlier, another archbishop of Canterbury, Oda (941–58), likewise came from an immigrant (in his case, Danish) family and likewise left his parents to find an educational grounding on home soil in England, this time in the company of a noble, Æthelhelm, before travelling abroad, to Rome, then returning to royal service before being elevated to the bishopric of Ramsbury and later to the archbishopric of Canterbury. Oda may have studied abroad, at the monastery of Fleury-sur-Loire (département Loire); he certainly dispatched there his nephew and protégé Oswald to learn more and we know of other expatriate Englishmen who took the same path in the tenth century. Æthelwold, future bishop of Winchester, who like Becket had received his formative education in an English town, also aspired to travel abroad but his ambitions were frustrated.[10] So here we have traces of a trajectory comparable to that later followed by Becket, made at a time when formal cultural and intellectual training available on both sides of the English Channel remained largely monastic, as did the goals of learning. We discern, however, the same sense of indebtedness to France and the same restlessness of aspirant individuals. Young men went to France to learn, and some, like Oda's nephew Oswald, won high office on their return, in his case ultimately the archbishopric of York (971–92).

Opportunities for intermediate and advanced education changed across western Europe between the ninth and twelfth centuries to a degree almost unimaginable in 900. The foundation of institutions of higher education on the Continent, the cathedral schools of the later tenth and eleventh centuries and the universities operating in the twelfth, enabled the creation of a reservoir of highly educated men, able to staff the papal, imperial and royal bureaucracies, but also available for high office in the Church. Although the details of the education offered are sometimes hard to construe, what is clear and is widely acknowledged is the great gulf between the learning of the monastic schools across Europe and the broader education of the cathedral schools and later the universities which developed initially on the Continent and then, by the twelfth century, in England.[11] The change is evident in England in the nature of the texts studied and copied. Anglo-Saxonists have noted the apparent

[10] *The Life of Oswald*, i.4–5, ii.4–5 (M. Lapidge, ed. and trans., *Byrhtferth of Ramsey: The Lives of St Oswald and St Ecgwine* (OMT; Oxford, 2009), pp. 16–27 and 38–43, esp. p. 39 n. 29). *The Life of St Æthelwold*, 6, 10 (M. Lapidge and M. Winterbottom, eds. and trans., *Wulfstan of Winchester, The Life of St Æthelwold* (OMT; Oxford, 1991), pp. 8–11, 18–19).

[11] Jaeger, *The Envy of Angels*, esp. p. 328; Thomson, *England*, XIV, XVIII–XIX.

abandonment of the canon of texts assembled from the remnants of late antiquity and used to teach in pre-Conquest England: the grammatical and rhetorical works essential for establishing the rudiments of Latin in a Germanic-speaking society and the cluster of late Latin poets who explicated Christian teaching through verse narratives, all apparently cease to be replicated for circulation to new readers.[12] In come different texts, suggesting changed methods if not priorities, initially patristic works and then Latin classics, both used for basic and intermediate instruction, and new compositions designed to educate.[13] Meanwhile, the advanced education available at the Continental schools brought profound intellectual and moral challenges. Components of the classical past were reconnected, through renewed freedom in the exploration of the secular poetic and philosophical inheritance in particular and via new exposure to lost texts of classical antiquity, newly discovered works of Greek philosophy and medicine recovered from Arabic translation by the efforts of scholars, a number of them Englishmen, like Adelard of Bath.[14]

But against this relatively well-documented and well-told story of twelfth-century attainment, we should set other versions of learning and training, admittedly much less well articulated in our sources and sometimes barely discernible. Universities, even grammar schools, were beyond the direct experience of the great majority in twelfth-century England, the literate as well as the illiterate. The secular elite, monks, their social inferiors, women, all were educated outside these structures. The monastic schools which were active in England throughout these centuries educated some destined for careers outside the institution, at least in the tenth and eleventh centuries. Wealthy women could apparently receive a monastic education without the expectation of permanent admission into the nunnery, among them Edith, sister of Harold Godwinesson, and Edith-Matilda, daughter of the Scottish king Malcolm III. Four noble boys attending the school at Ramsey *c.* 1000

[12] P. Lendinara, 'Instructional manuscripts in England: the tenth- and eleventh-century codices and the early Norman ones', in P. Lendinara *et al.*, eds., *Form and Content of Instruction in Anglo-Saxon England in the Light of Contemporary Manuscript Evidence* (Turnhout, 2007), pp. 59–113, at pp. 93–104.

[13] T. Webber, 'The patristic content of English book collections in the eleventh century: towards a continental perspective', in P. R. Robinson and R. Zim, eds., *Of the Making of Books. Medieval Manuscripts, Their Scribes and Readers: Essays Presented to M. B. Parkes* (Aldershot, 1997), pp. 191–205; Thomson, *England*, XIV, XVIII; M. Lapidge, 'Versifying the Bible in the Middle Ages', in Jill Mann and Maura Nolan, eds., *The Text in the Community: Essays on Medieval Monks, Manuscripts, Authors and Readers* (Notre Dame, 2006), pp. 11–40, at p. 28.

[14] C. Burnett, 'Mathematics and astronomy in Hereford and its region in the twelfth century', in D. Whitehead, ed., *Hereford: Medieval Art, Architecture, and Archaeology* (British Archaeological Society Conference Transactions 15; Leeds, 1995), pp. 50–9.

were spared punishment for a prank by a wise abbot who correctly predicted that being of noble birth they would reward the abbey handsomely in later life. One boy, at least, was a relative of the abbot, and others may have prospered in episcopal, rather than secular, careers, and until they are identified it is not safe to assume that they made their fortunes outside the Church.[15]

Outside formal education, however, there is evidence of a much wider network of informal teaching, sometimes, but not necessarily, involving literate skills. Churchmen taught their congregations and flocks, not least by example, and Dunstan thus was credited with the education of women as well as men.[16] Men and women of noble and sub-noble birth were trained in practical accomplishments appropriate to their gender and status. Elite behaviour had to be inculcated, and literacy, although prized and of course an essential component in formal education, was only one skill appropriate for the gentleman or gentlewoman to acquire.[17] Asser, King Alfred's biographer, famously boasted how the children at the court school in the late ninth century, noble and sub-noble alike, learned to read from books in Latin and English and learned composition, so that 'even before they had the requisite strength for manly skills (hunting, that is, and other skills appropriate to noblemen), they were seen to be devoted and intelligent students of the liberal arts' (*Life of Alfred*, §75). Asser's text may be read as a comment on the exceptional nature of the opportunities provided.

Indeed, without making assumptions about literacy levels, there is reason to believe that the acquisition of discipline and skill were essential components of growing up in England in these centuries. At every social level skills had to be learned, from fighting and hunting, to embroidery, to trades like stone-, metal- and gold-working, down to successful animal husbandry and the effective preparation, handling and preservation

[15] W. D. Macray, ed., *Chronicon Abbatiae Ramseiensis*, (RS; London, 1886) pp. 112–14. Discussed by Orme, *From Childhood*, pp. 60–1. Orme takes these to be secular nobles. Early Continental monastic schools rarely educated outsiders: J. L. Nelson, 'Parents, children and the church', in D. Wood, ed., *The Church and Childhood* (Oxford, 1994), pp. 95–6; K. O'Brien O'Keeffe, 'Goscelin and the consecration of Eve', *ASE*, 35 (2006), 251–70.

[16] *Life of St Dunstan*, §37 (W. Stubbs, ed., *Memorials of Saint Dunstan, Archbishop of Canterbury* (RS; London, 1874), pp. 49–50).

[17] Asser, *Life of Alfred*, §§22, 75 (S. Keynes and M. Lapidge, trans. *Alfred the Great: Asser's Life of Alfred the Great and Other Contemporary Sources* (Harmondsworth, 1983), pp. 75, 91–2); J. Crick, *Charters of St Albans* (Anglo-Saxon Charters 12; London, 2007), no. 7; M. Innes, '"A Place of Discipline": Carolingian courts and aristocratic youth', in C. Cubitt, ed., *Court Culture in the Early Middle Ages* (Turnhout, 2003), pp. 59–76; J. L. Nelson, 'Dhuoda', in P. Wormald and J. L. Nelson, eds., *Lay Intellectuals in the Carolingian World* (Cambridge, 2007), pp. 106–20.

of food. How such skills were acquired we often cannot say. Two main routes look the most probable: learning away from the natal household (with a master, at a school or court, or as an apprentice) and learning at home, from a parent or resident teacher. Both are documented, and the evidence will be discussed here. It has to be interpreted with considerable care. Literacy might be supposed to be the best-documented skill because by definition it documents itself, but literacy in the early Middle Ages comprised multiple skills – reading, comprehension, composition and penmanship – and few practitioners will have acquired expertise in all. Other crafts are mentioned only in passing in the written record; every item of material culture attests workmanship and training whose mode of acquisition can usually only be guessed at.[18]

LEARNING CRAFTS AND THE CRAFT OF LEARNING

Asser, in the passage describing Alfred's court school just quoted, reiterates the Latin word '*ars*' (art, skill, trade). The boys apply themselves to the liberal **arts** (*in liberalibus artibus*), but also to hunting and other **arts** (*ceteris artibus*) appropriate to nobles before they are physically capable of manly **arts** (*humanis artibus*). A century later, in a fictional conversation between a monastic teacher and his pupil, surviving as a Latin text with continuous Old English gloss, we find the same contrast between secular skills (*artes seculares/woruldcræftas*) and literate ones, this time embodied in the monk and his service to God.[19]

MASTER: I ask you (*indicating a particular pupil*), what do you say to me? What is your work?

'MONK': I am a professed monk, and every day I sing seven times with the brethren, and I am busy with reading and singing, but nevertheless between times I want to learn to speak the Latin language.

It becomes clear as the conversation unfolds that the monk's profession is considered as a trade to be acquired.

MASTER: What do your friends do?

'MONK': Some are ploughmen, some shepherds, some oxherds; some again, huntsmen, some fishermen, some fowlers, some merchants, some shoemakers, salters, bakers.

[18] For a rare discussion see P. Lendinara, 'The world of Anglo-Saxon learning', in M. Godden and M. Lapidge, eds., *The Cambridge Companion to Old English Literature* (Cambridge, 1991), pp. 264–81, at pp. 266–7, also Lendinara, 'Instructional manuscripts', p. 75.

[19] *Ælfric's Colloquy*, M. Swanton, ed. and trans., *Anglo-Saxon Prose* (rev. edn; London, 1993), pp. 169, 174.

After interviewing some of these workers the Master resumes his interrogation of the monk.

MASTER: Oh monk, you who are speaking to me. Now, I have found that you have good and very necessarily companions; and who are these, I ask you?
'MONK': I have craftsmen: blacksmiths, a goldsmith, silversmith, coppersmith, carpenters and workers in many other different crafts [*artium/cræfta*].

And it is of these crafts (*artes/cræftas*) that the service of God is judged the superior. Ælfric has constructed this most contrived of conversations in part to model basic Latin syntax and vocabulary for an audience of English monks grappling with the language just as it says here, for the advancement of their monastic profession. But his story has a deeper message and a wider resonance. In Old English the word *cræft* (craft) translates Latin *ars* and OE *cræft(i)ca* (craftsman) renders Latin *artifex* (artisan, craftsman).[20] Ælfric, like Asser before him, uses Latin *artes* to describe practical skills, those acquired in training and exercised in the pursuit of a profession or trade, including literate skills. The Anglo-Saxon schoolboy who comes to his lesson without writing implements is made to declare, 'No craftsman [*artifex*] can work well without tools.'[21] Likewise the Latin apparatus of formal education, from classical times described as arts – the *ars scribendi* (composition), the *ars grammatici* (language acquisition) – would all have been understood as crafts, as reflected in the Old English words for learning: *leornungcræft* and *wordcræft*.

The connection between craft, skill and cultural work suggested here is not just a semantic one. Learning was a skill and, for some, even a trade, if the practitioner was a man of the Church devoted to the word of God as conveyed to him in Latin texts or a professional remembrancer, of the sort increasingly rare in the west in these centuries.[22] Although the monk's position is an exceptional one, and the acquisition of literacy only one part of his job, for nobles, at least, with the luxury of learning more than one craft, the skills of reading and writing could be learned alongside other practical accomplishments. This was reportedly the case at the courts of Charlemagne and Alfred, where hunting and military skills

[20] S. Gwara, ed., and D. W. Porter, trans., *Anglo-Saxon Conversations: The Colloquies of Ælfric Bata* (Woodbridge, 1997), p. 199. Note Clanchy's observation: 'In non-literate cultures the skills of eye and hand are associated primarily with craftsmanship and the visual arts': Clanchy, *From Memory*, p. 278.

[21] *The Colloquies of Ælfric Bata*, §14 (Gwara, ed., and Porter, trans., *Anglo-Saxon Conversations*, pp. 112–13).

[22] Michael Richter has noted that these words translated *professio* – a profession, craft or skill; Richter, *The Formation of the Medieval West: Studies in the Oral Culture of the Barbarians* (Dublin, 1994), pp. 191–2.

were learned alongside literacy, and it remained true after the Norman Conquest, when noblemen and women continued to be judged and valued according to their acquisition of skills in many different spheres, whether in music, literature, hunting or, for men, fighting.[23]

EDUCATION AND UPBRINGING

Inherent within the modern vocabulary of education is the notion of upbringing and training, a taming process analogous to, or comparable with, that appropriate to animals. Thus in modern English a horse can be schooled; in modern French '*élève*' denotes a pupil but '*élèvage*' the rearing of animals; the modern English word 'education' is a post-medieval coinage which contains within it '*educatio*', (rearing, breeding or training). We find the same conceptual elements in Latin '*discere*', to learn, which contains notions of guidance and training, giving us 'pupils', '*discipuli*', but also '*disciplina*', a programme of study, yet also application to that study or correction. Both kinds of *disciplina* could be physical, as Asser and Einhard indicated.

The notion that education is a developmental process akin to physical growth, involving the acquisition of norms of proper adult behaviour, and correction of infringements of those norms by physical chastisement (as it does in training an animal), runs deep in medieval and late antique writing. *Grammatica*, the personification of grammar, is represented in the twelfth century, as in late antiquity, as a woman holding a whip.[24] Such sanctions were needed. In one account, Anglo-Saxon schoolboys resemble their Victorian successors not only in playing with hoops, but in thieving apples, raising cash from locals through black-market sales of stolen goods, larking about when they should have been working and generally failing in application to their studies.[25] But the analogy stops there. These were boys learning godliness, not manliness: learning to recite, read and write in the service of a higher authority. The account is fictional, part of another text modelling the Latin language for native English-speakers, but it is aimed at the boys whose behaviour is described and so

[23] Innes, '"A Place of Discipline"'; Orme, *From Childhood*, pp. 24, 142–210. On the physicality of learning to write see Matthew Hussey, 'Anglo-Saxon scribal *habitus* and Frankish aesthetics in an early uncial manuscript' (unpublished manuscript).

[24] S. Reynolds, *Medieval Reading: Grammar, Rhetoric and the Classical Text* (Cambridge, 1996), p. 18.

[25] *The Colloquies of Ælfric Bata*, §3, 5–7, 25, 28 (Gwara, ed., and Porter, trans., *Anglo-Saxon Conversations*, pp. 82–5, 89–95, 155–7, 164–5).

commands an element of credibility. But the physicality of learning had other dimensions. The term *gymnasium* was sometimes used to describe Anglo-Saxon monastic schools, a poetic synonym, perhaps, but a word which aptly combines the sense of exertion and regimentation inherent in education.[26] In the earlier and later Middle Ages education and moral correction were closely connected. And moral rectitude was a major concern of Anglo-Saxon education.

Alongside discipline, another idea deeply ingrained in our sources is that of nurturing and sustenance. Metaphors of nourishment flow through the language of education during our period. The tutors and nannies who bring up infants in the ninth century as in the twelfth are '*nutritores*' and '*nutrices*', also meaning wet nurse. Writers of the tenth-century reform relate how boys are nourished by the psalms, just as writers of the twelfth describe children digesting their elementary education like milk in preparation for the solid food of sacred texts.[27] Anglo-Latin writers made heavy use of the metaphor. Archbishop Dunstan sustains his pupils with the food of his teaching as they grow from youth to manhood. In the eleventh century pupils who are starved through lack of food for their souls celebrate the arrival of a master from overseas: '"Indeed we seek to taste of your bread and of the dishes of your laden table".' [28]

The process of intellectual and spiritual growth herein described has a literal physical corollary: these are children becoming adults. Accounts of growing up from late antiquity to the later Middle Ages commonly subdivide the period before puberty, distinguishing whether the child receives a formal education, is educated privately by tutors or, as later medieval sources indicate, learns a trade. All three types of education went on in our period, but the evidence for the acquisition of practical skills is sparse indeed, and although learning and training can be posited in a variety of situations, especially centres of population, surviving texts relate primarily to education in monastic schools. A scatter of accounts from many centuries and different parts of Europe suggest roughly the same stages of the acquisition of literacy, although the terminology varies: at about

[26] *The Life of St Oswald*, iv.4 (Lapidge, ed. and trans., *Byrhtferth of Ramsey*, pp. 100–3); Gwara, ed., and Porter, trans., *Anglo-Saxon Conversations*, p. 202.

[27] K. Dutton, '*Ad erudiendum tradidit*. The upbringing of Angevin comital children', *ANS* 32 (2009 (2010)), 24–39.

[28] *Colloquia difficiliora*, §§8, 12 (Gwara, ed., and Porter, trans., *Anglo-Saxon Conversations*, pp. 188–9, 194–7). For other examples see *Life of St Dunstan*, §22 (Stubbs, ed., *Memorials of Saint Dunstan*, p. 33), *The Life of St Oswald*, iv.1, *The Life of St Ecgwine*, i.8 (Lapidge, ed. and trans., *Byrhtferth of Ramsey*, pp. 96–9, 220–1); *The Life of St Æthelwold*, §5 (Lapidge and Winterbottom, eds. and trans., *Wulfstan of Winchester*, pp. 8–9).

seven a child is deemed ready to progress. Girls as well as boys learn the syllables and memorize the Psalter, and later a minority, predominantly male, can progress to higher learning.[29]

We know of perhaps a dozen named places where collective education could be found in pre-Conquest England, at nodal points of the Church like Canterbury and Winchester, in monasteries like Abingdon, Glastonbury, Ramsey, Æthelney, Ely and Westminster, at the seat of a bishopric like Dunwich or at the royal court. Where there were religious communities with offices to be sung, boys had to be trained, as was the pattern throughout the Middle Ages, both before and after our period, and all religious communities accepting oblates or novices will have offered such elementary training.[30]

At their most sophisticated, pre-Conquest schools taught intense engagement with the Latin traditions of Christian antiquity and of the fathers of the Anglo-Saxon Church: Bede and Aldhelm. But although pre-Conquest texts model classroom situations, and the word most often used to describe sites of collective learning is '*scola*' (school), the word signals a process of education rather than any particular system.[31] Alfred's court is described as a *scola* under the care of masters and offering bilingual education to a broad catchment, but these arrangements resemble not so much the arrangements in identifiable monastic schools of the period, as the more informal and practical training offered in post-Conquest noble households. Indeed, two levels of education were apparently available at Alfred's court. Alfred's elder son and daughter were reared at court by nannies and tutors ('*cum magna nutritorum et nutricum diligentia*') (*Life of Alfred*, §75) as Alfred himself had been, although Asser reports that his tutors and parents had neglected his education (*Life of Alfred*, §22). The implication is that the education of Alfred's elder children was different from the more formal bilingual education received by his younger

[29] For accounts see *Life of St Oswald*, iv.10, *Life of St Ecgwine*, i.8–9 (Lapidge, ed. and trans., *Byrhtferth of Ramsey*, pp. 118–21, 218–23) *Life of Christina of Markyate*, §§2–5 (*Vie de Christina de Markyate*, ed. and trans. P. L'Hermite-Leclercq and A.-M. Legras (2 vols.; Paris, 2007), i.74–81, ii.81–8).

[30] *Life of St Dunstan*, §15 (Stubbs, ed., *Memorials of Saint Dunstan*, pp. 25–6); *Life of St Oswald*, iv.4 (Stubbs, ed., *Memorials of Saint Dunstan*, pp. 100–3) *Liber Eliensis*, ii.91, iii.35 (J. Fairweather, trans., *Liber Eliensis, A History of the Isle of Ely from the Seventh Century to the Twelfth* (Woodbridge, 2005), pp. 191, 326–32); Goscelin, *Vita Wulfsini*, §§1–2, R. Love, ed. and trans., 'The life of St Wulfsige of Sherborne by Goscelin of Saint-Bertin: a new translation with introduction, appendix and notes', in K. Barker, D. A. Hinton and Alan Hunt, eds., *St Wulfsige and Sherborne: Essays to Celebrate the Millennium of the Benedictine Abbey 998–1998* (Bournemouth University School of Conservation Sciences, Occasional Paper 8; 2005), pp. 98–123, at p. 105.

[31] Jaeger, *The Envy of Angels*, p. 28. Compare Innes's discussion, '"A Place of Discipline"', pp. 59–61.

son and noble peers. In his youth their father had committed poems to memory, and practised hunting skills, though he had not learned to read until after twelve. His elder children applied themselves to 'other pursuits of this present life which are appropriate to the nobility', but also learned the psalms, the first step on the road to literacy, and they studied English books and poems.

Although the education of laymen is a process much more scantily documented in earlier centuries, the notion of learning in a domestic setting is a plausible one. Aristocrats often found learning outside the classroom in the post-Conquest period, either at home or at the household of a secular noble or an elite cleric, and Anglo-Saxon children, too, were farmed out for their upbringing. Alfred's biographer stresses that he was his parents' favourite, 'always brought up at the royal court and nowhere else, from infancy to boyhood' (Asser, *Life of Alfred*, §22) which allows for the possibility that others were sent away at this critical period. A century later Ælfric translated words commonly rendered into modern English as tutor, nurse and pupil (*nutritor, nutrix, alumnus*) as *fosterfæder, fostermoder, fostercild*.[32] The Anglo-Saxon Chronicle records that Cnut entrusted his son to Thorkell the Tall (ASC C s.a. 1023), an arrangement reminiscent of Norman dukes and kings Henry I and II, who regularly assigned their sons to trusted secular lieutenants, whom contemporaries described in Latin as a *paedagogus* or *tutor*. Anglo-Saxon writers recorded or envisaged the entrusting of princes to educators. Byrhtferth of Ramsey, writing *c.* 1000, records that Edgar's son Edward (r. 975–8) had been 'instructed in holy scripture' by Sidemann, bishop of Crediton (973–7), and the same writer, in a fictional account, imagines how an eighth-century bishop of Worcester acted as a 'wise instructor of princes' (*sagax pedagogus clytonum*) and educated the sons of the king of Mercia.[33] Although in neither situation is Byrhtferth clear about where the education took place, young men of noble birth certainly moved away from home to find an education. His biographers relate that as a youth (*adolescens*) the future bishop of Winchester Æthelwold (963–84) lodged in King Æthelstan's household, in the royal palace (*palati*[*um*]) in his natal town

[32] Julius Zupitza, ed., *Ælfrics Grammatik und Glossar: Text und Varianten*, foreword by Helmut Gneuss (Berlin, 1966), p. 300.

[33] *Life of St Oswald*, iv.18 (Lapidge, ed. and trans., *Byrhtferth of Ramsey*, pp. 138–9) Æthelred of Mercia by Ecgwine (*Life of St Ecgwine* ii.2 (Lapidge, ed. and trans., *Byrhtferth of Ramsey*, pp. 238–9)) Edward the Confessor at Ely: *Liber Eliensis*, ii.91 (Fairweather, trans., *Liber Eliensis*, p. 191) D. Bates, 'The Conqueror's adolescence', *ANS* 25 (2002 (2003)), 1–18. See also the examples collected in Wormald and Nelson, eds., *Lay Intellectuals*.

of Winchester, 'where he learned many useful things from the king's wise men'. The king later sent him to the bishop of Winchester to be educated, with whom he remained as a cleric, and later priest, again, presumably in his household, where he 'studiously attended to the teaching and example of his patron and *ordinator*' before pursuing more advanced formal study (grammar and metrics) at the monastery of Glastonbury. The term *ordinator*, literally one who puts in rank, is translated by Lapidge as 'ordainer', but its use in an unrelated context to describe the role of a ninth-century Continental mother and educator, Dhuoda (*ordinatrix*), illustrates that the term can have an extended meaning, presumably to do with the shepherding of a dependant.[34] Most remarkably, the future Archbishop Oda was sent away from his parents to the home of a *miles* dedicated to Christ, named Æthelhelm, usually interpreted as an unidentified layman, where he studied 'a number of books and the true discipline [*regulam*] of the catholic faith and the sacraments of the holy mother church'.[35]

Unspecified general education must have been available to many in the service of great men. Becket's biographer describes how he was chosen as tutor to Henry II's heir, the young Henry, who constituted only one of the young nobles entrusted to the chancellor, some of whom he retained for his own household. They would have learned manners and civility as well as reading and writing.[36] Dunstan, although a future abbot and archbishop of Canterbury, received his formal education at the monastery of which he later became abbot, but interrupted it apparently with a spell of involvement as an associate of the king, where the machinations of his own social group ('several of his own friends and [fellow?] courtiers', *nonnulli propriorum sodalium et palatinorum*), especially those who were his relatives, caused him to be exiled from the king's presence. Later he nearly lapsed into the life of secular noble by contemplating marriage, before being rescued by his relative, the bishop of Winchester, and becoming a monk, apparently at Winchester, and only later returning to Glastonbury to continue his education.[37]

The idea of learning by example is not an exclusively secular one. The notion of being entrusted to a superior to learn resounds around the

[34] Wulfstan, *Vita*, §7; Ælfric, *Vita*, §5 (Lapidge and Winterbottom, eds. and trans., *Wulfstan of Winchester*, pp. 10–11, 72). Nelson, 'Dhuoda', p. 113.

[35] *Life of St Oswald*, i.4 (Lapidge, ed. and trans., *Byrhtferth of Ramsey*, pp. 18–19, nn. 54–5).

[36] Barlow, *Thomas Becket*, p. 44; Robertson, ed., *Materials*, iii, pp. 22, 175–6; Orme, *From Childhood*, p. 56.

[37] *Life of St Dunstan*, §§5–12 (Stubbs, ed., *Memorials of Saint Dunstan*, pp. 19–20). For commentary see M. Lapidge, 'Dunstan [St Dunstan] (*d*. 988)', *ODNB*.

texts of the monastic reform movement of the tenth century, the pupils (*alumni*, *scholastici* and *discipuli*) who cluster around great ecclesiastical figures who teach by example. Ælfric, rendering Gospel parables into English for the consumption of the general populace *c.* 1000, regularly calls Christ's disciples '*leornung cnihtas*' – learning boys – which conveys a sense of youth, collective behaviour and learning by example which cannot have been unfamiliar to his audience.[38] Personal connections perpetuated principles and educational practice along chains of association, described by Michael Lapidge as *diachia*, and these are evident in the cathedral schools of the Continent as much as in pre-Conquest England. Likewise men were sent to learn the best monastic practice by personal experience, travelling abroad as necessary, like Oswald and Germanus, both sent to observe and memorize monastic custom abroad in order to teach their own people at home.[39] Undeniably such connections were jolted by changes to monastic structure and personnel, to be replaced by new networks of association, as after the Norman Conquest.

We should also remember how much training went on simply unrecorded. The skills practised by the monk's contemporaries in Ælfric's *Colloquy* – his friends the ploughmen, shepherds, oxherds, huntsmen, fishermen, fowlers, merchants, shoe-makers, salters and bakers – all would have learned by observation, presumably in later boyhood. Sometimes, knowledge would have been acquired from a relative – many such trades were no doubt inherited, and sometimes a kind of apprenticeship might have taken place. Recent research on Anglo-Saxon medical texts suggests that practitioners must have learned by practical experience at the hands of a master. Old English medical texts do not explain the basic skills required to make up a recipe: technical expertise is assumed. Just as a modern scientific paper documents processes and results only intelligible to and repeatable by those with advanced training and knowledge, so early medical texts presuppose knowledge acquired by experience. So we imagine a world in which technical knowledge passed between craftsmen and mates, masters and apprentices, but also parents and children. Many trades and professions were heritable: they passed down families. Bards were the sons of bards and priests followed their fathers, until

[38] References indexed by John C. Pope, ed., *Homilies of Aelfric: A Supplementary Collection* (EETS; Oxford, 1968), 11. On pupils in general see Wulfstan, *Vita*, §§9, 11; Ælfric, *Vita*, §6–7 (Lapidge and Winterbottom, eds. and trans., *Wulfstan of Winchester*, pp. 14–23, 72–73) *Life of St Dunstan*, §15 (Stubbs, ed., *Memorials of Saint Dunstan*, pp. 25–6).

[39] *Life of St Oswald*, ii.2–7 (Lapidge, ed. and trans., *Byrhtferth of Ramsey*, pp. 34–49). On chains of association, see Lapidge, 'Versifying the Bible' Jaeger, *The Envy of Angels*, ch. 4.

reform, when nephew followed uncles. Although the details of transmission are barely documented, skills must have been learned in the household. Certainly, other people's children were sent to the households of social superiors for this very reason.

This kind of informal education remained common, even the norm, throughout the Middle Ages, and there is no reason to associate it particularly with any one place or period.[40] There is some evidence that skills which we would instinctively associate with formal education were transmitted and practised outside formal settings in our period. The tenth-century noblewoman Æthelgifu manumitted the wife of her huntsman and her daughter, enjoining her and two other women to sing psalms every week for a year, presumably a skill learned outside any monastic school, most probably in a domestic situation. In the early thirteenth century the Cistercian John of Forde recorded how the hermit Wulfric of Haselbury (ob. 1154) had used the services of a local man trained as a scribe. This man, named Richard, was not a monk, although he worked in the monastery of Forde and later became a monk there. He had a son himself, and was the son of a priest. How he received his training is unknown, whether in a monastic school or in a household, even, perhaps, at home, in his case.[41]

IMPORTANCE OF WRITING IN THE VERNACULAR

We have no means of calibrating levels of knowledge and education among the population at large in the three centuries before 1200, but there is some evidence that learning reached surprisingly far down the social scale (see Chapter V.6). Texts would have reached most people through the ear, as listeners, but there is also evidence of an unusual degree of active participation in literacy, through writing. Critical to both developments was language. Two written vernacular languages emerged in these centuries, first English and then French. Each language acted like a switch, enabling the flow of knowledge in one direction, towards one constituency, and impeding it in others. In the first part of our period knowledge was

[40] For Continental examples see Nelson, 'Parents', pp. 96–7, 101–2, Innes, '"A Place of Discipline"', pp. 61–3; on the later Middle Ages in England, see P. H. Cullum, 'Learning to be a man, learning to be a priest in late medieval England', in Sarah Rees Jones, ed., *Learning and Literacy in Medieval England and Abroad* (Utrecht Studies in Medieval Literacy 3; Turnhout, 2003), pp. 135–53; see also Orme, 'Schools', pp. 1–3, Clanchy, *From Memory*, pp. 238–41.

[41] For Æthelgifu see Crick, ed., *Charters*, no. 7. For Wulfric, Maurice Bell, ed., *Wulfric of Haselbury by John of Ford* (Somerset Record Society, 47; 1933), pp. xxiv–vi, §§28–9, 77.

actively cultivated through the medium of English. Kings and educators consciously promoted its use as a means of communication down the command chain, with those within their spheres of political or moral authority. In this sense a centuries-old cultural rift began, temporarily, to close. Englishmen and women lived in a former Roman colony whose colonial inheritance was much more broken than in the Continental remnants of empire. In Spain, Gaul and Italy bishops and leaders could preach in Latin with reasonable expectation of being understood for perhaps three centuries after the ending of empire, although they were forced to simplify their diction as the languages spoken by their hearers evolved from Latin to Romance. The cultivation of Latin Christianity in the English-speaking parts of Britain, a region with no functioning linguistic heritage from classical antiquity, posed an entirely different pastoral problem. To reach an unlettered and non-Latinate population and to work moral change the Church needed a mechanism powerful enough to reach down into the population. In the absence of ecclesiastical structures intensive enough to educate the populace in the locality, pastors from at least the eighth century onwards used the vernacular, and in the tenth and eleventh centuries English challenged Latin as the carrier of a great variety of material – from notes and memoranda to matter of supreme ideological importance, including the Bible itself.

Educators struggled to harness the medium appropriately. Ælfric, who himself made translations from eight Old Testament books, one, the Book of Joshua, for the lay noble Æthelweard, feared the effect of 'naked narrative', allowing the ignorant access to biblical text unmediated by appropriate commentary. Elsewhere, in composing a Latin grammar in Old English for the consumption of young boys, Ælfric constructed another bridge to help his fellow countrymen to Christian enlightenment, by advancing their knowledge of scripture.[42] The colloquies frequently cited in this chapter model Latin for a monastic audience learning to comprehend and speak it, although sometimes painfully: the teacher curses a lazy pupil in the colloquy of Ælfric Bata, who in turn asks for him to speak more simply, because he cannot understand the complexity of his master's Latin.[43] Certainly, the kind of highly decorative Latin cultivated in tenth- and eleventh-century England could only be acquired by

[42] On Æthelweard: J. Wilcox, ed., *Ælfric's Prefaces* (Durham, 1994), pp. 37–44; nos. 4a–4b, pp. 116–19; S. Ashley, 'The lay intellectual in Anglo-Saxon England: Ealdorman Æthelweard and the politics of history', in Wormald and Nelson, eds., *Lay Intellectuals*, pp. 218–45.

[43] *The Colloquies of Ælfric Bata*, §25 (Gwara, ed., and Porter, trans., *Anglo-Saxon Conversations*, pp. 154–5).

specialist schooling and was only comprehensible to a closely connected and arguably inward-facing circle of scholars. But some nobles were ready to meet educators more than halfway, even if the mechanisms they used yielded unusual results. The eccentric vocabulary and singular syntax of the Latin rendering of the Anglo-Saxon Chronicle attributed to a lay noble, the same Ealdorman Æthelweard for whom Ælfric translated books of the Old Testament, were arguably influenced by the conventions of vernacular composition, whether this English noble composed the work himself, or whether he employed an amanuensis not only to commit it to the page but to construct the Latin.[44] Scribal resources were employed by an earlier tenth-century noble, the author of the lengthy Old English memorandum describing the progress and settling of a dispute concerning Fonthill, Wiltshire. Again, a secular author has been posited, but whoever composed and copied the document did not write as a scribe trained in a recognized centre, but as an amateur, struggling to master the rudiments of script.[45] Again, we have no received model for the kind of activity we are witnessing here.

Sometimes the precocity of the vernacular in tenth- and eleventh-century England is depicted as a problem, as it must have been for French-speakers attempting to govern the country after the Norman Conquest and to run its Church. But in many ways the development of the vernacular prefigured later ages just as much as did the advanced Latin education of the twelfth century.[46] English texts, both those translated from Latin and those composed for the moral education of the English population, were circulated in organized campaigns, produced in multiple copies to ensure they reached their target readership. Ælfric agonized about the advisability of translating the Bible for laymen (see above), concerned, like later Reformation commentators, that translation might expose the text to misinterpretation. Moreover there is evidence not only that the vernacular was a mature written language, but that, as the Fonthill memorandum illustrates, it was read and written beyond a narrow clerical circle. New research has identified in eleventh-century contexts the hands of a thousand different copyists and composers of

[44] A. Lutz, 'Æthelweard's *Chronicon* and Old English Poetry', *ASE*, 29 (2000), 177–214.

[45] On the author, see S. Keynes, 'The Fonthill Letter', in M. Korhammer, with K. Reichl and H. Sauer, eds., *Words, Texts and Manuscripts: Studies in Anglo-Saxon Culture Presented to Helmut Gneuss on the Occasion of His Sixty-Fifth Birthday* (Cambridge, 1992), pp. 53–97.

[46] D. A. Bullough, 'The educational tradition in England from Alfred to Ælfric: teaching *utriusque linguae*', in *La scuola nell'occidente latino dell'alto medioevo* (*Settimane di Studio del Centro Italiano di studi sull'alto medioevo*, 19; 2 vols.; Spoleto, 1972), pp. 453–94, at p. 493. On the problem presented to the Normans see Thomson, *England*, XVIII, esp. p. 29.

English, that is men and possibly women copying and annotating texts and books in their native language. They would have been educated in a period in which we know very little about formal educational provision, before the proliferation of the urban and cathedral schools documented after the Conquest; chance references to schools at places like Dunwich and Westminster, already mentioned, perhaps suggest that urban and cathedral schools were not necessarily without earlier precedent. These scribal campaigns, some short and many unprofessional, attest considerable and at present unexplained activity, as perplexing as the Latin attributed to Æthelweard or the Old English attributed the secular author of the Fonthill Letter. Let us put this figure into perspective. Petrucci, studying the most literate part of Europe on the eve of the Renaissance, counted 230 named scribes copying books with Italian texts in fifteenth-century Italy, and in a separate study identified 388 scribes writing Latin in seventh- and eighth-century Italy combined, a figure which he took as a sign of rising literacy in those centuries.[47] His scribes were named, while almost all of our eleventh-century English ones were anonymous, but in comparison with available figures from the most literate part of Europe the English evidence remains impressive: several times as many. Not all these writers were monastic; some were certainly clerics; none may have belonged to the laity, or to laity working outside monastic institutions. But the degree of engagement with the written word and the English language deserves to be registered.

A further enigma which hardly squares with the received model of education before or after the Norman Conquest is the volume of texts. More than a thousand different Old English texts survive, some in multiple copies, most committed to writing in the centuries addressed in this volume, the great majority before 1100, one would imagine.[48] Who do we envisage produced them and committed them to writing and where and for whom? Many can be assigned by their content or authorship to a restricted milieu, a monastic and clerical clique which initially crystallized around the royal court of the later tenth century, trained the educators and bishops of succeeding generations and were themselves exposed as adolescents not only to monastic education but to life at court. But this tiny cluster is unlikely to account for all the vernacular writing and composition which we observe.

[47] Armando Petrucci, *Writers and Readers in Medieval Italy: Studies in the History of Written Culture*, Charles M. Radding, ed. and trans. (London, 1995), p. 198 and, on literacy, pp. 92–4.

[48] Roberta Frank and Angus Cameron record more than 941 prose texts alone in *A Plan for the Dictionary of Old English* (Toronto, 1973), pp. 44–223.

But the flow of information in one direction impeded it in the other. Successive conquests in the eleventh century brought Norse- and French-speaking elites potentially deaf to the appeal of the native vernacular but who acted as patrons of performance, translation and composition in other languages, like the middle-ranking administrators who were the recipients of two early twelfth-century vernacular texts in French.[49] Moral instruction continued in the English vernacular but the breaking and tangling of chains of command and patronage, particularly after the Norman Conquest, and the overlay of education at parish level by twelfth-century urban foundations providing a very different kind of education produced a complex knot which is almost impossible to unpick. Written English emerges out of it in the later twelfth century but how exactly remains very difficult to discern.[50]

CONCLUSION

The educators and learners of the tenth, eleventh and twelfth centuries comprised a large sector of the population. All those in authority – kings, bishops, clergy, parents and heads of households – carried some measure of responsibility for the moral and social education of their subordinates. Many will have taught practical skills or modelled behaviour, but access to salvation required knowledge of texts, memorized or read. What imprint this left on the literacy of laymen is difficult to gauge. The sharp retraction of the English prelacy and the English aristocracy after 1066 will have checked the networks of vernacular learning which had begun to proliferate before the Conquest, when documents of governance migrated from Latin to English. We have more information about the acquisition of learning in domestic settings, at the households of kings or nobles, but the pattern matches the shreds of evidence which we have from before the Conquest, so there is reason to believe that the arrangements were not unprecedented, although they were more significant in range and scale. Our evidence does not allow us to gauge levels of exposure to written texts, but the fragmentary indications we do have are suggestive: in the

[49] Ian Short, 'Language and literature', in C. Harper-Bill and E. van Houts, eds., *A Companion to the Anglo-Norman World* (Woodbridge, 2003), pp. 191–213, at p. 208; M. Townend, 'Contextualizing the Knútsdrápur: skaldic praise-poetry at the court of Cnut', *ASE*, 30 (2001), 145–79.

[50] Godric of Finchale (d. 1170) may have acquired literacy using books in English: Ian Short, 'On bilingualism in Anglo-Norman England', *Romance Philology*, 33.4 (1980), 467–79, at 476, n. 33. On moral instruction in the vernacular see M. Swan, 'Ælfric's Catholic homilies in the twelfth century', in M. Swan and E. M. Treharne, eds., *Rewriting Old English in the Twelfth Century* (Cambridge, 2000), pp. 62–82.

will of Æthelgifu, composed in the tenth century, it is assumed that non-elite female satellites of a Christian household could recall the Psalter, the same rudimentary text later studied by the infant Christina of Markyate.

In these three centuries, as in the preceding and succeeding quarter-millennia, seismic cultural change took place. It makes no sense to deny that the French-speaking world of Thomas Becket was anything but utterly different from the Anglo-Danish sphere in which Archbishop Oda had been reared two centuries before. Huge intellectual changes were wrought by new monasticism and the cathedral schools, by Church reform, new learning and knowledge of the sheer intellectual wealth locked up in Continental libraries. The developing structures of formal education, particularly in the grammar schools, vastly increased potential capacity, both in terms of the numbers who could be educated and their levels of academic attainment. Nevertheless, certain continuities can be anticipated: the transmitting of information and knowledge within households, of practical skills between masters and boys, the education to be gained by placement in an elite household. All the time observation and repetition, begun in adolescence, if not in childhood, ensured the inculcation and successful replication of habits of mind, skills, both intellectual and practical, and spiritual and political knowledge.

Learning takes place at certain major sites: at home, at court or in households, in church, in institutions away from home, abroad, in combinations of all of these. Although the institutions themselves changed greatly in the second half of our period, all of these situations provided opportunities for social alignment and for the formation of networks of association. Throughout the period education brought reward: the prospect of salvation for many and the hope of more immediate advancement for the few. Tenth-century kings prized exquisitely arcane Latinity in their courtiers, just as in the twelfth century Henry I and II patronized lucid classicism in theirs, and all availed themselves of the connection between learning, government and governance, a message plain to all within the social reach of the court.[51] But herein lies the difference. The world of the educated tenth-century Englishman, at least as represented to us in contemporary texts, is shaped unashamedly by family connections. Dunstan's father gets him into the school at Glastonbury, his peers and

[51] For an early and exceptionally well-articulated example see David Pratt, *The Political Thought of Alfred the Great* (Cambridge, 2007), but the patronage of the tenth-century reform movement by Edgar, in particular, demonstrates the same tendencies: for example, Lapidge and Winterbottom, eds., *Wulfstan of Winchester*, pp. lxxxix–xci. Clanchy, *From Memory*, pp. 72–3 on the exchequer.

young relatives (*consanguinei*) have him thrown out of court, he is rescued from marriage by another relative (*propinquus*), the bishop of Winchester, who gets him ordained. Æthelwold and Oswald, the only other educated Englishmen of the tenth century whose lives are documented in narrative form, likewise rely on family connections at strategic moments in their careers. Becket, although tailed by a train of dependants and relatives during his exile in France, did not owe his career to them so much as to a network of friends and companions acquired during and after his education. The impecunious student is a character in twelfth-century texts, not in tenth-century ones. As the graph of social ascent became much steeper and much less stable, the prospect of success apparently lured many to invest more than they could easily afford in their education. The outcome must often have been no more than a modest appointment in a magnate's household, but for some it brought elevation above the rank of kings.

CHAPTER VI.2

Information and its retrieval

Nicholas Karn

The management and archiving of information are matters of relevance to historians in all periods, for archiving practices have structured the data available for modern analysis. It is rarer that such matters attain the status of a significant subject for debate and discussion among historians. In relation to England in the central Middle Ages this has come to pass largely through the work of M. T. Clanchy, presented in *From Memory to Written Record: England, 1066–1307*. The starting point of his work is the upwards trend in the amount of written material surviving from that period, which moves from the paucity of the mid-eleventh century to the relative abundance of the early fourteenth. This change had been observed before, but Clanchy imposed a new sense of structure on historians' understanding of these developments. He argued not only that the increase in surviving records marked expanding familiarity with writing, but also that archiving was in some sense a cause of literacy, because making records and keeping them familiarized many kinds of people with the practical and everyday uses of literacy, as opposed to solemn and ritual uses, and this familiarity over time turned into the habit of using documents.[1]

Clanchy's thesis is the most persuasive and influential analysis of the uses and social consequences of writing in England in the central Middle Ages. Its heart, however, lies in the period from the later twelfth into the thirteenth century, and the uses – especially lay uses – of writing in that period provide the baseline against which earlier centuries have been assessed. The treatment of earlier periods in *From Memory to Written Record* is more equivocal, however. The first edition used earlier centuries as a simple counterpoint to the thirteenth, while the second is more positive on pre-Conquest uses of literacy. But the basic message of the book

[1] M. T. Clanchy, *From Memory to Written Record: England, 1066–1307* (London, 1979; 2nd edn, Oxford, 1993), p. 2.

is consistent. It suggests that the relative lack of writing when contrasted with the thirteenth century indicates that, outside a few very particular subcultures, literacy was rare and of relatively less importance in most aspects of government and society.[2]

Clanchy's thesis contains a number of assumptions which are highly questionable, and which have been undercut by P. J. Geary's study of remembering in eleventh-century continental Europe.[3] The first problematic assumption is about the gulf between oral and written means of transacting business, and between oral and literate mentalities, when throughout this period oral and written means were so closely integrated that it is nearly meaningless to write of distinct mentalities. The second problematic assumption is that there is some clear and consistent relationship between the amount that was written at any given time and the amount that survives to the present day. This is highly questionable, primarily because it does not sufficiently allow for the processes of preservation or archiving, which inevitably involved a winnowing of records in accordance with a sense of their usefulness and importance.

The relationship between use of memory and use of records, and the consequences of that relationship for the form and content of archives, can best be approached through an example. In 1150, the monks of Bury St Edmunds found that one of their knights was accused of plotting against king Stephen, and so claimed that the liberties of the abbey – granted by charter in the middle of the eleventh century – meant that they had the right to try him:

The lord abbot took friends and monks and barons of the church to the lord king, showed him the privileges and charters of the church in this matter and made his supplication and request. To which the king replied: 'Let the privileges be put before my justice and the counties and be read out, and whatever right and liberty the barons of the counties will testify to belong to St Edmund in this matter or another this I grant and will that he shall have without reduction or diminution.' Consequently the privileges were put before the counties and publicly recited, and several people began to say several things. Seeing this, Hervey de Glanvill suddenly leapt forward and standing in the middle said: 'Honest and most prudent men! It is a long time since I first heard the charters of St Edmund's which were read here just now and they have always been authoritative unto this day. I would have you know that I am a very old man, as you can see, and I remember many things that happened in the time of King Henry and before, when justice and right, peace and fidelity flourished in England, whereas now,

[2] Clanchy, *From Memory*, p. 21.

[3] P. J. Geary, *Phantoms of Remembrance: Memory and Oblivion at the End of the First Millennium* (Princeton, 1994), p. 15.

under pressure of war, justice has fled and laws have fallen silent and the liberties of churches, like other good things, have been lost in many places; nonetheless I say for certain, testify and affirm that fifty years have passed since I first began to attend the hundred and shire courts with my father, before I had an estate of my own, and I have done so ever since. And every time a case arose in the shire courts involving any man of the eight-and-a-half hundreds, whosesoever man he was, the abbot of St Edmunds or his steward and officials took that case with them for hearing in the court of St Edmunds and, whatsoever the allegation or charge, with the exception of treasure trove and murder, it was dealt with there.' Having heard these words, the aforesaid bishops and barons agreed ...[4]

What is significant about this account is the manner in which the abbey's claim to jurisdiction is discussed and then defined. First, the charters themselves were read to the king, but he did not rule on the matter, perhaps because this circumstance was not directly covered by the charters. So, the charters were then read to the shire courts of Norfolk and Suffolk, but this was not enough to prove the abbey's right to the position that it claimed. Those attending the court – the landholding freemen of the two shires or their representatives – then broke into many different opinions as to the applicability of the charters to this case. This is wholly understandable given the sheer vagueness of royal writs and writ-charters, for they might do no more than confirm or regrant the liberties of the abbey, leaving the scope and nature of those liberties for local definition. In such settings, the written documents were only components in defining the abbey's rights, and relied upon being fleshed out by the men of the shire. Second, the raising of the claim generates dissension, as the account allows, even though one might expect that an account from the abbey's perspective might wish to convey a sense of uniform and unquestioned respect for the abbey's liberties. This cacophony of voices is not settled through reference to the documents themselves, because they were simply inadequate for this purpose, but rather through an impressive intervention by one of the abbey's leading barons. His testimony of course supported the claim of the monks, but it was buttressed in specific ways that were meant to gain the support of the court. He stressed not only his own antiquity, but also how often he had been in the court, as his father's son and then in his own right, how often he had heard these privileges recited and affirmed and how he had seen them respected in times more propitious than his own war-torn days. This intervention quashed the dissension, and the whole of the court then fell into line with the views of the

[4] R. C. Van Caenegem, *English Lawsuits from William I to Richard I* (Selden Society 106–7; London, 1990–1), i, pp. 288–91, no. 331.

abbot and the baron. Third, it was the men of the shire who determined the matter, not the charters, which emphasizes that even where (as often in Domesday Book) the settlement of a case is attributed to the men of a shire or hundred, there is some likelihood that such a form of words obscures the use of documents in determining a case.[5]

Clearly, the use of writing and its archiving cannot be examined alone, for memory, debate and documents were not regarded as separate realms – as is abundantly apparent from contemporary descriptions of the use of speech and writing in combination, as in Richard fitz Nigel's account of the operation of the exchequer in his *Dialogus de Scaccario* of the late 1170s and 1180s. The interdependence of speech and writing is moreover deducible from the forms of many documents from this period. This is apparent from the looseness of drafting in many twelfth-century charters, which contrasts greatly with the drafting of even the humblest private deed of the thirteenth century. For instance, Henry I could command: 'Know that I have given and conceded to Abbot Vincent the abbey of Abingdon, with all things pertaining to the same abbey',[6] without defining what the nature of the office was, or what the abbey might be thought to contain or have pertaining to it. Documents of this type could not be used by themselves to demand specific rights, but had value only in so far as they could be related to and interpreted by the testimony of authoritative individuals. For a definitive public statement of the rights and possessions of his church, Abbot Vincent would more naturally go to the men of the shire, or to the barons of his own honorial court. His archive lay as much in their recollections as in his own charters. The one was scarcely intelligible without the other, and it is probably safest to regard them as aspects of an integrated whole, where the interpretation and use of writing was merged into oral practices. Only in the early thirteenth century were documents themselves deemed essential for the demonstration of right to land.[7]

It was suggested above, following Geary, that the pattern and quantity of surviving written materials from England in the central Middle Ages need not have any significant relation to the pattern and quantity

[5] C. P. Wormald, 'Charters, law and the settlement of disputes in Anglo-Saxon England', in W. Davies and P. Fouracre, eds., *The Settlement of Disputes in Early Medieval Europe* (Cambridge, 1986), pp. 149–68; B. O'Brien, 'Forgery and the literacy of the early common law', *Albion*, 27 (1995), 1–18.

[6] *Historia ecclesie Abbendonensis*, ii. 235: J. Hudson, ed. and trans., *The History of the Church of Abingdon* (2 vols.; OMT; Oxford, 2002–7), ii, pp. 228–31.

[7] Clanchy, *From Memory*, p. 38.

of documents that were produced in the central Middle Ages. Clanchy suggested that the great rise in document survival from the eleventh to the thirteenth centuries reflected a rise in production, and that the relative shortage of written materials surviving from the tenth and eleventh centuries indicated that relatively little was produced then.[8] Students of later Anglo-Saxon England have, generally, not agreed. They have argued persuasively that the later Anglo-Saxon state was a sophisticated and powerful entity, compared against both its contemporaries and the Anglo-Norman state, basing their arguments on the surviving, fragmentary textual remains of Anglo-Saxon government, and inferring from those remains how much activity, and how much capacity to act, there might have been.[9] Such arguments might be described as 'maximalist' – that is, any one item of evidence is presented as though this were a rare survivor of a much commoner class, and that the techniques exposed in it were once standard.

It is, of course, hard to demonstrate that administrative and legal writings existed in large quantities in tenth- and eleventh-century England when the surviving remains are, by the standards of the later twelfth or thirteenth centuries, rather meagre. Nonetheless, there are large quantities of documents surviving from some major churches, and these demonstrate that organized archiving was possible; some, moreover, are forged documents which illustrate the use of those archives through incorporating phrases or data from older, genuine ones. Thus, over 180 original diplomas and writs survive through the archive of Christ Church, Canterbury, which collectively suggest what a major church might have held; still more compelling is the evidence from Worcester, where a cartulary formed from components of *c.* 1000 and the later 1090s shows how writings could be preserved and organized for use; and the same cartulary also mentions how the *scrinium* or archive of the church was broken open at the command of Bishop Wulfstan II.[10] Lest it be thought that archiving was characteristic only of major churches, it might be noted that, in the early twelfth century, William of Malmesbury explained that he took

[8] Clanchy, *From Memory*, p. 31.

[9] J. Campbell, 'Observations on English government from the tenth to the twelfth century', *TRHS* 5th ser., 25 (1975), 39–54, repr. in Campbell, *Essays in Anglo-Saxon History* (London, 1986), pp. 155–70.

[10] S. Keynes, *The Diplomas of King Æthelred 'the Unready', 978–1016: A Study in Their Use as Historical Evidence* (Cambridge, 1980), 1–4; F. Tinti, 'From episcopal conception to monastic compilation: Hemming's cartulary in context', *Early Medieval Europe*, 11 (2002), 233–61, esp. 242–3.

a letter from the *scrinium* of Milton Abbey in Dorset,[11] a relatively poor and obscure monastery, and from which hardly any records now survive. In such cases, it is not difficult to see why archives appeared and why they persisted. Institutional prosperity depended upon the management of knowledge and authority in relation to the past, and great churches possessed the resources and expertise for effective long-term archiving. Moreover, these institutions and others like them persisted over centuries, even, in the cases of Canterbury and Worcester, to the present day, albeit through closely related successors, so that their records are likely to have survived to modern times – more likely than family archives, more likely than the records of more transitory institutions and more likely than most monastic archives, which were usually broken up when the monasteries were shut down on the orders of Henry VIII in the sixteenth century.

It is easy to see why charters from great churches should survive, but, by any estimate, charters and great churches are special cases. Most categories of document did not have the same long-term utility; and most institutions were much less stable. Nevertheless, surviving writings can be found that were essentially ephemeral, and what is notable about them is that they survive by roundabout and improbable routes, which indicate something about the extensive destruction of records which archiving entails. For example, an early eleventh-century list survives which details items provided by the monks of Ely to the monks of Thorney for stocking their estates.[12] The matters with which it is concerned are relatively humble, for it deals with pigs by the dozen and sums of pennies, rather than great estates. It is written scrappily in four different hands, showing how the transaction between the two abbeys developed over time, and how far this was a real working document. And yet it survives by the most improbable means. It was cut up into sections, of which two were found in the binding of a sixteenth-century printed book; it has been conjectured that the list was first reused as a flyleaf for a medieval book before reaching the book trade in the sixteenth century. Clearly, this document was not intended for long-term preservation, as is apparent from its treatment and its form, but its later history shows how medieval institutions had a keen sense of how their archives needed to be managed, so that important items were kept carefully and others reused or destroyed. The

11 M. Winterbottom and R. M. Thomson, eds. and trans., *William of Malmesbury, Gesta pontificum Anglorum*, v: (2 vols.; OMT; Oxford, 2007), i, pp. 598–9.

12 J. Backhouse, D. H. Turner and L. Webster, eds., *The Golden Age of Anglo-Saxon Art, 966–1066* (London, 1984), p. 148, no. 150, with facsimile at p. 147. Transcription and translation in A. J. Robertson, *Anglo-Saxon Charters* (Cambridge, 1939), pp. 252–7, with notes at pp. 502–5.

Ely farming memoranda demonstrate the side of the process that is rarely seen elsewhere, so that it is very hard to see how much lost material may once have been comparable.

If certain kinds of record were likely to be destroyed, certain kinds of institution likewise were unlikely to preserve extensive archives. The most obvious case is that of the king's government, which preserved large amounts of material only from the second half of the twelfth century, when Pipe Rolls, judicial records and, at the very end of the century, chancery enrolments survive.[13] Before that, Domesday Book of course was preserved, but it is not clear whether there was much else besides. The king's government was not the only official maker of documents, however, even though it has had much – perhaps excessive – fascination for historians. Many of the most remarkable administrative records – such as the pre-Domesday assessments identified by Sally Harvey or the Northamptonshire geld roll[14] – seem rather to have originated in shire administration, which, after all, was responsible for most of the practical and mundane activities of government. What survives of shire documents has been preserved through its absorption into the archives of institutions which possessed more stable personnel, and more suitable facilities for preservation; that is, the great churches, which took copies of these records for their own purposes. It is only through such indirect means that evidence survives to illustrate the activities of the shire administrations, and it is notable that only a few great churches felt moved to obtain copies of such texts.

Throughout the tenth, eleventh and twelfth centuries, there are good indications that writing was used extensively for all kinds of business, and that archiving was undertaken in a thorough and organized manner. This involved not only the preservation of documents, which necessarily most impresses modern historians, but also the systematic destruction or reuse of vast amounts of writing. There may have been especially large-scale destruction in the later eleventh century, when after the Norman Conquest Latin supplanted English as the language of record, but the most significant developments in archiving that affected this period came later, when, from the end of the twelfth century, the king's government changed its own archiving practices, partly as a consequence

[13] N. Vincent, 'Why 1199? Bureaucracy and enrolment under John and his contemporaries', in A. Jobson, ed., *English Government in the Thirteenth Century* (Woodbridge, 2004), pp. 17–48.

[14] S. Harvey, 'Domesday Book and its predecessors', *EHR*, 86 (1971), 753–73; for the Northamptonshire geld roll see Robertson, *Anglo-Saxon Charters*, pp. 230–7, with notes at pp. 481–4.

of the new common law. Other institutions responded to this by reordering their own archives, a trend observable today in the great rise in cartulary-making from the end of the twelfth century onwards. A very large part of the extant evidence for England 900–1200 now survives through the reordered archives of that period, including a large proportion of the surviving legal and charter material from pre-Conquest England. In other words, records from this period were sifted in accordance with the priorities of a later age, so that it is now impossible to say what has been lost, what was once kept, or how far our reconstruction of the Anglo-Saxon past in particular has been skewed by the priorities of the Plantagenet age.

CHAPTER VI.3

Esoteric knowledge

Andy Orchard

The esoteric learning of England before 1200 is enshrined in an extensive manuscript record that, while it exhibits significant losses as a result of Viking depredations and later looting and loss, and if it appears dramatically broken-backed in its relative reflection of Latin and vernacular texts before and after the pivotal reign of King Alfred the Great (871–99), nonetheless demonstrates a consistent and continuing interest in hidden and obscure learning throughout the period. The fact that Aldhelm (who died in 709/10), writing in the late seventh century, should quote from an anonymous treatise on animal noises that also appears in a late-tenth-century manuscript, Cambridge, Trinity College, MS O. 1. 18 (1042), with strong associations with Archbishop Dunstan of Canterbury (who died in 988),[1] is as pertinent in this regard as that Dunstan should also be directly linked with a composite manuscript, Oxford, Bodleian Library, Auctarium F.4.32 (2176), that contains, alongside material in Breton and Welsh, notes on weights and measures in Greek and Latin, a runic alphabet and an extract from Ovid's *Ars amatoria* (Art of love).[2] The *Ars amatoria* is otherwise attested (likely second-hand!) by Bede, who died in 735, by Wulfstan of Winchester (who died early in the eleventh century) and by a further manuscript from early England, namely Paris, Bibliothèque Sainte-Geneviève, MS 2410 (a Canterbury manuscript from around the year 1000), which contains two lines alongside an odd catch-all collection

[1] The manuscript also contains on fols. 112v–113r an acrostic–telestic, in which the first letters of each line read, as does the first line, 'O PATER OMNIPOTENS, DIGNERIS FERRE DONANTI' ('O all-powerful father, may you deign to bring [rewards] to the dedicator [of this poem]'), while the final letters of each line read 'INDIGNVM ABBATEM DVNSTANVM XPE RESPECTES' ('Christ, may you respect the unworthy Abbot Dunstan'). The poem can be dated to the period of Dunstan's abbacy (940–*c.* 957). For further connections between Dunstan and Aldhelm's learning, see below, p. 387. See further M. Lapidge, *Anglo-Latin Literature, 900–1066* (London and Rio Grande, OH, 1993), pp. 133–5, 146–9.

[2] For more on both these manuscripts, see H. Gneuss, *Handlist of Anglo-Saxon Manuscripts. A List of Manuscripts and Manuscript Fragments Written or Owned in England up to 1100* (Tempe, AZ, 2001), nos. 188 and 538.

of diverse lore (including works by the poets Juvencus, Caelius Sedulius, Odo of Cluny and Alcuin, as well as, for example, a Greek litany and *Sanctus*, Greek numbers in Latin letters and a poem on the Four Keys of Wisdom) that characterizes the comprehensiveness of early English interests.[3]

Seen in this light, what at first might seem oddities, such as London, BL, MS Cotton Vespasian B. vi, fols. 1–103, a manuscript that mainly contains a text of Bede's *De temporum ratione*, to which has been added lists of Carolingian rulers and Byzantine emperors, while written in France in the second quarter of the ninth century, was certainly in Anglo-Saxon England by the beginning of the eleventh century; to this base manuscript has been added in modern times fols. 104–9, a hodgepodge of material from Mercia that can be closely dated to 805×14 and contains a series of notes on such diverse subjects as the Ages of the World and the Ages of Man, on the human body and the dimensions of the world, the Temple of Solomon, the Tabernacle, St Peter's in Rome, Noah's Ark, on the books of the Bible and on measurements of length, together with lists of popes, Christ's seventy disciples, Anglo-Saxon bishops and Anglian royal genealogies.[4] Similarly diverse interests are evident in a manuscript from the Winchester New Minster that can again be closely dated, this time to the period 1023×31 (London, BL, MS Cotton Titus D. xxvi and xxvii), which again in the context of a book of calendrical lore (in this case the Old English *De temporibus anni* by Ælfric) provides various notes in both Latin and Old English, including one in code, on such subjects as the names of the Seven Sleepers, the age of the Virgin Mary, the Ages of the World, the length of Christ's body, the rainbow, together with prognostics, a version of the celebrated *Somniale Danielis* (The dream-book of Daniel) and a medical recipe.[5] Indeed, it has been noted the extent to which prognostic texts in late Anglo-Saxon manuscripts often kept eclectic and (to modern eyes) surprising company.[6] It was precisely such an outward-looking pre-Conquest magpie mentality that set the stage for the consolidation of learning and lore from all quarters that is the hallmark of the twelfth-century renaissance in knowledge and appreciation of both classical and Arabic texts.

If Anglo-Saxons and their counterparts immediately after the Norman Conquest found themselves exercised by such nuggets as the number and

[3] Gneuss, *Handlist*, no. 903. [4] Gneuss, *Handlist*, nos. 384 and 385.

[5] Gneuss, *Handlist*, no. 380.

[6] R. M. Liuzza, 'Anglo-Saxon prognostics in context: a survey and handlist of manuscripts', *ASE*, 30 (2001), 180–230.

type of elements that went into the making of Adam (and his height and age when first formed), the number and form of the 'victories of the wind', the best way to get rid of a 'night-walker', the use of cryptography and different scripts to communicate clandestinely, the significance of dreams and visions, the most detailed description of a hippopotamus, the most efficient way to kill an elephant (or a rhinoceros, come to that, also known as a *unicornis*) on the one hand and on the other how to tackle an unruly dwarf or an aggravated elf or a supernatural sexual predator, the meanings and powers of various precious gems, then the solutions all survive at the edges of what is commonly considered the mainstream and most-studied texts of the period.[7] At the same time, what might have seemed enticing and portentous mumbo-jumbo in the context of an Anglo-Saxon spell can turn out to be embarrassingly obvious when it is realized that it is just ordinary Irish, or in a simple substitution-cipher (with most commonly vowels represented by the following consonant), and the activities of generations of commentators and glossators can make the mundane seem seriously monstrous.[8] A good example of the latter is found in the so-called Harley glossary (written around the year 1000), where in a distant echo of the Catiline conspiracies in Rome of the first century BC, the key players, Lentulus, Cinna and Sulla, find themselves, through confusion of the last-named with the monstrous and man-eating Scylla, linked with the dreadful man-slaying whirlpool Charybdis. In all these cases, what is at stake is knowledge of the world outside, the world beyond, a world of shadows and obscurity and esoteric or privileged information, and the avid collection and transmission and preservation of such oddities and arcana in England over the more than half a millennium that separates the earliest English texts from the close of the thirteenth century of itself bears potent witness to an intellectual curiosity that Viking raids and successive conquests by their heirs, the Danes and Normans, could not dim.

[7] See in general G. Storms, *Anglo-Saxon Magic* (The Hague, 1948); J. E. Cross, 'The elephant to Alfred, Ælfric, Aldhelm and others', *Studia Neophilologica*, 37 (1965), 367–73; N. Kiessling, *The Incubus in English Literature: Provenance and Progeny* (Washington, DC, 1977); P. Kitson, 'Lapidary traditions in Anglo-Saxon England: I, The background; the Old English Lapidary', *ASE*, 7 (1978), 9–60; P. Kitson, 'Lapidary traditions in Anglo-Saxon England: II, Bede's *Explanatio Apocalypsis* and related works', *ASE*, 12 (1983), 73–123; P. Dinzelbacher, *Vision und Visionsliteratur im Mittelalter* (Stuttgart, 1981); M. Bayless and M. Lapidge, eds., *Collectanea Pseudo-Bedae* (Scriptores Latini Hiberniae 14; Dublin, 1998); Liuzza, 'Anglo-Saxon prognostics'; A. Orchard, *Pride and Prodigies: Studies in the Monsters of the 'Beowulf' Manuscript* (rev. edn; Toronto, 2003); and A. Hall, *Elves in Anglo-Saxon England* (Woodbridge, 2007).

[8] See further H. Meroney, 'Irish in the OE Charms', *Speculum*, 20 (1945), 172–82 and (for an extremely sceptical view) R. I. Page, 'Anglo Saxon runes and magic', *Journal of the Archaeological Association*, 27 (1964), 14–31.

Early English knowledge of the outside world both literally and metaphysically was shaped by the triple influence of Ireland, the continental mainland and the more exotic sources to be found further south and east. As an island in the northwest, acutely conscious of its position at the extremities of the then-known world, and to some extent envious of Ireland's ability to circumvent the direct connection to Francia by striking south to Spain, and so North Africa and even sunnier sources still further south, in Anglo-Saxon England (and its reflex after the Conquest, when Continental influence was rather vigorously enforced), the thirst for knowledge, especially hidden knowledge, was always profound. Even *Cædmon's Hymn*, often regarded as the earliest English composition, contains in one of its two main versions a nod to the widely circulating Hebrew etymology of Adam as *eorðe* ('earth'), as mediated through Latin sources (where it appears as *terra*).[9] Other Hebrew etymologies, often showing the influence of Jerome's interpretations, appear more or less casually in Anglo-Saxon literature, but explain why, for example, the poet of the perhaps eighth-century poem *Daniel* (preserved in the so-called Junius manuscript (Oxford, Bodleian Library, MS Junius 11, written around the year 1000)) should be so keen to alliterate the name of his eponymous hero with the noun *dom* ('judgement') no fewer than six of the eleven times it appears, so signalling his awareness of Jerome's explanation of Daniel's name as *iudicium dei* ('the judgement of God').[10] A further mark of early English interest in expanding their biblical studies is their intense use of and interest in texts that were commonly labelled as deuterocanonical or apocryphal, and which were certainly not all approved by the most authoritative Church Fathers.[11]

In assessing the roots of the arcane and abstruse knowledge available in early Anglo-Saxon England, the twin evidence of Aldhelm (who died in 709/10) and Bede (who died in 735), both of whose works were widely known up to 1200, is key, since it addresses issues of education and influence from very different perspectives. Aldhelm, with his close connections to the royal families of both Wessex and Northumbria, had the benefit of both travelling to Rome and being educated twice, first under heavy Irish

[9] For Hebrew etymologies in the period in general, see M. Thiel, *Grundlagen und Gestalt der Hebräischkenntnisse des frühen Mittelalters* (Spoleto, 1973).

[10] R. F. Farrell, ed., *'Daniel' and 'Azarias'* (London, 1974); Daniel is named in lines **150**, 158, **163**, 168, 481, **531**, **547**, 593, **654**, **661** and 735 (lines in **bold** include the word '*dom*'). Aldhelm also knows of the etymology and mentions it when introducing Daniel in his prose *De uirginitate* (R. Ehwald, ed., *Aldhelmi Opera* (Monumenta Germaniae Historica Auctores Antiquissimi 15; Munich, 1919), p. 250/20).

[11] See further F. M. Biggs, ed., *Sources of Anglo-Saxon Literary Culture: The Apocrypha* (Instrumenta Anglistica Mediaevalia 1; Kalamazoo, MI, 2007).

influence at Malmesbury and quite probably Iona, and then at Canterbury by Archbishop Theodore, a Greek-speaking monk from Tarsus, and his friend and helper Abbot Hadrian, a skilled Latinist from North Africa.[12] Between them, Theodore and Hadrian founded a school that was the envy of the west, and had young Anglo-Saxons speaking Greek and Latin as fluently as their own language, according to the admiring witness of Bede himself (*Historia ecclesiastica gentis Anglorum* IV.1–2 and V.8).[13] Bede's own education at first seems distinctly insular, since there is no evidence that he ever left the monastery at Monkwearmouth-Jarrow, but it is evident that he had access to a very substantial library, evidently based on the extraordinary activity of its founder and first abbot, Benedict Biscop (who died in 689).[14] According to Bede's own account (*Historia abbatum* 1–13), Benedict was a frequent visitor to Rome and an avid collector of books; at all accounts, it has been estimated that Bede had access to more than 300 different texts (not counting biblical and liturgical books, but distinguishing individual passions of martyrs), all of which have left traces in his writings, although given the difficulties of demonstrating direct acquaintance, such ball-park figures should be used with caution.[15]

Where Bede is often extremely careful to cite and label his sources, Aldhelm, working further south and with a very different social and educational background, is more cavalier. While Bede favours orthodox authority, Aldhelm rarely relies on more than one source for long, preferring instead to revel in knowledge of texts that his Northumbrian counterpart would surely have seen as beyond the pale. Bede's corpus of known writings dwarfs that of Aldhelm, and his range of reference is much greater, but it is Aldhelm's reading, in so far as it can be measured by citations and allusions generally unparalleled elsewhere, that is truly striking: unlike Bede's often slavish reliance on these giants, Aldhelm echoes Jerome and Isidore in a very small number of very obvious places, nods towards Augustine briefly and in a cursory manner, notices Gregory even less and seems to ignore Ambrose almost completely. For

[12] M. Lapidge, 'The career of Aldhelm', *ASE*, 36 (2007), 15–69.

[13] B. Colgrave and R. A. B. Mynors, eds., *Bede's Ecclesiastical History of the English People* (Oxford, 1969); B. Bischoff and M. Lapidge, eds., *Biblical Commentaries from the Canterbury School of Theodore and Hadrian* (Cambridge Studies in Anglo-Saxon England 10; Cambridge, 1994); M. Lapidge, ed., *Archbishop Theodore: Commemorative Studies on His Life and Influence* (Cambridge Studies in Anglo-Saxon England 11; Cambridge, 1995); M. Lapidge, *Anglo-Latin Literature, 600–899* (London and Rio Grande, OH, 1996), pp. 93–168.

[14] See further P. Wormald, 'Bede and Benedict Biscop', in G. Bonner, ed., *Famulus Christi: Essays in Commemoration of the Thirteenth Centenary of the Birth of the Venerable Bede* (London, 1976), pp. 141–69.

[15] M. Lapidge, *The Anglo-Saxon Library* (Oxford, 2006), pp. 198–228.

Aldhelm, it is the poets who capture his imagination, and (again unlike Bede) he is not overly fussy about the frankly pagan provenance of some of his favoured authors: Aldhelm echoes and quotes not only the same Christian-Latin and classical poets noted above as Bede (with the more exotic additions of, for example, Corippus, Damasus, Ennius, Lucretius, Paulinus of Périgueux, Proba and Seneca, and Symphosius), but makes fuller and more frequent use of his prodigious poetic palette (Vergil, Caelius Sedulius, Venantius Fortunatus, Juvencus, Arator, Symphosius and parts of Ovid's *Metamorphoses* being particular favourites, it seems), even to the point of including such rarities as verses from Andreas Orator, Paulus Quaestor and Sisebut, the king of the Visigoths, as well as from the now-lost *Orpheus* attributed to Lucan, for each of whom Aldhelm's quotation is an important early witness.[16] Indeed, it is precisely the rarity of some of these citations that connects Aldhelm with some of the more curious texts from the early medieval period, such as the anonymous so-called *Liber monstrorum* (Book of monsters), which may indeed have been written by one of his students, or the extraordinary *Cosmographia* attributed to one Aethicus Ister; both these oddities also share an interest in the exotic travel literature associated with Alexander the Great that becomes a feature of several texts and collectors in early England, including the Old English *Letter of Alexander to Aristotle* and *Wonders of the East* that both feature in the so-called *Beowulf*-manuscript (London, BL, MS, Cotton Vitellius A. xv), written around 1000, as well as London, BL, MS, Royal 13. A. i, written around 1200, but which focuses exclusively on texts to do with Alexander.[17]

Aldhelm was first educated at Malmesbury and likely Iona, with a profoundly Irish influence on his teaching that is evident not only from his association with the works of Virgilius Maro Grammaticus (like Bede), but also with the poem 'Altus prosator' attributed to Columba and the bizarre collection of texts that modern editors have styled the *Hisperica famina* (a translation such as 'West-like speakifications' would almost capture the strangeness of the original).[18] But the coming of Theodore and Hadrian and the establishment of their school at Canterbury had a profound effect on Aldhelm, who promptly went back to school, learned subjects he had never known in such detail (he singles out metrics, law

[16] A. Orchard, *The Poetic Art of Aldhelm* (Cambridge Studies in Anglo-Saxon England 8; Cambridge, 1994), pp. 126–238; Lapidge, *The Anglo-Saxon Library*, pp. 178–91.

[17] Orchard, *Pride and Prodigies*, pp. 86–139, 173–320.

[18] See further A. Orchard, 'The *Hisperica famina* as literature', *Journal of Medieval Latin*, 10 (2000), 1–45.

and astrology), and proceeded to disparage what he had learnt before. Some of the odder elements in Aldhelm's list of known sources can be traced directly back to Canterbury, including his close acquaintance with the 100 *Enigmata* (Riddles) of Symphosius, a North African poet, knowledge of whose works was surely brought to England by the North African Hadrian. Symphosius's (nick-)name means 'banquet boy' or 'party animal', and his three-line *Enigmata*, allegedly composed in the course of an extended drinking-party, influenced Aldhelm and later generations of Anglo-Saxons to produce riddles in both Latin and Old English of their own; it is doubtful that without Symphosius we would now recognize one of the *Exeter Book* riddles as having the solution 'one-eyed garlic seller' (it is a pity that we no longer have vernacular versions of other *Enigmata* by Symphosius with the solutions 'gouty soldier' and 'tight-rope walker', respectively).[19] Another clear symptom of Aldhelm's schooling seems to be his echoing of the so-called *Versus sibyllae de iudicio* (Verses of the sibyl on judgement), a Latin rendering, likely produced in Anglo-Saxon England, of a Greek acrostic that Theodore may well have introduced. The fact that Theodore's epitaph, partly quoted by Bede, has so many connections to Aldhelm's own work (he may indeed have composed it), only ties him the more closely to the Canterbury school.

The combined legacy of learning of both Aldhelm and Bede for early England is immeasurable, conflating as it did elements from Latin teachings in Ireland and the Continent and more exotic material from the Greek-speaking world, and through the good offices of such enterprising Anglo-Saxons as Boniface (who died in 755) and Alcuin (who died in 804) this legacy was carried to the Continent, whence it could be brought back to England in the tenth and eleventh centuries, once the ferocity of the Viking raids died down. Such a route of transmission is particularly clear in the case of Aldhelm's assertion on uncertain authority that Satan utters the word *puppup*, a term echoed on the Continent by Hrabanus Maurus (d. 856), a student of Alcuin, and in England by Archbishop Dunstan (d. 988), who like many of the instigators of the so-called Benedictine reform both spent time on the Continent and was swayed by Continental influence. Dunstan's own hand has been identified as that of Scribe D in Oxford, Bodleian Library, MS Rawlinson C. 697, a manuscript written in Francia in the late ninth century, and in England by the mid-tenth

[19] A. Orchard, 'Enigma variations: the Anglo-Saxon riddle-tradition', in K. O'Brien O'Keeffe and A. Orchard, eds., *Latin Learning and English Lore: Studies in Anglo-Saxon Literature for Michael Lapidge* (2 vols.; Toronto, 2005), i, 284–304.

century, and which contains not only Aldhelm's prose and verse *De uirginitate* (including the word *puppup* in the acrostic–telestic preface to the verse version) his *Enigmata* (Riddles), as well as the distinctly arcane *Versus cuiusdam Scotti de alfabeto* (Verses on the alphabet by a certain Irishman), which seem verbally indebted to the *Enigmata* of both Aldhelm and Symphosius,[20] the *Psychomachia* (Battle of the soul) by Prudentius and an obscure acrostic–telestic poem in praise of King Æthelstan (who ruled 924/25–39), formerly attributed to John the Old Saxon (one of the scholars King Alfred, Æthelstan's grandfather, brought in to assist with his programme of educational reform), since the first letters of each line spell out ADALSTAN and the last letters spell out IOHANNES.[21]

Æthelstan was an avid collector of books and relics (including the sword of Constantine and the lance of Charlemagne, according to William of Malmesbury, the place where Æthelstan, who had a special fondness for the place, was buried), with a deeply international perspective: much traffic between Ireland and Brittany is attested, as well as with Scandinavia (King Hákon of Norway was his foster-son, and the Icelander Egill Skallagrímsson composed a poem in his honour that he may have recited in his presence). As Æthelstan extended his grasp much further than anything Alfred envisaged, he set his sights well beyond that of the traditional homeland of Wessex. Given such an international and intellectually curious background, it is perhaps unsurprising that several obscure and difficult texts showing a keen interest in arcane knowledge have been associated with both Æthelstan's reign and Dunstan's time, including the so-called *Dialogues of Solomon and Saturn* that exist in various versions in both prose and verse (with Solomon and Saturn representing biblical, which is to say Judaeo-Christian, lore and the 'false' learning of the classical world, respectively) and the extraordinary compilation of biblical and other lore attributed to Bede (who would surely have disowned it) and now known as the *Pseudo-Bede Collectanea*, which also includes *Enigmata* by both Aldhelm and

[20] Apart from clear verbal reminiscences in the *Versus cuiusdam Scotti de alfabeto* to the *Enigmata* of both Symphosius and Aldhelm, it is worth noting that each of the stanzas on separate letters of the alphabet is three lines long, as are each of the *Enigmata* of Symphosius, a scheme that is also echoed in the Old English *Rune Poem* from the now-burned portion of the eleventh-century manuscript, London, British Library, Cotton Otho B. x (as well as in, for example, the *Icelandic Rune Poem*).

[21] See Lapidge, *Anglo-Latin Literature, 900–1066*, pp. 60–71; for a different view, see G. R. Wieland, 'A new look at the poem "Archalis clamare triumuir"', in G. R. Wieland, C. Ruff and R. G. Arthur, eds., *'Insignis, sophiae arcator': Medieval Latin Studies in Honour of Michael Herren on His 65th Birthday* (Publications of the Journal of Medieval Latin 6; Turnhout, 2006), pp. 178–92.

Symphosius.[22] A related but likely later Old English text, also a dialogue found in a late eleventh- or twelfth-century manuscript, is now known as *Adrian and Ritheus*, but in fact represents a rendering of an original Latin series of forty-eight questions and answers put in the mouths, of the Roman emperor Hadrian and the Greek philosopher Epictetus respectively.[23] All these texts offer the same combination of Irish (mostly Hiberno-Latin), Continental and English sources found so prevalently in the pre-Alfredian tradition, suitably augmented and accreted.

Early English interest in prophetic and magico-medical texts is also well attested, with some of the seeming mumbo-jumbo to be uttered in the latter, often mangled in transmission, turning out to be simply Irish, Greek or Hebrew (a further indication of the elevated status of languages recognized in England as being in some way 'learned').[24] Many of the charms in both prose and verse that survive incorporate both words and actions in forms that can traced on the one hand to Christian ceremony, and on the other to folk belief and deliberate mystification; few true signs of what might be termed 'pagan' religious practices have been certainly identified. Still more exotic was knowledge of the Arab world, which in Anglo-Saxon England was limited, but far from absent altogether: the golden Kufic coin minted by King Offa of Mercia (who ruled 757–96), with its representations of Qu'ranic verses alongside an Islamic date AH 157 (AD 774) was presumably intended as a declaration of wider aspirations.[25] The post-Conquest period is often seen as an ascendency of Norman functionalism and anti-intellectualism, but in fact the Normans necessarily also instigated and encouraged an English engagement with the outside world. Among the many extraordinary authors who sparked a twelfth-century renaissance of learning was Adelard of Bath (*c.* 1080–*c.* 1152), who travelled widely and acted as midwife for many Arabic texts and translations of Greek works into English, introducing a number of then extraordinary concepts (such as the Arabic numerical system) that we now take for granted.[26]

Indeed, the increasing internationalism of Anglo-Saxon England was in the end the agent of its own demise: when King Æthelred (who ruled

[22] See now D. Anlezark, ed. and trans., *The Old English Dialogues of Solomon and Saturn* (Anglo-Saxon Texts 7; Cambridge, 2009); Bayless and Lapidge, eds., *Collectanea Pseudo-Bedae*.

[23] J. E. Cross and T. D. Hill, eds., *The 'Prose Solomon and Saturn' and 'Adrian and Ritheus'* (Toronto, 1982).

[24] Meroney, 'Irish in the OE charms'; Storms, *Anglo-Saxon Magic*.

[25] K. Scarfe Beckett, *Anglo-Saxon Perceptions of the Islamic World* (Cambridge Studies in Anglo-Saxon England 33; Cambridge, 2003).

[26] C. Burnett, *Adelard of Bath: An English Scientist and Arabist of the Early Twelfth Century* (London, 1987).

978–1016, with a period of exile from 1013–14 intervening) married the young Emma of Normandy, he sowed the seeds of a Conquest still to come, and when in the St Brice's Day Massacre of Friday, 13 November 1002 he is said to have attempted to purge England of the contamination of Danes (read Norse settlers, for discussion see Chapter IV.1), he succeeded only in antagonizing King Svein Forkbeard of Denmark, whose sister Gunhild was among the slaughtered, and who promptly invaded in 1003–4 alongside his young son Cnut, who would eventually acquire both England and Emma. The scene was thus set for the calamitous events of 1066 when Normandy and Norway vied for England, and England lost.

Events after the Conquest moved with a bewildering rapidity, as Arthur replaced Alexander the Great as the monster-slayer *par excellence*, and hard-won experience and travel to the Holy Land meant that the Saracens substituted for the Vikings as *bêtes noires* and objects of especial distaste. In much the same way, the eleventh and twelfth centuries saw a dramatic increase in interest in the other-world, whether mediated by visions of the afterlife or in an increase in popular piety. England, particularly Anglo-Saxon England, is often seen as peculiarly or reprehensibly insular, but in fact ever since the English arrived in the fifth century, their collective gaze was generally elsewhere. When Alfred the Great died in 899, he had on the one hand welcomed foreign scholars and expertise from beyond his own borders, and on the other reached a settlement with Viking raiders, traders and invaders that set the seal on English identity for generations to come. Over the period 900–1200, England came of age: the world that was once outside became one that had penetrated fully into the consciousness (and national borders!) of a nation that was itself only emerging into being after Alfred's death. Likewise the mysterious and the magical had through proliferation and repetition come to seem mostly mundane, part of a backdrop to romance and legend, more or less literary or antiquarian survivals of an age that was itself becoming more romanticized by twelfth-century historians and authors for whom Old England and ancient Britain before it had become increasingly mythical. By the time such writers as William of Malmesbury (*c.* 1080/95–*c.* 1143), Henry of Huntingdon (*c.* 1080–1160), Geoffrey of Monmouth (*c.* 1100–*c.* 55), Walter Map (1140–*c.* 1210) and Gerald of Wales (*c.* 1146–*c.* 1223) had had their say,[27] nothing seemed truly surprising or even unlikely, and the unfamiliar had come firmly home to stay.

[27] For thumbnail sketches of all these authors, see A. G. Rigg, *A History of Anglo-Latin Literature 1066–1422* (Cambridge, 1992), pp. 34–40, 41–7, 88–96.

CHAPTER VI.4

Medical practice and theory

Carole Rawcliffe

The practice of medicine in England before the late twelfth century and the theoretical assumptions that underpinned it have been subject to a comprehensive process of reassessment over the last three decades, with the result that sources formerly regarded as little more than 'magic gibberish' are now viewed in a far more positive light. Charles Singer's often-quoted dismissal of Anglo-Saxon medicine as the 'final pathological disintegration' of a once-great classical tradition was largely based upon his reading of Oswald Cockayne's influential edition of the principal medical texts of the tenth century.[1] Produced in the 1860s with a lengthy introduction that emphasized the 'superstitious' and 'irrational' element of works such as Bald's *Leechbook* and *The Old English Herbarium*, Cockayne's idiosyncratic and often inaccurate translations were embellished with archaisms designed to make them appear even more outlandish and primitive.[2] It is thus hardly surprising that, with a few exceptions, subsequent generations of medical historians tended to regard the years between 900 and 1150 as a dark age, when links with both the classical past and current intellectual developments on the Continent were lost through ignorance, and when healing was largely subsumed into folklore.

By returning to the original manuscript sources and the shared body of knowledge whence they sprang, more recent research presents a radically different picture of the intellectual *milieu* in which their compilers functioned. Far from being a stagnant backwater divorced from the rest of Europe, tenth- and eleventh-century England possessed centres of medical learning where Latin texts could be collected, translated into the vernacular and glossed as part of a coherent and well-organized project for the spread of accessible information among a lay as well as a clerical audience.

[1] J. H. G. Grattan and Charles Singer, *Anglo Saxon Magic and Medicine* (Oxford, 1952), p. 94.

[2] Anne Van Arsdall, *Medieval Herbal Remedies: The Old English Herbarium and Anglo-Saxon Medicine* (London and New York, 2002), chs. 1 and 2.

Figure 17 The use of cauteries illustrated in an early twelfth-century English manuscript owned by the monks of Durham.
Durham Cathedral Library, MS Hunter 100, fol. 119r; published by kind permission of Durham Cathedral

It has, for instance, been suggested that *The Old English Herbarium* and a companion text on the use of remedies from animals together represent a unique and highly original attempt to produce a common, working pharmacopoeia which could, where necessary, be modified in light of practical experience. The expert translators benefited from the close connections that bound English Benedictine houses, such as Winchester and Canterbury, to monasteries on the Continent, giving ready access to their libraries and scriptoria.[3]

The work of botanists and anthropologists has likewise prompted a sweeping reappraisal of the proficiency of medieval healers. It is now widely acknowledged that any system of therapeutics based largely on herbal remedies will rely heavily at all levels upon oral communication and practical demonstration, whereby expertise is passed from master to apprentice in an essentially 'hands-on' fashion. Textual information, although useful, will thus serve more as an *aide memoire*, or as a source of supplementary knowledge, and its authors may, by the same token, assume a relatively high level of expertise on the part of the reader. Far from reflecting their authors' ignorance or confusion, the terse, seemingly imprecise instructions for the preparation of most medicinal recipes in Old English manuscripts are, in fact, indicative of a society in which empirical skill generally developed independently of literary transmission. As the revered Greek physician Galen (d. 216) had observed, 'the best method of learning about drugs is by going out into the field, not through books'.[4]

Nor did recourse to the occult loom as large as was previously supposed. Some ostensibly 'superstitious' procedures for the collection and preparation of plants clearly had a sound practical basis. Thus, for example, instructions for the gathering of vervain on Midsummer Day reflect the fact that this particular herb will have just begun to flower, and will therefore be at its freshest and most efficacious, while prohibitions on the use of iron when processing certain plants indicate an awareness of the potentially harmful effects of ferrous metal on delicate roots and leaves. Investigation into the 'verifiable use' of specific herbs reveals, moreover, that a long-standing preoccupation with the magical elements of medieval medical practice has led historians to underestimate

[3] M. A. D'Aronco, 'Gardens on vellum: plants and herbs in Anglo-Saxon manuscripts', in Peter Dendle and Alain Touwaide, eds., *Health and Healing from the Medieval Garden* (Woodbridge, 2008), pp. 101–27.

[4] J. M. Riddle, 'Theory and practice in medieval medicine', *Viator*, 5 (1974), 159–84, at p. 165.

the physiological benefits involved. When prepared by a skilled herbalist, some remedies may well have ameliorated distressing symptoms. M. L. Cameron has estimated that, of the 186 plants itemized in *The Old English Herbarium*, at least 130 are still in medicinal use today, generally for the same purpose, as carminatives, contraceptives, diuretics, laxatives and so forth.[5]

By separating the 'rational' from the 'magical', and concentrating almost exclusively upon what are now deemed to be the scientifically valid aspects of specific procedures, historians nonetheless run the risk of adopting as narrow and anachronistic an approach as the one they seek to correct. Irrespective of whether they worked in a strictly biomedical sense, many remedies were valued because they appeared to harness the miraculous potential of particular plants and animals. As every practitioner knew, the efficacy of certain herbs would depend upon the ritual prayer, incantation or blessing that unlocked their God-given power. Remedies employing the body parts of animals such as rams, hares, swallows or boars might likewise seek to transmit through the forces of sympathetic magic the remarkable fertility, speed, sharp eyesight or strength for which these creatures were celebrated. In a dangerous and uncertain world charms, amulets and folkloric practices offered a measure of reassurance against the onslaught of disease that conventional medicine simply could not provide. The hazards of pregnancy and childbirth, the debilitating effects of diarrhoea and fever and the scourge of pestilence demanded special measures, more often than not invoking the support of celestial agents.

The teeming medical marketplace that operated in medieval England has often been described in terms of a 'hierarchy of resort', generally beginning in the home and progressing upwards through the ranks of herbalists, bone-setters, teeth-drawers, astrologers, wise-women, midwives, druggists and leeches until the patient reached the higher rungs of the profession in the person of the physician or surgeon. Since most of these individuals were illiterate and acquired their skills through the empirical processes described above, we know very little about them. Partly for this reason, research on the period between 900 and 1200 has concentrated upon medical provision in monastic houses and at the royal court, although it is important to stress that expertise was certainly not confined to these comparatively well-documented places. Fleeting references to

[5] M. A. D'Aronco and M. L. Cameron, *The Old English Illustrated Pharmacopoeia* (Copenhagen, 1998), pp. 61–4.

such figures as the Jewish physician who was killed by a mob at Bishop's Lynn in 1190, despite the admiration accorded him as a healer, reveal how much of the iceberg still lies hidden below the water line. Evidence of women's practice, in particular, remains elusive, and, when it survives, is often mediated through the voice of male writers who are at best dismissive of their skill or contemptuous of their resort to charms and incantations. An analysis of Old English gynaecological texts reveals, however, that a significant number of practical herbal remedies were devoted to childbirth, fertility and female maladies, being the product of a specifically female, and thus mainly oral, tradition.[6]

There can, on the other hand, be no doubt of the Church's dominant place in the hierarchy of resort, and of the unquestioning belief in the innate superiority of spiritual therapeutics over care for the human body with its manifest frailties and imperfections. What price the attainment of robust physical health if one's soul were consumed by disease? All too aware of the limitations of earthly medicine, chroniclers praised physicians who used their prognosticatory skills to prepare the patient for a 'good' death, so that he or she could expire in a state of grace. To a modern reader such conduct smacks of defeatism, whereas to their contemporaries these men demonstrated a proper subservience to divine will. Yet, notwithstanding the reservations expressed in some quarters about the impiety of attempting to cure those whom God had decided to test or punish, the assumption that the Church proved hostile or resistant to conventional medical practice requires considerable qualification. In the first place, Christ's obvious concern for the sick and physically disabled cast him in the role of a good physician, or *medicus*, whose selfless dedication to his patients provided a model for others. Significantly, the Rule of St Benedict (d. 550) enjoined those in authority to act as wise physicians, who might even resort to amputation in order to preserve the health of the community. In its stipulation that 'above all things care must be taken of the sick, so that they may be served in the very deed as Christ Himself', the Rule not only sanctioned the provision of medical facilities in monastic houses but also, implicitly, the study of relevant literature and the transmission of knowledge to others.[7]

On first reading, the lives of saints and the accounts of their healing miracles that proliferated between 900 and 1200 convey an impression

[6] Marijane Osborn, 'Anglo-Saxon ethnobotany: women's reproductive medicine in *Leechbook III*', in Dendle and Touwaide, eds., *Health and Healing*, pp. 145–61.

[7] Justin McCann, ed., *The Rule of St Benedict* (London, 1952), p. 258.

of distrust towards earthly practitioners, since so many cures reflect their powerlessness, if not overt incompetence and greed. The tale of the Oxford boy left as a corpse on his parents' table after the surgeon had fled in the middle of a bungled operation, or of the sacristan of Norwich Cathedral, who was struck down by St William for placing all his trust in the medical profession, certainly suggest a degree of antagonism on the part of twelfth-century hagiographers, especially towards those monks who foolishly 'sought refuge in the deceits of medicine'.[8] Yet the same men were anxious to display their newly acquired medical knowledge, and in the privacy of the monastic infirmary would almost certainly have benefited from the best attention that money could buy. William of Canterbury, one of Thomas Becket's first publicists, was clearly familiar with recent literature on the aetiology of disease, even citing Galen and other classical authorities when it suited his purpose. A growing interest in deontology (medical ethics and etiquette) reflects the fact that priests, as 'physicians of the soul', felt they had much to learn from their earthly counterparts. It is, moreover, apparent that many of the sick pilgrims who flocked to healing shrines benefited from a range of physical treatment that may well have accounted for their improved health. Medicinal baths, a routine prophylactic which relieved pain, as well as treating a number of skin conditions, seem to have been widely available. The biographer of Bishop Wulfstan of Worcester (d. 1095) provides an interesting account of one miracle performed by the saint but more probably attributable to the dramatic effects of the bath which one of his attendants gave to a filthy leper.[9]

Some unease still remained among the ecclesiastical elite, as we can see from the career of the renowned Italian physician Faritius, who became abbot of Abingdon in 1100. Having attended Queen Matilda's first confinement and gained her support, he established a lucrative practice among the Anglo-Norman elite, which marks him out as precursor of the successful society physician of later centuries. His easy charm, elegant manners and erudition (so necessary in an age when it was essential to win the confidence of the patient) did not, however, meet with universal approval. He was apparently denied the archbishopric of Canterbury because some of his critics considered it unseemly that 'a man who spent his time examining the urine of women' should hold such an exalted office.[10]

[8] Augustus Jessopp and M. R. James, eds., *Thomas of Monmouth, The Life and Miracles of St William of Norwich*, (Cambridge, 1896), pp. 174–7.

[9] Carole Rawcliffe, *Leprosy in Medieval England* (Woodbridge, 2006), pp. 171, 229–30.

[10] See C. H. Talbot and E. A. Hammond, *The Medical Practitioners in Medieval England: A Biographical Register* (London, 1965) for brief biographies of the practitioners discussed here.

Despite these reservations, some of England's most celebrated healers were Benedictines. Abbot Baldwin of Bury St Edmunds was initially summoned to England from Alsace by Edward the Confessor, who engaged him as his personal *medicus*. Having then been called to the bedside of the ailing Abbot Leofstan of Bury, he evidently impressed the monks so much that in 1065 they chose him to succeed the dying man. This was clearly a wise decision, as after the Conquest members of the Norman aristocracy, including the new king and Archbishop Lanfranc, sought to retain his professional services. His popularity may, in part, have been due to his remarkable skill in both medicine and surgery, for he was adept in the use of cauteries, which served to burn off infected or damaged skin, and were potentially lethal instruments. Surgical procedures were generally attempted as a last resort because of the pain, the risk of haemorrhage and the likelihood of post-operative complications. One of the posthumous miracles of St Edmund describes Baldwin's consummate expertise (guided by the celestial hand) in healing a serious eye injury, which, we are told, not even Hippocrates or Galen could have attempted. It was perhaps under his aegis that the Bury scriptorium produced the magnificent Latin herbal, now in the Bodleian Library, Oxford, which testifies to the interest in medicine long apparent in English monasteries.

Like other monk-physicians who combined high ecclesiastical office with a lucrative practice, Baldwin and Faritius ploughed much of their wealth back into monastic building projects, but others may have been less scrupulous. Fear that members of religious orders might be tempted 'to promise health in return for detestable money' prompted a series of ecclesiastical rulings in the 1130s, prohibiting monks and regular canons from the study of medicine for crude material gain. Often misunderstood by medical historians, these regulations did not curtail the activities of men such as Master Walter the physician, another Bury monk, who in the late twelfth century gave 'a large donation of money that he had made from his medical practice' toward the construction of a new infirmary, and thus avoided any allegations of personal acquisitiveness. Rather more restrictive in its consequences, a further decree of 1163 forbade professed monks to leave the cloister 'for pondering medical concoctions under the pretext of aiding the bodies of their sick brothers'.[11] As we shall see, this may have been a reaction against the increasingly complex and theoretical

[11] D. W. Amundsen, 'Medieval canon law on medical and surgical practice by the clergy', *Bulletin of the History of Medicine*, 52 (1978), 22–44, at 31.

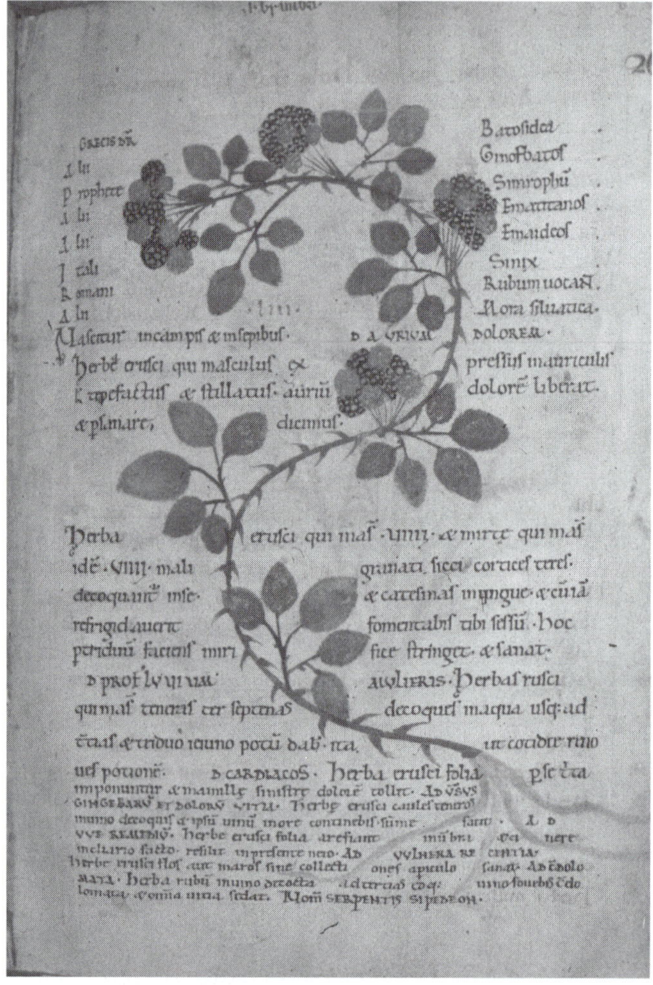

Figure 18 A late eleventh-century herbal produced at the abbey of Bury St Edmunds. Bodleian Library, Oxford, MS Bodley 130, fol. 26r; reproduced with kind permission of The Bodleian Libraries, University of Oxford

nature of academic medicine, and did *not* prevent monks from either studying or practising the healing arts in their own communities. From a long list of interesting examples we might cite the case of Ramelmus, a Cluniac canon and skilled *medicus* of Much Wenlock, who dispensed advice and treatment among the local poor, or of Thomas Northwick of Evesham Abbey, whose medical knowledge 'attracted the favour and grace of the whole surrounding countryside'. Not until 1215 did the papacy prohibit clergy in higher orders (both secular and religious) from practising surgery, as Abbot Baldwin had done, in part because of the danger of accidental homicide, but there was certainly no embargo before that date.

Because of their essentially pragmatic approach, Anglo-Saxon healers, and, indeed, the majority of those practising throughout the later Middle Ages, felt little need for a complex theoretical infrastructure that would provide detailed pathological or physiological explanations for tried and tested procedures. It was, indeed, this apparent disregard for 'scientific principles' that so exasperated Singer and his students. Written sources nonetheless reveal that at least some authors and their readers must have acquired a basic grasp of the holistic beliefs developed by the ancient Greeks. That health depended upon the preservation of a balance between the vital elements of heat, cold, moisture and aridity within the human body was understood in principle, as was the inherent danger of any excess or deficiency in one or more of the four humours. Such a universally applicable system offered an intelligible explanation for every human malady, as well as accounting for one's gender, character, appearance and behaviour.

Temperament	*Characteristic*	*Humour*	*Ruling organ*
Choleric	hot and dry	yellow bile/choler	gall bladder
Phlegmatic	cold and wet	phlegm	lungs
Sanguine	hot and wet	blood	liver
Melancholic	cold and dry	black bile	spleen

Humoral matter, which was generated from digested food and could thus be calibrated through diet, was also affected by a variety of external factors, such as the seasons, the climate, the moon and the stars. A more sophisticated awareness of the remarkable complexity of this relationship and its impact upon health was dependent upon the availability of texts that had long since disappeared from western libraries but still survived in the Arab world.

Already celebrated in the eleventh century for the empirical skill of its practitioners, Salerno in southern Italy became a magnet for those interested in studying the work of Muslim physicians and philosophers, newly translated into Latin by Constantine the African (d. by 1098) and his associates. The impact of this 'veritable explosion in thought and writing' was threefold.[12] First, it made available in the west a rapidly expanding corpus of material based upon classical Greek medical concepts, which was more theoretical, systematic and firmly rooted in natural science. This, in turn, gave rise to the creation of a syllabus of standard texts, known as the *Articella*, which, with a few variations, was widely adopted across Europe. Prominent in this curriculum were the *Isagoge* of Hunain ibn Ishāq (an introduction to medical theory), the *Aphorisms* attributed to Hippocrates and a selection of tracts on the pulse, fevers and diagnosis through the examination of urine. The study of medicine at the highest level thus became far more abstract and academic. Third, developments in surgery, pharmacy and therapeutics pioneered by Muslim practitioners stimulated Salernitan authors to produce their own works of synthesis, which combined the more formal, philosophical approach of the Arabs with their own inherently practical training. This process of fusion gave rise to such works as the *Antidotarium Nicholai* (on compound medicines), the *Circa instans* (an extended pharmacopoeia) and the *Trotula* (on gynaecology), each of which eventually became a canonical text. A new type of literature dealing with *questiones*, or medical debates, also began to circulate at this time. Adelard of Bath (d. *c.* 1152), one of many Englishmen drawn to Salerno, adopted this type of approach in his own philosophical and scientific writing.

The demand for these new works both reflected and promoted their growing influence. Shortly before 1153, for instance, a local physician presented the Benedictine monastery at Durham with his collection of twenty-six tracts, several of which were recent translations from Hebrew and Arabic made in Italy. They included short works on surgery, diagnostics and pharmacy, as well as two herbals. Significantly, the monks had already acquired a treatise on cauterization (Figure 17), the use of which had been greatly refined by Muslim surgeons.[13]

Not everyone was impressed by the growing fashion for study at one of the new Continental faculties of medicine. In his *Metalogicon* of 1159, John of Salisbury poured scorn upon the poorly educated scholars who,

> becoming cognizant of their inadequate grounding in philosophy, have departed to Salerno or Montpellier, where they have become medical students ... Stoked with fallacious empirical rules for healing various cases, they return after a brief interval to practice with sedulity what they have learned. Ostentatiously they

[12] Monica Green, ed., *The Trotula: A Medieval Compendium of Women's Medicine* (Philadelphia, 2001), pp. 2, 9–17.

[13] E. J. Kealey, *Medieval Medicus* (Baltimore and London, 1981), p. 44.

quote Hippocrates and Galen, pronounce mysterious words and have their aphorisms ready to apply to all cases. Their strange words serve as thunderbolts, which stun the minds of their fellow men.[14]

Of all the maxims now at their disposal, Salisbury dryly observes, they demonstrate a particular attachment to those concerning money. He would undoubtedly have agreed with the historian of pharmacy J. M. Riddle, who has described the rise of learned medicine in twelfth-century Europe as a retrograde development that inhibited rather than fostered the growth of clinical practice.[15] There can certainly now be little doubt that the 'dark age' of English medicine was notable for its robust tradition of empirical therapeutics, which flourished at all levels of society. The secondary position accorded to medical theory should not be equated with indifference, ignorance or the fog of superstition.

[14] D. D. McGarry, ed. and trans., *The Metalogicon of John of Salisbury* (Berkeley and Los Angeles, 1955), pp. 17–18.

[15] Riddle, 'Theory and practice', pp. 178, 183.

CHAPTER VI.5

Subversion

Martha Bayless

A tension between spiritual joy and earthly pleasures was a hallmark of the period in question, as it was of many other periods of history. On the whole, the 'official' culture of the Church regarded levity, eating, drinking and the enjoyment of the body, particularly the unruly and potentially immoral lower body, as profane and ungodly. These austere religious authorities shared an uneasy coexistence with more worldly forces, inside the Church as well as outside, which relished earthly delights, indulged the lower body and celebrated these exploits without shame. Occasionally such profane behaviour was purposefully blasphemous; at other times it was designed as satire, reproof for the abuses and hypocrisies of the Church and the age. Perhaps most often it was merely the product of high spirits, though those high spirits were commonly regarded as an offence to the dignity of the Church.

The period before 1200 recorded less frivolity, profanity and licence than later centuries, but this is indubitably an effect of limited literacy and the sombre bias of the written records. The situation of the modern scholar is much like that of Gerald of Wales, who described a dinner at Canterbury Cathedral Priory in 1180. Enjoined to solemnity, the monks were supposed to be keeping silence, but Gerald observed that in practice they were irrepressibly lively. Referring to himself in the third person, Gerald wrote that despite the monks' vow of silence,

> they overflowed with gesticulations of fingers and hands and arms and with whistling in place of speaking, more lightheartedly and freely than was proper, so that he seemed to be seated at theatrical performances or among actors and jesters.[1]

Like Gerald, we may note that official strictures called for serious and sombre behaviour, but that in practice violations of this were endemic.

[1] Gerald of Wales, *De rebus a se gestis*, III, cap. 5: J. S. Brewer *et al*, eds., *Giraldi Cambrensis opera*, (8 vols.; RS; London, 1861–91), i, p. 51.

And like Gerald, we may be sure that the subjects in question were merry, although we cannot hear their jokes.

Orthodox Christian teaching held that merriment and playfulness were permissible only when they foreshadowed the rejoicing in heaven, the *gaudium spirituale*, and thus were appropriate to the afterlife rather than to the earthly realm. Only the very saintly could properly express joy on earth, as they were actually enjoying a foretaste of heavenly joy; but for sinners, sorrow and seriousness were more fitting. This was affirmed by scriptural passages such as the saying addressed to the devout: 'The world shall rejoice, and you shall lament' (John 16:20). Thus official religious attitudes towards merriment were grudging at best, and the enjoyment of wit, mockery and sensual pleasures was commonly regarded as ungodly and subversive of pious rectitude.

However much religious authorities disapproved of merriment, it is striking that earthly pleasures continued to be enjoyed by clerics as well as the secular. In the tenth century King Edgar deplored the depravity of clerics, 'disgraceful in their words', who indulged in amusements when they should have been celebrating Mass. He complained that they

> expend themselves in feasting and drinking sessions, in beds and acts of shamelessness; so that now the houses of the clerics are considered brothels of prostitutes, gathering-places for performers. There gaming takes place, there dancing and singing, there people are awake until the middle of the night with loud noise and uncouth behaviour.[2]

He went on to censure clerics for their enjoyment of hounds, hawks and other 'ludicra', and suggested that even performers themselves satirized the loose practices of the clergy: 'The soldiers shout these things, the people mutter them, the actors [*mimi*] sing and dance about them.'[3]

Numerous other authorities denounced clerical misbehaviour, profane speech and excessive merrymaking. One letter of Ælfric warned against drinking and carousing in church; another admonished priests not to be *gligmenn* (entertainers, performers or minstrels).[4] The *Canons of Edgar* warned that no priest should be a *cerevisiarius*, and this is echoed by the Northumbrian Priests' Law, which warns of penalties should a priest be a drunkard, '*vel scurrilis aut cerevisiarius*', 'or fool-like or a beer-host'.[5] The

[2] Walter de Gray Birch, ed., *Cartularium Saxonicum*, (3 vols.; London, 1885–99), iii, p. 573.

[3] *Ibid.*

[4] B. Fehr, ed., *Die Hirtenbriefe Ælfrics in altenglischer und lateinischer Fassung*, (Hamburg, 1914, repr. Darmstadt, 1966), Letter I, no. 107, p. 24; Letter III, no. 188, p. 216.

[5] R. Fowler, ed., *Wulfstan's Canons of Edgar*, (EETS o.s. 266; Oxford, 1972), p. 14, no. 65 with parallel text on p. 15, no. 65; see also no. 58.

Seasons for Fasting, of the late tenth or early eleventh century, complained of priests who went straight from the Mass to the tapster (*tæppere*), seeking wine and oysters, and lied in telling the tapster that it was permissible to give him such dainties in the morning without sinning.[6]

Clerical life appeared to offer frequent such opportunities for carousal. Church-sanctioned feasting and drinking in community were widespread, and there is reason to believe that monastic practice often followed the patterns of secular feasting. This must have been especially true when monasteries hosted the local aristocracy, with whom they were eager to forge ties.

One of the principal witnesses to clerical merriment is the Cambridge Songs, a collection of Latin lyrics copied at St Augustine's, Canterbury, in the mid-eleventh century, from an exemplar most likely of German origin. The compilation includes hymns, political songs and other serious fare, but among the more light-hearted are love songs, religious humour and seven narratives of comic trickery which can lay claim to being the earliest surviving fabliaux. These serve as evidence that monastic taste at the most sophisticated levels might be more bawdy than ascetic. One of the fabliaux, the *Modus Liebinc* sequence, also provides a glimpse of the contemporary view of entertainers: while the merchant husband is abroad, the wife receives illicit visitors, and the song says succinctly: '*Mimi aderant*', 'Entertainers came.' Almost immediately the wife conceives an illegitimate child; the poem uses the mere presence of performers to signal licence and debauchery.

Although ribald entertainments were deplored by the moralizers within the Church, others countered licentiousness with risqué remarks of their own. In the twelfth-century *De nugis curialium* (1.24), Walter Map recounts a jibe of his own against monastic debauchery. A number of clerics and others, including Map himself and Gilbert Foliot, bishop of London, were discussing the miracles of Bernard of Clairvaux. A Cistercian abbot said he had been present when Bernard threw himself on a dead boy and prayed for him to be raised, but on that occasion Bernard's prayers had been unsuccessful. Map quipped to the company, 'That was the most unfortunate of monks, for I have never heard that when a monk lay on a boy, the boy didn't get up again right afterwards'. He adds: 'The abbot blushed, and many went out so they could laugh.'

Certain times of the year were particularly given to licence. Feast days seem to have provided special opportunities for indulgence, and Christmas

[6] E. V. K. Dobbie ed., *The Anglo-Saxon Minor Poems*, (ASPR 6; New York, 1942), lines 208–30.

may have been particularly favoured in this way. A tradition of extended leisure at Christmas had been established by 877, when the laws of Alfred granted servants holiday for the twelve days following Christmas Day.[7] At the royal court Christmas was evidently a time for special entertainments, as suggested by the records of one Roland le Petour, also called 'Roulandus le Fartere', who was granted a serjeanty, apparently of the late twelfth century. His grant is typical of that given to favoured entertainers as well as to others of service to the king. In his case it included the requirement of performing '*saltum, siffletum, pettum*', 'a jump, a whistle [and] a fart', before the king on Christmas Day.[8] The phrase was a stock expression and seems to represent standard buffoonery, the kind of thing that would constitute a jester's performance, and so it is likely that Roland the Farter was a royal jester and the fart his stock in trade.

Although not a religious holiday, New Year also served as an occasion for behaviour that displeased the Church. In the early eleventh century Wulfstan denounced 'the nonsense which is performed on New Year's Day in various kinds of sorcery'.[9] This is likely to refer to divination, which was common on New Year's Day in later centuries. In the late twelfth century the bishop of Exeter similarly railed against those who 'keep the New Year with pagan rites'.[10]

Disapproval was harshest for clerics who failed to conduct themselves soberly, but lay folk also came under censure for unseemly conduct. As with clerics, such conduct included merriment, drinking and the pleasures of the lower body. Homilies warned against 'frivolous speech and board games and drinking parties', activities forbidden at all times but, one homilist admonished, particularly on the Days of Rogation.[11] Insufficient reverence on the part of laymen could be sacrilegious. In the *Gesta pontificum Anglorum* (ii.75.30–1) William of Malmesbury tells of a group of laymen who were urged to forgo sex with their wives around Ash Wednesday, though such an interdiction was not formally commanded by the Church. The men responded respectfully except for one, who 'made the others laugh by cracking a joke: he was incapable, he said, of giving

[7] John Johnson, ed., *A Collection of the Laws and Canons of the Church of England*, (Oxford, 1850), i, p. 328.

[8] The documents are reproduced and discussed by Valerie Allen, *On Farting: Language and Laughter in the Middle Ages* (New York, 2007), pp. 168–77.

[9] *Councils and Synods*, i, 319–20.

[10] John T. McNeill and Helena M. Gamer, eds., *Medieval Handbooks of Penance*, (New York, 1938), p. 349.

[11] Homily for Monday in Rogationtide (no. xix), D. G. Scragg, ed. *The Vercelli Homilies and Related Texts* (EETS 300; Oxford, 1992), p. 320, lines 90–1.

up both wine and wife, which meant doing without sustenance and sex at the same time … he accentuated his folly by using an obscene and common expression'. He was reproved by the bishop for his irreverence and found dead in his bedroom the following morning. William adds pointedly: 'He had been strangled, possibly by the Devil.' The connection between wine, women, irreverence and eternal damnation was clear.

If merriment and recreation were contrary to pious rectitude, entertainers, those who fostered merriment as a profession, were especially ungodly. Ælfric tells a symbolic story about a *truð*, an entertainer usually associated with a *truð horn*, or trumpet. This particular *truð* sinfully ignores the Lenten fast and fails to attend Mass, instead gluttonously helping himself to food in the bishop's kitchen. Predictably, he is struck down as he gulps down the first bite.[12] Here the conflict between piety and the spiritual, on the one hand, and ungodliness, entertainment and the bodily, on the other, is made manifest. Several stories portray minstrels as potentially treacherous, a result of their identity as entertainers and also of the fact that they were often itinerant and therefore of unknowable origin and reputation. In the *Gesta regum Anglorum*, William of Malmesbury told the legend of King Alfred's sortie in the disguise of a minstrel, by which he gleaned the secrets of the Danish camp (ii.121). Later in the same volume he recounted the more ominous story of Anlaf, the Viking king of Northumbria, who infiltrated the English camp disguised as a minstrel. Geoffrey of Monmouth's *Historia regum Britannie* (ix.i), written in the 1130s, tells a similar story in which the enemy Saxon Baldulf infiltrates King Arthur's stronghold by disguising himself as a minstrel. Geffrai Gaimar's *L'Estoire des Engleis*, composed in the 1140s for an English patroness, associated the murder of Edward the Martyr in 978 with the treacherous disobedience of a dwarf jester at the royal court.[13] Minstrels and entertainers were worryingly unknowable, and their treachery could threaten the safety of the realm itself.

Although – or because – entertainers were associated with licence and sin, they were abundant in England of this period, and appear in both clerical and secular records. But professional entertainers were not necessary for carousal. Drinking fostered merriment, and the English were enthusiastic drinkers. In the *Gesta regum Anglorum* (ii.245), William of Malmesbury reports that the Anglo-Saxons were more interested in

[12] W. W. Skeat, ed., *Ælfric's Lives of Saints*, (EETS o.s. 76; London, 1881), p. 264 (no. 12, Ash Wednesday).

[13] I. Short, ed. and trans., *Geffrei Gaimar, L'Estoire des Engleis*, (Oxford, 2009), pp. 218–19, lines 3983–96.

communal feasting than in riches, and that 'drinking in company was a universal practice, and in this passion they made no distinction between night and day'. In the tenth century Ælfric inveighed against the drinking parties of countrywomen, where, he had heard, the women held *gebeorscipes* (drinking parties) in latrines, revelling, drinking and eating in the privy. 'No virtuous person ever does this', the scandalized Ælfric pronounced.[14] It is tempting to speculate on why these women would have chosen to have their drinking parties in private, and in such a disagreeable location. Ælfric identified it as a disregard for decency; but the women may have preferred the latrine simply because it was the only place off limits to male moralizers such as Ælfric.

Eating, drinking, the lower body and sin went together naturally in the eyes of the Church. The lower body was profane by nature, as if the sinfulness brought about by the Fall inhered especially in the lower regions. As such it was an offence to godliness. In the 1180s Walter Map told the story of Henry II and a monk called Dom Reric, who spotted a second monk tripping over a stone and falling on the road, exposing his rear. The king averted his gaze, but Reric commented wryly, 'Accursed the religion that unveils the backside!'[15] William of Malmesbury's *Gesta pontificum Anglorum* (v.275) told the story of an obscene jokester who lowered his breeches and broke wind at the relics of St Aldhelm. Only vigils, fasts and prayer cured him of the evil spirit that had seized him during the episode. The twelfth-century *Gesta Herewardi*, a legend of the historical Hereward the Wake, tells of a witch of the Fens who offended her pursuers by muttering incantations while baring her backside at them (ch. xxv). Yet although the pious were scandalized by such behaviour, the lowliness of the nether body also had great amusement value. The 'obscene' Old English riddles of the *Exeter Book*, highly suggestive of sexual parts, were clearly meant to be entertaining, and suggest that secular culture held a more mirthful view of the body than the abundance of religious strictures reveals. The case of Roland le Petour demonstrates the amusement value of the indignity of the lower body, a value not lost on others. In his twelfth-century *Policraticus* (i.viii) John of Salisbury complained that

> [jesters] are not barred from eminent houses, but even perform disgraceful acts with the obscene parts of their bodies before the eyes of all … More astonishing,

[14] Mary Clayton, 'An edition of Ælfric's *Letter to Brother Edward*', Elaine Treharne and Susan Rosser, eds. in *Early Medieval English Texts and Interpretations: Studies Presented to Donald G. Scragg*, (Tempe, AZ, 2002), pp. 262–83, at 282.

[15] M. R. James, ed. and trans., C. N. L. Brooke and R. A. B. Mynors, rev., *Walter Map, De Nugis Curialium: Courtiers' Trifles*, (OMT; Oxford, 1983), p. 102.

they are not even thrown out when, with a blast from their lower parts, they make the air stink with a series of noises … Could he possibly appear wise to you, if he keeps his eyes and ears open to these things? But who would not watch and laugh with pleasure when the arts of the performer are quashed by a dousing of urine, and when the power of discernment is restored to eyes that have been weakened by his wicked tricks? It is pleasant and does not detract from the honour of a worthy man to take delight in seemly lightheartedness, but it is disgraceful to erode his seriousness with frequent dissolute behaviour.

John cites a list of performers and entertainers, deploring their scurrility, and reminding his audience pointedly that the Fathers forbade actors and entertainers from taking the sacrament.

Though condemned by the high-minded, buffoonery also featured in the *comediae* emerging in the twelfth century. Three Latin examples, likely of English origin, make ample use of the humour of food and the body and serve as testimony to the amusements of the educated. The play *Babio*, full of puns, linguistic wit and comic violence, concerns a cuckolded man competing for love of his stepdaughter. *Baucis et Thraso* involves an alluring prostitute, a pompous knight and the bawd who arranges their liaison. The witty dialogue 'De clericis et rustico', possibly the work of the Englishman Geoffrey of Vinsauf, concerns two erudite students trying to beguile a cake out of a peasant; while the students philosophize, the peasant eats the cake.

Gerald of Wales noted that the poems attributed to the legendary glutton Golias had begun to circulate in his time, satirizing the pope and the papal curia as well as celebrating the pleasures and perils of drink. Such verses flourished in the later period, appearing most notably in the Bekynton Anthology (Oxford, Bodleian Library, Bodley Add. A.44), assembled around the year 1200. This contains the widely circulating tale of the Adulterous Monk, told in biblical prose, a number of satires and parodies extolling wine, an equal number focused on the gluttony of clerics and kitchen-humour celebrations of topics such as gorging and belching. The 'Case of the Salmon' involves the accusation and defence of a salmon which has caused the death of a gluttonous monk; the 'Martyrdom of the Game' uses pseudo-religious terms to describe the passion of animals martyred to provide an abbot's dinner. The satirical juxtaposition of supposedly lofty-minded clerics with the lowly and comic pleasures of the flesh proved to be endlessly amusing.

The twelfth century also saw the lowly used to satirical effect in texts such as the *Speculum stultorum*. Written by Nigel Wireker or Whiteacre (also known as Nigel de Longchamps), a monk of Christ Church,

Canterbury, this mock epic in Latin elegiacs satirizes clerical foolishness through the character of Brunellus, a donkey who goes to enormous lengths in his quest for a longer tail. Clerical folly might lead to reproof, but even reproof might take the form of entertainment. However earnest the thoughts of the high-minded, they were always shadowed by other elements in culture: the satirical, the amusing, the high-spirited and the gleefully dissolute.

Table 1 *Kings of England 871–1066*

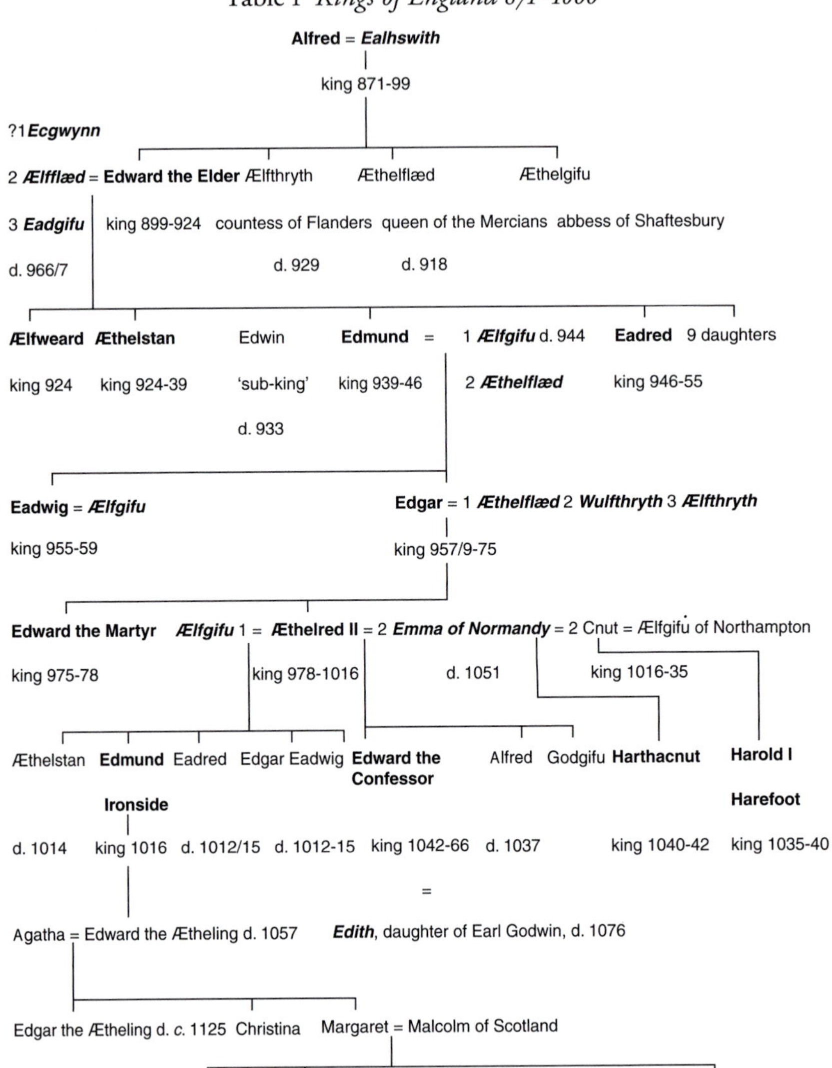

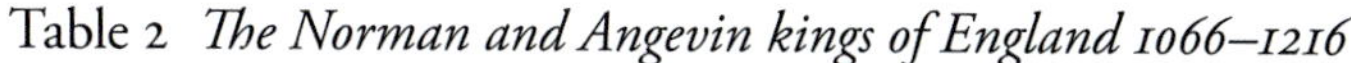

Table 2 *The Norman and Angevin kings of England 1066–1216*

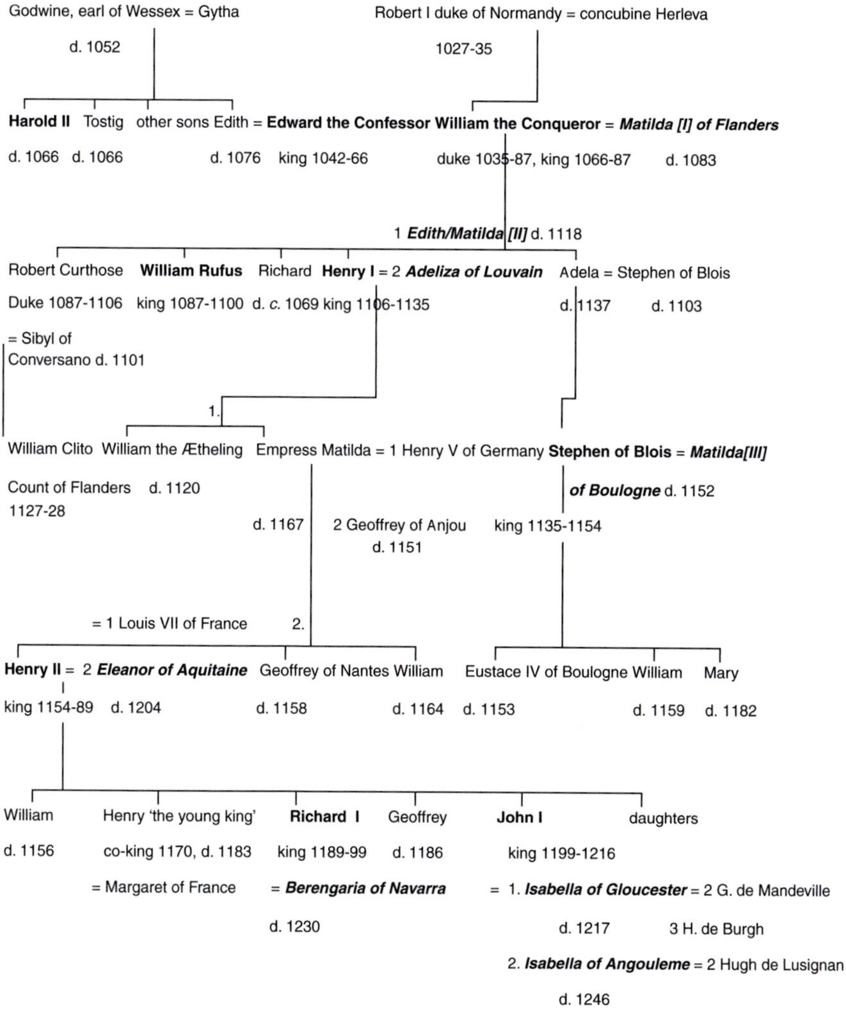

Godwine, earl of Wessex = Gytha
d. 1052

Robert I duke of Normandy = concubine Herleva
1027-35

Harold II d. 1066
Tostig d. 1066
other sons
Edith d. 1076 = **Edward the Confessor** king 1042-66

William the Conqueror duke 1035-87, king 1066-87 = ***Matilda [I] of Flanders*** d. 1083

Robert Curthose Duke 1087-1106 = Sibyl of Conversano d. 1101
William Rufus king 1087-1100
Richard d. *c.* 1069
Henry I king 1106-1135 = 1 ***Edith/Matilda [II]*** d. 1118 = 2 ***Adeliza of Louvain***
Adela d. 1137 = Stephen of Blois d. 1103

William Clito Count of Flanders 1127-28
William the Ætheling d. 1120
Empress Matilda d. 1167 = 1 Henry V of Germany
2 Geoffrey of Anjou d. 1151
Stephen of Blois king 1135-1154 = ***Matilda[III] of Boulogne*** d. 1152

Henry II king 1154-89 = 2 ***Eleanor of Aquitaine*** d. 1204 = 1 Louis VII of France
Geoffrey of Nantes d. 1158
William d. 1164
Eustace IV of Boulogne d. 1153
William d. 1159
Mary d. 1182

William d. 1156
Henry 'the young king' co-king 1170, d. 1183 = Margaret of France
Richard I king 1189-99 = ***Berengaria of Navarra*** d. 1230
Geoffrey d. 1186
John I king 1199-1216 = 1. ***Isabella of Gloucester*** d. 1217 = 2 G. de Mandeville 3 H. de Burgh
2. ***Isabella of Angouleme*** d. 1246 = 2 Hugh de Lusignan
daughters

Glossary

Abbreviations: Lat. = Latin; OE = Old English; ON = Old Norse; OF = Old French; Fr = French

acre (Lat. *acra*)	could be used as linear measure of 66 feet, or as square measure of 4 × 40 perches (*sub voce* literally, 'under this word', hereafter s.v.); a unit of assessment to geld
ætheling (OE *ætheling*)	royal prince
agnatic	belonging to the father's side of the family
allod (Lat. *alodium*)	property held free of service
amber	a liquid measure of sizeable volume
antecessor (Lat. *antecessor*)	In Domesday Book (s.v.) the preceding landholder, usually pre-Conquest, from whom the 1086 holder might claim legal title
antiphonary	book of antiphons and other choir chants for the Office
apostle	disciple of Christ
assize	legislation, or procedures arising from this legislation
ban	power of command over a region's people or resources (especially in France)
bannal	(exactions, rights, etc.) concerning or resulting from the ban (s.v.)
Benedictine Rule	set of rules, called after St Benedict of Nursia (6th c.), for monks

The Editors wish to acknowledge with gratitude the help received from Sarah Hamilton, and the use of the unpublished 'Glossary of key terms' compiled by Professor Christine Carpenter (Faculty of History, University of Cambridge).

benedictional	book containing blessings pronounced by bishop at Mass
bookland (OE *bocland*)	land held by royal charter (s.v.); bookland tenure gives prospect of freedom to dispose of the land
bordar (OF *borde*)	literally 'he who has a wooden hut'; a smallholder, usually a customary tenant (s.v.)
borough (from *burh* or *burgh*)	town, city or small trading place, usually with a market, often defended and often (from twelfth century) with a charter
burgage	unit of property in a borough (s.v.)
Burghal Hidage	tenth-century list of named fortifications with their hidage (s.v.) for people and resources to maintain their defence
burh (OE *burh*, Lat. *burgus*)	fortified town usually with market and garrison
canon law	ecclesiastical law
cartulary	register of charters (s.v.), sometimes accompanied by a narrative
carucate (Lat. *caruca*)	lit. 'plough land'; measure of land and fiscal assessment unit in Danelaw (s.v.)
cathedral	bishop's church
chapter	body of a collegiate or cathedral church
charter	document recording a juridical transaction (e.g. a gift of land or rights)
chirograph	a charter in two parts, each containing the same text, to be cut into halves (one for the grantor and one for the recipient)
churchscot (OE *ciric*, *sceat*)	church tribute; a custom of corn collected on St Martin's Day; extended to other similar contributions
cognatic	belonging to the mother's side of the family
confraternity	religious or charitable association
conversus, i (Lat.)	lay brother(s)
cottar (OE *kot*)	lit. 'he who has a cottage'; smallholder, usually a customary tenant (s.v.)

customary tenant	person whose obligations to his lord and terms of tenure are determined by custom and enforced in the manorial court (s.v.)
Danegeld	see heregeld; also term in modern parlance often used to describe tribute paid to Danes
Danelaw (OE *Dena laga*)	literally 'laws of the Danes'; area of northern and eastern England settled by Danes, referred to as such only from twelfth-century onwards
demesne (Lat. *dominium*)	agricultural land and/or manor kept by a lord for himself in his own direct power, although with peasant tenants working on it
diocese	ecclesiastical district ruled by a bishop, also known as see (s.v.)
Domesday Book	written record based on Domesday survey (s.v.) compiled in 1086
Domesday survey	royal survey of his lands and their resources commissioned by King William I in 1085/6
dower (Lat. *dos*)	gift associated with marriage; from late tenth century usually denoting land or income set aside by husband for his widow
dowry (Lat. *dos*)	land or money handed over with a bride by her family
ealdorman (OE *ealdorman*)	a nobleman with regional judicial and military powers, from eleventh century usually called earl (s.v.)
earl (OE or ON *jarl*)	a nobleman of the highest aristocracy in charge of an earldom
earldom	collection of shires (s.v.) under the control of an earl
encellullement (Fr)	literally 'breaking up in cells', i.e. fragmentation of political power around castles (especially in eleventh-century France)
endogamy	marrying within one's own social, religious or kin group

epistolary	book containing the Epistles, i.e. letters from the apostles (s.v.)
eucharist	the sacrament of the Lord's supper, i.e. the consecrated elements of the Mass (s.v.)
exchequer	the centre of the king's financial administration, first appearing in the early twelfth century
exemplar	manuscript from which a scribe makes a copy
exogamy	marrying outside one's own social, religious or kin group
farm (Lat. *firma*)	fixed payment or rent in return for land or the privilege of exercising an office (e.g. the sheriff's farm)
fief	a wide variety of aristocratic landholdings usually held from a superior and usually in return for some services
forest law	a form of law protecting the king's hunting rights and enforced in royal forests; it subjected whole areas, (not just the woods themselves) to more stringent royal authority
fyrd (OE *fyrð*)	military levy or host
gradual	book of responsorial chants for Mass
Gregorian reform movement	eleventh-century reform movement in the Christian Church, named after Pope Gregory VII (1073–85); it aspired to greater segregation between clergy and laity through clerical celibacy and preventing simony (s.v.)
guild/gild	association of traders or artisans in towns
hagiography	the writing of saints' biographies
haw (OE *haga*)	enclosure
here (OE *here*)	army
heregeld (OE)	annual tax raised to pay for standing army 1012–51
herepath	military road

hidage	see hide
hide	literally household; became a fiscal measurement; later meaning a measure of land of roughly 120 acres;
homily	edifying sermon
honour	lordship held directly by lord from king
honorial court	court where the lord of the honour does justice among his tenants
housecarl (ON *huscarl*)	member of royal household troops since time of King Cnut; possibly equivalent to a king's thegn (s.v.)
hundred (OE *hundred*)	notionally, and sometimes, actually, comprising 100 hides (s.v.); subdivision of English local government below the shire (s.v.)
hundred court	judicial session of hundred (s.v.)
incubus (Lat.)	devil in human shape
indulgence (Lat. *indulgentia*)	literally 'to be kind'; remission of temporal punishment granted by ecclesiastical authority to penitent sinners
inland (OE *inland*)	demesne (s.v.) land for which no service was due
knight's fee	land held owing service of a knight
landgable (OE *landgafol*)	fixed ground rent in towns and cities, usually 12d per year
liturgy	forms for public, as opposed to private, worship, hence the form and content of church services
loanland (OE *lænland*)	land held by lease, often for three lives (i.e. generations)
manor	a lordship, sometimes incorporating a vill (s.v.) but could be part of a vill or on occasion of several vills, usually having customary tenants and a manorial court (s.v.)
manorial court	lord's court of manor (s.v.), exercising justice over his tenants
manumission	grant of freedom to an unfree person
market (Lat. *mercatum*)	place or occasion licensed for the exchange of goods

Mass	eucharistic liturgical service
messuage (from OF *ménage*)	dwelling with its adjoining yards and outbuildings
minster	church
monastic cathedral	cathedral (s.v.) church headed by a bishop with a chapter (s.v.) consisting of prior and monks (specific to England)
Office	a church service
patrilinear	descending in the male line
patronym	name referring to one's father, or an ancestor in the male line
perch (OF *perche*)	measuring rod, commonly of 5½ yards
pontifical	book containing the forms for the rites and offices reserved to a bishop outside the eucharistic liturgy
port (Lat. *portus*)	trading-place or harbour (river or sea)
prebend	stipend of a cathedral canon
Psalter	book containing the Psalms
quadrivium	the second tier of the classical seven liberal arts (mathematics, astronomy, music and geometry), see also *trivium*
reeve (OE *gerefa*)	representative of royal (also private) authority with administrative responsibility, e.g. in charge of hundred (s.v.), port (s.v.) or (as sheriff, s.v.) of shire (s.v.)
rod	unit of measurement of 16½ feet
sacramentary	manuscript containing texts for Mass needed by the officiant
saltern	saltpan
salvific	concerning divine salvation
sceatta	small silver penny
scriptorium (Lat. writing place)	place where manuscripts are presumed to have been written, usually in a monastery or church
see	seat of a bishop, also diocese (s.v.)

serf	unfree person
sheriff (OE *scirgerefa*)	royal official or reeve (s.v.) responsible for all aspects of royal administration at the level of the shire (s.v.); originally he was the deputy of the ealdorman (s.v.) or earl (s.v.)
shire (OE *scir*)	county in England; from the 10th c. administrative, legal and military organization
shire court	place for exercise of justice in shire (s.v.)
simony	offence of purchase of spiritual gifts, especially an ecclesiastical office
soke (OE *soke*)	lordship of an area, possibly deriving from the inhabitants' obligation to attend a court held at a royal manor; the right to hold such a court
soulscot	payment for burial with priestly ministration in a holy place
staithe (OE *stæþ*)	bank or shore, hence landing stage or wharf
styca (OE *stycce*)	coin made of base silver especially in Northumbria in ninth and tenth centuries
succubus (Lat.)	devil in human shape
tenant	person who holds land from a superior
tenant-in-chief	tenant (s.v.) who holds directly from the king
thegn (OE *thegn*)	freeman of high status or minor nobleman
tithe (literally 'one tenth')	a tax to the church consisting of one tenth of one's income
toponym	name derived from, or referring to, a place-name
trivium	the first tier of the classical seven liberal arts (grammar, rhetoric and dialectic or logic)
vill (Lat. *uilla*)	village
virgate	quarter of a hide (approximately 30 acres)
wapentake (ON *vápnatak*)	unit of land in Danelaw (s.v.), equivalent to the hundred (s.v.)
warland (from OE *wara*)	land for which service was due

wergild (OE *wergild*)	'man money' or 'blood money', i.e. money paid in full if a person was killed or proportionally for injury; amount varied according to legal status
wic (Lat. *vicus*, OE *wic*)	trade enclave, usually accessible from the sea

Time line 900–1200

899	26 Oct.: death of King Alfred; Edward the Elder succeeds as king of the Anglo-Saxons; his sister and brother-in-law, Æthelflæd and Æthelred, hold power in Mercia
924/5	Æthelstan succeeds to the throne
927	Æthelstan receives the submission of the rulers of North and West Britain at Eamont, Cumbria
937	Æthelstan reasserts hegemony over the Scots and Norse in battle at *Brunanburh*
939	27 Oct.: death of King Æthelstan; Edmund succeeds
946	26 May: Edmund murdered at Pucklechurch, Glos.; Eadred succeeds
954	Death of Eric Bloodaxe, last Scandinavian king of York
955	23 Nov.: Eadred dies; Eadwig consecrated king
957	Edgar, his brother, made king of Mercia and Northumbria
959	Death of Eadwig; Edgar king of England
963	Æthelwold, reforming abbot of Abingdon, made bishop of Winchester
964	20 Feb.: expulsion of secular clerics from the New Minster, Winchester
973	11 May: Edgar consecrated King
975	8 July: death of Edgar; succession disputed between his sons Edward and Æthelred
978	18 May: murder of King Edward; succession of Æthelred
990s	Viking raids increase in ferocity and frequency
991	Battle of Maldon: Ealdorman Byrhtnoth of Essex defeated and killed by Danish raiding army
994	Unsuccessful attack on London by Swein Forkbeard, king of Denmark, and Olaf Tryggvasson, king of Norway
1001	Canonization of Edward 'the Martyr'
1002	13 Nov.: St Brice's Day massacre

1012	Payment of £48,000 tribute to Viking armies
1013	Swein Forkbeard, king of Denmark, acknowledged as king of all England
1014	3 Feb.: death of Swein Forkbeard; his son, Cnut, hailed as his successor but King Æthelred restored
1016	23 April: death of Æthelred 'the Unready'; succession of his son, Edmund Ironside
	18 Oct.: kingdom divided after defeat by Cnut at Battle of *Assundun*
	30 Nov.: Edmund Ironside dies; Cnut succeeds; exile of Æthelred's surviving descendants
1019	Cnut made king of Denmark
1019–20, 1022/3, 1025/6, 1026/7, 1027	Cnut absent from England in Denmark
1028	Cnut established as king of Sweden (by conquest); his son, Harthacnut, named as king of Denmark
1035	Death of Cnut; Harold I Harefoot chosen as regent of all England
1036	Murder of Æthelred's son, Alfred, on return from exile in Normandy
1040	17 March: death of Harold; accession of Harthacnut
1042	8 June: death of Harthacnut; accession of Edward the Confessor
1045	Marriage of Edward the Confessor to Edith, daughter of Earl Godwine of Wessex
1051/2	Earl Godwine and sons dispossessed and in exile; later restored at a council in London
1054	Malcolm Canmore established on throne of Scotland following invasion by Siward, earl of Northumbria
1057	Death of Edward, son of Edmund Ironside, on return from exile in Hungary
1065	Rebellion in Northumbria; Earl Tostig Godwinesson ousted
1066	4/5 Jan.: death of Edward the Confessor
	6 Jan.: Harold Godwinesson crowned king
	25 Sept.: Battle of Stamford Bridge; Tostig Godwinesson killed
	28/9 Sept.: Duke William of Normandy with fleet of some 800 ships lands at Pevensey

	14 Oct.: Battle of Hastings; death of King Harold; Edgar the Ætheling chosen by Archbishop Ealdred of York, the citizens of London and earls Edwin and Morcar
	Autumn: English nobility submits to King William
	25 Dec.: coronation of King William in Westminster Abbey
1067	Spring: King William returns to Normandy
	Dec.: King William back in England
1068	11 May: Matilda crowned queen at Westminster
1069	King Harold's sons from Ireland attack coast of Devon; Edgar the Ætheling goes to Scotland; punitive expedition to York
1070	Failed invasion of Sweyn of Denmark's brother Osbeorn and sons. King William completes subjugation of Fenland rebels including Hereward
1071	Earl Edwin is killed; Earl Morcar held in captivity in Normandy; coronation of King William by papal legate
1072	King William's expedition to Scotland; peace treaty of Abernethy
1073	King William's expedition into Maine (France)
1075	Revolt of earls Ralph de Gael, Roger son of William FitzOsbern and Waltheof;
	18 Dec.: Death of Queen Edith, widow of Edward the Confessor
1076	Earl Waltheof executed for treason
1079	Jan.: siege at Gerberoi, where King William faces his son Robert Curthose and King Philip of France
1081	King William's expedition to St David's in Wales
1082	Bishop Odo of Bayeux, earl of Kent, half-brother of King William, accused of treason and imprisoned
1083	2 Nov.: death of Queen Matilda
1084	Siege of Sainte-Suzanne (Maine)
1085	Threat of invasion by King Cnut IV of Denmark
1086	Domesday survey
1087	July: King William falls ill during attack on Mantes
	9 Sept.: death of King William; Robert Curthose becomes duke of Normandy
	26 Sept.: coronation of William Rufus; release of Bishop Odo of Bayeux from prison
1088	Rebellion against William Rufus led by Bishop of Odo of Bayeux
1092	Expedition of William Rufus to Carlisle

1096 Sept.: William Rufus to Normandy after paying mortgage for duchy which enabled Duke Robert Curthose to go on crusade

1099 May: William Rufus holds first court at new hall at Westminster

1100 2 Aug.: death of William Rufus, killed by arrow during hunt in New Forest

5 Aug.: coronation of Henry I

Sept.: return of Robert Curthose from Holy Land to Normandy

Marriage of Henry I and Edith-Matilda, daughter of King Malcolm of Scotland and Queen Margaret, herself a royal princess of the house of Wessex

1101 March: Anglo-Flemish treaty whereby Count Robert of Flanders promised the supply of 1,000 knights in return for Henry I's payment of £500 per annum

Aug.: failed invasion of England by Duke Robert Curthose; Treaty of Alton

1105 Henry I invades Normandy

1106 28 Sept.: Battle of Tinchebray; Robert Curthose, duke of Normandy taken into captivity; Henry I becomes duke of Normandy

c. 1108 King Henry I orders the Flemish to move from Cumbria to south Wales

1109 Marriage agreement of Empress Matilda and Emperor Henry V of Germany

Feb.: Matilda goes overseas and is educated at Trier

1110 Betrothal and marriage of Empress Matilda and Emperor Henry V; renewal of Anglo-Flemish treaty

1113 David, later king of Scotland, marries Matilda, widow of Simon of Senlis

1114 Royally sanctioned English expeditions into Wales

1115 Jan.?: Norman nobles accept William the Ætheling as Henry I's heir and successor in Normandy

1116 March: William the Ætheling accepted as Henry I's heir and successor in England

1118 1 May: death of Queen Edith-Matilda

1119 20 Aug.: Battle of Brémule; Henry I defeats King Louis VI of France

1120 June: marriage of William the Ætheling and Matilda of Anjou

25 Nov.: White Ship disaster in which William the Ætheling dies

1121	Early: marriage of King Henry I and Adeliza of Louvain
1125	Marriage of Stephen of Blois and Matilda of Boulogne
1126	Death of Henry V of Germany; his widow Empress Matilda returns to Normandy/England
1127	Jan.: King Henry I appoints Empress Matilda as his heir and successor
	22 May: betrothal of Empress Matilda and Geoffrey of Anjou
1128	10 June: Geoffrey of Anjou and thirty young men knighted at Rouen
	17 June: marriage of Empress Matilda and Geoffrey of Anjou
1133	25 March: birth of Henry, eldest son of Empress Matilda and Geoffrey, at Le Mans
1135	1 Dec.: death of King Henry I
	22 Dec.: coronation King Stephen
1136	First invasion of Normandy by Geoffrey of Anjou and Empress Matilda
	Sept.: second invasion of Normandy by Geoffrey of Anjou and Empress Matilda
c. 1136/7	Rumour that all French (or Normans) in England be killed by royal order
1137	March: King Stephen's only visit to Normandy
1138	Geoffrey of Anjou secure in Normandy
1139	Sept.: Empress Matilda arrives in England to challenge Stephen's right to the throne
1144	Henry, son of Empress Matilda, returns to Anjou; Geoffrey of Anjou becomes duke of Normandy
1148	Empress Matilda returns to Normandy
1149	Henry of Anjou knighted at Carlisle by King David of Scotland
1151	Aug./Sept.: peace conference of Geoffrey of Anjou, his son Henry and Louis VII of France; Henry accepted as duke of Normandy;
	14 Sept.: death of Geoffrey of Anjou
1152	March: dissolution of marriage of King Louis VII of France and Eleanor of Aquitaine; English bishops refuse King Stephen's request that his son Eustace be co-crowned
	May: death of Queen Matilda
	18 May: marriage of Duke Henry of Normandy and Eleanor of Aquitaine

1153 17 Aug.: death of Eustace, eldest son of Stephen and Matilda
birth of William, eldest son of Henry II
6 Nov.: peace between Duke Henry and King Stephen
Dec.: Treaty of Winchester whereby King Stephen appoints Duke Henry as his successor

1154 25 Oct.: Death of King Stephen
19 Dec.: coronation of King Henry II

1155 28 Feb.: birth of Henry, later the Young king

1156 King Henry subdues his brother Geoffrey's revolt and makes him count of Nantes

1157 King Henry II rescinds Treaty of Winchester's grants to Flemish
8 Sept.: Richard I born at Oxford

1158 King Henry II's expedition to Toulouse; death of William V of Warenne, son of King Stephen; death of Geoffrey, count of Nantes
23 Sept.: birth of Geoffrey, later duke of Brittany

1162 Thomas Becket, royal chancellor, appointed archbishop of Canterbury

1163 Renewal of Anglo-Flemish treaty

1164 30 Jan.: death of William of Anjou, brother of King Henry II, after Thomas Becket refused his marriage to Isabel of Warenne; marriage of Isabel of Warenne and Hamelin, half-brother of Henry II; Constitutions of Clarendon
Late autumn: Thomas Becket flees from Northampton to the Continent

1166 Inquest into knight service; Assize of Clarendon on jury inquest

1167 10 Sept.: death of Empress Matilda
24 Dec.: birth of John, later king

1169 Treaty of Montmirail: King Henry II designates Young Henry as heir and successor to England, Normandy and Anjou, Geoffrey as heir to Brittany and Richard to Aquitaine; Richard betrothed to Alice, daughter of Louis VII

1170 Summer: co-coronation of Henry the Young King
1 Dec.: Thomas Becket returns to England
29 Dec.: Thomas Becket murdered in Canterbury Cathedral

1172 Summer: Richard installed as duke of Aquitaine

1173–4 Rebellion of King Henry II's sons Henry the Young king, Richard and Geoffrey supported by their mother, Queen Eleanor

1174 Sept.: King Henry II accepts submission of his sons

1176 Assize of Northampton

1181 Marriage of Geoffrey and Constance, heiress of Brittany; Assize of Arms

1183 11 June: death of Henry the Young King

1184 Assize of the Forest

1186 Aug.: death of Geoffrey, duke of Brittany

1187 March: birth of Arthur, son and heir to Constance and the late Geoffrey; truce between King Henry II and King Philip Augustus of France

1188 21 Jan: Richard takes the cross but then postpones going on crusade

1189 4 July: Treaty of Azay-le-Rideau between King Henry II, his son Richard and King Philip Augustus

6 July: death of King Henry II at Chinon

20 July: Richard accepted as duke of Normandy

3 Sept.: coronation of King Richard I in London; rumour that king ordered all Jews to be killed

11 Dec.: Richard I leaves England

1190 March: massacre of Jews at York

4 July: Richard I and King Philip Augustus leave Vézelay to go on crusade

1191 Feb.: Queen Eleanor brings Berengaria of Navarra to her son Richard at Naples

12 May: marriage of King Richard and Berengaria at Limasol (Cyprus)

1192 Dec.: Richard on return from Holy Land to England captured by Leopold of Austria

1194 4 Jan.: Richard released after paying ransom

13 March: Richard arrives at Sandwich

12 May: Richard leaves England for Normandy

1197 Renewal of Anglo-Flemish treaty

1199 6 April: death of Richard I

27 May: coronation of Richard's brother John (d. 18/19 Oct. 1216)

Further reading

I.1 LAND USE AND PEOPLE

Audouy, M. and A. Chapman, *Raunds: The Origins and Growth of a Midland Village AD 450–1500* (Oxford, 2009).

Blair, J., 'Hall and chamber: English domestic planning 1000–1250', in G. Meirion-Jones and M. Jones, eds., *Manorial Domestic Buildings in England and Northern France* (London, 1993), pp. 1–21.

Booth, P., A. Dodd, M. Robinson and A. Smith, *The Thames through Time: The Archaeology of the Gravel Terraces of the Upper and Middle Thames. The Early Historical Period: AD 1–1000*, Oxford Archaeology Thames Valley Landscapes Monographs, 27 (Oxford, 2007).

Creighton, O. and R. Liddiard, 'Fighting yesterday's battle: beyond war or status in castle studies', *Medieval Archaeology*, 52 (2008), 161–9.

Cunliffe, B., *Excavations at Portchester Castle*, vol. II, *Saxon*, Reports of the Research Committee of the Society of Antiquaries of London, 33 (London, 1976).

Dyer, C., *Making a Living in the Middle Ages: The People of Britain 850–1520* (London and New Haven, 2002).

Fairbrother, J. R., *Faccombe Netherton: Excavations of a Saxon and Medieval Manorial Complex*, 2 vols., British Museum Occasional Papers, 74 (London, 1990).

Faith, R., *The English Peasantry and the Growth of Lordship* (London, 1997).

Fleming, R., 'Lords and labour', in Wendy Davies, ed., *From the Vikings to the Normans. The Short Oxford History of the British Isles,* (Oxford, 2003), pp. 107–38.

'The new wealth, the new rich, and the new political style in late Anglo-Saxon England', *Anglo-Norman Studies*, 23 (2000 (2001)), 1–22.

Fowler, P., *Farming in the First Millennium AD: British Agriculture between Julius Caesar and William the Conqueror* (Cambridge, 2002).

Gardiner, M. F., 'Implements and utensils in *Gerefa*, and the organization of seigneurial farmsteads in the High Middle Ages', *Medieval Archaeology*, 50 (2006), 260–7.

'Late Saxon settlement', in H. Hamerow, S. Crawford and D. Hinton, eds., *A Handbook of Anglo-Saxon Archaeology* (Oxford University Press, 2011).

'The origins and persistence of manor houses in England', in M. F. Gardiner and S. Rippon, eds., *Medieval Landscapes* (Macclesfield, 2007), pp. 170–82.

Hamerow, H., *Early Medieval Settlements: The Archaeology of Rural Communities in North-West Europe 400–900* (Oxford, 2002).

Hardy, A., B. M. Charles and R. J. Williams, *Death and Taxes: The Archaeology of a Middle Saxon Estate Centre at Higham Ferrers, Northamptonshire* (Oxford, 2007).

Hey, G., *Yarnton: Saxon and Medieval Settlement and Landscape*, Thames Valley Landscapes Monograph, 20 (2004).

Jones, R. and M. Page, *Medieval Villages in an English Landscape: Beginnings and Ends* (Macclesfield, 2006).

Lewis, C., P. Mitchell-Fox and C. Dyer, *Village, Hamlet and Field: Changing Medieval Settlements in Central England* (Manchester, 1997), pp. 77–118.

Loveluck, C., *Rural Settlement, Lifestyles and Social Change in the Later First Millennium AD: Anglo-Saxon Flixborough in Its Wider Context*, Excavations at Flixborough, 4 (oxford, 2007).

Oosthuizen, S., 'New light on the origins of open-field farming', *Medieval Archaeology*, 49 (2005), 165–93.

Rippon, S., *Beyond the Medieval Village: The Diversification of Landscape Character in Southern Britain* (Oxford, 2008), pp. 61–105.

Rippon, S., R. M. Fyfe and A. G. Brown, 'Beyond villages and open fields: the origins and development of a historic landscape characterised by dispersed settlement in south-west England', *Medieval Archaeology*, 50 (2006), 31–51.

Williams, A., 'A bell-house and a *burh-geat*: lordly residences in England before the Norman Conquest', in C. Harper-Bill and R. Harvey, eds., *Medieval Knighthood*, 4 (1992), pp. 221–40.

Williams, P. and R. Newman, *Market Lavington, Wiltshire: An Anglo-Saxon Cemetery and Settlement*, Wessex Archaeology Reports, 19 (Salisbury, 2006).

Williamson, T., *Shaping Medieval Landscapes: Settlement, Society, Environment* (Macclesfield, 2003).

1.2 WATER AND LAND

Barber, L. and G. Priestley-Bell, *Medieval Adaptation, Settlement and Economy of a Coastal Wetland. The Evidence from around Lydd, Romney Marsh, Kent* (Oxford, 2008).

Blair, J., ed., *Waterways and Canal Building in Medieval England* (Oxford, 2007).

Clarke, C., *Literary Landscapes and the Idea of England, 700–1400* (Woodbridge, 2006).

Crowson, A., T. Lane, K. Penn and D. Trimble, *Anglo-Saxon Settlement on the Siltland of Eastern England* (Sleaford, 2005).

Gardiner, M., 'The transformation of marshlands in Anglo-Norman England', *ANS* 29 (2006 (2007)), 35–50.

'The wider context', in L. Barber and G. Priestley-Bell, *Medieval Adaptation, Settlement and Economy of a Coastal Wetland. The Evidence from around Lydd, Romney Marsh, Kent* (Oxford, 2008), pp. 297–304.

Long, A., S. Hipkin and H. Clarke, *Romney Marsh: Coastal and Landscape Change through the Ages* (Oxford, 2002).

Rippon, S., 'Landscape change during the "long eighth century" in southern England', in N. J. Higham and M. J. Ryan, eds., *The Landscape Archaeology of Anglo-Saxon England* (Woodbridge, 2010), pp. 39–64.

'"Making the most of a bad situation"? Glastonbury Abbey, Meare, and the medieval exploitation of wetland resources in the Somerset Levels', *Medieval Archaeology*, 48 (2004), 91–130.

The Transformation of Coastal Wetlands: Exploitation and Management of Marshland Landscapes in North West Europe during the Roman and Medieval Periods (London, 2000).

I.3 FOREST AND UPLAND

Atherden, M., *Upland Britain. A Natural History* (Manchester, 1992).

Cox, J. C., *The Royal Forests of England* (London, 1905).

Rackham, O., 'The Abbey woods', in A. Gransden, ed. *Bury St Edmunds. Medieval Art, Architecture, Archaeology and Economy* (London, 1998), pp. 139–60, plates XXXIII–XXXIV.

Ancient Woodland. Its History, Vegetation and Uses in England, 2nd edn (Dalbeattie, 2003).

The History of the Countryside (London, 1986), esp. ch. 5, 'Woodland', ch. 6, 'Wood-Pasture' and ch. 14, 'Moorland'.

The Last Forest. The Story of Hatfield Forest (London, 1989).

Wager, S. J., *Woods, Wolds and Groves. The Woodland of Medieval Warwickshire*, British Archaeological Reports, British Series, 269 (Oxford, 1998).

I.4 MINERAL RESOURCES

Hooke, D., *The Anglo-Saxon landscape: The Kingdom of the Hwicce* (Manchester, 1985).

Loveluck, C., 'Wealth, waste and conspicuous consumption: Flixborough and its importance for Middle and Late Saxon rural settlement studies', in H. Hamerow and A. MacGregor, eds., *Image and Power in the Archaeology of Early Medieval Britain* (Oxford, 2001), pp. 78–130.

Metcalf, D.M., 'Regions around the North Sea with a monetised economy in the pre-Viking and Viking ages', in J. Graham-Campbell and G. Williams, eds., *Silver Economy in the Viking Age* (Walnut Creek, CA, 2007), pp. 1–11.

Parsons, D., ed., *Stone: Quarrying and Building in England AD 43–1525* (Chichester, 1990).

Spufford, P., *Money and Its Uses in Medieval Europe* (Cambridge, 1988).

I.5 HEALTH AND DISEASE

Cameron, M. L., *Anglo Saxon Medicine* (Cambridge, 1993).

Hagen, A., *A Handbook of Anglo-Saxon Food Processing and Consumption* (Pinner, 1994).

A Second Handbook of Anglo-Saxon Food and Drink: Production and Distribution (Hockwold-cum-Wilton, 1995).

Pearson, K. L., 'Nutrition and the early-medieval diet', *Speculum*, 72 (1997), 1–32.

Rawcliffe, C., *Leprosy in Medieval England* (Woodbridge, 2006).

Roberts, C. and M. Cox, *Health and Disease in Britain from Prehistory to the Present Day* (Stroud, 2003), chs. 4–5.

Roberts, C. and K. Manchester, *The Archaeology of Disease*, 2nd edn (Stroud, 1995).

II.1 AUTHORITY AND COMMUNITY

Abels, R., *Lordship and Military Obligation in Anglo-Saxon England* (Berkeley, CA, 1988).

Baxter, S., *The Earls of Mercia: Lordship and Power in Late Anglo-Saxon England* (Oxford, 2007).

Campbell, J., 'Some agents and agencies of the late Anglo-Saxon state', in J. C. Holt, ed. *Domesday Studies* (Woodbridge, 1987) pp. 201–18.

Faith, Rosamond, *The English Peasantry and the Growth of Lordship*, Studies in the Early History of Britain (London, 1997).

Fell, C., *Women in Anglo-Saxon England and the Impact of 1066* (London, 1984).

Fleming, R., *Britain after Rome*, c. *400–1050* (London, 2010).

Kings and Lords in Conquest England (Cambridge, 1991).

Hadley, D. M., *The Northern Danelaw: Its Social Structure*, c. *800–1100* (London, 2000).

Helmholz, R. H., *The Oxford History of the Laws of England*, vol. 1, *Canon Law and Ecclesiastical Jurisdiction from 597 to the 1640s* (Oxford, 2004), chs. 1 and 2.

Hudson, J., *The Formation of the English Common Law: Law and Society in England from the Norman Conquest to Magna Carta* (London, 1996).

Hyams, P., *Kings, Lords and Peasants in Medieval England: The Common Law of Villeinage in the Twelfth and Thirteenth Centuries* (Oxford, 1980).

Rancor and Reconciliation in Medieval England (Ithaca, NY, 2003).

Keynes, Simon, 'Crime and punishment in the reign of King Æthelred the Unready', in I. N. Wood and N. Lund, eds., *People and Places in Northern Europe, 500–1600: Studies Presented to Peter Hayes Sawyer* (Woodbridge, 1991), pp. 67–81.

The Diplomas of King Æthelred the 'Unready', 978–1016 (Cambridge, 1980).

McCarthy, C., *Marriage in Medieval England: Law, Literature and Practice* (Woodbridge, 2004).

Reynolds, A., *Late Anglo-Saxon England: Life and Landscape* (Stroud, 1999).

Rollason, D., *Northumbria, 500–1100: Creation and Destruction of a Kingdom* (Cambridge, 2003).
Stafford, P., 'Women and the Norman Conquest', *TRHS* 6th ser., 4 (1994), 221–49.
Thomas, H., *The English and the Normans: Ethnic Hostility, Assimilation, and Identity, 1066–*c. *1220* (Oxford, 2003).
White, G. J., *Restoration and Reform, 1153–1165: Recovery from Civil War in England* (Cambridge, 2000).
Williams, A, *The English and the Norman Conquest* (Woodbridge, 1995).
Wormald P., '*Engla Lond*: the making of an allegiance', *Journal of Historical Sociology*, 7 (1994), 1–24.
'Lordship and justice in the early English kingdom: Oswaldslow revisited', in W. Davies and P. Fouracre, eds., *Property and Power in the Early Middle Ages* (Cambridge, 1995), pp. 114–36.

II.2 LORDSHIP AND LABOUR

Aston, T. H., 'The origins of the manor in England', *TRHS* 5th ser., 8 (1958), 59–83; repr. with an important postscript in T. H. Aston, P. R. Cross, C. Dyer and J. Thirsk, eds., *Social Relations and Ideas: Essays in Honour of R. H. Hilton* (Cambridge, 1983), pp. 1–43.
Bartlett, R., *England under the Norman and Angevin Kings, 1075–1225* (Oxford, 2000), pp. 202–330.
Crouch, D., *The Birth of Nobility: Constructing Aristocracy in England and France, 900–1300* (London, 2005).
Dyer, C., *Making a Living in the Middle Ages: The People of Britain 850–1520* (London, 2002).
Green, J., *The Aristocracy of Norman England* (Cambridge, 1997).
Maitland, F. W., *Domesday Book and Beyond: Three Essays in the Early History of England*, new edn with foreword by J. C. Holt (Cambridge, 1987).
Miller, E. and J. Hatcher, *Medieval England: Rural Society and Economic Change, 1086–1348* (London, 1978).
Poly, J.-P. and E. Bournazel, *La mutation féodale, x[e]–xiie siècles*, 2nd edn (Paris, 1991), trans. C. Higgitt as *The Feudal Transformation* (New York, 1991).
Williams, A., *The World before Domesday* (London, 2008).

II.3 ORDER AND JUSTICE

English Lawsuits from William I to Richard I, ed. R. C. van Caenegem, 2 vols., Selden Society, 106, 107 (London, 1990–1).
Fleming, R., *Domesday Book and the Law* (Cambridge, 1998).
MacQueen, H. L., *Common Law and Feudal Society in Medieval Scotland* (Edinburgh, 1993).

O' Brien, B. R., *God's Peace and King's Peace: The Laws of Edward the Confessor* (Philadelphia, 1999).
Reynolds, A., *Anglo-Saxon Deviant Burial Customs* (Oxford, 2009).
Wormald, P., *Legal Culture in the Medieval West. Law as Text, Image, and Experience* (London, 1999).
The Making of English Law: King Alfred to the Twelfth Century, vol. 1, *Legislation and Its Limits* (Oxford, 1999).

II.4 WAR AND VIOLENCE

Barker, J., *The Tournament in England, 1100–1400* (Woodbridge, 1986).
Bartlett, R.J., *The Making of Europe* (Harmondsworth, 1993).
Bisson, T., *The Crisis of the Twelfth Century* (Princeton, 2009).
Kaeuper, R., *Chivalry and Violence in Medieval Europe* (Oxford, 1999).
Keen, M., *Chivalry* (New Haven, 1984).
Lawson, M. K., *The Battle of Hastings 1066* (Stroud, 2002).
Prestwich, J., *The Place of War in English History, 1066–1214* (Woodbridge, 2004).
Strickland, M. J., *War and Chivalry: The Conduct and Perception of War in England and Normandy, 1066–1217* (Cambridge, 1996).

II.5 FAMILY, MARRIAGE, KINSHIP

Bauduin, P., 'Désigner les parents: le champ de la parenté dans l'oeuvre des premiers chroniqueurs normands', *ANS* 24 (2001), 71–84.
Crick, J., 'Women, posthumous benefaction and family strategy in pre-conquest England', *Journal of British Studies*, 38 (1999), 399–422.
Green, J., *The Aristocracy of Norman England* (Cambridge, 1997).
Holt, J., Presidential addresses to the Royal Historical Society: Feudal society and the family in early medieval England: I. 'The revolution of 1066', *TRHS* 5th ser., 32 (1982), 193–212; II. 'Notions of patrimony', *TRHS* 5th ser., 33 (1983), 193–220; III. 'Patronage and politics', *TRHS* 5th ser., 34 (1984), 1–25; IV. 'The heiress and the alien', *TRHS* 5th ser., 35 (1985), 1–28.
Johns, S., *Noblewomen, Aristocracy and Power in the Twelfth-Century Anglo-Norman Realm* (Manchester, 2003).
Moore, J. S., 'The Anglo-Norman family: size and structure', *ANS* 14 (1991 (1992)), 153–96.
Stafford, P., '*La mutation familiale*: a suitable case for caution', in J. Hill and M. Swan, eds., *The Community, the Family and the Saint: Patterns of Power in Early Medieval Europe. Selected Proceedings of the International Medieval Congress, University of Leeds, 4–7 July 1994, 10–13 July 1995*, International Medieval Research, 4 (Turnhout, 1998), pp. 103–25.
Wareham, A., 'The transformation of kinship and the family in late Anglo-Saxon England', *Early Medieval Europe*, 10 (2001), 375–99.

II.6 POOR AND POWERLESS

Dyer, C. and P. R. Schofield, 'Recent work on the agrarian history of medieval Britain', in I. Alfonso, ed., *The Rural History of Medieval European Societies*, The Medieval Countryside, 1 (Turnhout, 2007), pp. 21–55.

Harvey, P. D. A., '*Rectitudines singularum personarum* and *Gerefa*', *EHR*, 108 (1993), 1–22.

Kemble, J. M., *The Saxons in England: A History of the English Commonwealth till the End of the Norman Conquest*, new edn, rev. Walter de Gray Birch, 2 vols. (London, 1876), II, pp. 497–517 (ch. 11, 'The poor').

Rawcliffe, C., *Leprosy in Medieval England* (Woodbridge, 2006).

III.1 TOWNS AND THEIR HINTERLANDS

Beresford, M. W., *New Towns of the Middle Ages: Town Plantation in England, Wales and Gascony* (London, 1967; repr. Stroud, 1988).

Blair, J., *The Church in Anglo-Saxon Society* (Oxford, 2005).

Britnell, R. H., *The Commercialisation of English Society, 1000–1500*, 2nd edn (Manchester, 1996).

Darby, H. C., *The Domesday Geography of England* (Cambridge, 1977).

Davies, W., ed., *From the Vikings to the Normans*, Short Oxford History of the British Isles (Oxford, 2003).

Dyer, C., *Everyday Life in Medieval England* (London, 2000).

Making a Living in the Middle Ages, the People of Britain 850–1520 (Yale, 2002).

Gerrard, C. and M. Aston, *The Shapwick Project, Somerset, a Rural Landscape Explored* (Leeds, 2007).

Giles, K. and C. Dyer, eds., *Town and Country in the Middle Ages, Contrasts, Contacts and Interconnections 1100–1500*, Society for Medieval Archaeology Monograph, 22 (Leeds, 2005).

Griffiths, D., R. A. Philpott and G. Egan, *Meols: The Archaeology of the North Wirral Coast* (Oxford, 2007).

Hall, R. A., ed., *Aspects of Anglo-Scandinavian York* (York, 2004).

Hill, D. and A. R. Rumble, *The Defence of Wessex: The Burghal Hidage and Anglo-Saxon Fortifications* (Manchester, 1996).

Hoskins, W. G., *The Making of the English Landscape* (London, 1955).

Jones, R. and M. Page, *Medieval Villages in an English Landscape: Beginnings and Ends* (Macclesfield, 2006).

Lewis, C., P. Mitchell-Fox and C. Dyer, *Village, Hamlet and Field: Changing Medieval Settlements in Central England* (Macclesfield, 1997, 2001).

Palliser, D. M., ed., *The Cambridge Urban History of Britain*, vol. 1, *600–1540* (Cambridge, 2000).

Rippon, S., *Beyond the Medieval Village* (Oxford, 2008).

Roberts, B. K., and S. Wrathmell, *An Atlas of Rural Settlement in England* (London, 2000).

Thomas, H. M., *The English and the Normans: Ethnic Hostility, Assimilation and Identity 1066–c. 1220* (Oxford, 2003).

Williamson, T., *Shaping Medieval Landscapes: Settlement, Society, Environment* (Macclesfield, 2003).

III.2 COMMERCE AND MARKETS

Britnell, R. H., 'English markets and royal administration before 1200', *EcHR* 2nd ser., 31 (1978), 183–96.

Haslam, J., *Anglo-Saxon Towns in Southern England* (Chichester, 1984).

Jones, S. R. H., 'Transaction costs, institutional change, and the emergence of a market economy in later Anglo-Saxon England', *EcHR*, 46 (1993), 658–78.

Maddicott, J. R., 'Trade, industry and the wealth of King Alfred', *P&P*, 123 (1989), 3–51.

Metcalf, D. M., *An Atlas of Anglo-Saxon and Norman Coin Finds, 973–1086* (London, 1998).

Sawyer, P. H., 'Early fairs and markets in England and Scandinavia', in B. L. Anderson and A. J. H. Latham, eds., *The Market in History* (London, 1986), pp. 59–77.

'The wealth of England in the eleventh century', *TRHS* 5th ser., 15 (1965), 145–64.

III.3 URBAN PLANNING

Baker, N. and R. Holt, *Urban Growth and the Medieval Church: Gloucester and Worcester* (Aldershot, 2004).

Barley, M. W., ed., *The Plans and Topography of Medieval Towns in England and Wales*, CBA Research Report, 14 (London, 1976).

Barrow, J., 'Churches, education and literacy in towns 600–1300', in D. M. Palliser, ed., *The Cambridge Urban History of Britain*, vol. 1, *600–1540* (Cambridge, 2000), pp. 127–52.

Bassett, S., 'The middle and late Anglo-Saxon defences of western Mercian towns', in S. Crawford and H. Hamerow, eds., *Anglo-Saxon Studies in Archaeology and History*, 15 (Oxford, 2008), pp. 180–239.

Brooks, N., 'The administrative background to the Burghal Hidage' in Brooks, *Communities and Warfare 700–1400* (Aldershot, 2000), pp. 114–37.

Crummy, P., 'The system of measurement used in town planning from the ninth to the thirteenth centuries', in S. C. Hawkes, D. Brown and J. Campbell, eds., *Anglo-Saxon Studies in Archaeology and History*, British Archaeological Reports, British Series, 72 (Oxford, 1979), pp. 149–64.

Fleming, R., 'Rural élites and urban communities in late-Saxon England', *P&P*, 141 (1993), 3–37.

Hinton, D., 'The large towns 600–1300', in D. M. Palliser, ed., *The Cambridge Urban History of Britain*, vol. 1, *600–1540* (Cambridge, 2000), pp. 217–43.

Palliser, D. M., T. R. Slater and E. P. Dennison, 'The topography of towns 600–1300', in D. M. Palliser, ed., *The Cambridge Urban History of Britain,* vol. I, *600–1540* (Cambridge, 2000), pp. 153–86.

Slater, T. R., 'Benedictine town planning in medieval England: evidence from St Albans', in T. R. Slater and G. Rosser, eds., *The Church in the Medieval Town* (Aldershot, 1998), pp. 155–76.

III.4 URBAN POPULATIONS AND ASSOCIATIONS

Bateson, M., 'The Law of Breteuil', *EHR*, 15 (1900), 305–6.

Biddle, M., ed., *Winchester in the Early Middle Ages: An Edition and Discussion of the Winton Domesday* (Oxford, 1976).

Campbell, J., 'Power and authority 600–1300', in D. M. Palliser, ed., *The Cambridge Urban History of Britain,* vol. I, *600–1540* (Cambridge, 2000), pp. 51–78.

Holt, R., 'Society and population 600–1300' in Palliser, ed., *The Cambridge Urban History of Britain*, vol. I, pp. 79–104.

Hutcheson, A., 'The French borough', *Current Archaeology*, 170 (2000), 64–68.

Keene, D., 'English urban guilds, *c.* 900–1300: the purposes and politics of association', in I. Gadd, ed., *Guilds and Association in Europe, 900–1900* (London, 2006), pp. 3–26.

Kowaleski, M., ed., *Medieval Towns: A Reader* (Peterborough, Ont., 2006).

Palliser, D. M., *Towns and Local Communities in Medieval and Early Modern England* (Aldershot, 2006).

Reynolds, S., 'English towns of the eleventh century in a European context', in P. Johanek, ed., *Die Stadt im 11. Jahrhundert* (Münster, 1995), pp. 1–12.

An Introduction to the History of English Medieval Towns (Oxford, 1977).

Kingdoms and Communities in Western Europe, 900–1300 (Oxford, 1984).

Reynolds, S., ed. C. van de Kieft, *Elenchus fontium historiae urbanae,* vol. II, *Great Britain and Ireland* (Leiden, 1988).

Rosser, G., 'The essence of medieval urban communities: the vill of Westminster', *TRHS* 5th ser., 34 (1984), 91–112.

Shaw, D. G., 'Social networks and the foundations of oligarchy in medieval towns', *Urban History*, 32 (2005), 200–22.

Wilcox, J., 'The St. Brice's Day massacre and Archbishop Wulfstan', in D. Wolfthal, ed., *Peace and Negotiation: Strategies for Coexistence in the Middle Ages and the Renaissance*, Arizona Studies in the Middle Ages and the Renaissance, 4 (Turnhout, 2000), pp. 79–92.

IV.1 INVASION AND MIGRATION

Abrams, L., 'King Edgar and the men of the Danelaw', in D. Scragg, ed., *Edgar, King of the English 959–975. New Interpretations* (Woodbridge, 2008), pp. 171–91.

Abrams, L. and D. Parsons, 'Place-names and the history of Scandinavian settlement in England', in J. Hines, A. Lane and M. Redknap, eds., *Land, Sea and Home* (London, 2004), pp. 379–431.

Barrow, G. W. S., *The Anglo-Norman Era in Scottish History. The Ford Lectures Delivered in the University of Oxford in Hilary Term 1977* (Oxford, 1980).

Bisson, T. N., 'The lure of Stephen's England: *tenserie*, Flemings and a crisis of circumstance,' in P. Dalton and G. J. White, eds., *King Stephen's Reign 1135–1154* (Woodbridge, 2008), pp. 171–81.

Crick, J., 'The Irish in England from Cnut to John: speculations on a linguistic interface', in E. Tyler, ed., *Conceptualizing Multilingualism, 800–1250* (Turnhout, in press).

Hadley, D. M. and J. D. Richards, eds., *Cultures in Contact. Scandinavian Settlement in England in the Ninth and Tenth Centuries* (Turnhout, 2000).

Innes, M., 'Danelaw identities: ethnicity, regionalism and political allegiance', in Hadley and Richards, eds., *Cultures in Contact*, pp. 65–88.

Jayakuma, S., 'Some reflections on the "foreign policies" of Edgar the "Peaceable"', *Haskins Society Journal*, 10 (2001), 17–37.

Lawson, M. K., *Cnut. The Danes in England in the Early Eleventh Century* (Harlow, 1993).

Lewis, C. P., 'The Norman settlement of Herefordshire under William I', *ANS* 7 (1984 (1985)), 195–213.

Oksanen, E., 'Anglo-Flemish treaties and Flemish soldiers in England *c.* 1101–1163', in J. France, ed., *Mercenaries and Paid Men: The Mercenary Identity in the Middle Ages. Proceedings of a Conference Held at the University of Wales, Swansea, 7th–9th July 2005* (Leiden, 2008), pp. 261–73.

Postles, D., 'Migration and mobility in a less mature economy: English internal migration *c.* 1200–1350', *Social History*, 25 (2000), 285–99.

Roesdahl, E., 'Denmark–England in the eleventh century: the growing archaeological evidence for contacts across the North Sea', in N. Lund, ed., *Seksogtyvende tværfaglige vikingesymposium Københavns Universitet 2007* (Aarhus, 2007), pp. 7–31.

Rumble, A., ed., *The Reign of Cnut: King of England, Denmark and Norway* (Leicester, 1994).

Thomas, H. M., *The English and the Normans. Ethnic Hostility, Assimilation and Identity, 1066–*c. *1220* (Oxford, 2003).

van Houts, E., 'The Flemish contribution to biographical writing in England in the eleventh century', in D. Bates, J. Crick and S. Hamilton, eds., *Writing Medieval Biography, 750–1250. Essays in Honour of Professor Frank Barlow* (Woodbridge, 2006), pp. 111–27.

'The vocabulary of exile and outlawry in the North Sea area around the first millennium', in L. Napran and E. van Houts, eds., *Exile in the Middle Ages. Selected Proceedings from the International Medieval Congress, University of Leeds, 8–11 July 2002*, International Medieval Research, 14 (Turnhout, 2004), pp. 13–28.

Williams, A., *The English and the Norman Conquest* (Woodbridge, 1995).

IV.2 ETHNICITY AND ACCULTURATION

Barrett, J., 'What caused the Viking Age?', *Antiquity*, 82 (2008), 671–85.

Foot, S., 'The making of *Angelcynn*: English identity before the Norman Conquest', *TRHS* 6th ser., 6 (1996), 25–49.

Frank, R., 'King Cnut in the verse of his skalds', in A. Rumble, ed., *The Reign of Cnut: King of England, Denmark and Norway* (Leicester, 1994), pp. 106–24.

Geary, P., 'Ethnic identity as a situational construct in the early Middle Ages', *Mitteilungen der Anthropologischen Gesellschaft in Wien*, 113 (1983), 15–26.

Hadley, D. M., *The Vikings in England. Settlement, Society and Culture* (Manchester, 2006).

Kershaw, P., 'The Alfred–Guthrum treaty: scripting accommodation and interaction in Viking Age England', in D. M. Hadley and J. D. Richards, eds., *Cultures in Contact. Scandinavian Settlement in England in the Ninth and Tenth Centuries* (Turnhout, 2000), pp. 43–64.

Lawson, M. K., 'Archbishop Wulfstan and the homiletic element in the laws of Ethelred II and Cnut', in A. Rumble, ed., *The Reign of Cnut: King of England, Denmark and Norway* (Leicester, 1994), pp. 141–64.

Reynolds, S., 'What do we mean by "Anglo-Saxon" and "Anglo-Saxons"?', *Journal of British Studies*, 24 (1985), 395–414.

Thomas, G. 'Anglo-Scandinavian metalwork from the Danelaw: exploring social and cultural interaction', in D. M. Hadley and J. D. Richards, eds., *Cultures in Contact. Scandinavian Settlement in England in the Ninth and Tenth Centuries* (Turnhout, 2000), pp. 237–55.

Townend, M., *Language and History in Viking-Age England. Linguistic Relations between Speakers of Old Norse and Old English* (Turnhout, 2002).

Whitelock, D., 'The dealings of the kings of England with Northumbria in the tenth and eleventh centuries', in P. Clemoes, ed., *The Anglo-Saxons: Studies in Some Aspects of Their History Presented to Bruce Dickins* (London, 1959), pp. 70–88.

IV.3 INTERMARRIAGE

Clark, C., 'Women's names in post-conquest England: observations and speculations', *Speculum*, 53 (1978), 223–51, repr. in *Words, Names and History. Selected Writings by Cecily Clark*, ed. P. Jackson (Cambridge, 1995), pp. 117–43.

Keats-Rohan, K., *Domesday People. A Prosopography of Persons Occurring in English Documents, 1066–1166*, vol. 1, *Domesday Book* (Woodbridge, 1999).

Searle, E., 'Women and the legitimization of succession at the Norman conquest', *Proceedings of the Battle Conference on Anglo-Norman Studies 1980* (Woodbridge, 1981), pp. 159–70, 226–9.

Stafford, P., 'Women and the Norman Conquest', *TRHS* 6th ser., 4 (1994), 221–49.

Thomas, H. M., *The English and the Normans: Ethnic Hostility, Assimilation and Identity, 1066–*c. *1220* (Oxford, 2003), pp. 138–60.

van Houts, E., 'Intermarriage in eleventh-century England', in D. Crouch and K. Thompson, eds., *Normandy and Its Neighbours, 900–1250. Essays Presented to David Bates* (Turnhout, 2010), forthcoming.

Williams, A., '"Cockles amongst the wheat": Danes and English in the western Midlands in the first half of the eleventh century', *Midland History*, 11 (1986), 1–22.

IV.4 THE JEWS

Dobson, R. B., *The Jews of Medieval York and the Massacre of March 1190*, Borthwick Papers, 45 (York, 1974).

Jacobs, J., ed., *The Jews of Angevin England* (New York, 1893; repr. New York, 1977).

Mundill, R. R., 'The medieval Anglo-Jewish community: organization and royal control', in C. Cluse, A. Haverkamp and J. Yuval, eds., *Jüdische Gemeinden und ihr christlicher Kontext in kulturräumlich vergleichender Betrachtung von der Spätantike bis zum 18. Jahrhundert* (Hannover, 2003), pp. 267–81.

Richardson, H. G., *The English Jewry under Angevin Kings* (London, 1960).

Skinner, P., ed., *Jews in Medieval Britain* (Woodbridge, 2003).

Stacey, R. C., 'Jewish lending and the medieval economy', in R. H. Britnell and B. M. S. Campbell, eds., *A Commercialising Economy. England 1086 to* c. *1300* (Manchester, 1995), pp. 78–92.

'Jews and Christians in twelfth-century England: some dynamics of a changing relationship', in M. A. Signer and J. Van Engen, eds., *Jews and Christians in Twelfth-Century Europe* (Notre Dame, 2001), pp. 340–54.

V.1 RELIGION AND BELIEF

Backhouse, J., *The Golden Age of Anglo-Saxon Art, 966–1066* (London, 1984).

Barlow, F., *The English Church, 1000–1066. A History of the Later Anglo-Saxon Church* (London, 1963).

The English Church, 1066–1154 (London, 1979).

Bartlett, R., *Gerald of Wales, 1146–1223* (Oxford, 1982).

Biller, P., 'Popular religion in the central and later Middle Ages', in M. Bentley, ed., *Companion to Historiography* (London, 1997), pp. 221–46.

Blair, J., *The Church in Anglo-Saxon Society* (Oxford, 2005).

Blair, J. and R. Sharpe, eds., *Pastoral Care before the Parish* (Leicester, 1992).

Brett, M., *The English Church under Henry I* (Oxford, 1975).

Brooke, C. N. L. and R. Brooke, *Popular Religion in the Middle Ages. Western Europe 1000–1300* (London, 1984).

Brown, A., *Church and Society in England, 1000–1500* (Basingstoke, 2003).

Burton, J., *The Monastic and Religous Orders in England,* c. *1000–1300* (Cambridge, 1994).

Colvin, H., 'The origins of chantries', *JMH*, 26 (2000), 163–73.

Cownie, E., *Religious Patronage in Anglo-Norman England 1066–1135* (London, 1993).

Crouch, D., 'The culture of death in the Anglo-Norman world', in C. Warren Hollister, ed., *Anglo-Norman Political Culture and the Twelfth-Century Renaissance: Proceedings of the Borchard Conference on Anglo-Norman History 1995* (Woodbridge, 1997), pp. 172–7.
Finucane, R. C., *Miracles and Pilgrims: Popular Beliefs in Medieval England* (London, 1977).
Foot, S., *Veiled Women*, 2 vols. (Aldershot, 2000).
Harper-Bill, C., 'The piety of the Anglo-Norman knightly class', *Proceedings of the Battle Conference of Anglo-Norman Studies*, 2 (1979), 63–77.
'Searching for salvation in Anglo-Norman East Anglia', in C. Harper-Bill, C. Rawcliffe and R. G. Wilson, eds., *East Anglia's History. Studies in Honour of Norman Scarfe* (Woodbridge, 2002), pp. 19–40.
Kieckhefer, R., *Magic in the Middle Ages* (Cambridge, 1989).
Le Goff, J., *The Birth of Purgatory*, trans. A. Goldhammer (London, 1984).
McGatch, M., *Preaching and Theology in Anglo-Saxon England: Aelfric and Wulfstan* (Toronto, 1977).
Murray, A., 'Confession before 1215', *TRHS* 6th series, 3 (1993), 51–81.
Ridyard, S., *The Royal Saints of Anglo-Saxon England: A Study of West Saxon and East Anglian Cults* (Cambridge, 1988).
Rollason, D., *Saints and Relics in Anglo-Saxon England* (Oxford, 1989).
Rubin, M., *Corpus Christi. The Eucharist in Late Medieval Culture* (Cambridge, 1991).
Southern, R. W., *St Anselm. A Portrait in a Landscape* (Cambridge, 1990).
Thompson, S., *Women Religious. The Founding of English Nunneries after the Norman Conquest* (Oxford, 1991).
Thompson, V., *Dying and Death in Later Anglo-Saxon England*, Anglo-Saxon Studies, 4 (Woodbridge, 2004).
Tinti, F., ed., *Pastoral Care in Late Anglo-Saxon England* (Woodbridge, 2005).

V.2 RITES OF PASSAGE AND PASTORAL CARE

Bedingfield, M. B., *The Dramatic Liturgy of Anglo-Saxon England*, Anglo-Saxon Studies, 1 (Woodbridge, 2002).
Greenfield, K., 'Changing emphases in English vernacular homiletic literature, 1060–1225', *JMH*, 7 (1981), 283–97.
Lucy, S. and A. Reynolds, eds., *Burial in Early Medieval England and Wales* (London, 2002).
Lynch, J. H., *Godparents and Kinship in Early Medieval Europe* (Princeton, NJ, 1986).
Paxton, F. S., 'Birth and death', in T. F. X. Noble and J. M. H. Smith, eds., *The Cambridge History of Christianity*, vol. III, *Early Medieval Christianities* c. *600*–c. *1100* (Cambridge, 2008), pp. 383–98.
Christianizing Death. The Creation of a Ritual Process in Early Medieval Europe (Ithaca, NY, 1990).
Pfaff, R. W., ed., *The Liturgical Books of Anglo-Saxon England*, Old English Newsletter Subsidia, 23 (Kalamazoo, MI, 1995).

Spinks, B. D., *Early and Medieval Rituals and Theologies of Baptism: From the New Testament to the Council of Trent* (Aldershot, 2006).
Stocker, D. and P. Everson, *Summoning St Michael. Early Romanesque Towers in Lincolnshire* (Oxford, 2006).
Tanner, N. P. and S. Watson, 'Least of the laity: the minimum requirements of a medieval Christian', *JMH*, 32 (2006), 395–423.
Thompson, V., *Dying and Death in Later Anglo-Saxon England*, Anglo-Saxon Studies, 4 (Woodbridge, 2004).
Warner, P., 'Shared churchyards, freemen church-builders and the development of parishes in eleventh-century East Anglia', *Landscape History*, 8 (1986), 39–52.
Zadora-Rio, E., 'The making of churchyards and parish territories in the early medieval landscape of France and England in the 7th–12th centuries: a reconsideration', *Medieval Archaeology*, 47 (2003), 1–19.

V.3 SAINTS AND CULTS

Crook, J., *The Architectural Setting of the Cult of Saints in the Early Christian West* c. *300*–c. *1200* (Oxford, 2000).
Foreville, R., *Thomas Becket dans la tradition historique et hagiographique* (London, 1981).
Hayward, P. A., 'Gregory the Great as "apostle of the English" in post-Conquest Canterbury', *JEH*, 55 (2004), 19–57.
'The *Miracula inuentionis beate Mylburge uirginis* attributed to "Ato, Cardinal Bishop of Ostia"', *EHR*, 114 (1999), 543–73.
The Politics of Sanctity in Anglo-Norman England (Oxford, in press).
Hollis, S., ed., *Writing the Wilton Women: Goscelin's* Liber confortatorius *and the Legend of Edith* (Turnhout, 2004).
Kemp, B. R., 'The hand of St James at Reading Abbey', *Reading Medieval Studies*, 16 (1990), 77–96.
Ridyard, S. J., *The Royal Saints of Anglo-Saxon England: A Study of West Saxon and East Anglian Cults* (Cambridge, 1988).
Rollason, D. W., *Saints and Relics of Anglo-Saxon England* (Oxford, 1989).
Webb, D., *Pilgrimage in Medieval England* (London, 2000).
Wilson, S. E., *The Life and After-Life of St John of Beverley: The Evolution of the Cult of an Anglo-Saxon Saint* (Aldershot, 2006).
Yarrow, S., *Saints and Their Communities: Miracle Stories in Twelfth-Century England* (Oxford, 2005).

V.4 PUBLIC SPECTACLE

Bailey, T., *The Processions of Sarum and the Western Church* (Toronto, 1971).
Biddle, M., 'Seasonal festivals and residence: Winchester, Westminster and Gloucester in the tenth to twelfth centuries', *ANS* 8 (1985 (1986)), 51–72.
Coss, P. and M. Keen, eds., *Heraldry, Pageantry and Social Display in Medieval England* (Woodbridge, 2002).

Cowdrey, H. E. J., 'The Anglo-Norman *Laudes regiae*', *Viator*, 12 (1981), 37–78.
Malone, C. M., *Façade as Spectacle: Ritual and Ideology at Wells Cathedral* (Boston, MA, and Leiden, 2004).
Nelson, J. L., 'Inauguration rituals', in P. H. Sawyer and I. N. Wood, eds., *Early Medieval Kingship* (Leeds, 1977), pp. 50–71.
'The rites of the conqueror', *ANS* 4 (1981 (1982)), 117–32.
'Ritual and reality in the early medieval *ordines*', in D. Baker, ed., *The Materials, Sources and Methods of Ecclesiastical History*, Studies in Church History 11 (Oxford, 1975), pp. 41–51.
Rollason, D. W., *Two Anglo-Saxon Rituals. The Dedication of a Church and the Judicial Ordeal*, Vaughan Papers, 33, Fifth Brixworth Lecture, 1987 (Brixworth, 1988).
Sharpe, R., 'The setting of St Augustine's translation, 1091', in R. Eales and R. Sharpe, eds., *Canterbury and the Norman Conquest. Churches, Saints and Scholars 1066–1109* (London and Rio Grande, OH, 1995), pp. 1–13.

V.5 TEXTUAL COMMUNITIES (LATIN)

Burnett, C., *The Introduction of Arabic Learning into England*, The Panizzi Lectures, 1996 (London, 1997).
Harper, J., *The Forms and Orders of Western Liturgy from the Tenth to the Eighteenth Century: A Historical Introduction and Guide for Students and Musicians* (Oxford, 1991).
Keynes, S., ed., *The Liber Vitae of the New Minster and Hyde Abbey Winchester: British Library Stowe 944 together with Leaves from British Library Cotton Vespasian A. VIII and British Library Cotton Titus D. XXVII*, Early English Manuscripts in Facsimile, 26 (Copenhagen, 1996).
Lapidge, M., 'Anglo-Latin literature', in S. B. Greenfield and D. G. Calder, eds., *A New Critical History of Old English Literature* (New York, 1986), pp. 5–37; repr. in M. Lapidge, ed., *Anglo-Latin Literature, 600–899* (London, 1996), pp. 1–35.
Lapidge, M. and M. Winterbottom, eds. and trans., *Wulfstan of Winchester, The Life of St Æthelwold*, OMT (Oxford, 1991).
Leedham-Green, E. and T. Webber, eds., *The Cambridge History of Libraries in Britain and Ireland*, vol. 1, *To 1640* (Cambridge, 2006), chs. 3–4.
Southern, R. W., 'The place of England in the twelfth-century renaissance', in Southern *Medieval Humanism and Other Studies* (Oxford, 1970), pp. 158–80.
Thomson, R. M., 'England and the twelfth-century renaissance', *P&P*, 101 (1983), 3–21.

V.6 TEXTUAL COMMUNITIES (VERNACULAR)

Clanchy, M. T., *From Memory to Written Record: England 1066 to 1307* (2nd edn, Oxford, 1993).
Conner, P., *Anglo-Saxon Exeter. A Tenth-Century Cultural History* (Woodbridge, 1993).

'Parish guilds and the production of Old English literature in the public sphere', in V. Blanton and H. Scheck, eds. *(Inter)Texts: Studies in Early Insular Culture Presented to Paul E. Szarmach* (Tempe, AZ, 2007), pp. 257–73.

Dean, R. J. with M. B. M. Bolton, *Anglo-Norman Literature: A Guide to Texts and Manuscripts*, Anglo-Norman Texts Society Occasional Publications, 3 (London, 1999).

Ker, N., *Catalogue of Manuscripts Containing Anglo-Saxon* (Oxford, 1957; repr. 1991 with supplement).

O'Donnell, D., ed., *Cædmon's Hymn: A Multi-Media Study, Edition and Archive* (Woodbridge, 2005).

Owen-Crocker, G., ed., *Working with Anglo-Saxon Manuscripts* (Exeter, 2009).

Townend, M., 'Skaldic praise-poetry at the court of Cnut', *ASE*, 30 (2001), 145–79.

Townend, M., ed., *Wulfstan, Archbishop of York: The Proceedings of the Second Alcuin Conference* (Turnhout, 2004).

Treharne, E., 'The life of English in the mid-twelfth century: Ralph D'Escures's Homily on the Virgin Mary', in R. Kennedy and S. Meecham-Jones, eds., *Writers of the Reign of Henry II. Twelve Essays* (New York, 2006), pp. 169–86.

'Producing a library in Late Anglo-Saxon England: Exeter 1050–1072', *Review of English Studies*, 54 (2003), 155–72.

Webber, T., *Scribes and Scholars at Salisbury Cathedral, c. 1075–1125* (Oxford, 1992).

VI.1 LEARNING AND TRAINING

Banniard, Michel, *Viva voce: communication écrite et communication orale du IVe au IXe siècle en Occident latin* (Paris, 1992).

Clanchy, M. T., *Abelard: A Medieval Life* (Oxford, 1997).

From Memory to Written Record: England, 1066–1307 (London, 1979; 2nd edn, Oxford, 1993).

Crick, J., 'English vernacular script', in R. Gameson, ed., *The Cambridge History of the Book in Britain*, vol. 1 (Cambridge, in press), pp. 00–00.

Cubitt, C., '"As the lawbook teaches": reeves, lawbooks and urban life in the anonymous Old English legend of the seven sleepers', *EHR*, 124 (2009), 1021–49.

Gillingham, J., 'Some observations on social mobility in England between the Norman Conquest and the early thirteenth century', in Gillingham, in his *The English in the Twelfth Century: Imperialism, National Identity and Political Values* (Woodbridge, 2000), pp. 259–76.

Gneuss, H., 'The origin of Standard Old English and Æthelwold's school at Winchester', *ASE*, 1 (1972), 63–83.

Godden, M., 'King Alfred's Preface and the teaching of Latin in Anglo-Saxon England', *EHR*, 117 (2002), 596–604.

Gretsch, M., *The Intellectual Foundations of the English Benedictine Reform* (Cambridge, 1999).

'Winchester vocabulary and Standard Old English: the vernacular in late Anglo-Saxon England', *Bulletin of the John Rylands University Library of Manchester*, 83 (2001), 41–87.

Gullick, M., 'Professional scribes in eleventh- and twelfth-century England', in P. Beal and J. Griffiths, eds., *English Manuscript Studies 1100–1700*, 7 (London, 1998), pp. 1–24.

Gwara, S., ed., and D. Porter, trans., *Anglo-Saxon Conversations: The Colloquies of Ælfric Bata* (Woodbridge, 1997).

Hudson, J., 'L'écrit, les archives et le droit en Angleterre (IXe–XIIe siècle)', *Revue historique*, 315 (2006), 3–35.

Keynes, S., 'The Fonthill Letter', in M. Korhammer, with K. Reichl and H. Sauer, eds., *Words, Texts and Manuscripts: Studies in Anglo-Saxon Culture Presented to Helmut Gneuss on the Occasion of His Sixty-Fifth Birthday* (Cambridge, 1992), pp. 53–97.

Lapidge, M., *Anglo-Latin Literature, 900–1066* (London and Rio Grande, OH, 1993).

The Anglo-Saxon Library (Oxford, 2006).

Lendinara, P., 'Instructional manuscripts in England: the tenth- and eleventh-century codices and the early Norman ones', in P. Lendinara, L. Lazzari and M. A. d'Aronco, eds., *Form and Content of Instruction in Anglo-Saxon England in the Light of Contemporary Manuscript Evidence* (Turnhout, 2007), pp. 59–113.

'The world of Anglo-Saxon learning', in M. Godden and M. Lapidge, eds., *The Cambridge Companion to Old English Literature* (Cambridge, 1991), pp. 264–81.

Orme, N., *From Childhood to Chivalry: The Education of the English Kings and Aristocracy 1066–1530* (London, 1984).

Rector, G., 'The *Romanz* psalter in England and northern France in the twelfth century: production, *mise-en-page*, and circulation', *Journal of the Early Book Society* (in press).

Reynolds, S., *Medieval Reading: Grammar, Rhetoric and the Classical Text* (Cambridge, 1996).

Scragg, D., *Handlist of Scribes* (Woodbridge, in press; see also www.arts.manchester.ac.uk/mancass/C11database/).

Southern, R. W., 'From schools to University', in J. I. Catto, ed., *The History of the University of Oxford*, vol. 1, *The Early Oxford Schools* (Oxford, 1984), pp. 1–36.

Thomson, R. M., *England and the Twelfth-Century Renaissance* (Aldershot, 1998).

Webber, T., 'Monastic and cathedral book collections in the late eleventh and twelfth centuries', in E. Leedham-Green and T. Webber, eds., *The Cambridge History of Libraries in Britain and Ireland*, vol. 1, *To 1650* (Cambridge, 2006), pp. 109–25.

Wilcox, J., 'The dissemination of Wulfstan's homilies: the Wulfstan tradition in eleventh-century vernacular preaching', in C. Hicks, ed., *England in the Eleventh Century. Proceedings of the 1990 Harlaxton Symposium* (Stamford, 1992), pp. 199–217.

Wormald, P., 'The uses of literacy in Anglo-Saxon England and its neighbours', *TRHS* 5th ser., 27 (1977), 95–114.

VI.2 INFORMATION AND ITS RETRIEVAL

Geary, P. J., *Phantoms of Remembrance: Memory and Oblivion at the End of the First Millennium* (Princeton, 1994).

Keynes, S., 'Royal government and the written word in late Anglo-Saxon England', in R. McKitterick, ed., *The Uses of Literacy in Early Medieval Europe* (Cambridge, 1990), pp. 226–57.

O'Brien, B., 'Forgery and the literacy of the early common law', *Albion*, 27 (1995), 1–18.

Vincent, N. 'Why 1199? Bureaucracy and enrolment under John and his contemporaries', in A. Jobson, ed., *English Government in the Thirteenth Century* (Woodbridge, 2004), pp. 17–48.

Wormald, C. P., 'Charters, law and the settlement of disputes in Anglo-Saxon England', in W. Davies, and P. Fouracre, eds., *The Settlement of Disputes in Early Medieval Europe* (Cambridge, 1986), pp. 149–68.

VI.3 ESOTERIC KNOWLEDGE

Anlezark, D., ed. and trans., *The Old English Dialogues of Solomon and Saturn*, Anglo-Saxon Texts, 7 (Cambridge, 2009).

Burnett, C., *Adelard of Bath: An English Scientist and Arabist of the Early Twelfth Century* (London, 1987).

Gneuss, H., *Handlist of Anglo-Saxon Manuscripts. A List of Manuscripts and Manuscript Fragments Written or Owned in England up to 1100* (Tempe, AZ, 2001).

Hall, A., *Elves in Anglo-Saxon England* (Woodbridge, 2007).

Liuzza, R. M., 'Anglo-Saxon prognostics in context: a survey and handlist of manuscripts', *ASE*, 30 (2001), 180–230.

Orchard, A., 'Enigma Variations: the Anglo-Saxon riddle-tradition', in K. O'Brien O'Keeffe and A. Orchard, eds., *Latin Learning and English Lore: Studies in Anglo-Saxon Literature for Michael Lapidge*, 2 vols. (Toronto, 2005), I, 284–304.

Pride and Prodigies: Studies in the Monsters of the 'Beowulf' Manuscript, rev. edn (Toronto, 2003).

Page, R. I., 'Anglo Saxon runes and magic', *Journal of the Archaeological Association*, 27 (1964), 14–31.

Rigg, A. G., *A History of Anglo-Latin Literature 1066–1422* (Cambridge, 1992).

Scarfe Beckett, K., *Anglo-Saxon Perceptions of the Islamic World*, Cambridge Studies in Anglo-Saxon England, 33 (Cambridge, 2003).

Storms, G., *Anglo-Saxon Magic* (The Hague, 1948).

VI.4 MEDICAL PRACTICE AND THEORY

Amundsen, D. W., *Medicine, Society and Faith in the Ancient and Medieval Worlds* (Baltimore and London, 1996).

Arsdall, A. van, *Medieval Herbal Remedies: The Old English Herbarium and Anglo-Saxon Medicine* (London and New York, 2002).

Cameron, M. L., *Anglo Saxon Medicine* (Cambridge, 1993).

Conrad, L. I., M. Neve, V. Nutton, R. Porter and A. Wear, *The Western Medical Tradition* (Cambridge, 1995).

Dendle, P. and A. Touwaide, eds., *Health and Healing from the Medieval Garden* (Woodbridge, 2008).

Getz, F., *Medicine in the English Middle Ages* (Princeton, 1998).

Meaney, A., 'The practice of medicine in England about the year 1000', *Social History of Medicine*, 13 (2000), 221–37.

Wallis, F., 'The experience of the book', in D. Bates, ed., *Knowledge and the Scholarly Medical Traditions* (Cambridge, 1995), pp. 101–26.

VI.5 SUBVERSION

Bate, K., ed., *Three Latin Comedies* (Toronto, 1976).

Bayless, M., 'Humour and the comic in Anglo-Saxon England', in S. Hordis and P. Hardwick, eds., *English Medieval Comedy* (Turnhout, 2007), pp. 13–30.

Map, W., *De nugis curialium: Courtiers' Trifles*, ed. and trans. M. R. James, rev. C. N. L. Brooke and R. A. B. Mynors, OMT (Oxford, 1983).

Mozley, J. H., trans., *A Mirror for Fools: The Book of Burnel the Ass* (Oxford, 1961).

Speculum Stultorum, ed. J. H. Mozley and R. R. Raymo (Berkeley, CA, 1960).

Ziolkowski, J., ed., *The Cambridge Songs (Carmina Cantabrigiensia)* (New York and Tempe, AZ, 1994).

Index

Bishops and abbots are indexed under their institutions unless they figure in the text as significant political actors in their own right (e.g. Æthelwold, Dunstan, Thomas Becket etc.)